Communications
in Computer and Information Science 322

Aboul Ella Hassanien   Abdel-Badeeh M. Salem
Rabie Ramadan Tai-hoon Kim (Eds.)

Advanced Machine Learning Technologies and Applications

First International Conference, AMLTA 2012
Cairo, Egypt, December 8-10, 2012
Proceedings

Springer

Volume Editors

Aboul EllaHassanien
Rabie Ramadan Cairo University, Egypt
E-mail:{aboitegypt, rabieramadan}@gmail.com

Abdel-Badeeh M. Salem
Ain Shams University, Cairo, Egypt
E-mail: abmsalem@yahoo.com

Tai-hoon Kim
University of Tasmania, TAS, Australia
E-mail: taihoonn@empal.com

ISSN 1865-0929   e-ISSN 1865-0937
ISBN 978-3-642-35325-3   e-ISBN 978-3-642-35326-0
DOI 10.1007/978-3-642-35326-0
Springer Heidelberg Dordrecht London New York

Library of Congress Control Number: 2012953006

CR Subject Classification (1998): I.2, H.3, H.4, C.2, I.4-5, F.1

Typesetting: Camera-ready by author, data conversion by Scientific Publishing Services, Chennai, India

Printed on acid-free paper

Springer is part of Springer Science+Business Media (www.springer.com)

Preface

The 1st International Conference on Advanced Machine Learning Technologies and Applications (AMLTA 2012) was held on the campus of Ain Sham University in Cairo, Egypt during 8–10 December 2012. Authors of 58 accepted scientific papers, chosen from among 103 submissions, had many fruitful discussions and exchanges that contributed to the success of the conference. Participants from 18 countries made the conference truly international in scope. The AMLTA 2012 proceedings contain 8 parts as follows: Rough Sets and Applications, Machine Learning in Pattern Recognition and Image Processing, Machine Learning in Multimedia Computing, Bioinformatics and Cheminformatics: Trends and Applications, Data Classification and Clustering: Theory and Applications, Cloud Computing and Recommender Systems, Case-Based Reasoning and Data Processing, Authentication, Digital Forensics and Plagiarism Detection.

There were three plenary lectures covering the different areas of the conference. The first talk, by Prof. Dipankar Dasgupta, Director of the Center for Information Assurance, and Professor of Computer Science at the University of Memphis, Tennessee, was entitled Genetic Learning Algorithms in Developing a Framework for Cloud Security Insurance. The second talk, by Prof. Guoyin Wang, College of Computer Science and Technology, Chongqing University of Posts and Telecommunications, and Institute of Electronic Information Technology, Chongqing Institute of Green and Intelligent Technology, was entitled Cloud Model – A Bidirection Cognition Model between Concept Extension and Intension. The final talk, by Prof. Shampa Chakraverty, Netaji Subhas Institute of Technology, Delhi University, New Delhi, was entitled A Fuzzy Cuckoo-Search Approach for Multiprocessor Embedded Systems Design.

There were three tutorials. The first was by Dr. Mohamed Medhat Gaber, Senior Lecturer at the University of Portsmouth, UK; Dr. Joao Gama, Associate Professor at the University of Porto and researcher at LIAAD-Inesc Tec.; and Dr Pedro Pereira Rodrigues, Invited Assistant Professor at the Health Information and Decision Sciences Department of the Faculty of Medicine of the University of Porto, Portugal. The tutorial focused on Machine Learning from Data Streams: Techniques and Applications. The second tutorial, by Dr. Waheedah Al Mayyan, Software Technology Research Laboratory (STRL), UK, was on Tutorial Multimodal Biometrics: Aspects and Challenges. The last tutorial, by Prof. Hussein Zedan, Software Technology Research Laboratory (STRL), UK, focused on Logic-Based Approaches for the Development of Dependable Computing Systems. We are thankful to all those who held these tutorials, for their support and cooperation.

There were also 10 special sessions focusing on the following subjects: Reconfigurable Computing Systems, Complex Adaptive Systems, Computational Intelligence and Wireless Sensor Networks, Machine Learning for Data Streams

Applications, Engineering Ubiquitous Systems, Soft Computing Techniques for Multimedia Applications, Machine Learning for Biometrics, Cloud Computing: A Security Perspective, Machine Learning in Information Security Applications, and Cloud Technologies and Applications. We thank all special session chairs for their hard work before and during the conference.

The editors would like to acknowledge the work of the members of the PC in reviewing and discussing the papers.The EasyChair conference system proved very helpful during the submission, review, and editing phases. We are thankful to Alfred Hofmann and the excellent CCIS team at Springer for their support and cooperation in publishing the proceedings as a volume of the Communications in Computer and Information Science series. Special thanks to the SERSC center for their technical support and the SERSC team for their support and cooperation.

October 2012

Aboul Ell Hassanien
Abdel-Badeeh M. Salem
Rabie Ramadan
Tai-hoon Kim

Organization

Honorary Chairs

Mohamed Fahmy Tolba, Egypt
Janusz Kacprzyk, Poland

General Co-chairs

Aboul Ella Hassanien, Egypt
Tai-hoon Kim, Korea

International Advisory Board

Ajith Abraham, USA
Christian Müller-Schloer, Germany
Dominik Slezak, Poland
Samy El-Ghoniemy, Egypt
Hiroshi Sakai, Japan
Lakhmi Jain, Australia

Nikhil R. Pal, India
Pawan Lingras, Canada
Qiangfu Zhao, Japan
Václav Snášel, Czech Republic
Zbigniew Suraj, Poland
Khaled Shaalan, Egypt

Program Co-chairs

Abdel-Badeeh Salem, Egypt
Rabie Ramadan, Egypt

Workshop and Special Session Chairs

Neveen Ghali, Egypt
Soumya Banerjee, India
Ahmed Abdel Nabi, Egypt

Publicity Co-chairs

Ahmad Taher Azar, Egypt
Jan Platos, Czech Republic
Kai Xiao, China

Mohamed Elwakil, Egypt
Nashwa El Bendary, Egypt
Tauseef Gulrez, Australia

Webmasters

Ahmed Hamdy, Egypt
Walaa Hussein, Egypt

Tutorial Chairs

Hala Shawki, Kuwait
Mohammed Abdel-Megeed, Egypt

Local Organizing Committee

Neveen Ghali, Egypt
Nashwa El Bendary, Egypt
Mostafa Salama, Egypt
Mohamed Mostafa, Egypt

Heba Eid, Egypt
Kareem Kamal, Egypt
Mohamed Tahoun, Egypt

International Program Committee

Adel M. Alimi, Tunisa
Siby Abraham, India
Ajith Abraham, USA
Ali Ismail Awad, Egypt
Anna Gomolinska, Poland
Aquil khan, India
Azizah Abd Manaf, Malysia
Barna Iantovics, Romania
Beata M Zielosko, Saudi Arabia
Beate Meffert, Germany
Christopher Henry, Canada
Davide Ciucci, Italy
Dayong Deng, China
Domenico Talia, Italy
Duoqian Miao, China
Emilio Corchado, Spain
Elena Nechita, Romania
Georg Peters, Germany
Guoyin Wang, China
Hala Own, Kuwait
Hongmei Chen, China
Hussein Zedan, UK
Ilias Maglogiannis, Greece
Jan Bazan, Poland

Jan Platoš, Czech Republic
Jerzy Grzymala-Busse, USA
Jiinn-Shiing Cheng, Taiwan
Jitender Deogun, USA
Joao Gama, Portugal
Jude Hemanth, India
Karray Hichem, Tunisia
Kazumi Nakamatsu, Japan
Kensuke Baba, Japan
Khaled Shaalan, United Arab Emirates
Krzysztof Cyran, Poland
Krzysztof Pancerz, Poland
Lech Polkowski, Poland
Li-Shiang Tsay, USA
Marcin Wolski, Poland
Masahiro Inuiguchi, Japan
Michinori Nakata, Japan
Mihir K. Chakraborty, India
Mohamed Medhat Gaber, UK
Mohammed Abdel-Megeed, Egypt
Mokhtar Beldjehem, Canada
Pawan Lingras, Canada
Pedro Pereira Rodrigues, Portugal
Pedro Rodrigues, Portugal

Qing Tan, Canada
Raghavendra Rao, India
Richard Jensen, UK
Robert C. Berwick, USA
Roman Neruda, Czech Republic
Roman Slowinski, Poland
Roumen Kountchev, Bulgaria
Ryszard Janicki, Canada
S. Arumugam, Australia
Samar Kamal, Egypt
Shampa Chakraberty, India
Shi Fuqian, China
Sławomir Zadrożny, Poland
Tsung-Chih Lin, Taiwan
Urszula Stańczyk, Poland

Vaclav Snasel, Czech Republic
Vadrevu Sree Hari Rao, India
Vijay Raghavan, India
William Zhu, China
Xiaodong Liu, China
Xun GONG, USA
Yan Yang, China
Bartosz Krawczyk, Poland
Yan Yang, China
Yiyu Yao, Canada
Yudith Cardinale, Venezuela
Nagwa Bader, Egypt
Zbigniew Suraj, Poland
Zbigniew W. Ras, USA
Wei-Chiang Hong, Taiwan

Table of Contents

Part I: Rough Sets and Applications

Part II: Machine Learning in Pattern Recognition and Image Processing

Part III: Machine Learning in Multimedia Computing

Part IV: Bioinformaticsand Cheminformatics Trends and Applications

Part V: Data Classification and Clustering Theory and Applications

Part VI: Cloud Computing and Recommender Systems

Part VII: Case-Based Reasoning and Data Processing

Part VIII: Authentication, Digital Forensics and Plagiarism Detection

Part I

Rough Sets and Applications

Rough Sets-Based Machine Learning over Non-deterministic Data: A Brief Survey*

Hiroshi Sakai[1], Mao Wu[1], Michinori Nakata[2], and Dominik Ślęzak[3,4]

[1] Faculty of Engineering, Kyushu Institute of Technology
Tobata, Kitakyushu 804, Japan
sakai@mns.kyutech.ac.jp, wumogaku@yahoo.co.jp
[2] Faculty of Management and Information Science
Josai International University
Gumyo, Togane, Chiba 283, Japan
nakatam@ieee.org
[3] Institute of Mathematics, University of Warsaw
Banacha 2, 02-097 Warsaw, Poland
[4] Infobright Inc.
Krzywickiego 34 pok. 219, 02-078 Warsaw, Poland
slezak@{mimuw.edu.pl,infobright.com}

Abstract. *Rough Non-deterministic Information Analysis* (*RNIA*) is a rough sets-based framework for handling tables with exact and inexact data. Under this framework, we investigated *possible equivalence relations, data dependencies, rule generation, rule stability, question-answering systems*, as well as *missing* and *interval values* as special cases of non-deterministic values. In this paper, we briefly survey *RNIA*, and report the state of its underlying software implementation. We also discuss to what extent *RNIA* can be seen as an example of a new emerging paradigm in machine learning.

Keywords: Machine learning, Rough sets, Data dependencies, Rule generation, Question-answering systems, Missing values, Interval values.

1 Introduction

Rough set theory offers a mathematical approach to vagueness [8]. It has many applications related to the areas of classification, feature reduction, rule generation, machine learning, data mining, knowledge discovery and others [9, 10]. Rough set theory is usually employed to deal with data tables with deterministic information, which we call *Deterministic Information Systems* (*DISs*). However, somewhat in parallel to the main stream of applications, rough set approaches to incomplete data systems have been investigated as well [2, 3].

---

* This work is supported by the Grant-in-Aid for Scientific Research (C) (No.22500204), Japan Society for the Promotion of Science. The fourth author was partially supported by the Polish National Science Centre grant 2011/01/B/ST6/03867.

A. Ell Hassanien et al. (Eds.): AMLTA 2012, CCIS 322, pp. 3–12, 2012.
© Springer-Verlag Berlin Heidelberg 2012

Table 1. An exemplary NIS Φ for the suitcase data set. The values of attributes *color, size, weight, price* are as follows: $V(color) = \{red, blue, green\}$, $V(size) = \{small, medium, large\}$, $V(weight) = \{light, heavy\}$, $V(price) = \{high, low\}$.

object	color	size	weight	price
1	{red,blue,green}	{small}	{light,heavy}	{low}
2	{red}	{small,medium}	{light,heavy}	{high}
3	{red,blue}	{small,medium}	{light}	{high}
4	{red}	{medium}	{heavy}	{low,high}
5	{red}	{small,medium,large}	{heavy}	{high}
6	{blue,green}	{large}	{heavy}	{low,high}

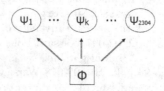

Fig. 1. An exemplary NIS Φ and 2304 derived $DISs$

In this paper, we focus on *Non-deterministic Information Systems* ($NISs$) and *Incomplete Information Systems* ($IISs$), which have been proposed for handling information incompleteness in $DISs$ [4, 6]. $NISs$ have been recognized as an important framework for handling information incompleteness in tables, and several theoretical works have been reported [2–7]. We followed this framework by developing algorithms and software tools, which can handle rough sets-based concepts in $NISs$. We call this direction of our research as *Rough Non-deterministic Information Analysis* ($RNIA$).

2   Issues in RNIA and an Exemplary NIS

In a standard table, each attribute value is fixed. In the case of a NIS Φ, each attribute value is given as a set. We may then assume that there is an actual value in each value set but we do not know which one it is. Let us consider a case when each set of attribute values is finite. We might then replace each set in Φ with an element in a set. In such a way, we would obtain a standard table. We call such tables as *derived DISs*. For Φ in Table 1, there are 2304 ($2^8 \times 3^2$) derived $DISs$ ψ_i ($1 \leq i \leq 2304$).

Generally, as illustrated by Figure 1, the number of derived $DISs$ may increase exponentially. For large data sets with relatively high level of non-determinism understood as cardinalities of value sets, creation of scalable methods of data analysis requires finding a way to handle Φ directly, with no need to considering all particular derived $DISs$. In the case of rule generation, we have solved this problem by using rough sets-based framework.

In our research, we have coped with the following challenges described in more detail in the subsequent sections:

A Management of possible equivalence relations [15];
B The minimum and the maximum degrees of data dependency [12];
C Certain and possible rules, and rule generation [13];
D Stability factor of rules and calculation [17];
E Management of missing values [13, 16];
F Management of an actual value by intervals [16];
G Management of numerical patterns and figures [14];
H Direct question-answering [17].

3 Management of Possible Equivalence Relations

In rough sets, we make use of equivalence relations and classes in a DIS. However in $NISs$, there may be several derived $DISs$, for example in Φ there are 2304 derived $DISs$. Namely in Φ, there are less than 2304 kinds of equivalence relations. We named such relations and classes *possible equivalence relations (pe-relation)* and *possible equivalence classes (pe-class)* in Φ, respectively. We may see each *pe*-class as a possible granule from a NIS.

In $LERS$ system [2] by Grzymała-Busse, equivalence classes defined by descriptors [*attribute*, *value*] are called *blocks*. We follow Grzymała-Busse's framework, and propose the following inf and sup blocks in $NISs$.

Inf and Sup Blocks of Descriptors
(1) For a descriptor $[A, \zeta]$,
$\quad inf([A, \zeta]) = \{x : object \mid attribute\ value\ of\ A\ is\ \{\zeta\}\}$,
$\quad sup([A, \zeta]) = \{x : object \mid attribute\ value\ of\ A\ includes\ \zeta\}$.
(2) For a conjunction of descriptors $\wedge_i [A_i, \zeta_i]$,
$\quad inf(\wedge_i [A_i, \zeta_i]) = \cap_i inf([A_i, \zeta_i])$, $sup(\wedge_i [A_i, \zeta_i]) = \cap_i sup([A_i, \zeta_i])$.

By using inf and sup, we can define *pe*-class $pe([A, \zeta])$ as follows.
$\quad pe([A, \zeta]) = inf([A, \zeta]) \cup M$ $(M \subseteq (sup([A, \zeta] \setminus inf([A, \zeta])))$.
In Φ, $inf([color, red]) = \{2, 4, 5\}$ and $sup([color, red]) = \{1, 2, 3, 4, 5\}$ hold, and we have the following.
$\quad pe([color, red]) = \{2, 4, 5\} \cup M_1$ $(M_1 \subseteq \{1, 3\})$,
$\quad pe([color, blue]) = M_2$ $(M_2 \subseteq \{1, 3, 6\})$, $pe([color, green]) = M_3$ $(M_3 \subseteq \{1, 6\})$,
By fixing M_1, M_2 and M_3 satisfying $M_1 \cup M_2 \cup M_3 = \{1, 3, 6\}$, we can obtain a *pe*-relation on color. We defined this issue as a constraint satisfaction problem, and implemented a program. Furthermore, we have implemented a program to merge *pe*-relations [15]. Namely, we first generate *pe*-relations for each attribute, then we merge them for generating *pe*-relations for a set of attribute. Like this, we have reduced the computational complexity. [12]

4 Minimum/Maximum Degrees of Data Dependencies

In a DIS, the *degree of dependency* for condition attributes CON to decision attributes DEC is a ratio

$deg(CON, DEC)=|\{x \in OB|\ x$ is consistent [8] for CON and DEC $\}|/|OB|$.
$OB : object\ set,\ |OB| : the\ number\ of\ objects.$

In a NIS, this degree depends upon each derived DIS, therefore we need to consider the minimum and the maximum degrees. The actual degree of dependency is between the minimum and the maximum degrees. If the difference between two degrees is small, the actual degree may not be influenced by the information incompleteness in a NIS.

By merging program, we obtain pe-relations on $CON=\{color, size, weight\}$, and we obtained 20 different pe-relations. Since there are 4 pe-relations on $DEC=\{price\}$, we can calculate each degree of dependency for 2304 derived $DISs$ by considering 80 ($=20\times4$) combinations. We have the following.

```
--- Dependency Check ------------
CRITERION 1(Num_of_Consistent_DISs/Num_of_All_DISs)
     Number of Derived DISs: 2304
     Number of Derived Consistent DISs: 1364
     Degree of Consistent DISs: 0.592
CRITERION 2(Total_Min_and_Max_Degrees)
     Minimum Degree of Dependency: 0.167
     Maximum Degree of Dependency: 1.000
EXEC_TIME=0.000(sec)
```

5   Certain and Possible Rules, and Rule Generation

This section considers rules at first, then we show NIS-apriori algorithm [13]. There may be some definitions of rules in $DISs$, and we employ a rule is an implication τ (defined by object x) satisfying appropriate constraint. A familiar constraint is defined by two values in the following:

$support(\tau)= |[x]_{CON} \cap [x]_{DEC}|/|OB|$,

$accuracy(\tau)=|[x]_{CON} \cap[x]_{DEC}|/|[x]_{CON}|$,

$[x]_{CON}$, $[x]_{DEC}$: equivalence classes on CON and DEC.

Similar to the previous sections, these values also depend upon derived $DISs$. Therefore, we defined the following two types of implications.

(Certain rule). $support(\tau) \geq \alpha$ and $accuracy(\tau) \geq \beta$ hold in each derived $DISs$.

(Possible rule). $support(\tau) \geq \alpha$ and $accuracy(\tau) \geq \beta$ hold in a derived DIS.

Generally, the number of derived $DISs$ increases exponentially, because the number of derived $DISs$ is a product of possible cases in each set. If we employ an *explicit* method, namely we sequentially examine the constraint in each derived DIS, we have a problem on the exponential order. Even in Φ, there are 2304 derived $DISs$ ($2^8 \times 3^2$). However, we could characterize the following by employing inf and sup blocks. (In reality there are three cases of τ, and the following is the simplest case.)

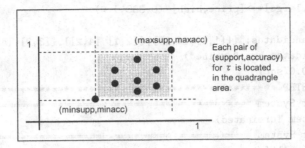

Fig. 2. A distribution of pairs (*support, accuracy*) for τ. There exists ψ_{min} which makes both *support*(τ) and *accuracy*(τ) the minimum. There exists ψ_{max} which makes both *support*(τ) and *accuracy*(τ) the maximum.

(1) $minsupp(\tau) = Min_\psi\{support(\tau)\} = |inf([CON, \zeta]) \cap inf([DEC, \eta])|/|OB|$,

(2) $maxsupp(\tau) = Max_\psi\{support(\tau)\} = \frac{|inf([CON,\zeta]) \cap inf([DEC,\eta])|}{|inf([CON,\zeta])| + |OUT|}$,

(3) $minacc(\tau) = Min_\psi\{accuracy(\tau)\} = |sup([CON, \zeta]) \cap sup([DEC, \eta])|/|OB|$,

(4) $maxacc(\tau) = Max_\psi\{accuracy(\tau)\} = \frac{|inf([CON,\zeta]) \cap sup([DEC,\eta])| + |IN|}{|inf([CON,\zeta])| + |IN|}$,

$OUT = [sup([CON, \zeta]) \setminus inf([CON, \zeta])] \setminus inf([DEC, \eta])$,

$IN = [sup([CON, \zeta]) \setminus inf([CON, \zeta])] \cap sup([DEC, \eta])$.

Furthermore, we have proved $minsupp(\tau)$ and $minacc(\tau)$ occur in the same derived *DIS* ψ_{min}. Similarly, $maxsupp(\tau)$ and $maxacc(\tau)$ occur in the same derived *DIS* ψ_{max}. Like this, we obtained the following chart.

According to Figure 2, we can consider the following tasks for rule generation.

(Certain rule generation task)
Find τ satisfying $minsupp(\tau) \geq \alpha$ and $minacc(\tau) \geq \beta$ hold.
(Possible rule generation task)
Find τ satisfying $maxsupp(\tau) \geq \alpha$ and $maxacc(\tau) \geq \beta$ hold.

We applied the above results to *Apriori* algorithm [1], and proposed *NIS-apriori* algorithm [13]. Since $minsupp(\tau), \cdots, maxacc(\tau)$ do not depend upon the number of derived *DISs*, the computational complexity of *NIS*-apriori is almost the same as the original *Apriori*. The following is real execution log for Φ (decision attribute: *price*).

```
File=[tcase5|p1] Support=0.3, Accuracy=0.8
***** 1st STEP *************************************************
===== Lower System =========================================
(Lower System Terminated)
===== Upper System =========================================
       :        :        :
[5] [color,green]==>[price,low]  (0.333,1.0)
[10] [size,medium]==>[price,high]  (0.667,1.0)
```

```
[12] [size,large]==>[price,high]  (0.333,1.0)
     :        :        :
The Rest Candidates: [[[1,1],[4,1]],[[2,1],[4,2]],[[3,2],[4,1]]]
(Next Candidates are Remained)
EXEC_TIME=0.0(sec)
***** 2nd STEP ***************************************************
===== Lower System =============================================
(Lower System Terminated)
===== Upper System =============================================
[2] [color,red]&[size,small]==>[price,high]  (0.5,1.0)
[4] [size,small]&[weight,heavy]==>[price,high]  (0.333,1.0)
The Rest Candidates: [[[1,1],[3,2],[4,1]]]
(Upper System Terminated)
EXEC_TIME=0.0(sec)
```

In the above execution, there is no implication satisfying certain rule constraint. However, we have some possible rules.

6 Stability Factor of Rules and Its Calculation

As for possible rules, we added the degree of derived $DISs$ supporting τ. We named this degree *stability factor* $SF(\tau, \Phi)$ [17]. For example in Φ, let us consider rules 10 and 12 in the 1st step. The following is real execution of stability factors.

```
?-sf([[size,medium]],[price,high]).
SF=0.456=(20/44)
EXEC_TIME=1.0(sec)
?-sf([[size,large]],[price,high]).
SF=0.25=(2/8)
EXEC_TIME=0.0(sec)
```

The above shows that there are 44 derived (restricted) $DISs$ related to rule 10. (As for attributes $\{size, price\}$, there are 48 ($=2^4 \times 3$) derived $DISs$, and rule 10 does not occur in 4 derived $DISs$.) Rule 10 satisfies constraints in 20 derived (restricted) $DISs$, which is about 45% of $DISs$. On the other hand, rule 12 is supported by 25% of $DISs$. Even though both rule 10 and rule 12 are possible, rule 10 is more reliable according to stability factor.

For the calculation of rule 10, we use $pe([size, medium])$ and $pe([price, high])$. Since $pe([A, \zeta]) = inf([A, \zeta]) \cup M$ ($M \subseteq (sup([A, \zeta] \setminus inf([A, \zeta]))$) holds,

$pe([size, medium]) = \{4\} \cup M_1$ ($M_1 \subseteq \{2, 3, 5\}$),

$pe([price, high]) = \{2, 3, 5\} \cup M_2$ ($M_2 \subseteq \{4, 6\}$).

There are 32 combinations for the calculation, which depends upon $2^{|sup-inf|}$. The calculation of stability factor takes much time.

7   Management of Missing Values

There are several important directions of research on $DISs$ with missing values or *Incomplete Information Systems*. For example, *LERS* system [2] by Grzymała-Busse and a framework of reduction based rule generation [3] by Kryszkiewicz are well known. In both cases, some interpretations are assumed for missing values, and rule extraction methods are investigated.

In [11], we are showing the execution logs on some data sets. In *Mammographic* data set in [18], there are 960 objects and 6 attributes (*assessment*, *age*, *shape*, *margin*, *density* and *severity*). The decision attribute is *severity*, and its attribute values are *benign* (0) and *malignant* (1). There are 2, 5, 31, 48 and 67 missing values (? is employed to denote them) on 5 remaining attributes, respectively. Since each set of attribute values is discrete and finite, we can convert this data set to a NIS by replacing each ? with a set of attribute values. The number of derived $DISs$ is more than 10 power 90, but NIS-$Apriori$ could handle such data sets easily [11].

Generally, a NIS-$Apriori$ rule generator is also applicable to $DISs$ with missing values. In most of tables with categorical data, each domain of attribute values is a finite set. Since any missing value is an element of this finite domain, we replace each missing value with this domain. Then, we can apply our rule generator to such an adjusted NIS. In our framework, the interpretation of missing values seems clear, but instead we needed to face the problem of exponential order of the number of derived $DISs$. We have solved this exponential order problem successfully in the NIS-$Apriori$ algorithm.

8   Management of an Actual Value by Using Intervals

We see an interval $[lower, upper]$ takes the role of non-deterministic information in numerical values. Namely, we see an actual value val^{actual} satisfies $lower \leq val^{actual} \leq upper$. By using this consideration, we can handle the information incompleteness in numerical values.

However, we have a problem for handling numerical attribute values. Namely, the concept defined in Fig. 1 is vague. A set of real numbers is infinite and uncountable. It is necessary to control the figure in a numerical value. We introduced the concept of *resolution* γ (>0) into numerical attributes. An interval $[lower, upper]$ is $definite$, if $(upper - lower) \leq \gamma$. Otherwise, we may have infinite number of derived interval $[lower', upper']$ ($lower \geq lower'$, $upper' \leq upper$ and $(upper' - lower') = \gamma$. By using resolutions, we can have a chart similar to Fig 1 for numerical values [16], but we have another problem. For each discrete set of attribute values VAL_A, we can naturally define a descriptor $[A, val]$ ($val \in VAL_A$). In a set of numerical attribute values, the definition of descriptors is vague. Even though we are currently specifying descriptors for numerical values, we need to consider what is the proper descriptors in a set of numerical attribute values.

In [11], we are showing an execution log for an exemplary data set, which consists of non-deterministic information and intervals.

9 Management of Numerical Patterns and Figures

Now, we consider information incompleteness for numerical values, again. Information incompleteness is a relative concept. For example, let us consider number π. The value 3.14 will be enough for students, but it will be too simple for researcher. This example will also be related to granularity and granular computing.

We introduced two symbols @ and #, which represent numeric from 0 to 9. A *numerical pattern* is a sequence of @ and #, for example @@@, @@#, @##, @@.@ and @#.#. Here, '.' denotes a decimal point, and @ does not occur after #. We see @@@, @@#, @## and ### have the same type ???. Three patterns @@.@, @@.# @#.# have the same type ??.?, too. Here, @ denotes a significant figure and # denotes a figure, which we do not care.

For example, students are seeing π by a numerical pattern @.@@##···, and researchers must be seeing π by a numerical pattern @.@@@@···. Furthermore in baseball games, we often see a season batting average higher than .300 is considered to be excellent player. In this case, we are seeing .300 by a numerical pattern .@##. If we see two players' averages 0.309 and 0.310 by .@##, these two players belong to the same equivalence class. However, if we employ a numerical pattern .@@#, the two players belong to the different equivalence class.

If we employ a fine numerical pattern (with much @ symbols), we obtain the large number of equivalence classes. On the other hand, if we employ a coarse numerical pattern (with less @ symbols), we obtain the small number of equivalence classes. Namely, numerical patterns control the size of equivalence classes, *support* and *accuracy* values. In [14], we coped with numerical patterns, and implemented a software tool.

10 Direct Question-Answering

If the condition $\wedge_i[A_i, val_i]$ matches with the condition part of an obtained certain or possible rule $\wedge_i[A_i, val_i] \Rightarrow [DEC, val_j]$, we have a decision $[DEC, val_j]$ with certainty or possibility.

However, if the condition $\wedge_i[A_i, val_i]$ does not match with the condition part of any obtained rules, we may not have decision from the data set, because $\wedge_i[A_i, val_i]$ may not conclude unique decision attribute value. In such case, we apply direct question-answering, and we know all $[DEC, val_j]$ with $minsupp(\tau_j)$, $minacc(\tau_j)$, $maxsupp(\tau_j)$ and $maxacc(\tau_j)$ which characterize the validity of val_j. Direct question-answering can provide all information for decision making in such case. The following is the real execution handling Table 1.

```
?-qa([[color,red]]).
----- Direct Question/Answering Mode --------
[1] [color,red]==>[price,low]
MINSUPP=0.000,MINACC=0.000,MAXSUPP=0.333,MAXACC=0.500
[2] [color,red]==>[price,high]
MINSUPP=0.333,MINACC=0.500,MAXSUPP=0.667,MAXACC=1.000
EXEC_TIME=0.0(sec)
yes
?-qa([[size,medium],[weight,heavy]]).
----- Direct Question/Answering Mode --------
[1] [size,medium]&[weight,heavy]==>[price,low]
MINSUPP=0.000,MINACC=0.000,MAXSUPP=0.167,MAXACC=1.000
[2] [size,medium]&[weight,heavy]==>[price,high]
MINSUPP=0.000,MINACC=0.000,MAXSUPP=0.500,MAXACC=1.000
EXEC_TIME=0.0(sec)
yes
```

The actual value of *support* is between *minsupp* and *maxsupp*, and the actual value of *accuracy* is between *minacc* and *maxacc*. The *support* and *accuracy* values give us the validity for deciding decision attribute value. In the first case, we will select [*price, high*] instead of [*price, low*]. Similarly in the second case, we know that there is no definite information, but the possibility of [*price, high*] is much high for the condition [*size, medium*]&[*weight, heavy*].

11   Concluding Remarks

This paper surveyed our framework for rough sets-based machine learning over non-deterministic data. In our approach, as illustrated by Figure 1, we need to cope with complexity of possible settings of actual values. We do it by employing the notions of the certainty and the possibility. Specifically, we employ a kind of granular computing method based on the *inf* and *sup* blocks. In particular, in the case of rule generation, our *NIS-Apriori* algorithm escaped from the exponential order problem.

Each of challenges described in this paper is just an entrance of more detailed research. In the next steps, among other requirements, we shall introduce inexact types of data into *NISs*. We also need to categorize algorithmic aspects of learning a *DIS* from a *NIS*.

References

1. Agrawal, R., Srikant, R.: Fast algorithms for mining association rules in large databases. In: Bocca, J.B., Jarke, M., Zaniolo, C. (eds.) VLDB 1994, pp. 487–499. Morgan Kaufmann (1994)

2. Grzymała-Busse, J.W.: Data with Missing Attribute Values: Generalization of Indiscernibility Relation and Rule Induction. In: Peters, J.F., Skowron, A., Grzymała-Busse, J.W., Kostek, B.z., Świniarski, R.W., Szczuka, M.S. (eds.) Transactions on Rough Sets I. LNCS, vol. 3100, pp. 78–95. Springer, Heidelberg (2004)
3. Kryszkiewicz, M.: Rules in incomplete information systems. Information Sciences 113(3-4), 271–292 (1999)
4. Lipski, W.: On databases with incomplete information. Journal of the ACM 28(1), 41–70 (1981)
5. Nakata, M., Sakai, H.: Applying Rough Sets to Information Tables Containing Possibilistic Values. In: Gavrilova, M.L., Tan, C.J.K., Wang, Y., Yao, Y., Wang, G. (eds.) Transactions on Computational Science II. LNCS, vol. 5150, pp. 180–204. Springer, Heidelberg (2008)
6. Orłowska, E., Pawlak, Z.: Representation of nondeterministic information. Theoretical Computer Science 29(1-2), 27–39 (1984)
7. Pawlak, Z.: Systemy Informacyjne: Podstawy Teoretyczne. WNT (1983) (in Polish; English translation: Information Systems: Theoretical Foundations)
8. Pawlak, Z.: Rough Sets: Theoretical Aspects of Reasoning About Data. Kluwer Academic Publishers (1991)
9. Peters, G., Lingras, P., Ślęzak, D., Yao, Y. (eds.): Selected Methods and Applications of Rough Sets in Management and Engineering. Springer (2012)
10. Polkowski, L., Skowron, A. (eds.): Rough Sets in Knowledge Discovery, Parts 1 & 2. Physica-Verlag (1998)
11. RNIA software logs, http://www.mns.kyutech.ac.jp/~sakai/RNIA
12. Sakai, H.: Possible Equivalence Relations and Their Application to Hypothesis Generation in Non-deterministic Information Systems. In: Peters, J.F., Skowron, A., Dubois, D., Grzymała-Busse, J.W., Inuiguchi, M., Polkowski, L. (eds.) Transactions on Rough Sets II. LNCS, vol. 3135, pp. 82–106. Springer, Heidelberg (2004)
13. Sakai, H., Ishibashi, R., Koba, K., Nakata, M.: Rules and Apriori Algorithm in Non-deterministic Information Systems. In: Peters, J.F., Skowron, A., Rybiński, H. (eds.) Transactions on Rough Sets IX. LNCS, vol. 5390, pp. 328–350. Springer, Heidelberg (2008)
14. Sakai, H., Koba, K., Nakata, M.: Rough sets based rule generation from data with categorical and numerical values. Journal of Advanced Computational Intelligence and Intelligent Informatics 12(5), 426–434 (2008)
15. Sakai, H., Okuma, A.: Basic Algorithms and Tools for Rough Non-deterministic Information Analysis. In: Peters, J.F., Skowron, A., Grzymała-Busse, J.W., Kostek, B.z., Świniarski, R.W., Szczuka, M.S. (eds.) Transactions on Rough Sets I. LNCS, vol. 3100, pp. 209–231. Springer, Heidelberg (2004)
16. Sakai, H., Nakata, M., Ślęzak, D.: A Prototype System for Rule Generation in Lipski's Incomplete Information Databases. In: Kuznetsov, S.O., Ślęzak, D., Hepting, D.H., Mirkin, B.G. (eds.) RSFDGrC 2011. LNCS, vol. 6743, pp. 175–182. Springer, Heidelberg (2011)
17. Sakai, H., Okuma, H., Nakata, M., Ślęzak, D.: Stable rule extraction and decision making in rough non-deterministic information analysis. International Journal of Hybrid Intelligent Systems 8(1), 41–57 (2011)
18. UCI Machine Learning Repository, http://mlearn.ics.uci.edu/MLRepository.html

A Role of (Not) Crisp Discernibility in Rough Set Approach to Numeric Feature Selection[*]

Dominik Ślęzak[1,2] and Paweł Betliński[1]

[1] Institute of Mathematics, University of Warsaw
Banacha 2, 02-097 Warsaw, Poland
[2] Infobright Inc.
Krzywickiego 34 pok. 219, 02-078 Warsaw, Poland

Abstract. We investigate the rough-set-based framework for feature selection in decision tables with numeric attributes. We compare functions evaluating subsets of attributes with respect to their potential in determining the distinguished decision attribute by means of two alternative methods: discernibility-based functions over discretized numeric data, as well as distance-based functions often used in the fuzzy-rough approaches to feature selection. In both cases, the idea is to compare objects belonging to different decision classes, by verifying whether they can be distinguished from each other by using discretized attributes or measuring distances between their values over original numeric attributes. We draw a correspondence between functions evaluating subsets of numeric attributes according to both methodologies. For a subset of numeric attributes, we consider a function measuring the amount of pairs of objects belonging to different decision classes that are not discerned by discretized attributes, averaged over all possible choices of binary discretization cuts over the attribute ranges. We prove that such a function can be rewritten by means of distances between the original numeric attributes. Namely, it is equal to the average fuzzy indiscernibility function computed by using the product t-norm combining indiscernibility degrees obtained over particular attributes.

Keywords: Feature selection, Rough sets, Discernibility, Numeric data.

1 Introduction

Decision support systems are based on models, which represent knowledge in a possibly compact form. The process of deriving decision models from data is often referred to as the knowledge discovery in databases (KDD). It consists of steps such as selection of the most representative features, analysis of dependencies between them, as well as extraction, evaluation and interpretation of the most meaningful patterns [5,6]. The data mining approaches utilized in KDD can be divided into *symbolic* and *non-symbolic* methods. Symbolic methods focus on finding relationships within data, often reported in a form of rules in a feature-value language. Non-symbolic methods are focused on classification properties of

[*] Supported by the Polish National Science Centre grant 2011/01/B/ST6/03867.

A. Ell Hassanien et al. (Eds.): AMLTA 2012, CCIS 322, pp. 13–23, 2012.

data rather than data patterns or if-then dependencies. Non-symbolic methods may achieve high accuracy but they are hard to understand by decision-makers. Symbolic methods may be easier to modify by involving domain knowledge. Therefore, many researchers attempt to combine advantages of both approaches within various types of hybrid decision models [13,29].

Depending on a problem's nature, the decision model can take various forms imposed by the applied methods. Prediction, segmentation and relationship discovering are the typical data mining tasks reflecting the users' needs. However, according to the principles of the KDD process, the prior step should always be related to feature selection [8,27], which leads to an increase of interpretability and usefulness of decision systems regardless of the choice of a specific data mining methodology. Even the most complicated methods yield clearer outcomes when applied to data with significantly less features. Sometimes it is even worth working with a number of less accurate sub-models learnt from far smaller feature subsets, in order to expose different aspects of the problem and the underlying data. It is worth doing even given an additional requirement of fusion of such sub-models into the final decision model [1,28].

We concentrate on feature selection techniques arising from the theory of rough sets [20,21], which were successfully applied within various hybrid decision systems [10,18]. The rough-set-based feature selection methodology is based on *decision reducts* – irreducible subsets of attributes, which determine specified decision classes. Subsets of attributes providing exactly the same degree of determination as the original set are often referred to as *crisp* decision reducts, in opposite to so called *approximate* decision reducts [17,24], where some controlled decrease of determination is allowed. It is often claimed that rough sets are not suitable for non-categorical data types because of a specific way of evaluating attributes. However, as clearly visible also in this paper, rough set methods of feature selection and decision model construction have been successfully applied to numeric data and some other types of data as well [7,26].

It is worth noting that during the decision model design phase one can choose which of the data mining techniques will be later applied in the model. Therefore, one may attempt to adjust the feature selection criteria to specific data mining algorithms to be used later. In the case of rough sets, the most typical optimization function refers to the feature subsets' cardinality, while the constraints of feature elimination often refer to the ability to discern pairs of objects belonging to different decision classes by the remaining attributes. However, the way of understanding discernibility between objects may vary with respect to the type of the data and the type of a decision algorithm. For instance, if one considers construction of a decision tree or forest for a numeric data set [9,19], then the feature selection criterion may relate to a function evaluating ability to discern objects by subsets of discretized attributes. We will refer to this approach as to the crisp discernibility. As another example, if a decision model is supposed to rely on distances or similarities defined over numeric feature domains, then the notion of discernibility utilized in rough-set-based feature selection might take a softer form based on, e.g., fuzzy indiscernibility relations [4,12].

In this paper, we compare the feature evaluation criteria based on crisp and fuzzy discernibility. We prove an interesting fact illustrating that criteria for determining decision classes basing on original discernibility over discretized attributes and fuzzy distance-based discernibility over original numeric attributes are not so far away. This shows that discernibility-based feature selection criteria provide a truly rich foundation for a mixture of symbolic and non-symbolic methods that can be used to discover knowledge from numeric data sets.

The paper is organized as follows. Section 2 outlines the basics of rough set approach to feature selection, focusing on the notions based on discernibility and fuzzy indiscernibility. Section 3 reports some already-known discernibility-based evaluation functions and related results developed within the theory of rough sets for single numeric features. Section 4 reports the above-mentioned mathematical link between crisp and fuzzy discernibility feature selection criteria, which generalizes the previous investigations onto the case of arbitrary subsets of numeric attributes and provides a common framework for handling categorical and numeric decision features. Section 5 concludes the paper.

2   Rough Sets and Feature Selection

Feature subsets can be searched using various approaches, following *filter, wrapper,* or *embedded* paradigms [8,16]. In the filter approach, the feature subset(s) are selected as a preprocessing step. Selected features or feature subsets are then used by a learning algorithm to construct a decision model. Feature subset evaluation is a part of the selection process and it does not depend on the learning algorithm. The phase of learning a decision model based on the previously found feature subset(s) may have nothing in common with the criteria and algorithms employed in the phase of feature selection.

The rough-set-based feature selection methods are usually regarded as an example of the filter approach, although sometimes they are interpreted as an embedded approach as well, especially if the derived subsets of attributes are utilized to construct rule-based classifiers. There are numerous rough-set-based algorithms aimed at searching for decision reducts, which are irreducible subsets of features that satisfy predefined criteria of (approximate) determination of decision features [21,28]. Those criteria are verified on the training data and can encode more or less directly the risk of misclassification by if-then rules with their left sides referring to the values of investigated feature subsets and their right sides referring to decisions. Discovered decision reducts can be followed by arbitrary learning algorithms [10,18]. The general focus on the space of feature subsets rather than on single features has resulted in a number of intelligent search techniques documented in rough set literature [2,30].

Let us use the standard notation of information systems to represent the data [20,21]. By an information system we mean a tuple $\mathbb{A} = (U, A)$, where U is a set of objects and A is a set of attributes. We treat attributes $a \in A$ as functions $a : U \to V_a$, V_a denoting a's domain. By a decision table we mean $\mathbb{A} = (U, A \cup \{d\})$, where $d \notin A$ is a distinguished decision attribute. The values

$v_d \in V_d$ usually correspond to decision classes that we want to describe using the values of A. However, one may consider the situations where decision values are numeric and the task is to approximate rather than classify them.

We say that subset $B \subseteq A$ discerns objects $u, u' \in U$, if and only if there exists $b \in B$ such that $b(u) \neq b(u')$. We say that $B \subseteq A$ is a decision reduct for $\mathbb{A} = (U, A \cup \{d\})$, if and only if it is an irreducible subset of attributes such that for each pair of objects $u, u' \in U$ satisfying inequality $d(u) \neq d(u')$, if they are discerned by A, then they must be also discerned by B. Surely, in the case of large real-world data sets there may be some weakened versions of the notion of a decision reduct considered. According to one of them, we may be interested in searching for irreducible subsets of attributes $B \subseteq A$, which discern almost all pairs of objects with different decision values that are discerned by A. As another example, we can consider decision tables with numeric attributes $a \in A$, where the whole notion of discernibility needs to be reconsidered, as operating with inequalities of the form $a(u) \neq a(u')$ does not make sense in practice.

Out of many approaches that extend the standard discernibility-based formulation of a decision reducts onto the case of numeric attributes, let us focus for a while on utilization of fuzzy indiscernibility relations [4,12], where the basic idea is to avoid pairs of objects from different decision classes with high degree of indiscernibility or fuzzy similarity. In other words, a given subset of attributes should be penalized for any of such pairs. Mathematically, we can express such a penalty measure as a kind of aggregation of the similarity quantities of the form

$$R_B(u, u') = \mathcal{T}_{b \in B}(R_b(u, u')) \tag{1}$$

over all pairs of objects $u, u' \in U$ such that $d(u) \neq d(u')$, where $\mathcal{T}$ denotes a fuzzy T-norm and the quantities of $R_b(u, u')$ are computed directly from the data as normalized similarities between the numeric values $b(u)$ and $b(u')$.

In the same way, in the case of numeric or fuzzy decision, we should avoid objects with low degree of indiscernibility with respect to decisions and high degree of indiscernibility with respect to an evaluated subset of attributes. For the sake of clarity, let us denote a numeric decision attribute as d^* and assume that there is given a fuzzy similarity measure of the form $R_{d^*}(u, u')$. Then, while searching for subsets of attributes that are able to approximate decision values we should pay attention to the quantities of the following form:

$$\mathcal{T}(1 - R_{d^*}(u, u'), R_B(u, u')) \tag{2}$$

The notion of an approximate decision reduct can be then reformulated as a minimal subset of attributes $B \subseteq A$ that keeps an aggregate value of the above quantities as not *significantly* higher than in the case of using the whole A.

The feature selection mechanisms based on the above fuzzy indiscernibility criteria seem to be especially useful in combination with the classification techniques relying on similarities between objects [1,11]. On the other hand, one may argue that operating with T-norms calculated for the pairs of objects may be not feasible for decision tables with large universes. Thus, let us also consider an alternative approach popular in the rough set literature – discretization of numeric attributes, i.e., their translation to symbolic features that are further utilized to build decision models [2,19].

For discretized data the above penalty functions simply refer to counting how many pairs belonging to different decision classes are not discerned by particular subsets of attributes. More precisely, let $\mathbb{A} = (U, A \cup \{d\})$ be a decision table, $B \subseteq A$ be a subset of numeric attributes, and $cut_B = \{(b, cut_b) : b \in B, cut_b \in (\underline{b}, \overline{b})\}$ be a set of cuts over the domains of attributes $b \in B$, where $\underline{b} = min_{u \in U} b(u)$ and $\overline{b} = max_{u \in U} b(u)$. For the sake of simplicity, we write cut instead of cut_B.

We say that two objects $u, u' \in U$ are discerned by cut over B, which we denote as $B(u) \parallel_{cut} B(u')$, if there is at least one $b \in B$ such that $min(b(u), b(u')) < cut_b < max(b(u), b(u'))$. Analogously, by $B(u) \not\parallel_{cut} B(u')$ we denote the fact that objects $u, u' \in U$ are *not* discerned by cut over B. For such a kind of binary discretization, the above penalty function takes the following form:

$$Ind(d/cut) = |\{(u, u') : d(u) \neq d(u'), B(u) \not\parallel_{cut} B(u')\}|. \qquad (3)$$

Although such a function is formulated over the pairs of objects as before, its computation depends on only cardinalities of indiscernibility classes defined by decision values and the cuts over numeric attributes. The question is, however, how to choose the cuts. In the literature, we can find a number of approaches spanning from intelligent heuristics to fully random cut generation. We can also find attempts to measure numeric attributes subsets quality via evaluating classifiers based on dynamic discretization of those attributes [14,22].

Let us also discuss how the discretization-based approach could be adapted to the case of numeric decision d^*. Consider the following function:

$$Ind(cut^*/cut) = |\{(u, u') : d^*(u) \parallel_{cut^*} d^*(u'), B(u) \not\parallel_{cut} B(u')\}|, \qquad (4)$$

where by $d^*(u) \parallel_{cut} d^*(u')$ we mean that the numeric values $d^*(u)$ and $d^*(u')$ are separated by $cut^* \in (\underline{d^*}, \overline{d^*})\}$, where $\underline{d^*} = min_{u \in U} d^*(u)$ and $\overline{d^*} = max_{u \in U} d^*(u)$. Consider a simple approach where we create an ensemble of classifiers learnt over attributes and decisions discretized in various random ways and then combine their outcomes by means of intersecting the decision ranges defined by intervals $(\underline{d^*}, cut^*)$ and $(cut^*, \overline{d^*})$ obtained from each of such classifiers. In this paper we investigate mathematical relationships between the expected quality of such classifiers and the measures of fuzzy indiscernibility of the form (1) and (2).

3 Discernibility Functions for Feature Evaluation

Naturally, discretization is more often used as a preprocessing step in the case of symbolic methods, than in the case of similarity-based methods mentioned in the previous section. What might be useful to perform before discretization is feature selection, that is choosing most promising attributes in the sense of ability to determine decision after their discretization - but de facto without performing any discretization, that is without any modification of attributes domain before their selection. In this section we remind some measures of quality for single numeric attribute, which try to release this idea.

Direct approach to rank attribute in the context of its further discretization is to estimate average attribute quality for randomly chosen cuts. We define this crisp discernibility measure for some given attribute a as follows:

$$Disc(d/a) = \frac{1}{\overline{a} - \underline{a}} \int_{\underline{a}}^{\overline{a}} Disc(d/cut)dcut, \tag{5}$$

where $Disc(d/cut)$ is the following natural measure of quality of the cut:

$$Disc(d/cut) = |\{(u, u') : d(u) \neq d(u'), \{a\}(u) \parallel_{cut} \{a\}(u')\}|. \tag{6}$$

It can be noticed, that in formula (5) there is one hidden assumption - random cuts are uniformly distributed over the range of attribute a. This is because of the fact that we do not assume any a priori knowledge about the placement of these cuts. Of course more general setting can be considered, where the distribution is modifiable according to user preferences. It turns out, that this measure is strongly correlated with the following fuzzy discernibility one:

$$Dist(d/a) = \sum_{u,u':d(u) \neq d(u')} \frac{|a(u) - a(u')|}{\overline{a} - \underline{a}}. \tag{7}$$

Measure $Dist(d/.)$ is high for such attribute, that pairs of objects from different decision classes are far away according to value of this attribute. The interesting property is that $Disc$ and $Dist$ are equivalent, that is for every $a \in A$:

$$Dist(d/a) = Disc(d/a). \tag{8}$$

This fact was first informally mentioned in [25], where it was utilized to design appropriate optimization functions for the task of searching for linear combinations of the original numeric features that would be the best in order to build a k-NN classifier [1,11]. The complete proof of the above fact was published a couple of years later in the PhD thesis of the first author [23]. This fact has a practical meaning - instead of calculating measure according to integral formula (5) we can perform equivalent and efficient calculation using formula (7).

In the next section we will consider more general forms of the following measures, which are in fact reversed versions of $Dist$ and $Disc$ respectively:

$$Sim(d/a) = \sum_{u,u':d(u) \neq d(u')} \left(1 - \frac{|a(u) - a(u')|}{\overline{a} - \underline{a}}\right), \tag{9}$$

$$Ind(d/a) = \frac{1}{\overline{a} - \underline{a}} \int_{\underline{a}}^{\overline{a}} Ind(d/cut)dcut, \tag{10}$$

where $Ind(d/cut)$ is like in (3) when putting $B = \{a\}$.

It is easy to see that property (8) is equivalent to the following one:

$$Sim(d/a) = Ind(d/a), \tag{11}$$

because $Dist(d/a) + Sim(d/a) = |\{(u, u') : d(u) \neq d(u')\}|$ and $Disc(d/a) + Ind(d/a) = |\{(u, u') : d(u) \neq d(u')\}|$.

All these measures and property (11) are only for single attribute, while analogical result for measures ranking arbitrary subsets of numeric features has been missing. This generalization is the topic of the next section. Obviously, ability of evaluating the subsets of features with respect to their joint discernibility potential is crucial for feature selection.

4   The Main Result

Let us recall that an (approximate) decision reduct is an irreducible subset of attributes that provide (almost) the same level of information about decision as the whole initial set of attributes. The level of information is usually described by a measure that estimates an ability to train an accurate classifier basing on the attributes in a given subset. In the previous sections, we mentioned that the rough set criteria for evaluating attribute subsets may borrow some analogies from other areas of data analysis. We also provided some measures for evaluation of single numeric attributes. Now, we are going to consider the discernibility-based feature subset evaluation functions that can be utilized to search for approximate decision reducts over numeric attributes.

Let $I_B = \times_{b \in B}[\underline{b}, \overline{b}]$. Let us define the following two measures:

$$Sim(d/B) = \sum_{u,u':d(u) \neq d(u')} \prod_{b \in B} \left(1 - \frac{|b(u) - b(u')|}{\overline{b} - \underline{b}}\right), \tag{12}$$

$$Ind(d/B) = \prod_{b \in B} \frac{1}{\overline{b} - \underline{b}} \int_{I_B} Ind(d/cut)dcut, \tag{13}$$

where $Ind(d/cut)$ takes the form of (3).

The fuzzy indiscernibility measure (12) is consistent with the general form presented in first section, each element of the sum is a special case of (1) for product T-norm and $R_b(u, u') = 1 - |b(u) - b(u')|/(\overline{b} - \underline{b})$, which is very popular in the literature [4,12]. As in the previous section, we assume uniform distribution of cuts. Our main result in this paper is as follows:

Theorem 1. $Sim(d/B) = Ind(d/B)$.

Proof. After simple reformulation, we need to prove that:

$$\int_{I_B} Ind(d/cut)dcut = \sum_{u,u':d(u) \neq d(u')} \prod_{b \in B} \left((\overline{b} - \underline{b}) - |b(u) - b(u')|\right). \tag{14}$$

$\int_{I_B} Ind(d/cut)dcut$ is equal to $\int_{I_B} \sum_{u,u':d(u) \neq d(u')} \chi_{\{cut:B(u)\varkappa_{cut}B(u')\}}dcut$ and then to $\sum_{u,u':d(u) \neq d(u')} \int_{I_B} \chi_{\{cut:B(u)\varkappa_{cut}B(u')\}}dcut$, where $\chi_{\{cut:B(u)\varkappa_{cut}B(u')\}}$ denotes a characteristic function of the set of all combinations of cuts over B, for which objects u and u' are not discerned.

It is now sufficient to show that for every $u, u' \in U$ the following holds:

$$\int_{I_B} \chi_{\{cut : B(u) \nparallel_{cut} B(u')\}} dcut = \prod_{b \in B} \left((\bar{b} - \underline{b}) - |b(u) - b(u')| \right). \qquad (15)$$

Denote by $L_{b(u) \nparallel b(u')} = [\underline{b}, min(b(u), b(u'))] \cup [max(b(u), b(u')), \bar{b}]$ the union of intervals, for which $cut_b \in (\underline{b}, \bar{b})$ does not discern u and u' over $b \in B$. Further, let us put $L_{B(u) \nparallel B(u')} = \times_{b \in B} L_{b(u) \nparallel b(u')}$. As both sides of the above equality (15) can be equivalently rewritten as $\int_{L_{B(u) \nparallel B(u')}} 1 dcut$, the proof is finished. $\square$

The above result can be also rephrased for the sake of the equality between the following measures that do not take into account the decision attribute:

$$Sim(B) = \sum_{u,u'} \prod_{b \in B} \left(1 - \frac{|b(u) - b(u')|}{\bar{b} - \underline{b}} \right), \qquad (16)$$

$$Ind(B) = \prod_{b \in B} \frac{1}{\bar{b} - \underline{b}} \int_{I_B} Ind(cut) dcut, \qquad (17)$$

where $Ind(cut) = |\{(u, u') : B(u) \nparallel_{cut} B(u')\}|$. Indeed, the proof of $Sim(B) = Ind(B)$ is analogous – it is enough to remove $d(u) \neq d(u')$ when applicable.

Furthermore, we can consider an analogous version of the above theorem for the case of numeric decision. For the sake of clarity, let us denote the numeric decision attribute by d^* in order to distinguish it from the symbolic decision attribute d. The question is how the classification problem specified for d could be translated to the approximation problem for d^*. The related question is how to define the measures of $Sim(d^*/B)$ and $Ind(d^*/B)$. In the first case, the idea is to focus particularly on the pairs of objects which have relatively distant decision values and relatively similar attribute values. The following measure is a special case of aggregation of quantities of the form (2) considered in Section 2:

$$Sim(d^*/B) = \sum_{u,u'} \frac{|d^*(u) - d^*(u')|}{\bar{d^*} - \underline{d^*}} \prod_{b \in B} \left(1 - \frac{|b(u) - b(u')|}{\bar{b} - \underline{b}} \right). \qquad (18)$$

In the second case, let us put

$$Ind(d^*/B) = \frac{1}{\bar{d^*} - \underline{d^*}} \prod_{b \in B} \frac{1}{\bar{b} - \underline{b}} \int_{I_B} \int_{\underline{d^*}}^{\bar{d^*}} Ind(cut^*/cut) dcut^* dcut, \qquad (19)$$

where $Ind(cut^*/cut)$ takes the form of (4) and where, as before, we assume a uniform distribution over the binary cuts of the decision attribute domain.

The following result shows the relationship analogous to Theorem 1. Actually, let us note that both in the case of $Sim(d^*/B)$ and $Sim(d/B)$, as well as $Ind(d^*/B)$ and $Ind(d/B)$, we deal with two versions of a more general attribute dependency formula defined for symbolic and numeric decisions, respectively.

Theorem 2. $Sim(d^*/B) = Ind(d^*/B)$.

Proof. It is enough to note that $Sim(d^*/B) = Sim(B) - Sim(B \cup \{d^*\})$ and $Ind(d^*/B) = Ind(B) - Ind(B \cup \{d^*\})$. $\square$

5   Conclusions

In this work we have considered two types of indiscernibility measures, together with their variations and generalizations. First type are fuzzy indiscernibility measures, where we refer directly to original values of numerical attributes. The second type are crisp indiscernibility measures, where evaluation is based on discretization. We have shown the equivalence of both types.

This result is important not only from a purely mathematical perspective. It also provides new intuition with regard to algorithms developed for searching for optimal feature subsets and interpretation of classifiers that are based on such subsets obtained using various criteria for determining decisions.

Thanks to the above equivalence, we have a free choice which measure to use for calculation. Fuzzy criteria can be efficiently utilized to perform attribute selection for relatively small data sets, while for larger data we can speed up both types of calculations by using, e.g., random cut generation.

This part of our future research is closely related to the topic of scalability of rough-set-based algorithms, which is particularly challenging with respect to fast heuristic evaluation of subsets of numeric attributes [14,15].

Another interesting aspect relates to the tasks involving numeric decision attributes – a special case of complex decision problems, where standard decision classes may be replaced by other some types of structures [3,7].

References

1. Bay, S.D.: Combining Nearest Neighbor Classifiers Through Multiple Feature Subsets. In: Proc. of ICML, pp. 37–45 (1998)
2. Bazan, J.G., Nguyen, H.S., Nguyen, S.H., Synak, P., Wróblewski, J.: Rough Set Algorithms in Classification Problem. In: Polkowski, L., Tsumoto, S., Lin, T.Y. (eds.) New Developments in Knowledge Discovery in Information Systems, pp. 49–88. Physica Verlag (2000)
3. Bazan, J.G., Skowron, A., Ślęzak, D., Wróblewski, J.: Searching for the Complex Decision Reducts: The Case Study of the Survival Analysis. In: Zhong, N., Raś, Z.W., Tsumoto, S., Suzuki, E. (eds.) ISMIS 2003. LNCS (LNAI), vol. 2871, pp. 160–168. Springer, Heidelberg (2003)
4. Cornelis, C., Jensen, R., Hurtado Martín, G., Ślęzak, D.: Attribute Selection with Fuzzy Decision Reducts. Information Sciences 180(2), 209–224 (2010)
5. Düntsch, I., Gediga, G., Nguyen, H.S.: Rough Set Data Analysis in the KDD Process. In: Proc. of IPMU, pp. 220–226 (2000)
6. Fayyad, U., Piatetsky-Shapiro, G., Smyth, P.: From Data Mining to Knowledge Discovery in Databases. AI Magazine 17(3), 37–54 (1996)
7. Greco, S., Matarazzo, B., Słowiński, R.: Rough Sets Theory for Multicriteria Decision Analysis. European Journal of Operational Research 129(1), 1–47 (2001)
8. Guyon, I., Elisseeff, A.: An Introduction to Variable and Feature Selection. Journal of Machine Learning Research 3, 1157–1182 (2003)

9. Ho, T.K.: The Random Subspace Method for Constructing Decision Forests. IEEE Transactions on Pattern Analysis and Machine Intelligence 20(8), 832–844 (1998)
10. Hung, Y.H.: A Neural Network Classifier with Rough Set-based Feature Selection to Classify Multiclass IC Package Products. Advanced Engineering Informatics 23(3), 348–357 (2009)
11. Jensen, R., Cornelis, C.: Fuzzy-Rough Nearest Neighbour Classification. In: Peters, J.F., Skowron, A., Chan, C.-C., Grzymala-Busse, J.W., Ziarko, W.P. (eds.) Transactions on Rough Sets XIII. LNCS, vol. 6499, pp. 56–72. Springer, Heidelberg (2011)
12. Jensen, R., Shen, Q.: New Approaches to Fuzzy-Rough Feature Selection. IEEE Transactions on Fuzzy Systems 17(4), 824–838 (2009)
13. Kovalerchuk, B., Vityaev, E., Yupusov, H.: Symbolic Methodology in Numeric Data Mining: Relational Techniques for Financial Applications. Computational Engineering, Finance, and Science Journal (2002)
14. Kowalski, M., Stawicki, S.: SQL-based Heuristics for Selected KDD Tasks over Large Data Sets. In: Proc. of FedCSIS (2012)
15. Kwiatkowski, P., Nguyen, S.H., Nguyen, H.S.: On Scalability of Rough Set Methods. In: Hüllermeier, E., Kruse, R., Hoffmann, F. (eds.) IPMU 2010, Part I. CCIS, vol. 80, pp. 288–297. Springer, Heidelberg (2010)
16. Lal, T., Chapelle, O., Weston, J., Elisseeff, A.: Embedded Methods. In: Guyon, I., Gunn, S., Nikravesh, M., Zadeh, L. (eds.) Feature Extraction, Foundations and Applications. Springer (2005)
17. Moshkov, M.J., Piliszczuk, M., Zielosko, B.: On Partial Covers, Reducts and Decision Rules. In: Peters, J.F., Skowron, A. (eds.) Transactions on Rough Sets VIII. LNCS, vol. 5084, pp. 251–288. Springer, Heidelberg (2008)
18. Nair, B.B., Mohandas, V.P., Sakthivel, N.R.: A Decision Tree- Rough set Hybrid System for Stock Market Trend Prediction. International Journal of Computer Applications 6(9), 1–6 (2010)
19. Nguyen, H.S.: Approximate Boolean Reasoning: Foundations and Applications in Data Mining. In: Peters, J.F., Skowron, A. (eds.) Transactions on Rough Sets V. LNCS, vol. 4100, pp. 334–506. Springer, Heidelberg (2006)
20. Pawlak, Z.: Rough Sets – Theoretical Aspects of Reasoning about Data. Kluwer (1991)
21. Pawlak, Z., Skowron, A.: Rudiments of Rough Sets. Information Sciences 177(1), 3–27 (2007)
22. Rudnicki, W.R., Kierczak, M., Koronacki, J., Komorowski, J.: A Statistical Method for Determining Importance of Variables in an Information System. In: Greco, S., Hata, Y., Hirano, S., Inuiguchi, M., Miyamoto, S., Nguyen, H.S., Słowiński, R. (eds.) RSCTC 2006. LNCS (LNAI), vol. 4259, pp. 557–566. Springer, Heidelberg (2006)
23. Ślęzak, D.: Approximate Decision Reducts. PhD Thesis, University of Warsaw, Poland (2002) (In Polish)
24. Ślęzak, D.: Degrees of Conditional (In)dependence: A Framework for Approximate Bayesian Networks and Examples Related to the Rough Set-based Feature Selection. Information Sciences 179(3), 197–209 (2009)
25. Ślęzak, D., Wróblewski, J.: Classification Algorithms Based on Linear Combinations of Features. In: Żytkow, J.M., Rauch, J. (eds.) PKDD 1999. LNCS (LNAI), vol. 1704, pp. 548–553. Springer, Heidelberg (1999)
26. Stepaniuk, J.: Approximation Spaces, Reducts and Representations. In: Polkowski, L., Skowron, A. (eds.) Rough Sets in Knowledge Discovery 2, pp. 109–126. Physica Verlag (1998)

27. Świniarski, R.W., Skowron, A.: Rough Set Methods in Feature Selection and Recognition. Pattern Recognition Letters 24(6), 833–849 (2003)
28. Widz, S., Ślęzak, D.: Rough Set Based Decision Support – Models Easy to Interpret. In: Peters, G., Lingras, P., Ślęzak, D., Yao, Y. (eds.) Selected Methods and Applications of Rough Sets in Management and Engineering, Springer (2012)
29. Wojna, A.: Combination of Metric-Based and Rule-Based Classification. In: Ślęzak, D., Wang, G., Szczuka, M.S., Düntsch, I., Yao, Y. (eds.) RSFDGrC 2005, Part I. LNCS (LNAI), vol. 3641, pp. 501–511. Springer, Heidelberg (2005)
30. Wróblewski, J.: Ensembles of Classifiers Based on Approximate Reducts. Fundamenta Informaticae 47(3-4), 351–360 (2001)

Learning a Table from a Table
with Non-deterministic Information:
A Perspective*

Mao Wu[1], Naoto Yamaguchi[1], Michinori Nakata[2], and Hiroshi Sakai[1]

[1] Faculty of Engineering, Kyushu Institute of Technology
Tobata, Kitakyushu 804, Japan
`wumogaku@yahoo.co.jp`, `KITYN1124@gmail.com`,
`sakai@mns.kyutech.ac.jp`
[2] Faculty of Management and Information Science
Josai International University
Gumyo, Togane, Chiba 283, Japan
`nakatam@ieee.org`

Abstract. *Rough Non-deterministic Information Analysis (RNIA)* is a rough sets-based framework for handling tables with exact and inexact data. In this framework, we have mainly investigated rough sets-based concepts in a table with non-deterministic information and some algorithms. This paper considers perspective on a new issue that how we estimate a table with actual information from a table with non-deterministic information by adding some constraint. This issue in *RNIA* slightly seems analogous to backpropagation in Neural Networks.

Keywords: Estimation of actual information, Constraint, Rough sets, Data dependency, Rules.

1 Introduction

Rough set theory offers a mathematical approach to vagueness [7]. It has many applications related to the areas of classification, feature reduction, rule generation, machine learning, data mining, knowledge discovery and others [8, 9]. Rough set theory is usually employed to deal with data tables with deterministic information, which we call *Deterministic Information Systems (DISs)*. *Non-deterministic Information systems (NISs)* [5, 6] and *Incomplete Information systems* [3, 4] have also been investigated in order to handle information incompleteness.

We have been interested in *NISs*, and investigated *possible equivalence relations, data dependencies, rule generation, rule stability, question-answering systems,* as well as *missing* and *interval values* in *NISs* [10–16]. In each aspect,

---

* This work is supported by the Grant-in-Aid for Scientific Research (C) (No.22500204), Japan Society for the Promotion of Science.

A. Ell Hassanien et al. (Eds.): AMLTA 2012, CCIS 322, pp. 24–32, 2012.

modal concepts are employed, and each aspect is extended to two modes, namely the *certainty* and the *possibility*, or the *minimum* value and the *maximum* value.

In this paper, we describe perspective on new issue in *RNIA*. Namely, we consider methods that we estimate a table with actual information from a table with non-deterministic information by adding some constraint. This paper is organized as follows: Section 2 recalls the foundations of *RNIA*. Section 3 proposes to estimate a *DIS* from a *NIS* by consistency, dependency and rules. Section 4 concludes this paper.

2   Foundations of RNIA

A *Non-deterministic Information System (NIS)* Φ is a quadruplet [5–7].

$\Phi = (OB, AT, \{VAL_A | A \in AT\}, g)$,
OB : *finite set whose elements are called objects,*
AT : *a finite set whose elements are called attributes,*
VAL_A : *a finite set whose elements are called attribute values,*
$g : OB \times AT \rightarrow P(\cup_{A \in AT} VAL_A)$ (*a power set of* $\cup_{A \in AT} VAL_A$).

Every set $g(x, A)$ is interpreted as that there is an actual value in this set but this value is not known [5–7]. Especially if the real value is not known at all, $g(x, A)$ is equal to VAL_A. This is called the *null value* interpretation or missing value [3, 4]. We usually consider a table instead of this quadruplet Φ. Table 1 is an exemplary *NIS* Φ_1.

Table 1. An exemplary *NIS* Φ_1 for the suitcase data sets. Here, $VAL_{Color}=\{red, blue, green\}$, $VAL_{Size}=\{small, medium, large\}$, $VAL_{Weight}=\{light, heavy\}$, $VAL_{Price}=\{high, low\}$. In Φ_1, $g(x_1, Color)=VAL_{Color}$, and this means there is no information about this attribute value.

Object	Color	Size	Weight	Price
x_1	$\{red, blue, green\}$	$\{small\}$	$\{light, heavy\}$	$\{low\}$
x_2	$\{red\}$	$\{small, medium\}$	$\{light, heavy\}$	$\{high\}$
x_3	$\{red, blue\}$	$\{small, medium\}$	$\{light\}$	$\{high\}$
x_4	$\{red\}$	$\{medium\}$	$\{heavy\}$	$\{low, high\}$
x_5	$\{red\}$	$\{small, medium, large\}$	$\{heavy\}$	$\{high\}$
x_6	$\{blue, green\}$	$\{large\}$	$\{heavy\}$	$\{low, high\}$

Now, we introduce a *derived DIS* from a *NIS*, and show the basic chart in *RNIA*. Since each VAL_A $(A \in AT)$ is finite, we can generate a *DIS* by replacing each non-deterministic information $g(x, A)$ with an element in $g(x, A)$. We named such a *DIS* a *derived DIS* from a *NIS*, and define the following.

$$DD(\Phi) = \{\psi \mid \psi \text{ is a derived DIS from a NIS } \Phi\}.$$

In Φ_1, there are 2304 ($=3^2 \times 2^8$) derived *DISs*. The following *DIS* ψ_1 is an element of $DD(\Phi_1)$, namely $\psi_1 \in DD(\Phi_1)$ holds.

Table 2. A derived *DIS* ψ_1 from Φ_1

Object	Color	Size	Weight	Price
x_1	red	small	light	low
x_2	red	small	light	high
x_3	red	small	light	high
x_4	red	medium	heavy	low
x_5	red	small	heavy	high
x_6	blue	large	heavy	low

Due to the interpretation of non-deterministic information, we see an actual *DIS* ψ^{actual} exists in this 2304 derived *DISs*. Like this, we usually consider a set $DD(\Phi)$ of derived *DISs* and the *basic chart* in Fig.1. We also coped with next modality.

(Certainty). If a formula α holds in every $\psi \in DD(\Phi)$, α also holds in ψ^{actual}. In this case, we say α *certainly holds* in ψ^{actual}.
(Possibility). If a formula α holds in some $\psi \in DD(\Phi)$, there exists such a possibility that α holds in ψ^{actual}. In this case, we say α *possibly holds* in ψ^{actual}.

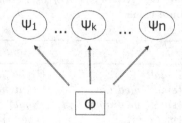

Fig. 1. An basic chart for Φ and a set $DD(\Phi)$ of derived *DISs*

Even if there exists the information incompleteness in Φ, we have the following decision making.

(1) If a formula α certainly holds, we think α holds under the uncertainty.
(2) If a formula α possibly holds, we think α may hold under the uncertainty.
(3) Otherwise, we think α does not hold under the uncertainty.

3   Learning a DIS from a NIS by Constraint

This section considers to estimate an actual DIS from a NIS.

3.1   A New Issue in RNIA

In the basic chart in Fig. 1, we considered $DD(\Phi)$ and defined the certainty and the possibility. We have already proposed some algorithms for handling them, and each algorithm is implicitly supposing some derived $DISs$ for concluding two modalities. Namely, our previous work in $RNIA$ took the following input and output.

(Previous Issue in $RNIA$)
Input: A NIS,
Output: Certain and possible conclusions with a set of supposed derived $DISs$.

In this paper, we consider the converse in output. Namely, we give constraint, and we estimate a set of supposed derived $DISs$.

(New Issue in $RNIA$)
Input: A NIS,
Output: A set of supposed derived $DISs$ for concluding given constraint.

In each constraint, we have a set M_γ (γ: constraint) of derived $DISs$, and we will estimate an actual DIS as an element of $\cap_\gamma M_\gamma$. In the following subsections, we enumerate constraint, and intuitively explain each manipulation by using Φ_1.

3.2   Constraint 1: An Equivalence Class

A *possible equivalence class* X in $ATR \subset AT$ is a set of objects whose attribute values in each $A \in ATR$ are the same in a DIS $\psi \in DD(\Phi)$. Therefore, we are implicitly obtaining ψ for generating X. We take the converse, namely we define constraint γ (an equivalence class X), and then we have a set M_γ.

Example 1. In Table 3, if constraint γ is $X_{\{Color\}} = \{x_2, x_3, x_4, x_5\}$, the attribute value *red* (underlined in Table 3) is fixed in x_3. If constraint γ is that x_4 and x_6 do not belong to the same equivalence class in *Price*, we conclude either $x_4 : low$ and $x_6 : high$ or $x_4 : high$ and $x_6 : low$.

3.3   Constraint 2: Data Dependency

Data recovery by data dependency is known well. Functional dependency and data dependency are often employed for recovering missing values. We fix each attribute value which makes the degree of dependency [7] to take the maximum value.

Table 3. A part of Φ_1

Object	Color	Price
x_1	$\{red, blue, green\}$	$\{low\}$
x_2	$\{red\}$	$\{high\}$
x_3	$\{\underline{red}, blue\}$	$\{high\}$
x_4	$\{red\}$	$\{low, high\}$
x_5	$\{red\}$	$\{high\}$
x_6	$\{blue, green\}$	$\{low, high\}$

Example 2. In Table 4, if constraint γ is that there is data dependency from $Size \Rightarrow Price$. In this case, if we fix the following attribute values (underlined in Table 4),

$x_2 : [medium, high]$, $x_3 : [medium, high]$, $x_4 : [medium, high]$,
$x_5 : [\{medium, large\}, high]$,

there are three candidates of $DISs$ according to the values of x_5 and x_6. Namely, we fix the following in $\psi' \in DD(\Phi_1)$,

$x_5 : [medium, high]$, $x_6 : [large, \{low, high\}]$.

The other candidate of a DIS $\psi' \in DD(\Phi_1)$ is the following,

$x_5 : [large, high]$, $x_6 : [large, high]$.

In any case, the degree of dependency is 1.0 (=6/6). Like this in Φ_1, we can estimate three candidates of $DISs$ with actual information.

Table 4. A part of Φ_1

Object	Size	Price
x_1	$\{small\}$	$\{low\}$
x_2	$\{small, \underline{medium}\}$	$\{high\}$
x_3	$\{small, \underline{medium}\}$	$\{high\}$
x_4	$\{medium\}$	$\{low, \underline{high}\}$
x_5	$\{small, \underline{medium, large}\}$	$\{\underline{high}\}$
x_6	$\{large\}$	$\{low, high\}$

In Example 2, this data set is very simple, and we could easily obtain the maximum degree of dependency from $Size \Rightarrow Price$. At first, we employed definite information in $x_1 : [small, low]$, then we fixed other attribute values. Namely, this procedure depends upon the validity of $x_1 : [small, low]$. However, this procedure may not be proper generally. In other cases, the ignorance of some definite information may make the degree maximum.

Generally, this calculation is translated to a combinatorial optimization problem, and the computational complexity is NP-hard [2]. Therefore, the calculation of the maximum degree for large data sets is not easy, and the estimation of attribute values may not be easy for large data sets, either.

3.4   Constraint 3: An Association Rule with Maximum Likelihood Estimation

In $RNIA$, we have proposed the following criteria for defining a rule τ.

(1) $minsupp(\tau) = Min_{\psi \in DD(\Phi)}\{support(\tau)\}$,
(2) $maxsupp(\tau) = Max_{\psi \in DD(\Phi)}\{support(\tau)\}$,
(3) $minacc(\tau) = Min_{\psi \in DD(\Phi)}\{accuracy(\tau)\}$,
(4) $maxacc(\tau) = Max_{\psi \in DD(\Phi)}\{accuracy(\tau)\}$.

Each criteria depends upon $DD(\Phi)$, and generally the number of $DD(\Phi)$ increases exponentially. Therefore, it will be difficult to calculate each criteria by enumerating each $\psi \in DD(\Phi)$. However, we have solved this problem by using two blocks inf and sup for each descriptor [13]. Furthermore, we have proved $minsupp(\tau)$ and $minacc(\tau)$ occur in the same derived DIS ψ_{min}. Similarly, $maxsupp(\tau)$ and $maxacc(\tau)$ occur in the same derived DIS ψ_{max}. Like this, we obtained the following chart [16].

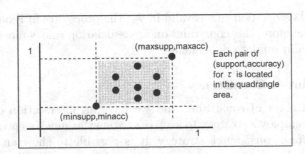

Fig. 2. A distribution of pairs ($support,accuracy$) for τ. There exists ψ_{min} which makes both $support(\tau)$ and $accuracy(\tau)$ the minimum. There exists ψ_{max} which makes both $support(\tau)$ and $accuracy(\tau)$ the maximum.

We also proposed NIS-$Apriori$ algorithm by using inf and sup. NIS-$Apriori$ algorithm implicitly handles $\psi \in DD(\Phi)$ for calculating four criterion values. We take the converse in NIS-$Apriori$ algorithm, namely we give an association rule as a constraint and we estimate a set of $\psi_{max} \in DD(\Phi)$. We fix attribute values according to ψ_{max}, and this is the application of maximum likelihood estimation with constraint by an association rule.

Example 3. In Table 5, if constraint γ is that an association rule $[Color, red] \Rightarrow [Price, high]$ holds. Then, we fix attribute values for satisfying γ according to the *maximum likelihood estimation*, i.e.,

$x_1 : [\{blue, green\}, low], x_3 : [red, high], x_4 : [red, high],$
$x_6 : [\{blue, green\}, \{low, high\}].$

Furthermore, if the next constraint γ' is that an association rule $[Color, green] \Rightarrow [Price, low]$ does not hold. Then, we can reduce the attribute values to the following.

$x_1 : [blue, low], x_3 : [red, high], x_4 : [red, high],$
$x_6 : [blue, \{low, high\}]$ or $[green, high].$

Table 5. A part of Φ_1

Object	Color	Price
x_1	$\{red, blue, green\}$	$\{low\}$
x_2	$\{red\}$	$\{high\}$
x_3	$\{red, blue\}$	$\{high\}$
x_4	$\{red\}$	$\{low, high\}$
x_5	$\{red\}$	$\{high\}$
x_6	$\{blue, green\}$	$\{low, high\}$

Since a specified association rule is valid in Φ_1, the procedure in Example 3 is always proper. Therefore, this constraint on an association rule is more convenient than the constraint on data dependency.

3.5   Constraint 4: Consistency

We have shown a set of constraint, and we have an intersection of $\cap_\gamma M_\gamma$. If $|\cap_\gamma M_\gamma| \geq 2$, we employ a strategy to keep consistency as much as possible, which we name *maximum consistency* strategy. It is possible to show an example to fix an attribute value. However, we are now considering the details of algorithms for this strategy.

3.6   An Example of Learning a DIS from a NIS

Now, we consider an exemplary NIS Φ_2 in Table 6.

Example 4. In Φ_2, we consider the first constraint

$\gamma_1 :$ *an association rule* $[Temperature, very\_high] \Rightarrow [Flu, yes],$

and we employ *maximum likelihood estimation*. Then, we have the following attribute values are reduced.

$x_2 : [very\_high, yes, \{yes, no\}, yes], x_3 : [very\_high, yes, yes, yes],$
$x_8 : [very\_high, yes, \{yes, no\}, yes].$

Table 6. An exemplary NIS Φ_2 for flu data sets. Here, $VAL_{Temperature}=\{normal,$ $high, very\_high\}$, $VAL_{Headache}=\{yes, no\}$, $VAL_{Nausea}=\{yes, no\}$, $VAL_{Flu}=\{yes,$ $no\}$.

Object	Temperature	Headache	Nausea	Flu
x_1	$\{high\}$	$\{yes, no\}$	$\{no\}$	$\{no\}$
x_2	$\{high, very\_high\}$	$\{yes\}$	$\{yes, no\}$	$\{yes\}$
x_3	$\{normal, high, very\_high\}$	$\{yes\}$	$\{yes\}$	$\{yes, no\}$
x_4	$\{high\}$	$\{yes\}$	$\{yes, no\}$	$\{yes, no\}$
x_5	$\{high\}$	$\{yes, no\}$	$\{yes\}$	$\{yes\}$
x_6	$\{normal\}$	$\{yes\}$	$\{yes, no\}$	$\{yes, no\}$
x_7	$\{normal\}$	$\{no\}$	$\{no\}$	$\{no\}$
x_8	$\{normal, high, very\_high\}$	$\{yes\}$	$\{yes, no\}$	$\{yes\}$

Table 7. An learned DIS ψ_2 from Φ_2

Object	Temperature	Headache	Nausea	Flu
x_1	high	no	no	no
x_2	very_high	yes	yes	yes
x_3	very_high	yes	yes	yes
x_4	high	yes	yes	yes
x_5	high	yes	yes	yes
x_6	normal	yes	yes	yes
x_7	normal	no	no	no
x_8	very_high	yes	yes	yes

We add the next constraint

γ_2 : *data dependency Headache $\Rightarrow$ Nausea,*

then we have the following attribute values are reduced.

x_1 : $[high, no, no, no]$, x_2 : $[very\_high, yes, yes, yes]$,

x_4 : $[high, yes, yes, \{yes, no\}]$, x_5 : $[high, yes, yes, yes]$,

x_6 : $[normal, yes, yes, \{yes, no\}]$, x_8 : $[very\_high, yes, yes, yes]$.

Finally, we add the third constraint

γ_3 : *an association rule $[Headache, yes] \wedge [Nausea, yes] \Rightarrow [Flu, yes]$.*

Then, each attribute values in Φ_2 is uniquely fixed, and we have a DIS ψ_2 in Table 7 from Φ_2.

4   Concluding Remarks

This paper described how we estimate a DIS with actual information from a NIS. In $RNIA$, we tried to conclude the certainty and the possibility from a NIS, and implicitly we obtained a set of $DISs$ supporting the conclusion. We take the converse of this framework, namely we estimated a set M_γ of $DISs$ by constraint γ.

We have just started this work, and we are now investigating the manipulation for each constraint and the manipulation to estimate $\psi^{actual} \in \cap_\gamma M_\gamma$. Such manipulation seems analogous to backpropagation [17] in neural networks.

References

1. Aldrich, J.: R.A. Fisher and the making of maximum likelihood 1912-1922. Statistical Science 12(3), 162–176 (1997)
2. Cook, W.J., Cunningham, W.H., Pulleyblank, W.R., Schrijver, A.: Combinatorial optimization. John Wiley & Sons (1997)
3. Grzymała-Busse, J.W.: Data with Missing Attribute Values: Generalization of Indiscernibility Relation and Rule Induction. In: Peters, J.F., Skowron, A., Grzymała-Busse, J.W., Kostek, B.z., Świniarski, R.W., Szczuka, M.S. (eds.) Transactions on Rough Sets I. LNCS, vol. 3100, pp. 78–95. Springer, Heidelberg (2004)
4. Kryszkiewicz, M.: Rules in incomplete information systems. Information Sciences 113(3-4), 271–292 (1999)
5. Orłowska, E., Pawlak, Z.: Representation of nondeterministic information. Theoretical Computer Science 29(1-2), 27–39 (1984)
6. Pawlak, Z.: Systemy Informacyjne: Podstawy Teoretyczne. WNT (1983) (in Polish; English translation: Information Systems: Theoretical Foundations)
7. Pawlak, Z.: Rough Sets: Theoretical Aspects of Reasoning About Data. Kluwer Academic Publishers (1991)
8. Peters, G., Lingras, P., Ślęzak, D., Yao, Y. (eds.): Selected Methods and Applications of Rough Sets in Management and Engineering. Springer (2012)
9. Polkowski, L., Skowron, A. (eds.): Rough Sets in Knowledge Discovery, Parts 1 & 2. Physica-Verlag (1998)
10. RNIA software logs, http://www.mns.kyutech.ac.jp/~sakai/RNIA
11. Sakai, H., Okuma, A.: Basic Algorithms and Tools for Rough Non-deterministic Information Analysis. In: Peters, J.F., Skowron, A., Grzymała-Busse, J.W., Kostek, B.z., Świniarski, R.W., Szczuka, M.S. (eds.) Transactions on Rough Sets I. LNCS, vol. 3100, pp. 209–231. Springer, Heidelberg (2004)
12. Sakai, H.: Possible Equivalence Relations and Their Application to Hypothesis Generation in Non-deterministic Information Systems. In: Peters, J.F., Skowron, A., Dubois, D., Grzymała-Busse, J.W., Inuiguchi, M., Polkowski, L. (eds.) Transactions on Rough Sets II. LNCS, vol. 3135, pp. 82–106. Springer, Heidelberg (2004)
13. Sakai, H., Ishibashi, R., Koba, K., Nakata, M.: Rules and Apriori Algorithm in Non-deterministic Information Systems. In: Peters, J.F., Skowron, A., Rybiński, H. (eds.) Transactions on Rough Sets IX. LNCS, vol. 5390, pp. 328–350. Springer, Heidelberg (2008)
14. Sakai, H., Koba, K., Nakata, M.: Rough sets based rule generation from data with categorical and numerical values. Journal of Advanced Computational Intelligence and Intelligent Informatics 12(5), 426–434 (2008)
15. Sakai, H., Okuma, H., Nakata, M., Ślęzak, D.: Stable rule extraction and decision making in rough non-deterministic information analysis. International Journal of Hybrid Intelligent Systems 8(1), 41–57 (2011)
16. Sakai, H., Nakata, M., Ślęzak, D.: A Prototype System for Rule Generation in Lipski's Incomplete Information Databases. In: Kuznetsov, S.O., Ślęzak, D., Hepting, D.H., Mirkin, B.G. (eds.) RSFDGrC 2011. LNCS, vol. 6743, pp. 175–182. Springer, Heidelberg (2011)
17. Werbos, P.J.: The roots of backpropagation: From ordered derivatives to neural networks and political forecasting. John Wiley & Sons, New York (1994)

Parameterised Fuzzy Petri Nets for Approximate Reasoning in Decision Support Systems

Zbigniew Suraj

Institute of Computer Science, University of Rzeszów, Poland
zsuraj@univ.rzeszow.pl

Abstract. The aim of this paper is to provide a new class of Petri nets called parameterised fuzzy Petri nets. The new class extends the generalised fuzzy Petri nets by introducing two parameterised families of sums and products, which are supposed to function as substitute for the t-norms and s-norms. The power and the usefulness of this model on the base of parameterised fuzzy Petri nets application in the domain of train traffic control are presented. The new model is more flexible than the generalised one as in the former class the user has the chance to define the parameterised input/output operators. The proposed model can be used for knowledge representation and approximate reasoning in decision support systems.

Keywords: parameterised fuzzy Petri nets, knowledge representation, approximate reasoning, decision support systems.

1 Introduction

Petri nets serve as a graphical and mathematical modelling tool applicable to many systems. The concept of a Petri net has its origin in C.A. Petri's dissertation [14]. In literature several extensions of Petri nets have been proposed [6],[10]. Currently, Petri nets are gaining a growing interest among people both in Artificial Intelligence due to its adequacy to represent the approximate reasoning process as a dynamic discrete event system [1]-[4],[9],[11]-[13],[15]-[17] as well as in Molecular Biology as a modeling tool to describe complex processes in developmental biology [5],[7].

In the paper [15], "*Generalised Fuzzy Petri Nets (GFPNs)*" for knowledge representation and approximate reasoning have been proposed. This model is a natural extension of fuzzy Petri nets introduced by C.G. Looney [9]. What is the main modification of this approach is that t-norms and s-norms are introduced to the model as substitutes of min and max operators. The latter ones generalise naturally AND and OR logical operators with the Boolean values 0 and 1.

The aim of this paper is to further improve the generalised fuzzy Petri net model. We propose a new class of Petri nets called "*Parameterised Fuzzy Petri Nets (PFPNs)*". The main difference between $GFPN$ model and the model proposed here is that $PFPN$ model accepts two parameterised families of sums and products, which are supposed to function as substitute for the t-norms and

A. Ell Hassanien et al. (Eds.): AMLTA 2012, CCIS 322, pp. 33–42, 2012.

s-norms. The new model is more flexible than the $GFPN$ one as in the former class the user has the chance to define the parameterised input/output operators. There has been intensive research in the field of logical operators carried out for the last three decades, which involves the development of parameterised families of sums and products [8]. The preliminary results of real-life data experiments using the proposed model are promising. In order to demonstrate the power and the usefulness of this model, an application of parameterised fuzzy Petri nets in the domain of train traffic control is presented.

The structure of this paper is as follows. Sect. 2 gives a brief introduction to generalised fuzzy Petri nets. In Sect. 3 parameterised fuzzy Petri nets formalism is presented. Sect. 4 describes an application of $PFPN$ model in the domain of train traffic control. In Sect. 5 conclusions are made.

2   Preliminaries

In this section, a definition of generalised fuzzy Petri nets [15] and basic notions related to them are recalled.

Let $[0, 1]$ be the closed interval of all real numbers from 0 to 1 (0 and 1 are included).

A t-norm is defined as $t : [0, 1] \times [0, 1] \rightarrow [0, 1]$ such that, for each $a, b, c \in [0, 1]$: (1) it has 1 as the unit element, i.e., $t(a, 1) = a$; (2) it is monotone, i.e., if $a \leq b$ then $t(a, c) \leq t(b, c)$; (3) it is commutative, i.e., $t(a, b) = t(b, a)$; (4) it is associative, i.e., $t(t(a, b), c) = t(a, t(b, c))$.

More relevant examples of t-norms are: the minimum $t(a, b) = min(a, b)$ which is the most widely used, the algebraic product $t(a, b) = a * b$, the Łukasiewicz t-norm $t(a, b) = max(0, a + b - 1)$.

An s-norm (or a t-conorm) is defined as $s : [0, 1] \times [0, 1] \rightarrow [0, 1]$ such that, for each $a, b, c \in [0, 1]$: (1) it has 0 as the unit element, i.e., $s(a, 0) = a$, (2) it is monotone, i.e., if $a \leq b$ then $s(a, c) \leq s(b, c)$, (3) it is commutative, i.e., $s(a, b) = s(b, a)$, and (4) it is associative, i.e., $s(s(a, b), c) = s(a, s(b, c))$.

More relevant examples of s-norms are: the maximum $s(a, b) = max(a, b)$ which is the most widely used, the probabilistic sum $s(a, b) = a + b - a * b$, the Łukasiewicz s-norm $s(a, b) = min(a + b, 1)$.

Definition 1. *A generalised fuzzy Petri net (GFP-net) is a tuple $N = (P, T, S, I, O, \alpha, \beta, \gamma, Op, \delta, M0)$, where: (1) $P = \{p_1, p_2, \ldots, p_n\}$ is a finite set of places, $n > 0$; (2) $T = \{t_1, t_2, \ldots, t_m\}$ is a finite set of transitions, $m > 0$; (3) $S = \{s_1, s_2, \ldots, s_n\}$ is a finite set of statements; the sets P, T, S are pairwise disjoint, i.e., $P \cap T = P \cap S = T \cap S = \emptyset$ and card(P) = card(S); (4) $I : T \rightarrow 2^P$ is the input function; (5) $O : T \rightarrow 2^P$ is the output function; (6) $\alpha : P \rightarrow S$ is the statement binding function; (7) $\beta : T \rightarrow [0, 1]$ is the truth degree function; (8) $\gamma : T \rightarrow [0, 1]$ is the threshold function; (9) Op is a finite set of t-norms and s-norms called the set of operators; (10) $\delta : T \rightarrow Op \times Op \times Op$ is the operator binding function; (11) $M0 : P \rightarrow [0, 1]$ is the initial marking, and 2^P denotes a family of all subsets of the set P.*

As for the graphical interpretation, places are denoted by circles and transitions by rectangles. The places are the nodes describing states (a place is a partial state) and the transitions depict the state changes. The function I describes the oriented arcs connecting places with transitions. It represents, for each transition t, fragments of the state in which the system has to be, before the state change corresponding to t can occur. The function O describes the oriented arcs connecting transitions with places. It represents, for each transition t, the fragments of the state in which the system will be after the occurrence of the state change corresponding to t. If $I(t) = \{p\}$ then a place p is called an *input place* of a transition t. Moreover, if $O(t) = \{p'\}$, then a place p' is called an *output place* of t. The initial marking $M0$ is an initial distribution of tokens in the places. It can be represented by a vector of dimension n of real numbers from $[0, 1]$. For $p \in P$, $M0(p)$ is the token load of place p and represents a partial state of the system described by a generalised fuzzy Petri net. This value can be interpreted as a truth value of a statement s bound with a given place p by means of the binding function α, i.e., $\alpha(p) = s$. Pictorially, the tokens are represented by means of the suitable real numbers placed inside the circles corresponding to appropriate places. We assume that if a truth value of a statement attached to a given place is equal to 0 then the token does not exist in the place. The number $\beta(t)$ is placed in a net picture over a transition t. Usually, this number is interpreted as a truth degree of an implication corresponding to a given transition t [2],[3]. The meaning of the threshold function γ is explained below. The operator binding function δ connects transitions with triples of operators $(op_{In}, op_{Out1}, op_{Out2})$. The first operator appearing in this triple is called the input operator, and two remaining ones are called the output operators. The input operator op_{In} belongs to one of the classes: t-norms or s-norms. It concerns the way in which all input places are connected to a given transition t (more precisely, statements corresponding to those places). Moreover, the output operator: op_{Out1} belongs to the class of t-norms and op_{Out2} belongs to the class of s-norms. Both of them concern the way in which the marking is computed after firing the transition t. This issue is explained more precisely below.

The generalised fuzzy Petri net dynamics defines how new markings are computed from the current marking when transitions are fired (the corresponding state change occurs). It describes the state changes of the decision support system modelled by the generalised fuzzy Petri net.

Let N be a *GFP*-net. A marking of N is a function $M : P \to [0, 1]$.

Let $N = (P, T, S, I, O, \alpha, \beta, \gamma, Op, \delta, M0)$ be a *GFP*-net, $t \in T$, $I(t) = \{p_{i1}, p_{i2}, \ldots, p_{ik}\}$ be a set of input places for a transition t, $\beta(t)$ be a value of the truth degree function β corresponding to t and $\beta(t) \in (0, 1]$ (0 is not included), $\gamma(t)$ be a value of threshold function γ corresponding to t, and M be a marking of N. Moreover, let op_{In} be an input operator and op_{Out1}, op_{Out2} be output operators for the transition t.

A transition $t \in T$ is *enabled* for marking M, if the value of input operator op_{In} for the transition t is positive and greater than or equal to the value of threshold function γ corresponding to t, i.e.,

$$op_{In}(M(p_{i1}), M(p_{i2}), \ldots, M(p_{ik})) \geq \gamma(t) > 0 \text{ for } p_{ij} \in I(t), j = 1, \ldots, k.$$

(*Mode 1*) If M is a marking of N enabling the transition t and M' the marking derived from M by firing t, then for each $p \in P$:

$$M'(p) = \begin{cases} 0 \text{ if } p \in I(t), \\ op_{Out2}(op_{Out1}(op_{In}(M(p_{i1}), M(p_{i2}), \ldots, M(p_{ik})), \beta(t)), M(p)) \\ \quad \text{if } p \in O(t), \\ M(p) \text{ otherwise.} \end{cases}$$

In this mode, a procedure for computing the marking M' is as follows: (1) Tokens from all input places of the transition t are removed (the first condition from M' definition). (2) Tokens in all output places of t are modified in the following way: at first the value of input operator op_{In} for all input places of t is computed, then the value of output operator op_{Out1} for the value of input operator op_{In} and the value of truth degree function $\beta(t)$ is determined, and finally, a value corresponding to $M'(p)$ for each $p \in O(p)$ is obtained as a result of output operator op_{Out2} for the value of output operator op_{Out1} and the current marking $M(p)$ (the second condition from M' definition). (3) Tokens in the remaining places of net N are not changed (the third condition from M' definition).

(*Mode 2*) If M is a marking of N enabling the transition t and M' the marking derived from M by firing t, then for each $p \in P$:

$$M'(p) = \begin{cases} op_{Out2}(op_{Out1}(op_{In}(M(p_{i1}), M(p_{i2}), \ldots, M(p_{ik})), \beta(t)), M(p)), \\ \quad \text{if } p \in O(t), \\ M(p) \text{ otherwise.} \end{cases}$$

The main difference in the definition of the marking M' presented above (*Mode 2*) concerns input places of the fired transition t. In *Mode 1* tokens from all input places of the fired transition t are removed (*cf.* the first definition condition of *Mode 1*), whereas in *Mode 2* all tokens from input places of the fired transition t are copied (the second definition condition of *Mode 2*).

Example 1. Consider a generalised fuzzy Petri net in Figure 1. For the net we have: the set of places $P = \{p_1, p_2, p_3, p_4, p_5\}$, the set of transitions $T = \{t_1, t_2\}$, the set of statements $S = \{s_1, s_2, s_3, s_4, s_5\}$, the input function I and the output function O in the form: $I(t_1) = \{p_1, p_2\}$, $I(t_2) = \{p_2, p_3\}$, $O(t_1) = \{p_4\}$, $O(t_2) = \{p_5\}$. Moreover, there are: the statement binding function $\alpha : \alpha(p_1) = s_1$, $\alpha(p_2) = s_2$, $\alpha(p_3) = s_3$, $\alpha(p_4) = s_4$, $\alpha(p_5) = s_5$, the truth degree function β: $\beta(t_1) = 0.7$, $\beta(t_2) = 0.8$, the threshold function γ: $\gamma(t_1) = 0.4$, $\gamma(t_2) = 0.3$, the set of operators $Op = \{max, min, *\}$, the operator binding function δ: $\delta(t_1) = (max, *, max)$, $\delta(t_2) = (min, *, max)$, and the initial marking $M0 = (0.6, 0.4, 0.7, 0, 0)$.

Transitions t_1 and t_2 are enabled by the initial marking $M0$. Firing transition t_1 by the marking $M0$ according to *Mode 1* transforms $M0$ to the marking $M' = (0, 0, 0.7, 0.42, 0)$ (Figure 2(a)), and firing transition t_2 by the initial marking $M0$ according to *Mode 2* results in the marking $M'' = (0.6, 0.4, 0.7, 0, 0.32)$ (Figure 2(b)).

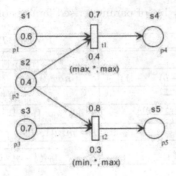

Fig. 1. A generalised fuzzy Petri net with the initial marking before firing the enabled transitions t_1 and t_2

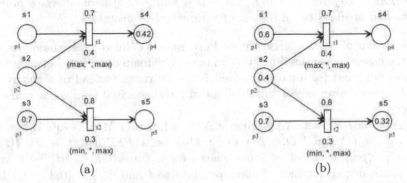

Fig. 2. An illustration of a firing rule: (a) the marking after firing t_1, where t_2 is disabled (*Mode 1*), (b) the marking after firing t_2, where t_1 and t_2 are enabled (*Mode 2*)

For more detailed information about *GFPNs* the reader is referred to [15] and [16].

3   Parameterised Fuzzy Petri Nets

Now we are ready to define a new class of Petri net model called parameterised fuzzy Petri nets. This model combines positive features of generalised fuzzy Petri nets and additional possibilities of parameterised families of sums and products [8]. This section presents the main contribution to the paper.

In Table 1 an exemplary list of parameterised families of sums and products is presented. For more details one shall refer to [8].

It is easy to observe that the first pair of parameterised families of sums $S(a, b, v)$ and products $T(a, b, v)$ from Table 1 for the parameter $v = 1$ correspond to the probabilistic sum $s(a, b) = a + b - a * b$ and the algebraic product $t(a, b) = a * b$, respectively.

Table 1. An exemplary list of parameterised families of sums and products

Sum $S(a,b,v)$	Product $T(a,b,v)$	Range v
$\frac{a+b-(2-v)*a*b}{1-(1-v)*a*b}$	$\frac{a*b}{v+(1-v)*(a+b-a*b)}$	$(0,\infty)$
$1-[max(0,(1-a)^{-v}+(1-b)^{-v}-1)]^{\frac{-1}{v}}$	$[max(0,a^{-v}+b^{-v}-1)]^{\frac{-1}{v}}$	$(-\infty,\infty)$
$\frac{a+b-a*b-min(a,b,1-v)}{max(1-a,1-b,v)}$	$\frac{a*b}{max(a,b,v)}$	$(0,1)$
$1-\log_v[1+\frac{(v^{1-a}-1)(v^{1-b}-1)}{v-1}]$	$\log_v[1+\frac{(v^a-1)(v^b-1)}{v-1}]$	$(0,\infty)$
$min[1,(a^v+b^v)^{\frac{1}{v}}]$	$1-min[1,((1-a)^v+(1-b)^v)^{\frac{1}{v}}]$	$(0,\infty)$
$\frac{1}{1+[(\frac{1}{a}-1)^{-v}+(\frac{1}{b}-1)^{-v}]^{\frac{-1}{v}}}$	$\frac{1}{1+[(\frac{1}{a}-1)^v+(\frac{1}{b}-1)^v]^{\frac{1}{v}}}$	$(0,\infty)$

Definition 2. *A parameterised fuzzy Petri net (PFP-net) is a tuple $N' = (P,T,$ $S,I,O,\alpha,\beta,\gamma,Op,\delta,M0)$, where (1) $P,T,S,I,O,\alpha,\beta,\gamma,\delta,M0$ have the same meaning as in Definition 1, and (2) Op is a finite set of parameterised families of sums and products called the set of parameterised operators.*

The behaviour of parameterised fuzzy Petri nets is defined in an analogous way as for the case of generalised fuzzy Petri nets. The main difference between these two models is that for a parameterised fuzzy Petri net instead of a concrete t-norm and s-norm we take a suitable pair of parameterised families of sums and products.

Let N' be a *PFP*-net. A marking of N' is a function $M : P \to [0,1]$.

Let $N' = (P,T,S,I,O,\alpha,\beta,\gamma,Op,\delta,M0)$ be a *PFP*-net, $t \in T$, $I(t) = \{p_{i1},p_{i2},\ldots,p_{ik}\}$ be a set of input places for a transition t, $\beta(t)$ be a value of the truth degree function β corresponding to t and $\beta(t) \in (0,1]$, $\gamma(t)$ be a value of threshold function γ corresponding to t, M be a marking of N', and v be a parameter value for a parameterised family of sums and products. Moreover, let op^v_{In} be an input parameterised operator and op^v_{Out1}, op^v_{Out2} be output parameterised operators with a parameter value v corresponding to t.

A transition $t \in T$ is *enabled* for marking M and a parameter value v, if the value of input parameterised operator op^v_{In} for the transition t is positive and greater than or equal to the value of threshold function γ corresponding to t and the parameter value v, i.e.,

$$op^v_{In}(M(p_{i1}),M(p_{i2}),\ldots,M(p_{ik})) \geq \gamma(t) > 0 \text{ for } p_{ij} \in I(t), j = 1,\ldots,k.$$

(Mode 1) If M with a parameter value v is a marking of N' enabling a transition t and M'_v the marking derived from M with v by firing t, then for each $p \in P$:

$$M'_v(p) = \begin{cases} 0 \text{ if } p \in I(t), \\ op^v_{Out2}(op^v_{Out1}(op^v_{In}(M(p_{i1}),M(p_{i2}),\ldots,M(p_{ik})),\beta(t)),M(p)) \\ \quad \text{if } p \in O(t), \\ M(p) \text{ otherwise.} \end{cases}$$

In this mode, a procedure for computing the marking M'_v is similar to appropriate procedure corresponding to generalised fuzzy Petri nets and *Mode 1* presented above. The difference is that present procedure needs to set a parameter value v at first. Remaining stages of the procedure are analogous to the previous procedure concerning *Mode 1*.

(*Mode 2*) If M with a parameter value v is a marking of N' enabling transition t and M_v' the marking derived from M with v by firing t, then for each $p \in P$:

$$M_v'(p) = \begin{cases} op_{Out2}^v(op_{Out1}^v(op_{In}^v(M(p_{i1}), M(p_{i2}), \ldots, M(p_{ik})), \beta(t)), M(p)) \\ \text{if } p \in O(t), \\ M(p) \text{ otherwise.} \end{cases}$$

The difference in the definitions of the marking M_v' presented above (*Mode 2*) and *Mode 1* is analogous to the case of generalised fuzzy Petri nets.

Example 2. Consider a parameterised fuzzy Petri net in Figure 3(a). For the net we have: the set of places P, the set of transitions T, the input function I, the output function O, the set of statements S, the binding function α, the truth degree function β, the threshold function γ and the initial marking $M0$ described analogously to Example 1. Moreover, there are: the set of operators $Op = \{S(.), T(.)\}$ and the operator binding function δ defined as follows: $\delta(t_1) = (S(.), T(.), S(.))$, $\delta(t_2) = (T(.), T(.), S(.))$ with a relevant parameter value v.

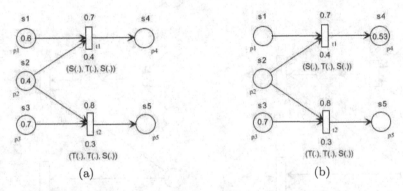

(a)   (b)

Fig. 3. (a) A parameterised fuzzy Petri net with the initial marking before firing the enabled transitions t_1 and t_2. (b) An illustration of a firing rule: the marking after firing t_1, where t_2 is disabled (*Mode 1*).

If we take, for instance, the first pair of parameterised families of sums $S(a, b, v)$ and products $T(a, b, v)$ from Table 1 and a parameter value $v = 1$, then $S(a, b, 1) = a+b-a*b$ and $T(a, b, 1) = a*b$. For the transition t_1 we have $S(0.6, 0.4, 1) = 0.6+0.4-0.24 = 0.76$ and $T(0.76, 0.7, 1) = 0.76*0.7 = 0.532$ by the initial marking $M0$ and $v = 1$. Because the global value for all input places of t_1 and $v = 1$ equals 0.76, hence it is positive and greater than $\gamma(t_1) = 0.4$. Thus, the transition t_1 is enabled by $M0$ and $v = 1$. Firing transition t_1 by the marking $M0$ and $v = 1$ according to *Mode 1* transforms $M0$ to the marking $M_1' = (0, 0, 0.7, 0.53, 0)$ (Figure 3(b)). It is easy to check that by the initial marking $M0$ and $v = 1$ the transition t_2 is not enabled.

4   Illustrating Example

In this section we present an application of *PFPN* in the domain of train traffic control [15].

The considered example is based on a simplified version of the real-life problem. We assume the following situation: a train B waits at a certain station for a train A to arrive in order to allow some passengers to change train A to train B. Now a conflict arises when the train A is late. In this situation, the following alternatives can be taken into consideration:

- Train B waits for train A to arrive. In this case, train B will depart with delay.
- Train B departs in time. In this case, passengers disembarking train A have to wait for a later train.
- Train B departs in time, and an additional train is employed for late train $A's$ passengers.

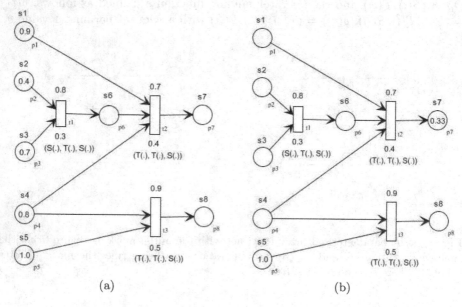

(a)   (b)

Fig. 4. (a) An example of *PFPN* model of train traffic control. (b) An illustration of a firing rule: the marking after firing a sequence of transitions $t_1 t_2$ (*Mode 1*)

To make a decision, several inner conditions have to be taken into account, for example: the delay period, the number of passengers changing trains, etc. The discussion regarding an optimal solution to the problem of divergent aims such as: minimization of delays throughout the traffic network, warranty of connections for the customer satisfaction, efficient use of expensive resources, etc. is disregarded at this point.

In order to describe the traffic conflict, we propose to consider the following three rules: (1) IF s_2 OR s_3 THEN s_6; (2) IF s_1 AND s_4 AND s_6 THEN s_7; (3) IF s_4 AND s_5 THEN s_8, where s_1: 'Train B is the last train in this direction today'; s_2: 'The delay of train A is huge'; s_3: 'There is an urgent need for the track of train B'; s_4: 'Many passengers would like to change for train B'; s_5: 'The delay of train A is short'; s_6: '(Let) train B depart according to schedule'; s_7: 'Employ an additional train C (in the same direction as train B)'; s_8: 'Let train B wait for train A'.

In Figure 4(a) the *PFPN* model corresponding to these rules, where the logical operators OR, AND are interpreted as the probabilistic sum $S(\cdot)$ and the algebraic product $T(\cdot)$, respectively, is shown. Note that the places p_1, p_2, p_3 and p_4 include the fuzzy values 0.9, 0.4, 0.7 and 0.8 corresponding to the statements s_1, s_2, s_3 and s_4, respectively. In this example, the statement s_5 attached to the place p_5 is the only crisp and its value is equal to 1. By means of evaluation of the statements attached to the places from p_1 up to p_5, we observe that the transitions t_1 and t_3 can be fired. Firing these transitions according to the firing rules for the *PFPN* model allows the computation of the support for the alternatives in question. In this way, the possible alternatives are ordered with regard to the preference they achieve from the knowledge base. This order forms the basis for further examinations and simulations and, in the end, for the dispatching proposal. If one chooses a sequence of transitions $t_1 t_2$ then they obtain the final value, corresponding to the statement s_7, equal to 0.33 (Figure 4(b)). In the second possible case (i.e., for the transition t_3 only), the final value, corresponding now to the statement s_8, equals 0.72.

5   Conclusions

In the paper a *PFPN* model has been proposed. This model combines the positive features of generalised fuzzy Petri nets and the additional possibilities of parameterised families of sums and products. Moreover, a *PFPN* formalism allows to handle complex and parameterised fuzzy rule bases. Using a simple real-life example suitability and usefulness of the proposed approach for the design and implementation of decision support systems have been shown. Success of the elaborated approach looks promising with regard to alike application problems that could be solved similarly.

One of the most important considerations in designing practical systems is the time representation, particularly in time-critical systems. Various approaches related to time within the context of Petri nets have been developed [1],[6],[10],[17]. In our further research we would like to consider a time factor together with the proposed net model and elaborate timed Petri net analysis methods.

Acknowledgment. The author is grateful to the anonymous referees for their critical comments and suggestions on the paper.

References

1. Cardoso, J., Camargo, H. (eds.): Fuzziness in Petri Nets. Springer, Berlin (1999)
2. Chen, S.M., Ke, J.S., Chang, J.F.: Knowledge representation using fuzzy Petri nets. IEEE Trans. on Knowledge and Data Engineering 2(3), 311–319 (1990)
3. Fryc, B., Pancerz, K., Suraj, Z.: Approximate Petri Nets for Rule-Based Decision Making. In: Tsumoto, S., Słowiński, R., Komorowski, J., Grzymała-Busse, J.W. (eds.) RSCTC 2004. LNCS (LNAI), vol. 3066, pp. 733–742. Springer, Heidelberg (2004)
4. Fryc, B., Pancerz, K., Peters, J.F., Suraj, Z.: On Fuzzy Reasoning Using Matrix Representation of Extended Fuzzy Petri Nets. Fundamenta Informaticae 60(1-4), 143–157 (2004)
5. Heiner, M., Donaldson, R., Gilbert, D.: Petri Nets for Systems Biology, ch. 3, pp. 61–97. Jones & Bartlett Learning, LCC (2010)
6. Jensen, K., Rozenberg, G.: High-level Petri Nets. Springer, Berlin (1991)
7. Kleijn, J., Koutny, M., Rozenberg, G.: Petri Nets for Biologically Motivated Computing. Scientific Annals of Computer Science 21, 199–225 (2011)
8. Klir, G.J., Folger, T.A.: Fuzzy Sets, Uncertainty and Information. Prentice-Hall, Englewood Cliffs (1988)
9. Looney, C.G.: Fuzzy Petri Nets for Rule-Based Decision-making. IEEE Trans. Syst., Man, Cybern. 18(1), 178–183 (1988)
10. Murata, T.: Petri Nets: Properties, Analysis and Applications. Proc. of the IEEE 77, 541–580 (1989)
11. Pedrycz, W.: Generalized fuzzy Petri nets as pattern classifiers. Pattern Recognition Letters 20(14), 1489–1498 (1999)
12. Pedrycz, W., Peters, J.F.: Learning in fuzzy Petri nets. In: Cardoso, J., Sandri, S. (eds.) Fuzzy Petri Nets. Physica-Verlag, Berlin (1998)
13. Peters, J.F., Skowron, A., Suraj, Z., Ramanna, S., Paryzek, A.: Modelling Real-Time Decision-Making Systems with Roughly Fuzzy Petri Nets. In: Proc. of the 6th European Congress on Intelligent Techniques and Soft Computing (EUFIT 1998), Aachen, Germany, September 7-10, pp. 985–989 (1998)
14. Petri, C.A.: Kommunikation mit Automaten. Schriften des IIM Nr. 2, Institut für Instrumentelle Mathematik, Bonn (1962); English translation: Technical Report RADC-TR-65-377, Griffiths Air Force Base, New York, vol. 1(suppl. 1) (1966)
15. Suraj, Z.: Generalised fuzzy Petri nets for approximate reasoning in decision support systems. In: Proc. of Int. Workshop on Concurrency, Specification, and Programming (CS&P 2012), September 28-30. LNCS (LNAI). Springer, Berlin (to appear, 2012)
16. Suraj, Z.: Knowledge Representation and Reasoning Based on Generalised Fuzzy Petri Nets. In: Proc. of the 12th Int. Conf. on Intelligent Systems Design and Applications (ISDA 2012), Kochi, India, November 27-29 (submitted, 2012)
17. Suraj, Z., Fryc, B.: Timed Approximate Petri Nets. Fundamenta Informaticae 71, 83–99 (2006)

New Method for Finding Rules in Incomplete and Distributed Information Systems Controlled by Reducts

Agnieszka Dardzinska Jolanta Pauk

Bialystok University of Technology Dept. of Mechanics and Applied Computer Science
ul.Wiejska 45C, 15351, Bialystok, Poland
a.dardzinska@pb.edu.pl

Abstract. We present a new method for extracting rules from incomplete Information Systems (IS) which are generalizations of information systems introduced by Pawlak [8],[9]. In this paper, a new extracting rule algorithm from more complete information system is proposed. First, we produce a covering on a domain according to attribute value of the objects, and then reducts are made on this covering. Second, we utilize rough sets model based on covering to predict some unknown values, so that an incomplete information system can be transformed to a more complete information system. From such system we extract all certain and possible rules. This algorithm was initially tested on children flat feet database, and the results are very promising.

Keywords: Covering, Rough sets, Incomplete information system, Rules.

1 Introduction

Each new database acquired for the purpose of data mining is a source of recurring problems with data. Some attributes are not clearly understood, some others can be understood in a specifically way, some of their values can be even missing [2],[3],[5],[6]. The users should treat such problems carefully, as serious misconceptions or misunderstandings will result when they understand attributes and their values differently from providers. Some of the knowledge extracted from such data may be misleading or even lost.

In many fields, such as banking, educational, medical or military similar databases are kept at many sites. Each database stores information about local treatments and uses attributes suitable for locally collected information. Since the local situations can be similar, the majority of attributes are compatible among databases [4],[10],[12]. Values of attributes are codes, such as disease or treatment code, patient category. They are nominal attributes with large numbers of values hiding plenty of information. An attribute may be missing in one database, while it occurs in many others. For instance, different but equivalent tests that measure a common medical condition may be applied in different hospitals. A doctor who researches effectiveness of a particular treatment may find it difficult to compare it in several hospitals, because they use different tests and because one test replaces another over the course of time. But if the relations between values of different tests can be discovered from data, many

A. Ell Hassanien et al. (Eds.): AMLTA 2012, CCIS 322, pp. 43–51, 2012.

attributes acquire a shared meaning and many datasets can be used together. Moreover, when we ask how values of attributes can be encoded, we find their definitions in terms of attributes which are more conductive to data analysis and KD process. With the use of its definition, one coded attribute can be replaced by several others, each with a small numbers of values and clear meaning. For instance, a code for broken bone indicates broken bone, the location, the type of fracture, etc.

There have been a lot of methods to extract rules from complete information system in the literature, while it is much more difficult to extract rules from incomplete information system. Chmielewski at al [1] proposed that incomplete data sets may be transformed into complete data sets before learning programs begin by removing objects with unknown values from data sets. Kryszkiewicz [7] used the indiscernibiity relations to characterize incomplete data.

The main purpose of this paper is to present a new method to extract rules from incomplete information system. The key point of the new algorithm is to form reducts on a domain according to the attribute value of an arbitrary object. We can estimate the unknown attribute value through the minimal description of objects after reducing the reduct. Then rules are extracted by transforming incomplete information system to more complete information system.

2   Basic Assumptions

In this section we recall definitions of an information system, incomplete information system, and distributed information system [8].

2.1   Information System

By an Information System we mean a triple $S = (X, A, V)$ where X is a nonempty, finite set of objects, A is a nonempty, finite set of attributes, $V = \bigcup \{V_a : a \in A\}$ is a set of values of attributes, where V_a is a set of values of attribute a, for any $a \in A$.

We also assume, that

$V_a \cap V_b = \varnothing$ for any $a, b \in A$ such that $a \neq b$,

$a : X \to V_a$ is a function for every $a \in A$.

Information systems can be seen as generalizations of decision tables. In any decision table together with the set of attributes a partition of that set into conditions and decisions is given.

2.2   Incomplete Information System

By an Incomplete Information System [3],[11] we mean $S = (X, A, V)$, as defined in Section 2.1. Additionally we assume that for each attribute $a \in A$ and $x \in X$,

$$a(x) = \{(a_i : i \in J_{a(x)} \wedge (\forall i \in J_{a(x)})[a_i \in V_a] or \ a = null\}$$

Null value assigned to an object is interpreted as all possible values of an attribute with equal confidence assigned to all of them.

2.3   Distributed Information System

By a distributed information system [10] we mean a pair $DS = (\{S_i\}_{i \in I}, L)$ where:
$S_i = (X_i, A_i, V_i)$ is an information system for $i \in I$ and $V_i = \bigcup \{V_{ia} : a \in A_i\}$
L is a symmetric, binary relation on the set I, I is a set of sites.

Let $S_i = (X_i, A_i, V_i)$ for any $i \in I$. From now on we use A to denote the set of all attributes in DS, $A = \bigcup \{A_i : i \in I\}$. Similarly, $V = \bigcup \{V_i : i \in I\}$. Distributed information system $DS = (\{S_i\}_{i \in I}, L)$ is object-consistent if the following condition holds:

$$(\forall i)(\forall j)(\forall x \in X_i \cap X_j)(\forall a \in A_i \cap A_j)$$

$$[(a_{[S_i]}(x) \subseteq a_{[S_j]}(x)) \ or \ (a_{[S_j]}(x) \subseteq a_{[S_i]}(x))],$$

where a_S denotes that a is an attribute in S.

We also assume that:

$S_j = (X_j, A_j, V_j)$ and $V_j = \bigcup \{V_{ja} : a \in A_j\}$, for any $j \in I$. The inclusion $(a_{[S_i]}(x) \subseteq a_{[S_j]}(x))$ means that the system S_i has more precise information about the attribute a in object x than system S_j.

Objects-consistency means that information about objects in one of the systems is either the same or more general than in the other. Saying other words, two consistent systems cannot have conflicting information about any object x which is stored in both of them. System in which the above condition does not hold is called objects-inconsistent.

2.4   Covering Reducts

Let us assume that $S = (X, A, V)$ is an information system and $V = \bigcup \{V_a : a \in A\}$. With every subset of attributes $B \subseteq A$, we associate an equivalence relation $ER(B)$, defined as follows:

$$ER(B) = \{(x, y) \in X \times X : \forall a \in B, a(x) = a(y)\}.$$

Assuming that both B_1, B_2 are subsets of A. We say that B_1 depends on B_2 if $ER(B_2) \subseteq ER(B_1)$. Also we say that B_1 is a covering of B_2 if B_2 depends on B_1 and B_1 is minimal. By a reduct of A in S we mean any covering of A denoted by $cov(a)$.

For any attribute $a \in A$, each object $x \in X$ is represented as a tuple (x, v), where v is a binary number 0 or 1. If the object xi has a certain value v_{ia} for $a \in A$ then $(x_i, 1)$ is put in the equivalence class, otherwise, $(x_i, 0)$ is put in each equivalence class. The object sets formed in this way are called incomplete equivalence classes.

3   New Algorithm

In this section we will present the idea of new method for finding decision rules, on the base of reducts.

First we collect all elements in the incomplete equivalence classes generated by all the condition attributes together. The set formed by above elements is a covering of domain X. For any object $x \in X$, $ER(x)$ can be obtained from the covering rough sets model. It follows from the condition attribute value that $ER(x)$ is an undistinguished minimal object set. If no more conditions other than the given condition attribute value exist, then the condition attribute value of all the objects in $ER(x)$ are identical.

In the incomplete information system, another important condition should be taken into consideration, which is the value of decision attribute. If the decision attribute value can be determined, the unknown value of classification attribute can be estimated in the following way:

If $x_i, x_j \in ER(x_k)$ and $(x_i, d) = (x_j, d)$ for decision attribute d, then all the condition attribute values of x_i and x_j can be transformed to the known value. If $x_i, x_j \in ER(x_k)$ and there exist decision attribute d such that $(x_i, d) \neq (x_j, d)$, then we assume x_i, x_j can be distinguished if there exists an estimate of the unknown attribute value, so that the classification attribute value is not identical. When an unknown attribute value of some object is estimated, the corresponding value 0 or 1 is displaced by it. Then the object with the new attribute value is compared with other objects in the common $ER(x)$. If the object can be distinguished with others, then it should be removed from $ER(x)$. We repeat the same steps up to the fixed point. In such way we can obtain the decision rules according to the objects and their decision attribute value.

Example
Let us assume incomplete information system given below.

Table 1. An incomplete information system

Objects	Attributes		
	a	b	d
x_1	N	H	-
x_2	H	L	-
x_3	N	H	+
x_4	L	L	0
x_5	L	H	+
x_6	L	N	+
x_7	L		0
x_8		H	-
x_9		N	-

Attributes a and b are classification attributes, and attribute d is a decision attribute. Classification attributes can be numerical or symbolical, decision attribute classifies objects into one from three classes. The algorithm consists of five main steps.

Step 1: Denote incomplete equivalence classes of all the

$$X / \{a\} = \{\{(x_2,1),(x_8,0),(x_9,0)\},\{(x_4,1),(x_5,1),(x_6,1),(x_7,1),(x_8,0),(x_9,0)\},$$
$$\{(x_1,1),(x_3,1),(x_8,0),(x_9,0)\}$$

$$X / \{b\} = \{\{(x_1,1),(x_3,1),(x_5,1),(x_7,0),(x_8,1)\},\{(x_2,1),(x_4,1),(x_7,0)\},$$
$$\{(x_6,1),(x_7,0),(x_9,1)\}$$

Step 2: Put all elements of each classification attribute of incomplete equivalence classes together.

$$\{\{(x_2,1),(x_8,0),(x_9,0)\},\{(x_4,1),(x_5,1),(x_6,1),(x_7,1),(x_8,0),(x_9,0)\},$$
$$\{(x_1,1),(x_3,1),(x_8,0),(x_9,0)\},\{(x_1,1),(x_3,1),(x_5,1),(x_7,0),(x_8,1)\},$$
$$\{(x_2,1),(x_4,1),(x_7,0)\},\{(x_6,1),(x_7,0),(x_9,1)\}\}$$

The $ER(x_i)$ is as follows:

$$ER(x_1) = \{x_1, x_3, (x_8,0)\} \qquad ER(x_2) = \{x_2\}$$
$$ER(x_3) = \{x_1, x_3, (x_8,0)\} \qquad ER(x_4) = \{x_4, (x_7,0)\}$$
$$ER(x_5) = \{x_5, (x_7,0), (x_8,0)\} \qquad ER(x_6) = \{x_6, (x_7,0), (x_9,0)\}$$
$$ER(x_7) = \{(x_7,0)\} \qquad ER(x_9) = \{(x_9,0)\}$$

Step 3: Simplify sets $ER(x_i)$. Note that $ER(x)$ is the minimal set of undistinguishable object according to the condition attribute value. In general, if $ER(x_j) \subseteq ER(x_i)$, then we delete $ER(x_j)$. For our example, the simplified $ER(x_i)$ is as follows:

$$ER(x_1) = \{x_1, x_3, (x_8, 0)\} \qquad\qquad ER(x_2) = \{x_2\}$$
$$ER(x_4) = \{x_4, (x_7, 0)\} \qquad\qquad ER(x_5) = \{x_5, (x_7, 0), (x_8, 0)\}$$
$$ER(x_6) = \{x_6, (x_7, 0), (x_9, 0)\}$$

Step 4: Evaluate the possible value of the unknown attribute according to the corresponding extracted rule. Since the decision attribute value of the object x_4 is consistent with that of the object x_7, we can evaluate that value of attribute b can be L. It is good to notice that the default attribute value of the object x_7 has been evaluated, and $ER(x_6) = \{x_6, (x_7, 0), (x_9, 0)\}$, then it follows that $(x_7, 0)$ in $ER(x_5) = \{x_5, (x_7, 0), (x_8, 0)\}$ is distinct from the other objects in $ER(x)$, then $(x_7, 0)$ can be deleted. Similarly, in $ER(x_3) = \{x_1, x_3, (x_8, 0)\}$ objects x_1 and x_8 have the same attribute values, thus we can evaluate possible value of attribute a in x_8 as N. In such case the value $(x_8, 0)$ in $ER(x_5) = \{(x_5, (x_8, 0)\}$ is deleted. In $ER(x_6) = \{x_6, (x_9, 0)\}$, objects x_6 and x_9 have different decision attribute, so the value of attribute a for object x_9 is still unknown. It means that for object x_9 we can have three values of attribute a with equal weights $1/3$: $((a, L), 1/3), ((a, N), 1/3), ((a, H), 1/3)$. The Table 1 changed into Table 2, and is shown below.

Table 2. More complete information system

Objects	Attributes		
	a	b	d
x_1	N	H	-
x_2	H	L	-
x_3	N	H	+
x_4	L	L	0
x_5	L	H	+
x_6	L	N	+
x_7	L	L	0
x_8	N	H	-
x_9		N	-

Step 5: Extract and simplify the rules. For extracting rules from such information system we use algorithm ERID [11], which is similar to LERS [5]. For the above example, the certain rules can be extracted as follows:

$$(a, N) * (b, N) \rightarrow (d, -) \qquad\qquad (a, H) * (b, L) \rightarrow (d, -)$$
$$(a, H) * (b, N) \rightarrow (d, -) \qquad\qquad (a, L) * (b, H) \rightarrow (d, +)$$
$$(a, L) * (b, L) \rightarrow (d, 0)$$

We can also obtain in a similar way all possible rules, and using given support and confidence we can evaluate all interesting possible rules as well.

4 Implementation and Testing

Our main goal is initial data analysis and data processing to explore different combinations of important factors leading to a significant recovery, and their relationships to different category of children flat foot problem. The human foot is a complex system which determines the interaction between the lower limbs and the ground during locomotion. Flat foot is the most common foot deformity known in children. In fact, 20% of children have flat foot [13]. Flat foot is a foot that does not have an arch when standing. In the medical world, flat feet are associated with pronated feet. Excessive pronation can lead to other medical problems such as: heel, knee, hip, or back pain, bunions, hammertoes, etc. Lack of an appropriate treatment may trigger additional complications including joint deformity, and gait instability. The one important characteristics of flat-foot is medial longitudinal arch, which describes the characteristic of body dynamic. The most important aspect of flat feet treatment is determining the exact type or underlying cause of flat feet, which is not always so obvious. There are many different treatment options [13]. Children may be treated with some type of support, whether it is molded insoles, special shoes, or braces. Without support to hold the foot in the correct position, the bones can develop abnormally, leading to future problems. The main goal of our work is how to predict which parameters such as age, body mass, gender, place of living, foot orthotics wedging, and playing sport, the arch height correction due to flat-foot can be essential and which of them and how can be changed. We analyzed the difference in arch height in 100 typical children (50 active children and 50 inactive children) aged from 9 to 10 years old. Records are grouped by similar foot orthotics wedging (in months) in the last two years, where these information of each patient is discretize into durations first, anchored from its initial treatment data. To reduce the number of values for numerical attributes in the database we used classical method based either on entropy or Gini index resulting in a hierarchical discretization. We explored the feasibility of predicting arch height correction. Our first results demonstrated that the arch height correction as age increased from 9 to 17 years. We also checked that flat feet children in age 7-15 years still need a correction. A significant difference was observed between the cities and countries populations. We observed that the arch height in girls from countries

(54.4%) was much higher than in boys (4.9%), and even more: it increased in active boys (38.8%) from countries and in active girls (36.1%) from cities. However, in active girls from counties the arch height decreased by 2.6%. This results suggests that in active flat feet children the arch height correction is higher than in inactive flat feet children.

The model suggests that the arch height correction is increased by increasing age and children activity. The arch height will increase by about 10% in boys and girls as the time of foot orthotics wedging increased from 0 to 22 months.

5   Conclusions

This paper put forward a new algorithm to extract rules from incomplete information system based on the reducts of rough sets models. The presented algorithm estimates some unknown condition attribute values and extract rules from the new, more complete information system. Presented method is simple for implementation and gives promising results during its testing on flat feet database.

Acknowledgment. This paper is supported by Bialystok University of Technology (S/WM/2/2008).

References

1. Chmielewski, M., Grzymala-Busse, J., Peterson, N., Than, S.: The rule induction system LERS-A version for personal computers. Found. Comput. Decision Sci. 18, 181–212 (1993)
2. Dardzinska, A., Ras, Z.: Rule-Based Chase Algorithm for Partially Incomplete Information Systems. In: Proceedings of the Second International Workshop on Active Mining (AM 2003), pp. 42–51 (October 2003)
3. Dardzinska, A., Ras, Z.: On Rule Discovery from Incomplete Information Systems. In: Proceedings: ICDM 2003 Workshop on Foundations and New Directions of Data Mining, pp. 31–35 (2003)
4. Dardzinska, A., Ras, Z.W.: Extracting Rules from Incomplete Decision Systems. In: Lin, T.Y., Ohsuga, S., Liau, C.-J., Hu, X. (eds.) Foundations and Novel Approaches in Data Mining. SCI, vol. 9, pp. 143–154. Springer, Heidelberg (2006)
5. Grzymala-Busse, J.: A new version of the rule induction system LERS. Fundamenta Informaticae 31(1), 27–39 (1997)
6. Giudici, P.: Applied Data Mining, Statistical Methods for Business and Industry. Wiley, West Sussex (2003)
7. Kryszkiewicz, M.: Rough set approach to incomplete information systems. Information Sciences, 39–49 (1998)
8. Pawlak, Z.: Rough sets. International Journal of Computer and Information Sciences 11, 341–356 (1982)
9. Pawlak, Z.: Rough sets-theoretical aspects of reasoning about data. Kluwer, Dordrecht (1991)

10. Ras, Z., Dardzinska, A.: Data security and null value imputation in distributed information systems, pp. 133–146. Springer (2005)
11. Ras, Z., Dardzinska, A.: Extracting Rules from Incomplete Decision Systems: System ERID, pp. 143–154. Springer (2005)
12. Sviridenok, A., Lashkovsky, V.: Biomechanical aspects of modern podiatrics development. In: International Conference in Biomechanics of Human Foot, pp. 4–11 (2008)
13. Tsumoto, S.: Automated extraction of medical expert system rules from clinical databases based on rough set theory. Information Sciences 112, 67–84 (1998)

Rough Sets-Based Rules Generation Approach: A Hepatitis C Virus Data Sets

Ahmed Zaki[1,*], Mostafa A. Salama[2,*], Hesham Hefny[1],
and Aboul Ella Hassanien[3,*]

[1] Department of Computer Sciences and Information, ISSR, Cairo University, Egypt
[2] Department of Computer Science, British University in Egypt, Cairo, Egypt
[3] Faculty of Computers and Information, Cairo University, Cairo, Egypt
http://www.egyptscience.net

Abstract. The risk of hepatitis-C virus is considered as a challenge in the field of medicine. Applying feature reduction technique and generating rules based on the selected features were considered as an important step in data mining. It is needed by medical experts to analyze the generated rules to find out if these rules are important in real life cases. This paper presents an application of a rough set analysis to discover the dependency between the attributes, and to generate a set of reducts consisting of a minimal number of attributes. The experimental results obtained, show that the overall accuracy offered by the rough sets is high.

Keywords: rough sets, rough reduct, rule generation, HCV.

1 Introduction

Medical informatics or Bioinformatics deals with the resources, devices, and methods required optimizing the acquisition, storage, retrieval, and use of information in health and biomedicine. Medical informatics tools include not only computers but also clinical guidelines, formal medical terminologies, and information and communication systems. It is applied to the areas of nursing, clinical care, dentistry, pharmacy, public health and (bio) medical research. As more data is gathered, medical doctors cannot use the tools for their own data analysis individually. User-centered universal tools should be applied for medical researchers to analyze their own data. An example of these researchers is the study in [1] has been started to discover the differences in the temporal patterns of hepatitis B (HBV) and C (HCV) which has not been clearly defined, and more importantly, to examine whether the methods applied can work well and be applied to other fields. Hepatitis is swelling and inflammation of the liver. It is not a condition, but is often used to refer to a viral infection of the liver. Hepatitis can be caused by: Immune cells in the body attacking the liver and causing autoimmune hepatitis Infections from viruses (such as hepatitis A, B, or C), bacteria, or parasites Liver damage from alcohol, poisonous mushrooms,

---

* Scientific Research Group in Egypt (SRGE).

A. Ell Hassanien et al. (Eds.): AMLTA 2012, CCIS 322, pp. 52–59, 2012.

or other poisons, medications, such as an overdose of acetaminophen, which can be deadly. Liver disease can also be caused by inherited disorders such as cystic fibrosis or hemochromatosis, a condition that involves having too much iron in your body (the excess iron deposits in the liver). The World Health organization (WHO) estimates that 170 million people, i.e. 3% of the world's population, are currently infected with the hepatitis-C virus (HCV) [2]. In majority of such cases, Symptoms are not appeared in the infected people for many years thus leaving them totally unaware of their condition. Liver damage is not caused by the virus itself but by the immune reaction of the body to the attack. This damage can be extremely serious, therefore resulting in liver failure and death of the patient. The indications of this type of hepatitis are normally less critical than hepatitis B. Hepatitis C spreads through contaminated blood or blood products, Sexual contact, contaminated intravenous needles. With some cases of Hepatitis C, no approach of transmission can be recognized. The current treatment for HCV, according to the United Kingdom's clinical guidelines, is with a combination therapy of two drugs: Interferon-alpha and Ribavirin [3]. A chief factor in prescribing combination therapy is that both drugs generate side effects in most inhabitants. The cost of combination therapy is between Ł3000 and Ł12,000 per patient per year. It is a general thinking that treating patients from pricey drugs with potentially severe side effects may be unsuitable unless there is a clear evident that patient has been infected from the virus. A liver biopsy is presently the only technique available to assess HCV activity. The biopsy involves removing a small core of tissue, which is approximately 15 mm in length and 2-3 mm in Diameter. This core is then goes on in paraffin wax, cut into pieces along its length and stained. At this level, a trained histopathology's will investigate the Samples under a light microscope and use his/her practice, Combined with a comprehensive definition, to evaluate the level of damage. The damage can usually be classified into two types and it is general to assign a numerical score relative to the level of damage for each type. One of the most widely used scoring methods is the Ishak system [4], which can be summarized as: Inflammation: assigned a necroinflammatory2 (activity) score from 0 to 18.

The rest of this paper is organized as follows: Section 2 gives an overview of the rough set theory and its techniques. Section 3 describe the proposed rule generation approach. Section 4 describes the experimental results and analysis, while the conclusion is presented in Section 5.

2   Rough Sets: A Brief Overview

Due to space limitations we provide only a brief explanation of the basic framework of rough set theory, along with some of the key definitions. A more comprehensive review can be found in sources such as [11,12,13].

Rough sets theory provides a novel approach to knowledge description and to approximation of sets. Rough theory was introduced by Pawlak during the early eighties [11] and is based on an approximation space-based approach to classifying sets of objects. In rough sets theory, feature values of sample objects are collected in what are known as information tables. Rows of a such a table correspond to objects and columns correspond to object features.

Let $\mathcal{O}, \mathcal{F}$ denote a set of sample objects and a set of functions representing object features, respectively. Assume that $B \subseteq \mathcal{F}, x \in \mathcal{O}$. Further, let $x_{\sim B}$ denote

$$x_{/\sim_B} = \{y \in \mathcal{O} \mid \forall \phi \in B, \phi(x) = \phi(y)\},$$

i.e., $x_{/\sim_B}$ (description of x matches the description of y). Rough sets theory defines three regions based on the equivalent classes induced by the feature values: lower approximation $\underline{B}X$, upper approximation $\overline{B}X$ and boundary $BND_B(X)$. A lower approximation of a set X contains all equivalence classes $x_{/\sim_B}$ that are proper subsets of X, and upper approximation $\overline{B}X$ contains all equivalence classes $x_{/\sim_B}$ that have objects in common with X, while the boundary $BND_B(X)$ is the set $\overline{B}X \setminus \underline{B}X$, i.e., the set of all objects in $\overline{B}X$ that are not contained in $\underline{B}X$. Any set X with a non-empty boundary is *roughly* known relative, i.e., X is an example of a rough set.

The indiscernibility relation $\sim_B$ (also written as Ind_B) is a mainstay of rough set theory. Informally, $\sim_B$ is a set of all classes of objects that have matching descriptions. Based on the selection of B (i.e., set of functions representing object features), $\sim_B$ is an equivalence relation that partitions a set of objects $\mathcal{O}$ into classes (also called elementary sets [11]). The set of all classes in a partition is denoted by $\mathcal{O}_{/\sim_B}$ (also by $\mathcal{O}/Ind_B$). The set $\mathcal{O}/Ind_B$ is called the quotient set. Affinities between objects of interest in the set $X \subseteq \mathcal{O}$ and classes in a partition can be discovered by identifying those classes that have objects in common with X. Approximation of the set X begins by determining which elementary sets $x_{/\sim_B} \in \mathcal{O}_{/\sim_B}$ are subsets of X.

3 Rule Generation Approach on Hepatitis C Virus Data Sets

With increasing sizes of the amount of data stored in medical databases, efficient and effective techniques for medical data mining are highly sought after. Applications of Rough sets [5, 6, 7]in this domain include inducing propositional rules from databases using Rough sets prior to using these rules in an expert system. Tsumoto [8] presented a knowledge discovery system based on rough sets and feature-oriented generalization and its application to medicine. Diagnostic rules and information on features are extracted from clinical databases on diseases of congenital anomaly. Experimental Results showed that the proposed method extracts expert knowledge correctly and also discovers that symptoms observed play important roles in differential diagnosis. Hassanien el al. [9] presented a rough set approach to feature reduction and generation of classification rules from a set of medical datasets. They introduced a rough set reduction technique to find all redacts of the data that contain the minimal subset of features associated with a class label for classification. To evaluate the validity of the rules based on the approximation quality of the features, a statistical test to evaluate the significance of the rules was introduced. Rough sets rule-based classifier performed with a significantly better level of accuracy than the other classifiers. Therefore, the use of reducts concept in combination with rule-based classification offers an improved solution for data set recognition. The medical diagnosis process can be interpreted as a decision-making process, during which the physician induces the diagnosis of a new and unknown case from an available set of clinical data and from clinical experience. This process can be computerized in order to present medical diagnostic procedures in a rational, objective, Accurate and fast way. In fact, during the last two or three decades, diagnostic decision support systems have become a well-established component of medical technology. Podraza et. al [10] presented an idea of complex data analysis and decision support System for medical staff based on rough set theory. The main aim of their system is to provide an easy to use, commonly available tool for efficiently diagnosing Diseases, suggesting possible further treatment and deriving unknown dependencies between different data coming from various patients' examinations. A blueprint of a possible architecture of such a system is presented including some example algorithms and suggested solutions, which may be applied during implementation. The unique feature of the system relies on removing some data through rough set decisions to enhance the quality of the generated rules. Usually such data is discarded, because it does not contribute to the knowledge acquisition task or even hinder it. In their approach, improper data (excluded from the data used for drawing Conclusions) is carefully taken into considerations. This methodology can be very important in medical applications as a case not fitting to the general classification cannot be neglected, but should be examined with special care.

One way to construct a simple model computed from data, easier to understand and with more predictive power, is to create a set of minimal number of rules. Some condition values may be unnecessary in a decision rule produced directly from the database. Such values can then be eliminated to create a more comprehensible minimal rule preserving essential information. The presented rough set approach for rule generation contains two phases (a) Discretization and (b) rule Generation. More details within the following subsections.

Discretization Based on RSBR. A real world data set, like medical data sets, contains mixed types of data including continuous and discrete valued data sets. The discretization process divides the attribute's value into intervals [11]. The discretization based on RS and Boolean Reasoning (RSBR) shows the best results in the case of heart disease data set. In the discretization of a decision table $S = (U, A \bigcap \{d\})$, where U is a non-empty finite set of objects and A is a non-empty finite set of attributes. And $V_a = [x_a, x_a)$ is an interval of real values x_a, w_a in attribute a. The required is to a partition P_a of V_a for any $a \in A$. Any partition of V_a is defined by a sequence of the so-called cuts $x_1 < x_2 < .. < x_k$ from V_a. The main steps of the RSBR discretization algorithm are provided in algorithm 1.

Algorithm 1. RSBR discretization algorithm

Input: Information system table (S) with real valued attributes A_{ij} and n is the number of intervals for each attribute.

Output: Information table (ST) with discretized real valued attribute.

1: **for** $A_{ij} \in S$ **do**
2:    Define a set of boolean variables as follows:

$$B = \{\sum_{i=1}^{n} C_{ai}, \sum_{i=1}^{n} C_{bi} \sum_{i=1}^{n} C_{ci}, ..., \sum_{i=1}^{n} C_{ni}\} \tag{1}$$

3: **end for**
    Where $\sum_{i=1}^{n} C_{ai}$ correspond to a set of intervals defined on the variables of attributes a
4: Create a new information table S_{new} by using the set of intervals C_{ai}
5: Find the minimal subset of C_{ai} that discerns all the objects in the decision class D using the following formula:

$$\Upsilon^u = \wedge\{\Phi(i,j) : d(x_i \neq d(x_j)\} \tag{2}$$

Where $\Phi(i,j)$ is the number of minimal cuts that must be used to discern two different instances x_i and x_j in the information table.

3.1 Rule Generating and Analysis Phase

Unseen instances are considered in the discovery process, and the uncertainty of a rule, including its ability to predict possible instances, can be explicitly represented in the strength of the rule [11]. The quality of rules is related to the corresponding reduct(s). We are especially interested in generating rules which cover largest parts of the universe U. Covering U with more general rules implies smaller size of a rule set. The main steps of the rule generation algorithm are provided in algorithm 2.

4 Experimental Works and Discussions

The data available at UCI machine [13] learning data repository Contains 19 fields with one output field. The output shows whether patients with hepatitis are alive or dead. The intention of the dataset is to forecast the presence or absence of hepatitis virus. Given the results of various medical tests carried out on a patient. The Hepatitis dataset contains 155 samples belonging to two different target classes. There are 19 features, 13 binary and 6 features with 6-8 discrete values. Out of total 155 cases, the class variable contains 32 cases that died due to hepatitis. In this section, an dataset table has been chosen and hybridization scheme that combines the advantages of PCA,and rough sets

---

Algorithm 2. Rule generation and classification

Input: reduct sets $R_{final} = \{r_1 \cup r_2 \cup .... \cup r_n\}$
Output: Set of rules

1: **for** each reduct r **do**
2:     **for** each correspondence object x **do**
3:         Contract the decision rule $(c_1 = v_1 \wedge c_2 = v_2 \wedge .... \wedge c_n = v_n) \longrightarrow d = u$
4:         Scan the reduct r over an object x
5:         Construct $(c_i, 1 \leq i \leq n)$
6:         **for** every $c \in C$ **do**
7:             Assign the value v to the correspondence attribute a
8:         **end for**
9:         Construct a decision attribute d
10:         Assign the value u to the correspondence decision attribute d
11:     **end for**
12: **end for**

---

in conjunction with statistical feature extraction techniques, have been applied to see their ability and accuracy to detect and classify the dataset into two outcomes: die or live.

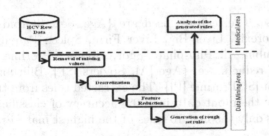

Fig. 1. Data mining services to the medical area

The architecture of the proposed rough sets approache is illustrated in figure 1. It is comprised of four fundamental building phases: In the first phase of the investigation, a preprocessing algorithm based on Normalizing data processing is presented. It is adopted to improve the quality of the data and to make the feature reducts phase more reliable. The set of features relevant to region of interest is extracted, and represented in a database as vector values. The third phase is rough set analysis. It is done by computing the minimal number of necessary attributes, together with their significance, and generating the sets of rules. Finally, a rough is designed to discriminate different regions of interest in order to separate them into die and live cases. These four phases are described in detail in the following section along with the steps involved and the characteristics

Table 1. The architecture of the proposed rough sets approache

Matches	Conditions	Class
86	(B=(-Inf,1.65)), (AP=(-Inf,131.5)) (P=(50.5,Inf))	2
77	(SP=(1.45,Inf)), (AP =(-Inf,131.5)) (P=(50.5,Inf))	2
52	(S=(58.5,Inf)), (P=(50.5,Inf))	2
46	(SP=(1.45,Inf)), (B=(-Inf,1.65)) (AP=(-Inf,131.5)), (S=(-Inf,58.5))	2
33	(AGE=(29.0,37.5)), (P=(50.5,Inf))	2
25	(AGE=(47.5,Inf)), (B=(-Inf,1.65)) (P=(50.5,Inf))	2
25	(AGE=(-Inf,29.0))	2
23	(AGE=(37.5,47.5)), (SP=(1.45,Inf)) (B =(-Inf,1.65)), (AP =(-Inf,131.5))	2
21	(AGE=(47.5,Inf)), (B=(-Inf,1.65)) (S=(-Inf,58.5))	2
19	(AGE=(47.5,Inf)), (SP=(1.45,Inf)) (P=(50.5,Inf))	2

feature for each phase. The features used are {Age, Sex, Steroid, Antivirals, Fatigue, Malaise, Anorexia, Liver Big, Liver Firm, Spleen Palpable, Spiders, Ascites, Varices, Bilirubin, Alk Phosphate, Sgot, Albumin, Protime, Histology}. The generated set of reducts are: {Age [A], Spiders [SP], Bilirubin [B], "Alk Phosphate" [AP], Sgot [S], Protime [P]}. The extracted rules from this data set, to successfully classify the input data in 100% accuracy of classification are 51 rules. Table (1) shows only the first 10 rules of the highest matches.

5   Conclusions and Future Works

In the steps of classification, discretization is one of the important steps in medical analysis. It partition the attribute value according to the classification problem. These cuts itself represents an importance in the medical field. It shows at which cut in the values the medical experts shows start to worry about the patient and what is the range of values that is considered as an alarm range. According to results after applying the reducts from the rough set theory and determining the rules, the classification accuracy resulted were 100. This implies that the generated rules are sufficient to classify the patient as If these rules are analyzed by experts in the field of medicine. It provides that the patients is in danger and the percentage of death is high. The future work here is to show this percentage in an accurate methodology.

References

1. Booth, J., OGrady, J., Neuberger, J.: Clinical guidelines on the management of hepatitis C, vol. 1, pp. 11–21 (2001)
2. Kedziora, P., Figlerowicz, M., Formanowicz, P., Alejska, M., Jackowiak, P., Malinowska, N., Fratczak, A., Blazewicz, J., Figlerowicz, M.: Comp utational Methods in Diagnostics of Chronic Hepatitis C. Bulletin of the Polish Academy of Sciences, Technical Sciences 53(3), 273–281 (2005)
3. Hodgson, S., Harrison, R.F., Cross, S.S.: An automated Pattern recognition system for the quantification of Inflammatory cells in hepatitis-C-infected liver biopsies. Image and Vision Computing 24, 1025–1038 (2006)
4. Ishak, K., Baptista, A., Histological, L.B., et al.: Histological grading and staging of chronic hepatitis. Journal of Hepatology 22, 696–699 (1995)
5. Pawlak, Z.: Rough Set. International Journal of Computer and Information Sciences 11, 341–356 (1982)
6. Wojcik, Z.: Rough approximation of shapes in pattern recognition. Computer Vision, Graphics, and Image Processing 40, 228–249 (1987)
7. Pal, S.K., Pal, B.U., Mitra, P.: Granular computing, rough entropy and object extraction. Pattern Recognition Letters 26(16), 2509–2517 (2005)
8. Tsumoto, S.: Automated Extraction of Medical Expert System Rules from Clinical Databases on Rough Set Theory. Journal of Information Sciences 112, 67–84 (1998)
9. Hassanien, A.E., Abraham, A., Peters, J.F., Schaefer, G., Henry, C.: Rough sets and near sets in medical imaging: A review. IEEE Trans. Info. Tech. in Biomedicine (2009), doi:10.1109/TITB.2009.2017017
10. Podraza, R., Dominik, A., Walkiewicz, M.: Decision Support System for Medical Applications. In: Proceedings of the IASTED International Conference on Applied Simulations and Modeling, Marbella, Spain, pp. 329–333. ACTA Press, Anaheim (2003)
11. Chao, S., Li, Y.: Multivariate interdependent discretization for continuous attribute. In: Proceeding of the 3rd International Conference on Information Technology and Applications, vol. 1, pp. 167–172 (2005)
12. Hameed, A.-Q., Ella, H.A., Ajith, A.: A Generic Scheme for Generating Prediction Rules Using Rough Sets Rough Set Theory: A True Landmark in Data Analysis, January 01, vol. 174, pp. 163–186 (2009)
13. UCI Machine Learning Repository,
   http://archive.ics.uci.edu/ml/datasets.html

Mammogram Segmentation Using Rough k-Means and Mass Lesion Classification with Artificial Neural Network

Vibha Bafna Bora[1], A.G. Kothari[2], and A.G. Keskar[3]

[1] G.H. Raisoni College of Engineering Nagpur-16, India
[2,3] Electronics Department, Visvesvaraya National Institute of Technology,
Nagpur-10, India

Abstract. The mammography is the most effective procedure for an early diagnosis of the breast cancer. Mammographic screening has been shown to be effective in reducing mortality rates by 30%–70%. In the analysis of Mammography images using Computer-Aided Diagnosis, Segmentation stage is one of the most Significant step, since it affects the accuracy of the Feature Extraction & Classification. In this paper, Rough k-means approach is used for segmentation of tumor from breast parenchyma. Pixel objects which definitely belong to the tumor region are classified under lower approximation, where as objects which possibly belong to the same are categorized as upper approximation. The difference of upper and lower approximation will result with objects in the rough boundaries. The segmentation algorithm has been verified on Mammograms from Mias database and the CICRI database. (Central India Cancer Research Institute, Nagpur, India). Geometrical and Textural features were calculated for segmented region. Once the features were computed for each region of interest (ROI), they are used as inputs to Artificial Neural Network (ANN) for classification as Benign or Malignant. Results of Rough k-means segmentation were compared with Otsu method of segmentation using ANN. Results indicate that Rough k-means method performs better than Otsu method in terms of classification accuracy up to 95% and can also reduces the number of biopsies required in the diagnostic process.

Keywords: Breast Cancer, Mammography, Rough k-means, Feature selection, Artificial Neural Network.

1   Introduction

Breast cancer is the leading cause of death in women. Currently the effective method for early detection and screening of breast cancers is Mammography [1]. Image processing techniques are used to assist radiologist for detecting tumors in Mammography. There is no doubt that evaluation and decisions of experts based on the data taken from patients are the most important factors in diagnosis, but objective, timely, detailed and precise computer-aided diagnosis(CAD) system, minimizing the possible errors caused by fatigued and inexperienced experts, also provide a great deal of help.

A. Ell Hassanien et al. (Eds.): AMLTA 2012, CCIS 322, pp. 60–69, 2012.
© Springer-Verlag Berlin Heidelberg 2012

Retrospective studies show that, in current breast cancer screenings, 10%–25% of the tumors are missed by the radiologists [2].

The significant steps in CAD system are 1) Image Segmentation; 2) Feature extraction; and 3) Mass Classification as shown in Fig.1. Segmentation involves partitioning an image into a set of homogeneous and meaningful regions so that the pixels in each partitioned region possess an identical set of properties or attributes. Extensive research has already been conducted in the field of detection of tumors in mammography. Many detection schemes involving tumor segmentation technique such as otsu thresholding [3], k-means clustering, fuzzy clustering [4] have been proposed. The challenges of k-means clustering are local minima and clusters having vague and imprecise boundaries. Such conditions of overlapping can be handled effectively by fuzzy or rough based techniques

In this paper, segmentation is done with rough k-means approach which assigns objects or pixels to more than one cluster. The set of objects which definitely belong to the cluster are classified under lower approximation, where as objects which possibly belong to the same are categorized as upper. The difference of upper and lower approximation will result objects in the rough boundaries. The results of rough k-means segmentation are compared with otsu segmentation.

The paper is organized as follows. Section 2 provides brief introduction of database and preprocessing. Section 3 presents segmentation using Otsu and Rough k-means algorithm on mammography images. Section 4 presents feature extracted from Otsu and Rough segmented region. Section 5 provides classification using Artificial Neural Network (ANN) followed by performance comparison of rough k-means with otsu. Section 6 presents Result and Conclusion with future work.

2   Database and Preprocessing

2.1   Database

The breast Mammography images used in this paper was taken from online Mias database. Few images from Central India Cancer Research Institute, Nagpur, India

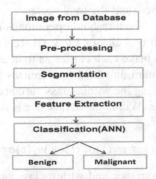

Fig. 1. CAD system for Classification of Mammography Image

were also considered for experimental purpose. The dataset consists of 84 cases, of which 32 are malignant and 52 are benign masses. All the diagnosis results of the cases were confirmed by biopsy.

2.2   Preprocessing

There are two steps involved in pre-processing the mammogram images and they are Noise reduction and Image enhancement. Noise may be accumulated during image acquisition. All the test images are subjected to median filtering. Many images have existing artifacts like written labels that need to be eliminate and this can done by cropping the images. In addition, the image enhancement step improves the quality of the image [5]. This is done by Histogram Equalization. It improves the distinct features in an image, by increasing the contrast range.

3   Segmentation Methods

A significant step in CAD algorithms is the segmentation of the mammographic image. The objective of this step is to extract one or more regions of interest (ROIs) from the background. This is not a trivial task, due to the vague borders, which make difficult their discrimination from the parenchyma's structures [6]. The accuracy of this process will affect strongly the following classification step. Segmentation methods can be divided into two main categories: edge-based methods and region-based. In edge-based methods, the local discontinuities are detected first and then connected to form longer, hopefully complete, boundaries. In region-based methods, areas of an image with homogeneous properties are found, which in turn give the boundaries. The threshold operation is regarded as the partitioning of the pixels of an image in two clusters.

3.1   Otsu Thresholding

This method is based on discriminant analysis. Let σ_w^2, σ_B^2 and σ_T^2 be the within-class variance, between-class variance, and the total variance, respectively. $\mu(1)$ and $\mu(2)$ be the means of class C0 & C1. The threshold operation is regarded as the partitioning of the pixels of an image into two classes C0 & C1. (e.g., objects and background). Threshold is set so as to try to make each cluster as tight as possible, thus minimizing their overlap [7, 8].Thus optimum threshold t maximizes the between-class variance, which is equivalent to minimizing the within-class variance, since the total variance is constant for different partitions .Within-class variance is defined as the weighted sum of the variances of each cluster.

$$\sigma_W^2(t) = w_1(t)\sigma_1^2(t) + w_2(t)\sigma_2^2(t) \tag{1}$$

Difference between the total variance and within-class variance is the between-class variance and is given by

$$\sigma_B^2(t) = \sigma_T^2 - \sigma_W^2(t) = w_1(t)w_2(t)[\mu_1(t) - \mu_2(t)]^2 \tag{2}$$

Thus the between-class variance is the weighted variance of the cluster means themselves around the overall mean. Fig 2 shows the results of Mammogram segmentation using Otsu thresholding.

3.2 Segmentation Using Rough k-Means

Clustering is an unsupervised classification of data patterns into homogeneous groups or clusters. Mostly used clustering algorithms used for image segmentation include k-means, Fuzzy C Means and Fuzzy Possibilstic c-means [9].

3.2.1 k-means Clustering

k-means is an iterative centre based algorithm to minimize the sum of point-to-centroid distances, summed over all k clusters. The objective is to assign n objects to k clusters [10]. k means algorithm proposed by Macqueen (1967) can be summarized as follows:

1. Choose initial centroid Ci for k cluster.
2. Assign objects xl with minimum distance $d(xl, Ci)$ to one of the clusters.
3. New updated centroid was obtained using the relation as

$$Ci = \frac{\sum_{xl \in C_i} xl}{|Ci|} \tag{3}$$

where $1 < i < k, 1 < l < n$ and $|Ci|$ is the cardinality of cluster.
4. Repeat step 2 and 3 until the updated centroid becomes stable.

The challenges of k-means clustering are vague and imprecise boundaries. Such conditions of overlapping can be handled by fuzzy or rough based techniques [11].

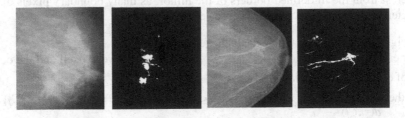

Fig. 2. Otsu segmentation (a) Original Image (mdb120) (b)Segmented Image (c) Original Image (cicri database) (d) Segmented Image

In many cases, the fuzzy degree of membership may be too descriptive for interpreting clustering results. Rough-set-based clustering gives a solution that is less restrictive than conventional clustering and less descriptive than fuzzy clustering.

3.2.2   Rough k-Means Segmentation

A rough set X is characterized by its lower and upper approximations $\underline{R}X$ and $\overline{R}X$ respectively. In rough context [12, 13] an object x_l can be a member of at most one lower approximation. If $x_l \in \underline{R}X$ of cluster X, then concurrently $x_l \in \overline{R}X$ of the same cluster. Whereas it will never belong to other clusters. If x_l is not a member of any lower approximation, then it will belong to two or more upper approximations. The following equation is used to calculate the centroids of clusters that need to be modified to include the effects of lower as well as upper bounds. The modified centroid calculations of cluster Ci are then given by [14]

- for $\underline{R}(Ci) \neq \phi$ and $Bnd(Ci) \neq \phi$

$$Ci = w_{low} \frac{\sum_{x_l \in \underline{R}(Ci)} x_l}{|\underline{R}(Ci)|} + w_{bnd} \frac{\sum_{x_l \in Bnd(Ci)} x_l}{|Bnd(Ci)|} \tag{4}$$

- for $\underline{R}(Ci) \neq \phi$ and $Bnd(Ci) = \phi$

$$Ci = w_{low} \frac{\sum_{x_l \in R(Ci)} x_l}{|\underline{R}(Ci)|} \tag{5}$$

where $w_{low} + w_{bnd} = 1$ and $1 < i < k$. The parameters w_{low} and w_{bnd} correspond to the relative importance of lower and upper bounds. $w_{low} < w_{bnd}$, $\underline{R}(Ci)$ signifies number of members in lower approximation of cluster Ci whereas $Bnd(Ci)$ signifies number of members present in rough boundary within two approximations. The next step is to design criteria to determine whether an pixel or object belongs to the upper and lower bound of a cluster.

- **Algorithm**

Rough k-means algorithm was applied to the leukocyte segmentation in microscopic images [11]. In Mammography images, rough k-means was applied to obtain region of interest from the ill defined borders of the tumor, as many boundary pixels display characteristics of ROI and parenchyma structures.[14]

1. Assign initial centroids Ci for the k clusters.
2. For each data object $x_l, 1 < l < n$, $d(x_l, Ci)$ the distance between itself and the centroid of cluster Ci is calculated.
3. If the $\frac{d(x_l, Cj)}{d(x_l, Ci)} \leq threshold$ where $1 \leq i, j \leq k$ and $d(x_l, Ci) = min_{1 \leq j \leq k} d(x_l, Cj)$ then

   $x_l \in \overline{R}(Ci)$ and $x_l \in \overline{R}(Cj)$ and x_l cannot be member of any lower approximation.
4. Else $x_l \in \underline{R}(Ci)$ such that Euclidean distance $d(x_l, Ci)$ is minimum over the k clusters.
5. Compute new updated centroid for each cluster Ci using equation (4 or 5).
6. Iterate till there are no more data members in the rough boundary.

The rough k-mean algorithm depends upon w_{low}, w_{bnd} and threshold (T). These parameters have to be suitably tuned for proper segmentation.

- **Practical Implementation**

Rough k-means algorithm was applied to mammograms obtained from mias & cicri database. The original image was resized to 220 x 220. For every pixel, gray level feature was recorded and feature data set X of size 48400 x 1 was prepared. Redundancy among data pattern was discarded. This reduced form of X with size Nx1 serves as an input for rough k-means. Three gray values were selected from X as initial clusters centers. Distance $d(x_1,Ci)$ between x_1 and each cluster center Ci $(1<i<k)$ was measured. Depending on the ratio of distances and threshold each pixel gray value was assigned to lower or upper approximation of corresponding clusters. This process was repeated till the upper approximation becomes empty. After remapping results are shown in Fig.3.

The values of w_{low}=0.8 & w_{bnd}=0.2. Threshold was varied between 0.5 to 4. As threshold increases, number of object or pixels in rough boundary increase. Through rigorous experimentation for the threshold in the range of 0.8 to 1.8, the mammography images were classified with good accuracy as benign and malignant.

4   Feature Extraction

A key stage in tumor classification is the feature extraction. The feature specifies some quantifiable property of an object or an image. Due to the diversity of normal tissues and the variety of abnormalities the feature space could be very large and complex [15]. Some features give geometrical information, other ones provides shape parameters & texture [5]. All of them are not suitable for lesion classification. From both ROIs, 15 features [16] extracted were mean, std_deviation, area, perimeter, compactness, uniformity, correlation, kurtosis, skewness, entropy, smoothness, mean_global, contrast, homogeneity, and energy. Table.1 shows the features extracted from Rough k-means segmented lesion.

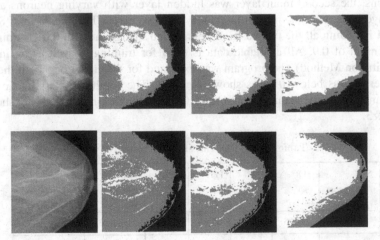

Fig. 3. Rough k-means Segmentation. From top to bottom are the cases of mdb120 and cicri database respectively.(a)Original image(b)Segmentation with T≤1.8 (c)T≤2.4(d) T≤3.2.

Table 1. Features extracted from Rough k-means ROI

filename	mean	std_deviation	area	perimeter	compactness	uniformity	correlation	kurtosis	skewness	entropy	smoothness	mean_global	contrast	homogeneity	energy
cicn1m.PNG	251.0541	32.92344915	2624	768	17.89653565	0.18808071	3398.3148	1.84E+10	228687470	-3.33153	0.0009217	173.7936713	36054.37	0.023263131	9.00E-06
cicn1n.PNG	249.5967	40.90563254	6336	1064	14.2258573	0.12652518	4941.92244	1.41E+11	1221312435	-3.35535	0.00059728	137.408936	38409.51	0.023254758	7.17E-06
cicn5n.PNG	250.8464	46.08051875	1536	516	13.80125398	0.23249308	1967.16864	2.99E+10	311383014	-2.96597	0.00047072	158.748088	42121.37	0.021232624	6.25E-06
cicn9m.PNG	249.0873	21.50276435	16640	1978	18.72016245	0.07562855	14629.9786	4.74E+10	603238421	-3.85081	0.00215811	171.9961534	95977.31	0.010063111	8.01E-06
cicn12m.PNG	249.9834	18.40927252	9728	2063	35.00159759	0.08689315	11550.1553	1.3E+10	206721029	-3.74107	0.00284203	189.4043406	32193.61	0.023359558	7.54E-06
cicn13n.PNG	251.265	42.10792434	1536	438	9.944143113	0.25217361	2428.11564	1.85E+10	224210374	-2.79619	0.00056367	172.1691702	47285.63	0.020579827	6.09E-06
cicn14m.PNG	251.3511	36.86637538	1664	594	16.58223451	0.18313565	2897.7147	1.68E+10	194945261	-3.21986	0.00073522	168.1443008	100979	0.009849822	8.00E-06
cicn14n.PNG	251.8058	50.57196952	896	312	8.649909008	0.30796452	1384.64869	1.91E+10	209030777	-2.62553	0.00389085	163.4524314	46969.71	0.020290404	6.09E-06
cicn15m.PNG	249.3542	33.22676149	1344	464	12.7540188	0.16448989	1680.56746	1.01E+10	122825662	-3.63861	0.0089655	171.990604	37940.35	0.023360264	7.41E-06
cicn20m.PNG	254.1696	70.62015048	896	286	7.258326319	0.69828703	2256.6481	3.19E+10	377645452	-1.20632	0.00220047	170.4749242	47990.45	0.020098673	6.11E-06
cicn21m.PNG	252.2751	39.6936855	4864	410	2.751594976	0.2015293	6278.95679	6E+10	677808685	-2.96915	0.00063428	165.9200443	45967.26	0.020250573	6.34E-06
mdb003.PNG	248.7121	28.91256976	19456	1734	12.30424554	0.07751124	13013.7013	1.76E+11	1991801824	-3.64926	0.00115483	145.8039708	67343.19	0.010315726	7.25E-06
mdb004.PNG	246.867	23.08959043	25280	2806	24.79754142	0.07007567	18340.9411	1.03E+11	1179414394	-3.91804	0.00187219	159.3354948	34029.45	0.022867722	7.14E-06
mdb005.PNG	252.8135	64.64025943	1984	289	3.351694126	0.4957076	3875.23296	6.99E+10	761229948	-1.86429	0.00229327	163.0643924	99470.83	0.012052333	6.32E-06
mdb010.png	250.5392	47.10078134	3776	826	14.38594745	0.21195295	4723.79117	8.03E+10	820077750	-2.98129	0.00045056	156.4474293	12210.1	0.023654338	7.45E-06
mdb013.png	249.3884	28.34083104	7232	1340	19.76754572	0.11002167	7074.13758	4.28E+10	497867081	-3.57323	0.00124347	166.3304343	95622.7	0.009750893	7.29E-06

5   Classification of Mass Lesion Using ANN

An Artificial neural network is a parallel distributed information processing structure consisting of processing elements (neurons). Neural networks can be trained using various learning algorithms classified as supervised and unsupervised learning algorithms. Gradient descent, Radial Basis Function (RBF), Learning vector quantization, Back propagation are some of the learning algorithms. Back propagation is one of the gradient descent supervised learning algorithm applied in feed forward neural networks. The knowledge gained by the learning experience is stored in the form of connection weights, which are used to make decisions on fresh input [17].

Back Propagation Neural Network (BPNN) has 3 layers; the first input layer with 15 neurons, the second input layer was hidden layer with varying neurons and the output layer was with one neuron to classify the two cases. The Database of 84 files was used including all the two cases of benign and malignant with 0.01 learning rate & momentum of 0.9. All available data is used for training as well as testing [18] (Resubstitution Method).The program was executed for different epochs till the mean squared error was below 0.05 as shown in Fig.4. The results of classification after training and testing the features from Otsu ROI and Rough k-means ROI are shown in Table 2 &3.

Table 2. Otsu ROI classification using BPNN

N/W Architecture (I-[H]-O)	TPR (%)	TNR (%)	FPR (%)	FNR (%)	Learning rate, Epochs	Accuracy (%)
15-45-1	79.15	64.31	35.69	20.85	0.01,85	72
15-25-1	75.78	53.57	46.43	24.22	0.01,98	65

Table 3. Rough ROI classification using BPNN

N/W Architecture (I-[H]-O)	TPR (%)	TNR (%)	FPR (%)	FNR (%)	Learning rate, Epochs	Accuracy (%)
15-45-1	93.56	95.65	4.35	6.44	0.01,265	95
15-25-1	68.81	79.45	20.55	31.19	0.01,367	74

6   Results, Conclusion and Future Work

An efficient way to compare the two techniques would be to measure the efficiency of methods in detecting malignant and benign cases. Malignant cases are the ones that can prove fatal to the patients and hence need immediate attention. Thus, to evaluate the performance, specificity and sensitivity of detection have been considered. Sensitivity and specificity are terms that show the significance of a method related to the presence or absence of the malignant cancer. Performance comparison is shown in Table 4.

MATLAB software package version 10 was used to implement the Otsu Segmentation, Rough k-means Segmentation & BP Neural Network. Otsu Segmentation technique has been proven to provide fast and easy way to perform the intensity segmentation on digital mammograms .The obtained accuracy of BPNN for Otsu ROI was 72% only whereas sensitivity & specificity was found out to be 79.15% and 64.31%respectively .While rough k-means gives accuracy upto 95% with sensitivity and specificity of 93.56% and 95.65% respectively at the cost of processing time. Thus the rough k-means is valuable to improve the accuracy of the diagnosis of breast cancer at low false positive rates and reduces the number of unnecessary biopsies.

Table 4. Performance Comparison

Method	Sensitivity	Specificity	Accuracy
Otsu	79.15 %	64.31 %	72 %
Rough k-means	93.56 %	95.65 %	95 %

Sensitivity = TPR/ (TPR + FNR),

Specificity= TNR/ (TNR + FPR)

Accuracy=(TPR+TNR)/(TPR+TNR+FNR+FPR)

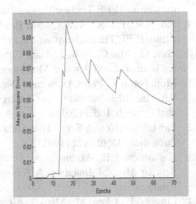

Fig. 4. Mean Square Error Plot

Furthermore, the detection results for some type of lesions which are characterized by texture may be improved if rough k-means clustering algorithm considers texture values in addition with gray value. Rough cluster quality index can be used to obtain optimum threshold for objects to be in lower bound or upper bound.

Acknowledgement. The authors would like to thanks Dr Suchitra Mehta, Central India Cancer Research Institute, Nagpur, India for providing labeled Mammography Images.

References

1. Sivaramakrishna, R., Gordon, R.: Detection of breast cancer at a smaller size can reduce the likelihood of metastatic spread: A quantitative analysis. J. Acad. Radiol. 4, 8–12 (1997)
2. Bird, R., Wallace, T., Yankaskas, B.: Analysis of cancer missed at screening mammography. J. Radiology 184, 613–617 (1992)
3. Gajanayake, G.M.N.R., Yapal, R.D., Hewawithana, B.: Comparison of Standard Image Segmentation Methods for Segmentation of Brain Tumors from 2D MRImages. In: 4th International Conference on Industrial and Information Systems, Sri Lanka, pp. 301–305 (2009)
4. Kanungo, T., Mount, D.M., Netanyahu, N.S., Piatko, C.D., Silverman, R., Wu, A.Y.: An efficient k-means clustering algorithm: analysis and implementation. IEEE Transactions on Pattern Analysis and Machine Intelligence 24, 881–892 (2002)
5. Gonzalez, R., Woods, R.: Digital image processing, 3rd edn. Prentice Hall, New York (2008)
6. Cascio, D., Fauci, F., Magro, R., Raso, G., Bellotti, R., De Carlo, F., Tangaro, S., De Nunzio, G., Quarta, M., Forni, G., Lauria, A., Fantacci, M.E., Retico, A., Masala, G.L., Oliva, P., Bagnasco, S., Cheran, S.C., Lopez Torres, E.: Mammogram Segmentation by Contour Searching and Mass Lesions Classification With Neural Network. IEEE Transactions on Nuclear Science 53, 2827–2833 (2006)
7. Otsu, N.: A Threshold Selection Method from Gray-Level Histogram. IEEE Transactions on Systems, Man, and Cybernetics 9, 62–66 (1979)
8. Cheriet, M., Said, J.N., Suen, C.Y.: A Recursive Thresholding Technique for Image Segmentation. IEEE Transactions on Image Processing 7, 918–921 (1998)
9. Pal, N.R., Pal, K., Keller, J.M., Bezdek, J.C.: A possibilistic fuzzy cmeans clustering algorithm. IEEE Transactions on Fuzzy Systems 13, 517–530 (2005)
10. Gan, G., Ma, C., Wu, J.: Data Clustering Theory, Algorithms, and Applications. Society for Industrial and Applied Mathematics (2007)
11. Mohapatra, S., Patra, D., Kumar, K.: Blood Microscopic Image Segmentation using Rough Sets. In: IEEE International Conference on Image Information Processing, pp. 1–6. Himachal Pradesh, India (2011)
12. Pawlak, Z.: Rough Sets –Theoritical Aspects of Reasoning about Data. Kluwer Academic Publishers, Dordrecht (1991)
13. Hassanien, A.E., Abraham, A., Peters, J.F., Schaefer, G., Henry, C.: Rough Sets and Near Sets in Medical Imaging: A Review. IEEE Transaction on Information Technology in Biomedicine 13, 955–968 (2009)
14. Lingras, P., Chen, M., Miao, D.: Rough Cluster Quality Index Based on Decision Theory. IEEE Transactions on Knowledge and Data Engineering 21, 1014–1026 (2009)
15. Shi, X., Cheng, H.D., Hua, L., Ju, W., Tian, J.: Detection and classification of masses in breast ultrasound images. J. Digital Signal Processing 20, 824–836 (2010)

16. Al-Shamlan, H., El-Zaart, A.: Feature Extraction Values for Breast Cancer Mammography Images. In: IEEE International Conference on Bioinformatics and Biomedical Technology, pp. 335–340 (2010)
17. Al-Timemy, A.H., Al-Naima, F.M., Qaeeb, N.H.: Probabilistic Neural Network for Breast Biopsy Classification. In: 2nd International Conference on Developments in eSystems Engineering, pp. 101–106. IEEE Computer Society (2009)
18. Jain, A.K., Duin, R.P.W., Mao, J.: Statistical Pattern Recognition: A Review. IEEE Transactions on Pattern Analysis and Machine Intelligence 22, 4–37 (2000)

Part II

Machine Learning in Pattern Recognition and Image Processing

Automatic Color Image Segmentation
Based on Illumination Invariant and Superpixelization

Muhammed Salem, Abdelhameed Ibrahim, and Hesham Arafat

Computers and Systems Engineering Department, Faculty of Engineering,
Mansoura University, Mansoura, Egypt
{afai79,h_arafat_ali}@mans.edu.eg

Abstract. Superpixel and invariant methods for color images are becoming increasingly popular in many applications of computer vision and image analysis. This paper presents an automatic segmentation based on illumination invariant and superpixelization methods. We develop an automatic superpixel generation method by automatically modifying the quick-shift parameters based on invariant images. The proposed method segments a color image into homogeneous regions by applying quick-shift method with initial parameters, and then automatically get the final segmented image by calculating the best similarity between the output image and the invariant image by changing the quick-shift parameters values. To reduce the number of colors in image that will be used in comparison, a quantization process is applied to the original invariant image. Changing parameters values in iterations instead of using a specific value made the proposed algorithm flexible and robust against different image characteristics. The effectiveness of the proposed method for a variety of images including different objects of metals and dielectrics are examined in experiments.

Keywords: Superpixel, invariant feature, color image, image representation, image segmentation.

1   Introduction

Illumination factors such as shading, shadow, and specular highlight, observed from object surfaces in a natural scene, affect seriously the appearance and analysis of the images. Therefore, image representation invariant to these factors was proposed for color and spectral images in several ways [1-2, 19-20]. These invariant representations play an important role in many applications such as feature detection, such as edge and corner detection, object recognition, and image retrieval. Ibrahim et al. [2] presents an invariant method that is independent of the geometric parameters and is invariant to highlights and shading. This representation is available for all material surfaces including dielectric and metal, observed under a general illumination environment including colored light source.

Image segmentation refers to the process of partitioning an image into homogeneous and connected regions or segments (sets of pixels, also known as superpixels). The goal is subdividing an image into its constituent regions or objects that have similar features according to a set of predefined criteria. It is also typically

A. Ell Hassanien et al. (Eds.): AMLTA 2012, CCIS 322, pp. 73–81, 2012.

used to locate objects and boundaries such as lines, curves, etc. Superpixel is commonly known as a perceptually uniform region in the image, so removing shadow and highlight make image features more adequate. The major advantage of using superpixels is computational efficiency. A superpixel representation greatly reduces the number of image primitives compared to the pixel representation. Moreover, superpixel segmentation provides the spatial support for computing region based features and change the representation of an image into another that is more meaningful and easier to analyze.

This paper uses quickshift [3] to extract superpixels from the illumination-invariant images. Unlike superpixelization schemes based on normalized cuts (e.g. [21]), the superpixels produced by quickshift are not fixed in approximate size or number. A complex image with many fine scale image structures may have many more superpixels than a simple one, and there is no parameter which puts a penalty on the boundary, leading to superpixels which are quite varied in size and shape. This produces segmentations consist of many small regions that preserve most of the boundaries in the original image.

The superpixels extracted via quickshift are controlled by three parameters of ratio, tradeoff between spatial consistency and color consistency, KernelSize, the standard deviation of the parzen window density estimator, and MaxDist, the maximum distance between nodes in the quickshift tree which used to cut links in the tree to form the segmentation. Fulkerson et al. [10] use the same parameters for all of their experiments where these values were determined by segmenting a few training images by hand until they found a set which preserved nearly all of the object boundaries and had the largest possible average segment size. In practice, the algorithm is sensitive to the choice of parameters, so a quick tuning by hand is not sufficient.

This paper presents an automatic color image segmentation based on illumination invariant representation [2] and superpixelization [3] methods. We develop an automatic superpixel generation method by automatically modifying the quick-shift parameters based on invariant images. The invariant method reduces shading, shadow, and specular highlight which affect seriously the appearance and analysis of the color images. The proposed method segments images into homogeneous regions by extract superpixels via quick-shift method through looking for the parameter set which achieve best similarity. To reduce the number of colors in image that will be used in comparison, a quantization process is applied to the original invariant image. Changing parameters values in iterations instead of using a specific value made the proposed algorithm flexible and robust against different image characteristics. The effectiveness of the proposed method for a variety of images including different objects of metals and dielectrics are examined in experiments.

The reminder of this paper is organized as follow: Section 2 briefly reviews the existing superpixel segmentation methods. In Section 3, the proposed automatic segmentation method is presented in details. Section 4 tests the proposed method for various images and shows the quickshift parameter values for best similarity with CPU time for the tested images. This paper ends with conclusions in Section 5.

2   Superpixel Segmentation Methods

We briefly review existing image segmentation methods and focus on their suitability for producing superpixels. Mainly according to [4,18], algorithms for generating superpixels can be broadly categorized as either graph-based or gradient-ascent-based methods.

2.1   Graph-Based Methods

NC05 – The Normalized cuts algorithm [5] recursively partitions a graph of all pixels in the image using contour and texture cues, globally minimizing a cost function defined on the edges at the partition boundaries. It produces very regular, visually pleasing superpixels. However, the boundary adherence of NC05 is relatively poor and it is the slowest among the methods (particularly for large images), although attempts to speed up the algorithm exist [6]. NC05 has a complexity of O $(N^{(3/2)})$ [7], where N is the number of pixels.

SL08 – Moore et al. propose a method to generate superpixels that conform to a grid by finding optimal paths, or seams, that split the image into smaller vertical or horizontal regions [8]. Optimal paths are found using a graph cuts method similar to Seam Carving [9]. While the complexity of SL08 is O $(N^{3/2} \log N)$ according to the authors, this does not account for the pre-computed boundary maps, which strongly influence the quality and speed of the output.

2.2   Gradient-Ascent-Based Methods

QS08 – Quick shift [3] also uses a mode-seeking segmentation scheme. It initializes the segmentation using a medoid shift procedure. It then moves each point in the feature space to the nearest neighbor that increases the Parson Density estimate. It has relatively good boundary adherence and the superpixels produced by QS08 are not fixed in approximate size or number. Previous works have used QS08 for object localization [10] and motion segmentation [11] where the parameters were manually determined by segmenting a few training images.

TP09 – Turbopixel method progressively dilates a set of seed locations using level-set based geometric flow [12]. The geometric flow relies on local image gradients, aiming to regularly distribute superpixels on the image plane. TP09 superpixels are constrained to have uniform size, compactness, and boundary adherence. TP09 relies on algorithms of varying complexity, but in practice, as the authors claim, has approximately O(N) behavior [12]. However, it is among the slowest algorithms examined and exhibits relatively poor boundary adherence.

SLIC10 – Simple linear iterative clustering (SLIC) is an adaptation of k-means for superpixel generation. Authors in [13] generates superpixels by clustering pixels based on their color similarity and proximity in the image plane. SLIC is similar to the approach used as a reprocessing step for depth estimation described in [14], which was not fully explored in the context of superpixel generation.

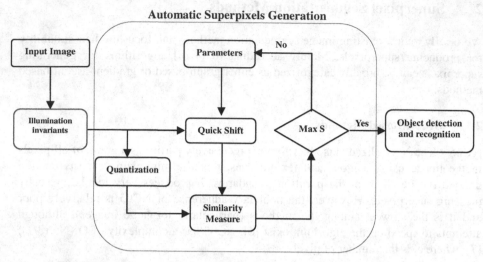

Fig. 1. Block diagram showing the proposed automatic segmentation method

gSLIC11 – gSLIC [22] is a parallel implementation of the Simple Linear Iterative Clustering (SLIC) superpixel segmentation by using GPU and the NVIDIA CUDA framework. Using a single graphic card, this implementation achieves speedups of 10x to 20x from the sequential implementation. This allow to use the superpixel segmentation method in real-time performance. The software is now online and is open source.

3   Proposed Automatic Segmentation Method

The proposed method block diagram is shown in Figure 1. The method aims to segment the input RBG images into homogenous regions by applying an automatic superpixels generation to be suitable for object detection and recognition. First, we eliminating the factors that may affect image acquisition such as shadow and highlight by applying an illumination invariant method [2]. Let $\mathbf{C}_S = \begin{bmatrix} C_S^{(R)} & C_S^{(G)} & C_S^{(B)} \end{bmatrix}^T$ be a 3D column vector representing the red, green, and blue sensor responses of a color imaging system observing the object. The invariant equation is given as

$$\hat{C}_S'^{(i)} = \frac{\hat{C}_S^{(i)} - \min\{\hat{C}_S^{(R)}, \hat{C}_S^{(G)}, \hat{C}_S^{(B)}\}}{\sqrt{\sum_{j \in \{R,G,B\}} \left(\hat{C}_S^{(j)} - \min\{\hat{C}_S^{(R)}, \hat{C}_S^{(G)}, \hat{C}_S^{(B)}\}\right)^2}}, \quad i \in \{R,G,B\} \tag{1}$$

This representation is available for all material surfaces including dielectric and metal, observed under a general illumination environment including colored light source.

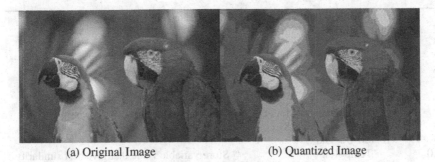

(a) Original Image   (b) Quantized Image

Fig. 2. Image Quantization [23]

Second, we reduce the number of colors of the invariant image that will be used in comparison as a reference image by quantization process [23]. Quantization involves reducing the number of colors in an image by dividing the RGB color cube into a number of smaller boxes, and then mapping all colors that fall within each box to the color value at the center of that box. Uniform quantization and minimum variance quantization are types of quantization and differ in the approach used to divide up the RGB color cube. With uniform quantization, the color cube is cut up into equal-sized boxes (smaller cubes) and with minimum variance quantization, the color cube is cut up into boxes (not necessarily cubes) of different sizes; the sizes of the boxes depend on how the colors are distributed in the image.

In minimum variance quantization, the method specify the maximum number of colors in the output image's color map. The number specified determines the number of boxes into which the RGB color cube is divided. Figure 2 shows an example of the importance of the quantization. Minimum variance quantization works by associating pixels into groups based on the variance between their pixel values. For example, a set of blue pixels might be grouped together because they have a small variance from the center pixel of the group. Kim et al. [24] presents a scene-adaptive color quantization method which eases this constraint by determining the number of representative colors automatically.

Then, we apply the quickshift [3] to extract superpixels from the invariant images to be compared with quantized invariant images. Quickshift exploits kernel methods to extend both mean-shift and the improved medoid-shift to a large family of distances, with complexity bounded by the effective rank of the resulting kernel matrix, and with explicit regularization constraints. Quick shift explicitly trades off under- and over fragmentation and operates in non-Euclidean spaces in a straightforward manner.

The superpixels are controlled in the proposed automatic method by three parameters of ratio, KernelSize, and MaxDist. Initial parameters values are set, then the similarity between segmented image and quantized invariant image is calculated. We repeat the previous steps several times automatically with changing the parameters values till reaching the highest similarity (Max S) as shown in Fig.1. The accuracy of the segmentation results between the segmented image and the quantized invariant images is numerically demonstrated by the similarity measure with a suitable window size for labeled images [25]. Figure 3 shown the overall algorithm for producing the final segmented image.

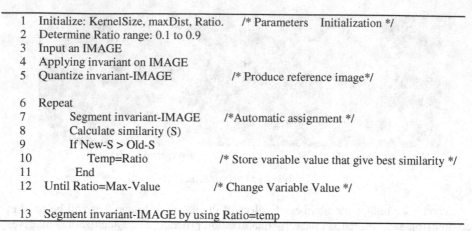

1   Initialize: KernelSize, maxDist, Ratio.   /* Parameters   Initialization */
2   Determine Ratio range: 0.1 to 0.9
3   Input an IMAGE
4   Applying invariant on IMAGE
5   Quantize invariant-IMAGE   /* Produce reference image*/

6   Repeat
7   Segment invariant-IMAGE   /*Automatic assignment */
8   Calculate similarity (S)
9   If New-S > Old-S
10   Temp=Ratio   /* Store variable value that give best similarity */
11   End
12   Until Ratio=Max-Value   /* Change Variable Value */

13   Segment invariant-IMAGE by using Ratio=temp

Fig. 3. Algorithm: automatic image segmentation

4   Experiments

We have examined the performance of the proposed segmentation method for color images of natural scenes of different objects. Figure 4 illustrates different stages of the proposed method. Figure 4 (a) shown four different color images which containing metals and dielectric objects, Img1(409x312), Img2(173x174), Img3(173x174), and Img4(276x175). Figure 4(b) presents the illumination-invariant representation of such images. The color quantization of the invariant images is shown in Fig. 4(c). Figure 4 (d) shows the final segmentation result.

We note that the final segmented image by the proposed automatic method is better than the invariant image and very similar to the quantized invariant image. The edges of the proposed segmented images are more sharpen, however, the invariant images are look noisy. Note that, for image Img2, our result is the best.

To get the optimum similarity value, we had to do some experiments on the values of quickshift parameters; which are kernel size, maximum distance and ratio. For example, after doing some experiments on image Img1, a sample results are shown in Table.1. Table 1 shows that the best similarity of 91.25% for image Img1 is produced within CPU time of 21.47s and the best parameters values are Ratio=0.2, KernelSize=4, and MaxDist=30. Higher similarity value indicates that the final segmented image is looks like the quantized invariant image. The experiments are run on CPU Intel Core2 Due 2GHz with 2G memory using Matlab.

The quickshift parameters values, best similarity, and CPU time for the other tested images in Fig.4. are shown in Table 2. In our experiments, we note that the best values for most of the images are KernelSize=2 and MaxDist =10 but the ratio is different from image to another according to the nature of image and objects within it.

(a)   (b)   (c)   (d)

Fig. 4. Illustrates different stages of the proposed algorithm; (a) Original image, (b) Invariant image, (c) Quantized invariant image, (d) Proposed segmented image

Table 1. Sample results for image Img1

Ratio	KernelSize	MaxDist	Similarity	CPU-Time (s)
0.2	2.0	10.0	0.85126	12.00
0.2	2.0	20.0	0.8865	13.66
0.2	2.0	30.0	0.9053	18.05
0.2	4.0	10.0	0.8649	15.37
0.2	4.0	20.0	0.8955	17.55
0.2	**4.0**	**30.0**	**0.9125**	**21.47**
0.9	2.0	10.0	0.8373	11.29
0.9	2.0	20.0	0.8811	14.27
0.9	2.0	30.0	0.9018	17.87
0.9	4.0	10.0	0.8554	15.18
0.9	4.0	20.0	0.8920	17.77
0.9	4.0	30.0	0.9096	21.64

Table 2. Quickshift parameters values, best similarity, and CPU time for the tested images in Fig.4

Image Name	Ratio	KernelSize	MaxDist	Similarity	CPU-Time (s)
Img1	0.2	4	30	0.9125	21.47
Img2	0.1	2	10	0.90030	2.71
Img3	0.1	2	10	0.83832	2.83
Img4	0.1	2	10	0.84417	4.35

5   Conclusion

This paper proposed a flexible and robust method for image segmentation based on superpixelization and illumination invariant with considering of an automatic modification of quickshift parameters. We developed an automatic superpixel generation method by automatically modifying the quick-shift parameters based on invariant images. The proposed method segmented color images into homogeneous regions by applying quick-shift method with initial parameters, and then automatically get the final segmented image by calculating the best similarity between the output image and the quantized invariant image. The effectiveness of the proposed method for a variety of images including different objects of metals and dielectrics are examined in experiments. Overall object detection and recognition are left as future works.

References

1. Ibrahim, A., Tominaga, S., Horiuchi, T.: Invariant representation for spectral reflectance images and its application. EURASIP Journal on Image and Video Processing, 1–12 (June 2011)
2. Ibrahim, A., Tominaga, S., Horiuchi, T.: Illumination-invariant representation for natural color images and its application. In: IEEE Southwest Symposium on Image Analysis and Interpretation (SSIAI 2012), USA (2012)
3. Vedaldi, A., Soatto, S.: Quick Shift and Kernel Methods for Mode Seeking. In: Forsyth, D., Torr, P., Zisserman, A. (eds.) ECCV 2008, Part IV. LNCS, vol. 5305, pp. 705–718. Springer, Heidelberg (2008)
4. Achanta, R., Shaji, A., Smith, K., Lucchi, A., Fua, P., Susstrunk, S.: SLIC Superpixels, EPFL Technical Report 149300 (June 2010)
5. : Normalized cuts and image segmentation. IEEE Transactions on Pattern Analysis and Machine Intelligence (PAMI), 888–905 (2000)
6. Cour, T., Benezit, F., Shi, J.: Spectral segmentation with multiscale graph decomposition. In: IEEE Computer Vision and Pattern Recognition, CVPR 2005 (2005)
7. Levinshtein, A., Stere, A., Kutulakos, K., Fleet, D., Dickinson, S., Siddiqi, K.: Turbopixels: Fast superpixels using geometric flows. IEEE Transactions on Pattern Analysis and Machine Intelligence, PAMI (2009)
8. Moore, A., Prince, S., Warrell, J., Mohammed, U., Jones, G.: Superpixel Lattices. In: IEEE Computer Vision and Pattern Recognition, CVPR (2008)
9. Avidan, S., Shamir, A.: Seam carving for content-aware image resizing. ACM Transactions on Graphics (SIGGRAPH) 26(3) (2007)

10. Fulkerson, B., Vedaldi, A., Soatto, S.: Class segmentation and object localization with superpixel neighborhoods. In: IEEE 12th International Conference on Computer Vision (ICCV), pp. 670–677 (2009)
11. Ayvaci, A., Soatto, S.: Motion segmentation with occlusions on the superpixel graph. In: Workshop on Dynamical Vision, Kyoto, Japan (October 2009)
12. Levinshtein, A., Stere, A., Kutulakos, K., Fleet, D., Dickinson, S., Siddiqi, K.: Turbopixels: Fast superpixels using geometric flows. IEEE Transactions on Pattern Analysis and Machine Intelligence, PAMI (2009)
13. Achanta, R., Shaji, A., Smith, K., Lucchi, A., Fua, P., Ssstrunk, S.: SLIC Superpixels. Tech. Rep., EPFL (2010)
14. Zitnick, C.L., Kang, S.B.: Stereo for image-based rendering using image over-segmentation. International Journal of Computer Vision (IJCV) 75, 49–65 (2007)
15. Geusebroek, J.-M., Boomgard, R., Smeulders, A.W.M., Geerts, H.: Color invariance. IEEE Trans. Pattern Analysis and Machine Intelligence 23(12), 1338–1350 (2001)
16. Gevers, T., Smeulders, A.W.M.: Color based object recognition. Pattern Recognition 32(3), 453–464 (1999)
17. van de Sande, K.E.A., Gevers, T., Snoek, C.G.M.: Evaluating color descriptors for object and scene recognition. IEEE Trans. Pattern Analysis and Machine Intelligence 32(9), 1582–1596 (2010)
18. Achanta, R., Shaji, A., Smith, K., Lucchi, A., Fua, P., Süsstrunk, S.: SLIC Superpixels Compared to State-of-the-art Superpixel Methods. IEEE Transactions on Pattern Analysis and Machine Intelligence, PAMI (May 2012)
19. Tan, R.T., Ikeuchi, K.: Separating reflection components of textured surface using a single image. IEEE Trans. Pattern Analysis and Machine Intelligence 27(2), 178–193 (2005)
20. Mallick, S.P., Zickler, T.E., Kriegman, D.J., Belhumeur, P.N.: Beyond Lambert: reconstructing specular surfaces using color. In: IEEE Proc. Computer Vision and Pattern Recognition (CVPR 2005), vol. 2, pp. 619–626 (2005)
21. Ren, X., Malik, J.: Learning a classification model for segmentation. In: Proc. IEEE International Conference on Computer Vision, ICCV (2003)
22. Yuheng Ren, C., Reid, I.: gSLIC: a real-time implementation of SLIC superpixel segmentation, University of Oxford, Department of Engineering Science (June 2011)
23. Periasamy, P.S., Athi Narayanan, S., Duraiswamy, K.: A Hybrid Method for Image Quantization 5(D09) (December 2009)
24. Kim, N., Kehtarnavaz, N.: DWT-based scene-adaptive color quantization. Real-Time Imaging 11, 443–453 (2005)
25. Horiuchi, T.: Similarity measure of labelled images. In: Proc. IAPR 17th International Conference on Pattern Recognition (ICPR 2004), vol. 3, pp. 602–605 (2004)

CBARS: Cluster Based Classification for Activity Recognition Systems

Zahraa Said Abdallah[1,4], Mohamed Medhat Gaber[2], Bala Srinivasan[1], and Shonali Krishnaswamy[1,3]

[1] Centre for Distributed Systems and Software Engineering
Monash University, Melbourne, Australia
{zahraa.said.abdallah,srini}@monash.edu
[2] School of Computing, University of Portsmouth
Portsmouth, Hampshire, England, PO1 3HE, UK
mohamed.gaber@port.ac.uk
[3] Institute for Infocomm Research (I2R), Singapore
shonali.krishnaswamy@monash.edu
[4] Faculty of Computer and Information Science
Ain Shams University, Cairo, Egypt

Abstract. Activity recognition focuses on inferring current user activities by leveraging sensory data available on today's sensor rich environment. Supervised learning has been applied pervasively for activity recognition. Typical activity recognition techniques process sensory data based on point-by-point approaches. In this paper, we propose a novel Cluster Based Classification for Activity Recognition Systems, *CBARS*. The novel approach processes activities as clusters to build a robust classification framework. *CBARS* integrates supervised, unsupervised and active learning and applies hybrid similarity measures technique for recognising activities. Extensive experimental results using real activity recognition dataset have evidenced that our new approach shows improved performance over other existing state-of-the-art learning methods.

Keywords: Activity recognition, Cluster based classification, Hybrid similarity measure.

1 Introduction

There is a general consensus on the need for effective automatic recognition of user activities to enhance the ability of a pervasive system to properly recognise activities and react to circumstances. Recognizing human activities based on sensory data has recently drawn much research interest from the pervasive computing community. Activity recognition system focuses on inferring the current activities of users by leveraging the rich sensory environment. Sensor readings are collected and interpreted to recognise various human activities. Systems that can recognise human activities from sensory data opened the door to many important applications in the fields of healthcare, social networks, environmental monitoring, surveillance, emergency response and military missions.

A. Ell Hassanien et al. (Eds.): AMLTA 2012, CCIS 322, pp. 82–91, 2012.

Activity recognition (AR) is typically viewed as a classification problem where many traditional machine learning techniques can be applied [1]. In most existing supervised learning approaches in AR, the training data is collected, a classification model is generated offline from the collected data, and finally the obtained model is deployed to recognise the activity. A wide range of classification models has been used for activity recognition such as Decision Trees, Naive Bayes and Support Vector Machines. A typical activity recognition system builds the learning model with annotated data to recognise new data and predict human activity type based on the learning model.

We propose a novel cluster based classification method for robust activity recognition across users. We coined our technique *CBARS*, which stands for *Cluster Based Activity Recognition System*. *CBARS* adapts hybrid similarity measure classification for both accurate activity recognition and active learning for the new/unlabelled sensory data. Our proposed technique extends the state-of-the-art in AR by providing the following advantages.

- *Adaptability to the nature of activity recognition data:* People perform activities in a sequential manner (i.e., performing one activity after another). Therefore, activity recognition data stream typically composites of sequence of chunks that represents various activities. Different from other activity recognition systems, *CBARS* is a cluster based classification that deals with activities as clusters rather than processing each point. The novel approach is adapted for activity recognition data nature. Therefore, computation and processing time are conserved when dealing with the entire cluster instead of processing each point.
- *Hybrid similarity measure:* Learning model in *CBARS* contains clusters that represent different activities. When new cluster is emerged, hybrid similarity measure is deployed to match up similarities of the new cluster/activity with the existing ones. These measures are namely distance, density, gravity and within cluster standard deviation (*WICSD*). Applying the aforementioned similarity measures for activity recognition shows superiority over the use of individual ones, and therefore enhances the system robustness across users.
- *Combination of modelling techniques:* The system combines supervised, unsupervised and active learning all in one data stream model. We initially build the learning model with supervised learning. When new data received, unsupervised learning is deployed to cluster activities. Active learning is also employed in the event of confusion on cluster labels.
- *Framework for adapted model and evolving data stream:* One of the characteristics of *CBARS* framework is the flexibility to be updated as the data evolves. Therefore, the updated model is personalised and adapted to the most recent changes detected in the user's activities. In this paper, we present the framework that allows adaptation over time. However, the implementation of the adaptation is not in the scope of this paper.

To the best of our knowledge, no other existing activity recognition system addresses all aforementioned points in a single framework. The rest of the paper is organised as follows. Section 2 provides a discussion of the research context. Explanation of the proposed framework and its details are presented in Section 3. Section 4 reports the experimental results and analysis. Finally, Section 6 concludes the paper with a summary.

2   Research Context

An efficient approach based on data mining has been recently proposed in a number of research projects considering the activity recognition from the machine learning perspective. Methods commonly used for activity classification were reviewed in [1]. Supervised learning has been deployed pervasively for activity recognition. One example system is explained in [2]. In this system, three classification techniques from WEKA [3] are used to induce models for predicting the user activities. Some other systems used fuzzy classifiers for activity recognition as in [4] and [5]. Few studies considered unsupervised learning techniques for activity recognition and change detection. In [7], the feasibility of applying a specific type of unsupervised learning to high-dimensional, heterogeneous sensory input was analysed. The correspondence between clustering output and classification input was proposed as well. Typically there is only a small set of labelled training data available in addition to a substantial amount of unlabelled training data. Therefore, some studies considered labelling only profitable samples of data or continue learning while system is running. Longstaff et al. Longstaff et al. [8] investigated methods of further training classifiers after a user begins to use them using active and semi-supervised learning.

To the best of our knowledge, none of these techniques has considered combining supervised, unsupervised and active learning for building a robust activity recognition system across users. Typical activity recognition stream is formed from a sequence of data chunks representing activities. Therefore, we propose a novel approach that treats data input as a stream and uses clustering to avoid having to respond to each input data point. As the stream evolves, there is a need to assess old and new clusters and this is handled with a hybrid similarity measure.

3   *CBARS*: Cluster Based Classification for Activity Recognition Systems

CBARS mainly composites of three consecutive phases. Illustration of the different phases is presented in this section.

3.1   Phase 1: Build Learning Model

Initially, supervised learning is applied on labelled data to train and generate the learning model. The generated model consists of set of clusters. Each cluster represents one of the labelled activities that applied while training the model.

CBARS creates k clusters of k activities in the training data. The cluster label is the majority label among cluster instances. Training examples typically contain outliers and noisy data that might affect the quality of the model directly. Therefore, we add a filtration step that aims to purify clusters and therefore build more accurate learning model.

Model Purification: While creating new cluster from training data, cluster is purified by considering only true-labelled instances inside the cluster and ignoring other mis-clustered examples (instances with different labels). Building on the purified clusters, characteristics are extracted for each cluster and all raw points are then dismissed.

CBARS extracts features from each cluster and dismisses all raw data at the end of this phase. Cluster characteristics are the basic information describes the cluster. Characteristics of a cluster include basically the cluster centroid, density, within cluster standard deviation and boundaries. The learning model is formed from set of clusters/activities that are deployed in training. The extracted features represent clusters/activities and raw data is dismissed.

3.2   Phase 2: Unsupervised Learning for New Data

This step aims to create clusters of various activities exist in data received. When unlabelled data emerged, we apply clustering on data to generate clusters of the performed activities . Various clustering techniques such as k-means, Expectation Maximisation and DBScan [9] have used and compared to reach the best performance. Clusters Characteristics are extracted and all raw data is dismissed similar to the learning model building procedure. The output of this phase is the set of clusters'/activities' characteristics ready for the recognition phase.

3.3   Phase 3: New Activity Recognition

As the stream evolves, we assess new and learning model clusters to predict new clusters' labels. This is handled with a hybrid similarity measure approach. As raw data has been dismissed, characteristics of the new cluster are compared to the existing learning model ones. The predicted label is based on the characteristics of the most similar cluster in the learning model. Clusters are similar if they match based on the hybrid similarity measure approach. For each new formed cluster, the algorithm checks how similar it is to other clusters already exist in the learning model. We apply various measures to test similarities among clusters. Each measure votes for its own " candidate" cluster from the measure respective. The predicted label is the candidate cluster with the majority of votes among all measures, while the true label of a cluster is the majority label among cluster instances. There are three cases expected from the voting procedure as follows.

1. *Correct prediction:* This case occurs when the majority of votes have chosen the candidate cluster/activity with the true label.

2. **Active learning:** In case of equal votes are assigned to a specific two clusters, user input is required to label the cluster. In this case, equal votes are assigned for exactly two clusters. The algorithm inquires about the correct label from user in an active learning mode with either of the labels of the two nominated clusters.
3. **Incorrect prediction:** The cluster is incorrectly classified when a total confusion with lowest confidence among all measures for candidate clusters or when voting for an incorrect cluster.   •

Hybrid similarity measure technique implements four measures namely distance, density, gravitational force and within cluster standard deviation. We concern in these measures about the distance among the cluster centroids, clusters density, how strong is the gravitational force among clusters and the cohesion inside the cluster. Learning model **LM** consists of n clusters/ activities.

$$LM = \{C_1, C_2, C_3, ...C_n\} \tag{3.1}$$

When new cluster C_{new} arrives, the algorithm deploys the various similarity measures to choose the best candidate cluster C_i from n clusters of LM. The four measures are:

– **Distance:** Cluster centroid is an n dimensional array of mean n- dimensional instances inside the cluster. C_i is the candidate cluster from distance perspective if distance between C_{new} and C_i centroids is the shortest among n clusters in LM.
– **Density:** Each cluster has its own density that distinguishes it from other clusters. Cluster density reflects the distribution of data points inside the cluster. It is described by the Formula 3.2 :

$$ClusDens = \frac{SizeOfCandidate}{AvgDist} \tag{3.2}$$

$$AvgDist = \frac{\sum_{i=1}^{m}(P_i - ClusCntr)}{m} \tag{3.3}$$

Where (m) is the number of points in the cluster, (P) is a n- dimensional data point inside the cluster and $(ClusCntr)$ is the cluster centroid. the average Distance($avgDis$)is the within-cluster sum of the distances between cluster's examples and respective cluster centroid divided by the number of examples within cluster.Two clusters are similar from density perspective if they have the smallest difference in density. C_i is the candidate cluster if the difference between C_{new} and C_i density is the minimum among n clusters in LM.
– **Gravitational force:** Gravitational force has been previously applied in machine learning such as in [10] , [11], and [12] . There exists a natural attraction force between any two objects in the universe and this force is called gravitation force. According to Newton universal law of gravity, the strength of gravitation between two objects is in direct ratio to the product

of the masses of the two objects, but in inverse ratio to the square of distance between them. The law is described in Equation 3.4:

$$F_g = G\frac{m_1 m_2}{r^2} \tag{3.4}$$

Where F_g is the gravitation between two objects (clusters); G is the constant of universal gravitation; m_1 is the mass of object 1 (size of cluster 1); m_2 is the mass of object 2 (size of cluster 2); r the distance between the two objects (Euclidean distance between clusters' centroids) .

According to Equation 3.4, each cluster generates its own gravitational force created from its weight. The bigger the weight of the candidate the stronger the gravitational force produced around it. Therefore, the probability it could attract more data object would be increased. When the gravitational force between $Cnew$ and C_i is bigger than with other clusters existing in LM, then C_i is the candidate cluster from gravitational force perspective.

- **WICSD (Within Cluster Standard Deviation):** This measure considers the cohesion inside each cluster. Standard deviation of n dimensional points inside the cluster is calculated as the equation 3.5.

$$WICSD = \sqrt{\frac{\sum_{i=1}^{m} EDistance(P_i, ClusCntr)^2}{m}} \tag{3.5}$$

Where $EDistance$ is the Euclidean Distance, (m) is the number of points into the cluster, (P) is a n- dimensional data point inside the cluster and $(ClusCntr)$ is the cluster centroid.

Clusters that have similar standard deviation are more likely to present the same activity/label. C_i is the candidate cluster form $WICSD$ perspective if it has the smallest difference in standard deviation measure with C_{new} among n clusters in LM.

4 Experimental Study

This section reports the experiments conducted to study how $CBARS$ performs in practice. Activity recognition systems deal with high-dimensional, multi-modal streams of data. In the recently started European research project [13], the OPPORTUNITY dataset has been recorded to recognise complex activities. The dataset has labels for five users across five segments with annotated activities such as (sitting, walking and running) streaming form accelerometer sensors attached to the user's body.

Let F_c = total existing class instances correctly classified, F_a = total existing class instances trigger active learning, F_i = total existing class instances misclassified, S = total instances the dataset. We use the following performance metrics to evaluate our technique. M_c: % of class instances correctly classified = $\frac{F_c * 100}{S}$, M_a: % of class instances requires active learning = $\frac{F_a * 100}{S}$, and ERR: % of misclassification class instances = $\frac{F_i * 100}{S}$.

CBARS is tested on the OPPORTUNITY dataset. Part of the data is used to build the learning model; other new date is applied for testing. Testing data is a new data that has not used for training the model. Learning and testing data could be for the same user but different segments or for different users.

4.1   Cluster Purification and Learning Model

Model purification is an essential step for pruning and refining the learning model. It has a superior advantage of building a robust model that filters outliers and wrong-labelled examples. Therefore, purified model represents activity of majority label with high confidence. Figures 1 and 2 show the effect of model purification on M_c with different runs N. Different runs are for different combinations of training and testing datasets for same user (N= 1,2) or various users (N= 3,4,5,6). As shown in figure 1, model purification shows better performance for most of the runs.

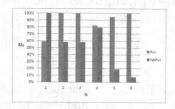

Fig. 1. Cluster Purification and Recognition accuracy

The impact of the purification step on the various measures is shown in Figure 2. Eliminating outliers and wrong-labelled instances affects the position of clusters' centroids. Therefore, purification boosts measures that rely mainly on the coordinates of centroids. That include distance, gravity and WICSD as shown in Figure 2(a)(b)(d). On the other hand, purification might eliminate instances belong to low dense clusters that seemed to be outliers. Therefore, density might be affected badly with purification as showed in Figure 2(c). Although, purification has not enhanced the performance of all the measures, it has an overall positive effect on M_c when combining all of these measures as explained in Figure 1.

We evaluate *CBARS* performance with various clustering techniques deployed in phase 2. The algorithm implements Weka [3] clustering techniques, namely *k-means*, *EM* and *DBScan*. Experimentally, clustering accuracy has a direct influence on the system performance. Therefore, we apply the EM clustering in all our experiments unless otherwise stated.

4.2   Combining Various Measures

In the recognition phase, we apply a hybrid similarity measure technique for predicting new cluster's label. For the four similarity measures implemented in

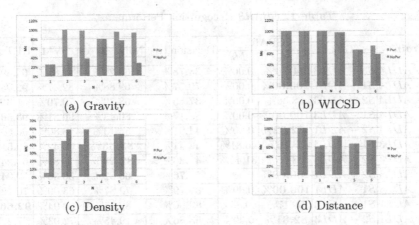

(a) Gravity   (b) WICSD

(c) Density   (d) Distance

Fig. 2. Cluster Purification and Measures accuracy

CBARS, each has its own average accuracy for correct prediction M_c of cluster's label. Distance measure has the best average accuracy of 68.48 % followed by the *WICSD* measure accuracy of 61.46%. Gravitational force and density measures come next with average accuracy of 54.17% and 53.13% respectively.

Combining the four measures benefits from the strengths of each one and eliminates encountered problems of using an individual measure and therefore helps enhancing the performance of single similarity measure techniques. Four different measure combinations showed the best performance. The four combinations are as follow. $Comb_1$ is for only the top accurate individual measures (distance, *WICSD*). Applying measures in $Comb_1$ attained a metrics of $M_c= 79.76\%$, $M_a= 20.24\%$. The recognition accuracy, M_c increased to 86.84%, while M_a decreased to 13.16% using $Comb_2$. This combination adds density to the before mentioned combination ($Comb_1$). $Comb_3$ includes gravity, distance and *WICSD*. Applying $Comb_3$ had the performance metrics of $M_c= 85.96\%$, $M_a= 10.21\%$. The highest correct recognition percentage attained when combining all measures in $Comb_4$. It has the recognition performance of $M_c= 89.36\%$ and $M_a= 6.81\%$. As active learning percentage becomes higher, more frequent requests are sent to user to label confusing clusters. Therefore, the large percentage of active learning such as in $Comb_1$ and $Comb_2$ makes the system inefficient. Although *ERR* increases by 3.83% when combining all measures, this increase is not from the correct recognition rather than active learning percentage.

4.3   *CBARS* and Other Classification Techniques

Table 1 illustrates the performance of *CBARS* across various learning and testing datasets in comparison to other iconic classifications techniques. Names of different datasets indicate the subject number such as *S1, S2, S3* followed by segment no such as *ADL1, ADL2, ADL3*.

Decision tree and the other classification techniques shows a good accuracy when the testing and training data are for the same user. However, testing data

Table 1. *CBARS* Recognition Performance

Train	*Test*	CBARS		DecisionTree	Naive Bayes	SVM	RFTree
		M_c	M_a				
$S1 - ADL4$	$S3 - ADL3$	**94.70%**	0.00%	34.78%	60.20%	47.83%	64.59%
$S1 - ADL4$	$S1 - ADL1$	**100.00%**	0.00%	79.57%	69.88%	82.47%	92.03%
$S1 - ADL4$	$S2 - ADL3$	68.56%	0.00%	37.86%	53.79%	70.70%	**74.32%**
$S1 - ADL4$	$S1 - ADL3$	**100.00%**	0.00%	88.17%	86.43%	90.31%	93.50%
$S1 - ADL4$	$S2 - ADL1$	**72.92%**	0.00%	44.51%	54.13%	58.80%	64.56%
$S3 - ADL3$	$S1 - ADL4$	53.19%	46.81%	42.41%	**83.53%**	66.42%	59.55%
$S3 - ADL3$	$S2 - ADL3$	68.56%	31.44%	48.36%	**82.24%**	58.87%	61.24%
$S3 - ADL3$	$S2 - ADL1$	**100.00%**	0.00%	51.76%	66.82%	56.36%	59.94%
$S3 - ADL3$	$S1 - ADL1$	**100.00%**	0.00%	39.79%	72.87%	65.09%	76.72%
$S1 - ADL1$	$S1 - ADL3$	59.17%	40.83%	83.90%	89.35%	90.94%	**92.66%**
$S1 - ADL1$	$S2 - ADL3$	**82.31%**	0.00%	53.86%	79.45%	72.93%	77.22%
$S1 - ADL1$	$S3 - ADL3$	**94.70%**	0.00%	40.27%	58.07%	51.70%	58.18%
Average		**79.75%**	15.64%	53.77%	71.40%	67.70 %	72.88%

across users confuses the decision tree and therefore has a negative impact on the recognition accuracy. On the other hand, *CBARS* shows stable high accuracy in recognising new activities either for the same or across users. The recognition accuracy (100%) in *CBARS* means that "all" new activities/clusters formed in testing phase have been successfully assigned a correct label. In case of active learning, *CBARS* is confused between two clusters labels . Therefore, user input is required to assign the true activity label. Figure 3 shows the percentage of incorrect prediction in *CBARS* and other classification techniques on various runs. Different runs are for different combinations of training and testing datasets for same user or across users. As shown in Figure 3, *CBARS* has the lowest *ERR* among all other techniques for all runs.

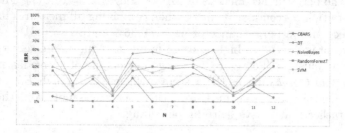

Fig. 3. Incorrect Recognition for *CBARS* and other Classification techniques

5   Conclusion

In this paper we present a novel classification framework for activity recognition (*AR*) systems, named *CBARS*. This framework integrates supervised, unsupervised and active learning to build a robust and efficient recognition system. In comparison to state-of-art models, *CBARS* provides high performance results with the minimum error rate especially when dealing with recognition of activities across users.

References

1. Preece, S.J., Goulermas, J.Y., Kenney, L.P.J., Howard, D., Meijer, K., Crompton, R.: Activity identification using body-mounted sensors: a review of classification techniques. Physiological Measurement 30(4), 1–33 (2009)
2. Kwapisz, J.R., Weiss, G.M., Moore, S.A.: Activity recognition using cell phone accelerometers. SIGKDD Explor. Newsl. 12, 74–82 (2011)
3. Witten, I.H., Frank, E.: Data Mining: Practical Machine Learning Tools and Techniques, 2nd edn. Morgan Kaufmann, San Francisco (2005)
4. Helmi, M., Almodarresi, S.M.T.: Human activity recognition using a fuzzy inference system. In: IEEE International Conference on Fuzzy Systems, pp. 1897–1902 (2009)
5. Yang, J.-Y., Chen, Y.-P., Lee, G.-Y., Liou, S.-N., Wang, J.-S.: Activity Recognition Using One Triaxial Accelerometer: A Neuro-fuzzy Classifier with Feature Reduction. In: Ma, L., Rauterberg, M., Nakatsu, R. (eds.) ICEC 2007. LNCS, vol. 4740, pp. 395–400. Springer, Heidelberg (2007)
6. Dempster, A.P., Laird, N.M., Rubin, D.B.: Maximum likelihood from incomplete data via the EM algorithm. Journal of the Royal Statistical Society B 39, 1–38 (1977)
7. Li, F., Dustdar, S.: Incorporating unsupervised learning in activity recognition. In: Workshops at theAAAI Conference on Artificial Intelligence (2011)
8. Longstaff, B., Reddy, S., Estrin, D.: Improving activity classification for health applications on mobile devices using active and semi supervised learning. In: Pervasive Computing Technologies for Healthcare (PervasiveHealth) 2010, pp. 1–7 (2010)
9. Ester, M., Peter Kriegel, H., Jörg, S., Xu, X.: A density-based algorithm for discovering clusters in large spatial databases with noise, pp. 226–231. AAAI Press (1996)
10. Peng, L., Yang, B., Chen, Y., Abraham, A.: Data gravitation based classification. Inf. Sci. 179(6), 809–819 (2009)
11. Abdallah, Z.S., Gaber, M.M.: Ddg-clustering: A novel technique for highly accurate results. In: Proceedings of the IADIS European Conference on Data Mining (2009)
12. Abdallah, Z.S., Gaber, M.M.: Kb-cb-n classification: Towards unsupervised approach for supervised learning. In: Proceedings of the IEEE Symposium on Computational Intelligence and Data Mining, CIDM 2011, pp. 283–290 (2011)
13. Roggen, D., Förster, K., Calatroni, A., Holleczek, T., Fang, Y., Tröster, G., Lukowicz, P., Pirkl, G., Bannach, D., Kunze, K., Ferscha, A., Holzmann, C., Riener, A., Chavarriaga, R., del R. Millán, J.: Opportunity: Towards opportunistic activity and context recognition systems. In: Proc. 3rd IEEE WoWMoM Workshop on Autononomic and Opportunistic Communications (2009)

Wavelet Based Statistical Adapted Local Binary Patterns for Recognizing Avatar Faces

Abdallah A. Mohamed[1,2] and Roman V. Yampolskiy[1]

[1] Computer Engineering and Computer Science,
University of Louisville, Louisville, KY USA
[2] Department of Mathematics, Menoufia University,
Shebin El-Koom, Menoufia Egypt
{aamoha04,rvyapm01}@louisville.edu

Abstract. In this paper, we propose a novel face recognition technique based on discrete wavelet transform and Local Binary Pattern (LBP) with adapted threshold to recognize avatar faces in different virtual worlds. The original LBP operator mainly thresholds pixels in a specific predetermined window based on the gray value of the central pixel of that window. As a result the LBP operator becomes more sensitive to noise especially in near-uniform or flat area regions of an image. To deal with this problem we propose a new definition to the original LBP operator not based only on the value of the central pixel of a certain window, but based on all pixels values in that window. Experiments conducted on two virtual world avatar face image datasets show that our technique performs better than original LBP, wavelet LBP, adaptive LBP and wavelet adaptive LBP in terms of accuracy.

Keywords: Avatar, face recognition, LBP, SALBP, wavelet transform.

1 Introduction

Face recognition is one of the biometric traits that received a great attention from many researchers during the past few decades because of its potential applications in a variety of civil and government-regulated domains [1]. Face recognition however is not only concerned with recognizing human faces, but also with recognizing faces of non-biological entities or avatars. To address the need for a decentralized, affordable, automatic, fast, secure, reliable, and accurate means of identity authentication for avatars, the concept of Artimetrics has emerged [2, 3]. Artimetrics is a new area of study concerned with visual and behavioral recognition and identity verification of intelligent software agents, domestic and industrial robots, virtual world avatars and other non-biological entities [2, 3].

Extracting discriminant information from a facial image is one of the key components for any face recognition system [1]. There are many different algorithms proposed to extract features, such as Principal Component Analysis (PCA) [4], Linear Discriminant Analysis (LDA) [5] and Local Binary Pattern (LBP) [6].

LBP was applied to face recognition for the first time by Ahonen et al. [7]. But the original LBP method worked as a local descriptor to capture only local information [8]. It thresholds all pixels in the neighborhood based on the gray value of the central

A. Ell Hassanien et al. (Eds.): AMLTA 2012, CCIS 322, pp. 92–101, 2012.

pixel. As a result the original LBP becomes more sensitive to noise specially in near uniform or flat areas [9]. One solution to this problem is to threshold all the pixels automatically based on the available data.

Most of the work done so far on face recognition has focused on humans. Research on recognizing virtual world's avatars has not received due attention. Some methods developed LBP further for either recognizing human faces or avatar faces. For example, Yang et al. [10] applied LBP for face recognition with Hamming distance constraint. Chen et al. [11] used Statistical LBP for face recognition. Mohamed et al. [2] applied hierarchical multi-scale LBP with wavelet transform to recognize avatar faces. Mohamed et al. [12] applied wavelet transform as well but with adapted local binary patterns and direction statistical features to recognize avatar faces.

In this paper, we propose a novel LBP face recognition technique to recognize avatar faces from different virtual worlds. In this approach, we combine the idea of discrete wavelet transform with new definition of the original LBP operator, Statistical Adapted Local Binary Pattern (SALBP) operator. The efficiency of our proposed method is demonstrated by experiments on two different avatar datasets from Second Life and Entropia Universe virtual worlds.

The rest of this paper is organized as follows; Section 2 briefly provides an introduction to wavelet decomposition. In Section 3, an overview of the LBP is presented. Section 4 presents SALBP operator. Wavelet Statistical Adapted Local Binary Pattern (WSALBP) operator is described in section 5. Section 6 reports experimental results which followed by conclusions in Section 7.

2   Discrete Wavelet Transform

Wavelet Transform (WT) or Discrete Wavelet Transform (DWT) is a popular tool for analyzing images in a variety of signal and image processing applications including multi-resolution analysis, computer vision and graphics. It provides multi-resolution representation of the image which can analyze image variation at different scales.

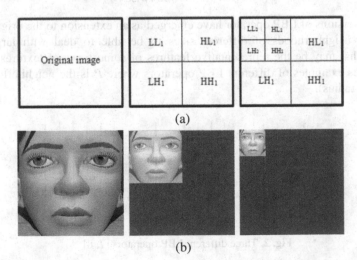

(a)

(b)

Fig. 1. (a) Wavelet coefficient structure [14] (b) Original image, One and two levels wavelet decomposition for an image

WT was applied in image decomposition for many reasons [13]: it reduces the computational complexity of the system, decomposes images into sub-images corresponding to different frequency ranges and this can lead to reduction in the computational overhead of the system and allows obtaining the local information in different domains (space and frequency). Thus it supports both spatial and frequency characteristics of an image at the same time.

WT decomposes facial images into approximate, horizontal, vertical and diagonal coefficients. Approximate coefficient of one level is repeatedly decomposed into the four coefficients of the next level of decomposition [13]. Decomposing an image with the first level of WT provides four sub-bands LL_1, HL_1, LH_1 and HH_1 as in Fig. 1.

3   Local Binary Pattern

LBP operator, proposed by Ojala et al. [6], is a very simple and efficient local descriptor for describing textures. It labels the pixels of an image by thresholding the pixels in a certain neighborhood of each pixel with its center value, multiplied by powers of two and then added together to form the new value (label) for the center pixel [15]. The output value of the LBP operator for a block of 3x3 pixels can be defined as follows [15]:

$$LBP_{P,R} = \sum_{p=0}^{7} 2^p S(g_p - g_c)$$ (1)

where g_c corresponds to the gray value of the central pixel, g_p ($p = 0,1,2,..,7$) are the gray values of its surrounding 8 pixels and $S(g_p - g_c)$ can be defined as follows:

$$S(g_p - g_c) = \begin{cases} 1, & g_p \geq g_c \\ 0, & otherwise \end{cases}$$ (2)

Later new versions of LBP operator have emerged as an extension to the original one. They used neighborhoods of different sizes to be able to deal with large scale structures that may be the representative features of some types of textures [8, 16]. (Fig. 2 gives examples of different LBP operators where P is the neighborhood size and R is its radius).

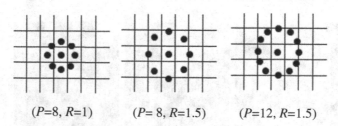

(P=8, R=1)   (P= 8, R=1.5)   (P=12, R=1.5)

Fig. 2. Three different LBP operators [7, 8]

4   Statistical Adaptive Local Binary Pattern (SALBP)

Using the central pixel value of the neighborhood of any pixel as a threshold has a negative effect on how the LBP method can deal with noise especially in near uniform or flat areas. To obtain good results, we propose a novel LBP operator, SALBP, which overcomes the high sensitivity of LBP to noise. The SALBP's threshold is not fixed but is computed automatically from the available image data using simple statistics. To minimize the effect of noise, we propose the following equation by which differences between the central pixel value of any local patch and its surrounding pixels values can be reduced. The reduction resulting from computing the weight for each pixel in a local patch by using the following equation and then that weight can be used to redefine a new value for each pixel.

$$J = (g_c(i,j) - \sum_{q=1}^{P} w_q g_q(i,j))^2 \tag{3}$$

where g_c corresponds to the central pixel, g_q to the surrounding pixels, w_q is the weight for any pixel q and $\sum_{q=1}^{P} w_q = 1$.

By deriving both sides of equation 3 with respect to the weight for any pixel p and assign the result to zero we get:

$$\frac{\partial J}{\partial w_p} = -2g_p(i,j)(g_c(i,j) - \sum_{q=1}^{P} w_q g_q(i,j)) = 0$$

then:

$$g_c(i,j) = \sum_{\substack{q=1 \\ q \neq p}}^{P} w_q g_q(i,j) + w_p g_p(i,j) \tag{4}$$

From equation 4 we can obtain the value of w_p using the following equation:

$$w_p = \frac{g_c(i,j) - \sum_{\substack{q=1 \\ q \neq p}}^{P} w_q g_q(i,j)}{g_p(i,j)} \tag{5}$$

where p is any pixel we currently compute its weigh where q is any pixel other than p in the surrounding.

For more explanation about how we can compute w_p for different pixels in the neighborhood we have to follow the following steps:

1- Initialization $w_p = 1/P$ for every $p = 1,2,....,P$
2- Use the updated equation 5
   Repeat
      For p = 1 : P
         Update w_p with the new value and each time when we compute the new value of w_p for any pixel we use this value to compute the w_p for the next pixels.
      end

After applying these steps we would have the weights for all pixels in the neighborhood and thus we can define the SALBP operator as following:

$$SALBP = \sum_{p=0}^{P-1} s(g_p * w_p - k * std_p) 2^p \qquad (6)$$

And so the obtained binary code can be seen as:

$$s(g_p * w_p - k * std_p) = \begin{cases} 1, & if \quad g_p * w_p \geq k * std_p \\ 0, & otherwise \end{cases} \qquad (7)$$

where std_p is the standard deviation of all pixels values in an image patch and k is a scaling factor such that $0 < k \leq 1$. For more explanation about how this new LBP operator works see   Fig. 3 below shows the result of applying the proposed technique in a local image area with $k = 0.3$.

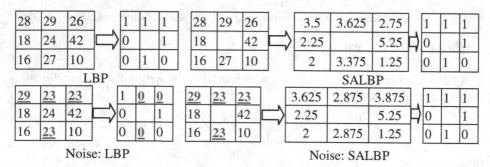

Fig. 3. Comparison of LBP and SALBP operators. First row: original encodings. Second row: encodings with noise. The bold underlined red pixels are changed with noise.

5   Wavelet Statistical Adaptive Local Binary Pattern (WSALBP)

The proposed algorithm has three steps: preprocessing, feature extraction and recognition or classification:

5.1   Preprocessing Facial Images

We followed some of preprocessing operations to improve the efficiency of extracting the face features. First, the input images are manually cropped to pure face images by removing the background which is not useful in recognition. Second, these pure face images have to be normalized and then decomposed using the first level of wavelet decomposition to obtain the pure facial expression images. Detailed images resulting from applying wavelet decomposition contain changes which represent the difference of face images. So considering only the approximation images will enhance the common features of the same class of images and at the same time the differences will be reduced. For this reason, we decomposed only the approximation images resulted from the first level of wavelet decomposition to obtain the second level of decomposition. So, our experiments were concerned only with the approximation images resulted from the second level of wavelet decomposition and which we used in training and testing to evaluate the performance of the proposed algorithm.

5.2   Extracting Facial Features Using SALBP

The choice of the threshold is very important to obtain good results in any face recognition system. One of the best ways for choosing the proper threshold is by automatically computing this threshold using the local statistics of the available images pixels. So, we have used the SALBP operator, defined by equation 6, to provide the new value for each pixel of the approximation facial image obtained from the second level of decomposition.

In order to compute the SALBP binary code for each pixel we have to follow:

- Compute the local weight for each pixel in an image patch by using equation 5 and then multiply this weight by its pixel to produce a new pixel value.
- Compute standard deviation of all old pixels values in the image patch including the central pixel value.
- Choose a scaling factor k which has a value between 0 and 1 and multiply k with the computed standard deviation to obtain new threshold. (there is no fixed value for k but we have to try different values till we obtain a proper one since its value affects the obtained binary code and then affects also the accuracy rate, during our experiments we used $k = 0.3$).

Use our threshold with the new pixels values to compute the SALBP binary code for each pixel (see Fig. 3 as an example of how we can use the SALBP operator).

5.3   Dissimilarity Measure

The last stage of our proposed technique is to classify each facial image to its subject. To this end we have used chi-square distance to compute the dissimilarity between each input image and the training model as in the following equation [8]:

$$D_{LBP}(X,Y) = \sum_{n=1}^{N} \frac{(X_n - Y_n)^2}{X_n + Y_n} \tag{8}$$

where X is the testing image, Y is the training model and N is the number of bins.

6   Experimental Results and Analysis

In this section, we verify the performance of the proposed algorithm on two different types of avatar datasets: the first type is the Second Life (SL) dataset and the second is the Entropia Universe (ENT) dataset (Fig. 4 gives an example of a subject from each dataset). The proposed method is compared with other single scale techniques such as, the original LBP, wavelet LBP (WLBP), adaptive LBP (ALBP) and Wavelet ALBP.

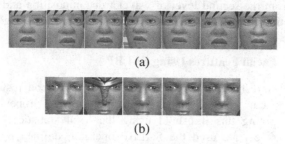

(a)

(b)

Fig. 4. Samples of one subject of facial images from: a) Second Life dataset b) Entropia dataset

6.1   Experimental Setup

To evaluate our proposed technique, we have used two facial image datasets.

The first dataset was acquired from a large collection of SL virtual world avatar face dataset [17]. This dataset contains 847 gray scale images with size 1280 x 1024 each to represent 121 different avatars. Each avatar subject has 7 different images for the same avatar with different frontal pose angle (front, far left, mid left, far right, mid right, top and bottom) and facial expression.

The second dataset was collected from ENT virtual world [18]. ENT dataset contains 545 gray scale images with size 407 x 549 pixels. These images were organized in 109 subjects (avatars). Each subject has different 5 images for the same avatar with different frontal angle and facial details (with and without a mask).

In order to compare the performance of our technique against other techniques we added two types of noise to each image in both datasets and then obtain the recognition rate after applying each technique. These two types of noise are noise Gaussian noise and Salt & Pepper noise. We used the default parameters for each one of the two types of noise.

The facial part of each image in SL and ENT datasets was manually cropped from the original images based on the location of the two eyes, mouth and the nose. The new size of each facial image in SL dataset is 260 x 260 pixels while in ENT dataset each facial image was resized to 180 x 180 pixels. After applying the second level of wavelet decomposition the resolution of each facial image was reduced to 65 x 65 pixels and to 45 x 45 pixels for SL dataset and ENT dataset respectively.

Each of the two datasets was split in two independent sets. One set is used for training and the second set for testing. For training we used four image from each subject in the SL dataset and three images from each subject in the ENT dataset. All training images were randomly chosen while the rest were used for testing.

6.2   Experimental Results

To ensure the efficiency of using our new definition of the LBP operator with noisy facial images, we compared WSALBP with the original LBP, ALBP, WLBP and

WALBP with several experiments. First we got the performance of WSALBP, LBP, ALBP, WLBP and WALBP with different LBP operators applied on Gaussian noisy facial images from the two datasets (SL and ENT) and then on Salt & Pepper noisy facial images.

We applied all techniques with R = 1, 2, 3 and P = 8, 16, 24. It is evident in figures 5 and 6 that changing the LBP operator affects the recognition rate for all techniques. Also the recognition rate for the same technique and LBP operator changes from one dataset to another.

In case of Gaussian noise, the performance of the WSALBP technique is better than the performance of other techniques with most of all LBP operators and with both SL and ENT datasets. In the SL dataset, the WSALBP recognition rate is greater than that of its closest competitor, WALBP, by about 3% in average. The highest recognition rate obtained (when the LBP operator is (16, 3)) is 92.37%. In the ENT dataset, the WSALBP recognition rate is greater than that of its closest competitor, WALBP, by more than 4% in average. The highest recognition rate obtained (when the LBP operator is (16, 2)) is 81.63%.

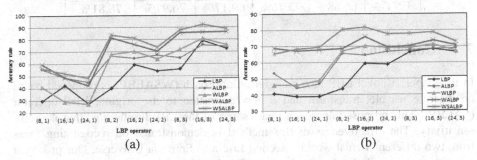

Fig. 5. Recognition rate for the SL dataset and ENT dataset with Gaussian noise: a) SL dataset b) ENT dataset

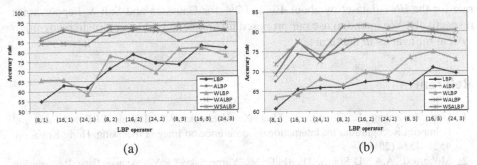

Fig. 6. Recognition rate for the SL dataset and ENT dataset with Salt & Pepper noise: a) SL dataset b) ENT dataset

There was no great difference in performance of the WSALBP technique on the Gaussian and the Salt & Pepper noisy images. That is, performance of the WSALBP is better if compared to most other techniques. The closest competitor to The

WSALBP technique on the Salt & Pepper noisy images is the ALBP technique (in case of the SL dataset). The increase in the recognition rate is 3% in average and the highest recognition rate is 94.77% obtained when the LBP operator is either (16, 3) or (24, 3). In case of the ENT dataset, the closest competitor to the WSALBP technique is the WALBP with difference of about 2% in average to the side of the WSALBP technique. The highest recognition rate is 81.63% when the LBP operator is either (16, 2) or (8, 3) (see table 1 which shows the average recognition rate for all techniques where SL_G stands for SL dataset with Gaussian noise and SL_{SP} stands for SL dataset with Salt & Pepper noise and the same for ENT_G and ENT_{SP}).

Table 1. Average recognition rate for different algorithms

Dataset	Techniques				
	LBP	ALBP	WLBP	WALBP	WSALBP
SL_G	51.14%	62.56%	58.59%	70.73%	**73.92%**
SL_{SP}	71.44%	89.29%	72.69%	8920%	**92.29%**
ENT_G	53.57%	60.70%	61.67%	70.28%	**74.77%**
ENT_{SP}	66.68%	75.76%	69.17%	76.97%	**78.81%**

7   Conclusion

In this paper, a novel LBP face recognition approach (WSALBP) is proposed based on discrete wavelet transform and a new definition to the original LBP operator (SALBP). This proposed approach treats some of the LBP limitations, that is, noise sensitivity. The effectiveness of this method is demonstrated on recognizing faces from two different virtual worlds, Second Life and Entropia Universe. Our proposed technique improved the recognition rate for the SL dataset by about 3% for both Gaussian and Salt & Pepper noise when compared to LBP, ALBP, WLBP and WALBP and different LBP operators. Also, our technique improved the recognition rate for the ENT dataset by about 4% and 2% for Gaussian and Salt & Pepper noise respectively. We intend to use our proposed technique to build a complete recognition system for avatars in the future.

References

1. Guo, Z., Zhang, L., Zhang, D., Mou, X.: Hierarchical Multiscale LBP for Face and Palmprint Recognition. In: International Conference on Image Processing, Hong Kong, pp. 4521–4524 (2010)
2. Mohamed, A.A., D'Souza, D., Baili, N., Yampolskiy, R.V.: Avatar Face Recognition using Wavelet Transform and Hierarchical Multi-scale LBP. In: 10th IEEE International Conference on Machine Learning and Applications, Honolulu, Hawaii, pp. 194–199 (2011)
3. Gavrilova, M.L., Yampolskiy, R.V.: Applying Biometric Principles to Avatar Recognition. In: International Conference on Cyberworlds, Singapore, pp. 179–186 (2010)

4. Turk, M., Pentland, A.: Face Recognition using Eigenfaces. In: IEEE Conference on Computer Vision and Pattern Recognition, Maui, HI, pp. 586–591 (1991)
5. Lu, J., Plataniotis, K.N., Venetsanopoulos, A.N.: Face Recognition Using LDA Based Algorithms. IEEE Transactions on Neural Networks 14(1), 195–200 (2003)
6. Ojala, T., Pietikainen, M., Harwood, D.: A comparative study of texture measures with classification based on featured distributions. Pattern Recognition 29(1), 51–59 (1996)
7. Ojala, T., Pietikainen, M., Maenpaa, T.: Multiresolution Gray-Scale and Rotation Invriant Texture Classification with Local Binary Patterns. IEEE Transactions on Pattern Analysis and Machine Intelligence 24(7), 971–987 (2002)
8. Ahonen, T., Hadid, A., Pietikainen, M.: Face Description with Local Binary Patterns: Application to Face Recognition. IEEE Transactions on Pattern Analysis and Machine Intelligence 28(12), 2037–2041 (2006)
9. Akhloufi, M.A., Bendada, A.: Locally Adaptive Texture Features for Multispectral Face Recognition. In: IEEE International conference on Systems Man and Cybernetics, Istanbul, Turkey, pp. 3308–3314 (2010)
10. Yang, H., Wang, Y.D.: A LBP-based Face Recognition Method with Hamming Distance Constraint. In: 4th International Conference on Image and Graphics, Sichuan, China, pp. 645–649 (2007)
11. Chen, L., Wang, Y.H., Wang, Y.D., Huang, D.: Face Recognition with Statistical Local Binary Patterns. In: 8th International Conference on Machine Learning and Cybernetics, Baoding, China, pp. 2433–2439 (2009)
12. Mohamed, A.A., Gavrilova, M.L., Yampolskiy, R.V.: Artificial Face Recognition using Wavelet Adaptive LBP with Directional Statistical Features. In: 12th International Conference on Cyberworlds, Darmstadt, Germany (2012)
13. Mazloom, M., Ayat, S.: Combinational Method for Face Recognition: Wavelet, PCA and ANN. In: International Conference on Digital Image Computing: Techniques and Applications, Canberra, pp. 90–95 (2008)
14. Garcia, C., Zikos, G., Tziritas, G.: A Wavelet-based Framework for Face Recognition. In: 5th European Conference on Computer Vision, Freiburg, Allemagne, pp. 84–92 (1998)
15. Meng, J., Gao, Y., Wang, X., Lin, T., Zhang, J.: Face Recognition based on Local Binary Patterns with Threshold. In: IEEE International Conference on Granular Computing, San Jose, CA, pp. 352–356 (2010)
16. Wang, W., Chang, F., Zhao, J., Chen, Z.: Automatic facial expression recognition using local binary pattern. In: 8th World Congress on Intelligent Control and Automation, Jinan, China, pp. 6375–6378 (2010)
17. Second Life, http://www.secondlife.com
18. Entropia Universe, http://www.entropiauniverse.com

Solving Avatar Captchas Automatically

Mohammed Korayem[1,3], Abdallah A. Mohamed[2,4],
David Crandall[1], and Roman V. Yampolskiy[2]

[1] School of Informatics and Computing, Indiana University
Bloomington, Indiana USA
{mkorayem,djcran}@indiana.edu
[2] Computer Engineering & Computer Science, Speed School of Engineering
University of Louisville, Louisville, Kentucky USA
{aamoha04,roman.yampolskiy}@louisville.edu
[3] Department of Computer Science,
Fayoum University, Fayoum Egypt
[4] Department of Mathematics,
Menoufia University, Shebin El-Koom, Menoufia Egypt

Abstract. Captchas are challenge-response tests used in many online systems to prevent attacks by automated bots. Avatar Captchas are a recently-proposed variant in which users are asked to classify between human faces and computer-generated avatar faces, and have been shown to be secure if bots employ random guessing. We test a variety of modern object recognition and machine learning approaches on the problem of avatar versus human face classification. Our results show that using these techniques, a bot can successfully solve Avatar Captchas as often as humans can. These experiments suggest that this high performance is caused more by biases in the facial datasets used by Avatar Captchas and not by a fundamental flaw in the concept itself, but nevertheless our results highlight the difficulty in creating Captcha tasks that are immune to automatic solution.

1 Introduction

Online activities play an important role in our daily life, allowing us to carry out a wide variety of important day-to-day tasks including communication, commerce, banking, and voting [1, 9]. Unfortunately, these online services are often misused by undesirable automated programs, or "bots," that abuse services by posing as human beings to (for example) repeatedly vote in a poll, add spam to online message boards, or open thousands of email accounts for various nefarious purposes. One approach to prevent such misuse has been the introduction of online security systems called Captchas, or Completely Automated Public Turing tests to tell Computers and Humans Apart [1]. Captchas are simple challenge-response tests that are generated and graded by computers, and that are designed to be easily solvable by humans but that are beyond the capabilities of current computer programs [17]. If a correct solution for a test is received, it is assumed that a human user (and not a bot) is requesting an Internet service.[1]

---

[1] This paper is an expanded version of a preliminary paper [13] that appeared at the ICMLA Face Recognition Challenge [19].

A. Ell Hassanien et al. (Eds.): AMLTA 2012, CCIS 322, pp. 102–110, 2012.
© Springer-Verlag Berlin Heidelberg 2012

Three main categories of Captchas have been introduced [4]. *Text-based Captchas* generate distorted images of text which are very hard to be recognized by state-of-the-art optical character recognition (OCR) programs but are easily recognizable by most humans. *Sound-based Captchas* require the user to solve a speech recognition task, while others require the user to read out a given sentence to authenticate that he/she is a human. Finally, *image-based Captchas* require the user to solve an image recognition task, such as entering a label to describe an image [9]. Other work has combined multiple of these categories into multi-modal Captchas [2], which can increase security while also giving users a choice of the type of Captcha they wish to solve.

The strength of a Captcha system can be measured by how many trials an attacking bot needs on average before solving it correctly [4]. However, there is a tension between developing a task that is as difficult as possible for a bot, but is still easily solvable by human beings. This is complicated by human users who may have sensory or cognitive handicaps that prevent them from solving certain Captchas. The best Captcha schemes are thus the ones which are easy for almost any human to solve but that are almost impossible for an automated program.

Recently, a novel image-based system was proposed called *Avatar Captcha* [6] in which users are asked to perform a face classification task. In particular, the system presents a set of face images, some of which are actual human faces while others are avatar faces generated by a computer, and the user is required to select the real faces. The designers of the scheme found that humans were able to solve the puzzle (by correctly finding all human faces) about 63% of the time, while a bot that randomly guesses the answers would pass only about 0.02% of the time.

In this paper, we consider how well a bot could perform against this Captcha if, instead of random guessing, it used computer vision algorithms to try to classify between human and avatar faces. Through experiments conducted on the human and avatar face images released by the authors of [6], we test a variety of modern learning-based recognition algorithms, finding that this task is surprisingly easy, with some algorithms actually *outperforming* humans on this dataset. While these results indicate that Avatar Captcha is not as secure as the authors had hoped, our results suggest that the problem may not be in the idea of Avatar Captcha, but instead in the way the avatar facial images were generated, allowing the recognition algorithms to learn subtle biases in the data.

2   Background and Related Work

As noted above, text-based Captchas are currently the most common systems on the web, and have been successfully deployed for almost a decade [1]. In order to increase the level of security against increasingly sophisticated OCR algorithms, text-based Captchas have had to increase the degree of distortion of the letters or numbers and hence may become so difficult that even humans are unable to recognize all of the text correctly. To address this problem, Captcha systems using image-based labeling tasks have been proposed [4, 7, 16]. No distortion is required for many of these tasks because humans can easily identify thousands of objects in images, while even state-of-the-art computer vision algorithms cannot perform this task reliably, especially when the set of possible classes is drawn from very large datasets [6]. While image-based

Fig. 1. Sample avatar faces (top) and human faces (bottom) from our dataset

Captchas are still never completely secure, they are thought to widen the success rate gap between humans and non-humans.

Avatar Captcha. The authors of [6] proposed Avatar Captcha as a specific type of image-based task. In their approach, the system presents 12 images organized into a two-by-six matrix, with each image either a human face from a face dataset or a synthetic face from a dataset of avatar faces. The relative number of human and avatar faces and their arrangement is chosen randomly by the system. The user's task is to select all (and only) the avatar images among these 12 images by checking a checkbox under each avatar image. The user is authenticated as a human if he/she correctly completes the task, and otherwise is considered a bot. Using brute force attack, a bot has a success rate of 50% for each of the 12 images, since each image is either a human or avatar, so the probability of correctly classifying all 12 images is just $0.5^{12} = 1/4096$. Humans, on the other hand, were found to complete the task correctly about 63% of the time. In this paper, we show that a bot can achieve significantly higher performance than random guessing, and even outperform humans, using object recognition and machine learning.

3 Methods

We apply a variety of learning-based recognition approaches to the task of classifying between human and avatar faces. For data, we used a publicly-available dataset released by the authors of [6] as part of the Face Recognition Challenge held in conjunction with the International Conference on Machine Learning and Applications (ICMLA 2012) conference [19]. This dataset consists of 200 grayscale photos, split evenly between humans and avatars. The human dataset consists of frontal grayscale facial images of 50 males and 50 females with variations in lighting and facial expressions. The avatar dataset consists of 100 frontal grayscale facial images collected from the Entropia Universe and Second Life virtual worlds. All images were resampled to a uniform resolution of 50x75. Figure 1 shows sample images from the dataset.

Each of our recognition approaches follows the same basic recipe: we use a particular choice of visual feature which is used to produce a feature vector from an image, we learn a 2-class (human vs avatar) classifier using labeled training data, and then apply the classifier on a disjoint set of test images. We now describe the various visual features and classifiers that we employed.

3.1   Naïve Approaches

As baselines, we start with three simple approaches using raw pixel values as features.

Raw Images. These feature vectors are simply the raw grayscale pixel values of the image, concatenated into a $50 \times 75 = 3750$ dimensional vector.

Summary Statistics. As an even simpler baseline, we use a 1D feature that consists only of the mean grayscale value of the image. A second baseline represents each image as a vector of five dimensions, consisting of the maximum pixel value, the minimum pixel value, the average pixel value, the median pixel value, and the sum of all pixel values.

Grayscale Histograms. This feature consists of a simple histogram of the grayscale values in the image. We tested different quantizations of the histogram, in particular testing histograms with 256, 128, 64, 32, 16, 8, 4, and 2 bins.

3.2   Histograms of Oriented Gradients (HOG)

Histograms of Oriented Gradients (HOG) features have become very popular in the recognition community for a variety of objects including people [5]. Computing these features consists of 5 stages: (1) global image normalization to reduce effect of changing illumination, (2) computing the image gradient at each pixel, (3) dividing the image into small 8x8 pixel cells, and then computing histograms over gradient orientation within each cell, (4) normalization of the histograms within overlapping blocks of cells, and (5) creating a feature vector, by concatenating all normalized histograms for all cells into a single vector. For the images in our dataset, this procedure yields a 2268 dimensional feature vector.

3.3   GIST

The GIST descriptor [15] was originally developed for scene recognition but has become popular for other recognition problems as well. This feature applies a series of filters to an image, each of which responds to image characteristics at different scales and orientations. The image is divided into a 4x4 grid of regions, and the average response of each filter is calculated within each region. This yields a descriptor that captures the "gist" of the scene: the orientation and scale properties of major image features at a coarse resolution, yielding a 960 dimensional vector.

3.4   Quantized Feature Descriptors

Another popular technique in recognition is to detect a sparse set of highly distinctive *feature points* in an image, calculate an invariant descriptor for each point, and then represent an image in terms of a histogram of vector-quantized descriptors. The Scale-Invariant Feature Transform (SIFT) [14] and Speeded-Up Robust Features (SURF) [3] are two commonly-used descriptors; we use the latter here. We use SURF to detect features points and calculate descriptors for each point, and then use k-means to produce a set of 50 clusters or "visual words." We then assign each descriptor to the nearest visual word, and represent each image as a histogram over these visual words, yielding a 50 dimensional feature vector. Figure 2 illustrates some detected SURF features.

Fig. 2. Detected SURF features for a human face (left) and avatar face (right)

3.5 Local Binary Pattern-Based Features

Four-Patch Local Binary Pattern (FPLBP). The local binary pattern (LBP) descriptor examines each pixel in a small neighborhood of a central pixel, and assigns a binary bit depending on whether the grayscale value is greater than or less than that of the central pixel. The bits that represent the comparison are then concatenated to form an 8-bit decimal number, and a histogram of these values is computed. FPLBP is an extension to the original LBP where for each pixel in the image we consider two rings, an inner ring of radius r_1 and an outer one of radius r_2 (we use 4 and 5, respectively), each centered around a pixel [18]. T patches of size $s \times s$ (we use $s = 3$) are spread out evenly on each ring. Since we have T patches along each ring then we have $T/2$ center symmetric pairs. Two center symmetric patches in the inner ring are compared with two center symmetric patches in the outer ring, each time setting one bit in each pixels code based on which of the two pairs are more similar, and then calculate a histogram from the resulting decimal values.

Local Difference Pattern Descriptor. We also introduce a simple modification to the above approach which we call Local Difference Pattern. We divide the image into $n x n$ ($3x3$) windows and compute a new value for the center of each window based on the values of its neighbors. We compute the new value as the average of the differences between the center and all other pixels in the window (instead of computing the binary window and converting it into its decimal value as in LBP). We tried using both absolute and signed differences. Figure 3 illustrates this feature. Finally we compute a histogram for these new values.

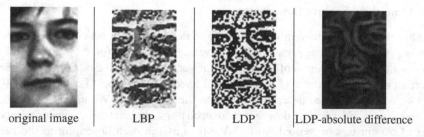

original image   LBP   LDP   LDP-absolute difference

Fig. 3. Illustration of LBP and LDP features for a human face

3.6 Classifiers and Feature Selection Methods

For learning the models from each of the above feature times, we applied two different types of classifiers: Naïve Bayes [11,12], and LibLinear with L2-regularized logistic regression [8]. We used Correlation-based Feature Selection (CFS) [10] to reduce feature dimensionality.

4 Results

Table 1 presents the results on the face-versus-avatar classification task for our simplest features (the Naïve features based on raw pixel values) and our simplest classifier (Naïve Bayes). All results presented here were evaluated using 10-fold cross-validation. The best classification rate obtained in this set of experiments is 93%, when raw grayscale pixel values concatenated into a vector are used as features. Interestingly, even much simpler techniques give results that are significantly better than random guessing (which would yield 50% accuracy). The 128-dimensional grayscale histograms achieve 92%

Table 1. Classification results using Naïve features and Naïve Bayes classifiers

Method	Accuracy	Precision	Recall	F-measure
Pixel-values	**93%**	**93.2%**	**93%**	**93%**
Histograms(256-Bins)	89%	89.8%	89%	88.9%
Histograms(128-Bins)	92%	92.3%	92.%	92%
Histograms(64-Bins)	77%	77.3%	77%	76.9%
Histograms(32-Bins)	78%	78.2%	78%	78%
Histograms(16-Bins)	75%	75.1%	75%	75%
Histograms(8-Bins)	77%	77.9%	77%	76.8%
Histograms(4-Bins)	69%	69.1%	69%	69%
Histograms(2-Bins)	52%	52.1%	52%	51.7%
Average-mean-pixel	57%	57.4%	56%	53.8%
Avg_Min_Max_Sum_Median	61%	62.9%	61%	59.5%

Table 2. Classification accuracy using different features and classifiers, with feature dimensionality in parentheses

Method	LibLinear	Naïve Bayes	Naïve Bayes + FS
Raw pixels	**100% (3750f)**	93% (3750f)	98% (54f)
Histogram	60% (256f)	**89% (256f)**	82% (24f)
GIST	84% (960f)	88% (960f)	**90% (24f)**
HOG	**99% (2268f)**	94% (2268f)	95% (44f)
FPLBP	94% (240f)	89% (240f)	**95% (26f)**
SURF codebook	**97% (50f)**	96% (50f)	94% (22f)
LDP (absolute differences)	94% (256f)	99% (256f)	**100% (61f)**
LDP (differences)	96% (256f)	98% (256f)	**99% (75f)**
LBP	**98% (256f)**	95% (256f)	98% (31f)

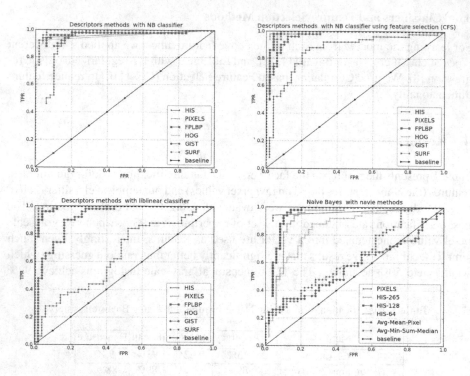

Fig. 4. ROC curves for the human versus avatar classification task. *Top left:* Naïve Bayes classifiers, *Top right:* feature selection and Naïve Bayes, *Bottom row:* LibLinear classifiers.

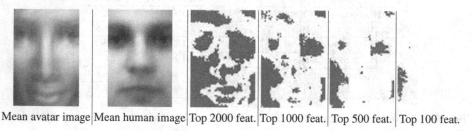

Mean avatar image | Mean human image | Top 2000 feat. | Top 1000 feat. | Top 500 feat. | Top 100 feat.

Fig. 5. *From left:* Mean face images, and positions of top features according to information gain

accuracy, but even 4-dimensional histograms achieve almost 70% accuracy. Our simplest method, which encodes an image as a single dimension corresponding to its mean pixel value, gives an accuracy of 56%.

The fact that such simple recognition tools yield surprisingly high results suggests that there may be some unintended biases in the Avatar Captcha dataset that the classifiers may be learning. These biases could probably be removed relatively easily, by for example applying grayscale intensity and contrast normalization so that the histograms and summary statistics of human and avatar images would be identical. Figure 5 shows the most informative locations in the raw grayscale pixel features, and suggests that the key differences between avatars and humans are in the cheek lines and around the eyes.

We next tested more sophisticated techniques which may be much more difficult to guard against. Table 2 shows results for the more sophisticated features and classifiers that we tested. Each row of the table shows a different feature type, while the columns show results for classification using LibLinear, Naïve Bayes (NB), and Naïve Bayes with feature selection (NB+FS). Perfect recognition results (100% accuracy) are achieved by both the LibLinear classifier using raw pixel values, and the local difference pattern (LDP) descriptor using Naïve Bayes with feature selection. HOG features also produced excellent results (99% correct accuracy), while SURF and the local binary pattern variants all yielded accuracies above 95% for at least one of the classifiers. GIST and grayscale histogram features performed relatively poorly at around 90%, but this is still a vast improvement over the random baseline (50%). Figure 4 presents ROC curves for the different classifiers and features.

5 Discussion and Conclusion

Our experimental results indicate that the current Avatar Captcha system is not very secure because relatively straightforward image recognition approaches are able to correctly classify between avatar and human facial images. For example, several of our classifiers achieve 99% accuracy on classifying a single image, which means that they would achieve $(0.99)^{12} = 88.6\%$ accuracy on the 12-face classification Captcha proposed in [6]. This results is actually better than the human performance on this task (63%) reported in [6]. Our classifiers work better than baseline even on surprisingly simple features, like summary statistics of an image. These results suggest that there may be substantial bias in the library of face images used in the current system, and that a new dataset without such biases would yield a much more secure system. Our work thus highlights the difficulty of creating image-based Captcha systems that do not suffer from easily-exploitable biases, and how to prevent such biases (and ideally to prove that they do not exist) is a worthwhile direction for future work.

References

1. von Ahn, L., Blum, M., Hopper, N.J., Langford, J.: CAPTCHA: Using Hard AI Problems for Security. In: Biham, E. (ed.) EUROCRYPT 2003. LNCS, vol. 2656, pp. 294–311. Springer, Heidelberg (2003)
2. Almazyad, A., Ahmad, Y., Kouchay, S.: Multi-modal captcha: A user verification scheme. In: Proceedings of International Conference on Information Science and Applications (ICISA), pp. 1–7. IEEE (2011)
3. Bay, H., Tuytelaars, T., Van Gool, L.: SURF: Speeded Up Robust Features. In: Leonardis, A., Bischof, H., Pinz, A. (eds.) ECCV 2006, Part I. LNCS, vol. 3951, pp. 404–417. Springer, Heidelberg (2006)
4. Chandavale, A., Sapkal, A., Jalnekar, R.: A framework to analyze the security of text based captcha. International Journal of Computer Applications 27(1), 127–132 (2010)
5. Dalal, N., Triggs, B.: Histograms of oriented gradients for human detection. In: Computer Vision and Pattern Recognition, pp. 886–893 (2005)
6. D'Souza, D., Polina, P., Yampolskiy, R.: Avatar captcha: Telling computers and humans apart via face classification. In: Proceedings of IEEE International Conference on Electro/Information Technology (EIT). IEEE (2012)

7. Elson, J., Douceur, J., Howell, J., Saul, J.: Asirra: a CAPTCHA that exploits interest-aligned manual image categorization. In: In Proceedings of the 14th ACM Conference on Computer and Communications Security, CCS 2007, pp. 366–374 (2007)
8. Fan, R., Chang, K., Hsieh, C., Wang, X., Lin, C.: Liblinear: A library for large linear classification. Journal of Machine Learning Research 9, 1871–1874 (2008)
9. Gao, H., Yao, D., Liu, H., Liu, X., Wang, L.: A novel image based CAPTCHA using jigsaw puzzle. In: Computational Science and Engineering (CSE), pp. 351–356 (2010)
10. Hall, M.: Correlation-based feature selection for machine learning. PhD thesis, The University of Waikato (1999)
11. Hall, M., Frank, E., Holmes, G., Pfahringer, B., Reutemann, P., Witten, I.: The WEKA data mining software: an update. ACM SIGKDD Explorations Newsletter 11(1), 10–18 (2009)
12. John, G., Langley, P.: Estimating continuous distributions in bayesian classifiers. In: Uncertainty in Artificial Intelligence, pp. 338–345 (1995)
13. Korayem, M., Mohamed, A., Crandall, D., Yampolskiy, R.: Learning visual features for the avatar captcha recognition challenge (2012)
14. Lowe, D.: Object recognition from local scale-invariant features. In: International Conference on Computer Vision, pp. 1150–1157 (1999)
15. Oliva, A., Torralba, A.: Modeling the shape of the scene: A holistic representation of the spatial envelope. International Journal of Computer Vision 42(3), 145–175 (2001)
16. Von Ahn, L., Blum, M., Langford, J.: Telling humans and computers apart automatically. Communications of the ACM 47(2), 56–60 (2004)
17. Wang, L., Chang, X., Ren, Z., Gao, H., Liu, X., Aickelin, U.: Against spyware using CAPTCHA in graphical password scheme. In: Proceedings of IEEE International Conference on Advanced Information Networking and Applications (AINA), pp. 760–767. IEEE (2010)
18. Wolf, L., Hassner, T., Taigman, Y.: Descriptor based methods in the wild. In: ECCV Workshop on Real-Life Images (2008)
19. Yampolskiy, R.: ICMLA Face Recognition Challenge, http://www.icmla-conference.org/icmla12/

Comparative Analysis of Image Fusion Techniques in Remote Sensing

J. Jayanth[1], T. Ashok Kumar[2], and Shivaprakash Koliwad[3]

[1] VTU-RRC, Dept. of ECE, GSSSIETW, Mysore, Karnataka, India
[2] VCIT, Puttur (DK), Karnataka, India
[3] Dept. of ECE, VCIT, Puttur (DK), Karnataka, India
jayanth.j123@gmail.com

Abstract. The study is to compare the performance of different image fusion techniques for the enhancement of an urban features and coastal data. The goal is to obtain high resolution multispectral image which combines the spectral characteristic of low resolution data with high the spectral resolution of the panchromatic image. For the data fusion, IHS (Intensity-Hue-Saturation), DWT (Discrete Wavelet Transformation), PCA (Principal Component Analysis),BT (Brovey Transform), MT (Multiplicative Transform) and DWT-HIS. Visual and statistical analyses prove that the techniques present here is clearly better for preserving the spectral properties with improve spatial data.

Keywords: Data fusion, multi-source, PAN.

1 Introduction

Most of the earth observation satellite provides a means for locating, identifying and mapping certain coastal zones features and assessing of spatio- temporal changes. The Mangalore coastal zone of is a mosaic of complex interacting ecosystems, exposed to dramatic changes due to natural and anthropogenic causes.Due to huge quantities of satellite image are available from many different earth observation sites, moreover thanks to a growing number of satellite sensors, the acquisition frequency of a same scene is permanently increasing. Furthermore, the difference in spatial resolution between panchromatic and the multispectral mode can be measured by the ratio of the ground sampling distance and vary between 1:3 and 1:5. The objective of the image fusion is to combine the high spatial and multispectral information to form a fused multispectral image that retains the spatial resolution from the high resolution panchromatic image and the spectral characteristics of the lower resolution multispectral image.

Image fusion has been applied to digital imagery to achieve a number of objectives, such as: image sharpening; improve geometric correction; provide stereo-viewing capabilities for stereophotogrammetry feature enhancement; Complement data sets for improved classification; detect changes using multi-temporal data; Substitute missing information (e.g. clouds-VIR, shadows-SAR) in one image with signals from another sensor image; and, replace effective data.

A. Ell Hassanien et al. (Eds.): AMLTA 2012, CCIS 322, pp. 111–117, 2012.
© Springer-Verlag Berlin Heidelberg 2012

2   Test Site

2.1   Data Source

In this study, for the landuse/landcover change detection in coastal region have a practical significance studies, an image of 16 March 2008 and LISS IV image of 20 March 2008 have been used. The data have four multispectral bands (B1: 0.45-0.52um, B2: 0.52-0.60um; B3: 0.63-0.69um) and one panchromatic band (Pan: 0.45-0.9um). The spatial resolution is 2.5m for the panchromatic image, while it is 5.8m resolution for the multispectral bands. All images are merged with panchromatic image with 1m ground sampling distance (GSD) using image fusion techniques. As we calculate the average deviation per pixel measured as digital number (DN) which is based on 8-bit or 16-bit range, depending on the resolution of employed imagesAs a test site, Mangalore city has been selected. Mangalore city is situated in the south east part of Karnataka state. Although the city is extended from the west to the east about 30km, and from the north to the south about 20 km, the study area is chosen for the present study covers a very small portion (it is about 3.15km from the west to the east and about 2.15km from the north to the south). Subsets are of a coastal area at Mangalore area and include vegetated areas, sandy beach and water. Subsets were selected in order to include a variety of land use categories i.e. buildings, roads, sea, vegetation, grass and bare soil, delimited by multioriented edges.

2.2   Co-registration of Images

In this study, the intensity images of IRS P5/P6 and LISSIV have been used. Therefore, there is no need to apply special procedure to extract grayscale images from the LISSIV images. Generally, in order to perform accurate data fusion, high geometric accuracy between the images is needed. As a first step, the IRSP5 images was georeferenced to a map projection using three ground control points (GCPs) defined from a field survey. For transformation, a second order transformation and nearest neighbour resampling approach were applied and the related root mean square error (RMSE) was 1.06 pixels. The errors of less than 1.5m were considered as acceptable for further studies.

3   Image Fusion

The concept of image is the integration of different digital images in order to create new image and obtain more information that can be separately derived from any of them. In this study data fusion has been performed at pixel level and the following techniques were applied: Each of these techniques is briefly discussed below:

Principal Component Analysis: It is a linear orthogonal transformation that projects the multivariate data on a subspace spanned by the principal axes. Thus, the principal components are obtained by projecting the multispectral image on the principal axes (eigenvectors) estimated from the sample covariance matrix. In PCA based sharpening, the PAN image replaces the first principal component, before an inverse principal component transform is performed.

Intensity-Hue-Saturation Method: The HIS system offers the advantage that the separate channels outline certain colour properties, namely intensity (I), hue (H), Saturation (S). This specific colour space is chosen because the visual cognitive system of human beings tends to treat the three components as roughly orthogonal perceptual axes.

Multiplicative Technique (MT): The MT is grouped under the arithmetic method which uses the four possible arithmetic methods (addition, subtraction, division and multiplication) to incorporate an intensity image into an achromatic image. The MT algorithm is based on the following relation

$$DN_{R\,(new)} = DN_R * DN_{PAN}; \; DN_{G\,(new)} = DN_G * DN_{PAN}; \; DN_{B\,(new)} = DN_B * DN_{PAN}$$

Brovey Transform: This is a simple numerical method used to merge different digital data sets. The algorithm based on a brovey transform uses a formula that normalises multispectral bands used for a red, green, blue colour display and multiplies the result by high resolution data to add the intensity or brightness components of the image.

Wavelet-Based Fusion: The wavelet transform decomposes the signal based elementary functions so called the wavelets. By using this, an image is decomposed into a set of multi-resolution images with wavelet coefficient. For each level, the coefficients contain spatial difference between two successive resolution levels. In general, a wavelet based image fusion can be performed by either replacing some wavelet coefficients of the low-resolution image with the corresponding coefficients of the high-resolution image or by adding high resolution coefficient to the low resolution data.

IHS and Wavelet Integrated Fusion: Combining wavelet with IHS transformation makes it easy to preserve the colour information, because the transformation is done only in one channel, while generally wavelet transform is done on three channels separately.

The wavelet and IHS fusion process can be performed in the following steps: Transform the multi-spectral image into the IHS components (forward IHS transform); Apply histogram match between panchromatic image and Intensity component (I), and get new panchromatic image (new Pan); Decompose the histogram-matched panchromatic image and Intensity component (I) to wavelet planes respectively; Partially replace the LL^P in the panchromatic decomposition with the LL^I of the intensity decomposing resulting in LL', LH^P, HH^P and HL^P; Perform an inverse wavelet transform, and generate a new intensity; Transform the new intensity, together with the hue and saturation components back into RGB colour space (inverse IHS transform).

4   Quality Assessment

Quality refers to both the spatial and spectral quality of fused images. This work aims at the evaluation of data fusion methods applied to satellite data with pixel level image fusion through a set of various indicators. Beside subjective quality assessment employing the human visual system (HSV) model, the successful quality measure is the quality assessment using mathematically defined for quantitative evaluation in both spatial and spectral content of the fused images. With references to the ground truth data discussion on fusion method and evaluation indicators help users to select the appropriate data fusion method to enhance the spectral and spatial resolution to meet the requirements of the specific application, and examine for the comparative evaluation for coastal zone change detection analysis in sharpening the multispectral images.

4.1   Spectral Fidelity

The basic principal of spectral fidelity is that the low spatial frequency information in the high resolution image should not be absorbed to the fusion image, so as to preserve the spectral content of original MS image. The indexes which can reflect fidelity of fusion image include:

Standard Deviation: It is an important index to a weight the information of image; it reflects the deviation degree of values relative to the mean of image. The greater SD is, the more dispersible the distributing of the gray grade is in the statistical theory.

$$\sigma = (1/1\text{-}n \ \Sigma(MS_{i,j} - MS_{mean})^2)^{1/2} \tag{1}$$

Where σ is the SD, MS is the multi-spectral data, n is the bands of MS.

4.2   Spatial Criterion

Maximization of spatial details in terms of maximizing the correlation coefficient between the high frequency component of the fusion product and the original PAN image as in eq

$$CC = \frac{\sum_{i=1}^{n} (xi - x)(yi - y)}{\sqrt{\sum_{i=1}^{n} (xi - x)^2} \sqrt{\sum_{i=1}^{n} (yi - y)^2}} \tag{2}$$

Where n is the number of pixels, xi, yi are the grey values of homologous pixels in the two images (bands under comparison), and x and y are the mean grey values of both the images.

The Relative Difference of Means: Relative Difference of Means between the fused product and the original low spatial resolution multispectral image. The value is given relative to the mean value of the original image. The ideal value is zero. Let F refers to the fused image

$$RMD = 1 - \frac{F_{Mean}}{MS_{Mean}} \tag{3}$$

5   Evaluation Results for Image Fusion Technique

In this work, objective image quality measures have been examined for the comparative evaluation of pixel-based fusion techniques used for coastal zone change detection analysis in sharpening the multispectral images. In order to understand the performance of image fusion algorithms, multiple criteria and statistical indicators regarding different aspects of image quality are presented for objective and quantitative evaluation of the fused images. ERDAS IMAGINE 9.1 software and algorithms have been used. With references to the ground truth data discussion on fusion method and evaluation indicators help users to select the appropriate data fusion method to enhance the spectral and spatial resolution to meet the requirements of the specific application, and examine for the comparative evaluation.

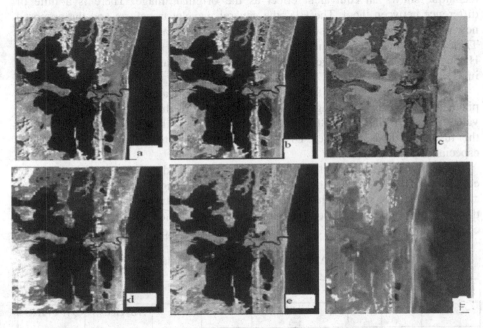

Fig. 1. Results of Image Fusion (a) DWT (b) Multiplicative (c) PCA (d) BT (e) HIS (f) DWT-IHS

5.1   Visual Analysis

In all of these images is possible to differentiate the beach ridges from the surrounding areas. Comparing to the color composites these fusion produce images, which are more sharpened because in all cases, the multi-spectral images have been fused with a high resolution image. From figure1 we can observe that BT, HIS and PCA techniques plays much more emphasis on the spatial information than the spectral information. They can achieve higher spatial results but preserve less spectral fidelity. The HPF and MT methods cause large spectral distortion and achieve lower spatial information. Unlike the BT method, the spectral quality of fused images with the HPF and MT method if the spectral difference between the panchromatic image and the multispectral image is large. The wavelet transform+IHS method can achieve a very close color to the original image. It can control the trade off between the spectral information and the spatial structure by adjusting the wavelet decomposition level. However it involves complicated and time consuming frequency decomposition and reconstructing processing.

5.2   Statistical Analysis

The same (0-255) standard stretching method was applied to all these images for the display as shown in Table1. The mean bias is the difference between the means of the original image and the fused image. It is given in percentage relative to the mean of the original image. The idea value is zero for mean bias. The fused image with PCA technique shows an equivalent effect as the original image. There is a little of difference between them. The HIS, the general wavelet transform and the proposed new method produces images with a much closer mean values as the original images. Their average intensities are nearly equivalent. However, the brovey, the MT and the HPF technique produce images with lower mean value than the original image. These images look darker.

The standard deviation of the difference globally indicates the level of error at any pixel. It is given in percentage relative to the mean of the original image. The idea value is zero for SDD. The SDD of the proposal new method is the lowest among all the fusion methods, and then HPF technique. Other methods have higher SDD, especially the HIS method.

The correlation coefficient of two images is often used to indicate their degree of correlation. If the correlation coefficient of two images approaches one, their correlation is very strong. The correlation coefficient between the fused image with the HPF technique and the original images are the highest. The lowest correlation coefficient exist in the BT, the PCA and the HIS techniques. The correlation

Table 1. Statistical Assessment result of different Image fusion methods

Index	Band	TM	Method					
			BT	MT	HIS	PCA	Wavelet	DWT+IHS
Mean Bias	R	0.00	39.43	58.60	-1.11	-0.02	-2.20	0.22
	G	0.00	38.12	52.78	-2.40	-.0002	7.74	2.20
	B	0.00	38.92	53.20	-1.84	-0.007	1.77	2.59
Standard deviation	R	0.00	38.10	26.49	46.97	47.97	25.08	17.47
	G	0.00	35.18	21.19	46.61	38.83	21.53	16.89
	B	0.00	37.66	23.86	48.33	43.86	25.27	17.56
CC	R	1.00	0.47	0.88	0.50	0.30	0.83	0.91
	G	1.00	0.34	0.85	0.40	0.42	0.82	0.88
	B	1.00	0.41	0.87	0.46	0.41	0.81	0.90

coefficient reflects the consistency of the change tendency of the corresponding pixel DN value in two images. The HPF technique has a good consistency regarding to the change tendency. However, its mean bias is much higher.

6   Conclusion

To reduce the colour distortion and improve the fusion quality, an simple spectral preserve fusion approach based on IHS and wavelet integrated is presented. This approach utilizes the HIS transform to fuse high-resolution spatial information into the low-resolution multispectral images, and uses the wavelet transform to reduce the colour distortion, in the way of generating a new high-resolution panchromatic image that highly correlates to the intensity image of the IHS transform. The fusion results are compared with this conventional exsisitnig technique by statistical analysis. The results demonstrate that the new technique proposed in this paper does significantly reduce the colour distortion and gains a higher spatial detail comparing to the conventional methods.

A final validation of fusion techniques shows that there is no superior method. Instead the best technique has to be chosen on a case by case.

Acknowledgment. We would like to thank Dr. K.S. Sreedhara Dept of CSE, UBDTCE, Davangere, Jude Hemanth for giving this Opportunity and MCF Hassan for compiling and maintaining the database. This work has been partially supported by the Dept of ECE, GSSSIETW, Mysore.

References

[1] Carper, W.J., Lillesand, T.M., Kiefer, R.W.: The use of Intensity-Hue-Saturation transformations for merging SPOT Panchromatic and multispectral image data. Photogrammetric Engineering and Remote Sensing 56(4), 459–467 (1990)

[2] Chavez Jr., P.S., Sides, S.C., Anderson, J.A.: Comparison of three different methods to merge multiresolution and multispectral data: TM & SPOT pan. Photogrammetric Engineering and Remote Sensing 57(3), 295–303 (1991)

[3] Dallemand, J.F., Lichtenegger, J., Kaufmann, V., Paudyal, D.R., Reichert: Combined analysis of ERS-1 SAR and visible/infrared RS data for land cover/land use mapping in tropical zone: a case study in Guinea. In: Proc. First ERS-1 Symposium Space at the Service of our Environment, ESA SP, Cannes, France, November 6-8, vol. 359, pp. 555–561 (1992)

[4] Harris, J.R., Murray, R., Hirose, T.: IHS transform for the integration of radar imagery with other remotely sensed data. Photogrammetric Engineering and Remote Sensing 56(12), 1631–1641 (1990)

[5] Pohl, C., van Genderen, J.L.: Multisensor fusion: Optimization and operationalization for mapping applications. In: Proc. of SPIE Conf. Signal Proc., Sensor Fusion, and Target Recognition III, Orlando-FL-USA, April 4-6, vol. 2232, pp. 17–25 (1994)

[6] Pohl, C., van Genderen, J.L.: Image fusion of microwave and optical remote sensing data for map updating in the Tropics. In: Proc. Conference on Image and Signal Processing for Remote Sensing, Paris, France, September 25-29 (1995)

[7] Remote sensing handbook for tropical coastal management. UNESCO publishing/coastal management sourcebook 3 (2000)

Density Based Fuzzy Thresholding for Image Segmentation

Jianli Li[1], Bingbin Dai[1], Kai Xiao[1,*], and Aboul Ella Hassanien[2]

[1] School of Software, Shanghai Jiao Tong University, China
{tk1307993,magictracy,showkey}@sjtu.edu.cn
[2] Information Technology Department, Cario University, Egypt
aboitcairo@gmail.com

Abstract. In this paper, we introduce an image segmentation framework which applies automatic threshoding selection using fuzzy set theory and fuzzy density model. With the use of different types of fuzzy membership function, the proposed segmentation method in the framework is applicable for images of unimodal, bimodal and multimodal histograms. The advantages of the method are as follows: (1) the threshoding value is automatically retrieved thus requires no prior knowledge of the image; (2) it is not based on the minimization of a criterion function therefore is suitable for image intensity values distributed gradually, for example, medical images; (3) it overcomes the problem of local minima in the conventional methods. The experimental results have demonstrated desired performance and effectiveness of the proposed approach.

Keywords: Segmentation, Histogram thresholding, Fuzzy density.

1   Introduction

Image segmentation is an indispensable preprocessing task in most image processing, recognition and analysis applications. As the most intuitive and least computation-intensive approach, segmentation methods using global threshoding separate objects and background pixels into non-overlapping regions [1]. The key of applying this type of method is to find an appropriate threshold. Gray level of the pixels under or higher than this value are assigned respectively into two different groups [2].

Most previous works on various thresholding techniques are good at particular kinds of images. Otsu's method [3] automatically perform histogram shape-based image thresholding. Some previous works are based on information theorem which suggests that entropy is a measure of the uncertainty of an event [4], [5]. In these methods, rather than maximizing the inter-class variance, the inter-class entropy is maximized in order to find the optimal thresholds.

Fuzzy set theory is suitable to be applied on image thresholding to partition the image into meaningful regions. The nature of the fuzziness in image arises from the

---

[*] Corresponding author.

A. Ell Hassanien et al. (Eds.): AMLTA 2012, CCIS 322, pp. 118–127, 2012.

uncertainty present and provides a new tool for image segmentation [6] – [12]. Fuzzy clustering is an important application of the theory and becomes popular in the recent decades [14] – [16]. To apply fuzzy set theory on quick image segmentation, several researchers have investigated fuzzy based thresholding techniques. Li et al. [6] combined the fuzzy set theory and information theorem to develop a criterion of maximum fuzzy entropy to obtain the threshold. Chaira and Ray [7] [8] applied four types of methods, i.e. fuzzy divergence proposed in [7], linear and quadratic indices of fuzziness, fuzzy compactness and fuzzy similarity. This type of method minimizes the fuzzy divergence or the separation between the actual and the ideal thresholded image. In [9] [10], Tobias et.al introduced a method based on criterion of similarity between gray levels instead of using a criterion function to be minimized with the use of Zadeh's S-function. Lopes et.al [11] further developed this method to make it fully automatic through a statistical approach with image equalization. Further improvement by Prasad et.al [12] uses $\pi-$function instead of S-function to produce more accurate and reliable results compared to the algorithm proposed in [10], the πfunction is chosen as one standard deviation of the arithmetic mean to locate the intensities of the misclassification regions. Huang et.al [13] further improved Tobias' algorithm by fixing boundary value on medical images.

In this paper, we propose an automatic image thresholding method based on fuzzy set theory, i.e. fuzzy density model. The framework with the use of this method applies different types of fuzzy membership function to be suitable for images of unimodal, bimodal and multimodal histograms.

2   Fuzziness and Fuzzy Density in Image

2.1   Fuzzy Set Theory

On the basis of the principles of uncertainty, ambiguity and vagueness, Zadeh introduced the fuzzy set theory in 1965 [17]. A fuzzy set is a class of objects with a continuum of grades of membership.

Let us assume X be a space of points, this is also called the universe. In X, its elements are denoted as x, that is, $x_i : X = \{x_1, x_2, ..., x_n\}, 0.0 \leq x_i \leq 1.0$. A fuzzy set A in X is formally defined as

$$A = \{(x_i, \mu_A(x_i))\}, x_i \in X, i = 1,2 \cdots, n \qquad (1)$$

where $\mu_A(.)$ is termed as the characteristic or membership function of the elements in the set.

In a fuzzy set, the membership function functions can be viewed as mappings of diverse human choices to an interval [0,1]. Thus, a fuzzy set is a more generalized set where the membership values lie between 0 and 1.There are a numerous membership functions described in the literature as monotonic and non-monotonic families [18].

2.2 Fuzzy Density Model

The mass density or density of a material is defined as its mass per unit volume. In [19], Wang introduced the neighborhood counting, a general methodology for devising similarity functions (NCM) used in the framework of kNN algorithm, to find the nearest neighbors. To introduce this concept, here we first consider an example. Fig. 1a and Fig. 1b show a 2D data space along with some data points respectively. To simplify, let us assume these points are all on average distribution, that is, at a same radius of r (we use circle for its boundary here, see Fig. 1a and Fig. 1b), the centroids of these points are at the same coordinate but with different distance to its centroid. In this case, although these points both have the same centroid, but in fuzzy density model we say Fig. 1a has a high density in its fuzzy region. We could describe this character with the help of fuzzy membership function, that is, a closer distance to the centroid would get a higher fuzzy value so its fuzzy average would also be higher. It is intuitively sensible that the higher this value, the more similar these points are. When the radius become larger, that is, R > r (see Fig. 1a), there are no effect that we assume no more point is at the region between r and R. It is obvious that a small region would have a high value of fuzzy density under the same situation. To quantify this intuition, we could use the Euclidean distance (see Fig. 1).

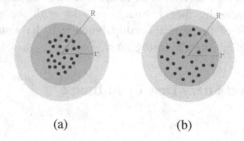

(a)   (b)

Fig. 1. An example of fuzzy density model. (a) has a higher fuzzy density in the same region at the radius of *r* than it in (b).

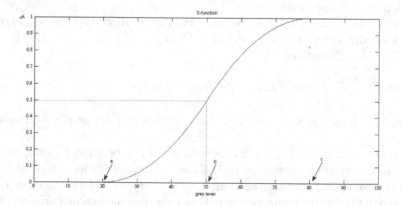

Fig. 2. S-membership function. *a, b, c* are the three control points and μ_a is membership value.

Using the notion of fuzzy density model, we now state the above intuition formally. Let U be a data space, and *fdm(r,p)* be the function to calculate the fuzzy density, where r denotes the region and p is the points within this region of boundary. The higher the *fdm(r,p)*, the more similar these points are. When taking image into account, in a simple manner, the gray scale is divided into two parts by a selected value X. X is the boundary to both parts and we could get two regions at the same time, i.e. [*Min,X*], [*X,Max*], where *Min, Max* denotes the minimum and maximum gray scale respectively. Pixels under this partition are these points in p. We could use gray level to express the distance of pixels. As a whole, we calculate *fdm(r,p)* at the selected value of X to choose a proper threshold.

Although there are many other membership functions, in this work, we use three different types of formula to calculate the membership function according to the distance in its fuzzy density region.

a). Zadeh's S-membership function [10]

Such a function is defined as

$$\mu_S(x) = S(x,a,b,c) = \begin{cases} 0, x < a \\ 2[(x-a)/(c-a)]^2, a < x \le b \\ 1 - 2[(x-c)/(c-a)]^2, b < x < c \\ 1, x > c \end{cases} \quad (2)$$

where a, b, and c, are the three parameters as shown in Fig.2. b denotes the crossover point and could be any value between a and c. Here we define b by b = (a+c)/2 with $\mu_A(b) = 0.5$. For a = Xmin, c = Xmax, the membership function plot is shown in Fig.2 for a normalized set.

b). Gamma membership function [7]

The general formula for the probability density function of the Gamma distribution is:

$$f(x) = \frac{\left(\left(\frac{x-\mu}{\beta}\right)^{\gamma-1}\right)\exp\left(-\left(\frac{x-\mu}{\beta}\right)\right)}{\Gamma(\gamma)}, x \ge \mu, \gamma, \beta > 0 \quad (3)$$

where γ is the shape parameter, μ is the location parameter, β is the scale parameter and Γ is the Gamma function.

when $\mu \ne 0, \beta = 1, \gamma = 1$, the Gamma distribution takes the form

$$\mu(x) = \exp(-c \cdot |x - \mu|) \quad (4)$$

It may be pointed out that in the membership function, the constant 'c' has been taken to ensure membership value of the gray level feasible in the range [0,1] and would explain how to chose in the following section.

c). Gaussian membership function [18]

$$\mu(x) = \exp\left(-\frac{(x-m)^2}{2\sigma^2}\right), m = mean \quad (5)$$

3   Threshold Selection Method

We introduce the key idea in section 2, that is, by combining fuzzy set theory we could use fuzzy density model to calculate the character of image which can is illustrated in Fig.3 as below.

The histogram consists by two groups of pixels, dark part and light part. The target is to split the image histogram into two crisp subsets, namely, object subset O and background subset B, $O \cup B = A$. Firstly, we get two initial fuzzy subsets, denoted by L and R, are associated with initial histogram intervals located at the beginning and the end regions of the histogram, i.e. *[Xmin,Xl], [Xr,Xmax]*, and we assume there are both enough initial points that the two parts contain. For bright objects $R \subset O, L \subset B$, for dark objects $L \subset O, R \subset B$. The place between *[Xl,Xr]* is called fuzzy region. In order to get a proper threshold value, we continuously choose gray level in *[Xl,Xr]*, Xi denotes. Every time we calculate the fuzzy density of *[Xl,Xi],[Xi,Xr]* respectively, then a comparison between them is made as described in Equation (6):

$$\begin{cases} IF\big(fdm(Xmin,Xi) > fdm(Xi,Xmax)\big), THEN\ Xi \subset L \\ IF\big(fdm(Xmin,Xi) < fdm(Xi,Xmax)\big), THEN\ Xi \subset R \end{cases} \tag{6}$$

Note that in the proposed framework the fuzzy density model is used, where a fuzzy set with a high value of fuzzy density indicates its elements is much closer, or similar. And with its region get large, its value would become low normally (see Fig.3).

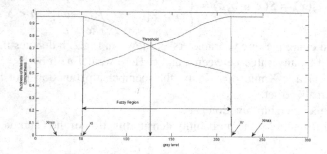

Fig. 3. Base idea of the fuzzy density model thresholding method. *Xmin, Xmax* denotes the minimum and maximum gray level that has pixels in the histogram of the image respectively.

Since the key of the proposed classification method is the comparison of fuzzy density value, normalization to the L or R region is needed. We take the trivial method proposed in [9] by first computing the initial subsets L or R to get a normalization factor α according to formula listed below and then normalize the value at every round, take L region that needed be normalized as example:

$$\alpha = \frac{fdm(R)}{fdm(L)} \tag{7}$$

A way to calculate the fdm(r,p) is by making a little change to the index of fuzziness [18]. The index of fuzziness is defined as:

$$I(A) = \frac{2}{n^k} \cdot d(A,\bar{A}) \tag{8}$$

where $d(A,\bar{A})$ denotes the distance between image A and its nearest ordinary image $\bar{A}$.

There are two types of indices of fuzziness:(a) linear and (b) quadratic. These are defined as:

1, If k = 1, d becomes the Hamming distance, the linear index of fuzziness may be rewritten as:

$$I(A) = \frac{2}{n}[\sum_{i=1}^{n}|\mu_A(x_i) - \mu_{\bar{A}}(x_i)|] \tag{9}$$

2, If k =2, d becomes the Euclidean distance, then the quadratic index of fuzziness is defined as:

$$I(A) = \frac{2}{n^{1/2}}[\sum_{i=1}^{n}|\mu_A(x_i) - \mu_{\bar{A}}(x_i)|^2]^{1/2} \tag{10}$$

We take the centroid of pixels in each region to be the origin of $\bar{A}$. So the closer points to centroid would get a higher value in each membership function thus making more contribution to its fuzzy density value.

This is the basic idea of the approach. The concept presented above sounds attractive but has some limitations concerning the initialization of the seed subsets thus it sometimes needs manually operations to select initial boundary. More general, it runs not well in low contrast images. The work proposed in [11] overcomes a similar problem in [10] by a procedure with statistical parameters P1 and P2. In fact, the initial subsets are defined automatically and they are large enough to accommodate a minimum number of pixels defined at the beginning of the process. The minimum number of pixels of each set i.e. object or background depends on the shape of the histogram and it is a function of the number of pixels in the gray level intervals [0,127] and [128,255].

$$MinPix_{Bseed(Wseed)} = P_1 \sum_{i=0\,(128)}^{127\,(255)} h(x_i) \tag{11}$$

where $P1 \in [0,1]$ and $h(x_i)$ denotes number of occurrences at gray level x_i. If $P1$ is too high, the fuzzy region between the initial intervals will be small and the values are gray levels for thresholds are limited, on the other hand if the $P1$ is too low the initial subsets are not representative and the method does not converge. For low contrast images, popular histogram equalization is performed to bring minimum number of pixels into the region with poor number of pixels. If the number of pixels belonging to either side of the histogram from the intensity 128 is smaller than $P_{min} = P2 * MN$, where $P_2 \in [0.1]$ and M * N are the total number of pixels in the image, then histogram equalization is recommended. Finally the $P1$ and $P2$ are estimated as 39.64% with standard deviation 13.37% and 20% with standard deviation 14.30% respectively.

Now the whole approach can be summarized in the following algorithm:

```
Let B,W describe individually the Background and Object.
Assume that Object is the white region.
  Input: An image
  Output: Thresholding Value
  Preliminary Step:
  1, Determine if image needs to equalization through P2
  2, Calculate the initial region boundary X1,Xr through P1
  3, Get the normalization factor α
  Basic Step:
```

```
for i =  (Xl + 1) to (Xr - 1)
     compute LEFT = fdm([Xmin,Xi]);
     compute RIGHT = fdm([Xi,Xmax]);
     if LEFT * α is larger than RIGHT
            Set Xi belongs to B
     else
            Set Xi belongs to W
     end
end
```

4   Experimental Results and Analysis

In order to validate the proposed algorithm, various types of images with the use of different membership functions discussed in the Section 2 are listed. Two other results based on minimal criterion methods, i.e. Fuzzy divergence [7], Otsu's method [3], are also presented.

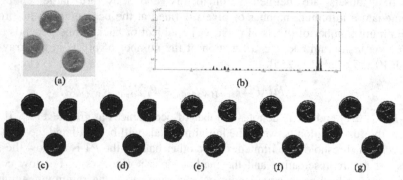

Fig. 4. (a) Input image 'coin', (b) its histogram and thresholded using (c) Fuzzy Divergence[7], (d) Otsu's method[3], (e) S-membership function, (f) Gamma membership function, (g) Gaussian membership function. Image copied from [13].

As we mentioned before, our method is good at segmenting images with ambiguous objects or gradually distributed intensity. Fig. 4 and Fig. 5 are two unimodal images (See their histograms). In Fig. 4, the image 'coin' with size 252 x 252 particularly demonstrates this kind of advantage. It obtains more details of information located with the center of coin stamp (See Fig. 4(e), (f), (g)) while the two other methods don't (See Fig.4 (c), (d)). And in Fig. 5, the image 'block' with size 200 x 200 has four block regions directly shown in different gray level that needs to be fully partitioned. By choosing Gaussian membership function in our framework (See Fig. 5(e)), it successfully obtains the right result while the two other methods fail (See Fig. 5(c), (d)). Because the proposed membership function is originally distributed in values and could easily be selected by testing the most suitable one for given kinds of images, under such particular condition which need more details around objects or images with intensities distributed in gray level, the proposed approach is more flexible and useful.

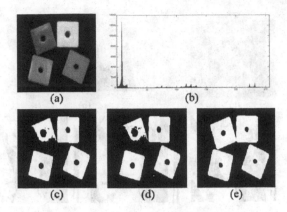

Fig. 5. (a) Input image 'block', (b) its histogram and thresholded using (c) Fuzzy Divergence[7], (d) Otsu's method[3], (e) Gaussian membership function.

Fig. 6 shows a typical bimodal image (See its histogram) 'blood' of size 272 x 265. All the five results are satisfactory that we can accept for correctly dividing the object. In details, we could notice that Fig. 6(c) and Fig. 6(d) get a similar partition because they both find the minimum value of criterion function, however, our approach gets more details around the region between background and object region. Fig. 6(b), (c), (d) get different contours in the middle of blood clot, different weights of its membership function are in accordance with its intensity which gradually change at that place. It can be seen that the threshold using Gamma membership function, S-membership function and Gaussian membership function obtains outer contour, inner contour, and region between contour and outer contours, respectively. It is flexible to choose the more suitable one by switching membership function.

When comes to the object and background of the input image has some overlapping regions in the histogram. In Fig. 7, the typical multimodal image 'lena' of size 512 x 512 shows a result. Our approach also works well comparing to these methods of finding an absolute minimum of the histogram (See Fig. 7(e)).

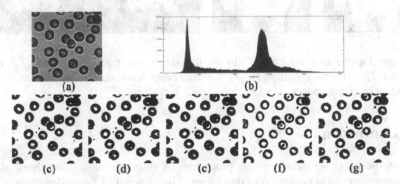

Fig. 6. (a) Input image 'blood', (b) its histogram and thresholded using (c) Fuzzy Divergence[7], (d) Otsu's method[3], (e) S-membership function, (f) Gamma membership function, (g) Gaussian membership function.

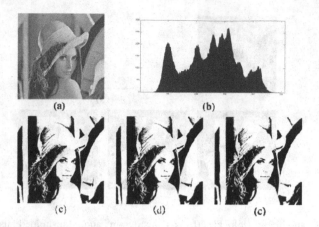

Fig. 7. (a) Input image 'lena', (b) its histogram and thresholded using (c) Fuzzy Divergence[7], (d) Otsu's method[3], (e) Gamma membership function

For a particular series of medical image, a desired threshold can be obtained from our proposed method, while the other two do not (See Fig. 8 (c), (d), (e)), such as getting the sacroiliac bone region. Fig. 8 shows the experimental results by using S-membership function and manually setting the boundary value of $a = X_{min} + 10$ and $c = X_{max} - 10$ each time.

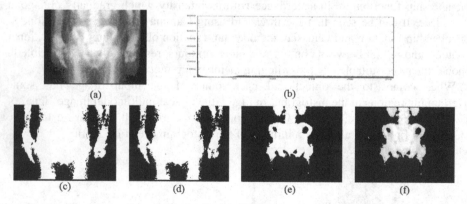

Fig. 8. (a) Input image 'sacroiliac', (b) its histogram and thresholded using (c) Fuzzy Divergence[7], (d) Otsu's method[3], (e) S-membership function, (f) the final result from thresholding and input images.

5   Conclusion

Based on the fuzzy set theory, a new procedure of automatic histogram threshold for image segmentation is presented in this paper. The concept of fuzzy density model is developed to choose the proper threshold for object extraction. The threshold level is obtained by its combined method and in such case yields optimal segmentation of the objects from the background. It is fully automatic that no prior knowledge of the image is required and not based on the minimization of a criterion function thus good at coping some kinds of images with gray level distributed gradually in illumination. Comparative experimental results suggest that the proposed method is suitable some medical image segmentation tasks. It is also applicable for real-time applications owing to the its less computation-intensiveness.

References

1. Sijbers, J., Verhoye, M., Scheunders, P., der Linden, A.V., Dyck, D.V., Raman, E.: Watershed-based Segmentation of 3D MR Data for Volume Quantization. Magnetic Resonance Imaging 15(6), 679–688 (1997)
2. Clarke, L.P., Velthuizen, R.P., Camacho, M.A., Heine, J.J., Vaidyanathan, M., Hall, L.O., Thatcher, R.W., Silbiger, M.L.: MRI Segmentation: Methods and Applications. Magnetic Resonance Imaging 13(3), 343–368 (1995)
3. Otsu, N.: A Threshold Selection Method from Gray Level Histograms. IEEE Trans. Sys., Man, Cybern. 9(1), 62–66 (1979)
4. Brink, A.D.: Minimum Spatial Entropy Threshold Selection. IEEE Proc. Vis. Image Signal Process. 142(3), 128–132 (1995)
5. Sahoo, P.K., Soltani, S., Wong, K.C., Chen, Y.C.: A Survey of Thresholding Techniques. Computer Vision, Graphics, and Image Processing 41, 233–260 (1988)
6. Li, X., Zhao, Z., Cheng, H.D.: Fuzzy Entropy Threshold Approach to Breast Cancer Detection. Information Sciences 4, 49–56 (1995)
7. Chaira, T., Ray, A.K.: Segmentation Using Fuzzy Divergence. Pattern Recognition Letters 24, 1837–1844 (2003)
8. Chaira, T., Ray, A.K.: Threshold Selection Using Fuzzy Set Theory. Pattern Recognition Letters 25, 865–874 (2004)
9. Tobias, O.J., Seara, R., Soares, F.A.P.: Automatic Image Segmentation Using Fuzzy Sets. In: Proc. 38th Midwest Symp. Circuits and Systems, vol. 2, pp. 921–924 (1996)
10. Tobias, O.J., Seara, R.: Image Segmentation By Histogram Thresholding Using Fuzzy Sets. IEEE Trans. Image Process. 11 (2002)
11. Lopes, N.V., Modadouro do Couto, P.A., Bustince, H., Melo-Pinto, P.: Automatic Histogram Threshold Using Fuzzy Measures. IEEE Trans. Image Process. 19(1) (2010)
12. Prasad, M.S., Divakar, T., Rao, B.S., Raju, N.: Unsupervised Image Thresholding Using Fuzzy Measures. International Journal of Computer Applications 27(2) (2011)
13. Huang, J.-Y., Tsai, M.-F., Kao, P.-F., Chen, Y.-S.: Automatic Computer-aided Sacroiliac Joint Index Analysis for Bone Scintigraphy. Computer Methods And Programs in Biomedicine 98, 15–26 (2010)
14. Chuang, K.-S., Tzeng, H.-L., Chen, S., Wu, J., Chen, T.-J.: Fuzzy C-Means Clustering with Spatial Information for Image Segmentation. Computerized Medical Image and Graphics 30, 9–15 (2006)
15. Jawahar, C.V., Biswas, P.K., Ray, A.K.: Investigations on Fuzzy Thresholding Based on Fuzzy Clustering. Pattern Recogn. 30(10), 1605–1613 (1997)
16. Ahmed, M.N., Yamany, S.M., Mohamed, N., Farag, A.A., Moriarty, T.: A Modified Fuzzy C-Means Algorithm for Bias Field Estimation and Segmentation of MRI Data. IEEE Trans. on Medical Imaging 21(3), 193–199 (2002)
17. Zadeh, L.A.: Fuzzy Sets. Information and Control 8, 338–353 (1965)
18. Chaira, T., Ray, A.K.: Fuzzy Image Processing and Applications with MATLAB. CRC Press (2009)
19. Wang, H.: Nearest Neighbors by Neighborhood Counting. IEEE Trans. on Pattern Analysis and Machine Intelligence 28(6), 942–953 (2006)

Subjectivity and Sentiment Analysis of Arabic: A Survey

Mohammed Korayem[1,3], David Crandall[1], and Muhammad Abdul-Mageed[2]

[1] School of Informatics and Computing, Indiana University
Bloomington, Indiana USA
{mkorayem,djcran}@indiana.edu
[2] Department of Linguistics &
School of Library & Information Science,
Indiana University, Bloomington, USA
mabdulma@indiana.edu
[3] Department of Computer Science,
Fayoum University, Fayoum, Egypt

Abstract. Subjectivity and sentiment analysis (SSA) has recently gained considerable attention, but most of the resources and systems built so far are tailored to English and other Indo-European languages. The need for designing systems for other languages is increasing, especially as blogging and micro-blogging websites become popular throughout the world. This paper surveys different techniques for SSA for Arabic. After a brief synopsis about Arabic, we describe the main existing techniques and test corpora for Arabic SSA that have been introduced in the literature.

1 Introduction

The web has become a read-write platform where users are no longer strictly consumers of information but also producers. User-generated content, in the form of unstructured free text, is becoming an integral part of the web mainly because of the dramatic increase of social network sites, video sharing sites, online news, online reviews sites, online forums and blogs. Because of this proliferation of user-generated content, Web content mining is gaining considerable attention due to its importance for many businesses, governmental agencies and institutions. Subjectivity and sentiment analysis (SSA) is an important sub-area of Web content mining.

In natural language, *subjectivity* refers to aspects of language used to express opinions, feelings, evaluations, and speculations [14], including sentiment. The process of subjectivity classification refers to the task of classifying texts as either *objective* (e.g., *The new iPad was released*) or *subjective* (e.g., *The new iPad is cool*). Subjective text can further be classified by its *sentiment* and *polarity*. For sentiment classification, the task consists of identifying whether a subjective text is *positive* (e.g., *Egyptians inspired the world with their revolution!*), *negative* (e.g., *The bloodbaths in Syria are horrifying!*), *neutral* (e.g., *Obama may sign the bill*), or *mixed* (e.g., *The iPad is cool, but way too expensive*). These various types of SSA are gaining increasing attention because they provide an automated way to summarize vast quanitities of text (including reviewers, blogs, Twitter feeds, etc.) into the opinions that they express. This data is of

A. Ell Hassanien et al. (Eds.): AMLTA 2012, CCIS 322, pp. 128–139, 2012.

use to businesses and institutions who want to monitor feelings about their products and services. Private citizens can also benefit from this information to be able to compare sentiments about competing products, for example. Following a considerable body of related literature, we will henceforth use the terms *subjectivity and sentiment analysis* and *sentiment analysis* interchangeably.

Sentiment analysis can thus be viewed as a classification process that aims to determine whether a certain document or text was written to express a positive or a negative opinion about a certain object (e.g., a topic, product, or person). This process regards each document as a basic information unit. The process has been referred to as 'document level-sentiment classification' where the document is seen as an opinionated artifact. The more fine-grained problem of identifying the sentiment of every sentence has also been studied [30]. Sentiment analysis is typically performed using one of two basic approaches: *rule-based classifiers*, in which rules derived from linguistic study of a language are applied to sentiment analysis [15, 16, 18, 24], and *machine learning classifiers* in which statistical machine learning algorithms are used to learn signals of sentiment automatically [2, 26, 27, 30, 33, 34].

Currently, most of the systems built for sentiment analysis are tailored for the English language [26, 30], but there has been some work on other languages. This paper reviews efforts to build SSA systems for Arabic, a Semitic language. After a brief discussion of the properties of Arabic in Section 2, we review resources and test corpora for Arabic in Section 3. Section 4 then reviews various approaches that have been employed for Arabic SSA.

2 Arabic

As the official language of 22 countries, Arabic is spoken by more than 300 million people, and is the fastest-growing language on the web (with an annual growth rate of 2,501.2% in the number of Internet users as of 2010, compared to 1,825.8% for Russian, 1,478.7% for Chinese and 301.4% for English) [1]. There are about 65 million Arabic-speaking users online, or about 18.8% of the global Internet population [1].

Arabic is a Semitic language [35] and consists of many different regional dialects. While these dialects are true native language forms, they are typically used only in informal daily communication and are not standarized or taught in schools [22]. There is one formal written standard that is commonly used in written media and education throughout the Arab world called *Modern Standard Arabic* (MSA). There is a large degree of difference between MSA and most Arabic dialects, and, interestingly, MSA is not actually the native language of any Arabic country or group. MSA is syntactically, morphologically, and phonologically based on Classical Arabic (CA) [22], which is the language of the Qur'an (Islam's Holy Book).

Arabic has a very rich inflectional system and is considered one of the richest languages in terms of morphology [23]. Arabic sentential forms are divided into two types, nominal and verbal constructions [21]. In the verbal domain, Arabic has two word order patterns (i.e., Subject-Verb-Object and Verb-Subject-Object). In the nominal domain, a normal pattern would consist of two consecutive words, a noun (i.e., subject) then an adjective (subject descriptor).

3 Corpora and Lexicons

The availability of annotated corpora for training and testing is very important to enable progress on sentiment recognition systems. Collecting this data (and particularly the annotations) can be very labor-intensive. Fortunately, a number of research groups have developed and released Arabic sentiment analysis corpora, and we review this work here.

AWATIF is a multi-genre, multi-dialect corpus for Arabic SSA built by Abdul-Mageed and Diab [4, 7]. AWATIF is extracted from three different resources: the Penn Arabic Treebank (PATB), which is an existing collection of news wire stories in different domains (e.g. sports, politics, finance, etc.), Wikipedia user talk pages covering a variety of topics, and conversation threads from web forums on seven different sites. In annotating the corpus they used two different procedures, one that used untrained annotators via crowd sourcing technologies to give a coarse sentiment label (positive, negative, or neutral) to each sentence, and then one that used annotators trained with some linguistic background to label each sentence. The authors also manually created an adjective polarity lexicon, giving coarse labels (again positive, negative or neutral) to each of nearly 4,000 Arabic adjectives. In a related work, Abdul-Mageed and Diab [5] use a machine translation procedure to translate available English lexicons (e.g., from [20] and [9]) into Arabic. They retrieve 229,452 entries, including expressions commonly used in social media.

Opinion corpus for Arabic (OCA) is a corpus of text from movie review sites by Rushdi-Saleh *et al.* [34], and includes a parallel English version called EVOCA. The corpus consists of 500 reviews, half negative and half positive. The raw reviews contained a number of challenges which the authors attempted to fix manually, including filtering out spurious and unrelated comments, romanization of Arabic, multi-language reviews, differing spellings of proper names, and movie reviews that were more opinions of the cultural and political themes of a movie than the film itself. (As an example of the latter issue, the movie "Antichrist" has a rating of 6.7 in IMDB but a rating of 1 in the reviews on the Arabic blog.) OCA and EVOCA performed standard pre-processing on the corpus, including correcting spelling mistakes and deleting special characters, and also have made available unigram, bigram, and trigrams for the dataset.

MPQA subjective lexicon & Arabic opinion holder corpus: Another corpus for Arabic opinion holder and subjectivity lexicon is proposed by Elaranoty et al. [18], who created an Arabic news corpus. They crawled 150 MB of Arabic news and manually annotated 1 MB of the corpus for opinion holder. The opinion holder corpus was annotated by three different people. Any conflict emerging because of different annotations was solved using majority voting. For preprocessing the corpus, the Research and Development International (RDI) tool (http://www.rdi-eg.com) was used to handle the morphological analysis of Arabic sentences and assign parts of speech (POS) tags. Finally, semantic analysis of the words were done. Arabic Named Entity Recognition (ANER) [3] was used for extracting names from documents. The proposed Arabic subjectivity lexicon contains strong as well as weak subjective clues by manually translating the MPQA lexicon [37].

An **Arabic Lexicon for Business Reviews** was proposed by Elhawary and Elfeky [19]. Elhawary and Elfeky [19] used the similarity graph to build an Arabic lexicon.

The similarity graph is a type of graph where the two words or phrases have an edge if they are similar on polarity or meaning. The weight of the edge represents the degree of similarity between two nodes. Usually, this graph is built in an unsupervised manner based on lexical co-occurrences from large Web corpora. Here, the researchers initially used a small set of seeds and then performed label propagation on an Arabic similarity graph. For building the Arabic similarity graph, a list of seeds for positive, negative and neutral are used. The Arabic lexicon created from the similarity graph consists of two columns where the first column is the word or phrase and the second column represent the score of the word which is the sum of the scores of all edges connected to this node (word/phrase). They applied filtering rules to avoid both the sparseness of the data and garbage nodes. Garbage nodes caused the top 200 positive words to be non-positive. They removed nodes with a high number of weighted edges and kept the 25 top ranked synonyms of the word. The top 25 synonyms of positive words are 90% positive. This ratio became 50-60% when considering all synonyms. The sentiment of the review is computed based on the sentiment of the sentences. That is, sentence boundary detection is used, and negation is also used, to flip the sentiment score from positive to negative and vice versa. There are around 20 Arabic words for negation. Sentences greater than 120 character are ignored. The results show that the created Arabic lexicon has high precision but has low recall.

Another subjectivity lexicon is proposed by El-Halees [17]. This lexicon is built manually based on two resources, the SentiStrength project and an online dictionary. They translated the English list from SentiStrength project and then manually filtered it. Common Arabic words were added to the lexicon.

4   Subjectivity and Sentiment Analysis Systems and Methods for Arabic

We now turn to reviewing the different methods for Arabic subjectivity and sentiment analysis that have been proposed in the literature. First, we describe language-independent feature selection/extraction methods applied to Arabic. Then, we discuss the systems employing standard IR methods (e.g., TF*IDF) and hybrid classifiers. Finally, we discuss systems employing Arabic-specific features and those tailored for extracting opinion holders.

4.1   Language-Independent Feature Selection and Extraction

One way of building sentiment analyses for languages other than English or building systems that work for multiple languages is to extract and select features that do not depend on the language itself. Different approaches have been followed to select and extract these features, including: (1) Entropy Weighted Genetic algorithms [2], (2) Feature Subsumption [38], (3) Local grammar-based methods [11, 12], (4) Positional features [32] and (5) Common seeds word methods [25]. Among these methods, we are aware of only two that have been applied to Arabic: entropy weighted genetic algorithms and local grammar methods.

Abbasi *et al.* [2] used genetic algorithms to select language features for both Arabic and English. Genetic Algorithms (GA) are a general class of techniques that apply the concept of evolution to general optimization problems. Entropy Weighted Genetic Algorithms (EWGA) combine genetic algorithms with information gain (IG) to perform the feature selection. In particular, IG is used to select the initial set of features for the initial stage of the GA, and is also applied during the cross-over and mutation stages. EWGA is applied to select features for sentiment analysis in a corpus of Web forum data containing multiple languages [2]. They used two types of features, stylistic features and lexical features. They avoided semantic features because they are language dependent and need lexicon resources, while the limitation of their data prevent using of linking features.

The paper evaluates the proposed system on a benchmark testbed consisting of 1000 positive and 1000 negative movie reviews. Their system that uses feature selection outperforms several previous systems [28, 29, 31, 36]. Using this system, they achieved an accuracy rate of 91% while other systems achieved accuracy rates between 87-90% on the movie review data set. They were also able to achieve 92% accuracy on Middle Eastern forums and 90% on US forums using the EWGA feature selection method.

Use of Local Grammar is another method that can be used to extract sentiment features [11]. Ahmed *et al.* [12, 13] applied this approach to documents from the financial news domain. They identified domain-specific key words by looking for words that occurred often in a corpus of financial news but relatively infrequently in a general corpus. Using the context around these words they built a local grammar to extract sentiment-bearing phrases. They applied their approach to Arabic, English and Chinese. They evaluated the system manually and achieved accuracy rates between 60-75% for extracting the sentiment bearing phrases. Importantly, the proposed system could be used to extract the sentiment phrases in financial domain for any language.

4.2   Standard IR and Hybrid Classifiers

Here we describe systems employing standard IR methods (e.g., TF*IDF) and hybrid classifiers.

The work of Rushdi *et al.* [33, 34] builds machine learning classifiers using both the OCA and EVOCA corpora. They use both Support Vector Machines (SVMs) and Naive Bayes (NB) classifiers, reporting 90% *F*-measure on OCA and 86.9% on EVOCA using SVMs. They show that SVMs outperform the NB classifier, which is common in text classification tasks. Results also show that there is no difference between using term frequency (tf) and the slightly more complicated term frequency-inverse document frequency (tf-idf) as weighting schemes. Experiments also show that stemming words before feature extraction and classification nearly always degrades the results.

Elhawary and Elfeky [19] present a system for sentiment analysis on Arabic business reviews, with the specific goal of building a web search engine that would automatically annotate returned pages with sentiment scores. The system has several components. The first component classifies whether an Internet page is a review or not. For this component, they extend an in-house multi-label classifier to work for Arabic such that its task is to assign a tag from the set {*review, forum, blog, news, shopping store*} to a document. To build an Arabic review classifier data set, 2000 URLs were collected and more than 40% of them were found to be reviews through manual labeling. This data set was collected by searching the web using keywords that usually exist in reviews (such as "the camera is very bad"). The authors translated the lists of keywords collected and add to them a list of Arabic keywords that usually appear in opinionated Arabic text. The final list contained 1500 features and was used to build an AdaBoost classifier, using 80% of the data for training and the rest for testing. After a document is classified as belonging to the Arabic review class or not, a second component of the system analyzes the document for its sentiment. They build an Arabic lexicon based on a similarity graph for use with the sentiment component. The final component of the system is designed to provide the search engine with an estimate of the sentiment score assigned to a document during the search.

A combined classification approach is proposed by El-Halees [17] for document level sentiment classification. He applied different classifiers in a sequential manner. A lexicon-based classifier is first used to estimate the sentiment of a document based on an aggregation of all the opinion words and phrases in the document. However, because some documents lack enough opinion words to use this lexicon-based classifier, a second phase uses a maximum entropy classifier. All classified documents from first classifier are used as the training set for this maximum entropy classifier, which is then used to compute the probability that a given document belongs to a certain sentiment class. In particular, if the probability is greater than a threshold of 0.75, then the document is assigned a class, and otherwise the document is passed to the next stage. The final stage is a k-nearest neighbors (KNN) classifier that finds the nearest neighbors for the unannotated document using the training set coming from the previous two classifiers.

The corpus used for evaluation consisted of 1134 documents collected from different domains (e.g., education, politics, and sports), with 635 positive documents (with 4375 positive sentences) and 508 negative documents (with 4118 negative sentences). Preprocessing is applied to filter HTML tags and non-textual contents are removed. Alphabets are normalized and some misspelled words are corrected. Sentences are tokenized, stop words are removed, and an Arabic light stemmer is used for stemming the words, and *TF-IDF* is used for term weighting. The paper reports an f-measure of 81.70% averaged over all domains for positive documents and 78.09% *F*-measure for negative documents. The best *F*-measure is obtained in the education domain (85.57% for the positive class and 82.86% for the negative class).

4.3   Arabic-Specific, Social Media, and Genre-Specific Features

Other techniques use the linguistic features of Arabic in order to perform sentiment analysis, by analyzing the grammatical structure of Arabic [21] and Arabic-specific morphological features [4, 6–8].

Farra *et al.* [21] proposed Arabic sentence-level sentiment classification, considering two different approaches: a grammatical approach and a semantic approach. The grammatical approach is based on Arabic grammatical structure and combines the verbal and nominal sentence structures in one general form based on the idea of actor/action. In this approach, the subjects in verbal and nominal sentences are actors and verbs are actions. They manually label action and actor tags in sentences and used these tags as features. Their feature vector constitutes the following dimensions: sentence type (verbal or nominal), actor, action, object, adjective, type of pronoun and noun, transition (the type of word linking the current sentence with the previous sentence), word polarity (positive, negative, neutral) and sentence class.

The second approach proposed by Farra *et al.* [21] combined syntactic and semantic features by extracting some features like the frequency of positive, negative, and neutral words, the frequency of special characters (e.g., "!"), the frequency of emphasis words (e.g., "really" and "especially"), the frequency of conclusive and contradiction words, etc. For extracting the semantics of the words, the paper builds a semantic interactive learning dictionary which stores the semantic polarity of word roots extracted by stemmer. The system asks the user for the polarity of a word if it has not yet been learned.

For evaluation of the grammatical approach, only 29 sentences are annotated manually with part-of-speech tags. They report 89.3% accuracy using an SVM classifier with 10-fold cross validation. Sentences from 44 random documents are used for evaluating the semantic and syntactic approach using a J48 decision tree classifier. They report 80% accuracy when the semantic orientation of the words extracted and assigned manually is used, and 62% when the dictionary is used. They also classified the documents by using all sentence features and chunking the document into different parts, reporting 87% accuracy with an SVM classifier when documents divided into 4 chunks and neutral class excluded.

Abdul-Mageed et al. [4, 6–8] created sentence-level annotated Arabic corpora and built subjectivity and sentiment analysis systems exploiting them. In their systems these authors use various types of features, including language independent features, Arabic-specific morphological features, and genre-specific features. In [6,8], they classify MSA news data at the sentence level for both subjectivity and sentiment. They use a two-stage SVM classifier, where a subjectivity classifier is first used to separate subjective from objective sentence. In a second stage, subjective sentences are classified into positive and negative cases, with an assumption that neutral sentences will be treated in a future system. These authors make use of both language-independent and Arabic-specific features. The language independent features include a feature indicating the domain of the document (e.g., politics, sports) from which a sentence is derived, a *unique* feature where all words occuring less than four times are replaced by the token "UNIQUE", *N-gram* features including all *N*-grams of frequency less than 4, and an *adjective* feature for adjectives indicating the occurrence of a polarized adjective based on a pre-developed polarity lexicon of 3982 entries. Classification accuracy of 95.52% are reported. The results showed that the adjective feature is very important, as it improved the accuracy by more than 20% and the unique and domain features are also helpful.

Other work by Abdul-Mageed *et al.* [10] presents SAMAR, an SVM-based system for Subjectivity and Sentiment Analysis (SSA) for Arabic social media genres. They tackle a number of research questions, including how to best represent lexical information, whether standard features are useful, how to treat Arabic dialects, and whether genre specific features have a measurable impact on performance. The authors exploit data from four social media genres: Wikipedia Talk Pages, Web forums, chat, and Twitter tweets. The corpus includes data in both Modern Standard Arabic and dialectal

Arabic. These authors break down their data into 80% training, 10% development, and 10% testing and exploit standard SSA features (e.g., the "unique" feature, a wide coverage polarity lexicon), social and genre features (e.g., the gender of a user), and a binary feature indicating whether a sentence is in MSA or dialectal Arabic. They are able to significantly beat their majority class baselines with most data sets. The results suggest that they need individualized solutions for each domain and task, but that lemmatization is a feature in all the best approaches.

Table 1 summarizes the SSA systems which are described above.

Table 1. Summary of different Arabic SSA systems

System	Type	Features	SSA level	Corpus	Advantages	Disadvantages
[2]	ML	Stylistic + LF	Doc	Movie reviews, web forums	– Language independence – Effective feature selection	– High computational cost
[12, 13]	NC	domain-specific lexical features	Phr	Financial news	– Simple method – Language independence	– No sentiment classification (only phrase extraction)
[33, 34]	ML	LF	Doc	Web reviews	– Simple features – Introduces OCA corpus	– No Arabic-specific features
[19]	ML	LF	Doc	Business reviews	– Builds large-scale lexicon – Computes soft sentiment score (in addition to hard classification)	– No Arabic-specific features
[17]	LC+ML	LF	Doc	Multi-domain	– Combines lexical and ML – Multi-domain	– No Arabic-specific features
[21]	ML	Syntactic & LF	Sen+Doc	News	– Combines LF & syntactic	– Evaluated on small dataset
[4, 6–8]	ML	LF, syntactic & genre-specific, social media features	Sen	News, social media	– Combines language-independent and Arabic-specific features – Incorporates dialectal Arabic – Employs a wide-coverage polarity lexicon	–Some genre and social media features are costly to acquire

Legend

Classification types: ML=Machine Learning, CL=Rule or lexicon-based classifiers, NC=No classification.
Features: LF=Lexical features.
SSA level: Doc=Document-level, Phr=Phrase-level, Sen=Sentence-level classification.

4.4 Opinion Holder Extraction

Different approaches for extracting the opinion holder in Arabic are proposed in [18]. Their approach is based on both pattern matching and machine learning. They extract three different types of opinion holders. The first type of opinion holder is opinion holder for speech events, which is defined as a subjective statement said directly by someone or claimed to be said by someone. In this way, they combine the direct speech event and indirect speech event in this type. The second type of opinion holder is defined as related to an opinion holder that expresses sentiment towards certain opinion subject. The third type is defined as related to expressive subjective elements (e.g., emotions, sarcasm) expressed implicitly. Definitely the third type is the hardest type to extract because it depends on the meaning of the words rather than the structures. The first approach used in [18] to extract opinion holders is based on pattern matching. They manually extract 43 patterns where the morphological inflections of the words are neglected. Examples of these patterns are "And <holder> expressed his objection about ....", or "And adds <holder>...." A pattern-based opinion holder classifier is built using the extracted patterns. The following rule to extracting an opinion holder is followed: the opinion holder is retrieved if it contains a subjective statement or a named entity and it contains a statement that is classified as objective or subjective using a high-precision classifier.

While the first approach is based on pattern matching, the second and third approaches are based on machine learning. The authors formulate the opinion holder problem as a classification problem where each word in the corpus is classified as "Begining of a holder (B-holder)", "Inside a holder (I-holder)" or "Non holder". A conditional random field (CRF) probabilistic discriminative model is used for classification. The authors build the CRF classifier based on a set of lexical, morphological, and semantic features. Pattern matching is used as a source for additional features for training the classifier in the third approach. Syntactic features are not used because of a lack of a robust general Arabic parser. The lexical features used are the focus word itself and window of size 3 around it (i.e., previous and next three words). The second type of features, i.e., semantic field features, are generated by grouping the semantically related words and giving them the same probability. In that way the handling of a missing word of the group in training data will not affect the performance if any word of the group appeared in the test data. The third feature type used is POS Tags generated by the RDI morphological analyzer. The set of tags generated by the RDI analyzer is reduced to a small set of tags and this small set are used as features. In addition, base phrase chunk and named entity recognition features are used. Finally, a feature based on pattern matching is used such that it is detected whether any word is part of the patterns extracted manually in the first approach or not.

Experimental results on the Arabic Opining Holder corpus show that machine learning approaches based on CRF achieve better results than the pattern matching approach. The authors report 85.52% precision, 39.49% recall, and 54.03% F-measure. Authors justify the performance degradation of the system by stating that it is due to the lower performance of Arabic NLP tools compared to those of English as well as the absence of a lexical parser.

5   Conclusion

To conclude, we surveyed the different methods for building subjectivity and sentiment analysis systems for Arabic. The available resources for Arabic sentiment analysis are introduced. Here, it is suggested that a nuanced method to be followed in building a sentiment analysis system for Arabic employs not only language-independent, but also Arabic-specific features; exploits wide-scale, domain-specific polarity lexicons; and leverages genre- and social media-specific features. While it is costly to build resources tailored to Arabic and acquire certain types of features (e.g., genre- and social media-specific features), this route yields high performance and brings interesting insights to the classification task. Alternatives to this method would be transferring the sentiment knowledge from English into the Arabic language or to use language independent methods.

References

1. Internet world stats, http://www.internetworldstats.com/stats7.htm
2. Abbasi, A., Chen, H., Salem, A.: Sentiment analysis in multiple languages: Feature selection for opinion classification in Web forums. ACM Transactions on Information Systems (TOIS) 26(3), 12 (2008)
3. AbdelRahman, S., Elarnaoty, M., Magdy, M., Fahmy, A.: Integrated machine learning techniques for arabic named entity recognition. International Journal of Computer Science Issues, IJCSI 7(4), 27–36 (2010)
4. Abdul-Mageed, M., Diab, M.: AWATIF: A Multi-Genre Corpus for Modern Standard Arabic Subjectivity and Sentiment Analysis. In: Proceedings of the Eight International Conference on Language Resources and Evaluation (LREC 2012). European Language Resources Association, ELRA (2012)
5. Abdul-Mageed, M., Diab, M.: Toward building a large-scale Arabic sentiment lexicon. In: Proceedings of the 6th International Global Word-Net Conference, Matsue, Japan (2012)
6. Abdul-Mageed, M., Diab, M., Korayem, M.: Subjectivity and sentiment analysis of modern standard Arabic. In: Proceedings of the 49th Annual Meeting of the Association for Computational Linguistics: Human Language Technologies, vol. 2, pp. 587–591. Association for Computational Linguistics (2011) (short papers)
7. Abdul-Mageed, M., Diab, M.T.: Subjectivity and sentiment annotation of modern standard arabic newswire. In: Proceedings of the 5th Linguistic Annotation Workshop, LAW V 2011, pp. 110–118 (2011)
8. Abdul-Mageed, M., Korayem, M.: Automatic Identification of Subjectivity in Morphologically Rich Languages: The Case of Arabic. In: Proceedings of the 1st Workshop on Computational Approaches to Subjectivity and Sentiment Analysis (WASSA), pp. 2–6 (2010)
9. Abdul-Mageed, M., Korayem, M., YoussefAgha, A.: Yes we can?: Subjectivity annotation and tagging for the health domain. In: Proceedings of the International Conference Recent Advances in Natural Language Processing, RANLP, Hissar, Bulgaria (2011)
10. Abdul-Mageed, M., Kuebler, S., Diab, M.: Samar: A system for subjectivity and sentiment analysis of arabic social media. In: Proceedings of the 3rd Workshop in Computational Approaches to Subjectivity and Sentiment Analysis, pp. 19–28. Association for Computational Linguistics (2012)
11. Agić, Ž., Ljubešić, N., Tadić, M.: Towards sentiment analysis of financial texts in croatian. In: Proceedings of the Seventh International Conference on Language Resources and Evaluation, LREC 2010 (2010)
12. Ahmad, K., Cheng, D., Almas, Y.: Multi-lingual sentiment analysis of financial news streams. In: Proceedings of the 1st International Conference on Grid in Finance (2006)
13. Almas, Y., Ahmad, K.: A note on extracting sentiments in financial news in English, Arabic & Urdu. In: Proceedings of Workshop on Computational Approaches to Arabic Script-based Languages (2007)

14. Banfield, A.: Unspeakable sentences: Narration and representation in the language of fiction. Routledge & Kegan Paul Boston (1982)
15. Brooke, J., Tofiloski, M., Taboada, M.: Cross-linguistic sentiment analysis: From English to Spanish. In: Proceedings of the 7th International Conference on Recent Advances in Natural Language Processing, Borovets, Bulgaria, pp. 50–54 (2009)
16. Denecke, K.: Using SentiWordNet for multilingual sentiment analysis. In: IEEE 24th International Conference on Data Engineering Workshop, ICDEW, pp. 507–512. IEEE (2008)
17. El-Halees, A.: Arabic Opinion Mining Using Combined Classification Approach. In: Proceedings of the International Arab Conference on Information Technology, ACIT (2011)
18. Elarnaoty, M., AbdelRahman, S., Fahmy, A.: A Machine Learning Approach For Opinion Holder Extraction Arabic Language. CoRR, abs/1206.1011 (2012)
19. Elhawary, M., Elfeky, M.: Mining Arabic Business Reviews. In: Proceedings of International Conference on Data Mining Workshops (ICDMW), pp. 1108–1113. IEEE (2010)
20. Esuli, A., Sebastiani, F.: Sentiwordnet: A publicly available lexical resource for opinion mining. In: Proceedings of the 5th Conference on Language Resources and Evaluation (LREC 2006), vol. 6, pp. 417–422. Citeseer (2006)
21. Farra, N., Challita, E., Assi, R., Hajj, H.: Sentence-Level and Document-Level Sentiment Mining for Arabic Texts. In: Proceedings of International Conference on Data Mining Workshops (ICDMW), pp. 1114–1119. IEEE (2010)
22. Habash, N.: Introduction to Arabic natural language processing. Synthesis Lectures on Human Language Technologies 3(1), 1–187 (2010)
23. Habash, N., Rambow, O., Roth, R.: Mada+ tokan: A toolkit for arabic tokenization, diacritization, morphological disambiguation, POS tagging, stemming and lemmatization. In: Proceedings of the 2nd International Conference on Arabic Language Resources and Tools (MEDAR), pp. 242–245 (2009)
24. Kim, J., Jung, H., Lee, Y., Lee, J.: Conveying Subjectivity of a Lexicon of One Language into Another Using a Bilingual Dictionary and a Link Analysis Algorithm. International Journal of Computer Processing of Oriental Languages 22(2), 205–218 (2009)
25. Lin, Z., Tan, S., Cheng, X.: Language-independent sentiment classification using three common words. In: Proceedings of the 20th ACM International Conference on Information and Knowledge Management, pp. 1041–1046. ACM (2011)
26. Liu, B.: Sentiment analysis and subjectivity. In: Handbook of Natural Language Processing, pp. 627–666 (2010)
27. Mihalcea, R., Banea, C., Wiebe, J.: Learning multilingual subjective language via cross-lingual projections. In: Proceedings of the 45th Annual Meeting of the Association of Computational Linguistics, vol. 45, pp. 976–983. Association for Computational Linguistics (2007)
28. Mullen, T., Collier, N.: Sentiment analysis using support vector machines with diverse information sources. In: Proceedings of Conference on Empirical Methods in Natural Language Processing, EMNLP, vol. 4, pp. 412–418 (2004)
29. Pang, B., Lee, L.: A sentimental education: Sentiment analysis using subjectivity summarization based on minimum cuts. In: Proceedings of the 42nd Annual Meeting on Association for Computational Linguistics, p. 271. Association for Computational Linguistics (2004)
30. Pang, B., Lee, L.: Opinion mining and sentiment analysis. Foundations and Trends in Information Retrieval 2(1-2), 1–135 (2008)
31. Pang, B., Lee, L., Vaithyanathan, S.: Thumbs up?: Sentiment classification using machine learning techniques. In: Proceedings of Conference on Empirical Methods in Natural Language Processing, pp. 79–86. Association for Computational Linguistics (2002)
32. Raychev, V., Nakov, P.: Language-independent sentiment analysis using subjectivity and positional information. In: Proceedings of the International Conference Recent Advances in Natural Language Processing, RANLP, pp. 360–364 (2009)

33. Rushdi-Saleh, M., Martín-Valdivia, M., Ureña-López, L., Perea-Ortega, J.: Bilingual Experiments with an Arabic-English Corpus for Opinion Mining, pp. 740–745 (2011)
34. Rushdi-Saleh, M., Martín-Valdivia, M., Ureña-López, L., Perea-Ortega, J.: Oca: Opinion corpus for Arabic. Journal of the American Society for Information Science and Technology 62(10), 2045–2054 (2011)
35. Versteegh, K., Versteegh, C.: The Arabic Language. Columbia University Press (1997)
36. Whitelaw, C., Garg, N., Argamon, S.: Using appraisal groups for sentiment analysis. In: Proceedings of the 14th ACM International Conference on Information and Knowledge Management, pp. 625–631. ACM (2005)
37. Wilson, T., Wiebe, J., Hoffmann, P.: Recognizing contextual polarity in phrase-level sentiment analysis. In: Proceedings of the conference on Human Language Technology and Empirical Methods in Natural Language Processing, pp. 347–354. Association for Computational Linguistics (2005)
38. Zhai, Z., Xu, H., Li, J., Jia, P.: Feature Subsumption for Sentiment Classification in Multiple Languages. In: Zaki, M.J., Yu, J.X., Ravindran, B., Pudi, V. (eds.) PAKDD 2010, Part II. LNCS, vol. 6119, pp. 261–271. Springer, Heidelberg (2010)

Part III

Machine Learning in Multimedia Computing

Support Vector Machine Approach for Detecting Events in Video Streams

Ahlem Walha, Ali Wali, and Adel M. Alimi

REGIM: REsearch Group on Intelligent Machines,
University of Sfax, ENIS, BP W, 3038, Sfax, Tunisia
{walha.ahlem,ali.wali,adel.alimi}@ieee.org

Abstract. The object recognition is an important topic in image processing. In this paper we present an overview of a robust approach for event detection from video surveillance. Our events detecting system consists of three modules, learning, extraction and detection. The extraction part of the video characteristics is based on MPEG 7. Meanwhile, in the detection part we use SVMs for the recognition of events.

1 Introduction

The multimedia information retrieval is becoming increasingly useful for many applications. The existence of networks of excellence (PASCAL, Muscle, DELOS, etc..), European projects (with Media, etc..), pro-grams tested (TRECVid, ImagEVAL, etc..) and the involvement of large industrials (Google, IBM, etc..) are clear evidence of an emerging market for multimedia search tools. These tools generally follow the same pattern that is on the one hand by extracting content visual characteristics of raw materials, and on the other hand by exploiting these characteristics to solve a spot of a more or less generic research. We usually distinguish between two types of video indexing systems. There is a part called generic systems that enables a classification of different available movies without taking into account contextual information. These systems allow classifying the different movies depending on the stage (internal or external), camera (static or moving), etc... The other part is called specific systems which allow only indexing a particular type of video such as TV news, surveillance video, sporting events such as football or tennis, etc.

Although their use is limited to one type of movie, however, the specific systems can respond to many requests from users of video indexing systems. The goal of this paper is to continue this genericity improvement models in the context of kernel methods. Figure (1) shiws a positive example of the type event of interest which is presented once or more in this video, while Figure (2) show a negative example of the type "event of interest which is not presented in this video" [6]. The problem is similar to find-ing weakly supervised objects in images, which are examples of the type "object of interest which is present once or more in this picture. Having held our expertise in this area, only a work of adaptation to the context will be conducted on the general principle of detector

A. Ell Hassanien et al. (Eds.): AMLTA 2012, CCIS 322, pp. 143–151, 2012.
© Springer-Verlag Berlin Heidelberg 2012

Fig. 1. Positive example for the event PersonRun

Fig. 2. Negative example for the event PersonRun

construction. By cons-level management of real-time detection in the flow, significant work remains to be conducted [8]. A new detection method is iterative development, which will update the detection results after each arrival of a new frame; this is based on the results obtained during previous iterations [18].

The indexing of video sequences can be viewed as a binary classification of all images, whether the sequence of images corresponds to the predefined event, or not. The problem is then to detect predefined events in video sequences or scenarios as in [3]. The ideal tool in the field of indexing according to a given problem is software that would work in two stages. After a learning phase of video sequences where the events are not predefined, a recognition step would classify each sequence of images into two classes: those that meet the predefined event and those that do not match. This recognition step is of course based on the learning process conducted initially [12]. In [21] a technique for detection of events based on a generic learning system called M-SVM (Multi-SVM) is proposed. The objective of this method is allows the detector to make different types of event by presenting an incremental way a significant number of examples. Examples of application of this technique are the intelligent video surveillance of airports and shopping spaces. In [22] a hybrid method that combines HMM with SVM to detect semantic events in video is proposed. The advantage of this method that is suitable to the temporal structure of event thanks to Hidden Markov Models (HMM) and guarantees high classification accuracy thanks to Support Vector Machines (SVM).

In this paper we describe our approach of event detection in video streams for surveillance applications. The following part of this paper is organized as follows: In Section 2, a description of our detection method is provided. The results are presented and commented in Section 3. Finally, concluding remarks are drawn in Section 4.

2   Support Vector Machine: A Brief Background

Support vector machine is a concept related to supervised learning. It is based on statical learning theory. The main idea of SVM algorithm is to adjust sigmoid kernel function in order to achieve the optimal use of input data for separation. Support vector machine constructs an N-dimensional hyperplane that optimally separates the input data into two classes. SVM uses alternative training method for linear, polynomial, radial basis function, and multi-layer perceptron classifiers. The input of SVM is a set of vectors, with each vector belongs to one of the two classes. For linear kernel function, the optimal goal is to find the hyperplane that leaves largest number of cases of the class at the same side. The linear separating hyperplane is defined by equation (1).

$$yi(w.xi + b) >= 1 \tag{1}$$

Where w is a normal weight and b is a bias which will satisfy the inequalities. X_i is the input space, y belongs -1,1, which is the corresponding class. SVM selects the hyperplane, which leave the maximum distance which is $\frac{1}{w}$. The closed cases are called support vectors. The value $\frac{2}{w}$ quantity is called margin. For non separable data optimization, problem is solved by introducing error and penalization for misclassified cases. Here, the problem is minimizing, as shown in equation (2).

$$min(1/2(w)^2 + C\sum_{i=1} e \tag{2}$$

With this constraint, the separation equation is changed to equation (3).

$$yi(w.xi + b) >= 1 - e, e > 0 \tag{3}$$

The parameter C is the tradeoff between training set and the error in the separation. The are other widely used kernel functions, such as polynomial kernel function and gaussian kernel function, as shown in equation (4) and equation (5), respectively.

$$k(x', x'') = (x'\Delta x'' + 1)p, \tag{4}$$

$$k(x, x) = exp(-\frac{x - x}{sigma}) \tag{5}$$

3   Approach

The system of video surveillance is characterized by the event detection in un-controlled environments. It has one main problem: the enormous diversity of an event seen from different angles, at different scales and with different degrees. The proposed approach has mainly three major phases which are visual feature extraction, learning by SVM and detection of event. These three phases are described in detail in this section along with the steps involved and the charac-teristics feature for each phase. Figure (3) shows an overview of event detection approach.

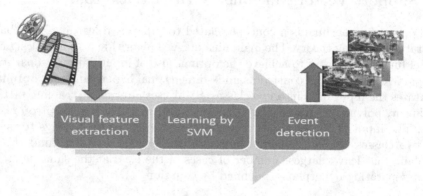

Fig. 3. The proposed event detection approach phases

3.1   Extracting Descriptors

A video sequence can be decomposed into a hierarchy of plans. A plan is a video taken from camera which continues for a given event. Then each shot video can be characterized by one or more keyframes extracted from video plan. These images are useful for the learning module [12]. The next step is to define the descriptors of each image. We will use the standard MPEG7 to obtain these de-scriptors. We should obtain, for each image, the following characteristics (1) Color Descriptors (2) Shape Descriptors, (3) Texture Descriptor, and (4) Motion Descriptors.

The extraction of information contained in an image requires a choice be-tween different types of possible de-scriptors: color, motion, shape and texture. A descriptor is a vector of values calculated from an image, which summarizes information contained in the image (color, shape, texture ...). Each descriptor MPEG7 is a summary of the characteristics of the image. The following descrip-tors had the top overall performance [16]:

- **LayoutColor:** is obtained by sampling the image for a block of 8x8 pixels. The information of the 3 color channels of the block is treated separately to obtain decomposition into baseband signals by applying the DCT.

- **StructureColor:** this descriptor is mostly used for image retrieval. It expresses local color structure in an image [3].
- **ScalableColor:** the Scalable Color Descriptor is a Color Histogram in HSV Color Space, which is encoded by a Haar transform [3].
- **DominantColor:** is obtained by vector quantization of color in the image into classes. The percentage of pixels associated with each class and the value of the 3 color components of each class is the SFD [3]. The descriptor "dominant colors" is constructed as follows: We have to note that each color the image is represented by three parameters what are dominant color, the percentage of this class in the image, and the variance of color in the class
- **Variance:** characterizes the texture, we use gray level of pixels (the V of HSV). For each pixel, we then calculate the variance of all pixels contained in a neighborhood of size $n \times n$ around the pixel (n = 3, 5, 7 ...). We then take the histogram of these variances as a descriptor of the image.
- **The co-occurrence matrices** that contains the average space of second order. Fourteen indices (defined in Haralick) which correspond to the descriptive characteristics of textures can be calculated from these matri-ces. We have only listed six of these indices: Uniformity, Contrast, Entropy, Correlation, Directivity and Con-sistency.
- **Contour shape:** the descriptor uses the closed contour of an object or a 2D uniform in color. It consists of a list of points (coordinate pair) defining the contour of the object [18].
- **Région Shape:** the shape of an object may consist of either a single region or a set of regions as well as some holes in the object.
- **Keypoint descriptor:** the local image gradients are measured at the selected scale in the region around each keypoint [4] [5]. These are transformed into a representation that allows for signi?cant levels of local shape distortion and change in illumination [7].
- **Optical flow:** is the pattern of apparent motion of objects, surfaces, and edges in a visual scene caused by the relative motion between camera and scene [6] [12] [13].

Figure (4) shows the optical flow results calculated for two successive images.

Fig. 4. Optical flow calculated for two successive images

3.2 Learning by SVM

Support Vector Machines (SVM) is a set of supervised learning techniques to solve problems of discrimination and regression. The SVM is a generalization of linear classifiers. The SVMs have been applied to many fields (bio-informatics, information retrieval, computer vision, finance, etc.) [1,2]. According to the data, the performance of SVM is similar to a neural network or a Gaussian mixture model. They directly implement the principle of structural risk minimization and work by mapping the training points into a high dimensional feature space, This module begins by making learning with SVM. We will use picture types for each event from which we are going to define a vector descriptor. This vector is a combination of different values of descriptors. After obtaining all vectors that characterize each event we move to the next stage of testing events. In our approach, we aim at building two models for each class: a model for the be-ginning of events and another for the end. We will work with the 6 events:

3.3 Detection of Events

In this module, we detect the event from different angles. Each image tested by the learning module has a class of membership; it is to calculate the probability of each event presented by the sequence of image and we choose the closest event without exceeding a definite threshold [12].

4 Experimental Results

The dataset consists of surveillance camera which was acquired at London Gatwick airport; it is provided by TREC Video Retrieval Evaluation (TRECVid) [20]. The

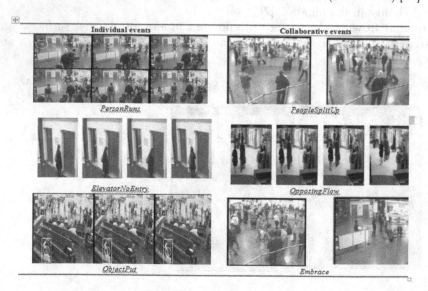

Fig. 5. Event treated results

dataset is large in scale, an approximately 100 hour video dataset, which consists of videos from five fixed-view surveillance cameras in the airport.

We aim at treating six events which are grouped into two categories (1).

The experiment is to apply our detection algorithm on a set of 1282 subsequences of 6 events, "PersonRuns", "OpposingFlow", "ElevatorNoEntry", "PeopleMeet", "Embrace", and "PeopleSplitUp" extracted manually that we knew their classes.

Table 1 shows our event detection result and a comparison between other systems [19], where #Ref is the number of annotated events, Sys# is the number of events detected, #Cordet is the number of correct detections, #Fa is the number of false detections and #Miss is the number of missed events. From the result, we can see that we have obtained a good performance in event PersonRun, PeopleSplitUp and ObjectPut. However, the action OpposingFlow, Embrace and EvaluatorNoEntry are relatively low. We consider that SVM classifier model does not have enough discrimination ability.

Table 1. Event Detection Scoring Analysis Report (**??**)

PersonRun	#Ref	# Sys	#Cordet	#Fa	#Miss
Our System	107	20	7	13	8
Informediatrecvid 2010	107	532	19	513	88
OpposingFlow	#Ref	# Sys	#Cordet	#Fa	#Miss
Our System	150	24	4	20	9
PeopleSplitUp	#Ref	# Sys	#Cordet	#Fa	#Miss
Our System	187	32	6	26	9
eSur@trecvid 2009	187	198	7	191	180
eSur@trecvid 2010	187	167	16	136	171
Embrace	#Ref	# Sys	#Cordet	#Fa	#Miss
Our System	187	23	5	17	10
eSur@trecvid 2009	175	80	1	79	174
eSur @ trecvid 2010	175	925	6	71	169
EvaluatorNoEntry	#Ref	# Sys	#Cordet	#Fa	#Miss
Our System	30	0	0	0	3
ObjectPut	#Ref	# Sys	#Cordet	#Fa	#Miss
Our System	621	9	7	2	8
IPG-BJTU @ Trecvid 2010	621	8	1	7	620

5 Conclusions and Future Works

We have presented a method to detect events in video recordings. This technique has applications for very large video surveillance indexing and detection of specific events (human intrusion into a prohibited area, or someone leaving a package, etc...) in a video database. The main idea of this method is to extract the various descriptors of the image and then learn the desired event with a number of relevant examples presented by the user. It also provides the "lifelike" sequences more and then take the test for the entire database.

References

1. Li, H., Lei, B., Zan, G., Arnold, O., Wei, L., Long-Fei, Z., Shoou-I, Y., Ming-Yu, C., Florian, M., Alexander, H.: Informedia@TRECVID (2010), http://www-nlpir.nist.gov/projects/tvpubs/tv10.papers/cmu-informedia.pdf
2. Kaihua, J., Zhipeng, H., Zhongwei, C., Guochen, J., Ten, X., Qiong, H., Guangcheng, Z., Yaowei, W., Lei, Q., Yonghong, T., Xihong, W., Wen, G.: PKU-IDM @ TRECVid 2010: Pair-Wise Event Detection in Surveillance Video (2010), http://www-nlpir.nist.gov/projects/tvpubs/tv10.papers/pku-idm.pdf
3. Swain, M., Ballard, D.: Color Indexing. Int. Journal of Computer Vision 7(1), 11–32 (1991)
4. Lowe, D.G.: Distinctive Image Features from Scale-Invariant Keypoints. The International Journal of Computer Vision 60(2), 91–110 (2004)
5. Ming-Yu, C., Huan, L., Alexander, H.: Informedia@TRECVID2009:Analyzing Video Motions (2009), http://www-nlpir.nist.gov/projects/tvpubs/tv9.papers/cmu.pdf
6. Masaki, T., Yoshihiko, K., Mahito, F., Masahiro, S., Noboru, B., Shin'ichi, S.: NHK STRL at TRECVID 2009: Surveillance Event Detection and High-Level Feature Extraction (2009), http://www-nlpir.nist.gov/projects/tvpubs/tv9.papers/nhkstrl.pdf
7. Lowe, D.G.: Object recognition from local scale-invariant eatures. In: Proc. ICCV 1999, vol. 2, pp. 1150–1157 (1999)
8. Viola, P., Jones, M.: Robust Real-time Object Detection. International Journal of Computer Vision 57(2), 137–154 (2004)
9. Han, F., Shan, Y., Cekander, R.: A Two-Stage Approach to People and Vehicle Detection with HOG-Based SVM. In: PerMIS Proceeding, pp. 133–140 (2006)
10. Scholkopf, B., Plat, J.C., Shawe-Taylor, J., Smola, A.J., Williamson, R.C.: Estimating the support of a high-dimensional distribution. Neural Computation 13, 1443–1471 (2001)
11. Chen, P.H., Lin, C.J., Scholkopf, B.: A tutorial on-support vector machines. Applied Stochastic Models in Business and Industry 21, 111–136 (2005)
12. Weilong Y., Tian L., Greg, M.: SFU@TRECVid2009: Event Detection, http://www.sfu.ca/~wya16/trecvid/trecvid.html
13. Efros, A.A., Berg, A.C., Mori, G., Malik, J.: Recognizing action at a distance. In: IEEE International Conference on Computer Vision, October 13-16, pp. 726–733. California Univ., Berkeley (2003)
14. Wali, A., Alimi, A.M.: Event detection from video surveillance data based on optical flow histogram and high-level feature extraction. In: IEEE DEXA Workshops 2009, pp. 221–225 (2009)
15. Macan, T., Loncaric, S.: Hybrid optical flow and segmentation technique for lv motion detection. In: Proceedings of SPIE Medical Imaging, San Diego, USA, pp. 475–482 (2001)
16. Xiaokang, Y., Yi, X., Rui, Z., Erkang, C., Qing, Y., Bo, X., Zhou, Y., Ning, L., Zuo, H., Cong, Z., Xiaolin, C., Anwen, L., Zhenfei, C., Kai, G., Jun, H., Tong, S.J.: University participation in high-level feature extraction and surveillance event detection at TRECVID 2009 (2009), http://www-nlpir.nist.gov/projects/tvpubs/tv9.papers/sjtu-iicip.pdf
17. Wali, A., Ben Aoun, N., Karray, H., Ben Amar, C., Alimi, A.M.: A New System for Event Detection from Video Surveillance Sequences. In: Blanc-Talon, J., Bone, D., Philips, W., Popescu, D., Scheunders, P. (eds.) ACIVS 2010, Part II. LNCS, vol. 6475, pp. 110–120. Springer, Heidelberg (2010)

18. Chan, T., Vese, L.: An Active Contour Model without Edges. In: Nielsen, M., Johansen, P., Fogh Olsen, O., Weickert, J. (eds.) Scale-Space 1999. LNCS, vol. 1682, pp. 141–151. Springer, Heidelberg (1999)
19. Yuan, S., Ping, G., Shu, W., Lin, Y., Haifeng, D., Liang, L., Zhenjiang, M.: Event detection: IPG-BJTU Trecvid (2010),
    http://www-nlpir.nist.gov/projects/tvpubs/tv10.papers/ipg_bjtu.pdf
20. National Institute of Standards and Technology (NIST): TRECVID 2009 Evaluation for Surveillance Event Detection (2009),
    http://www.nist.gov/speech/tests/trecvid/2009/   and   http://www.itl.nist.gov/iad/mig/tests/trecvid/2009/doc/eventdet09-evalplan-v03.htm
21. Wali, A., Alimi, A.M.: Incremental Learning Approach for Events Detection from large Video dataset. In: Seventh IEEE International Conference on Advanced Video and Signal Based Surveillance, AVSS, pp. 555–560 (2010)
22. Bae, T.M., Kim, C.S., Jin, S.H., Kim, K.-H., Ro, Y.M.: Semantic Event Detection in Structured Video Using Hybrid HMM/SVM. In: Leow, W.-K., Lew, M., Chua, T.-S., Ma, W.-Y., Chaisorn, L., Bakker, E.M. (eds.) CIVR 2005. LNCS, vol. 3568, pp. 113–122. Springer, Heidelberg (2005)

Study of Feature Categories for Musical Instrument Recognition

Glenn Eric Hall[1], Hassan Ezzaidi[1], and Mohammed Bahoura[2]

[1] Université du Québec à Chicoutimi,
555, boul. de l'Université, Chicoutimi, Qc, Canada, G7H 2B1
{glennerichall,hezzaidi}@uqac.ca
[2] Université du Québec à Rimouski,
300, allée des Ursulines, Rimouski, Qc, Canada, G5L 3A1
Mohammed_Bahoura@uqar.ca

Abstract. Timbre conveys powerful perceptive attribute for musical identification and has been subject of several researches. Several spectro-temporal parameters have been proposed and compared. The main research content in this paper is to examine some topic often ignored in lastly works. Several features inspired by both the psychoacoustic and perceptive knowledges are reexamined to explore the efficiency of the timbre dimension contribution for each feature and each category (similar processing and representation form), on a large database. Also, the impact of the normalization, time duration decomposition (short term vs. long term) and three feature selection algorithms are examined. Using the Real World Computing (RWC) music database, results shown that using 7 envelope features, the score is better than using 14 LPC coefficients and lower than using 13 MFCC coefficients. After applying Sequential Forward Selection (SFS) reduction technique to the observation vectors composed of all the 38 proposed features, 5 envelope features are retained when only 7 and 11 features are kept for MFCC and LPC, respectively.

Keywords: instrument, features, psychoacoustic, SFS, multimedia.

1 Introduction

Music information retrieval (MIR) has numerous commercial avenues. Several everyday life applications can benefit from MIR: similarity searches, copyright verification, musical thumbnailing, automatic karaoke generation, etc. Professional systems use this information in quality enhancement (time alignment of instrumental tracks, effects at key locations such as choruses, etc.). With the identification of musical instruments, queries on the orchestration can be performed but in addition, the extraction of the number of musical sources can be used to adapt parametric audio coding to instrumental content.

Musical instrument's sound is generally characterized by pitch, loudness and timbre. Timbre is considered to be distinctive between two instruments playing the same note with the same pitch and loudness. Therefore, timbre is viewed as

A. Ell Hassanien et al. (Eds.): AMLTA 2012, CCIS 322, pp. 152–161, 2012.

one of the most important features to convoy the identity of musical instrument. The previous works have opted for representing the timbre with several descriptors exploiting different assumptions related to human perception. In principle, the acoustical signal components that are censed to determinate timbre dimensions are estimated from the spectral envelope, temporal envelope, Mel Frequency Cepstral Coefficients (MFCC), Linear Predictive Coding (LPC), statistical moments of the spectral/temporal representation, pitch and onset. This variety of parameters offers evidence that it is not possible with the technical tools currently available to represent the tone by one single common descriptor for different musical sounds. However, the challenge becomes to determine which attribute characterize best the multidimensional perceptual timbre.

In part, it is possible to draw analogies and similarities between speech recognition and musical analysis. Identifying musical instruments is comparable to speaker identification though very different in practice. The task of musical instruments recognition is comparable to that of speaker recognition. While the identity of the speaker is represented, in almost all speaker identification systems, by a small set of MFCC as features and Gaussian Mixture Model (GMM) as classifier [1], in the case of the musical instrument, features and models vary according to contextual factors (musician, instrument manufacturer, tuning, etc.) [2]. There is no consensus for the best features determining the signature of musical instruments comparatively to speaker recognition, in despite of using MFCC combined with other features to build the multidimensional vector space timbre. In general, musical instrument recognition focuses, until now, on the extraction of pertinent features to characterize each musical attribute, and on dimension reduction algorithms.

This paper re-examine some several features inspired by both psychoacoustic and perceptive knowledges to explore the efficiency of the timbre dimension contribution for each feature and each category (similar processing and representation form), on a large database. Different processing and strategies are explored to highlight the impact of dimension reduction algorithm, data normalization, algorithm estimation, and components contribution based on music category. Using a large database (RWC), the results show that features envelope conveyed a powerful and salient contribution as MFCC and LPCC for timbre characterization.

The paper is organized as follow. In section 2, a state of art of timbre music and instrument recognition is explored. Section 3 presents the selected database. In section 4, the methodology regarding the selected classifiers and features used in current work is explained. The results concerning the impact of normalization, the feature selection and the frame decomposition are discussed in section 5.

2   State of Art

Sound is characterized by pitch, loudness and timbre. Timbre is considered to be distinctive between two instruments playing the same note with the same pitch and loudness [3]. Determining which attributes characterizes best the multidimensional perceptual timbre is nevertheless a challenge. Psycho-acousticians sketch timbre as a geometric construction built from similarity ratings. Multidimensional scaling is generally used to find sound attributes that correlate best with the perceptual dimensions (brightness, smoothness, compactness, etc.) [4,5]. From the same idea, research in musical instrument identification began with the construction of a vector space describing the timbre or commonly named the space timbre [6,7]. The main idea is to reduce the dimension of the feature vectors while preserving the natural topology of the instrument timbre; a practical interpretation should emerge. De Poli and Prandoni [8] used a 6 MFCC coefficients vector as input to a Kohonen self-organizing map (SOM) in order to build timbre spaces. Besides constructing timbre spaces, they have investigated different approaches on automatic instrument recognition.

Martin [9] used 1023 notes from 15 different instruments contained in the MUMS database [10,11] to investigate hierarchical classification. Eronen and Klapuri [12,13] reused the hierarchical classification strategy proposed by Martin [9]. Their experiment showed similar results to those of Martin [9] for hierarchical classifiers, but managed to get better results with direct classification. The difference in the number of the used instruments makes unfortunately the comparison difficult between these systems.

Hall et al. [14] used 6698 notes with the hierarchical classification proposed by Martin [9] and constructed a system where the feature vector is dynamic and changes depending on each level and each node of the hierarchical tree. The feature vector was thus optimized and determined with the Sequential Backward Selection (SBS) algorithm. Using a large database (RWC), the results showed a score gain in musical instrument recognition performances.

Kitahara et al. [15,16] used pitch-dependent algorithms as an F0-dependent multivariate normal distribution, where each element of the mean vector is represented by a function of F0. Using 6247 notes of 19 musical instruments, their results showed an improvement of the recognition rate.

Agostini et al. [17] employed only spectral characteristics of 1007 notes from 27 musical instruments classified with support vector machines and quadratic discriminate analysis. The most relevant features were to be the in harmonicity, the spectral centroid, and the energy contained in the first partial.

3   Database

The chosen database (RWC Music Database for Musical Instrument Sound) provides multiple records for each instrument (three variations for each instrument: three manufacturers, three musicians and three different dynamics) [18]. For each instrument, the musician is playing each note individually at an interval of a semitone over the entire possible range of the instrument. In terms of string instruments, the full range for each chord is played. Dynamics is also varied with intensities strong, mezzo and piano (see Table 1 for used instruments).

In all experiments of this work, a cross-validation containing 90% training data and 10% of test data was used.

Table 1. Database Description

Instrument	Notes	Instrument	Notes
Accordion	282	Acoustic Guitar	463
Alto Sax	198	Banjo	208
Baritone Sax	198	Bassoon (Fagotto)	240
Cello	377	Clarinet	240
Cornet	62	Electric Bass	676
Electric Guitar	468	English Horn	60
Flute	148	French Horn	218
Harmonica	168	Mandolin	283
Oboe	132	Pan Flute	74
Piccolo	200	Pipe Organ	56
Recorder	150	Soprano Sax	198
Tenor Sax	196	Trombone	194
Trumpet	141	Tuba	180
Ukulele	144	Viola	360
Violin	384		
Total : 6 698			

4   Methodology

4.1   Classifiers

The popular k-nearest neighbor (k-NN) algorithm and gaussian mixture model (GMM) are used in the classification and decision task. The metric used for the k-NN classifier is the Euclidean distance and the number of neighbors was set to 4, value determined by empirical testing. The number of components for the GMM classifier was set to 4, value also determined by empirical testing.

4.2   Parameters

The proposed parameter vector in this work was built from 38 features, according to [14,19,20] as follow: 1) MFCC and LPC features are the most popular used in speaker identification system. In principle, lower order features are censed to capture a description of spectral shape (formant). Previous works in musical instrument shows a good performance [14,19,20]. A total of the first 13 MFCC and 14 LPC coefficients were extracted. 2) Spectral centroid is computed as the first moment from the spectrum. 3) Spectral spread is computed from the second moment (variance) of the spectrum and measures the spectral dispersion from the centroid. 4) Spectral kurtosis is a statistical measure that computes the flatness of spectral shape. 5) Spectral skewness corresponds to a statistical measure that computes the symmetry of spectral shape. 6) Zero-crossing rate (ZCR), calculates the rate of the signal crossing a fixed threshold. 7) Envelope slope, centroid, spread and skewness means the estimation respectively of attack period, centroid, spread, symmetrical aspect of the spectral envelope of audio signal.

5   Results

In despite that the 38 parameters proposed in this paper have been yet used in last works but not once at time except [14], they were never examined in other perspectives such as: normalization, parameter reduction and salient components. In the following, we will review step by step the repercussions of each perspective and, eventually by deduction, determine and evaluate the performance of the optimal parameter vector.

5.1   Impact of Normalization

Typically, normalizing the feature vectors is assumed to give best results by compressing the interval range related to the feature vectors. For this reason, experiments were performed with the following normalization: standardization mu-sigma (equation 1), min-max (equation 2) and without normalization.

$$\widetilde{x}_{i,j} = \frac{x_{i,j} - \widetilde{x}_j}{\sigma_j} \tag{1}$$

$$\widetilde{x}_{i,j} = \frac{x_{i,j}}{\max |x_{i,j}|} \tag{2}$$

Results show that the mu-sigma normalization enhances recognition performance with about 2%. Therefore, only experiments based on this normalization are presented at the next sections.

5.2   Features Selection

Techniques attempting to use some transformations to convert a set of correlated feature parameters into a set of uncorrelated parameters are another important quality factor in recognition systems. Here, three algorithms are investigated to study impact of dimension reduction on the recognition performance. The set of all proposed features (38) are used with Principal Component Analysis (PCA), Sequential Forward Selection (SFS) [21] and Sequential Backward Selection (SBS) algorithms [21]. Results illustrated in Fig. 1 shows that SFS and SBS increase slightly (4%) the recognition rate. Score gain is related to the fact that the redundant and insignificant feature parameters are removed from the feature set.

5.3   Training Based Frames and Mean Frames

We also assessed the recognition rate for a system trained with data composed of all frames and data representing the average frames for each instrument. In fact, classification with all frames offers best performances for both GMM and k-NN classifiers. However, a 6% gain in performance is observed at the cost of a time consuming that is inappropriate for real-time applications.

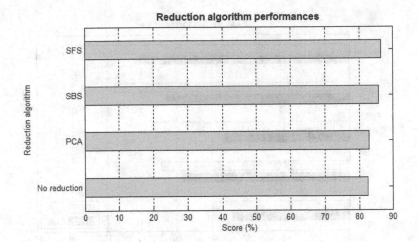

Fig. 1. Performances of reduction algorithms using mu-sigma normalization and k-NN classifier

5.4   Comparison of Features

Descriptor performances in aggregated and individual forms for direct k-NN classification and mu-sigma normalization are shown in Fig. 2. Evidently, the best performance is attributed to the combination of all feature parameters. However, if the recognition score by category is taken in account, MFCC coefficients and envelope derived features mainly contributes for global performance. Note that with only 5 components of envelope, the recognition rate is better than all the 14 LPC coefficients. MFCC on the other hand is composed of 13 components. After applying Sequential Forward Selection (SFS) reduction technique to observation vectors composed of all the proposed features (38), 5 envelope features are retained when only 7 and 11 features are kept respectively for MFCC and LPC.

Another important aspect is shown in Fig. 3, where the same envelope derived features are extracted from different envelope extraction algorithm and are combined to form one parameter vector. In this case, the performance increases at 60% comparatively to 67% for MFCC. This phenomenon enforces the idea that features related to envelope are powerful and interesting for timbre characterization. Again, results depend on the used feature extraction methods, which can mask certain attributes or conversely highlights them.

Finally, the selected parameters from all proposed features in the direct classification scheme using SFS algorithm are: 7 MFCC coefficients, 9 LPC coefficients, centroid, spread, spectral, centroid, spread, skewness, kurtosis, slope and zero-crossing (frame-decomposed). With this approach the instrument recognition, the family recognition and the articulation recognition rates are 86.56%, 94.33% and 99.28%, respectively. Results are illustrated in Table 2 with more details for each instrument. As can be seen in Table 2, recognition rate for instruments and

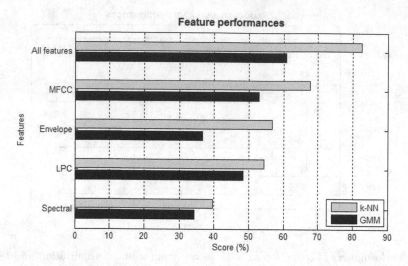

Fig. 2. Performances of feature categories using mu-sigma normalization

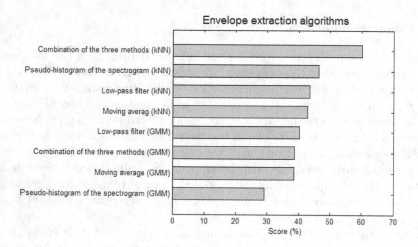

Fig. 3. Performances of envelope extraction algorithms

families is not uniform. The pipe organ is the easiest instrument to recognize. At the opposite, the cornet is the hardest instrument to recognize as it is often mistaken with the trumpet. The number of available cornet occurrences may be the cause of this high misclassification rate. Nevertheless, cornet has been classified in the correct family most of the times, as it is not the case for the oboe and the violin. In fact, reeds and strings are difficult families to classify.

Table 2. Instrument confusion matrix using SFS, k-NN and mu-sigma normalization. Rectangles distinguish families (from left to right: Brass, Flutes/Piccolo, Reeds and Strings).

86,56%	Trumpet	Cornet	Trombone	Tuba	French Horn	English Horn	Baritone Sax	Tenor Sax	Alto Sax	Soprano Sax	Piccolo	Flute	Pan Flute	Recorder	Clarinet	Pipe Organ	Oboe	Bassoon (Fagotto)	Accordion	Harmonica	Acoustic Guitar	Electric Guitar	Electric Bass	Banjo	Ukulele	Mandolin	Cello	Violin	Viola
Trumpet	115	7	3							1	3	1			2		2		1	1								1	4
Cornet	16	31	9		3				1			1					1												
Trombone		1	186		3	1									1		2												
Tuba				180																									
French Horn		2	24		190	1									1														
English Horn	1	3	2			49									1	4													
Baritone Sax	1		1		2		186	1	1								1											1	4
Tenor Sax	1				1		12	156	9			2			1					1							2	6	5
Alto Sax	5	3	3				7	17	141	1		1	5							1								9	5
Soprano Sax	5	1	7			1	1	1	2	161	2						8	1	4									1	3
Piccolo	4										193	2					1												
Flute	5	1	2						2	1	9	126																	2
Pan Flute						1	1			3	10	7	41	5						1	1						1	1	2
Recorder											1	2	2	139	2					2									2
Clarinet	3	1	4						2	3	4			1	211		4		1								2	3	1
Pipe Organ																54			1									1	
Oboe	9	6	1			12			1		2	2		1	6		86		1									2	3
Bassoon (Fagotto)		2	2	4										3				228								1			
Accordion	3		3	3	2						5	5	2	3	3				225		2					2	3	17	4
Harmonica							2	2	3		3			3			4			129	1						8	8	5
Acoustic Guitar																	2	3			427	9	2	7	3	7			3
Electric Guitar																					7	453	3			5			
Electric Bass																					17	3	656						
Banjo													1				1				17	1	2	165	13	4	2		2
Ukulele																					6	1	1	11	125				
Mandolin											2		1				1	3			28	10	2	4	3	226	1		2
Cello								5	1						4						2						346	9	10
Violin	2					1	3	5	1		9	1		1	3		5		10	2	1					1	5	303	31
Viola			1					2	1			2	4		2		2	3	1	5	1						9	57	270

6 Conclusion

In this paper, the problem of timbre characterization for musical instrument is investigated. We focused principally on comparing the contribution of sub-class features belonging to the same category (based on the same estimation method) to global vector composed from several component computed with different processing techniques. Features inspired from both psychoacoustic and perceptive knowledges are re-examined to explore for each one the efficiency of the contribution timbre dimension. In addition, the impact of the normalization, reduction algorithms, frame decomposition (short term vs. long term) are examined. As well, three algorithms for parameter vector reduction were compared. Using a large database (RWC), the results shows that using 7 envelope features, the score is better than using 14 LPC coefficients and slightly lower than using 13 MFCC coefficients. After applying Sequential Forward Selection (SFS) reduction technique to observation vectors composed of all the 38 proposed features, 5 envelope features are retained when only 7 and 11 features are kept respectively for MFCC and LPC.

The presented system performs 86.56% recognition rate for individual instrument, 94.33% for instrument family, and 99.45% for articulations (pizzicato vs. sustained). Envelope derived features have a significant impact on the overall performances since they have a major contribution on the recognition of articulation. The combination of MFCC coefficients and envelope derived features mainly contributes for global performance while LPC and spectral features are less performing than the formers.

References

1. Reynolds, D.A., Rose, R.C.: Robust Test-Independent Speaker Identification Using Gaussian Mixture Speaker Models. IEEE Transactions on Speech and Audio Processing 3, 72–83 (1995)
2. Houtsma, A.J.M.: Pitch and timbre: Definition, meaning, and use. Journal of New Music Research 26, 104–115 (1997)
3. American National Standard psychoacoustical terminology. ANSI S3.20-1973, New York (1997)
4. Grey, J.M.: Multidimensional perceptual scaling of musical timbres. Journal of the Acoustical Society of America 61(5), 1270–1277 (1977)
5. Martin, K.D., Kim, Y.E.: Musical instrument identification: A pattern-recognition approach. Presented at the 136th meeting of the Acoustical Society of America (1998)
6. McAdams, S.: Recognition of sound sources and events. In: McAdams, S., Bigand, E. (eds.) Thinking in Sound: the Cognitive Psychology of Human Audition, pp. 146–198. Oxford University Press, Oxford (1993)
7. Caclin, A., McAdams, S., Smith, B.K., Winsberg, S.: Acoustic correlates of timbre space dimensions: A confirmatory study using synthetic tones. Journal of the Acoustical Society of America 118, 471–482 (2005)
8. De Poli, G., Prandoni, P.: Sonological models for timbre characterization. Journal of New Music Research 26, 170–197 (1997)
9. Martin, K.D.: Sound-Source Recognition: A Theory and Computational Model. PhD thesis, Department of Electrical Engineering and Computer Science, Massachusetts Institute of Technology, Cambridge, MA (1999)
10. Opolko, F., Wapnick, J.: McGill University Master Samples. McGill University, Montreal (1986)
11. Eerola, T., Ferrer, R.: Instrument library (MUMS). Music Perception 25, 253–255 (2008) (revised)
12. Eronen, A., Klapuri, A.: Musical instrument recognition using cepstral coefficients and temporal features. In: The IEEE International Conference of Acoustics, Speech, and Signal Processing, pp. 753–756 (2000)
13. Eronen, A.: Comparison of features for musical instrument recognition. In: IEEE Workshop on the Applications of Signal Processing to Audio and Acoustics, pp. 19–22 (2001)

14. Hall, G.-E., Ezzaidi, H., Bahoura, M.: Hierarchical parametrization and classification for instrument recognition. In: The 11th International Conference on Information Science, Signal Processing and their Applications (ISSPA), Montreal, Canada, July 2-5, pp. 1066–1071 (2012)
15. Kitahara, T., Goto, M., Okuno, H.G.: Musical instrument identification based on F0-dependent multivariate normal distribution. In: IEEE International Conference on Acoustics, Speech, and Signal Processing (ICASSP 2003), April 6-10, vol. 5, pp. 421–424 (2003)
16. Kitahara, T., Goto, M., Okuno, H.G.: Pitch-Dependent Identification of Musical Instrument Sounds. Applied Intelligence 23, 267–275 (2005)
17. Agostini, G., Longari, M., Pollastri, E.: Musical instrument timbres classification with spectral features. EURASIP Journal on Applied Signal Processing, 5–14 (2003)
18. Goto, M., Hashiguchi, H., Nishimura, T., Oka, R.: RWC Music Database: Music Genre Database and Musical Instrument Sound Database. In: The 4th International Conference on Music Information Retrieval (ISMIR 2003), Baltimore, Maryland, October 26-30, pp. 229–230 (2003)
19. Eronen, A.: Automatic Musical Instrument Recognition. Master's thesis, Department of Information Technology, Tampere University of Technology, Tampere, Finland (2001)
20. Brown, J.C., Houix, O., McAdams, S.: Feature dependence in the automatic identification of musical woodwind instruments. Journal of the Acoustical Society of America 109, 1064–1072 (2001)
21. Liu, H., Motoda, H.: Feature Selection for Knowledge Discovery and Data Mining. Kluwer Academic Publishers (1998)

Towards a Characterization of Musical Timbre Based on Chroma Contours

Hassan Ezzaidi[1], Mohammed Bahoura[2], and Glenn Eric Hall[1]

[1] Université du Québec à Chicoutimi,
555, boul. de l'Université, Chicoutimi, Qc, Canada, G7H 2B1
{hezzaidi,glennerichall}@uqac.ca
[2] Université du Québec à Rimouski,
300, allée des Ursulines, Rimouski, Qc, Canada, G5L 3A1
Mohammed_Bahoura@uqar.ca

Abstract. Chroma conveying mainly a tonal content is considered as powerful representation that is widely used in musical information retrieval applications. In this paper, a new musical timbre description based only on the chromagram contours is investigated allowing the identification of both tonal content and particularly the instrument timbre (identity). After some steps of pre-processing and transformation, four methods are investigated as classifiers: support vector machine (SVM), neural network, invariant moments, and template matching based cross-correlation. All methods use only one pattern in training phase. Results are very promising and the graphical analysis demonstrates that contours are dependent on the music instrument. As first investigation, performance of about 70% is obtained with template matching and SVM classification techniques.

Keywords: instrument, recognition, chroma, contour, multimedia.

1 Introduction

The explosion of mass media, particularly the Internet and digital audio format, and the large amounts of musical contents available on the public and private media generate new needs as: maintenance, classification and authentication tasks. One way to accomplish these tasks is by extracting from raw audio signal some compact and pertinent descriptors that can be used as basic prototypes for matching techniques. The musical sound is generally characterized by pitch, loudness and timbre. Timbre is considered to be distinctive between two instruments playing the same note with the same pitch and loudness. Timbre descriptors are viewed as one of the most important features to convey the identity of musical instrument. It is possible to notice some analogies and similarities between speech recognition and musical analysis systems. Identifying musical instruments is comparable to speaker identification though very different in practice. The identity of the speaker is represented, in the majority of speaker identification systems, by a set of Mel Frequency Cepstral Coefficients (MFCC)

A. Ell Hassanien et al. (Eds.): AMLTA 2012, CCIS 322, pp. 162–171, 2012.
© Springer-Verlag Berlin Heidelberg 2012

as features and Gaussian Mixture Models (GMM) as classifier. In the case of the musical instrument, features and models varies considerably according to contextual factors (musician, instrument manufacturer, tuning, etc.). Until now, there is no consensus for attributes determining the exact signature of musical instruments comparatively to speaker recognition systems in which only MFCC features without any others parameters aggregation achieve the best performance. The previous works have opted for the representation of the musical timbre, by the concatenation of several descriptors exploiting different assumptions related to human perceptive dimension or psycho-acoustical knowledge. In principle, the components estimated form acoustical signal, censed to determinate dimension of timbre, are estimated generally from the spectral envelope, temporal envelope, MFCC, Linear Predictive Coding (LPC), statistical moments, pitch and onset. Psycho-acousticians sketches timbre as a geometric construction built from similarity ratings. Multidimensional scaling is generally used to find sound attributes that correlate best with the perceptual dimensions (brightness, smoothness, compactness, etc.) [1,2]. This variety of parameters validates evidence that it is not possible with the available technical tools to represent the tone by unique single feature based instrument and therefore common descriptor based family for different musical sounds. However, the challenge becomes to determine which attributes characterize best the multidimensional perceptual timbre.

In this work, the main research content is to propose and investigate a new and single representation describing and characterizing the musical timbre without any concatenation. This approach consists to extract multi-level contours from chromagram called chromatimbre that seems to be unique for each family instrument and conveys both tonal content and identity information. Classical feed-forward neural network (NN), Support Vector Machine (SVM), template matching using cross-correlation principle and the statistical invariants moments were proposed as classifiers in experiment of this work. Results show a great potential and promising approach for future work.

2   State of Art

All proposed features in the last years attempt to describe the multidimensional vector representing the perceptive human sensation into the timbre space. Since several decades, various parameters derived from time attack, time release, spectral centroid, harmonic partials, onset and frequency cutoff exhibit relevant information to characterize quality attributes of timbre instruments as orchestral instruments, bowed string, brightness, harmonic and inharmonic structure, etc [1,2,3]. Recently, many features related to characterize the sound source excitation and the resonant instrument structure extracted from transformed correlogram were suggested in [4]. All the 31 features extracted from each tone based statistical measures are related to pitch, harmonic structure, attack, tremolo and vibrato proprieties. They are assumed to capture a partial information of tone color (timbre). In addition, assuming that the human auditory perception system is organized and recognizes sounds in a hierarchical manner, a similar classification scheme was suggested and compared in the same work [4]. Results show a score improvement about of 6% for individual instrument and 8% for instrument family recognitions. Instead, Eronen [5] exploited the psychoacoustic knowledge to determine features parameters describing the timbre music. Essentially, statistical measures based pitch, onset, amplitude modulation, MFCC, LPC and their derivatives are investigated as parameters. Results show that the MFCC and derivatives extracted from the onset and steady state segment give mainly the best performance comparatively to others aggregated features. Performance comparison between direct and the hierarchical classification techniques was examined in [4,6] showing a particular interest with the last technique. Particularly, Hall et al. [6] used 6698 notes with the hierarchical classification proposed in [5] and constructed a system where the feature vector is dynamic and changes depending on each level and each node of the hierarchical tree. The feature vector was thus optimized and determined with the Sequential Forward Selection (SFS) algorithm. Using the Real World Computing (RWC) music database, the results showed a score gain in musical instrument recognition performance [7]. Kitahara et al. [8,9] used pitch-dependent algorithms as an F0-dependent multivariate normal distribution, where each element of the mean vector is represented by a function of F0.

3   Database

The "RWC Music Database for Musical Instrument Sound" [7] is chosen in this work. In this database, each audio file contains the signal of a single instrument played with isolated notes. The use of isolated notes, that is only one note at a time, has significant advantages for feature extraction: sophisticated acoustic descriptors are hardly calculable from a continuous flow of notes, which are likely to overlap. The database provides multiple records for each instrument: different manufacturers for the same instrument and different musicians took part to generate records and provide a range of several instrumental signatures. For each instrument, the musician is playing each note individually at an interval of a semitone over the entire possible range of the instrument. In terms of string instruments, the full range for each chord is played. Dynamics is also varied with intensities strong, mezzo and piano. In this experiment, 9 instruments (no duplicated pitch instances for each instrument) were selection with various notes for a total of 50 notes: accordion (reeds), acoustic guitar (steel string), electric guitar (string), clarinet (reeds), alto sax (brass), piano (string), violin (string), flute and trumpet (brass).

4   Proposed System

4.1   Chromagram Estimation

Chromagram is defined as the whole spectral audio information mapped into one octave. Each octave is divided into 12 bins representing each one semitone.

The same strategy based on instantaneous frequency (IF), presented in [10], is adopted in this work to compute the features chroma. The audio signal, with sampling frequency of 11025 Hz, is split up into frames (1024 points) interlaced over 512 points. Motivation behind the IF is to track only real harmonics.

4.2 Chromagram Contour or Chromatimbre Estimation

Each two-dimensional chroma matrix is associated with time axis and bin frequency axis (semitone note). We utilize the *contour* function of MATLAB, which determines 10-level contours by using a linear interpolation. Each contour tracking represent the intensity variation with respect to a fixed threshold for yielding a segmentation of chromagram representation (image) producing several regions. Hence, contours delimiting the frontiers give some description equivalent to the acoustical scene auditory activity. To deal with variability level, all contours are set to the same intensity. This is similar to transforming a color image to black and white. This binary encoding approximation is used just to accelerate and facilitate the continuation of this exploratory study. Fig. 1 and Fig. 2 illustrate both the chroma representation (left side) and the timbre description for flute and piano instruments playing different tones. According to geometrical shape contours, it is clear that chroma shows a great energy concentrated at small interval centred at bin number 4 for the two different note mode (C4 and C6). The same effect is obtained with the piano instrument playing G4 and G6 pitch interval what confirm that chroma preserve mainly the tonal content. On the other side, the contours representation (right side in Fig. 1 and Fig. 2) with the same instrument, exhibit rather than the tonal content, a particular pattern shape assumed to characterize timbre information. Illustrations beside patterns shapes seem to keep and conserve the same geometrical propriety when an instrument played different notes. An additional illustration is given in Fig. 3, where 6 instruments are inspected. Other graphical analysis reveals several visual attributes that can be targeted to characterize instrument identity from the chromatimbre image. Pizzicato is especially clearly visible and there is no ambiguity to distinguish sustained instruments from pizzicato instruments. The chromatimbre of the accordion is especially easy to recognize because of its unique signature. However, the shapes of chromatimbre are not trivial and it would be difficult to enumerate all the characteristics that can have each instrument. In addition, the chromatimbre can take many forms for a single instrument. Being a projection into the time-frequency plane, the chromatimbre provides an overview of the envelope and the spectrum of the note. We can easily see on the chromatimbre pattern the spectrum spread, amplitude and frequency modulations, attack time, sustain and release of the note. In this context, the need to elaborate simplified methods to explore the potential of chromatimbre approach is crucial.

4.3 Contour Pattern Normalization

The first challenge with contour parametrization is to deal with the time speed variation (stretching and compression), the frequency hopping and/or spread

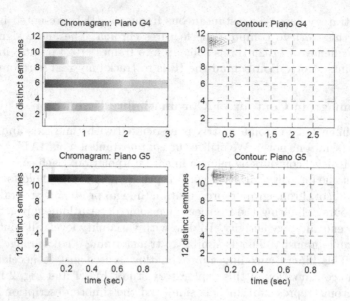

Fig. 1. Description by chromagram and the proposed chromatimbre: Piano instrument playing C4 and C6 notes

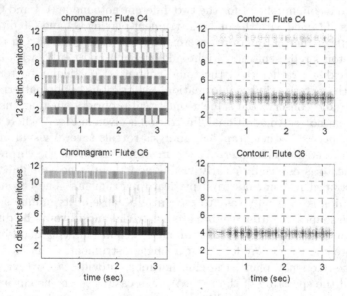

Fig. 2. Description by chromagram and the proposed chromatimbre: Flute instrument playing C4 and C6 notes

related by the change of playing different tones. Hence, all chromatimbre descriptions are transformed to the Portable Gray Map (PGM) Format yielding a matrix size of 315x420. Here, frequency octave is represented by 315 points and the time axis by 420 points assuring the invariance of the time length duration

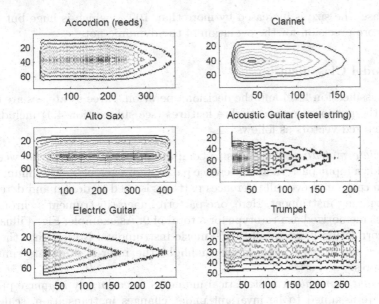

Fig. 3. Spectro-temporel description transformed to the Portable Gray Map (PGM) Format (315x420 matrix): Intervariability chromatimbre instruments notes

variability. The appearance and presence of secondary contours represented a second challenge to take into account. So, extracting the dominant contour can simply effectuated by first projecting the temporal contour variation among 12 bins tones axis to form an histogram (distribution). Then by using both zero crossing and the maximum value over histogram, the secondaries contours patterns were eliminated.

4.4   Preparation of Train and Test Data and Features Estimation

Assuming that the chromatimbre is characteristic for timbre, the entire pattern contours are computed to extract suitable features for representing timbre instrument identity. In one case, only the contours localized at the attack time phase of the signal have been proposed as a template for identifying the timbre of 9 musical instruments. These contours extracted for each instrument are represented by a matrix of 50x54 points. Hence, no clustering algorithm was necessary for partitioning the data into clusters. This constitutes the first type of features proposed in this experiment. In second case, the entire image is taken into consideration by splinting it into rectangular window moving horizontally and vertically. Each fragmentation yields a small image with size of 50x54 points. The idea behind this, is to cover all phases of the dynamic rating (attack, release, and sustain). Images with contour points (on pixels) less than a rate 15% are ignored and considered as silence images. This preparation corresponds to the second type of features presented to systems recognition. Notice, that the size of the first set of pattern features is 9 one for each type of instrument. In the second case, the size is increased by more than 100%, which is huge but allows having more precision for the evolution of the dynamic note.

4.5 Model Classification

At the classification level and the decision operation, three strategies are examined for the proposed chromatimbre features (see sub-section 4.4) including or not normalized vectors as follows:

- *Template matching*: it consists to compute a cross correlation between the unknown input pattern and reference pattern for each note. Maximum correlation computed over all references patterns is used to design and determine the winning instrument. Here, one pattern image (instrument's chromatimbre) is memorized as prototype for a total of 9. As example, Fig. 4 illustrates the correlation between all the 50 music instruments. Notice, that the diagonal is set to zero, in order to highlight the inter-instruments similarity measures.
- *Invariant moments*: the statistical moments, used largely in image processing, are assumed to be invariant under changes in translation, scale, and rotation are computed for each pattern instrument and stoked as codewords [11]. Each codeword has a vector composed from the seven statistical invariant moments. Nearest neightbour (k-NN) algorithm determines the decision of classification. The same training data as template matching method is used for invariant moments.
- *Support vector Machine* (SVM): this technique has shown better performance for recognition systems [12]. Dichotomy classification as the original proposition of SVM is proposed in this work using quadratic programming algorithm.
- *Neural network* (NN): feed-forward network including a set of 200 cells in the hidden layers is investigated as another tool for chromatimbre identification and classification.

In both case, SVM and NN, the second set with many features is used in training and testing session. Recall that our ambition is principally to explore meaningful information convoyed by chromatimbre to identify the musical instrument.

5 Results

As mentioned previously, the invariant moments and template matching techniques used the first feature set composed from a few data (one pattern by cluster) in training session. The remainder classification techniques employed the second feature set with huge data training. In all training sessions, only nine different instruments were presented but in the testing session 50 notes originating from the nine instruments were used. The result obtained by the invariant moments was the lowest score. Therefore, this technique was simply ignored without searching any amelioration issue. On the other hand, the template matching

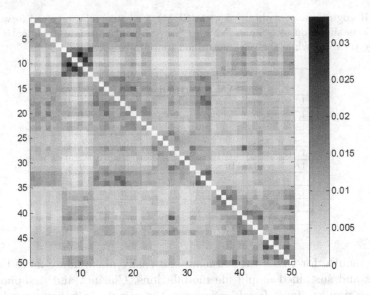

Fig. 4. Cross-correlation matrix between 50 different tone instruments (9 families)

based cross-correlation gave the highest score (69.7 %) using only a few normalized features. Comparatively, a similar score was obtained with SVM (69.4 %) and NN (67.7 %) classifiers. Both systems were trained with data size more than 100 % of those used for template matching technique. Details of all the performance results are given in Table 1 where the NN1 column gives results obtained with training data patterns that are presented sequentially from each image contours. In the NN2 column presents those obtained with training data selected randomly. I1 to I9 lines correspond to the performance recorded by the following instruments family: I.1= flute, I.2= piano, I.3= trumpet (brass), I.4=violin (string), I.5= accordion (reeds), I.6= clarinet; I.7= alto sax (brass), I.8= acoustic guitar (steel string) and I.9 = electric guitar (string). It was observed that clarinet was the trickiest instrument to recognize using template matching. SVM and NN recognize perfectly some instruments to the detriment of other instruments. The use of a larger database would probably enhance score performances. However, template matching based cross-correlation remained the most efficient one due to the almost balanced performance between different instruments, and principally for using a complete pattern of instrument chromatimbre. Uniform pattern fragmentation process may cause a forget factor on the temporal coordination of the original image. It should be added that the used approximations can disregard some details often useful to discriminate between similar instruments by their timbre properties. Finally, it was reported that with training data all the proposed systems obtained a perfect score.

With used database, some instruments had clearly mutual distinctive chromatimbre. This was especially true with the guitar, the piano and the accordion, since their excitation source is much less variable than with wind instruments

Table 1. Recognition rates obtained with (SVM), Cross-correlation, feed-forward network (NN) classification techniques: NN1 is trained by data presented sequentially from each image contour, while the NN2 is trained by data randomly

Patterns	Classifiers methods (score %)			
	SVM	Correlation	NN1	NN2
I.1 (6 notes)	67	84	100	100
I.2 (6 notes)	84	100	34	50
I.3 (6 notes)	50	67	50	34
I.4 (5 notes)	100	80	40	60
I.5 (5 notes)	20	60	60	40
I.6 (5 notes)	100	40	100	100
I.7 (6 notes)	100	50	84	84
I.8 (5 notes)	20	80	20	40
I.9 (6 notes)	84	67	77	84
mean	69.4	69.7	63.7	67.7

blown by mouth, for which the musician can easily make many more intensity variations and sustained amplitude modulations. Clarinet and saxophone will have rather similar shapes (reed instruments), particularly if they are calculated with only 12 bins. Using more bins in the calculation of the chromagram makes it easier to distinguish the inharmonicity and the frequency shifts of the attack. For example, the clarinet seemed to always have a frequency up shifting in the attack and a frequency down shifting upon release of note, maybe due to the reed transients. With more bins, the clarinet was easily distinguishable, at least visually. The impact of the number of bins in the classification implied that more bins increased significant distinctive details but made it harder to extract a single contour, since the chromatimbre shape will spread into multiple bins. Ultimately, an efficient system using chromatimbre features will have to use more than 12 bins per octave to seek contours. Characterization of timbre by chromatimbre (representation contours) appears to be a very promising approach that can be refined in the future to determine more robust encoding approaches for the contours representation.

6   Conclusion

The main topic research in this work is to present a set of new features to identify musical timbre. Features are extracted from contours of chromagram with some post-treatment and transformation. In fact, chroma is considered to exhibit mainly a tonal content and was used as powerful representation for many musical information retrieval applications. The proposed chromatimbre contours based shape demonstrates an interesting alternative representation allowing the identification of both tonal content and particularly the instrument timbre (identity). In addition, no concatenation is necessary; treatment is very simple, compatible and implemental for applications in real-time. The invariant moments, template matching, support vector machine, feed-forward Neural network have been proposed for the classification task. Contrary to what is usually done in practice, here only 18% of data were used during learning phase. In despite of little data used in the training phase as well as the several approximations effectuated on the original image, the performances scores remain close to 70% for the three proposed techniques. Particularly, template matching based cross-correlation and SVM give better performance. In fact, the SVM classification operates by dichotomy that can present new challenge for finding optimal arrangement of the class sequences. In our case, a class order was adopted randomly. The results are very promising given that visual graphic analysis have also convincingly the relevance of the proposed approach. However, several challenges remain to remove on effective treatments to extract and encode the contours.

References

1. Beauchamp, J.W.: Time-variant spectra of violin tones. Journal of the Acoustical Society of America 56(3), 995–1004 (1974)
2. Freedman, M.D.: Multidimensional perceptual scaling of musical timbres. Journal of the Acoustical Society of America 41(4A), 793–806 (1967)
3. Grey, J.M.: Multidimensional perceptual scaling of musical timbres. Journal of the Acoustical Society of America 61(5), 1270–1277 (1977)
4. Martin, K.D., Kim, Y.E.: Musical instrument identification: A pattern-recognition approach. Presented at the 136th Meeting of the Acoustical Society of America (1998)
5. Eronen, A.: Automatic Musical Instrument Recognition. Master's thesis, Department of Information Technology, Tampere University of Technology, Tampere, Finland (2001)
6. Hall, G.-E., Ezzaidi, H., Bahoura, M.: Hierarchical parametrization and classification for instrument recognition. In: The 11th International Conference on Information Science, Signal Processing and their Applications (ISSPA), Montreal, Canada, July 2-5, pp. 1066–1071 (2012)
7. Goto, M., Hashiguchi, H., Nishimura, T., Oka, R.: RWC Music Database: Music Genre Database and Musical Instrument Sound Database. In: The 4th International Conference on Music Information Retrieval (ISMIR 2003), Baltimore, Maryland, October 26-30, pp. 229–230 (2003)
8. Kitahara, T., Goto, M., Okuno, H.G.: Pitch-Dependent Identification of Musical Instrument Sounds. Applied Intelligence 23, 267–275 (2005)
9. Kitahara, T., Goto, M., Okuno, H.G.: Musical instrument identification based on F0-dependent multivariate normal distribution. In: IEEE International Conference on Acoustics, Speech, and Signal Processing (ICASSP 2003), April 6-10, vol. 5, pp. 421–424 (2003)
10. Ellis, D.: Classifying Music Audio with Timbral and Chroma Features. In: The 8th International Conference on Music Information Retrieval (ISMIR 2007), Vienna, Austria, September 23-30, pp. 339–340 (2007)
11. Hu, M.K.: Visual pattern recognition by moment invariants. IRE Transactions on Infomation Theory 8, 179–187 (1962)
12. Vapnik, V.N.: Statistical learning theory. John Wiley & Sons, Inc., New York (1998)

Augmenting Interaction Possibilities between People with Mobility Impairments and Their Surrounding Environment

Maurizio Caon, Stefano Carrino, Simon Ruffieux, Omar Abou Khaled,
and Elena Mugellini

University of Applied Sciences of Western Switzerland of Fribourg, Switzerland
{Maurizio.Caon,Stefano.Carrino,Simon.Ruffieux,Omar.AbouKhaled,
Elena.Mugellini}@Hefr.ch

Abstract. Disability is manifested when person-environment interactions result in low participation in daily life activities, which involves interaction with the environment. We present a smart Bluetooth power strip that enables the implementation of convenient interaction paradigms in order to facilitate the interaction between people with reduced mobility and their surrounding environment. In particular, two gestures-based interaction paradigms are presented: a specific application for smartphones and a natural deictic gesture paradigm. The usability test conducted with 13 users assessed the enhanced accessibility provided by these interaction paradigms for the control of electrical appliances present in the users' surrounding environment. The gestural approach scored 84 points out of 100 in the Brooke's system usability scale; the smartphone approach scored 91.

Keywords: Universal accessibility, Assistive technology, Human Computer Interaction.

1   Introduction

Reaching a physical switch on the household appliances is a quite difficult and tiring task for physically impaired people on wheelchair. On the other hand, building smart homes with a centralized system is very expensive and often requires a technical engineer. Nowadays, portable devices like smartphones are ubiquitous and quite democratic. They offer rich interfaces and connection capabilities opening the way to novel interaction approaches.

In this paper, we describe a comprehensive system for remote control of closely localized electric appliances. Our system enhances the interaction possibilities of people with reduced mobility in a twofold fashion: firstly, it enables the interaction with dumb appliances, for instance any standard electrical appliance; secondly, it supports two different interaction modalities suitable for people with movement impairments.

The proposed approach is based on a new device (we named it "BTSwitch") enabling direct remote control of multiple electric plugs. Users can interact with devices in the environment alternatively using a smartphone or using pointing gesture, as shown

A. Ell Hassanien et al. (Eds.): AMLTA 2012, CCIS 322, pp. 172–181, 2012.

Fig. 1. Interaction paradigms: on the left using the touch screen integrated in the smartphone and on the right through natural deictic gesture

in Fig. 1. The smartphone has a rich user interface, whereas the pointing gesture is based on the natural interaction paradigm [1].

The goal of the proposed system is to fill a gap between the houses with fragmented systems composed of independent household appliances and the intelligent and centralized systems of the near future.

The rest of the paper is structured as following: Section 2 presents the related work; Section 3 describes the system, whereas Section 4 is dedicated to the hardware. Section 5 presents the interaction paradigms and the relative usability test is discussed in Section 6. Section 7 contains the conclusion and shows the future work.

2   Related Work

2.1   Home Automation and Remote Control

An overview of the existing home automation systems should help providing a clearer view of the advantages and disadvantages of the proposed system. The currently available systems allowing the remote control of household appliances largely vary in prices, complexity of installation and functionalities.

The simplest systems use passive infrared sensors. A specific remote controller sends signals to the receptors controlling the state of electric appliances. These remote controllers are however not capable of receiving information from the appliances and each button must be programmed manually to control one specific appliance. Using a single remote controller for many appliances may be complex due to the 1-to-1 relation between the number of appliances and buttons.

An emerging solution is the adoption of low power radio frequency (RF) systems such as ZigBee, Z-Wave, INSTEON and other IP-based technologies [2]. Those technologies use high-level communication protocols providing wireless communication among small radios. The main advantages of those systems are the absence of cables, the high reliability of the transmissions and the low power consumption. However, those low-power frequency systems are currently not widely available on user's personal devices.

Another type of system widely used for home automation is the X-10 Power Line Carrier (PLC) [3]. This system is based on a communication protocol that uses the alternating current to transmit data between emitters and receivers. The main advantage of this system is that there is no need to add new cables to control the devices as it uses the existing electric network cables. This system requires the installation of different modules in the house as well as specific receivers to be able to use RF remote controllers.

Our approach merges three main concepts: a simple plug-and-play installation, a local system solution and a smart global remote controller already available on the user side. The project takes inspiration from the simple infrared solutions for its simplicity, and from the more complex solutions providing a smart and centralized control system for all devices. Similarly to [4] and [5], our solution uses the Bluetooth radio frequency standard protocol since it is widely available on all current handheld devices and PCs. Such a choice allows the users to directly control the system through their own personal smartphones and to have implicit localization of the devices surrounding the users. The active communication mechanism enables data exchange in order to provide information and real-time feedback from the controlled appliances on the user's smartphone. This system aims the automation of small and localized setups rather than full home automation.

2.2 Natural Interaction for Physically Impaired People

Gray et al. stated that social policies, conceptual models and classification systems have embraced the idea that disability is manifested when person-environment interactions result in low or no participation in major life activities [6]. In particular, we focus on the mobility disability, defined by individuals' ability to move about effectively in their surroundings, which predicts the onset of disability in tasks essential to living independently in the community and caring for oneself [7]. The research community and some niche companies are working hard to facilitate the interaction between physically impaired people and the surrounding environment, and to grant universal accessibility to information [8]. In fact, several works presented different infrastructural solutions for systems that can monitor and help people with physical disabilities [9]. Other works are focused on opportunistic interaction modalities and aim to eliminate the digital divide introduced by the obsolete design paradigms [8]. Specific disabilities can prevent the person from using common interfaces and computer peripherals. For example, [10] presented a camera mouse system based on a visual face tracking technique that allows users to interact with personal computers through head and face gestures. A wearable system based on a magnetic tracer for the tongue gestures recognition that helps people with severe disabilities to control their surrounding environment has been presented in [11]. The authors of [12] developed a head gesture controlled electric wheelchair and in [13] the same wheelchair is controlled through shoulders gestures. All the aforementioned examples involve the use of gestures for the interaction with the surrounding environment.

The system that we introduce offers two interaction paradigms through gestures. The first one consists of an application for smartphones with sensitive touch screen that transforms the device in a universal remote controller for electrical appliances. The second paradigm is based on natural interaction and especially on deictic gestures: the user has only to point at the electric appliance that he wants to interact with and the system contextually turns it on or off.

Smartphones can simplify certain daily living tasks but a universally accessible design of the interface is crucial to enable impaired people to comfortably interact with these devices. Since being able to use these devices can be the key to integration [14], some works focused on specific accessible design for smartphones, as in [15] and [16].

"Natural interaction is defined in terms of experience: people naturally communicate through gestures, expressions, movements, and discover the world by looking around and manipulating physical stuff" [1]. From this definition we can deduce firstly that the natural interaction is strictly dependent upon the user experience and, secondly, that its main advantage is the high learning rate. The first statement comports that humans will interact with a machine through the same modalities that they will use in the human-human interaction, the most used in the daily life (such as gestures, voice, emotions, etc.). The second statement brought interaction designers to define interfaces that are invisible to users; invisible means that since the user's culture, age, education and social context guide him to use those means of communications with almost no effort.

Gestures play an important role in the interaction. Guesgen and Kessell demonstrated that gesture interfaces can help physically impaired people to make use of household appliances by gesture [17]. The deictic (pointing) gesture is of special interest in the interaction with smart environments and for impaired people [17, 18].

3   System Overview

The system is presented in Fig. 2. A user on a wheelchair can control his surrounding environment using one of the two paradigms detailed in Section 5: using simple touch gestures on a smartphone or using natural interaction by pointing at a device. With the smartphone paradigm, the information is sent directly to the BTSwitch from the smartphone and the user has a direct, rich feedback on his screen. With the natural pointing, a specific computer tracks the user through a Microsoft Kinect camera. When a command is detected, it is sent to the BTSwitch and the user receives an acoustic feedback. Dumb appliances are directly plugged into the BTSwitch.

Both interaction paradigms can be used separately or simultaneously according to the user preferences and to the availability of each device: the smartphone paradigm involves the presence of the handheld device; the natural interaction paradigm is limited to the Kinect camera field of view.

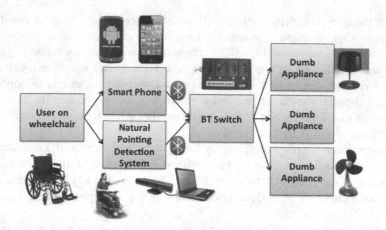

Fig. 2. Overview of the system

4   Hardware

The BTSwitch power strip prototype has been developed with the requirements to offer a simple and low cost solution to control dumb appliances while providing a plug-and-play installation system when used in conjunction with most smartphones available on the market. To fulfill these requirements, the choice of protocol has rapidly been oriented toward Bluetooth, being widely available on most smartphones and personal computers. This protocol also provides an interesting limitation: its medium range, which provides an implicit approximate localization of the controlled devices.

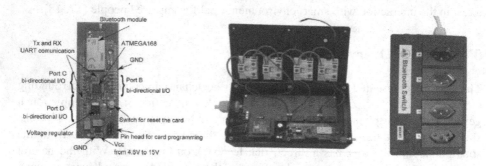

Fig. 3. Prototype of the Bluetooth switch: on the left, the custom electronic board and on the right the final prototype

The development of the prototype started with the creation of a specific electronic board, which is a smaller, cheaper and simplified version of the "ArduinoBT" electronic board [19]. Specific software has been developed for the electronic board to handle the simultaneous exchange of messages between up to 7 Bluetooth remote controllers and a BTSwitch. The power consumption has also been minimized through a sleep mode mechanism optimizing the power consumption when idle.

The BTSwitch power strip prototype is shown in Fig. 3; it controls up to four plugs and turns them on or off using mechanical relays. The electronic board is directly powered through the current used to supply the plugs. A LED indicates when remote communication occurs and a physical button provides the possibility to turn all plugs off manually.

5   Interaction Paradigms

5.1   Smartphone

The authors of [20] found that users prefer a global remote controller for instant control when studying interaction in a smart-home with interactive house-hold objects such as lamps, curtains, and information appliances. Nowadays, the technology embedded in smartphones can provide several connection possibilities and the software flexibility to implement a fully customizable universal remote controller. Therefore, an application has been developed for the three main platforms existing on the public market (iOS, Android and Windows Mobile). This application automatically discovers the surrounding BTSwitch modules and displays the discovered appliances. Within the application, the user can configure each plug and power strip with custom names and images. The display and configuration interfaces for the Android platform are illustrated in Fig. 4. As shown in the screenshot on the right in Fig. 4, the graphical interface can be customized according to user preference with a particular focus on size and position of the buttons. On the main interface of the application (Fig. 4, left), each button has different colors to indicate its state; the green color indicates that the plug is on; the red color indicates that the plug is off and the orange color indicates the transition while the message is being processed. Note that in normal conditions, the time to process a message is less than 200 milliseconds. To control an appliance, the user simply selects the desired BTSwitch power strip; then, the corresponding appliances are shown in the interface. The desired appliance is turned on or off in real-time by tapping on the corresponding button.

5.2   Natural Interaction

Along with the interaction performed through the smartphone, we provide to the users some possibilities of interaction through natural interaction and in particular through deictic gestures. The interaction idea is simple: pointing at a device to contextually switch its state on or off. For instance, pointing at a lamp will make turn it on if it was off and vice-versa.

In order to allow the interaction with the augmented objects, we created a virtual representation of the room. Virtual entities in the digital space represent the appliances connected to the BTSwich modules. The virtual interface allows making complete abstraction of the real connections in the room. In fact, a user willing to interact with a lamp has only to point at one of the virtual entities representing the lamp. The correct placement of the entities is highly flexible and can play a key role for disabled people. In fact, through the deictic interaction there is no need of a direct physical manipulation of any object or appliance, avoiding physically challenging interactions (e.g., switches that are inaccessible or uncómfortably reachable from a wheelchair). In addition, entity position in the room should reduce to the minimum the cognitive load of the interaction. For example, a user may point directly at the lamp to turn it on or point at the switch on the wall to turn on all the lamps in the room. We used the approach described by Carrino et al. [21] in order to model the virtual world according to the real one and to place the virtual entities in the more appropriate position. This procedure must be done once and, if an object is moved, just its virtual counterpart should be repositioned.

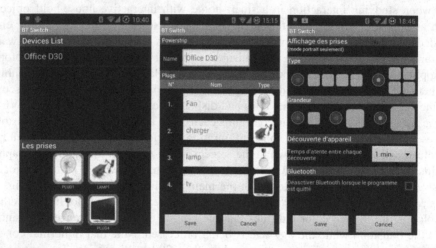

Fig. 4. The interfaces of the application: on the left, the main interface to interact with the appliances; in the center the interface to configure a particular power strip; on the right, the interface application configuration

Our system recognizes the deictic gesture using depth data and skeleton information coming from a Microsoft Kinect camera. A user is assumed to perform a pointing gesture if the arm chosen for the pointing is almost stretched. A preliminary experimentation with four people proved that the angle shoulder-elbow-wrist should be bigger than 160° to represent a good tradeoff between easiness to perform and a low number of false positives. In order to further reduce the false positives, we introduced a pointing temporal constraint: an object should be pointed continuously for at least 1 second in order to be selected. We chose the straight line crossing the user shoulder and his dominant hand as direction of pointing. The ray casting solution has been adopted to select the targeted device [22].

6   Usability Test

6.1   Participant and Procedure

We set up a scenario in an office context as shown in Fig. 5. The user is the first person entering in his work office; therefore, he has to turn the light on, to power on his personal computer and to start working. After a while, the office temperature raises and the user decides to turn the fan on for some freshness. He continues working for some time, then, before leaving his office, he turns all the electrical appliances off.

We tested the system with 13 users (1 person with reduced mobility on his own wheelchair and 12 able-bodied subjects on an electric wheelchair) with age ranging from 21 to 34. The experiment was composed of two phases; one phase involved the user following the office scenario controlling the electrical appliances through the smartphone paradigm. The other phase consisted in accomplishing the same scenario controlling the electrical appliances through the natural interaction paradigm. The order of the two phases was randomly chosen for each subject. After each phase the subject had to fill in a system usability scale (SUS) questionnaire [23]. At the end of the whole experiment, we gave to the subject a questionnaire with five open questions: which interaction paradigm he preferred and the advantages and the disadvantages of each interaction paradigm.

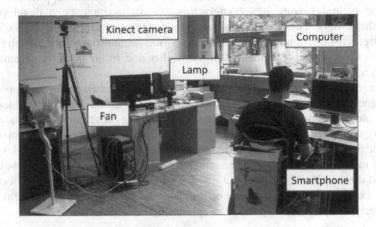

Fig. 5. Office scenario

6.2   Usability Results and Discussion

The users' evaluations assessed the smartphone interaction paradigm usability as excellent with an average SUS score of 91.3 points and a standard deviation of 7.5 points. The system with the natural interaction paradigm usability obtained an average SUS score of 84.2 with a standard deviation of 7.6.

According to users' feedbacks written in the questionnaires, the main advantages of the smartphone interaction paradigm are that it is reliable, intuitive, requires minimal effort, and that all the controllable appliances are visible on the screen with direct visual feedback of their state. The main disadvantages have been identified as the required precision to press a button on the touch screen and the need of carrying a handheld device. The main advantages of the natural interaction paradigm are that it is very intuitive, provides a natural interaction mechanism (absence of handheld device) and a direct visual feedback from the physical appliances. The main disadvantages are the need to move the wheelchair to control specific appliances, and the potential fatigue caused by the deictic gestures.

The subject with impaired mobility preferred the smartphone interaction paradigm. He specially emphasized the fact that most electric wheelchair users already have a smartphone attached to their wheelchair and the convenience of such a system for people with reduced mobility of the upper limbs. On the other hand, he also identified the advantage of the natural interaction paradigm for people with reduced mobility of the fingers that could find the smartphone interaction more troublesome. He also stated that, for both cases, a vocal modality could be a great additional feature.

7   Conclusion

In this paper, we presented and discussed a comprehensive system improving the interaction possibilities of people with reduced mobility. A novel prototype of Bluetooth-controlled power strip enables remote activation of dumb appliances. Smartphone and natural gesture based interaction paradigms have been developed and tested with 13 users. The first paradigm involves the use of subtle gestures and reduces the fatigue for the control of the appliances; the second paradigm exploits deictic gestures in order to improve the system flexibility and to enhance the interaction of people with specific hands disability.

Users evaluation concluded that the combination of the two paradigms provide an added value answering the needs of different kinds of users. Moreover, able-bodied people could also benefit from this system implementing these interaction paradigms.

As next step we plan to enhance the BTSwitch capabilities in order to control complex house appliances such as a TV or a media center. Moreover, we are making these interfaces multimodal. In fact, we are integrating the speech recognition in both paradigms and this improvement does not involve adding new devices. Indeed, the smartphone will exploit the integrated microphone and the deictic gesture paradigm system will use the microphones array that is integrated in the Kinect device.

References

1. Valli, A.: Natural interaction white paper (July 13, 2012),
   http://www.naturalinteraction.org/images/whitepaper.pdf
2. Gomez, C., Paradells, J.: Wireless home automation networks: A survey of architectures and technologies. IEEE Communications Magazine 48, 92–101 (2010)
3. Zuberi, K.H.: Powerline Carrier (PLC) Communication Systems. M.S: thesis, Department of Microelectronics and Information Technology, IMIT, Royal Institute of Technology, KTH, Sweden (2003)
4. Piyare, R., Tazil, M.: Bluetooth based home automation system using cell phone. In: 2011 IEEE 15th International Symposium on Consumer Electronics (ISCE), pp. 192–195 (2011)

5. Potts, J., Sukittanon, S.: Exploiting Bluetooth on Android mobile devices for home security application. In: 2012 Proceedings of IEEE Southeastcon, pp. 1–4 (2012)
6. Gray, D.B., Hollingsworth, H.H., Stark, S.L., Morgan, K.A.: Participation Survey/Mobility: Psychometric Properties of a Measure of Participation for People With Mobility Impairments and Limitations. Archives of Physical Medicine and Rehabilitation 87(2), 189–197 (2006)
7. Fried, L.P., Bandeen-Roche, K., Chaves, P.H., et al.: Preclinical mobility disability predicts incident mobility disability in older women. J. Gerontol A Biol. Sci. Med. Sci. 55A, M43–M52 (2000)
8. Newell, A.F.: Accessible Computing – Past Trends and Future Suggestions. ACM Transactions on Accessible Computing 1, 1–7 (2008)
9. Stefanov, D.H., Bien, Z., Bang, W.-C.: The smart house for older persons and persons with physical disabilities: structure, technology arrangements, and perspectives. IEEE Transactions on Neural Systems and Rehabilitation Engineering: a Publication of the IEEE Engineering in Medicine and Biology Society 12, 228–250 (2004)
10. Tu, J., Huang, T., Tao, H.: Face as Mouse Through Visual Face Tracking. In: The 2nd Canadian Conference on Computer and Robot Vision (CRV 2005), pp. 339–346. IEEE (2005)
11. Kim, J., Huo, X., Ghovanloo, M.: Wireless control of smartphones with tongue motion using tongue drive assistive technology. In: Conference Proceedings: Annual International Conference of the IEEE Engineering in Medicine and Biology Society. IEEE Engineering in Medicine and Biology Society Conference, pp. 5250–5253 (2010)
12. Reahman, S., Raytchev, B., Yoda, I., Liu, L.: Vibrotactile rendering of head gestures for controlling electric wheelchair. In: 2009 IEEE International Conference on Systems, Man and Cybernetics, pp. 413–417. IEEE (2009)
13. Sato, N., Yoda, I., Inoue, T.: Shoulder gesture interface for operating electric wheelchair. In: 2009 IEEE 12th International Conference on Computer Vision Workshops, ICCV Workshops, pp. 2048–2055. IEEE (2009)
14. Ling, R.: The Mobile Connection: The Cell Phone's Impact on Society. Elsevier, San Francisco (2004)
15. Verstockt, S., Decoo, D., Van Nieuwenhuyse, D., De Pauw, F., Van de Walle, R.: Assistive smartphone for people with special needs: The Personal Social Assistant. In: 2009 2nd Conference on Human System Interactions, pp. 331–337 (2009)
16. Olwal, A., Lachanas, D., Zacharouli, E.: OldGen. In: Proceedings of the 2011 Annual Conference on Human Factors in Computing Systems - CHI 2011, p. 3393. ACM Press, New York (2011)
17. Guesgen, H.W., Kessell, D.: Gestural Control of Household Appliances for the Physically Impaired. In: Florida Artificial Intelligence Research Society Conference (2012)
18. Karam, M.: A framework for research and design of gesture-based human computer interactions. Ph.D. thesis, Faculty of Engineering, Science and Mathematics, School of Electronics and Computer Science, University of Southampton, United Kingdom (2005)
19. ArduinoBT (July 13, 2012), http://arduino.cc/en/Guide/ArduinoBT
20. Koskela, T., Vaananen-Vainio-Mattila, K.: Evolution towards smart home environments: empirical evaluation of three user interfaces. Personal and Ubiquitous Computing 8, 234–240 (2004)
21. Carrino, S., Péclat, A., Mugellini, E., Abou Khaled, O., Ingold, R.: Humans and smart environments: a novel multimodal interaction approach. In: Proceedings of the 13th International Conference on Multimodal Interfaces - ICMI 2011, p. 105. ACM Press, New York (2011)
22. Dang, N.: A survey and classification of 3D pointing techniques. Research. Innovation and Vision for the Future, 71–80 (2007)
23. Brooke, J.: SUS-A quick and dirty usability scale. Usability evaluation in industry, 189–194 (1996)

A Genetic-CBR Approach for Cross-Document Relationship Identification

Yogan Jaya Kumar[1,2], Naomie Salim[2], and Albaraa Abuobieda[2]

[1] Faculty of Information and Communication Technology,
Universiti Teknikal Malaysia Melaka, 76100, Melaka, Malaysia
yogan@utem.edu.my
[2] Faculty of Computer Science and Information Systems,
Universiti Teknologi Malaysia, 81310, Skudai, Johor, Malaysia
naomie@utm.my, albarraa@hotmail.com

Abstract. Various applications concerning multi document has emerged recently. Information across topically related documents can often be linked. Cross-document Structure Theory (CST) analyzes the relationships that exist between sentences across related documents. However, most of the existing works rely on human experts to identify the CST relationships. In this work, we aim to automatically identify some of the CST relations using supervised learning method. We propose Genetic-CBR approach which incorporates genetic algorithm (GA) to improve the case base reasoning (CBR) classification. GA is used to scale the weights of the data features used by the CBR classifier. We perform the experiments using the datasets obtained from CSTBank corpus. Comparison with other learning methods shows that the proposed method yields better results.

Keywords: Cross-document structure theory (CST), Case based reasoning, Genetic algorithm, Supervised learning method, Feature weighting.

1 Introduction

Multi document analysis has sparked concerns among researchers to discover useful information from documents so that it could be beneficial to many related applications e.g. information retrieval, text summarization and etc. One of such analysis is the study on cross-document relationships. This study was pioneered by Radev [1] who came up with Cross-document Structure Theory (CST). The CST model is based on the idea that topically related documents often contain semantically related textual units such as words, phrases or sentences. In this work, we concentrate on identifying the CST relationships between sentences across documents. For example the relation between two sentences can be "Identity", "Contradiction", "Overlap", and etc.

We consider the task to identify the CST relationships as a multiclass classification problem. Supervised learning method is one of the widely sought methods for

A. Ell Hassanien et al. (Eds.): AMLTA 2012, CCIS 322, pp. 182–192, 2012.

multiclass classification problems. In this paper, we model the case based reasoning (CBR) method to perform the classification task. CBR is an instance based learning method in which its similarity function is very sensitive to the relevance of features used. In existing setting, all features are assumed to hold equal importance (weight) by the learning algorithm. Scaling the relevance of each feature is thus crucial for the success of the learning method. Therefore in this paper, we propose Genetic-CBR method which integrates feature weighting using genetic algorithm.

Past literatures show that there have been efforts to learn the CST relationships in texts. Zhang et al. [3] used boosting, a classification algorithm to identify the presence of CST relationships between sentences. It is an adaptive algorithm which works by iteratively learning previous weak classifiers and adding them to a final strong classifier. Their classifier was able to identify sentence pairs with no relationship very well, but showed poor performance in classifying the other CST relationship types.

In another related work, Miyabe et al. [4] investigated on the identification of CST relationship types by using cluster-wise classification with SVM classifier. They used a Japanese cross-document relation corpus annotated with CST relationships. The authors used the detected "Equivalence" relations to address the task of "Transition" identification. They obtained F-measure of 75.50% for equivalence and 45.64% for transition classes. However, their approach is limited to the two aforementioned relations.

The benefits of using CST have also been addressed by a number of researchers. Zahri and Fukumoto [5] determined five types of CST relation between sentences using SVM where they used the identified CST relations to determine the directionality between sentences for PageRank [6] computation. The impact of CST on summarization system have been studied by [2, 7], where they use CST to select sentences that maximize total number of CST relationships in the final summary. The major limitation of these works is that the CST relationships need to be manually annotated by human experts.

The rest of this paper is organized as follows: Section 2 outlines the proposed approach i.e. using Genetic-CBR method for the CST relationships identification. The experimental results and discussion are given in Section 3. Finally we end with conclusion in Section 4.

2   Genetic-CBR Approach

2.1   Overview of Approach

In this section, we will discuss the overview of our proposed Genetic-CBR approach for identifying the CST relationships between sentences pairs. Among the relationship types that we aim to identify are "Identity", "Subsumption", "Description" and "Overlap". The descriptions of these relations are given in Table 1. Further details with examples can be found in [2].

Table 1. Descriptions of CST relationships to be identified

Relationship	Description
Identity	The same text appears in more than one location
Subsumption	S1 contains all information in S2, plus additional information not in S2
Description	S1 describes an entity mentioned in S2
Overlap (partial equivalence)	S1 provides facts X and Y while S2 provides facts X and Z; X, Y, and Z should all be non-trivial.

Case based reasoning (CBR) is a type of supervised learning method which finds solutions for new problems based on its similarity to existing problems i.e. by assigning the solution of the known problem to the new ones. There are four major phases in a CBR process namely Retrieve, Reuse, Revise, and Retain [8]. These phases form the CBR cycle where first the most similar cases (problems) will be retrieved from the casebase and then the solution from the retrieved cases will be reused for the new case. If no similar cases are found in the casebase, the solution for the new case will be revised and finally retained into the casebase.

Based on the CBR process described above, we construct a CBR model for CST relationship identification. The following features were first extracted from each sentence pairs:

Cosine Similarity – Cosine similarity is used to measure how similar two sentences (S) are. Here the sentences are represented as word vectors with tf-idf as its element (i) value:

$$\cos(S_1, S_2) = \frac{\sum S_{1,i} \cdot S_{2,i}}{\sqrt{\sum (S_{1,i})^2} \cdot \sqrt{\sum (S_{2,i})^2}} \tag{1}$$

Word Overlap – This feature represents the measure based on the number of overlapping words in the two sentences. This measure is not sensitive to the word order in the sentences [5]:

$$overlap(S_1, S_2) = \frac{\# commonwords(S_1, S_2)}{\# words(S_1) + \# words(S_2)} \tag{2}$$

Length Type of S_1 – this feature gives the length type of the first sentence when the lengths of two sentences are compared:

$$lengtype(S_1) = 1 \quad \text{if} \quad length(S_1) > length(S_2),$$
$$-1 \quad \text{if} \quad length(S_1) < length(S_2), \tag{3}$$
$$0 \quad \text{if} \quad length(S_1) = length(S_2)$$

NP Similarity – this feature represents the noun phrase (NP) similarity between two sentences. The similarity between the NPs is calculated according to Jaccard coefficient as defined as in the following equation:

$$NP(S_1, S_2) = \frac{NP(S_1) \cap NP(S_2)}{NP(S_1) \cup NP(S_2)} \tag{4}$$

VP Similarity – this feature represents the verb phrase (VP) similarity between two sentences. The similarity between the VPs is calculated according to Jaccard coefficient as defined as in the following equation:

$$VP(S_1, S_2) = \frac{VP(S_1) \cap VP(S_2)}{VP(S_1) \cup VP(S_2)} \tag{5}$$

Each sentence pairs will then be represented as feature vectors (having the values of the above five features) with their respective outputs (CST relationship types). These pairs represent the cases in the casebase. Next, to identify the relationship type of a new case, the model will compare the input feature vector of the new case with existing cases in casebase. We use cosine similarity measure, where the cosine similarity between two cases (X, Y) is defined as following:

$$cos(X, Y) = \frac{\sum_{k=1}^{5} x_k \times y_k}{\sqrt{\sum_{k=1}^{5} x_k^2} \times \sqrt{\sum_{k=1}^{5} y_k^2}}, \tag{6}$$

However in this work we will assign weights to the features so that the performance of the CBR classification model can be improved. Thus, this gives us the weighted cosine similarity measure as the following:

$$wcos(X, Y) = \frac{\sum_{k=1}^{5} w_k x_k \times w_k y_k}{\sqrt{\sum_{k=1}^{5} (w_k x_k)^2} \times \sqrt{\sum_{k=1}^{5} (w_k y_k)^2}}, \tag{7}$$

where w_k is the weight of the kth feature. In order to obtain the weights for the features, we have integrated feature weighting using genetic algorithm (detailed description of genetic algorithm implementation is explained in Section 2.2).

Now using the weighted similarity measure, similar cases from the casebase can be retrieved. If the similarity value of the new case is more than the predefined threshold value, the model will reuse the solution (i.e. the relationship type of the sentence pair). However if the similarity value is less than the threshold value, the model will revise the new case as "No relation" type and retain the revised new case into the casebase. The overall process is illustrated in Figure 1.

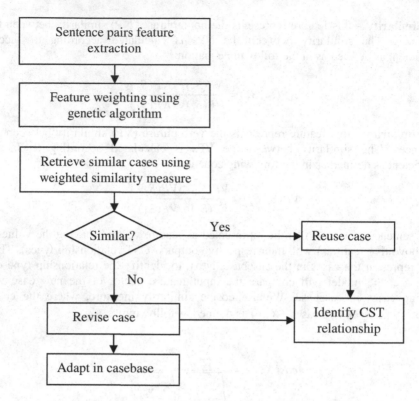

Fig. 1. Genetic-CBR approach for CST relationship identification

2.2   GA for Feature Weighting

As described in Section 2.1, after the feature extraction phase, each extracted features will be weighted before supplying them to the CBR model. In this section, we will discuss how genetic algorithm (GA) can be used to determine the weights of these features. GA is a well known optimization technique used in various fields of research and applications [9-11]. It is based on the evolution theory with the analogy that better solution can be build if we somehow combine the "good" parts of other solutions to generate the new ones. The GA procedure is shown in Figure 2.

Chromosome and Initial Population Construction. The first step in GA requires the construction of initial population which is composed of chromosomes. Each individual chromosome represents a potential solution to the given problem - in our case, the weights of the features. Since we have five features to be weighted, we construct five dimensional weight vectors by randomly initializing it with values between 0 and 1. These are known as real-valued population. To create a random population of N chromosomes, we have for example:

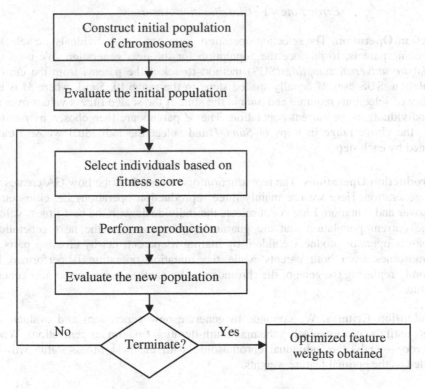

Fig. 2. Genetic algorithm procedure

$$Population = \begin{matrix} 0.25 & 0.08 & 0.74 & 0.53 & 0.26 \\ 0.77 & 0.67 & 0.03 & 0.22 & 0.31 \\ 0.07 & 0.35 & 0.20 & 0.75 & 0.68 \\ & & \cdots\cdots\cdots & & \\ 0.54 & 0.87 & 0.52 & 0.45 & 0.33 \end{matrix} \quad \begin{matrix} \leftarrow & \text{individual 1} \\ \leftarrow & \text{individual 2} \\ \leftarrow & \text{individual 3} \\ & \\ \leftarrow & \text{individual N} \end{matrix}$$

where each row represents the individual chromosome while each column value represents the weight of each feature.

Fitness Function Design. The next thing we need to provide to GA model is the fitness function, i.e. the function that needs to be optimized. Fitness function is used to evaluate the quality of each individual chromosome in the population by computing its fitness value. In this work we use our CBR model classification accuracy to evaluate the fitness of individuals. The classification accuracy is given by:

$$Classification\ Accuracy = \frac{c}{t} \qquad (8)$$

where c is the number of sentence pairs correctly classified and t is the total number of sentence pairs in the set. Since GA minimizes its fitness function, we use the classification error rate as the fitness function:

$$Error\ Rate = 1 - Classification\ Accuracy \tag{9}$$

Selection Operation. The selection operation describes how individuals are selected to become parents, to produce the population for the next generation. We used the *Stochastic universal sampling* (SUS) method to select the parents from the current population. SUS uses M equally spaced steps in the range [0, Sum], where M is the number of selections required and Sum is the sum of the scaled fitness values over all the individuals in the current population. The M parents are then chosen by moving along the above range in steps of Sum/M and select the individual whose fitness spanned by each step.

Reproduction Operations. The reproduction operations describe how GA creates its next generation. Here we use mainly three reproduction operations i.e. elite count, crossover and mutation. Elite count selects the individuals with the best fitness values in the current population that are guaranteed to survive to the next generation. Crossover operator produces children by mating its parent, i.e. by crossing parts of chromosomes from both parents while the mutation operation is performed by randomly replacing the gene of the chromosome by another to produce a new genetic structure.

Termination Criteria. We continue to generate new generations and evaluate its fitness until the process reaches the maximum iteration (maximum generation). When the process ends, the individual chromosome with the best fitness value will be selected as the optimal feature weights.

3   Results and Discussion

3.1   Experimental Settings

To experiment the identification of CST relationship, we used the dataset obtained from CSTBank [13] – a corpus consisting clusters of English news articles annotated with CST relationships. We collected 582 sentence pairs having the relationship types Identity, Subsumption, Description and Overlap. We also manually selected 100 pairs of sentences that pose no CST relations. At first we perform text preprocessing on each of these sentence pairs. This involves stop word removal and word stemming. After preprocessing, the features (as described in Section 2.1) will be extracted. These features will then form the instances for the training set where each instance is represented as feature vector with its corresponding CST relationship type.

We then use the training set and run the genetic algorithm to find the optimized weights for the features. The initial population consists of 20 chromosomes which were randomly initialized with real values between 0 and 1. To evaluate the fitness function i.e. the CBR classification error rate, each individual chromosome fitness value was obtained using the average classification accuracy by running 10 hold-out cross validation on the training set. Selected chromosomes were then reproduced, resulting 2 elite child, 11 crossover child and 7 mutation child in each generation. We run 100 generations (to allow the fitness to converge) before we terminate the process.

Once we obtain the optimized feature weights, we evaluate the performance of our Genetic-CBR model. Here we selected 476 sentence pairs for training and 206 sentence pairs for testing. We employ the evaluation measures commonly used in classification tasks – Precision, Recall and F-measure. Given the actual class (CST relation type) and the predicted class, we measure the following:

$$Precision = \frac{number\ of\ sentence\ pairs\ correctly\ labeled\ as\ class\ A}{total\ number\ of\ sentence\ pairs\ labeled\ as\ class\ A} \qquad (10)$$

$$Recall = \frac{number\ of\ sentence\ pairs\ correctly\ labeled\ as\ class\ A}{total\ number\ of\ sentence\ pairs\ actually\ belong\ to\ class\ A} \qquad (11)$$

$$F\text{-}measure = 2 \times \frac{precision \times recall}{precision + recall} \qquad (12)$$

3.2   Results

The result of feature weighting using genetic algorithm is shown in Figure 3. The optimal weights obtained are 0.18374, 0.94211, 0.81638, 0.61879 and 0.00631, representing the weights for cosine similarity, length type, word overlap, noun phrase similarity and verb phrase similarity, respectively. Table 2 and Figure 4 show the precision, recall, and F-measure of Genetic-CBR classification.

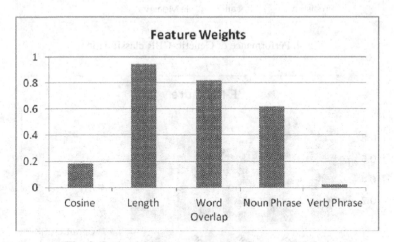

Fig. 3. Optimal feature weights after feature weighting

With the motivation to compare the performance of our proposed technique, we also evaluated the classification accuracy for CST relationship identification using CBR (without feature weighting), neural network (NN) and support vector machine (SVM). NN and SVM are two popular machine learning techniques used for classification tasks [12]. The parameters of NN and SVM were tuned to give optimal results. The result of this comparison is shown in Figure 5 and 6.

Table 2. Precision, recall, and F-measure of Genetic-CBR classification

CST Type	Precision	Recall	F-Measure
No relation	0.96	0.8	0.872727
Identity	1	0.966667	0.983050
Subsumption	0.837209	0.72	0.774193
Description	0.760869	0.921053	0.833333
Overlap	0.730158	0.793103	0.760330

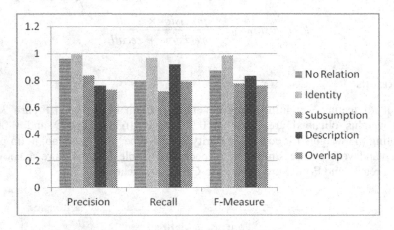

Fig. 4. Performance of Genetic-CBR classification

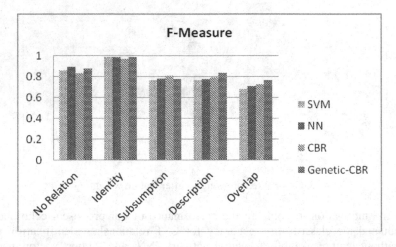

Fig. 5. Comparison of F-measures between SVM, NN, CBR and Genetic-CBR

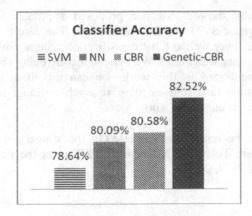

Fig. 6. Accuracy comparison between SVM, NN, CBR and Genetic-CBR

3.3   Discussion

This section discusses the results presented in the previous section. It can be observed that through feature weighting, the significance of the features varies. The feature weighting algorithm was able to differentiate the importance of each feature (with respect to the classification task), and assign it a suitable weight. The graph depicted in Figure 3 shows that features: length type, word overlap and noun phrase similarity are more important compared to features: cosine similarity and verb phrase similarity.

From the evaluation of Genetic-CBR technique, as given in Table 2, we can observe that it gives good (>90%) precision in identifying the relationship type "Identity" and "No Relation" while the other relations came close to 80%. This result is probably due to the characteristics of "Identity" type sentences which have high similarity in terms of words and length while "No Relation" possesses the complete opposite characteristics.

It can be seen from Figure 5 and 6 that overall, the proposed Genetic-CBR technique yields better results compared to CBR, NN and SVM. Genetic-CBR achieved the highest accuracy i.e. 82.52%. This shows that integrating GA with CBR can improve the classification results. Here genetic algorithm was able to optimize the set of weights that can maximize the CBR classification accuracy. Such approach is suitable when the features are not of equal relevance.

4   Conclusion

This work involves a study on cross document relationship (CST relation) identification, in particular, relationships between sentences across topically related documents, where we attempt to identify four CST relationship types i.e. "Identity", "Subsumption", "Description" and "Overlap". A novel approach has been outlined, that is using Genetic-CBR approach. The fundamental idea behind this approach is that performing feature weighting with respect to CBR classification can improve the classification performance as CBR classifier heavily rely on similarity-based selection (between feature vectors) to retrieve similar cases. In this work, genetic algorithm has been employed to optimize the weights of the features.

Experimental results showed that our proposed approach was effective and outperformed the popular SVM and NN techniques. The results also indicate that feature weighting does improve the CBR classification accuracy when we compared with CBR (without feature weighting). We believe that by being able to well identify the CST relations mentioned in this work, we can use them to facilitate multi document summarization task (our ongoing research) without relying on human experts. We regard this as our future work.

Acknowledgements. This research is supported by the Ministry of Higher Education (MOHE) and Universiti Teknologi Malaysia (UTM) under the Research University Grant No. Q.J130000, 7128, 00H74.

References

1. Radev, D.R.: A Common Theory of Information Fusion from Multiple Text Sources Step One: Cross-Document Structure. In: Proceeding of SIGDIAL, vol. 10, pp. 74–83 (2000)
2. Zhang, Z., Blair-Goldensohn, S., Radev, D.R.: Towards CST-Enhanced Summarization. In: Proceedings of AAAI/IAAI, pp. 439–446 (2002)
3. Zhang, Z., Otterbacher, J., Radev, D.R.: Learning cross-document structural relationships using boosting. In: Proceedings of CIKM, pp. 124–130 (2003)
4. Miyabe, Y., Takamura, H., Okumura, M.: Identifying cross-document relations between sentences. In: Proceedings of IJCNLP, pp. 141–148 (2008)
5. Zahri, N.A.H.B., Fukumoto, F.: Multi-document Summarization Using Link Analysis Based on Rhetorical Relations between Sentences. In: Proceedings of CICLing, vol. 2, pp. 328–338 (2011)
6. Erkan, G., Radev, D.R.: LexPageRank: Prestige in multi-document text summarization. In: Proceedings of EMNLP, pp. 365–371 (2004)
7. Jorge, M.L.C., Pardo, T.S.: Experiments with CST-based Multidocument Summarization. In: Workshop on Graph-based Methods for Natural Language Processing, pp. 74–82. ACL, Uppsala (2010)
8. Aamodt, A., Plaza, E.: Case-based reasoning: foundational issues, methodological variations and system approaches. AI Communications 7, 39–59 (1994)
9. Paszkowicz, W.: Genetic Algorithms, A Nature-inspired Tool: Survey of Applications in Materials Science and Related Fields. In: Mat. Man. Proc., vol. 24, pp. 174–197 (2009)
10. Scott, M.T.: An introduction to genetic algorithms. Journal of Computing Sciences in Colleges 20, 115–123 (2004)
11. Anita, T., Rucha, D.: Article: Genetic Algorithm - Survey Paper. In: IJCA Proceedings on NCRTC, vol. 5, pp. 25–29. Foundation of Computer Science, New York (2012)
12. Kotsiantis, S.B.: Supervised Machine Learning: A Review of Classification Techniques. Informatica Slovenia 31, 249–268 (2007)
13. CSTBank PhaseI, http://tangra.si.umich.edu/clair/CSTBank/

Improved Action Recognition Using an Efficient Boosting Method

Mohamed Abouelenien and Xiaohui Yuan

Computer Science and Engineering Department,
University of North Texas, Denton, Texas, USA
{mohamed,xiaohui.yuan}@unt.edu

Abstract. Creating an intelligent environment relies heavily on the automated recognition of different actions. Addressing this issue can advance many applications such as smart homes, automatic crime detection, controversial judgment in sports, etc. However, Action Recognition (AR) has yet to receive satisfactory performance. The massive amount of video data and the problems associated with traditional ensemble methods introduce a big challenge to the improvement in this field. We introduce a Diversity-Based ensemble learning method that efficiently learns from the AR data by selecting a representative subset at each iteration. The algorithm avoids boosting problems and introduces a weight control function that guarantees a diverse set of instances to be trained and eliminates outliers and noise. This provides better capability of successfully differentiating between different actions. Based on our experimental results, it is evident that our method achieves superior performance compared to traditional methods.

Keywords: Action Recognition, Ensemble learning, Sampling.

1 Introduction

Recently, growing number of applications relies on the performance of Action Recognition (AR). The task of action recognition is to classify different types of motions. Action recognition suffers from the massive amount of video data that keeps increasing as well as increasing number of actions. Moreover, the similarity between actions such as waving, clapping, and boxing, further complicates the process. Improving the process of automated action recognition results in more reliable applications. It can create an intelligent environment that saves time, money, and energy. Applications utilizing the task of AR include interactive applications like human computer interactions and gaming, security surveillance tasks like watching over neighborhoods, sports and entertainment, smart homes, and many others.

The process of AR requires two main phases: feature selection and classification. Feature selection can be divided into global and local representation. Global representation deals with images as a whole entity by extracting important information from a region of interest (ROI). Local representation deals with

A. Ell Hassanien et al. (Eds.): AMLTA 2012, CCIS 322, pp. 193–202, 2012.

independent patches of the data to extract local information. Local representation involves two main steps: salient point detection and feature description. Interesting points are detected first from videos. Then they are described by feature descriptors to provide discriminatory information between different actions. In this paper, we use local representation of the video data owing to its robustness to occlusion, illumination and other problems compared to global representation. Although the main focus of this paper is on the learning process, we employ a combination of points detected by Harris 3D and periodic methods. 3D SIFT method is used to describe the neighborhood of the detected points. Details are provided in section 2. The large number of features described are then clustered into words and quantitized into a word frequency histogram following the famous bag of words method [10].

In our previous work [1] we introduced the idea of combining sampling with boosting for improved efficiency. In this paper we provide a full analysis of the weighted error and a novel analysis of the instances weights updating process. The analysis lead us to introduce a Diversity-Based boosting method (D.Boost) which uses a weighted sampling mechanism for efficient training. Also by a combination of sampling and an extreme weight control function, the algorithm avoids early termination, eliminates training outliers, and guarantees a diverse set of instances trained in each iteration for a more confident and improved boosting performance.

The rest of this paper is organized as follows. In section 2 we review different feature selection methods and the most famous boosting techniques. In section 3 our analysis and algorithm are proposed. Experimental results and discussion are provided in section 4. Finally concluding remarks are provided in section 5.

2 Related Work

Two main steps are involved in the local representation process; salient point detection and feature description. Harris detector [7] analyzes local changes in patches of images using a Taylor expansion approximation and eigenvalues analysis to detect interesting points. Laptev and Lindeberg [8] introduced a space-time extension to Harris detector (Harris3D). Using spatial and temporal scales, Harris3D maximizes a normalized spatio-temporal Laplacian operator for better interesting points detection. Dollar et al. [4] proposed a periodic detector where a block of video data referred to as "cuboid" is processed using principal component analysis and clustering to create a codebook. Willems et al. [15] detected a scale-invariant, spatio-temporal interesting points that densely covers the video data using a scale-space theory.

Detected points are then described using feature descriptors. HOG [3] uses a histogram of gradient orientation in local patches of images. Speeded Up Robust Feature SURF [2] uses integral images for image convolutions and 2D Haar wavelet responses for an efficient feature description. David Lowe [9] introduced SIFT which, based on a Gaussian scale space, efficiently matches key points using an Euclidean distance metric. Based on SIFT, Scovanner et al. [14] proposed a

3D SIFT descriptor to capture the spatio-temporal aspects of the video data. Surveys on action recognition techniques can be found in [5, 11].

Boosting methods and in particular AdaBoost [6] achieved a wide success in machine learning and computer vision applications. The algorithm successively trains weak classifiers with training data using a weighted error minimization scheme. The method successfully improves accuracy but mostly on expense of efficiency. AdaBoost was proposed for binary classification and was later extended for multiple class classification. Freund and Schapire introduced a series of multi class extensions [6, 12] that converted the multiple class problem to a series of binary classifications. The methods suffered from strict termination conditions and degradation in efficiency. Zhu et al [17] introduced a simple extension to AdaBoost, Stage-wise Additive Modeling using Multi-class Exponential loss function SAMME, that modifies the loss function to ease termination conditions. Attempts on applying AdaBoost for AR is provided in [16].

3 Methodology

3.1 Analysis of the Weighted Error

We start by providing an insight on the early termination problem. First we provide a weighted error analysis that determines the reason for early termination of the boosting methods. We then introduce a novel analysis of the instances weights updating process. Based on the analysis we introduce a Diversity-Based boosting algorithm that solves the early termination problem and guarantees a diverse set of instances available for training at each iteration.

In traditional boosting methods, the algorithm is trained with the same training data every iteration. The chances of having the same misclassified instances is high especially with stable classifiers. Once this occurs, the weighted error increases enough to reach the error bound and terminate the algorithm. The analysis shows that boosting methods terminates rapidly if a set of one or more instances are repeatedly misclassified. The analysis employs SAMME algorithm and can easily be converted to AdaBoost and AdaBoost.M1.

Given a training set $(x_1, y_1), \ldots, (x_N, y_N)$, where $x_i \in \mathcal{X}$ and $y_i \in \mathcal{Y} = \{1, \ldots, C\}$. The instances are initialized with a weight of $w_1(i) = 1/N$. The total number of classes and instances are denoted by C and N respectively. We assume that after the first iteration, we have m misclassified instances, $m \in \{1, \ldots, N\}$. The weighted error is then calculated according to $\epsilon_1 = \frac{m}{N}$. We assume that after the second iteration, all the m instances are misclassified again. The weights for the m misclassified instances are updated to

$$w_2 = \frac{e^{\alpha_1}}{NW_2} \tag{1}$$

The weights for the are correctly classified instances are updated to

$$w_2 = \frac{e^{-\alpha_1}}{NW_2} \tag{2}$$

α is the weight assigned to the weak classifier according to its performance and W_2 presents a normalization factor. $W_2 = \sum_1^N w_2 = \frac{m}{N}e^{\alpha_1} + \frac{N-m}{N}e^{-\alpha_1}$.

$$\alpha_1 = \frac{1}{2}\log(\frac{1-\epsilon_1}{\epsilon_1}) + \frac{1}{2}\log(C-1) \tag{3}$$

Then the weighted error after the second training is

$$\epsilon_2 = \frac{\frac{m}{N}e^{\alpha_1}}{\frac{m}{N}e^{\alpha_1} + e^{-\alpha_1} - \frac{m}{N}e^{-\alpha_1}} = \frac{e^{2\alpha_1}}{e^{2\alpha_1} + \frac{N}{m} - 1} \tag{4}$$

The weighted error after we substitute with the values of α_1 and ϵ_1 is

$$\epsilon_2 = \frac{[\frac{N}{m}-1][C-1]}{[\frac{N}{m}-1][C-1] + \frac{N}{m} - 1} \tag{5}$$

The weighted error will then be

$$\epsilon_2 = 1 - \frac{1}{C} \tag{6}$$

When C is substituted with 2 as in AdaBoost or when the term $\log(C-1)$ is excluded as in AdaBoost.M1, the weighted error will convert to 0.5. Hence, all boosting algorithms terminate due to the increased weighted error which exceeds thier error conditions.

3.2   Analysis of Instances Weights

In this section we provide a novel analysis of the instances weights updating process. The analysis provides an expression for the number of instances n that are allowed to be misclassified after being correctly classified in the first iteration in terms of the weighted error.

We assume m instances are misclassified after the first iteration. The weighted error will be $\epsilon_1 = \frac{m}{N}$. The example weights for the misclassified and the correctly classified instances are updated according to equations (1) and (2) respectively. Now after the second iteration we assume we have a set of misclassified instances that consists of a fraction $d \in [0,1]$ of the m misclassified instances and n newly misclassified instances. The weighted error after the second training is updated to

$$\epsilon_2 = \frac{\frac{dm}{N}e^{\alpha_1} + \frac{n}{N}e^{-\alpha_1}}{\frac{m}{N}e^{\alpha_1} + e^{-\alpha_1} - \frac{m}{N}e^{-\alpha_1}} \tag{7}$$

ϵ_2 can be simplified by substituting with the values of α_1 and ϵ_1 to

$$\epsilon_2 = \frac{dm[\frac{N}{m}-1][C-1] + n}{m[\frac{N}{m}-1][C-1] + [N-m]} \tag{8}$$

Therefore, n can be represented as

$$n = [N-m][C\epsilon_2 - d(C-1)] \tag{9}$$

Equation (9) presents the number of instances that are allowed to be misclassified after being correctly classified in the first iteration in order for the weighted error not to reach the error bound and terminate the boosting method.

3.3   Diversity-Based Boosting

Based on our analysis we developed a novel Diversity-Based multiple class boosting algorithm (D.Boost) that integrates weighted sampling with a weight control function in order for the algorithm to achieve higher efficiency, avoid early termination, and guarantee a diverse set of instances to be trained in different iterations for improved and confident performance. In a typical boosting algorithm, the example weights are updated after each iteration according to the weak classifier evaluation. The misclassified instances achieve higher weights while the correctly classified instances achieve lower weights. This allows the algorithm to focus on hard to classify examples. However, using the same training set might result in having repeatedly misclassified instances which lead to early termination as discussed above. Moreover, for large data sets any improvement in the prediction accuracy will be on the expense of the efficiency. In D.Boost, the training set is down sampled to a specific size S for each iteration. After training,

---

Algorithm 1. Diversity-Based Boosting

1: initialize data distribution with $w_1(i) = 1/N$
2: **for** $j = 1, \ldots, J$ **do**
3:     Select a subset $S \subseteq D$ according to the instances weights
4:     Train a weak classifier f_j with S

$$f_j = \arg\min_{f_j \in F} \sum_{i=1}^{N} w_j(i) \mathcal{L}[y_i \neq f_j(x_i)]$$

5:     **if** $\epsilon_j \geq \frac{C-1}{C}$ **then**
6:         $\alpha_j = 0$
7:         Call algorithm 2
8:     **end if**
9:     Compute α_j for current weak classifier

$$\alpha_j = \frac{1}{2}[\log(\frac{1 - \epsilon_j}{\epsilon_j}) + \log(C - 1)]$$

10:    Update the data distribution weights

$$w_j \Leftarrow w_j e^{\alpha_j \mathcal{I}[y_i \neq f_j(x_i)]}$$

11:    Normalize w_j
12: **end for**
13: Combine classifiers f_j into $F(x)$

$$F(x) = \arg\max_y \sum_{t=1}^{T} \alpha_j f_j(x)$$

Algorithm 2. Weight Control Function

1: Define w^M as the weights of the m instances group.
2: Define w^N as the weights of the n instances group.
3: **if** Repeatedly m instances are misclassified **then**
4:     $w_j|_{w_j=max(w_j,w_j \in w^M), f_1(x_i) \neq y_i} = min(w(i))$
5: **else if** $n \geq (N-m)(C-1)(1-d)$ **then**
6:     $w_j|_{w_j=max(w_j,w_j \in w^N), f_j(x_i) \neq y_i} = min(w(i))$
7: **else**
8:     $w_j|_{w_j=max(w_j)} = min(w(i))$
9: **end if**

---

the whole training set is evaluated and their weights are updated. The sampling process depends on the weights of the instances. Accordingly, the misclassified instances have a higher probability of being selected. Once the weights of some misclassified instances increase to a certain limit, the weighted error reaches the allowed bound and the algorithm terminates. There are three reasons for this termination. First, the repetition of the same misclassified instances as shown in section 3.1. Second, the increase in the number of newly misclassified instances that were originally correctly classified as shown in section 3.2. For that, we substitute ϵ with the maximum error bound in algorithm (2). Third, the overall increase in the weights of different instances after several iterations. In our algorithm, once this increase in weights occurs, the algorithm calls a function that checks which of these reasons causes the termination. The determined reason specifies the group of instances causing the error increase. The algorithm then finds the one or more instances with the highest weights of this group and forces them to have the minimum weight. The new weights will assign a very small probability of these particular instances to be selected for the next iteration. After several iterations, some repeatedly misclassified instances are no longer valuable to the classification process. They could simply represent noise or outliers. D.Boost also allows the boosting algorithm to run for elongated number of iterations and guarantees a diverse set of instances to be selected.

The combination of the weighted sampling with the control of the extremes in instances weights results in a robust boosting method that achieves more confident and accurate decisions. Majority voting scheme is then used to combine the weak classifiers decisions. The boosting algorithm and the extreme weights control function are presented in algorithms (1) and (2) respectively. $\mathcal{I}[.]$ is an indicator function that results in 1 if true and -1 otherwise. $\mathcal{L}[.]$ is an indicator function that results in 1 if true and 0 otherwise.

4   Experimental Results

4.1   KTH Dataset

For our experiments, we processed the famous KTH action recognition data set [13]. KTH consists of six human actions that were performed by 25 persons. Each

Fig. 1. KTH dataset. Actions represented are Boxing, Clapping, Waving, Running, Walking, and Jogging respectively.

individual performed each action in 4 different ways. The actions are boxing, clapping, waving, jogging, running, and walking. Based on reported researches [14], we removed the jogging action from the experiments as jogging and running are basically the same. The processing of the KTH data set starts by extracting interesting points from the videos. Although the main focus of this paper is the learning process but we propose using a union of points detected by Harris 3D and periodic detectors. Preliminary experiments showed this strategy can extract better discriminatory information between different actions. 3D SIFT is then used to describe the spatial temporal regions around the detected points. The description vectors are quantized using K-means clustering. In our experiments we used 1000 clusters. Increasing the number of clusters resulted in better overall accuracy but on expense of processing time. Using the bag-of-words method, The centers of the clusters are referred to as words. A frequency histogram is then created. Each video is represented as a vector consisting of the frequency of the descriptors matched to the words vocabulary. Test videos are matched to the existing clusters to create their own frequency histogram. In our experiments, early pruned Decision Trees DT were used as the base classifiers in a 2-fold cross validation scheme. DT employed information gain as the splitting criterion. Diversity-Based boosting down sampled the training set to 15 (D.Boost-15), 25 (D.Boost-25), and 35 (D.Boost-35). The results were compared with AdaBoost.M1 and SAMME using a training set of 50 videos in ensemble sizes of 10, 50, and 100.

4.2 Discussion

Figure (2) presents the average error rate of all methods with all ensemble sizes. The results show a very close performance of AdaBoost.M1 and SAMME. Using D.Boost, a significant improvement in performance was observed. The decrease in the error rate compared to AdaBoost.M1 and SAMME reaches up to 44% using D.Boost-15 trained for 100 iterations. For D.Boost, further improvement is observed as the ensemble size increases. The only exception is D.Boost-35 where there was less than 1% degradation after increasing the ensemble size from 10 to 50. It can also be seen that as the number of iterations increases, the smaller sample sizes achieve faster improvement in performance than the larger sizes. For example, The best observed performance is D.Boost-15 using 100 iterations. Training only 10 iterations, D.Boost-15 had higher error rate than D.Boost-25 and D.Boost-35.

The very close performance of AdaBoost.M1 and SAMME using different ensemble sizes is illustrated in table 1. The average number of effective weak classifiers for the 2-fold cross validation, denoted by (EWC) is very low. The

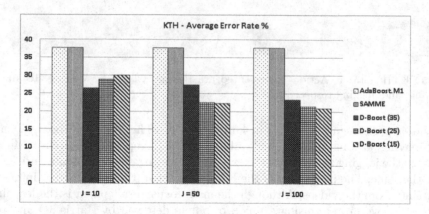

Fig. 2. KTH dataset. Action represented are Boxing, Clapping, Waving, Running, Walking, and Jogging respectively.

Table 1. Number of training Iterations (J), approximated individual class average error rate in %, approximated Time in minutes, and the average number of effective weak classifiers (EWC) for the KTH Action data set

KTH	AdaBoost.M1			SAMME			D.Boost-35			D.Boost-25			D.Boost-15		
J	10	50	100	10	50	100	10	50	100	10	50	100	10	50	100
Box%	44	43	43	43	44	43	39	24	25	37	29	29	35	29	27
Clap%	40	40	40	40	40	40	28	32	28	31	30	31	39	24	33
Wave%	39	39	39	39	39	39	27	32	28	34	27	28	35	28	28
Run%	31	31	31	31	31	31	21	26	18	14	13	8	16	18	7
Walk%	36	36	35	36	35	36	19	21	16	27	12	9	23	11	7
Time	3.4	17	35	3.4	17	35	2.4	12	24	1.9	9.2	18	1.4	6.1	12
EWC	1.5	1.5	4	2	1.5	4	10	39	89.5	10	45	83	9.5	43.5	85

classifiers with zero or very close to zero weights are neglected. EWC shows a maximum of 4 effective classifiers for all ensemble sizes. The low number is attributed to the early termination problem due to repetition of misclassified instances discussed earlier. For D.Boost, the maximum number of ineffective weak classifiers was 17 out of 100 for D.Boost-25. The table shows that the hardest classes to classify are the Box, Clap, and wave classes. This can be attributed to the similarity in performing the actions. Using D.Boost with all sample sizes the difficulty was lowered significantly compared to the other methods. Easier classes like running and walking were significantly improved with D.Boost-15 down to an error rate of 7%. Same trend was observed for individual classes where, as the number of iterations increases the performance is improved. A significant improvement in efficacy is observed using D.Boost as illustrated in the Time (in minutes) row. The improvement in efficiency using the best performing algorithm, D.Boost-15 trained for 100 iterations, compared to AdaBoost.M1 and SAMME is around 65%. It can be concluded that selecting smaller training subsets for longer number of iterations achieves better performance.

5 Conclusion

Action Recognition is a relatively growing field owing to its many applications that can create an intelligent environment that saves time and energy. Despite of its importance, this field has yet to achieve satisfactory performance and suffers the massive size of available data that requires a lot of processing. In this paper we proposed an efficient Multi-class Diversity-Based boosting method (D.Boost) for Action recognition. We First processed the Action Recognition data set using a union of interesting points detected by Harris 3D and periodic detector. The points were then described using 3D SIFT and clustered into a vocabulary of words using the famous Bag-of Words method. Each video was presented with a word frequency histogram. The processed videos were then trained using our proposed algorithm.

D.Boost is an efficient ensemble learning algorithms that avoids traditional problems experienced with other boosting methods. It avoids early termination due to repetition of misclassified instances by selecting a representative subset of the whole training set. It then guarantees a diverse set of instances to be trained in each iteration using a weight control function that eliminates selection of noisy and outlying instances that contribute to the early termination problem. The diversity achieved ensures that the algorithm can learn actions performed in different ways or by different individuals. Moreover, the new algorithm is very efficient by training only a subset of the whole training set at each iteration. Based on our experimental results, it is evident that our method achieves massive improvement in both accuracy and efficiency compared to the traditional boosting methods.

In future work we will further improve our method to be able to better differentiate between actions that have high degree of similarity. This can be achieved by creating a measure that allows selection of the most discriminatory instances from the training set.

References

1. Abouelenien, M., Yuan, X.: Sampleboost: Improving boosting performance by destabilizing weaklearners based on weighted error analysis. In: ICPR 2012, Proceedings of the 21st International Conference on Pattern Recognition (November 2012)
2. Bay, H., Tuytelaars, T., Van Gool, L.: SURF: Speeded Up Robust Features. In: Leonardis, A., Bischof, H., Pinz, A. (eds.) ECCV 2006, Part I. LNCS, vol. 3951, pp. 404–417. Springer, Heidelberg (2006)
3. Dalal, N., Triggs, B.: Histograms of oriented gradients for human detection. In: IEEE Computer Society Conference on Computer Vision and Pattern Recognition, CVPR 2005, vol. 1, pp. 886–893 (June 2005)
4. Dollar, P., Rabaud, V., Cottrell, G., Belongie, S.: Behavior recognition via sparse spatio-temporal features. In: 2nd Joint IEEE International Workshop on Visual Surveillance and Performance Evaluation of Tracking and Surveillance, pp. 65–72 (October 2005)

5. Forsyth, D.A., Arikan, O., Ikemoto, L., O'Brien, J., Ramanan, D.: Computational studies of human motion: part 1, tracking and motion synthesis. Found. Trends. Comput. Graph. Vis. 1(2-3), 77–254 (2005)
6. Freund, Y., Schapire, R.E.: A decision-theoretic generalization of on-line learning and an application to boosting. Journal of Computer and System Sciences 55, 119–139 (1997)
7. Harris, C., Stephens, M.: A combined corner and edge detector. In: Proc. of Fourth Alvey Vision Conference, pp. 147–151 (1988)
8. Laptev, I., Lindeberg, T.: Space-time interest points. In: Proceedings of the Ninth IEEE International Conference on Computer Vision, ICCV 2003, vol. 2, p. 432. IEEE Computer Society, Washington, DC (2003)
9. Lowe, D.G.: Distinctive image features from scale-invariant keypoints. Int. J. Comput. Vision 60(2), 91–110 (2004)
10. Niebles, J.C., Wang, H., Fei-Fei, L.: Unsupervised learning of human action categories using spatial-temporal words. In: Proc. BMVC (2006)
11. Poppe, R.: A survey on vision-based human action recognition. Image Vision Comput. 28(6), 976–990 (2010)
12. Schapire, R.E., Singer, Y.: Improved boosting algorithms using confidence-rated predictions. In: Machine Learning, pp. 80–91 (1999)
13. Schuldt, C., Laptev, I., Caputo, B.: Recognizing human actions: a local svm approach. In: ICPR 2004, Proceedings of the 17th International Conference on Pattern Recognition, vol. 3, pp. 32–36 (August 2004)
14. Scovanner, P., Ali, S., Shah, M.: A 3-dimensional sift descriptor and its application to action recognition. In: Proceedings of the 15th International Conference on Multimedia, MULTIMEDIA 2007, pp. 357–360. ACM, New York (2007)
15. Willems, G., Tuytelaars, T., Van Gool, L.: An Efficient Dense and Scale-Invariant Spatio-Temporal Interest Point Detector. In: Forsyth, D., Torr, P., Zisserman, A. (eds.) ECCV 2008, Part II. LNCS, vol. 5303, pp. 650–663. Springer, Heidelberg (2008)
16. Zhang, T., Liu, J., Liu, S., Ouyang, Y., Lu, H.: Boosted exemplar learning for human action recognition. In: 2009 IEEE 12th International Conference on Computer Vision Workshops (ICCV Workshops), September 27-October 4, pp. 538–545 (2009)
17. Zhu, J., Zou, H., Rosset, S., Hastie, T.: Multi-class adaboost. Statistics and Interface 2(3), 349–360 (2009)

Towards Smart Egypt – The Role of Large Scale WSNs

Rabie A. Ramadan

Computer Engineering Department, Faculty of Engineering, Cairo University,
Cairo, Egypt

Abstract. Egypt is currently going through new era where the face of Egypt is expected to be changing to much better environment. After the 25th revolution, the Egyptian people are excited to see new Egypt. However, such change faces many challenges including the utilization of technology in every aspect of Egyptians' life. Throughout this paper, a strategic view to the required technology and the role of Wireless Sensor Networks (WSNs) in developing *"New Egypt"* is presented. This paper is considered as guidelines to the developing countries as well as to the established countries in using new technologies. In addition, we stress on the role of WSNs in smartening our environment and propose a framework for the best utilization of WSNs.

Keywords: Smart Egypt, Smart city, WSN.

1   Introduction

In 25th of January 2011, Egyptians surprised the world by their revolution. The revolution led to changing the governed regime that was controlling the country for more than 30 years. The revolution was not a target by itself but it was a way of expressing the urgent need to change the face of Egypt. However, after the revolution, there is a need to start a new era in developing the country. We believe that technology is the right vehicle at this time to build up advanced and smart cities.

Egypt has many resources that if they are used properly, it might become one of the advanced countries in a short period of time. For instance, Egypt is well known as one of the oldest agriculture civilization; the amazing Nile River allowed sedentary agriculture society to develop thousands of years ago. However, Egypt has no effective rainfall to depend on it in agriculture. Therefore, the reliable water supply comes from the High Dam in Aswan and it is governed by the water-sharing treaty with the countries of the Nile Basin under which 55.5 billion m^3 per annum is allocated to Egypt [14]. Thus, the importance of smart water monitoring system and its distribution as well as its quality is urgently needed for best exploiting the water resources. Another example on the Egypt resources is the arable land where more than 90% of Egypt is desert. The agricultural land is about 3.5 million ha (8.4 million feddan) which is 3.5% of the total area. Planning to utilize such areas, again, requires smart water distribution and monitoring system.

With the advances in MEMS, WSNs have attracted many people from the academia and industry alike. Thus, WSNs became the base for smart applications. Sensor

A. Ell Hassanien et al. (Eds.): AMLTA 2012, CCIS 322, pp. 203–212, 2012.
© Springer-Verlag Berlin Heidelberg 2012

nodes are tiny devices that interact with the environment and measure its parameters. Figure 1 shows the basic architecture of WSN where nodes are deployed either manually or randomly in the monitored field. Sensors cooperate together to form a wireless ad hoc and multi-hop network; this network is usually report its data to a centralized node named "sink" node. Then, information is flowed to the end user through the Internet after analysis. WSNs are used in many applications including water monitoring [25], pollution detection [10], battle field monitoring [3], health care [11] and many others. However, sensors suffer from scarce energy sources, limited processing capabilities, and small memory footprint. Such sensors are required to live unattended for long time. Such restrictions pose many challenges to the designer of WSNs. Therefore, many of the researchers are targeting the minimization of energy consumption at different layers of the sensor's stack.

The paper is organized as follows: the following section explains our smart monitoring framework; section 3 elaborates on smart Egypt applications; finally the paper concludes in section 4.

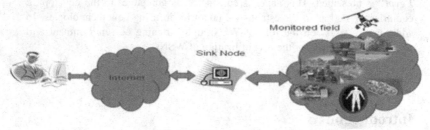

Fig. 1. WSN architecture

2   Smart Monitoring Framework

This section explains our view to the suitable monitoring framework for Egypt as well as any developing country. The framework consists of six phases as shown in Figure 2.

Phase 1: Choosing Appropriate Sensors
In the first phase, appropriate sensors are chosen where WSNs are application based. Each application has its own suitable types of sensors. For example, air pollution application might require temperature, humidity, Gas, and pressure sensors while battle field monitoring application might require motion and image sensors. In addition, some of the applications require dummy sensors while others require smart sensors. Smart sensor, in this context, means sensors with five basic units as given in Figure 3. The sensing unit consists of the sensing devices in which the type of sensor is defined based on. A sensor might sense only one feature from the monitored field or it might sensor multiple features. A sensor with single sensing device onboard is named "single modal" sensor while a sensor sensing multiple features is named "multimodal" sensor [8] [15]. The sensing unit also contains Analog to Digital Converter (ADC) where the sensed analog data is converted to digital.

The second main component of a sensor is the power unit where a sensor may depend only on AA batteries. Such limited energy source poses harsh constraints on the sensor's operation. The processing unit is the third unit of a wireless sensor where a processor/microcontroller is used. The memory constraints lead to the usage of tiny operating systems with limited capabilities such as TinyOS [12], Contiki [6], and MANTIS [1]. The communication unit is another component of a smart sensor where different standards are utilized such as ZigBee and Bluetooth. The other two units are considered optional in which Location Finding unit is usually needed for outdoor applications while the Mobility Support unit is required for mobile WSNs.

It is worth mentioning that Location Finding Unit is not recommended to be based on Global Positioning System (GPS). GPS is expensive in terms of energy consumption and it might not be available everywhere which limits the usage of sensors. Many other location estimation methods are invented for WSNs [22].

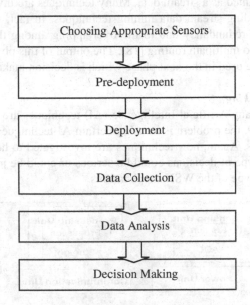

Fig. 2. Smart monitoring framework

Phase 2: Pre-Deployment
Since WSNs are used in many critical applications such as health care and battle field monitoring, the collected information is considered sensitive. Therefore, it is required to apply certain security algorithms where security keys, in most cases, might be pre-installed [24]. In addition, a node configuration and some software are required to be installed before deployment. So this phase is designated for such operations.

Phase 3: Deployment
Node deployment methods could be classified into deterministic and random. In deterministic deployment, nodes are usually placed manually in the monitored field. This type of deployment is suitable to indoor application when number of nodes are

not that large as well as the deployment environment is accessible such as in smart classroom applications [13] [19].

Phase 4: Data Collection
WSNs operation could be classified into reporting-based networks and query-based networks. In reporting-based networks, nodes transfer their sensed data through single or multi-hop to a centralized node (sink). On the other hand, in query-based networks, the sink queries the nodes and whoever has the answer to the query will replies back to the sink node. Based on this classification, different routing and data storage protocols are invented especially for sensor networks such as Directed Diffusion [4].

Phase 5: Data Analysis
After the data reaches the sink node, the node has to analyze the received data. In fact, such type of data is named as a stream data. Many techniques are investigated to handle to such data including stream data mining techniques. In fact, the received data usually contains huge redundancy due to the overlapping among the nodes sensing ranges as well as due to multipath routing [18]. The output of this phase is meaningful information that can be used in the next phase which is decision making phase.

Phase 6: Decision Making
Here, in this phase, many Artificial Intelligence (AI) techniques are utilized for decision making. However, the problem is in using certain AI techniques due to the limitations of sensor nodes. Again, new techniques are investigated to help in taking network decisions. The type of decisions could be serious or could be just controlling an actuator based on the type of the WSNs applications.

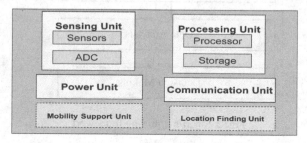

Fig. 3. Sensor node architecture

3   Smart Egypt Applications

For smart Egypt, there are many WSNs applications are required. These applications could be classified based on their relationship to each other as follows (shown in Figure 4): 1) Smart city, 2) Smart waterways, 3) Smart home, and 4) Smart grid. In this paper, we explore the smart city class only and study its requirements due to the space limitations. However, these classes of applications should be built over smart infrastructure including wired and wireless networks as well as intelligent information processing system. Information processing could be done over specialized server or over private cloud.

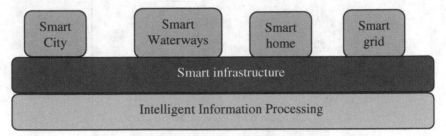

Fig. 4. Smart Egypt applications

3.1 Smart City

There are almost 41 cities in Egypt, shown in Figure 5; each one has special characteristics and requires special treatment in terms of changing it to smart city. Smart city could be defined as new regulations and generations of services based on information and communication technology. Smart cities should be easy to use, efficient, responsive, open and sustainable for the environment. Since smart city, as depicted in Figure 4, is based on smart infrastructure, we could declare that few of these cities could be smart. Cairo, Alexandria, Luxor, and Giza might be the best cities for smart city prototyping. Others might be planned for future development. However, we believe that the selected cities could enhance Egypt economy and lead to true revolution in information and communication technology.

In order for the four cities to be smart, we propose the framework presented in Figure 6. As can be seen in the Figure, there are some basic components that they have to cooperate together. Six components need to be built on the top of four agencies. The components are Smart Sensing, Smart Networks, Smart Transportation, Security and Surveillance, Artificial Intelligence, and Cloud computing and Human Behavior.

Smart sensing does not only mean using of smart sensors to monitor the environment parameters but also means efficient deployment to such sensors. In terms on node deployment, there are two main methods which are deterministic deployment [17] and random deployment [16]. In deterministic deployment, nodes are manually placed in monitored field. In this case, the monitored field is assumed accessible and the number of the deployed nodes is manageable to be placed manually. On the other hand, with large number of nodes and/or due to the inaccessibility of the monitored field, random deployment is preferred. Nodes might be deployed using helicopter or flaying robots in this case. The deployment problem could be also classified based on the deployment objectives. For instance, sensor nodes might be deployed targeting the coverage of the monitored field [20]. However, nodes might be deployed for network connectivity [13].

In fact, there are many deployment methods target saving nodes energy during the deployment phase. Some other objectives are considered in the literature such as

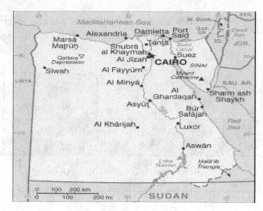

Fig. 5. Egypt cities

k-coverage and k-connectivity. Deployment problem is not limited to the deployment of sensor nodes but also extended to the deployment of a sink node. In other words, some researches were targeting the best position of the sink node for efficient operation to the WSN [23]. This problem is extended to include multiple sink nodes in large scale WSNs [7].

Smart network includes smart network architecture in terms of operation and communication. In addition, smart network means the availability of network security, re-configurability, and energy efficiency. In fact, these are issues of any wireless networks. For example, WSN security is a big issue since the capability of the node is very limited and cannot run regular algorithms such as DES [2] or RSA [9]. Moreover, with large number of nodes WSN suffers from scalability problem since nodes have to report their data to a centralized node and a message may transfer through large number of hops. Therefore, smart network is one of the major components of any smart city project.

The science of Artificial Intelligence (AI) is the science of engineering making machine intelligence. It is related to using computers to understand human intelligence but it does not have to confine itself to methods that are biologically observable. The main problems of AI include reasoning, knowledge, learning, planning, communication, and perception. In the context of smart city, AI is mostly related to event detection, behavior analysis, and emergency response. There are many related AI techniques that utilized in various smart application such as Neural Networks and Fuzzy Logic techniques.

Smart transportation is another important component of a smart city. However, transportation in Egypt is a special case and might need unusual methods to be solved due to many issues including the strange drivers' behavior. For example, there is a lake in efficient public transportation where 54% of public transportation is informal through micro-buses. In addition, roads have high accident rate due to many reasons including the quality of the roads. Moreover, there is no addressing to the disabled people in Egypt transportation system. Nevertheless, Egypt transportation institutions are weak and fragment. It is also worth mentioning that the new expansion and new cities is adding new problems to the transportation network in Egypt. Figure 7 shows the new expansions to Cairo.

However, smart transportation, in this context, does not mean vehicles transportation but also includes underground metros, railways, and flight transportation. Smart transportation component deals with traffic monitoring and access control. In fact, smart transportation cannot be separated from the Cloud Computing and Human Behavior and Security and Surveillance components. There are over 200 million cameras deployed worldwide while very few of them are in Egypt. These public cameras are used for safety and enforcing safer driving practices. A suggested structure like NetVI, shown in Figure 8, could be a suitable monitoring environment. This structure could be used for crime detection, event management, and pedestrian traffic monitoring.

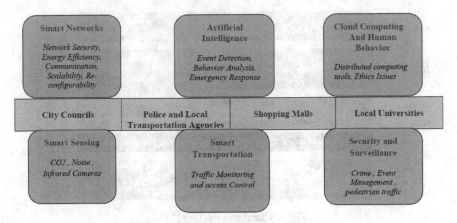

Fig. 6. Smart city framework

Cloud Computing and Human Behavior Component is another important component due to the huge amount of data that needs to be processed in a smart city. Cloud includes many of distributed computing tools for the operation on the collected data. A simplified architecture of a cloud is depicted in Figure 9. As can be seen, the cloud resources are hidden from the end user by a virtual machine layer. Above this layer, there is an application hosting platform for cloud running applications and a cloud user-level middleware which is an interface layer for handling the user requirements.

The previously mentioned components would not work efficiently unless the following agencies are cooperating: 1) city councils, 2) police and local transportation agencies, 3) shopping malls, and 4) local Universities. From the first glance, one might think that shopping malls and local Universities have no relation to smart city. However, local Universities have two important roles; first, they can provide an accurate research solutions and prototypes for different smart city problems. Second, the place of a university may have a serious effect on the transportation and services that needed to be offered to students which certainly affect the operation of a smart city. At the same time, shopping malls attract many people and they need large parking areas; therefore, their positions and accessibility will have a great effect of the operations of a smart city as well.

Finally, to conclude our vision to Egypt smart cities, there are some research challenges the need to be talked. These challenges are presented in Figure 10. These areas

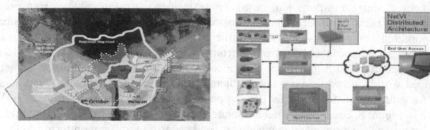

Fig. 7. Expansion of Cairo   **Fig. 8.** NetVI architecture

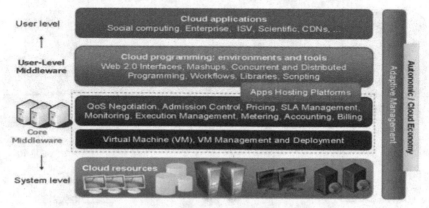

Fig. 9. Cloud architecture [5]

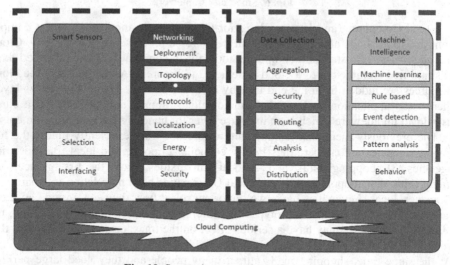

Fig. 10. Smart city research challenges

are very beneficial for researchers and industrial people to target. These areas include smart sensors technology, networking, data collection, and machine intelligence. All of these areas have to take into account the cloud computing and the distribution of the application.

4   Conclusion

In this paper, we introduced to the role of WSNs towards smartening Egypt. The paper started by introducing a smart monitoring framework. The suitability of this framework is also explained. Then, smart Egypt applications are explored. Some of these applications are smart city, smart waterway, smart home and smart grid. The paper focuses only on smart city applications such as smart sensing, smart network, and smart transportation networks. In addition, the paper introduced the important research areas that need to be investigated for building smart Egypt.

References

1. Bhatti, S., Carlson, J., Dai, H., Deng, J., Rose, J., Sheth, A., Shucker, B., Gruenwald, C., Torgerson, H.R.: Mantis OS: An Embedded Multithreaded Operating System for Wireless Micro Sensor Platforms. Mob. Netw. Appl. 10, 563–579 (2005)
2. Biham, E., Shamir, A.: Differential Cryptanalysis of DES-like Cryptosystems. Journal of Cryptology 4(1), 3–72 (1991)
3. Bokareva, T., Hu, W., Kanhere, S., Ristic, B., Gordon, N., Bessel, T., Rutten, M., Jha, S.: Wireless Sensor Networks for Battlefield Surveillance. In: Proceedings of the Land Warfare Conference (LWC 2006), Brisbane, Australia (October 2006)
4. Intanagonwiwat, C., Govindan, R., Estrin, D., Heidemann, J., Silva, F.: Directed diffusion for wireless sensor networking. IEEE/ACM Trans. Netw. 11(1) (February 2003)
5. Cloud architecture, accessed from
   http://texdexter.wordpress.com/2009/09/09/the-structure-of-the-new-it-frontier-cloud-computing-%E2%80%93-part-i/
6. Dunkels, A., Gronvall, B., Voigt, T.C.: A Lightweight and Flexible Operating System for Tiny Networked Sensors. In: Proceedings of the 9th Annual IEEE International Conference on Local Computer Networks, Washington, DC, USA, pp. 455–462 (October 2004)
7. Oyman, E.I., Ersoy, C.: Multiple sink network design problem in large scale wireless sensor networks. In: Proceedings of the IEEE International Conference on Communications (ICC), vol. 6, pp. 3663–3667 (2004)
8. Medhat, F., Ramadan, R., Talkhan, I.: Smart Clustering for Multimodal WSNs. In: Eventh International Conference on Broadband and Wireless Computing, Communication and Applications, Vectoria, Canada, November 12-14 (2012)
9. Kaliski, B.: Growing Up with Alice and Bob: Three Decades with the RSA Cryptosystem. RSA Security (April 7, 2006)
10. Khedo, K.K., Perseedoss, R., Mungur, A.: Wireless sensor Network Air pollution Monitoring system. International Journal of Wireless and Mobile Networks, IJWMN 2(2) (May 2010)
11. Ko, J., Lu, C., Srivastava, M.B., Stankovic, J.A., Terzis, A., Welsh, M.: Wireless sensor networks for healthcare. Proceedings of IEEE 98, 1947–1960 (2010)
12. Levis, P., Madden, S., Polastre, J., Szewczyk, R., Whitehouse, K., Woo, A., Gay, D., Hill, J., Welsh, M., Brewer, E., Culler, D.T.: An Operating System for Sensor Networks (2007)
13. Woehrle, M., Brockhoff, D., Hohm, T.: A new model for deployment coverage and connectivity of Wireless Sensor Networks, TIK Report, ETHZ (2007)

14. El-Nahrawy, M.A.: Country Pasture/Forage Resource Profiles. FAO (2011),
    `http://www.fao.org/ag/AGP/AGPC/doc/Counprof/PDF%20files/`
    `Egypt.pdf` (accessed)
15. Abdel-All, M.O., Ramadan, R.A., Shaaban, A.A., Abdel-Meguid, M.Z.: An Efficient Data
    Reduction Technique for Single and Multi-Modal WSNs. In: The 7th International Confe-
    rence on Intelligent Environments - IE 2011 (2011)
16. Ramadan, R.A., Ramadan, S.A.: Efficient Deployment of Connected Sensing Devices Us-
    ing Circle Packing Algorithms. In: International Conference on Autonomous and Intelli-
    gent Systems, AIS (2010)
17. Ramadan, R.A., Zewier, F.: Structured and Real Time Heterogeneous Sensor Deployment
    in Preferential Areas. In: International Workshop on Advanced Topics in Mobile Compu-
    ting for Emergency Management: Communication and Computing Platforms (2009)
18. Ramadan, R.A.: Agent Based Multipath Routing in Wireless Sensor Networks. In: IEEE
    Symposium Series on Computational Intelligence (2009)
19. Ramadan, R.A., Hagras, H., Nawito, M., El Faham Bahaa Eldesouky, A.: The Intelligent
    Classroom: Towards an Educational Ambient Intelligence Tesbed. In: 6th International
    Conference on Intelligent Environments - IE 2010 (2010)
20. Ramadan, R., Abdelghany, K., El-Rewini, H.: Optimal and Approximate Approaches for
    Deployment of Heterogeneous Sensing Devices. EURASIP JWCN Journal, Special Issue
    in Mobile Multi-Hop Ad Hoc Networks (2007)
21. Hakilo, S., Adnan, A., Hosseini, G.H.: Distributed WSN Data Stream Mining based on
    Fuzzy Clustering. In: The Sixth International Conference on Ubiquitous Intelligence and
    Computing, St Lucia, Brisbane, Australia, July 7-9 (2009)
22. Zheng, Y., Niu, R., Varshney, P.K.: Closed-Form Performance for Location Estimation
    Based on Quantized Data in Sensor Networks. In: Proc. of the 13th International Confe-
    rence on Information Fusion, Edinburgh, Scotland, UK (July 2010)
23. Hu, Y., Xue, Y., Li, Q., Liu, F., Keung, G.Y., Li, B.: The Sink Node Placement and Per-
    formance Implication in Mobile Sensor Networks. Mob. Netw. Appl. 14(2), 230–240
    (2009)
24. Li, Z., Gong, G.: A Survey on Security in Wireless Sensor Networks. Department of Elec-
    trical and Computer Engineering. University of Waterloo, Canada (2011)
25. Rasin, Z., Abdullah, M.R.: Water Quality Monitoring System Using Zigbee Based Wire-
    less Sensor Network. The International Journal of Engineering & Technology IJET 9(10),
    24–28 (2010)

Arabic Sign Language Recognition System Based on Adaptive Pulse-Coupled Neural Network

A. Samir Elons and Magdy Aboull-Ela

Scientific Computing Department
Faculty of Computer and Information Sciences, Ain Shams University
ahmed.new80@hotmail.com

Abstract. Many feature generation methods have been developed for object recognition. Some of these methods succeeded in achieving the invariance against object translation, rotation and scaling but faced problems of the bright background effect and non-uniform light on the quality of the generated features. This problem has objected recognition systems to work in free environment. This paper proposes a new method to enhance the features quality based on Pulse-Coupled Neural Network (PCNN). An adaptive model is proposed that defines continuity factor is as a weight factor of the current pulse in signature generation process. The proposed new method has been employed in a hybrid feature extraction model that is followed by a classifier and was applied and tested in Arabic Sign Language (ASL) static hand posture recognition; the superiority of the new method is shown.

Keywords: Pulse-Coupled Neural Network (PCNN), Mult-Layer Perceptron (MLP), Continuity Factor, Arabic Sign Language (ASL), Discrete Fourier Transform (DFT).

1 Introduction

Many recognition systems are based on saliency techniques which depend mainly on the segmentation step, which is very critical. A new trend for pattern recognition has been discovered that mainly depends on image understanding without segmentation. To skip the segmentation step, we need a transformation that expresses the contents of the image without segmentation. PCNN has the ability to convert a 2D image into a 1D periodic time series [1] which represents "Image Signature". PCNN is a biologically inspired neural network model that is proposed in 2000 by Eckhorn [2]. It has been acquired from the study of synchronous pulse bursts in the cat visual cortex. From this start, a different PCNN algorithm has been developed to simulate the exact model and have all the assumptions for dimension decreasing of image recognition. Examples of these modifications are: Modified PCNN, Feedback PCNN, Fast Linking PCNN and Optimized PCNN. PCNN is applied to image filtering, smoothing, segmentation and fusion [3]. PCNN also generates a unique one-Dimensional time series (image signature) based on computing the global pulsing behavior [4]. The idea of image signatures stems from biological research performed by McClurken et al. [5]

A. Ell Hassanien et al. (Eds.): AMLTA 2012, CCIS 322, pp. 213–221, 2012.

they measure the neural response of a macaque to checkerboard style patterns. The creation of signatures and using it in object recognition with the PCNN was first proposed by Johnson [6]. This paper proposes adding weight factor which is calculated every iteration (*continuity factor*). This factor permits a sufficient number of iterations and also minimizes the interference effect.

The rest of this paper is organized as follows: Section (2) discusses the sign language recognition system as a kind of gestures in general and reviews some recent and related published works. Section (3) discusses the mathematical background of the PCNN Models. Section (4) discussed the proposed Arabic Sign Language Recognition System in details. A set of experiments are then presented in Section (5), followed by some conclusions in Section (6).

2   Sign Language Recognition

Sign language as a kind of gestures is one of the most natural means of exchanging information for most deaf people. The aim of sign language recognition is to provide an efficient and accurate mechanism to transcribe sign language into text or speech. Sign language is a visual and manual language, made up of signs created with the hands, facial expressions, and body posture and movement [7,19]. Sign language conveys ideas, information, and emotion with as much range, complexity, and versatility as spoken languages. B. Bauer and H. Hienz [8] in 2000 developed a GSL (German Sign Language) recognition system that uses colored cloth gloves in both hands. The system is based on Hidden Markov Models (HMM) with one model of each sign. A lexicon of 52 signs was collected form one signer both for training and classification. A 94% recognition percentage was achieved. N. Tanibata et al. [9] -in 2001- proposed a method of extraction of hand features and recognition of JSL (Japanese Sign Language) words. For tracking the face and hand, they could recognize 64 out of 65 words successfully by 98.4%. J. Zieren et al. [10] presented two systems for isolated recognition: the first is for recognizing GSL, on a vocabulary of 152 signs achieving a rate of 97%, using HMM, but the rate decreases for the group of signs that contain overlaps in either hands or face and hands. A more recent approach in 2009 by Kelly et al. [11] also incorporates a non-manual feature, namely head movement; a detection ratio of 95.7% could be achieved. Compared to other sign languages, not much has been done in the automation of the Arabic sign language, except few individual attempts. Assaleh et al. [12] used colored gloves for collecting a varying size data samples for 30 manual alphabet of Arabic sign language. Polynomial classifiers were used as a new approach for classification. In a recent (2005) work in Arabic Sign Language, in 2011, Nashwa El bendart et al [13], recognized Arabic static alphabets with recognition accuracy 90%. When Microsoft released "Kinect" in November 2010, Fig 1, it was mainly targeted at consumers owning a Microsoft Xbox 360 console, allowing the user to interact with the system using gestures and speech. The device itself features an RGB camera, a depth sensor and a multi-array microphone, and is capable of tracking users' body movement.

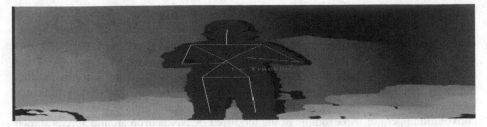

Fig. 1. Kinect in sign language recognition

This new technology encourages researchers in sign language recognition to customize it in real-time recognition. Unfortunately, due to low resolution of Kinect cameras, hands details and shapes in fast time animation are indistinguishable.

3 PCNN Models

A pulse-coupled neural network (PCNN) is a model of a biological network, specifically, a model of fragment of cat's sight network. It is a single-layer network [14] composed of neurons. Each of them is linked to one pixel of the input image. Each neuron contains two input compartments: the feeding and the linking. The feeding receives an external stimulus as well as local stimulus while the linking only receives local stimulus [14]. The local stimulus comes from the neurons within feeding radius. This local stimulus is hereafter called the firing information. The external stimulus is the intensity from the corresponding pixel in the picture. The feeding and linking are combined in a second order fashion to create the potential which then decides together with the output whether the neuron should fire or not.

3.1 Modified PCNN

There are several differences between the algorithms for the modified PCNN neuron and the exact physiological pulse coupled neuron. The differences are due to several simplifications made to the calculations, while still keeping the main features of the general theory. Each neuron in the modified PCNN could be described by the following set of equations [14]:

$$L(i) = L(i-1) \cdot e^{(-\alpha L)} + VL \cdot (R*Ysur(i-1)) \tag{1}$$

$$F(i) = S + F(i-1) \cdot e(-\alpha F) + VF \cdot (R*Ysur(i-1)) \tag{2}$$

$$U(i) = F(i) \cdot [1 + \beta \cdot L(i)] \tag{3}$$

$$\theta(i) = \theta(i-1)e^{-(\alpha q)} + V\theta \, Yout(i-1) \tag{4}$$

$$U > \theta(i) => Yout = 1 \text{ (Firing Condition)} \quad \text{otherwise} => Yout = 0 \tag{5}$$

Where L(i) is input linking potential, F(i) is input feeding potential and S represents the intensity of given image element. U(i) is the activation potential of neuron, θ(i) is threshold potential of neuron and (i) is iteration step. Parameters (αL), (αF) and (αq) decay coefficients, (β) is linking coefficient and parameters (VL) and (VF) are coefficients of the linking and threshold potential. Ysur is the firing information that indicates whether the surrounding neurons have fired or not and (Yout) indicates whether this neuron fires or not. (R) is the matrix of weight coefficients and * is convolution operator. An example of the modified PCNN neuron architecture is shown in Fig 2 as a schematic block diagram of the modified PCNN neuron as described through (1) - (5).

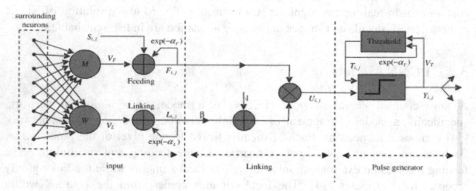

Fig. 2. A modified model of PCNN neuron

3.2 Optimized PCNN

The main aim of Optimized PCNN was to reduce the number of generated features to reach a high image recognition performance. The optimization was based on the PCNN with modified primary input (MPCNN).

The feeding potential F(i) is defined by the intensity pixel (Sij) only as in case of Modified-PCNN. The linking potential L(i) is defined only by the convolution matrix K(i) that is calculated by term:

$$K(i) = R*(Xsur (i-1).Ysur (i-1)) \tag{6}$$

$$L(i) = K(i) \tag{7}$$

$$U(i) = F(i) \times [1 + \beta \cdot L(i)] \tag{8}$$

$$X(i) = \frac{1}{1 + e^{\Theta(i-1) - U(i)}} \tag{9}$$

$$X(i) > 0.5 \Rightarrow Yout = 1 \text{ (firing Condition) otherwise} \Rightarrow Yout = 0 \tag{10}$$

where Y(i) is output quantity based on step-function and X(i) is output quantity based on sigmoid function.

3.3   Features Generation Methods

PCNN generates a unique one-dimensional time series (image signature) based on computing the global pulsing behavior [14]. The idea of image signatures stems from biological research done by McClurken et al. [5], and they measure the neural response of a macaque to checkerboard style patterns. The creation of signatures and using it in object recognition with the PCNN was first proposed by Johnson [6]. This experiment has worked well for single objects without a background. The standard approach of feature generation G(n) for specific iteration (i) is based on a series of virtual binary image generation. It is calculated as sum of output quantities *(Yi)* of activated neurons in the given iteration step [14]:

$$G(n)=\sum_{i=0}^{n} Y(i) \tag{11}$$

Through influence of geometrical transforms, it is very important for standardization of the generated features by standard equation.

$$g(n)=\frac{G(n)}{\max{(G)}} \tag{12}$$

Where max (G) is the function that returns the maximal value in the feature space for the first impulse of function G(n).The feature with maximal value is a feature with maximal information value for image recognition process. Equation (12) results one at this feature which makes this value irrelevant. To overcome this problem, a modification can be applied to (12), such that:

$$g(n)=\frac{G(n)}{\sum_{ij} S_{ij}} \tag{13}$$

Where (S_{ij}) is the intensity of a given image pixel (i,j); the previous equation achieves the standardization, but it does not satisfy the condition of $0 \le g(n) \le 1$. $0 \le g(n)$ is always guaranteed, but $g(n) \le 1$ is not valid in all the cases. This is because the sum of values Y(i) in the given iteration step i may be higher than the sum of values Sij (pixel intensity). Froge [14] proposed a new form of feature generation by introducing a new equation for feature value calculation g(n):

$$g(n)=\frac{\sum_{i=1}^{n} X(i) \times Y(i)}{\sum_{ij} S_{ij}} \tag{14}$$

Besides, Froge checked the validity of the standardization condition $0.5<(X(i) \times Y(i))<1$, and he showed the invariance against non-standard cases, and did not investigate the effect of lighting conditions and background brightness on his method.

4   Proposed Arabic Sign Language Recognition System

The idea of the proposed method is to weight each pulse by "Continuity factor". This factor mainly depends on how the surrounding pixels are fired in the same iteration. This factor has its maximum value when the pulse shows dense scene, and has its minimum value when the pulse shows holes and sparse scene. Figure 3 showed 2 pulses, the first showed a sparse pulse which will take a small weighting factor while the second contains a dense one for the same image which will have a relatively higher value.

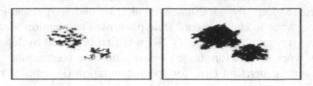

Fig. 3. A shows a sparse pulse, b-shows a dense pulse

First, we define an operator which is sensitive to the pixel intensity change, the operator happens to be the gradient. If the image is regarded as a function of two variables A(x,y), then the gradient is defined as:

$$\nabla x2A = A(x + 1, y) - A(x - 1, y) \tag{15}$$

$$\nabla y2A = A(x, y + 1) - A(x, y - 1) \tag{16}$$

$$Cr = \sqrt{(\nabla x2)^2 + (\nabla y2)^2} \tag{17}$$

$\nabla x2$ *and* $\nabla y2$ take either 0 or 1 so the continuity response values are 0, 1 and 1.414. The value of the response can be summed then normalized and producing the Continuity Factor, at a given pulse (i) by computing the following formula:

$$CF(i) = \frac{\Sigma(Cr)}{(1.414) \times N} \tag{18}$$

Where N is the number of pixels in the input image, the value 1.414 is the maximum value Cr can take.

$$g(n) = \frac{\sum_{i=1}^{n} (X(i) \times Y(i) \times CF(i))}{\Sigma_{ij} S_{ij}} \tag{19}$$

Figure 4 illustrates an example for two images for the same posture but with different background size and lighting conditions.

Fig. 4. Two images of the same posture but different in background size

Figure 5 illustrates the corresponding image features generated by eq(12), eq(14) and eq(15) for both images. Using eq(15) gave a more accurate signature for the distorted image.

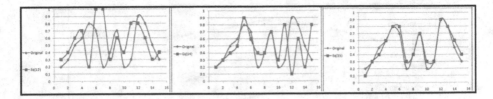

Fig. 5. Image signatures of 2 images using eq(12), eq(14) and eq(19)

This paper proposes a hybrid model for image features generation based on PCNN image signature. This model consists of two parts: PCNN layer to generate the image signature, eq.19 is the used model to generate the signature. Applying Discrete Fourier Transform (DFT) on the signature and choose the maximum (K) coefficients. Figure 6 illustrates the proposed feature extraction model. The main reason for the popularity of DFD coefficients is their behavior under common geometric transformations, such as translation, scaling and rotation. Neural networks are applicable in virtually every situation in which a relationship between the predictor variables (independents, inputs) and predicted variables (dependents, outputs) exists, even when that relationship is very complex and not easy to articulate in the usual terms of "correlations" or "differences between groups". The most popular network used in classification problems is "Multi-Layer erceptron"(MLP) [15- 17]. Back propagation is used to train the network.

5   Experimental Results

This research applies the proposed method to recognize 158 ASL static postures through exposing the image of size (600X 450) to OM-PCNN and evaluates the image signature. The image signature values are then classified using Multi-Layer Perceptron (MLP) network [18], each posture is represented by 10 exemplars: 6 of them used as training set, the object pixels percentage inside the image varies from 40% to 80%. The implementation details of the PCNN are: $\beta=0.1, \alpha L=1.0, \alpha q=0.8$, VL=0.25, VF=0.6 and V$\theta$=20. The implementation details of the MLP network are: Step size = 0.001, Number of iterations = 1000, 1 hidden layer has been used and Sigmoid Activation function was used. This study aims to enhance the feature calculation and compare previous methods results using eq.(11), eq.(14) and the proposed method result. The comparison is presented according to the same recognition environment. Figure (6) illustrates the superiority of the proposed system.

The input layer of MLP consists of 11 neurons; each is assigned for a feature extracted from DFT. The hidden layer consists of 18 neurons; which has been determined by experimental sensitivity analysis was conducted. The proposed method achieves 90% recognition accuracy which was obtained when the maximum 11 features are used which mainly is a problem field dependent factor.

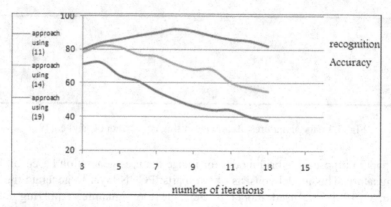

Fig. 6. The recognition accuracy against the number of features from DFT of the 3 methods

6   Conclusions

Different approaches have been developed in feature generation using PCNN. These approaches could not achieve the invariance against light conditions or bright background. The results of experiments of the proposed hybrid approach confirmed that the usage of continuity factor and DFT as an enhanced form of feature generation. The proposed feature generation approach permits the calculation of sufficiently long image signature with minimal interference effect. While the long output image signature keeps the interference in its minimum, it gives more detailed features needed in large background or non-uniform lighting cases. It was applied to ASL system which recognized the Arabic sign static postures and achieved 90% recognition accuracy, and showed invariance against geometrical transforms, bright background and light conditions.

References

1. Ranganath, H.J., Kuntimad, G., Johnson, J.L.: Pulse Coupled Neural Networks for Image Processing. In: PCNN International Workshop, Huntsville, Alabama (April 5, 1995)
2. Eckhorn, R., Reitboeck, H.J., Arndt, M., Dicke, P.: Feature linking via synchronization among distributed assemblies: Simulations of results from cat visual cortex. Neural Computation 2(3), 293–307 (1990)
3. Zhang, D., Mabu, S., Hirasawa, K.: Image de-noising using pulse coupled neural network with an adaptive Pareto genetic algorithm. IEEJ Transactions on Electrical and Electronic Engineering 6(5), 474–482 (2011)
4. Johonson, J.L.: Pulse-Coupled Neural Nets: translation, rotation, scale, distortion, and intensity signal invariance for images. Appl. Opt. 33(26), 6239–6253 (1994)
5. McClurkin, J.W., Zarbock, J.A., Optican, L.M.: Temporal Codes for Colors, Patterns and Memories. In: Peters, A., Rockland, K.S. (eds.) Cerebral Cortex, vol. 10, p. 443. Plenum Press, NY (1994)

6. Ranganath, H.S., Kuntimad, G., Johnson, J.L.: Pulse coupled neural networks for image processing. In: Proceedings of Southeast Conference on Visualize the Future, Raleigh, pp. 37–43 (1995)
7. Abdel-Wahab, M.S., Abul-Ela, M., Samir, A.: Arbic Sign Langugae Recognition using Neural Network and Graph Matching Techniques. In: AIC 2006 Proceedings of the 6th WSEAS International Conference on Applied Informatics and Communications (2006)
8. Bauer, B., Hienz, H.: Relevant Features for Video-Based Continuous Sign Language Recognition. In: Proceedings of the Fourth IEEE International Conference on Automatic Face and Gesture Recognition, pp. 64–75 (2000)
9. Tanibata, N., Shimada, N., Shirai, Y.: Extraction of Hand Features for Recognition of Sign Language Words. In: Proceedings of the 15th International Conference on Vision Interface, Calgary, Canada (2001)
10. Zieren, J., Kraiss, K.-F.: Robust Person-Independent Visual Sign Language Recognition. In: Proceedings of Pattern Recognition and Image Analysis, Second Iberian Conference, Estoril, Portugal (2005)
11. Kelly, D., McDonald, J., Markham, C.: Continuous recognition of motion based gestures in sign language. In: 2009 IEEE 12th International Conference on Computer Vision Workshops (ICCV Workshops), pp. 1073–1080 (2009)
12. Assaleh, K., Al-Rousan, M.: Recognition of Arabic Sign Language Alphabet Using Polynomial Classifiers. EURASIP Journal on Applied Signal Processing Society (13), 2136–2145 (2005)
13. El-Bendary, N., Zawbaa, H.M., Daoud, M.S., Hassanien, A.E., Nakamatsu, K.: ArSLAT: Arabic Sign Language Alphabets Translator. International Journal of Computer Information Systems and Industrial Management Applications 3, 498–506 (2011) ISSN 2150-7988
14. Forgá, R.: Feature Generation Improving by Optimized PCNN. In: 6th International Symposium on Applied Machine Intelligence and Informatics, SAMI 2008, January 21-22, pp. 203–207 (2008)
15. Ali, A.S., Hussien, A.S., Tolba, M.F., Youssef, A.H.: Visualization of large time-varying vector data. In: 3rd IEEE International Conference on Computer Science and Information Technology, art no. 5565176, pp. 210–215 (2010)
16. Khalifa, A.S., Ammar, R.A., Tolba, M.F., Fergany, T.: Dynamic online allocation of independent task onto heterogeneous computing systems to maximize load balancing. In: 8th IEEE International Symposium on Signal Processing and Information Technology, art. no. 4775659, pp. 418–425 (2008)
17. Tolba, M.F., Abdel-Wahab, M.S., Taha, I.A., Anbar, A.A.: Directed acyclic graphs scheduling in grid computing environments. In: International Conference on Internet Computing, pp. 260–266 (2004)
18. Khattab, D.R., El-Latif, Y.M.A., Wahab, M.S.A., Tolba, M.F.: Efficient face-based non-split connectivity compression for quad and triangle-quad meshes. In: 3rd International Conference on Computer Graphics Theory and Applications (GRAPP), pp. 31–38 (2008)
19. Fahmy Tolba, M., Saied Abdel-Wahab, M., Aboul-Ela, M., Samir, A.: Image Signature Improving by PCNN for Arabic Sign Language Recognition. Canadian Journal on Artificial Intelligence, Machine Learning & Pattern Recognition 1(1) (March 2010)

Surface Mining Signal Discrimination Using Landsat TM Sensor: An Empirical Approach

Richa N.K. Sharma[1], Roheet Bhatnagar[2], and A.K. Singh[3]

[1] Department of Remote Sensing, BIT Mesra Ranchi,
Ranchi, Jharkhand, India
[2] Department of Computer Science & Engineering, Manipal University Jaipur
Thikaria, Off Jaipur-Ajmer Highway, Jaipur, Rajasthan, India
[3] Department of Civil Engineering, BIT Mesra, Ranchi, Extension Center Deoghar
Jharkhand, India
richa_13@hotmail.com, roheet.bhatnagar@jaipur.manipal.edu,
aksingh@bitmesra.ac.in

Abstract. In Chotanagpur plateau of Jharkhand State in India, mining is a prominent activity. Sample sites of three such ores, viz. Bauxite, Hematite and Uranium were taken up for the present study wherein the first two are extracted through surface mining, leaving their signatures on the earth's surface, while the third one, extracted through underground mining process, leaves its trail in tailing-pond, after its beneficiation, because of the higher degree of its radioactive property (half-life of Uranium is around 4,500 million years [1]). The Study attempts to statistically discriminate mining signals that were picked up as DN (digital number) values of the first four spectral bands of TM (Thematic Mapper) sensor, displayed on the graphic screen as the additive colour composite, using three primary colours namely red, green and blue (RGB) as standard FCC (false colour composite) of Landsat satellite-image. The said discrimination were based on application of two independent statistical algorithm on these values, one being paired-sample Student's t-Test (at 95% confidence level and 3°of freedom) through SPSS (ver. 19) software and the second, subsequently, ANOVA (Analysis of Variance) test (at 95% confidence level), in order to further discriminate the signals based on parameters like spectral bands and nature of mineral being mined. According to the first algorithm Bauxite was found to be clearly discriminated, both from Uranium as well as Hematite, while Hematite could only be distinguished from Bauxite but not from Uranium. Performance of ANOVA test on the DN values discriminated the surface mining signals pertaining to these three different ores and it showed a high variance between the spectral bands both within the same ore group emphasising that different bands of the satellite sensors specifically identify features and also between the different ore groups.

Index Terms: Standard False Colour Composite (FCC), DN (Digital Number) Values, Paired-sample Student's t-Test, ANOVA (Analysis of Variance,) Landsat TM (Thematic Mapper) sensor.

1 Introduction

Jharkhand, meaning the land of forest, is the Ruhr of India. Many minerals are mined here. Through a displayed standard FCC of the satellite-image on RGB colour

A. Ell Hassanien et al. (Eds.): AMLTA 2012, CCIS 322, pp. 222–233, 2012.
© Springer-Verlag Berlin Heidelberg 2012

composite display, surface mining features related to some minerals can be discriminated through elements of image interpretation, while some of them look similar. The present paper discriminates surface mining features of three such mineral ores namely Bauxite, Hematite and Uranium which are difficult to distinguish in an analogue form or on the graphic screen (all show a cyan colour). In doing so the present study attempts, following an empirical approach, uses two standard statistical tests, the paired-sample Student's t-Test and ANOVA (Analysis of Variance) test, on the DN (digital number) values that were derived from the satellite data acquired from Landsat TM (Thematic Mapper) sensor of resolution 30m, corresponding to these mineral ores. While paired-sample Student's t-test is able to clearly discriminate pairs of Bauxite-Hematite and Bauxite-Uranium, it does not discriminate between the pairs of Hematite and Uranium. A further application of the ANOVA test is able to discriminate all the three mineral ores. The ANOVA test also shows variance between the spectral bands as significant, both within the same mineral ore group and between the different mineral ore group.

2   Study Area

Study area comprises of the mining locations of Bauxite, Hematite and Uranium in the districts of Lohardaga, West Singhbhum and East Singhbhum respectively in the State of Jharkhand lying between longitude 83.15°E and 85.45 °N and latitude 22°N to 25°N, India Fig 1. Satellite image displayed in the standard FCC format are depicted in Fig 2 and Fig 3 pertaining to the two mineral ores of Bauxite and Hematite respectively. Similar characteristics are for Uranium too.

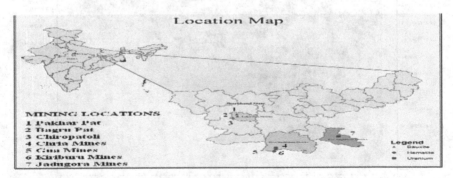

Fig. 1. Study Area

The surface mining activity is seen in cyan colour for all the three minerals. For display of the standard FCC spectral bands 2, 3 and 4 [2] are used. The reflectance values of the first four bands of the Landsat TM sensor used to derive the DN values are summarized in Table 1.

Standard FCC : Surface Mining of Bauxite Ore

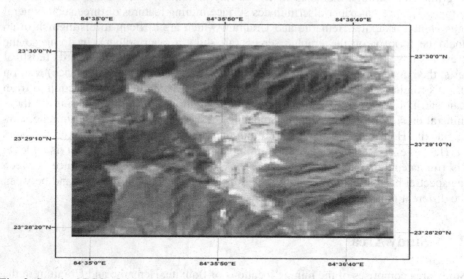

Fig. 2. Standard FCC of the satellite image showing surface mining activity related to Bauxite ore in cyan colour

Standard FCC : Surface Mining of Hematite Ore

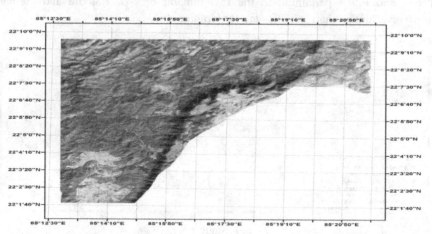

Fig. 3. Standard FCC of the satellite image showing surface mining activity related to Heamatite ore in cyan colour

Table 1. Spectral resolution of the Landsat TM bands used in the present Study

Band	B1	B2	B3	B4
Spectral range	0.45 - 0.52 µm	0.52 – 0.60µm	0.63 - 0.69 µm	0.76 - 0.90µm

3   Methodology

Bauxite and Hematite, in Jharkhand, are extracted through opencast mining, Uranium is mined   underground. Uranium mining started in the early sixties in the state. However, because of the higher degree of its radioactive property, Uranium gives a surface expression through the tailing ponds where the tailings are stored after its beneficiation process. Half-life (t1/2) period of Uranium is roughly 4,500 million years [3], thereby letting it leave its signatures in the tailing pond that are visible in remote sensing images. Usage of many statistical tests are made in remote sensing and GIS data analyses in order to discriminate similar looking features in Satellite images [4]. ANOVA (Analysis of Variance) has been used for discriminating various vegetation species in mangrove forest based on their leaf reflectance [5]. Use of paired sample Student's t-Test is also known to have been used in remote sensing images in monitoring landslide disaster [6]. The Test has also been used to compare models generated from remotely sensed data and forest data in estimation of tree parameters to establish the null hypothesis [7] and to discriminate vegetation species as sensed through remote sensing [8], [9] and empirically. While testing the equality of means from two independent normally distributed populations, classical paired sample Student's t-Test is recommended even for a small data, given that the variances of them are unknown and being assumed to be equal [10,11]. Entire process of the test is available in many statistical texts and research papers, [11], [12] [13]. Since this is a standard statistical test, its applications are vast and varied. In the present Study, attempts have been made to distinguish three mineral ores, from each other, through the application of paired sample Student's t-Test and ANOVA test.

DN values of Bauxite were acquired from three mining sites namely Pakhar Pat, Bagru Pat and Chiropatoli in Lohardaga district. Within each mine seven locations were available pertaining to this surface mining activity. DN values of Hematite were acquired from three mining sites namely Chria Mines, Gua Mines and Kiribru mines in West Singhbhum District. Within Chria Mines and Gua Mines each mine had three locations available pertaining to the surface mining activity from Kiriburu mines six locations were obtained DN values of Uranium were acquired from the tailing pond at Jadugora six locations were available pertaining to the surface mining activity in case of Uranium Table 2. This table also gives the geographical locations of these sites from where the surface mineral signatures were taken. The software used to extract the DN Values was ERDAS Imagine version 9.1. Duly geo-coded Satellite data procured for the present Study was a free ware from the USGS web site belonging to Landsat TM sensor that pertained to the year 1989 [14], [15], [16]. For the present study data was based on the availability of the images pertaining to the same time with respect to all these three mineral ores.   Pair wise Student's t-Test The data used for pair wise student's T- Test is given under Table 2 and the methodology used in discrimination of the DN values is as given in Fig. 4.

Table 2. Data used for Pair wise Student's t-Test DN Values and locations identified from the graphic screen on a standard FCC display of Landsat TM data

Sl.NO		LOCATION		DN VALUES			
		LOCATIONS OF BAUXITE FROM LOHARDAGA DISTRICT (All the data used is of the year 1989)					
	PLACE	**LONGITUDE**	**LATITUDE**	**B1**	**B2**	**B3**	**B4**
1	PAKHAR PAT	84°35'52.00" E	23°33' 47.74"N	92	52	75	81
2		84°35'46.18"E	23°34' 21.03"N	58	26	32	39
3		84°36'15.25"E	23°22' 22.17"N	72	38	58	57
4		84°36'22.83"E	23°32'26.17"N	66	37	60	56
5		84°36'28.04"E	23°32'29.16"N	69	41	67	68
6		84°36'30.74"E	23°32'22.94"N	69	38	59	63
7		84°36'07.58"E	23°31'19.31"N	68	38	60	55
	PLACE	**LONGITUDE**	**LATITUDE**	**B1**	**B2**	**B3**	**B4**
8	BAGRU PAT	84°35'48.47"E	23°29'13.10"N	76	44	64	76
9		84°35'58.70"E	23°29'24.87"N	78	43	71	66
10		84°36'10.02"E	23°29'24.32"N	76	43	69	66
11		84°36'09.88"E	23°29'12.25"N	71	46	74	68
12		84°36'06.45"E	23°29'08.87"N	79	50	84	78
13		84°36'06.64"E	23°29'05.00"N	87	53	82	73
14		84°35'59.28"E	23°29'00.56"N	87	73	51	68
	PLACE	**LONGITUDE**	**LATITUDE**	**B1**	**B2**	**B3**	**B4**
15	CHROPATOLI	84°28'06.12"E	23°22'49.34"N	69	40	69	64
16		84°28'05.84"E	23°22'51.87"N	72	40	66	61
17		84°2816.13"E	23°22'41.25"N	69	42	69	72
18		84°28'11.83"E	23°22'38.22"N	67	40	71	71
19		84°28'09.10"E	23°22'37.12"N	68	42	70	69
20		84°29'44.39"E	23°22'25.76"N	69	41	63	59
21		84°29'32.09"E	23°22'22.18"N	65	37	55	65
		LOCATIONS OF HAEMETITE FROM WEST SINGHBHUM DISTRICT					
	PLACE	**LONGITUDE**	**LATITUDE**	**B1**	**B2**	**B3**	**B4**
22	CHIRIA MINES	85°16'04.77"E	22°17'20.37"N	70	27	36	37
23		85°16'13.40"E	22°16'34.59"N	70	30	37	39
24		85°16'11.73"E	22°16'24.57"N	73	30	35	32

Table 3. *(continued)*

		LOCATION		DN VALUES			
	PLACE	LONGITUDE	LATITUDE	B1	B2	B3	B4
25	GUA MINES	85°21'51.89"E	22°12'44.16"N	75	32	41	40
26		85°21'20.18"E	22°12'36.54"N	75	32	40	40
27		85°20'58.46"E	22°12'17.77"N	70	29	31	41
		LOCATION		DN VALUES			
28	KIRIBURU MINES	85°16'07.05"E	22°04'29.78"N	68	30	36	33
29		85°15'55.77"E	22°04'01.31"N	69	27	31	26
30		85°15'24.45"E	22°04'01.81"N	71	30	35	33
31		85°15'12.81"E	22°03'35.71"N	69	29	38	23
32		85°15'15.12"E	22°03'07.36"N	68	27	28	41
33		85°15'42.09"E	22°03'23.59"N	67	28	27	39
LOCATIONS OF URANIUM FROM EAST SINGHBHUM DISTRICT							
	PLACE	LONGITUDE	LATITUDE	B1	B2	B3	B4
34	JADUGORA MINES	86°20'17.06"E	22°39'28.365"N	109	52	59	53
35		86°20'19.64"E	22°39'25.98"N	99	48	53	48
36		86°20'05.32"E	22°39'29.31"N	91	43	51	47
37		86°20'20.87"E	22°39'21.98"N	95	44	51	47
38		86°20'04.92"E	22°39'28.55"N	89	41	41	36
39		86°19'44.93"E	22°39'32.98"N	83	41	46	46

After display of the data, in standard FCC format, 39 locations relating to available signatures of ore extraction of these three minerals were identified from the graphic screen. Associated DN Values of four spectral bands, termed as B1, B2, B3 and B4, were recorded This data was collected using Digital Image Processing S/w Erdas Imagine (Ver. 9.1).

Student's t-Test was applied to the DN values associated with all above locations of surface mining activities. The advantage of Student's t-Test distribution is that it may be applied to a smaller sample size to compare the calculated value of t (t_{CAL}) with its tabular value (t_{TABLE}) at certain level of significance and degrees of freedom, 'df'. If t_{CAL} exceeds t_{TABLE} the value of t is significant and null hypothesis is rejected, i.e. all the samples come from different population. [17], [18]. Given the two paired sets X_i and Y_i of 'n' measured values, the paired sample Student's t-Test determines as to whether they differ from each other in a significant way or not, under a pre-conceived assumption that the paired differences are independent and identically normally distributed.

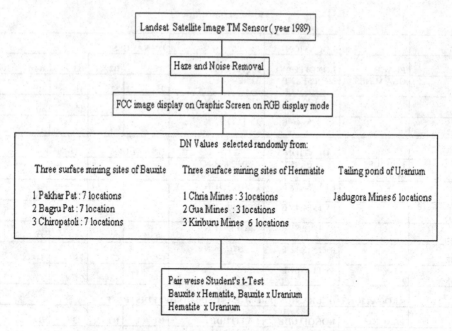

Fig. 4. Methodology used for Pair wise Student's t- Test

To apply the test, let

$$\hat{X}_i = (X_i - \bar{X}) \tag{1}$$

$$\hat{Y}_i = (Y_i - \bar{Y}) \tag{2}$$

Then, t is defined by eq. (3)

$$\text{i.e., } t = (\bar{X} - \bar{Y})\sqrt{\frac{n(n-1)}{\sum_{i=1}^{n}(\hat{X}_i - \hat{Y}_i)^2}} \tag{3}$$

This statistic has degrees of freedom. A table of Student's *t*-distribution confidence intervals is used to determine the significance level at which two distributions differ. This statistical approach was taken up to distinguish the features which look same on the graphic screen.

A. ANOVA Test

ANOVA test was performed to compare variations between parameters of the surface mining features of these three minerals assuming that the Null Hypothesis is true, i.e. all surface mining activities correspond to a single mineral with 95% confidence. The data pertaining to the test is summarized in Table 3.

Table 3. ANOVA Test Data - DN Values and locations identified from the graphic screen on a standard FCC display of Landsat TM data

Sl. No.	LOCATIONS w.r.t. THE SIGNATURES OF BAUXITE MINING IN LOHARDAGA DISTRICT						
		Location		DN Values			
	Place	LONGITUDE	LATITUDE	B1	B2	B3	B4
1	Bagru *Pat*	84°35'48.47"E	23°29'13.10"N	76	44	64	76
2		84°36'09.88"E	23°29'12.25"N	71	46	74	68
3		84°36'06.64"E	23°29'05.00"N	87	53	82	73
	LOCATIONS w.r.t. THE SIGNATURES OF HAEMETITE MINING IN WEST SINGHBHUM DISTRICT						
	PLACE	LONGITUDE	LATITUDE	B1	B2	B3	B4
4	CHIRIA MINES	85°16'04.77"E	22°17'20.37"N	70	27	36	37
5		85°16'13.40"E	22°16'34.59"N	70	30	37	39
6		85°16'11.73"E	22°16'24.57"N	73	30	35	32
		LOCATION		DN VALUES			
	LOCATIONS w.r.t. THE SIGNATURES OF URANIUM MINING EAST SINGHBHUM DISTRICT						
	PLACE	LONGITUDE	LATITUDE	B1	B2	B3	B4
7	JADUGORA MINES	86°20'17.06"E	22°39'28.365"N	109	52	59	53
8		86°20'19.64"E	22°39'25.98"N	99	48	53	48
9		86°20'05.32"E	22°39'29.31"N	91	43	51	47

There were three groups of mineral ores, i.e. Bauxite, Hematite and Uranium. Each of these mineral has 3 locations corresponding to three different geographical place. The test was performed both within the groups and then amongst the group. The structure of the ANOVA is summarized in Table 4.

Table 4. V: Structure of ANOVA table

Structure of ANOVA Table

Sources of Variations	Degrees of Freedom	Sum of Squares	Variance	Variance Ratio
1 Between Places				
2 Locations within Places				
3 Between Bands				
4 Places x Bands				
5 Error Contribution				

In the table the variance is calculated by dividing the Sum of squares by the degrees of freedom. The variance ratio is compared with the Table value of F ratio. If the calculated F value exceeds the Table value then the null hypothesis is rejected and there exists a significant difference between the variables.

4   Result and Discussions

The results of pair wise Student's t- Test is summarized in Table 5.

Table 5. Surface mining signals discriminated on the basis of paired sample Students t-Test

Sl. No.	Pairs between minerals	Pairs tested between Locations	No. of Pairs tested between Locations	Pairs showing $t_{cal} > t_{table}$ at 95% confidence level	% of pairs discriminated	Overall discriminitation among minerals
1	Bauxite with Uranium	Pakhar Pat with Jadugora mines	42	36	85.71	95.24%
		Bagru Pat with Jadugora mines	42	42	100	
		Chiropatolit with Jadugora mines	42	42	100	
2	Hematite with Uranium	Chria mines Jadugora mines	18	2	11.11	11.11%
		Gua mines with Jadugora mines	18	3	16.67	
		Kiriburui with Jadugora mines	36	3	8.33	
3	Bauxite with Hematite	Pakhar Pat with Chria mines	21	18	85.71	79.37%
		Pakhar Pat with Gua mines	21	18	85.71	
		Pakhar Pat with Kiriburu mines	42	36	85.71	
	Bauxite with Hematite	Bagru Pat with Chria mines	21	9	42.86	
		Bagru Pat with Gua mines	21	16	76.19	
		Bagru Pat with Kiriburu mines	42	19	45.23	
	Bauxite with Hematite	Chiropatoli with Chiria mines	21	21	100	
		Chiropatoli with Gua mines	21	21	100	
		Chiropatoli with Kiriburu mines	42	42	100	

Three set of pairs were tested for null hypothesis.

(1) 126 pairs of Bauxite with Uranium were tested out of which 120 pairs (95.24%) $t_{CAL} > 0.05$ indicated they are drawn from different populations.
(2) 72 pairs of Hematite with Uranium were tested out of which 7 pairs (11.11%) $t_{CAL} > 0.05$ indicated they are drawn from different populations.
(3) 252 pairs of Bauxite with Hematite were tested out of which 200 pairs (79.37%) $t_{CAL} > 0.05$ indicated they are drawn from different populations.

Table 6. ANOVA between Bauxite locations (within Bauxite group) (* highly significant results)

Sl no	Sources of Variations between	Degrees of Freedom	Sum of Squares	Variance	Variance Ratio
1	Places	2	1714.3570	857.179	4.6
2	Location within places	18	3349.9286	186.107	11.896
3	Bands	3	11428.7024	3809.567	242.9726*
4	Places and Bands	6	240.4048	40.067	2.56
5	Error Contribution	54	846.6428	15.679	-
6	Total	83	17580.0357	211.808	-

Table 7. ANOVA between Hematite locations (within Hematite group) (* highly significant results)

Sl no	Sources of Variations between	Degrees of Freedom	Sum of Squares	Variance	Variance Ratio
1	Places	2	187.2222	93.8611	7.3939
2	Location within places	6	76.1667	12.6945	1.7332
3	Bands	3	9750.3056	3250.10185	443.7544*
4	Places and Bands	6	125.61113	20.9352	2.8584
5	Error Contribution	18	131.8333	7.3241	-
6	Total	35	10271.6389	134.8149	-

Table 8. ANOVA between Bauxite, Hematite and Uranium. (Between groups of Bauxite, Hematite and Uranium group) (*highly significant results)

Sl no	Sources of Variations between	Degrees of Freedom	Sum of Squares	Variance	Variance Ratio
1	Places	2	4130.3889	2065.1945	288.3701*
2	Location within places	6	429.6667	71.6111	5.3
3	Bands	3	8414.75	2804.9167	207.77*
4	Places and Bands	6	2024.5000	337.4167	24.9938
5	Error Contribution	18	243.0000	13.5	-
6	Total	35			-

Table 6, Table 7 and Table 8 are summarizing the results of ANOVA analysis within and between the groups.

Comparisons of calculated variance ratio with standard F - distribution table values indicate the following that within groups or between the groups the variance between the bands is very significant. This is indicative of the fact that identification of features through remote sensing images is distinctly based on their spectral characters which are distinct in characteristic. The results of ANOVA within minerals indicate that there is not much significance difference within the groups of same minerals. Calculated variance values between the three different mineral groups are very high. This is indicative of the fact that there is a significant variation between the minerals as the variance ratio exceeds the table values, i.e between Bauxite, Hematite and Uranium.

5   Conclusions

Paired sample Student's t-Test could discriminate the surface mining signals between pairs of Bauxite with Uranium and Bauxite with Hematite. The Hematite ore could not be distinguished from Uranium based on the surface mining signals (DN Values). Application of ANOVA test further refined the results whereby a significant variance was observed between the bands in all the cases of within or between the groups of minerals. Statistical analysis of variance was able to discriminate between minerals, through ANOVA test. Though on the graphic screen the surface mining activity does not distinguish the mineral ores. ANOVA test discriminates surface features at the first instance, yet the interpretation of the results can further be corroborated by supplementing it with geologic information. This study may be found useful for the organisation like Indian Bureau of Mines (IBM) and their various counterparts in different countries involved in assessment of different types and categories of minerals. Further, the same analogy could be applied to all similar looking objects on the graphic screen but having differences in reality on ground. The use of image on an IHS (intensity, hue, saturation) [19] transformation and the use of hyperspectral data will further be a refinement to the study in future [20].

References

1. Nelkon, M., Parker, P.: Advanced level physics, 6th edn. Gulab Vazirani, New Delhi (1990)
2. Jensen, J.R.: Introductory digital image processing, 2nd edn. Prentice Hall, New Jersey (1996)
3. Pillai, R.N.S., Bhgavathi: Practical statistics. S. Chand and company, New Delhi (2010)
4. Le, W., Sousa Wayne, P.: Distinguishing mangrove species with laboratory measurements of hyperspectral leaf reflectance. Int. J. of Remote Sensing 30(5), 1267–1281 (2009)
5. Ihse, M.: Vegetation mapping and landscape changes. GIS-modelling and analysis of vegetation transitions, forest limits and expected future forest expansion. Norwegian J. of Geography 64(1), 76 (2010)
6. Zhang, W., Wang, W.: 'Landslide occurring probability decision based on remote sensing and quantification theory. In: The Int. Archives of the Photogrammetry, Remote Sensing and Spatial Information Sciences, Beijing, vol. XXXVII, Part B8 (2008)
7. Hassan, E.A., Elmar, C.: Integration of remote sensing, GIS and terrestrial forest inventory in estimation of acacia senegal tree parameters. In: Reuter, R. (ed.) Remote Sensing for Science, Education and Natural and Cultural Heritage. EARSeL (2010)

8. Cho, M.A., Sobhan, I., Skidmore, A.K., de Leeuw, J.: Discriminating species using hyperspectral indices at leaf and canopy scales. In: The Int. Archives of the Photogrammetry, Remote Sensing and Spatial Information Sciences, Beijing, vol. XXXVII, Part B7, pp. 369–376 (2008)
9. Vaiphasa, C.: Remote sensing techniques for mangrove mapping. Ph D thesis, ITC, The Neatrerlands (2006)
10. Lane, D.M.: Hyperstat online statistics textbook, http://davidmlane.com/hyperstat/.2007
11. Clark, M., Cooke, D.: A basic course in statistics. ELBS, Great Britain (1992)
12. Gupta, S.C., Kapoor, V.K.: Fundamental of Mathematical Statistics. S. Chand and Sons, New Delhi (1980)
13. Das, N.C.: General computational relation between t and F-Ratios. J. of the Bihar Mathematical Soc. 18, 18–22 (1997)
14. USGS 2009, Global Land Survey, 1975 TM 30m scene L4139045_04519890110 USGS, Sioux Falls, South Dakota
15. USGS 2009, Global Land Survey, 1975 TM 30m scene L4141044_04419890124 USGS, Sioux Falls, South Dakota
16. USGS 2009, Global Land Survey, 1975 TM 30m scene P141r045_5dt19891031_z44 USGS, Sioux Falls, South Dakota
17. Bancroft, G., O'Sullivan, G.: Maths and statistics for accounting and business studies, 2nd edn. McGraw-Hill Book Company, London (1988)
18. Reed III, J.F.: Contributions to two-sample statistics. J. Applied Statistics 32(1), 37–44 (2005)
19. Lillesand, T.M., Kiefer, R.W.: Remote sensing and image interpretation, pp. 579–584. John Willey and sons, Inc., New York (1994)
20. Vaiphasa, C., Ongsomwang, S., Vaiphasa, T.: Tropical mangrove species discrimination using hyperspectral data: A laboratory study. Estuarine, Coastal and Shelf Science 65, 371–379 (2005)

Design Space Exploration for High Availability drFPGA Based Embedded Systems

S. Chakraverty[1], Anubhav Agarwal[1], Amogh Agarwal[1], Anil Kumar[2], and Abhinav Sikri[1]

[1] Netaji Subhas Institute of Technology, Delhi University, New Delhi, India
{shampa,anubhav929,amogh.aggarwal,abhinavsikri23}@gmail.com
[2] Igate Computer Systems Ltd. NSEZ Noida, India
anil.ksingh@igate.com

Abstract. Dynamically reconfigurable FPGAs are being deployed for real time systems that not only adapt to run-time changes in the system load but also reconfigure their resources to minimize the adverse impact of faults. In this paper, we propose a systematic methodology for conducting a *Design Space Exploration* (DSE) of high availability mission-critical real time systems. Armed with abundant reconfigurable resources on the FPGA estate, the central challenge in this system design problem is to endow each task with the right degree of fault tolerance so as to sustain the most important services throughout the mission's life.

Our scheme employs a two-stage strategy to tackle faults online: A suite of passive online *Fault Tolerant* (FT) techniques provide immediate mitigation when faults strike in order to sustain the required functionality. Next, a pre-planned fault diagnosis and repair procedure analyzes the faulty modules offline to localize them and, if required utilizes spare resources to recover from hard faults. The repaired modules are re-engaged to restore the original FT configurations. We employ a *Genetic Algorithm* (GA) to evolve a population of chromosomes representing a set of FT architectures for the given application. Experiments conducted on large representative task graphs reveal that the DSE system is able to steer the population towards high availability architectural solutions with potential tradeoff between area usage and availability.

Keywords: Reconfigurable computing, Fault tolerance, Availability, Diagnosis and Repair, Design Space Exploration, Genetic Algorithm.

1 Introduction

With Moore's Law serving as beacon light, leaps and bounds in VLSI technology has re-embellished the FPGA real estate with a denser array of reconfigurable resources. Mission-critical systems utilize dynamically reconfigurable FPGAs (drFPGA) to support their complex functionality and to maximum system availability. FPGAs are vulnerable to *Single Event Effects* (SEEs) that occur when high-energy ionic particles that are produced by radiation, strike on the FPGA surface [1]. The challenge lies in designing an intelligently tailored computing system so that crucial services remain available even in the presence of faults. In this paper, we propose a *Design Space*

A. Ell Hassanien et al. (Eds.): AMLTA 2012, CCIS 322, pp. 234–243, 2012.
© Springer-Verlag Berlin Heidelberg 2012

Exploration (DSE) methodology that scans through alternative FT architectures in a guided manner and automatically endows the right degree of fault tolerance to each functional module of a real time application, keeping in view the user's availability prioritization of various services in the fully as well as partly functional states.

We give a bird's eye view of related prior work in section 2. In section 3, we present the design environment. In section 4, we elaborate upon the FT techniques and the diagnostic-repair process utilized by the fault management system. We describe the working of the GA-based DSE tool in section 5. We present experimental results in section 6 and conclude in section 7.

2   Prior Work

Fault tolerance in FPGAs is a richly researched area. Parris and Sharma give a classification of the range of FPGA FT techniques garnered from the literature and compare them in terms of FPGA area overheads, impact on throughput, fault detection latency and recovery time [2]. The authors have classified user-initiated FT techniques into passive methods such as online *Triple Modular Redundancy* (TMR), and active methods that either depend upon pre-planned allocation of resources [3, 4] or entail dynamic resource allocation [5].

Emmert *et al.* provide logic fault tolerance by first detecting faulty logic in a column/row intersection area by carrying out online *Built In Self Test* (BIST) using roving *Self Test Areas* (STARs) and then circumventing the detected faults by either reusing faulty logic or by trying out alternative reconfigurations or by stealing area from the STARs themselves [5]. In [6], the authors use a top-level software layer to monitor the performance of the underlying FPGA self-healing layer and make runtime decisions about the degree of fault tolerance needed to counter the prevalent environmental fault rate. In [7], the authors propose EAC/EVC (Empty Area/Volume Compactness) heuristics to efficiently utilize free area between permanently damaged FPGA areas during task placement, thereby improving computation density. In [8], the authors generate a tree-type database of FT structures on FPGAs and assess their structural reliability for air-craft applications. In [9], the authors propose a GA driven scheme for fault tolerant evolvable hardware design by employing process level, structural and multi-version redundancy. In [10] Brian Pratt *et al.* use multiple pipelined TMRs that vote at higher frequency in order to recuperate from higher *Multiple Independent Upset* (MIU) rates to achieve higher reliability than what is possible by simple TMR.

From the above discussion, it is clear that a plethora of FT techniques exist for drFPGA based system design. Most authors have either utilized passive methods such as TMR or active methods such as dynamic spare allocation to cope with faulty conditions. There is a need to analyze how different techniques can be profitably used in conjunction for a set of real time tasks with varying criticality levels and at given fault rates so as to boost overall system availability. Mission-oriented systems also need to plan beforehand what proportion of the reconfigurable resources should be reserved as replacement spares to suffice their lifetime. We address these critical issues in this paper.

3   Design Environment

The FT drFPGA system's design environment comprises the target application, its qualitative requirements, fault characteristics and the available FPGA area.

A) **Application Model:** The application is modelled as an acyclic, periodic, partially ordered *Task Precedence Graph* (TPG). The nodes of the TPG represent its functional tasks and its edges represent the communication tasks. The node and edge weights represent the execution times and data transfer times respectively. The primary outputs represent the services of the application. Their deadlines and availability importance are specified. A hierarchical task graph that we experimented on is shown in Figure 3b.

B) **Fault Model:** We assume that faults arise only due to external disturbances, called *Single Event Effects* (SEE). Fault occurrences are *i.i.d.* Poisson distributed random variables spaced apart enough in time to allow timely repairs. The most common SEEs are *Single Event Upsets* (SEUs) which are *Soft* errors that can be recovered by *scrubbing* [1]. Soft errors can lead to *Single Bit Upsets* (SBUs) that affect a single module or they may cause *Multiple Bit Upsets* (MBUs) whose effect can span nearby modules. *Hard* SEEs (H) cannot be recovered and must be *repaired by replacement* with spare resources [1]. Other than these stable faults, transient faults (T) may occur.

C) **Availability Model:** A Continuous Time Markov Chain (CTMC) describes the system states and probabilistic transitions between them. Initially, the system exists in the *Fully Operational (FO)*. On encountering faults the system may (i) still retain its full functionality but reduce its ability to tolerate another fault - such a state is *Fully Functional (FF)*(ii) enter a *Partially Functional (PF)* state in which some of its primary outputs (services) may become unavailable and its FT capabilities may degrade as well. After due repairs, the system finally returns to its *FO* state.

Each service has an associated *Importance-of-Availability IoA$_{po}$*. The availability of the system in state k is :

$$IoA_k = \frac{\sum_{x:\, po_x\, is\, available}(IoA_k(po_x))}{IoA_{FO}} \tag{1}$$

D) **Task Failure Rates:** The failure rate of a specific task on the FPGA depends upon its area and its active period. Let us denote the environmental fault rate as $\lambda_{env}^x : x \in \{T, SBU, MBU, H\}$. Let $T_{turnaround}$ be the total time for one complete invocation of the TPG and let η_{safety} denotes a safety margin to accommodate a larger than average fault striking rate. Let the area occupied by a *single* module of task k be $area_k$ and its total execution time be Tex_k. Then the per unit failure rate λ_k of task k is given by the formula below:

$$\lambda_k^x = \lambda_{env}^x \times \frac{area_k}{Area_{FPGA}} \times \frac{Tex_k}{T_{turnaround}} \times \eta_{safety} \tag{2}$$

The total single fault rate λ_k^S is the sum of the rates for all sources of single faults *viz.* transient, SBU and hard faults:

$$\lambda_k^S = \lambda_k^T + \lambda_k^{SBU} + \lambda_k^H \tag{3}$$

MBUs are the only source of multiple faults. A sequence of MBU faults can affect co-located replicated modules of a task in TMR configuration. The failure rate of multiple faults for task k is λ_k^{MBU}.

E) **Task Area:** A task is a composite functional unit that occupies a rectangular area on the drFPGA and has a fixed execution time. The total area of the task depends upon its assigned FT configuration and includes all its redundant units (modules), voter/comparator circuits, pre-allocated local spare resources and internal routing. A task's configuration bit-map is stored in the Flash ROM along with its pre-computed Cyclic Redundancy Check - the *golden CRC*.

4   Fault Management System (FMS)

The FMS performs the following three functions:

1. *Fault detection:* Faults must be detected as soon as possible after occurrence.
2. *Ad-hoc mitigation:* This step provides immediate mitigation from the deleterious effects of faults.
3. *Recovery:* This step locates and diagnoses fault ridden modules and repairs them in offline mode to restore the original fully operational state.

4.1   Fault Detection and Ad-Hoc Mitigation Techniques

The DSE system decides one of the following FT techniques for each task to perform the first two functions of the FMS.

A. *TMR with one Spare (TMR-S):* Three hardware implementations of the same task forward their results to a majority-voter which outputs the majority result. A fourth spare module is kept reserved as a standby and is switched in only when one of the three active modules fails. Figure 1a depicts the CTMC state transitions triggered by an SBU fault. The top line inside each state indicates the system's state and the bottom line indicates the affected task's FT status. The failure rate is initially trebled when there are three active modules. After an SBU occurs, the spare unit is switched in. The system remains fully functional but without any spare. Subsequent repair of the faulty module returns the task to TMR-S.

Figure 1b shows the CTMC transitions triggered by MBU faults. The first fault brings the task's FT level down one level to simple TMR. The next upset degrades the task's FT level to *Duplicate-and-Compare* (DC). Since now there are only two active modules, the fault rate is double that for a single module. Another upset on one of these two active modules causes the system to *remove* the task and all its dependents from the system. As a result some of the primary outputs become unavailable thereby leading the system to a PF state. From each of these states, repair probabilistically returns the system to its previous state.

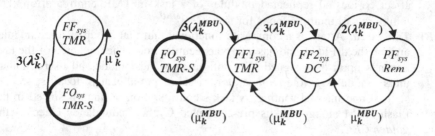

Fig. 1a. State transitions for single faults on task with TMR and one spare

Fig. 1b. State transitions for fault causing MBU errors on task with TMR and one spare

B. *TMR:* A circuit in TMR configuration masks a single SBU so that the system remains *Fully Functional* (FF), but degrades to DC. When an MBU sequence strikes the co-located modules of a TMR task, it first reduces from TMR to DC and then gets isolated from the system. Correspondingly, the system transits from the *Fully Operational* (FO) state to an FF state and then to a PF state. Repair causes transitions in the reverse direction.

C. *Duplicate and Compare (DC):* Two replicated modules of the same task pass their outputs to a comparator that generates an error signal whenever the two results vary. This error signal is utilized to block the erroneous output from propagating to dependent tasks, thus ensuring fail safe system operation. As a result some of the primary outputs that are derived from the affected task remain unavailable. Hence the system enters a *Partially Functional* (PF) state.

4.2   Fault Diagnosis and Repair Procedures

A faulty module is isolated and diagnosed in an offline mode while the remaining system functions normally. The system follows a planned, step by step diagnosis and repair procedure for single and multiple faults.

A. *Planning spare resources for the mission:* Whereas soft faults are recovered by scrubbing, hard faults can be recovered only by replacement. To provision enough spare resources for each task, we need to estimate the number of hard faults it will encounter during the mission's lifetime. Let us assume that the mission time is $T_{mission}$ and the mean time between hard faults is *MTBHF*. Then, the ratio $T_{mission}/MTBHF$ is the average number of times hard faults strikes the FPGA. Depending upon its *total* area $Area_k$ and execution time

Tex_k, a task will encounter a proportionate number of hard faults. The number of spares to be reserved for task k is therefore given by:

$$spares_k = \frac{T_{mission}}{MTBHF} \times \frac{Tex_k}{T_{turnaround}} \times \frac{Area_k}{Area_{FPGA}} \times \eta_{safety} \qquad (4)$$

B. *Diagnosis & repair process for single faults:* The three types of single faults *i.e.* Transient, SBU and Hard faults must be identified and treated separately.

Step 1-Readback: The diagnosis process begins by conducting a partial readback of the affected task, calculating its CRC and comparing it with its stored golden CRC. If this comparison reveals no differences then the fault was obviously transient and repair is not required, otherwise the procedure proceeds to step 2. The time taken for readback of task k is: t_k^{RB}.

Step 2-Partial Scrub and Readback: If a variance is found between the readback CRC and golden CRCs in step 1, the fault is stable. An attempt is now made to remove soft errors by scrubbing the faulty task followed by another readback [12]. The time t_k^{SCRUB} taken to scrub a task k depends on its size. The time to diagnose and repair an SBU is:

$$t_k^{SBU} = 2t_k^{RB} + t_k^{SCRUB} \qquad (5)$$

Step 3-Repair by Replacement: If the second readback in Step 2 still shows a difference between the readback CRC and the golden CRC, then fault is diagnosed to be a non-recoverable hard fault which must be repaired by replacement. Let the time required to replace a faulty resource by a spare one be t_k^{REPL}. The time incurred to diagnose and repair a hard fault is:

$$t_k^H = 2t_k^{RB} + t_k^{SCRUB} + t_k^{REPL} \qquad (6)$$

Overall repair time: Let P_{TRN} and P_{SBU} be the probabilities of occurrence of transient and SBU faults respectively. The average time to diagnose and repair single faults is:

$$t\_rep_k^S = t_k^{RB} + (1 - P_{TRN}).\left((t_k^{RB} + t_k^{SCRUB}) + (1 - P_{SBU}).t_k^{REPL}\right) \qquad (7)$$

The average single fault repair rate μ_k^S is the inverse of $t\_rep_k^S$.

C. *Diagnosis and repair process for multiple faults (MBUs):* MBUs are soft faults. The time taken to locate and recover MBUs in a task is the same as that for repairing an SBU because a single scrub of the task can repair all accumulated bit errors. Therefore:

$$t\_rep_k^{MBU} = 2t_k^{RB} + t_k^{SCRUB} \qquad (8)$$

The *average* MBU repair rate μ_k^M is the inverse of $t\_rep_k^{MBU}$.

D. *System Availability:* A composite CTMC containing all types of transitions discussed afore gives a system of linear equations for steady state operation. This set of simultaneous liner equations is solved to generate the state availabilities $\{A_k\}$. The overall availability of the system is:

$$Avail_{sys} = \sum_{k=1}^{NumStates} A_k \times IoA_k \tag{9}$$

5 GA Based FT Architecture Optimization

Genetic Algorithm is a meta-heuristic that mimics the process of natural evolution of populations of species [13]. They have been used successfully for solving a variety of multidimensional and multi-objective optimization problems [14]. We encode each gene of a chromosome with numeric codes representing the specific fault tolerant scheme adopted for a specific task. An initial population of randomly initialized feasible chromosomes represents a set of alternative FT implementations for the given application. The population is evolved through successive generations using Elitism, Ranking and Generation-gap selection methods and applied single point crossover and mutation.

Constraints and Objectives: A static, non-preemptive, 1dimensional variable-width columnar scheduler that uses deadline laxity based priorities, assigns start times to the tasks and places them on the drFPGA. All deadlines constraints must be fulfilled.

Each chromosome has its own CTMC model which is solved to yield the system availability as given by equation 8. The maximum width of the columns occupied by the task graph at any time during one full invocation of the task graph divided by the FPGA width gives the application's area usage:

$$Area_{sys} = \frac{max_t\{\sum_{i=1}^{N_t} w_{i,t}\}}{W_{FPGA}} \tag{10}$$

Where $w_{i,t}$ is the width of the ith column and N_t is the total number of columns occupied at time t and W_{FPGA} is the total width of the FPGA.

The objective of the DSE system is to maximize the availability of fully functional states and minimize the availability of partly functional states with least area usage. Using input weights W_1, W_2 and W_2, the overall objective function is:

$$OF = W_1 \times Avail_{FF} - W_2 \times Avail_{PF} - W_3 \times Area_{sys} \tag{11}$$

6 Experimental Results

We implemented the DSE scheme using Python programming language and executed the code on an Intel Quad core processor under Windows 7. The experiments were conducted on two artificially synthesized task graphs representative of distinct categories of applications. Task graph TPG_{15} shown in Figure 5 represents a hierarchical application. For a bigger application, we used a highly concurrent task graph TPG_{42}

comprising 42 tasks configured as three loosely coupled applications. The execution times of the tasks, the area of their basic unit and the data volumes transferred between communicating tasks were generated randomly.

A) *Route-to-optimization for TPG$_{42}$:* Using TPG$_{42}$ as input, the GA was launched with a population size of 100, a crossover rate of 0.9, a mutation rate of 0.2 and the objective function *OF* given by Equation 10. The variation of the best fitness and the average fitness values through successive generations is shown in Figure 2a. Elitism ensures that the best fitness remains non-decreasing throughout the evolution process. It reaches convergence at around the 26th generation, giving a best fitness value of 0.873.

B) *Tradeoff between Availability and Area usage:* A plot of *System Availability versus* normalized *Area usage* is shown in Figure 2b. It indicates three non-inferior solutions. While solution 1 yields the best solution in terms of availability but falls short on area usage, solutions 2 and 3 occupy progressively lesser area on the FPGA, but with corresponding reduction in system availability. This shows that the design exploration process yields variegated solutions with tradeoff possibilities between different objectives.

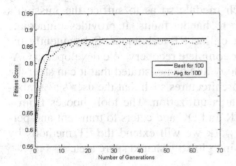   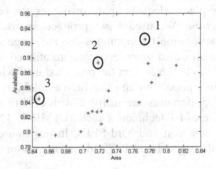

Fig. 2a. Route to optimization showing best and average fitness values along generations for the Task graph TPG$_{42}$

Fig. 3b. Non inferior solutions in terms of *Availability* and *Area usage*, identified in the final population for Task graph TPG$_{42}$

C) *Allocation of FT Levels in TPG$_{15}$:* The aim of this experiment is to investigate how the DSE tool endows each task with its appropriate FT level for high availability applications. We ran the DSE tool for TPG$_{15}$. We first experimentally tuned the genetic parameters. For example Figure 3a shows the optimization routes for two population sizes: 20 and 100. The later clearly gives better results. We derived the best parameters for TPG$_{15}$ to be a population size 100, crossover rate 0.7 and mutation rate 0.4.

Figure 3b shows the FT levels assigned to each task of TPG$_{15}$ for the best chromosome obtained at the end evolution. It illustrates that the tasks responsible for generating the most important outputs were all assigned TMR with spares whereas the remaining tasks contributing to less important services were assigned simple TMR. Thus the DSE system is able to distinguish between services of different criticality.

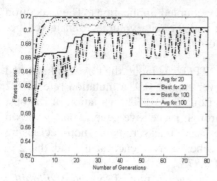 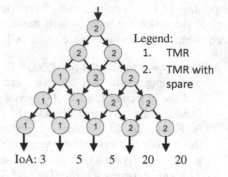

Fig. 3a. Optimization paths for TPG₁₅ for population sizes 100 and 20

Fig. 3b. Assignment of FT levels to the tasks of TPG15 for given IoA weights

7   Conclusion

We presented a DSE scheme that scans through the design space of FT techniques on drFPGAs for realizing mission-oriented real time applications. The system judiciously pre-plans adequate spare resources for each module so as to suffice the mission's lifetime. We used a two-pronged approach to handle faults. It provides immediate amelioration by tapping a diverse range of online FT techniques. Subsequently the pre-allocated spare resources are utilized for complete recovery. We developed a GA-driven tool based on the proposed methodology and demonstrated that it can steer the initial population towards high availability architectures such that the user's availability preferences are fulfilled with effective area utilization. The tool chooses from a suite of FT techniques such as TMR-S, TMR and DC and caters to transient and permanent soft and hard SEEs. In our future work we will extend the FT methods by including online BIST and task migration using globally shared spare area.

References

1. White, D.: Considering surrounding single error events in ASICs, FPGAs and processors, Xilinx WP 402, v1.0 (September 12, 2011)
2. Parris, M.G., Sharma, C.A.: Progress in automatic fault recovery in Field Programmable Gate Arrays. ACM Computing Surveys V(N), Article A (April 2010)
3. Mitra, S., Huang, W.J., Saxena, N.R., Yu, S., McCluskey, E.J.: Reconfigurable computing for autonomous self repair. IEEE Design and Test of Computer 21(3), 228–240 (2004)
4. Lach, J., Mangione-Smith, W.H., Potkonjak, M.: Efficiently supporting fault-tolerance in FPGAs. In: Proceedings of the 1998 ACM/SIGDA Sixth International Symposium on Field Programmable Gate Arrays (FPGA 1998). ACM, New York (1998)
5. Emmert, J.M., Stroud, C.E., Abromovici, M.: Online Fault Tolerance for FPGA Logic Blocks. IEEE Trans. on Very Large Scale Integration (VLSI) Systems, 216–226 (February 2007)

6. Al-Haddad, R., Oreifej, R., Ashraf, A., DeMara, R.F.: Sustainable Modular Adaptive Redundancy Technique Emphasizing Partial Reconfiguration for Reduced Power Consumption. International Journal of Reconfigurable Computing 2011, Article ID 430808, 25 pages (2011), doi:10.1155/2011/430808

7. Iturbe, X., Benkrid, K., et al.: Enabling FPGAs for future deep space exploration missions: improving fault tolerance and computational density with R3TOS. In: Proc. 2011 NASA/ESA Conf. on Adaptive Hardware Systems-AHS 2011, pp. 104–112 (2011)

8. Kharchenku, V.S., Tarasenko, V.V.: The multiversion design technology of an onboard fault tolerant fPGA devices. In: 2001 MAPLD. Johns Hopkins University, Laurel (2001)

9. Shanthi, A.P., Parthasarathi, R.: Exploring FPGA structures for evolving fault tolerant hardware. In: Proc. of the 2003 NASA/Dod Conf. on Evolvable Hardware. IEEE (2003) ISBN 0-7695-1977-6/03

10. Pratt, B., Caffrey, M., et al.: TMR with more frequent voting for improved FPGA reliability. In: Proc. of International Conference on Engineering of Reconfigurable Systems and Algorithms (July 2008)

11. Nace, W., Coopman, P.: A Graceful Degradation Framework for Distributed Embedded Systems. Research showcase. Carnegie Mellon Univ., Inst. for Software Research, http://repository.cmu.edu/isr/668/

12. Wang, Y.C.: Virtex 5QP External configuration management. Xilinx application note XAPP588, v1.0 (January 19, 2012)

13. Goldberg, D.E.: Genetic Algorithms in Search, Optimization, and Machine Learning. Addison-Wesley, Reading (1989)

14. Yang, J., Yang, J.: Intelligence Optimization Algorithms: A Survey. International Journal of Advancements in Computing Technology 3(4) (May 2011)

Part IV

Bioinformatics and Cheminformatics Trends and Applications

LWDOSM: Language for Writing Descriptors of Outline Shape of Molecules

Hamza Hentabli[1,*], Naomie Salim[1], Ammar Abdo[2], and Faisal Saeed[1,3]

[1] Faculty of Computer Science and Information System, Universiti Teknologi Malaysia, Malaysia
[2] Computer Science Department, Hodeidah University, Hodeidah, Yemen
[3] Information Technology Department, Sanhan Community College, Sana'a, Yemen
Hentabli_hamza@yahoo.fr

Abstract. The basic idea underlying similarity searching is the similar property principle, which states that structurally similar molecules will exhibit similar physicochemical and biological properties. In this paper a new language for writing 2D molecular descriptor based on outline shape (LWDOSM) is introduced. LWDOSM is a new method of obtaining a rough description of 2D molecular structure from its 2D connection graph in the form of character string. LWDOSM allows rigorous structure specification using very small and simple-rule. In this paper, we study the possibility of using the textual descriptor for describing the 2D structure of the molecule. Simulated virtual screening experiments with the MDDR database show clearly the superiority of the LWDOSM descriptor compared to many standard descriptors tested in this paper.

Keywords: Molecular database retrieval, Moleculardescriptor, Molecularsimilarity, Structures and substructure searching.

1 Introduction

Graph comparison was used in the early chemical information systems, for structure and substructure searching [1-2]. Structure searching involves searching a chemical database for a particular query structure with the aim of retrieving all the molecules with an exact match to the query structure whereas substructure searching retrieves all molecules that contain the query structure. The equivalence (similarity) between two structures can be achieved by using a graph whilst the substructure searching can be done using sub-graph isomorphism algorithms.

Various isomorphism algorithms have been developed for efficient performance, but they are still too slow for large chemical databases due to their combinational complexities [3]. However, structure and substructure searching were later complemented by another searching mechanism called similarity searching [4]. Similarity searching methods may be the simplest tools for ligand based virtual screening. The basic idea underlying similarity searching is the similar property principle, which states that structurally similar molecules will exhibit similar physicochemical and biological properties [5].Over the years, many ways of measuring the structural

---

* Corresponding author.

A. Ell Hassanien et al. (Eds.): AMLTA 2012, CCIS 322, pp. 247–256, 2012.

similarity of molecules have been introduced [6]. 2D similarity methods can be divided into two classes. The first class is the graph-based similarity methods and the second class is the fingerprint-based similarity methods. The graph-based similarity methods directly compare the molecular structures with each other and identify the similar (or common) substructures. These methods relate the parts of one molecule to parts of the other molecule. They generate a mapping or alignment between molecules. The maximum common substructure (MCS) method is an example of the graph based similarity methods. Another example of a graph based similarity method is the feature tree. Feature trees were introduced by Rarey and Dixon in [7] and are the most abstract way of representing a molecule by means of a graph. A feature tree represents the hydrophobic fragments and functional groups of the molecule and the way these groups are linked together. Each node in the tree is labeled with a set of features representing the chemical properties of the part of the molecule corresponding to the node. The comparison of feature trees is based on matching the sub-trees of two feature trees onto each other. Feature trees allow for similarity searching to be performed against a large database, when combined with fast mapping algorithms [8]. However, the most common similarity approaches use molecules characterized by 2D fingerprints that encode the presence of 2D fragment substructures in a molecule. The similarity between two molecules is then computed using the number of substructure fragments common to a pair of structures and a simple association coefficient [9].

The shape similarity between two molecules can be determined by comparing the shapes of those molecules, finding the overlap volume between them and then using a similarity measure (e.g. Tanimoto) to calculate the similarity between the molecules. However, most of the works in shape-based similarity approaches have depended on the 3D molecular shape [10]. Recently, the use of field-based or shape-based approacheshas been increased [11]. The shape comparison program Rapid Overlay of Chemical Structures (ROCS) [12] is used to perceive similarity between molecules based on their 3D shape. The objective of this approach is to find molecules with similar bioactivity to a target molecule but with different chemotypes, i.e. scaffold hopping. However, a disadvantage of 3D similarity methods is that the conformational properties of the molecules should be considered and therefore these methods are more computationally intensive than methods based on 2D structure representation. The complexity increases considerably if conformational flexibility is taken into account. In 2D structure representation, the molecular structure is represented by a large number of structural descriptors in a numerical form (integer or real). Among these, descriptors computed based on a molecule graph are widely used in modeling physical, chemical, or biological properties. The simplest 2D descriptors are based on simple counts of features such as hydrogen donors, hydrogen bond acceptors, ring systems (such as aromatic rings) and rotatable bonds, whereas the complex 2D descriptors are computed from complex mathematical equations such as 2D fingerprints and topological indices [13-14]. Theycharacterize molecular structures according to their size, degree of branching and overall shape where the structural diagram of molecules is considered as a mathematical graph, but not the contour of molecule shape.

Due to the multi-faceted nature of biological activities, there is a high possibility that there are no single and best molecular descriptor that can uniquely represent the molecules [15].This possibility has encouraged many researchers to continue to develop new molecular descriptors. Therefore, developing new molecular descriptors that can give a comparable or better result than the existing descriptors for drug discovery programmers is highly desirable.

In this paper, we introduced a new shape-based molecular descriptor (LWDOSM) that was inspired by research in information retrieval on the use of contour-based shape descriptor for image retrieval systems [16]. LWDOSM is a new method to obtain a rough description of the 2-D molecular structure from its outline shape. LWDOSM is a textual descriptor which allows rigorous structure specification by use of a very small and natural grammar.

2   Materials and Methods

The new descriptor LWDOSM is a textual descriptor using printable characters for representing molecules based on their shapes. In this paper, the outline shape (for the whole molecule) and the internal region (inside molecule rings) are exploited to calculate a rough description of the 2-D structure molecule. The proposed method uses a connection table to extract the information needed to represent the molecule shape. A specific language has been developed to describe the shape features; descriptors written in this language are invariants to scale change and rotation. LWDOSM is a true language, albeit with a simple vocabulary (atom and bond symbols) and only a few grammar rules. However, part of the power of the LWDOSM is that it is highly sensitive to molecular structure changes. In this work, the graph denotes the 2D molecular structure. This is essentially the 2D image chemists draw to describe the molecule. Here, only the labeled molecular graph (i.e. atoms and bonds) and all possible paths between every atom pair are taken into account.

A corresponding shape to a 2D molecule structure is generally composed by a main region (representing the outline shape) and one or many internal regions (representing areas inside rings) obtained after visiting all the atoms in the connection table of a molecule. In addition to the geometry of its outline, we take into account the geometry and the position of its internal regions. This additional information for shape description is important to identify and represent the molecule rings in the LWDOSM descriptor context. It is also very useful for shape comparison in the similarity calculation between two molecules from their 2D graph.

The process of generating the shape descriptor of any molecule starts with determining the top left atom in the molecule graph. The atom name is represented in the descriptor as the grammar described below. Then, we move in a clockwise direction to the next atom. The bond type and direction of the movement are represented before we visit and represent the next atom. The same procedure is repeated until we visit again the starting atom.

Once the starting atom is visited again, the description of the outline shape of the molecule graph is completed. The atoms and bonds within the internal regions (rings) need to be visited again to represent the internal region. However, the process of generating the LWDOSM is composed of a number of specification rules as explained below.

The language used for writing the LWDOSM descriptor consists of a series of characters and symbols. There are five generic encoding rules corresponding to the specification of atoms, bonds, ring closure, direction angle and disconnected parts. Some of these rules are similar to the rules used in SMILES strings [17]. Atoms are represented by their atomic symbols, usually two characters. The second character of the atomic symbol must be entered in lower case. If the atomic symbol is just one letter we add a blank space to the end of the atomic symbol, e.g., "Br", "C1","N ", "O ".

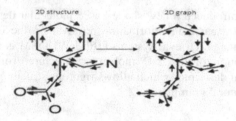

Fig. 1. The external and internal visiting movement in a 2D graph

The single, double, and triple bonds are represented by the symbols "-", "=", and "#", respectively. The internal regions (rings or cycles structures) are specified by enclosing their description in parentheses (Figure 2 for example).

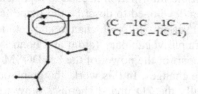

Fig. 2. Example of the representation of internal regions (cyclic structures)

The direction angle of the molecule shape boundary can be calculated using four directions ranges between 0 and 3 based on the value of the angle, as shown in Figure 3.

Angle Degree	Symbols	Example
0 ° -90°	0	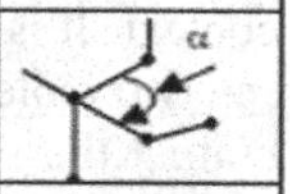
91- 180°	1	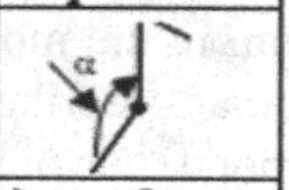
181 ° - 270	2	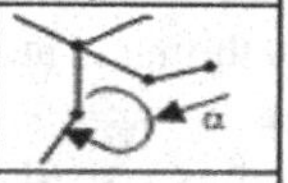
271 ° - 360 °	3	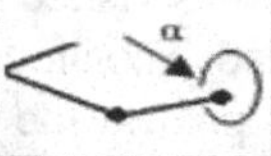

Fig. 3. Angle Direction

If the molecule graph is composed of more than one part (disconnected structures), the description of the disconnected compound is written as individual structures separated by "." (Period) as shown in Figure 4.

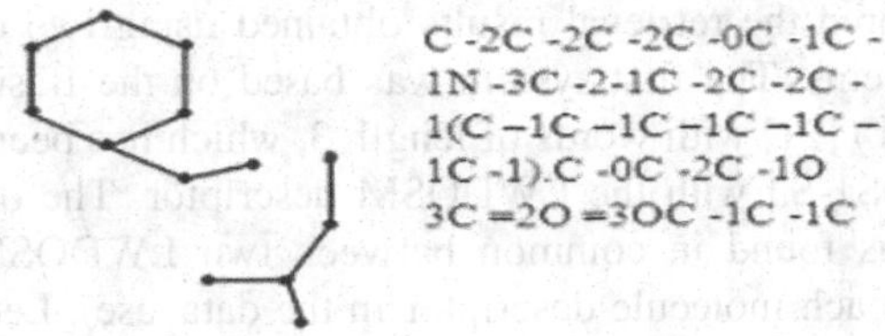

```
C -2C -2C -2C -0C -1C -
1N -3C -2-1C -2C -2C -
1(C -1C -1C -1C -1C -
1C -1).C -0C -2C -1O
3C =2O =3OC -1C -1C
```

Fig. 4. The disconnect parts representation

3   Experimental Design

In this section, we present experiments that show the usefulness of the new descriptor LWDOSM, when used for similarity-based virtual screening. To evaluate the LWDOSM descriptor, LWDOSM was compared with six different descriptors (fingerprints) from Scitegic's Pipeline Pilot[18] and PaDEL-descriptor [19]software. These were 120-bit ALOGP, 166-bit MACCS and 1024-bit Path fingerprints (EPFP4) from Scitegic's Pipeline Pilot and 1024-bit CDK (CDKFP), 1024-bit CDK graph only (GOFP), and 881-bit Pubchem fingerprints (PCFP) from the PaDEL software.

Experiments were conducted over the most popular cheminformatics database: the MDL Drug Data Report (MDDR) [11] which has been used in our previous studies [20]. This database consisted of 102516 molecules and contains 11 activity classes, which involve structurally homogeneous and heterogeneous actives, as shown in Table 1. Each row in the tables contains an activity class, the number of molecules belonging to the class, and the diversity of the class, which was computed as the mean pairwise Tanimoto similarity calculated across all pairs of molecules in the class.

Table 1. MDDR Activity Classes for MDDR Data Set

Activity Index	Activityclass	Active molecules	Pairwise similarity mean
31420	renin inhibitors	1130	0.290
71523	HIV protease inhibitors	750	0.198
37110	thrombin inhibitors	803	0.180
31432	angiotensin II AT1 antagonists	943	0.229
42731	substance P antagonists	1246	0.149
06233	substance P antagonists	752	0.140
06245	5HT reuptake inhibitors	359	0.122
07701	D2 antagonists	395	0.138
06235	5HT1A agonists	827	0.133
78374	protein kinase C inhibitors	453	0.120
78331	cyclooxygenase inhibitors	636	0.108

This study compared the retrieval results obtained using two different similarity-based screening systems. The first system was based on the Basic Local Alignment Search Tool (BLAST) [21] with words of length 3, which has been used to search the different data sets DS1-S3 with the LWDOSM descriptor. The output of BLAST is the number of words found in common between two LWDOSM descriptors (e.g. query molecule and each molecule descriptor in the database). Let A∩B and A∪B is the number of words in common and the total number of words in descriptors of molecules A and B, respectively. The similarity score SA;B for molecules A and B is then given by:

$$S_{A,B} = \frac{A \cap B}{A \cup B - A \cap B} \tag{1}$$

The second screening system was based on the Tanimoto (TAN) coefficient, which has been used for ligand based virtual screening for many years and which can hence be considered as a reference standard. TAN was used with six types of descriptors (fingerprints) in this study.

The screening experiments were performed with 10 reference structures selected randomly from each activity class. The recall results were averaged over each such set of active molecules, where the recall is the percentage of the actives retrieved in the top-1% or the top-5% of the ranked list resulting from a similarity search.

4   Results and Discussion

The main objective of this work is to identify the possibility of using the LWDOSM descriptor in similarity-based virtual screening and then identifying the retrieval effectiveness of using such a descriptor. In this study, we compared the retrieval effectiveness of LWDOSM against six different types of descriptors on the MDDR database. Selecting the best descriptors is based on their use in predicting the property/activity of a molecule from another molecule that is considered similar to it, either by using a certain similarity method, clustering or using its k-nearest neighbours [22].For those descriptors, and for predicting the activity class of molecules, the best descriptors are those yielding the highest number of correct predictions (molecules with similar activity class), taking into account the total number of molecules having that activity class in the database used.The results for the searches of MDDR are shown in Tables 2-3, using cutoffs of both 1% and 5% respectively.

Each row in a table corresponds to one activity class; shows the recall for the top 1% and 5% of a sorted ranking when averaged over the ten searches for this activity class. The penultimate row in a table corresponds to the mean value for that descriptor when averaged over all of the activity classes for a dataset. The descriptor with the best recall rate in each row is strongly shaded, and the recall value is bold-faced, any descriptor with an average recall within 5% of the value for the best descriptor is shown lightly shaded. The bottom row in a table corresponds to the total number of shaded cells for each descriptor type across the full set of activity classes.

Table 2. Retrieval results of top 1% for data set MDDR

Activity Index	LWDOSM	GRFP	PCFP	ALOGP	MACCS	EPFP4	CDKFP
31420	73.21	12.17	26.13	22.06	28.65	34.75	41.8
71523	20.4	8.68	9.61	13.72	14.71	14.29	19.6
37110	12.18	14.89	12.38	9.26	17.99	18.8	18.74
31432	36.03	15.12	15.55	16.52	24.52	22.81	25.75
42731	14.34	7.71	9.63	6.05	8.18	10.08	12.27
6233	9.36	5.58	6.8	7.98	8.8	8.35	9.47
6245	5.98	3.94	4.11	3.66	4.94	5.61	7.21
7701	8.98	4.19	4.62	5.86	7.39	6.75	7.77
6235	8.23	4.37	4.27	6.22	6.91	6.55	8.29
78374	11.66	6.88	13.16	7.81	6.02	8.01	10.64
78331	4.79	3.94	5.13	4.11	6.33	4.94	5.72
Mean	18.65	7.95	10.13	9.39	12.22	12.81	15.21
Shaded	7	0	1	0	2	1	5

Table 3. Retrieval results of top 5% for data set MDDR

Activity Index	LWDOSM	GRFP	PCFP	ALOGP	MACCS	EPFP4	CDKFP
31420	94.23	30.59	45.95	45.08	55.41	76.76	80.27
71523	43.5	20.17	19.73	33.38	29.97	33.31	37.92
37110	23.8	27.83	27.99	26.71	34.7	39.96	37.26
31432	68.18	33.91	33.73	39.37	48.29	41.01	51.46
42731	27.51	14.92	19.32	12.91	19.36	20.71	23.2
6233	16.32	14.34	17	20.47	24.07	20	19.92
6245	14.92	9.89	10.08	10.59	11.06	12.65	17.88
7701	24.31	9.92	11.62	13.6	22.34	17.69	18.86
6235	21.42	13.84	13.51	14.71	20.33	17.82	19.21
78374	20.4	13.74	18.1	14.71	11.73	12.59	15.11
78331	12.98	8.87	11.23	9.97	14.35	9.37	10.55
Mean	33.42	18	20.75	21.95	26.51	27.44	30.15
Shaded	7	0	0	0	2	1	1

Visual inspection of the recall values and the number of shaded cells in Tables 1 and 2 enables comparisons to be made between the effectiveness of the LWDOSM descriptor and the various other descriptors. In addition, a more quantitative approach using the Kendall W test of concordance was used to determine which of the descriptors performed best [23]. This test was developed to quantify the level of agreement between multiple sets of rankings of the same set of objects, here and in previous works [20]. We used this approach to rank the effectiveness of different descriptor types. In the present context, the activity classes were considered as judges and the recall rates of the various descriptor types as objects. The outputs of the test are the value of the Kendall coefficient and the associated significance level, which indicates whether this value of the coefficient could have occurred by chance. If the value is significant (for which we used cut-off values of (0.01 or 0.05), then it is possible to give an overall ranking of the objects that have been ranked. The results of the Kendall analyses are reported in Table 4 and describe the top 1% and 5% ranking for the various descriptor types. In Table 5, the columns show the data set type, the value of the coefficient, the associated probability, and the ranking of the descriptor. The descriptors are ranked in decreasing order of screening effectiveness (if two descriptors have the same rank then they are ordered on the basis of the mean recall, i.e. the mean values from the main tables of results). We shall use the 5% MDDR results (in Table 4) to illustrate the processing that took place. Here, the mean figures suggest that the LWDOSM descriptor has the best overall performance at the 5% cut-off. In addition, according to the total number of shaded cells in Table 4, LWDOSM is the best performing descriptor across the 11 activity classes. We can hence conclude that the overall ranking of the seven descriptors are: LWDOSM>CDKFP>MACCS>EPFP4>ALOGP>CFP>GRFP.

Table 4. Rankings of various types of descriptors Based on Kendall W Test Results: Top 1 & 5%

Recall type	W	P	Ranking
Top 1 %	0.642	<0.01	DKFP>LWDOSM >EPFP4>MACCS>PCFP>ALOGP>GRFP
Top 5%	0.473	<0.01	LWDOSM>CDKFP>MACCS>EPFP4>ALOGP>PCFP>GRFP

Table 5. Numbers of Shaded Cells for Mean Recall of Actives Using Different Descriptors: Top 1% and 5%

	LWDOSM	GRF	PCFP	ALOGP	MACC	EPFP	CDKF
Top 1 %	7	0	1	0	2	1	5
Top 5%	7	0	0	0	2	1	1

The good performance of LWDOSM is not restricted to the top 5% for MDDR, since it also gives one of best results for the top-1% for MDDR. Using the mean recall value as an evaluation criterion could be impartial to some descriptor type but not others, and that is because some of the activity classes may contribute disproportionally to the overall value of mean recall. To avoid this bias, the effectiveness performance of different descriptors has been further investigated based on the total number of shaded cells for each descriptor across the full set of activity classes, as shown in the bottom rows of Tables 4. These shaded cell results are listed in Table 5.

Visual inspection of the results in Table 5 (left-hand column) shows very clearly that the LWDOSM descriptor can provide a level of performance that is generally superior to the other descriptors. Finally, it should be noted here in this paper that the main purpose of using several types of descriptor in the experiments was not a performance comparison, but to show that our new descriptor LWDOSM is capable of representing and characterizing the molecule structure, and to show the possibility and feasibility of its use for similarity-based virtual screening. However, the retrieval performance for any descriptor depends on the type of similarity approach used. Hence, we believe that using different text similarity searching approaches with the LWDOSM descriptor will yield different results which may be much better than the current results.

5   Conclusions

In this paper, we present a new shape-based 2D molecular descriptor, LWDOSM that represents a rough description of 2D molecular structure from its outline shape in a textual form. Experiments with the MDDR database show clearly the superiority of the LWDOSM compared to many standard descriptors tested in this study. Experiments also show that the LWDOSM allows for an effective screening search to be carried out.

Acknowledgment. This work is supported by Ministry of Higher Education (MOHE) and Research Management Centre (RMC) at the UniversitiTeknologiMalaysia (UTM) under Research University Grant Category (VOT Q.J130000.7128.00H72).

References

1. Christie, B.D., Leland, B.A., Nourse, J.G.: Structure searching in chemical databases by direct lookup methods. J. Chem. Inf. Comput. Sci. 33, 545–547 (1993)
2. Fisanick, W., Lipkus, A.H., Rusinko, A.: Similarity searching on CAS Registry substances. 2. D structural similarity. J. Chem. Inf. Comp. Sci. 34, 130–140 (1994)
3. Figueras, J.: Substructure Search by Set Reduction. J. Chem. 12, 237–244 (1972)
4. Willett, P., Barnard, J.M., Downs, G.M.: Chemical Similarity Searching. J. Chem. Inf. Comput. Sci. 38, 983–996 (1998)
5. Johnson, M.A., Maggiora, G.M.: Concepts and Application of Molecular Similarity. John Wiley, New York (1990)
6. Sheridan, R.P., Kearsley, S.K.: Why do we need so many chemical similarity search methods? Drug Discov. Today 7, 903–911 (2002)
7. Rarey, M., Dixon, J.S.: Feature trees: A new molecular similarity measure based on tree matching. J. Comput. Aided Mol. Des. 12, 471–490 (1998)
8. Rarey, M., Stahl, M.: Similarity searching in large combinatorial chemistry spaces. Journal of Computer-Aided Molecular Design 15(6), 497–520 (2001)
9. Leach, A.R., Gillet, V.J.: An Introduction to Chemoinformatics. Kluwer, Dordrecht (2003)
10. Wild, D.J., Willett, P.: Similarity Searching in Files of Three-Dimensional Chemical Structures. Alignment of Molecular Electrostatic Potential Fields with a Genetic Algorithm. J. Chem. Inf. Comput. Sci. 36, 159–167 (1996)
11. Kirchmair, J., Distinto, S., Markt, P., Schuster, D., Spitzer, G.M., Liedl, K.R., Wolber, G.: How to Optimize Shape-Based Virtual Screening: Choosing the Right Query and Including Chemical Information. J. Chem. Inf. Model. 49, 678–692 (2009)
12. Rush, T.S., Grant, J.A., Mosyak, L., Nicholls, A.: A Shape-Based 3-D Scaffold Hopping Method and Its Application to a Bacterial Protein–Protein Interaction. J. Med. Chem. 48, 1489–1495 (2005)
13. Warr, W.A.: Representation of chemical structures. Wiley Interdisciplinary Reviews: Computational Molecular Science 1, 557–579 (2011)
14. Hall, L.H., Kier, L.B.: Issues in representation of molecular structure: The development of molecular connectivity. J. Mol. Graph. 20, 4–18 (2001)
15. Kogej, T., Engkvist, O., Blomberg, N., Muresan, S.: Multifingerprint Based Similarity Searches for Targeted Class Compound Selection. J. Chem. Inf. Model. 46, 1201–1213 (2006)

16. Larabi, S., Bouagar, S., Trespaderne, F.M., de la Fuente Lopez, E.: LWDOS: Language for Writing Descriptors of Outline Shapes. In: Bigun, J., Gustavsson, T. (eds.) SCIA 2003. LNCS, vol. 2749, pp. 1014–1021. Springer, Heidelberg (2003)
17. Weininger, D.: SMILES, A chemical language and information system. 1. Introduction to methodology and encoding rules. J. Chem. Inf. Comp. Sci. 28, 31–36 (1988)
18. SciTegicAccelrys Inc.
19. Yap, C.W.: PaDEL-descriptor: An open source software to calculate molecular descriptors and fingerprints. J. Comput. Chem. 32, 1466–1474 (2011)
20. Abdo, A., Chen, B., Mueller, C., Salim, N., Willett, P.: Ligand-Based Virtual Screening Using Bayesian Networks. J. Chem. Inf. Model. 50, 1012–1020 (2010)
21. Altschul, S.F., Madden, T.L., Schäffer, A.A., Zhang, J., Zhang, Z., Miller, W., Lipman, D.J.: Gapped BLAST and PSI-BLAST: a new generation of protein database search programs. Nucleic Acids Res. 25, 3389–3402 (1997)
22. Brown, R.D., Martin, Y.C.: Use of Structure-Activity Data To Compare Structure-Based Clustering Methods and Descriptors for Use in Compound Selection. J. Chem. Inf. Comput. Sci. 36, 572–584 (1996)
23. Siegel, S., Castellan, N.J.: Nonparametric Statistics for the Behavioral Sciences. McGraw-Hill, New York (1988)

Web Service Based Approach for Viral Hepatitis Ontology Sharing and Diagnosing

Galal AL-Marzoqi, Ibrahim F. Moawad, and Abdel-Badeeh M. Salem

Faculty of Computer and Information Sciences, Ain Shams University, Abbasia, Cairo, Egypt
galalalmarzoqi@gmail.com, ibrahim_moawad@cis.asu.edu.eg,
abmsalem@yahoo.com

Abstract. Liver viruses are the most dangerous cause for liver problems, because they last for a long time and lead to serious complications like liver inflammation. In our previous research, a Viral Hepatitis Ontology was developed using Ontology of Biomedical Reality framework for the A, B, C and D viruses, which are the most widely spread among males and females. This Ontology is represented in the Web Ontology Language (OWL) that has become recently the standard language for the semantic web. The Viral Hepatitis Ontology, in its current format, can be accessed by the computer science specialists only. In this paper, we present a Web Service based approach to share the Viral Hepatitis Ontology among physicians, students of medicine, and intelligent systems. In addition, the proposed approach enables physicians, and students of medicine to differentially diagnose the Viral Hepatitis diseases. To show how the approach is very beneficial for physicians and students of medicine, we developed a system prototype to present different usage case studies.

Keywords: Ontology sharing, Web Services, Biomedical Ontology, Viral Hepatitis Ontology, Viral Hepatitis Diagnosis.

1 Introduction

Ontology is a kind of controlled vocabulary of well defined terms with specified relationships between those terms, capable of interpretation by both humans and computers [1]. Medical Ontologies are interested in solving important issues such as the reusing and sharing of medical data. The unambiguous communication of complex and detailed medical concepts is now a crucial feature of medical information systems [2].

Liver is the largest solid organ in the human body, and has been affected by different kinds of diseases [3]. There are many viruses that cause liver diseases (Hepatitis A, B, C, and D). Liver viruses are the most dangerous cause for liver problems. For example, Hepatitis A Virus (HAV) is an important cause of infectious disease worldwide. According to the World Health Organization (WHO), 1.5 million clinical cases occur worldwide a year [4].

In this paper, we present a Web Service based approach to share the Viral Hepatitis Ontology among physicians, students of medicine, and intelligent systems. This ontology is represented by the Web Ontology Language (OWL) that has become

A. Ell Hassanien et al. (Eds.): AMLTA 2012, CCIS 322, pp. 257–266, 2012.

recently the standard language for the semantic web. Besides, the proposed approach can be exploited in diagnosing the Viral Hepatitis diseases. To show how the approach is very beneficial, a prototype has been implemented to present some of case studies for Viral Hepatitis Ontology sharing and diagnosing.

The rest of this paper is organized as follows. Section 2 reviews the background and related work. Section 3 introduces the Viral Hepatitis Ontology in pathology domain for the A, B, C and D viruses. Section 4 depicts the architecture of the proposed approach, while section 5 describes the required web service operations and their different usage scenarios. Section 6 presents the prototype implementation and how it is used in different case studies. Finally, section 7 concludes the most important points in this paper.

2   Related Work

Medical Ontologies are interested in solving important issues such as the reusing and sharing of medical data.The unambiguous communication of complex and detailed medical concepts is now a crucial feature of medical information systems [2]. There are medical Ontologies developed to facilitate this purpose. The Open Biomidical Ontology (OBO) is the library of medical Ontologies in different medical domains [5]. The Ontologies in OBO are designed to serve as controlled vocabularies for expressing the results of biological science [6]. NCBO's BioPortal is an open repository of biomedical Ontologies that provides access via Web browsers and web services to Ontologies [7]. Unified Medical Language System (UMLS) is a set of files and software that brings together many health and biomedical vocabularies and standards to enable interoperability between computer systems [8].

Many research works have been achieved to build specific domain Ontologies for different diseases. For example, Vanja Lukovic, et al [9] developed the OBR-Scolio application Ontology for the pathology domain of spine. Also, Abdel-Badeeh Salem, et al [10] built domain Ontology for lung cancer. Although the Viral Hepatitis (VH) diseases cause great complications to humans, there is no enough work done to facilitate the Viral Hepatitis diseases sharing and diagnosing. In this paper, a Web Service based approach is proposed to share the Viral Hepatitis Ontology among physicians, students of medicine, and intelligent systems. Besides, it enables physicians, and students of medicine to differentially diagnose the Viral Hepatitis diseases.

3   The Viral Hepatitis Ontology

In our previous research [11, 12], the Viral Hepatitis Ontology in pathology domain was developed using Ontology of Biomedical Reality framework for the A, B, C and D viruses. This Ontology is represented by the Web Ontology Language (OWL) that has become recently the standard language for the semantic web. Figure (1) shows the classes and relations of the Viral Hepatitis diseases integrated in the Ontology of Biomedical Reality in OWL. In addition, figure (2) shows the classes and relations of the Viral Hepatitis symptoms, signs and lab-findings. We classified the symptoms and signs according to the Viral Hepatitis disease causing them. For example, the "Symptom" class includes three subclasses: "HCV Symptom", "HDV Symptom", and "HCV, HBV, HAV, HDV Symptom". The "HCV Symptom" class represents the symptoms caused by the HCV disease only. Also, the "HDV Symptom" class represents the symptoms caused by the HDV disease only. The "HCV, HBV, HAV, HDV Symptom" class represents the common symptoms caused by the HAV, HBV, HCV and HDV diseases. Additionally, the "Lab Result" class includes three subclasses: the "Serology Test", "LFTs", and "Immunological assay" classes.

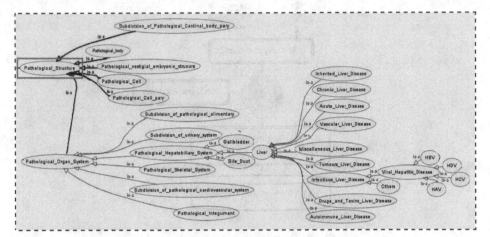

Fig. 1. The OBR Viral Hepatitis Diseases Hierarchy

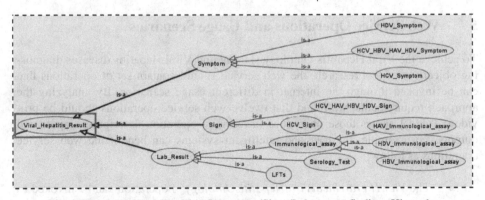

Fig. 2. The OBR Viral Hepatitis Symptoms/Signs/Laboratory-findings Hierarchy

4   Approach Architecture

Figure (3) shows the architecture of the proposed Viral Hepatitis Ontology Sharing Web Service approach. The main module of this approach is the Viral Hepatitis Ontology sharing Web Service that accesses the Viral Hepatitis OWL Ontology to share its primitives (concepts and properties) among physicians, students of medicine, and intelligent systems. The Viral Hepatitis Ontology Sharing Web Service includes the service operations needed for Ontology sharing and for Viral Hepatitis diseases diagnosing. The OWL Viral Hepatitis Ontology contains the Viral Hepatitis diseases and their signs, symptoms, and laboratory-findings. To exploit the Viral Hepatitis Ontology Sharing Web Service, physicians, students of medicine, and intelligent systems can invoke the web service operations through the internet in different usage scenarios.

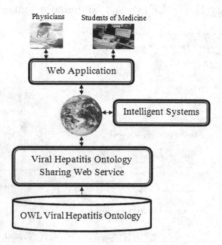

Fig. 3. The Approach Architecture

5   Web Service Operations and Usage Scenarios

To achieve the Viral Hepatitis Ontology sharing and Viral Hepatitis diseases diagnosing objectives of this research, the web service should contain set of operations that can be invoked through the internet in different usage scenarios. By analyzing the approach requirements, we found that twelve web service operations should be provided. Table 1 shows those operations in terms of operation description, inputs and outputs. For example, the user and intelligent systems can benefit the web service operations as follow: -

- The *ViewHierarchicalViralHepatitisOntology( )* operation can be invoked to return the Viral Hepatitis Ontology in OWL file.
- The *QueryForSymptomsSingsOrLaboratory-findings( )* operation can be invoked to return a list of symptoms, sings, or laboratory-findings for the input disease.
- The *QueryForCommonSymptomsOrSings( )* operation can be invoked to return a list of common symptoms and signs for the input set of diseases.
- The *RetrieveLaboratory-findingsForDisease( )* operation can be invoked to return a laboratory-findings list for the input disease.

Table 1. The Web Service Operations

Web Service Operation	Description	Input	Output
ViewHierarchicalViral HepatitisOntology	Returns the whole Viral Hepatitis Ontology file.	--	OWL File
QueryForCommonDiseasesOfSymptomsOrSings	Returns list of the common diseases for symptoms or sings.	List of symptoms or sings	List of diseases
RetrieveCommonDiseasesForSymptoms	Returns list of diseases causing the input symptoms.	List of symptoms	List of diseases
RetrieveCommonDiseasesForSigns	Returns list of diseases causing the input signs.	List of signs	List of diseases
QueryForSymptomsSingsOrLaboratory-findings	Returns symptoms, signs and laboratory-findings for a specific disease.	A disease	List of symptoms, sings, and laboratory-findings
RetrieveSymptomsForDisease	Returns a list of symptoms for a specific disease.	A disease	List of symptoms
RetrieveSingsForDisease	Returns a list of signs for a specific disease.	A disease	List of sings
RetrieveLaboratory-findingsForDisease	Returns a list of laboratory-findings for a specific disease.	A disease	List of laboratory-findings
QueryForCommonSymptomsOrSings	Returns the common symptoms or signs for set of diseases.	List of diseases	List of symptoms and signs
RetrieveCommonSymptomsForDiseases	Returns the common symptoms for set of diseases.	List of Diseases	List of symptoms
RetrieveCommonSingsForDiseases	Returns the common sings for set of diseases.	List of diseases	List of sings
DiagnoseSymptomsAndSigns	Retrieve the causing diseases for the input symptoms and signs	List of symptoms and sings	A disease

Many different usage scenarios can be achieved by the physicians, students of medicine, and intelligent systems to exploit the web service operations in different ways. By analyzing the needs of both physicians and students of medicine by asking domain expert, we found that there are important usage scenarios for learning and diagnosing: "Query for Common Diseases", "Query for Symptoms, Sings or Laboratory-findings", "Query for Common Symptoms or Sings", and "Diagnose Viral Hepatitis Diseases".

- **Scenario 1: Query for Common Diseases**

This scenario aims to help the physicians, students of medicine, and intelligent systems to retrieve the common diseases for specific symptoms or signs. As shown in figure (4), the scenario workflow is initiated by invoking the *QueryOfCommonDiseasesForSymptomsOrSings()* operation, which then invokes the *RetrieveCommonDiseasesForSymptoms()* or *RetrieveCommonDiseasesForSings()* operation that returns the common diseases for the input symptoms, or signs respectively. This scenario can be repeated if the physician, students of medicine, or intelligent systems wants to add more symptoms or signs. For example, if the user query about the diseases causing the "Abdominal Pain" symptom, the HBV and HCV diseases will be returned.

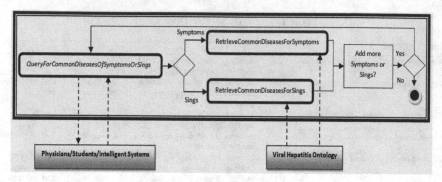

Fig. 4. Query for Common Disease

- **Scenario 2: Query for Symptoms, Sings or Laboratory-Findings**

This scenario aims to help the physicians, students of medicine, or intelligent systems to retrieve the symptoms, signs, or laboratory-findings for a specific disease. As shown in figure (5), the scenario workflow is initiated by invoking the *QueryForSymptomsSingsOrLaboratory-findings()* operation, which then invokes the *RetrieveSymptomsForDisease(), RetrieveSingsForDisease(), or RetrieveLaboratory-findingsForDisease()* operation that returns the symptoms, signs, or laboratory-findings for the input disease respectively. For example, if the user query for the symptoms of the HAV disease, the Diarrhea, Fatigue, Headache, Loss of Appetite, Nausea, Sore Muscle, Vomiting, Jaundice, and Abdominal Pain symptoms will be returned.

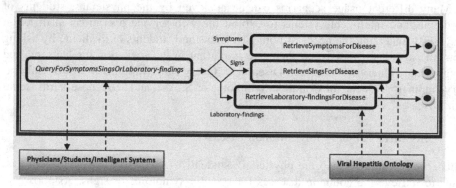

Fig. 5. Query for Symptoms, Sings or Laboratory-findings

- **Scenario 3: Query for Common Symptoms or Sings**

This scenario aims to help the physicians, students of medicine, or intelligent systems to retrieve the common symptoms or signs for set of diseases. As shown in figure (6), the scenario workflow is initiated by invoking the *QueryForCommonSymptomsOrSings()* operation, which then invokes the *RetrieveCommonSymptomsForDiseases()* or *RetrieveCommonSingsForDiseases()* operation that returns the common symptoms or signs for the input diseases respectively. For example, if the user query for the common symptoms

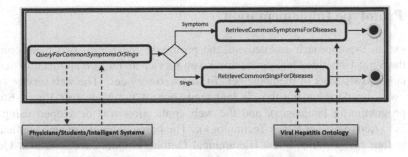

Fig. 6. Query for Common Symptoms or Sings

of the HAV and HBV diseases, the Diarrhea, Fatigue, Headache, Loss of Appetite, Nausea, Sore Muscle, Vomiting, Jaundice and Abdominal Pain symptoms will be returned.

- **Scenario 4: Diagnose Viral Hepatitis Diseases**

This scenario aims to help the physicians or students of medicine to differentially diagnose the Viral Hepatitis diseases. As shown in figure (7), the scenario starts with invoking the *RetrieveCommonDiseasesForSymptoms()* operation to retrieve the common diseases causing the input symptoms, and then the *RetrieveCommonDiseases-ForSigns()* operation is invoked to retrieve the common diseases causing the input signs. This step is repeated if the physicians (or students of medicine) want to add more symptoms/signs. After that, the *DiagnoseSymptomsAndSigns()* is invoked to diagnose the current input symptoms and signs. Finally, the *RetrieveLaboratory-findingsForDisease()* is invoked to confirm the diagnosis result by retrieving the laboratory-findings caused by the diagnosed disease. For example, if the user query for the symptom and sing ("Abdominal Pain", "Aching Limbs", "Cirrhosis", "Chills", and "Diarrhea"), the HAV, HBV, HCV and HDV diseases will be returned as the common diseases causing those symptoms and signs, but the HCV disease will be diagnosed as a final diagnosis. Also, the laboratory-findings for HCV disease can be returned to confirm the final diagnosis.

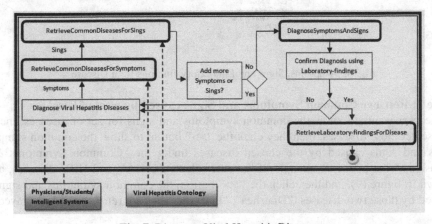

Fig. 7. Diagnose Viral Hepatitis Diseases

6   Prototype Implementation

As shown in the approach architecture, the prototype consists of two main components: the Viral Hepatitis Ontology sharing web service and a web application that let physicians and students of medicine benefit this web service. The web service component was developed using the C# language (one of the Microsoft Visual Studio .NET programming languages), and the web application was developed using the ASP.NET (Active Server Pages Technology). The home page of the web application contains four menu items: View Hierarchical Ontology, Query for Diseases, Query for Symptoms and Signs, and Diagnose Viral Hepatitis. In the following, sample of different usage case studies for the system prototype are presented.

Case 1: Retrieve Symptoms, Signs, and Laboratory-findings caused by a specific Disease

If the user wants to know what are the symptoms and signs caused by a specific disease, they can click the "Query for Symptoms and Signs" menu item. After that, they select the desired disease and click the ">>" button to show all symptoms and signs caused by this disease. For example, as shown in figure (8), when the user selects the HAV disease, and clicks the ">>" button, a list of symptoms and signs (Depression, Diarrhea, etc.) is retrieved and displayed. Finally if the user wants to show the laboratory-findings of the HAV disease, he clicks the "Lab" button, the Laboratory-Findings list caused by the HAV disease (Anti HAV IgG and Ant HAV IgM) is displayed.

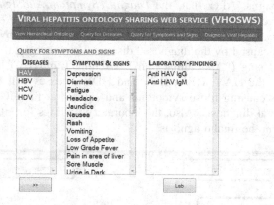

Fig. 8. Symptoms, Signs and Laboratory-findings for a Disease

Case 2: Retrieve Common Symptoms and Signs caused by a set of Diseases

If the user wants to know the common symptoms and signs for set of diseases, they can select those diseases, then they click the ">>" button to show the common symptoms and signs caused by the chosen diseases under the "Common Symptoms & Signs List" list box. For example, if the user selects the HAV and HBV diseases, as shown in figure (9), and then click the ">>" button, the common symptoms and signs caused by those two diseases ("Diarrhea", "Fatigue", etc) are retrieved and displayed.

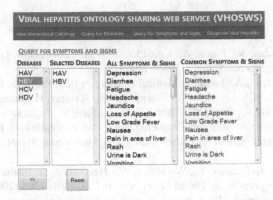

Fig. 9. Common Symptoms and Signs for set of Diseases

Case 3: Diagnose Viral Hepatitis Diseases

As shown in figure (10), if physicians and students want to diagnose the "Abdominal Pain", "Aching Limbs", "Cirrhosis", "Chills", and "Diarrhea" symptoms and signs, they can select them and click on the ">>" button, the HAV, HBV, HCV and HDV diseases will be displayed under the "Common Diseases" list box. After that, the user can click the "Diagnosis" button to retrieve the final diagnosis result, which is the HCV disease. Finally, to confirm the final diagnosis, the laboratory-findings for HCV disease can be retrieved and displayed when the user clicks the "Lab" button as shown in figure (10).

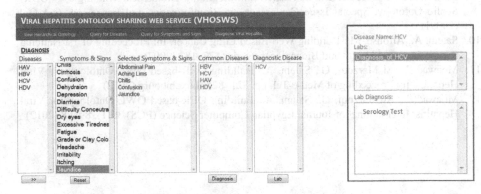

Fig. 10. Viral Hepatitis Differential Diagnosis

7   Conclusion

In this paper, a new Web Service based approach to share the Viral Hepatitis Ontology among physicians, students of medicine, and intelligent systems was presented. The approach enables physicians and students of medicine also to differentially diagnose the Viral Hepatitis diseases. In addition, a system prototype was developed to show how the approach is very beneficial for physicians and students of medicine by presenting different usage case studies.

References

1. Cicortas, A., Iordan, V., Fortis, A.: Considerations on Construction Ontologies. Journal Annals Computer Science Series 1, 79–88 (2009)
2. Sánchez, D., Moreno, A.: Learning Medical Ontologies from the Web. In: Riaño, D. (ed.) K4CARE 2007. LNCS (LNAI), vol. 4924, pp. 32–45. Springer, Heidelberg (2008)
3. Mofrad, F., Zoroofi, R., Chen, Y., Tehrani-Fard, A., Sato, Y., Furukawa, A.: Evaluation of Liver Shape Approximation and Characterization. In: Processing of Fifth International Conference on Intelligent Information Hiding and Multimedia Signal, vol. 2, pp. 2297–1300 (2009)
4. Lu, P., Euler, G., Hennessey, K., Weinbaum, C.: Hepatitis A accination coverage among adults aged 18-49 years in the United States. Vaccine 27, 1301–1305 (2009)
5. Marquet, G., Mosser, J., Burgun, A.: A method exploiting syntactic patterns and the UMLS semantics for aligning biomedical ontologies: the case of OBO disease ontologies. In: Proceeding of Epub., vol. 76, pp. 5353–5361 (2007)
6. Smith, B., Ceusters, W., Klagges, B., Köhler, J., Kumar, A., Lomax, J., Mungall, C., Neuhaus, F., Rector, A., Rosse, C.: Relations in biomedical ontologies. Genome Biology 6 (2005)
7. Bail, S., Horridge, M., Parsia, B., Sattler, U.: The Justificatory Structure of the NCBO BioPortal Ontologies. In: Aroyo, L., Welty, C., Alani, H., Taylor, J., Bernstein, A., Kagal, L., Noy, N., Blomqvist, E. (eds.) ISWC 2011, Part I. LNCS, vol. 7031, pp. 67–82. Springer, Heidelberg (2011)
8. Paul, C., Geller, J., Halper, M., Perl, Y.: The Neighborhood Auditing Tool: A hybrid interface for auditing the UMLS. Journal of Biomedical Informatics 42, 468–489 (2009)
9. Luković, V., Milošević, D., Devedžić, G.: Integrating Biomedical Ontologies - OBR-Scolio Ontology. Special Issue Conference on Bioinformatics and Image, pp. 664–669 (2009)
10. Salem, A., Alfonse, M.: Building Web-Based Lung Cancer. In: Proceeding of 1st National Symposium on e-Health and Bioengineering, pp. 177–182 (2007)
11. Moawad, I., Al Marzoqi, G., Salem, A.: Building OBR-based OWL Ontology for Viral Hepatitis. In: Proceeding of Med-e-Tel, pp. 821–825. Luxembourg (2012)
12. Moawad, I., Al Marzoqi, G., Salem, A.: Building OBR-based OWL Ontology for Viral Hepatitis. International of Journal Egyptian Computer Science (ECS) 36(1), 89–98 (2012)

Analysis of Scintigraphic Renal Dynamic Studies: An Image Processing Tool for the Clinician and Researcher

Yassine Aribi[1], Ali Wali[1], Fatma Hamza[2], Adel M. Alimi[1], and Fadhel Guermazi[2]

[1] REGIM: REsearch Groups on Intelligent Machines, University of Sfax, National School of Engineers (ENIS), BP 1173, Sfax, 3038, Tunisia
[2] Department of Nuclear Medecine, CHU BOURGUIBA, Sfax, 3029, Tunisia
{aribi.yassine,wali.ali}@gmail.com, adel.alimi@ieee.org,
{guermazifadhel,fatma.hamzamaaloul}@yahoo.fr

Abstract. The objective of this work is to develop a platform-independent tool for analysis of Scintigraphic renal dynamic studies. It allowing quantification kidney, from a series of Scintigraphic images in the format provided DICOM. This tool allows an automatic or manual drawing of regions of interest and the kidney in renal background even if small kidney and / or little functional kidney, drawing the isotopic nephrogram corrected for background noise (activity curves kidney) and determining the renal function on according to the method of the integral. This developed tool allows obtaining semi-automatic so reproducible results on page relevant information to the physician to assess the functional status of each kidney: the isotopic nephrogram, viewing dynamic images and the relative function that users can calculate renal function through the regions of both kidneys. This tool is a step forward towards standardization as a suitable tool for education, research, and for receiving distant expert's opinions.

Keywords: automatic region of interest, DICOM, quantifying renal dynamic algorithm for medical image processing.

1 Introduction

Dynamic renal scintigraphy is injected intravenously a tracer of low activity, having the property of being eliminated by glomerular filtration (99mTc-DTPA) and tubular secretion (99mTc-MAG3 a tracer used in nuclear medicine, during renography, when labelled with technetium-99m. It enables the function and drainage of each kidney to be assessed, giving similar results to DTPA with a lower dose of ionizing radiation.) and monitor its transit in the urinary tract by detecting using a gamma camera the gamma radiation emitted. The purpose of this review is to examine the quality of excretion and estimate the purification function (clearance) for each kidney. This is achieved by acquiring a time series of images after injection of a radiopharmaceutical. The quantification is based on the tracing of defining regions of interest from which each kidney are obtained, versus time, curves metering activity of the tracer (renogram). Determining the clearance was calculated from these curves after various

A. Ell Hassanien et al. (Eds.): AMLTA 2012, CCIS 322, pp. 267–275, 2012.

corrections eliminating components vascular and interstitial renal superimposed to the signal and at least partially correcting the attenuation phenomena and scattering of radiation. The current study presents a system treatment of functional images from dynamic studies. The aims of this paper is to integrate a robust method to automatically detect boundaries from renal dynamic studies, trace automatically curves of renal function, calculate a relative function automatically and renal clearance and provide portability of the software.

The rest of this paper is organized as follows: section (2) discuses the related state-of-the-art. The detailed overview of the proposed system is given in Section (3). Conclusions and future work are discussed in Section (4).

2   State-of-the-Art

Drawing regions of interest (ROIs) over the kidneys and for background subtraction is one of the most debated issues in the literature. Computer-derived kidney ROIs have been suggested as a more reproducible alternative to manual ROIs. These techniques included factor analysis, cluster analysis, fuzzy logic, artificial neural networks and image registration [1-2]. Factor analysis had been the most popular mathematical tool for separating dynamic renal structures and identifying the kidneys [1-3]. A totally automatic method for defining renal ROIs using factor analysis has been limited by the inclusion of spurious non-physiological pixels outside the kidneys due to image noise which require operator intervention to eliminate and/or to incorporate prior information such as physiological constraints [3].

AUTOROI is a program that provides an automated approach for detecting renal ROI for the extraction of the advanced quantitative MAG3 renograms from patients with suspected renal obstruction [4]. Semi-automated methods to define renal ROIs have also been developed and shown to significantly reduce operator variability in evaluating renal function in a small population [5]. Nevertheless, a recent study showed that, by using conventional techniques, a semi-automated method failed to detect the renal borders in 30% of kidneys. The failure always occurred in kidneys with poor function [6].

Nowadays, nuclear medicine professionals want to have (on hand) a complete software image processing for analyzing renal studies. In this direction, a project was launched in 2011 to develop a software platform called *IAEA renal dynamic analysis program* [7]. This software aimed at enhancing the routine implementation of advanced computational operation, including those introduces recently through the consensus committee for the definition of renal drainage parameters. An effort was made to introduce instruments of quality assurance at the various levels of the program's execution. These instruments include visual inspection, automatic detection, correction of patient's motion, automatic placement of regions of interest around the kidneys, cortical regions, and placement of reproducible background region on both primary dynamic and on postmicturition studies. Thus user can calculate the differential renal function through two independent methods, the integral or the Rutland-Patlak approaches.

3   Overview of the Proposed System

Figure (1) illustrates the architecture of the image processing system for the analysis of scintigraphic renal dynamic studies. It contains of two main stages: (1) Images acquisition; and (2) Image Processing. These two phases are described in detail in the following section along with the steps involved and the characteristics feature for each phase.

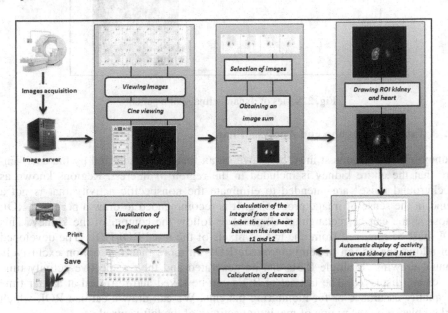

Fig. 1. Global Overview of the System

3.1   Images Acquisition Phase

The initial objective of the introduced system is to allow viewing images of a dynamic series stored on a server DICOM (Digital Imaging Communication in Medicine) [9]. Each digital image is a set of values corresponding to the number of a_{ij} strokes counted in a set of pixels identified by (i,j) represented in matrix form by $\{(i, j, a_{ij})\}$. Due to the radioactive decay of the marker and the biological decay caused by the elimination of metabolism, the image is not constant over time and becomes a function, sometimes complex. The system only displays images with a positive number of counts per minute. To ensure quality control, the system offers the user the ability to see the images in cine dynamic.

Figure (2) displaying a series of dynamic image of a patient also indicates the cine images. A cine presentation of the dynamic study facilitates the visual assessment of tracer kinetics, size position, and regional drainage of the tracer in multiphase dynamic studies (eg, 1-second frames followed by 15 seconds).

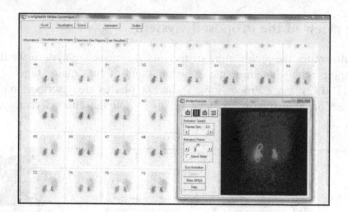

Fig. 2. Series of dynamic image of a patient

3.2   Image Processing and Analysis Phase

Kidney regions of interest must be drawn on an image sum selected by the user. Ensure that the entire kidney is included in the region of interest. Regions known as "background noise" are intended to eliminate the nonspecific activity that is not a sound in the sense of image processing. It is recommended to draw a perirenal ROI, whose shape can be rectangular, elliptical or follow the contour of the kidney. This ROI must be removed from one to two pixels of the renal ROI [10]. The developed tool allows the design of semi-automatic ROIs in more than one option exclusively manual drawing. Multiple ROIs can be generated and their respective activity time curves are displayed. The last set of ROIs can be saved and retrieved at a later time for quality assurance or for monitoring patients. We can draw a cardiac ROI, which will be placed on the region of maximum activity of the left ventricle.

The Image Sum: From a dynamic series the manipulator has the ability to choose those that are more meaningful sum to create an image called "composite". The composite image will be used later to draw the different regions of interest (kidney, renal

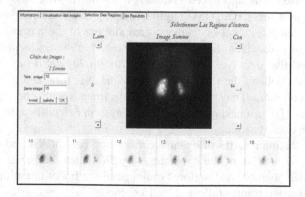

Fig. 3. Example of an image sum after selecting five successive images (10-15)

background, heart) either manually or automatically. Figure (3) shows an example of an image sum after selecting five successive images.

Drawing Renal ROI: We have tested several algorithms to achieve the ROI drawn automatically. Constraints were essentially the requirement of separation between the right kidney and left kidney, so the problem is how to define multiple ROIs, and obtain geometry and statistical data about the ROIs? REGION_GROW is the algorithm that gave the most satisfactory results. Region growing has shown to be a very useful and efficient segmentation technique in image processing [11, 12]. Region growing in its simplest sense is the process of joining neighboring points into larger regions [13] based on some condition or selection of a threshold value. Seeded region growing starts with one or more seed points and then grows the region to form a larger region satisfying some homogeneity constraint. The homogeneity of a region can be dependent upon any characteristic of the region in the image: texture, color or average intensity. One specific approach to region growing is described in the next section. The main steps of the REGION_ GROW algorithm are given as follows:

The REGION_ GROW algorithm

> **Step-1:** Select the seed pixel (a single pixel)
> **Step-2:** Check the neighboring pixels
> **Step-3: If** they are similar to the seed **Then**
> **Step-4:** Add them to the region
> > **Else** Go to **Step-1**
> > **Repeat**
> Steps 2-4 for each of the newly added pixels;
> > **Until** if no more pixels can be added.

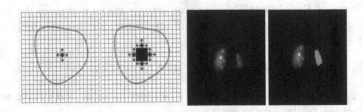

Fig. 4. A descriptive diagram of the algorithm REGION_ GROW with an illustrative example showing the right kidney segmented

Figure (4) shows a descriptive diagram of the algorithm REGION_ GROW with an illustrative example showing the right kidney segmented with 8 neighbors.

By displaying the contour around the kidney and not a region, that's why we have tried to extract the contour from segmented kidney. Figure (5) illustrate the construction of contour from a region, and if the kidney is not well surrounded by the contour, the introduced system provides the ability to automatically change the cursor with a THRESHOLD to have a good contour.

Fig. 5. Construction of contour from a region

Drawing Background ROI: The liver can sometimes affect the detection of regions of interests of the kidneys and distort the result. To overcome this problem, we should calculate the background noise and subtract from the initial region to have a net result. The background noise should be a small region below the kidney region. Our system would allow the user to draw the background noise manually or automatically. Figure (6) shows the generated background noise region of interest automatically

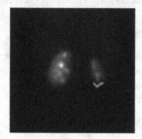

Fig. 6. Background noise ROI generated automatically

Activity Curve of Renal Net: The net renal activity curve expresses the number of shots images dynamically with time. To plot this curve, we should simply apply the following formula:

$$RAnet(k) = RA(k) - ABN(k) * S(k) \qquad (1)$$

Where *RAnet(k)* is renal activity net, *RA(k)* is activity of renal, *ABN* is the activity of background noise, while *S* is the surface.

After drawing the ROI and the background noise of each kidney, we could recall the number of counts kidney from the background in renal activity, the number of counts from the background noise which is the activity of background noise and we have also the surface of the kidney. Figure (7) shows the activity curve of renal net.

Final Report: The final report can be saved or printed, it contains the following information including (1) Basic patient information (includes: name, date of examination, patient id, body surface area, age, and sex; (2) Displaying the relative renal

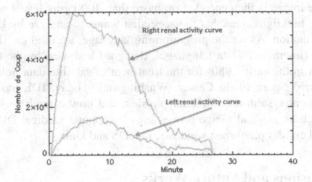

Fig. 7. Activity curve of renal net

function and renal clearance; (3) Sum image with the contours of both kidneys; (4) The curves of activity and renal net maximum value of each curve; (5) The renal clearance for each kidney; and (6) Summed image series (i.e., the user has the option of changing the interval of 3 images summed up to 60 frames). An example screen-shot of the final report is shown in Figure (8).

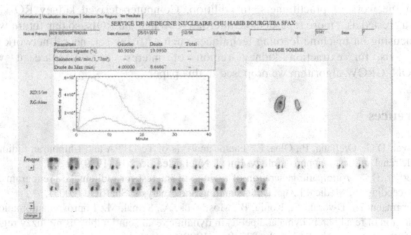

Fig. 8. Example of final report

The software has been extensively tested using Windows, Mac and Unix and developed to be portable and multi-platform. The current version can read different types of DICOM [8] formats (ie, Digital Imaging and Communications in Medicine) and wild-type files (eg, Nuclear Diagnostics). Tools are provided to rotate and flip the dynamic images. The DICOM is the standard method used in medical field. It allows by its structure to provide the medical digital images across a network. DICOM provides on the one hand the digital image and on the other the text information on the review. The image is then encoded on more than 4000 gray levels per pixel. It is also possible to highlight areas that the specialist wants to analyze by keeping high-resolution information. As for the programming language, we used the IDL programming language (Interactive Data Language), designed and used by the solar physics group at NASA in the early 1980s for the treatment of satellite data Solar Maximum Mission (Goddard Space Flight Center, Washington). Today, IDL has become the universal treatment system used in solar physics, and now extends to its success to other areas, such as medical image processing. It supports medical DICOM format and supports all current platforms: windows, macOS and Unix.

4   Conclusions and Future Works

Through this work, it became possible to make a multiplatform application of medical image format 'DICOM' for the case of dynamic renal scintigraphy. In this paper, we had presented initially the main objectives of our application based on the needs of the staff of the nuclear medicine department. Subsequently we had explained the different modules used in our application with an explanation of the algorithm REGION_ GROW that we have used for semi-automatic tracing of ROI.

This work can be improved in the future by the addition of other tools that can help benefit the work of practitioners. In addition, Computer-derived kidney ROIs has been suggested as a more reproducible alternative to manual ROIs, so our future work will focusing on machine learning techniques such as fuzzy set, neural network and rough sets for extraction kidney region of interest and compare it with REGION_GROW algorithm we proposed in this paper.

References

1. Pavel, D.G., Orellana, P., Olea, E.: Factor analysis of Tc-DTPA and I-hippuran radionuclide renal studies in nephro-urology. Eur. J. Nucl. Med. 15, 514 (1989)
2. Barber, D.C.: Automatic generation of regions of interest for radionuclide renograms. In: Proceedings of Medical Image Understanding and Analysis, Sheffield (2003)
3. Bergmann, H., Dworak, E., Konig, B., Mostlbeck, A., Samal, M.: Improved automatic separation of renal parenchyma and pelvis in dynamic renal scintigraphy using fuzzy regions of interest. Eur. J. Nucl. Med. 26, 837–843 (1999)
4. Garcia, E.V., Folks, R., Pak, S., Taylor, A.: Totally Automatic Definition of Renal Regions-of-Interest from Tc-99m MAG3 Renograms: Validation in Patients with Normal Kidneys and in Patients with Suspected Renal Obstruction. Nucl. Med. Commun. 31(5), 366–374 (2010)
5. Inoue, Y., Yoshikawa, K., Yoshioka, N., Watanabe, T., Saigua, S., Kaneko, Y., Yokoyama, I., Ohtomo, K.: Evaluation of renal function with 99m-Tc-MAG3 using semiautomated regions of interest. J. Nucl. Med. 41, 1947–1954 (2000)
6. Halkar, R.K., Chrem, Y., Galt, J.R.: Interoperator variability in quantitating the MAG3 renal uptake based on semiautomated and manual regions of interest. J. Nucl. Med. 37, 293P (1996)

7. Zaknun, J.J., Rajabi, H., Piepsz, A., Roca, I., Dondi, M.: The International Atomic Energy Agency Software Package for the Analysis of Scintigraphic Renal Dynamic Studies: A Tool for the Clinician, Teacher, and Researcher. Seminars in Nuclear Medicine 41(1), 73–80 (2011)
8. DICOM (Digital Imaging and Communications in Medicine), Supplement 23: Structured Reporting, NEMA, Rossyln VA (2000)
9. Revet, B.: DICOM Cook Book for Implementations in Modalities. PHILIPS Medical Systems (1997)
10. Sapirstein, L.A., Vidt, D.C., Mandel, M.J., et al.: Volumes of distribution and clearances of intravenously injected creatinine in the dog. Am. J. Physiol. 181, 330–336 (1955)
11. Jain, R., et al.: Machine Vision. McGraw-Hill, Inc. (1995)
12. Sonka, M., Hlavac, V., Boyle, R.: Image Processing, Analysis, and Machine Vision. Brooks/Cole Publishing Company (1998)
13. Zucker, S.W.: Region growing: Childhood and adolescence. Computer Graphics and Image Processing 5, 382–399 (1976)

Combining Multiple Individual Clusterings of Chemical Structures Using Cluster-Based Similarity Partitioning Algorithm

Faisal Saeed[1,2,*], Naomie Salim[1], Ammar Abdo[3], and Hamza Hentabli[1]

[1] Faculty of Computer Science and Information Systems, Universiti Teknologi Malaysia, Malaysia
[2] Information Technology Department, Sanhan Community College, Sana'a, Yemen
[3] Computer Science Department, Hodeidah University, Hodeidah, Yemen
alsamet.faisal@gmail.com

Abstract. Many types of clustering techniques for chemical file structures have been used in the literature, but it is known that any single method will not always give the best results for all types of applications. Recent work on consensus clustering methods is motivated because of the successes of combining multiple classifiers in many areas and the ability of consensus clustering to improve the robustness, novelty, consistency and stability of clustering. In this paper, Cluster-based Similarity Partitioning Algorithm (CSPA) was examined for improving the quality of chemical structures clustering. The effectiveness of clustering was evaluated based on the ability to separate active from inactive molecules in each cluster and compared with the Ward's clustering method. The chemical dataset MDL Drug Data Report (MDDR) database was used for experiments. The results were obtained by combining multiple individual clusterings with different distance measures. Experiments suggest that the effectiveness of consensus partition depends on the consensus generation step so that the effective individual clusterings with different distance measures can obtain more robust and stable consensus clustering.

Keywords: Consensus Clustering, Distance Measures, Graph Partitioning, Molecular Datasets, Ward's Clustering.

1 Introduction

Generally the main objective of clustering is to organize a collection of data items into some meaningful clusters, so that the items within a cluster are more similar to each other than items in the other clusters. There are many ways of grouping the clustering methods based on the problem they intend to solve, the general strategy they use, or others. For example, the clustering methods can be grouped into five opposing approaches which are agglomerative verses divisive, hard verses fuzzy or soft, monothetic verses polythetic, deterministic verses stochastic, incremental verses non incremental [1], and recently individual verses consensus methods.

---

* Corresponding author.

A. Ell Hassanien et al. (Eds.): AMLTA 2012, CCIS 322, pp. 276–284, 2012.
© Springer-Verlag Berlin Heidelberg 2012

However, many different methods of clustering techniques for chemical file structures have been used in the literature [2-13]. Brown and Martin [13] considered the Ward's clustering method to be the most efficient clustering method in compound clustering. However, as it is known, no clustering method is capable of correctly finding the best clustering results for all datasets and applications. So, the idea of combining different clustering results (consensus clustering) is considered as an alternative approach for improving the quality of the individual clustering algorithms [14].

Consensus clustering involves two main stages: (i) partitions generation and (ii) combination using the consensus function. In the first stage, as many as possible individual partitions will be generated. There are no constraints about how the partitions must be generated. Hence, different generation mechanisms can be applied including: (i) different object representations; (ii) different individual clustering methods; (iii) different parameters initialisation for clustering methods; and (iv) data resampling. In the second stage, there are two main approaches, i.e. the objects co-occurrence-based and the median partition-based approaches. Graph based consensus clustering is widely used for the first approach.

Topchy et al. [15] and Fred and Jain [16] summarised the main advantages of using consensus clustering which are robustness (the combination process must have better average performance than the single clustering algorithms), consistency (result of the combination should be somehow, very similar to all combined single clustering algorithm results), novelty (cluster ensembles must allow finding solutions unattainable by single clustering algorithms) and stability (results with lower sensitivity to noise and outliers).

In chemoinformatics, it is most unlikely that any single method will yield the best classification under all circumstances, even if attention is restricted to a single type of application [17]. The combination procedure, data fusion, has been used in virtual screening [18-25], and the fused search provides a high level of consistency that is better than that obtainable from any individual screening method [20].

Chu, et al. [17] used consensus similarity matrix clustering methods on sets of chemical compounds represented by 2D fingerprints (ECFP_4) and concluded that consensus methods can indeed out-perform the Ward's method, the current standard clustering method for chemoinformatics applications. However, based on the implemented methods, it was not the case if the clustering is restricted to a single consensus method. In this paper, we examined the use of the graph-based consensus clustering methods, CSPA, for clustering of MDDR dataset. Different representations of chemical dataset and different individual clustering techniques that use different similarity measures were used to evaluate the effectiveness of consensus clustering for chemical structures clustering.

2   Materials and Methods

2.1   Dataset

Experiments were conducted over the MDL Drug Data Report (MDDR) database [26]. This database consists of 102516 molecules. The subset (DS1) was chosen from the MDDR database which has been used for many virtual screening experiments [27-29]. The DS1 dataset contains eleven activity classes (8294 molecules), which involves homogeneous and heterogeneous (i.e., structurally diverse) actives. Details of this dataset are listed in Table 1. Each row in the table contains an activity class, the number of molecules belonging to the class, and the diversity of the class, which was computed as the mean pairwise Tanimoto similarity calculated across all pairs of molecules in the class. For the clustering experiments, two 2D fingerprint descriptors were used which were developed by Scitegic's Pipeline Pilot [30]. These were 120-bit ALOGP and 1024-bit ECFP_4 fingerprints.

Table 1. MDDR Activity Classes for DS1 Data Set

Activity Index	Activity class	Active molecules	Pairwise similarity
			Mean
31420	Renin Inhibitors	1130	0.290
71523	HIV Protease Inhibitors	750	0.198
37110	Thrombin Inhibitors	803	0.180
31432	Angiotensin II AT1 Antagonists	943	0.229
42731	Substance P Antagonists	1246	0.149
06233	Substance P Antagonists	752	0.140
06245	5HT Reuptake Inhibitors	359	0.122
07701	D2 Antagonists	395	0.138
06235	5HT1A Agonists	827	0.133
78374	Protein Kinase C Inhibitors	453	0.120
78331	Cyclooxygenase Inhibitors	636	0.108

2.2   Partitions Generation

Every consensus clustering method is made up of two steps: partitions generation and consensus functions. For the purpose of this paper, two levels of generation mechanism were used. In the first level, the partitions (also called ensembles) were generated by using four individual clustering algorithms on each 2D fingerprint. These algorithms were single-linkage, complete linkage, average linkage and weighted average distance agglomerative clustering methods. The thresholds of 500, 600, 700, 800, 900 and 1000 were used to generate partitions with different sizes (number of clusters). Every individual clustering method was applied by using six distance measures in order to generate six ensembles for each 2D fingerprint (each ensemble includes 4 partitions). In the second level, all generated partitions for each 2D fingerprint (obtained in the first level) were combined into one ensemble (each ensemble includes 24 partitions).

The distance measures, which were used with each clustering technique, were Correlation, Cosine, Euclidean, Hamming, Jaccard and Manhattan measures.

2.3   Cluster-Based Similarity Partitioning Algorithm

The graph-based consensus clustering algorithm, CSPA, proposed by Strehl and Gosh [31], was used to obtain the consensus partition from ensembles generated in the partitions generation step. The algorithm was developed based on transforming the set of clusterings into a hyper-graph representation. By using this algorithm, the clustering signifies a relationship between objects in the same cluster and can thus be used to establish a measure of pairwise similarity (similarity matrix).

The similarity matrix is generated so that each two objects have a similarity of 1 if they are in the same cluster and a similarity of 0 otherwise. The process is repeated for each clustering (4 and 24 times). A $n \times n$ binary similarity matrix $\mathbf{S}$ can be created where n is the total number of objects in the dataset. The entries of $\mathbf{S}$ are divided by r, which is the number of clusterings. Now, we can use the similarity matrix to recluster the objects using any reasonable similarity-based clustering algorithm. Here, we view the similarity matrix as graph (vertex = object, edge weight = similarity) and partition it using METIS [32], because of its robust and scalable properties, in order to obtain the consensus partition.

2.4   Performance Evaluation

The results were evaluated based on the effectiveness of the methods to separate active from inactive molecules using Quality Partition Index (QPI) measure, which was devised by Varin et al. [33]. As defined by [17], an active cluster is a non-singleton cluster for which the percentage of active molecules in the cluster is greater than the percentage of active molecules in the dataset as a whole. Let p be the number of actives in active clusters, q be the number of inactives in active clusters, r be the number of actives in inactive clusters (i.e., clusters that are not active clusters) and s be the number of singleton actives. The high value occurs when the actives are clustered tightly together and separated from the inactive molecules. The QPI is defined to be:

$$QPI = \frac{p}{p+q+r+s} \tag{1}$$

3   Results and Discussion

The generation process was carried out on two steps (or levels). In the first step, the results that were obtained by individual clusterings using each distance measures were combined together (4 partitions for each ensemble). Then, all partitions, obtained previously in the first step, were combined into one ensemble (24 partitions for each ensemble). This process was done for each fingerprint (ALOGP and ECFP_4).

The mean of QPI values were averaged over the eleven activity classes of the dataset. Tables 2-3 show the effectiveness of clustering of MDDR dataset using ALOGP and ECFP_4 fingerprints. The best QPI value of consensus clustering methods for each column was bold-faced for ease of reference.

Table 2. Effectivenss of clustering of MDDR dataset: ALOGP Fingerprint

Clustering Method			No. of clusters					
			500	600	700	800	900	1000
Consensus (CSPA)	CSPA	Correlation	44.44	47.59	48.46	48.97	48.27	51.22
		Cosine	44.80	46.85	47.36	48.17	48.57	52.01
		Euclidean	44.95	46.74	47.41	47.66	50.01	52.87
		Hamming	53.06	55.61	57.08	57.60	56.98	61.95
		Jaccard	52.86	53.53	**57.90**	57.41	**58.76**	**64.61**
		Manhattan	**53.80**	55.49	56.07	**59.20**	57.95	61.02
		All Measures	51.37	**55.71**	55.96	56.01	56.69	60.37
Individual	Ward's method		52.33	54.86	56.90	59.00	61.33	63.17

Table 3. Effectivenss of clustering of MDDR dataset: ECFP_4 Fingerprint

Clustering Method			No. of clusters					
			500	600	700	800	900	1000
Consensus (CSPA)	CSPA	Correlation	67.99	70.66	72.00	72.91	71.67	76.04
		Cosine	68.23	70.72	71.72	73.03	72.23	74.60
		Euclidean	62.16	63.24	67.26	68.08	69.31	72.71
		Hamming	62.00	62.62	66.97	69.01	69.45	73.27
		Jaccard	**68.80**	**70.78**	72.02	72.97	71.84	74.54
		Manhattan	62.00	62.62	66.97	69.01	69.45	73.27
		All Measures	68.03	70.65	**73.03**	**73.41**	**74.12**	**77.96**
Individual	Ward's Method		75.83	79.88	83.34	84.25	86.49	88.25

Visual inspection of QPI values in Tables 2-3 enables comparisons to be made between the effectiveness of consensus clustering of MDDR dataset and the Ward's method. In addition, the results of two levels of consensus clustering were shown in order to study the effectiveness of consensus clustering with different ensemble generation mechanisms.

For clustering of MDDR dataset which represented by ALOGP fingerprint, Table 2, the performance of consensus clustering that used Jaccard, Hamming and Manhattan distance measures gives better results compared with those given by Euclidean Cosine and Correlation in the first step. Moreover, when all individual clusterings were combined into one ensemble, the performance of consensus clustering outperformed the Ward's clustering method.

The results in Table 3 show that, when ECFP_4 fingerprint is used, the consensus clustering gives robust results better than the overall individual clusterings performance. The effectiveness of consensus clustering obtained from ensembles gives similar results using all distance measures, especially for Hamming and Manhattan. In the second level, when all partitions were combined into one ensemble, the performance of consensus clustering become more robust (better than the overall performance of first level consensus clustering) and closer to the performance of the Ward's clustering method.

Moreover, consensus clustering (CSPA) provides stable clusters by decreasing the sensitivity to noise and outliers. The average percentages of singleton clusters of individual clusterings compared to consensus clustering are shown in Tables 4-5 for both fingerprints. The results show that the consensus clustering partitions the dataset with average percentage of singleton equal to zero, which is better than individual clusterings and Wards' method.

Table 4. The percentages of singleton clusters for MDDR dataset: ALOGP fingerprint

Clustering Method		No. of clusters					
		500	600	700	800	900	1000
	Correlation	1.88	2.27	2.73	3.17	3.66	4.16
	Cosine	1.85	2.23	2.71	3.15	3.63	4.12
Individual Methods	Euclidean	1.90	2.31	2.76	3.15	3.51	3.97
(Avg)	Hamming	1.37	1.64	1.98	2.29	2.65	3.06
	Jaccard	1.18	1.45	1.74	2.14	2.52	2.84
	Manhattan	1.59	1.88	2.22	2.57	2.99	3.44
	Ward	0.11	0.14	0.17	0.20	0.25	0.33
Consensus Methods (Avg)		0.00	0.00	0.00	0.00	0.00	0.00

Table 5. The percentages of singleton clusters for MDDR dataset: ECFP_4 fingerprint

Clustering Method		No. of clusters					
		500	600	700	800	900	1000
	Euclidean	1.10	1.46	1.86	2.22	2.57	2.95
	Jaccard	1.13	1.51	1.90	2.25	2.59	3.03
Individual Methods	Cosine	1.22	1.56	1.83	2.17	2.57	3.00
(Avg)	Correlation	1.21	1.54	1.81	2.16	2.55	2.97
	Manhattan	1.16	1.52	1.94	2.29	2.64	3.08
	Hamming	1.21	1.54	1.81	2.16	2.55	2.97
	Ward	0.00	0.00	0.00	0.00	0.00	0.01
Consensus Methods (Avg)		0.00	0.00	0.00	0.00	0.00	0.00

4   Conclusion and Future Work

The results of the experiments show that graph-based consensus clustering, CSPA, can improve the effectiveness of chemical structures clustering. The performance of consensus clustering out-performs the Ward's method when ALOGP fingerprint is used and gives results that are closer to the performance of Ward's method for ECFP_4 fingerprint. In addition, the consensus clustering provides more stable clustering with lower sensitivity to outliers than individual clusterings and Ward's method. The experiments reported here suggest that consensus clustering depends on the consensus generation mechanism so that the more effective individual clusterings with different distance measures are used, the more robust and stable consensus clustering are obtained. In the future work, more graph-based consensus clustering methods will be examined with different partitions generation mechanisms.

Acknowledgment. This work is supported by Ministry of Higher Education (MOHE) and Research Management Centre (RMC) at the Universiti Teknologi Malaysia (UTM) under Research University Grant Category (VOT Q.J130000.7128.00H72). We also would like to thank MIS-MOHE for sponsoring the first author.

References

1. Jain, A.K., Murty, M.N., Flynn, P.J.: Data Clustering: a review. ACM Computing Surveys 31 (1999)
2. Adamson, G.W., Bush, J.A.: A method for the automatic classification of chemi-cal structures. Information Storage and Retrieval 9, 561–568 (1973)
3. Downs, G.M., Barnard, J.M.: Clustering of Chemical Structures on the Basis of Two-Dimensional Similarity Measures. Journal of Chemical Information and Computer Science 32, 644–649 (1992)
4. Willett, P.: Similarity and Clustering in Chemical Information Systems. Research Studies Press, Letchworth (1987)
5. Downs, G.M., Willett, P., Fisanick, W.: Similarity searching and clustering of chemical-structure databases using molecular property data. J. Chem. Inf. Comput. Sci. 34, 1094–1102 (1994)
6. Brown, R.D., Martin, Y.C.: The information content of 2D and 3D structural de-scriptors relevant to ligand–receptor binding. J. Chem. Inf. Comput. Sci. 37, 1–9 (1997)
7. Borosy, A., Csizmadia, F., Volford, A.: Structure Based Clustering of NCI's Anti-HIV Library. Presented at First Symposium of the European Society of Combinatorial Science, Budapest, Hungary (2001)
8. Downs, G.M., Barnard, J.M.: Clustering methods and their uses in computational Chemistry. In: Lipkowitz, K.B., Boyd, D.B. (eds.) Reviews in Computational Chemistry, vol. 18. John Wiley (2002)
9. Wild, D.J.: Advanced Chemoinformatics Methods. Chemical Engineering: Introduction to Chemoinformatics Lesson 6 (2003)
10. Holliday, J.D., Rodgers, S.L., Willet, P.: Clustering Files of chemical Structures Using the Fuzzy k-means Clustering Method. Journal of Chemical Information and Computer Science 44, 894–902 (2004)
11. Plewczynski, D., Spieser, S.A.H., Koch, U.: Assessing Different Classification Methods for Virtual Screening. Journal of Chemical Information and Computer Science 46, 1098–1106 (2006)

12. Varin, T., Bureau, R., Mueller, C., Willett, P.: Clustering files of chemical structures using the Székely–Rizzo generalization of Ward's method. Journal of Molecular Graphics and Modelling 28(2), 187–195 (2009)
13. Brown, R.D., Martin, Y.C.: Use of structure-activity data to compare structure-based clustering methods and descriptors for use in compound selection. J. Chem. Inf. Comput. Sci. 36, 572–584 (1996)
14. Vega-Pons, S., Ruiz-Schulcloper, J.: A survey of clustering ensemble algorithms. International Journal of Pattern Recognition and Artificial Intelligence 25(3), 337–372 (2011)
15. Topchy, A., Jain, A.K., Punch, W.: A mixture model of clustering ensembles. In: SIAM Int. Conf. Data Mining, pp. 379–390 (2004)
16. Fred, A.L.N., Jain, A.K.: Combining multiple clustering using evidence accumulation. IEEE Trans. Patt. Anal. Mach. Intell. 850, 835–850 (2005)
17. Chu, C.-W., Holliday, J., Willett, P.: Combining multiple classifications of chemical structures using consensus clustering. Bioorganic & Medicinal Chemistry (March 10, 2012)
18. Feher, M.: Consensus Scoring for Protein-Ligand Interactions. Drug Discovery Today 11, 421–428 (2006)
19. Salim, N., Holliday, J.D., Willett, P.: Combination of Fingerprint-Based Similarity Coefficients Using Data Fusion. J. Chem. Inf. Comput. Sci. 43, 435–442 (2003)
20. Willet, P.: Enhancing the Effectiveness of Ligand-Based Virtual Screening Using Data Fusion. QSAR Comb. Sci. 25, 1143–1152 (2006)
21. Hert, J., Willett, P., Wilton, D.J., Acklin, P., Azzaoui, K., Jacoby, E., Schuffenhauer, A.: New Methods for Ligand-Based Virtual Screening: Use of Data Fusion and Machine Learning to Enhance the Effectiveness of Similarity Searching. J. Chem. Inf. Model. 46, 462–470 (2006)
22. Whittle, M., Gillet, V.J., Willett, P.: Analysis of data fusion methods in virtual screening: Similarity and group fusion. J. Chem. Inf. Model. 6, 2206–2219 (2006)
23. Chen, B., Mueller, C., Willett, P.: Combination Rules for Group Fusion in Similarity-Based Virtual Screening. Mol. Inf. 29, 533–541 (2010)
24. Rivera-Borroto, O.M., Marrero-Ponce, Y., García de la Vega, J.M., Grau-Ábalo, R.C.: Comparison of combinatorial clustering methods on pharmacological data sets represented by machine learning-selected real molecular descriptors. J. Chem. Inf. Model. 51(12), 3036–3049 (2011)
25. Svensson, F., Karlen, A., Skold, C.: Virtual Screening Data Fusion Using Both Structure- and Ligand-Based Methods. J. Chem. Inf. Model. (2011)
26. Moffat, K., Gillet, V.J., Whittle, M., Bravi, G., Leach, A.R.: A Comparison of Field-Based Similarity Searching Methods: CatShape, FBSS, and ROCS. J. Chem. Inf. Model. 48, 719–729 (2008)
27. Abdo, A., Chen, B., Mueller, C., Salim, N., Willett, P.: Ligand-Based Virtual Screening Using Bayesian Networks. J. Chem. Inf. Model. 50, 1012–1020 (2010)
28. Abdo, A., Salim, N.: New Fragment Weighting Scheme for the Bayesian Inference Network in Ligand-Based Virtual Screening. J. Chem. Inf. Model. 51, 25–32 (2011)
29. Abdo, A., Saeed, F., Hentabli, H., Ali, A., Salim, N., Ahmed, A.: Ligand expansion in ligand-based virtual screening using relevance feedback. Journal of Computer-Aided Molecular Design 26, 279–287 (2012)
30. Sci Tegic Accelrys Inc. (September 1, 2012), http://www.http//accelrys.com/

31. Strehl, A., Ghosh, J.: Cluster Ensembles - A Knowledge Reuse Framework for Combining Multiple Partitions. J. Machine Learning Research 3, 583–617 (2002)
32. Karypis, G., Kumar, V.: A fast and high quality multilevel scheme for partitioning irregular graphs. SIAM J. Scient. Comput. 20, 359–392 (1998)
33. Varin, T., Saettel, N., Villain, J., Lesnard, A., Dauphin, F., Bureau, R., Rault, S.J.: Enzyme Inhib. Med. Chem. 23, 593 (2008)

SampleBoost for Capsule Endoscopy Categorization and Abnormality Detection

Mohamed Abouelenien and Xiaohui Yuan

Computer Science and Engineering Department,
University of North Texas, Denton, Texas, USA
{mohamed,xyuan}@unt.edu

Abstract. Analyzing Capsule Endoscopy videos is an expensive process that requires considerable human effort and time. The massive amount of data limits the usage of ensemble learning methods. In this paper SampleBoost, a boosting method that employs novel intelligent sampling, is proposed to learn from capsule endoscopy data. SampleBoost intelligently selects a subset of the training set at each iteration and evens imbalanced classes. Experimental results show a great improvement in both accuracy and efficiency as well as avoidance of early termination for both the balanced images categorization and the imbalanced abnormality detection.

Keywords: Classification, Boosting, Sampling, Capsule Endoscopy.

1 Introduction

In computer-aided endoscopy diagnosis, automatic detection of diseases, e.g., internal bleeding and tumors, is becoming extremely important given the massive amount of endoscopy videos. The key is to achieve satisfactory accuracy and efficiency. Wireless capsule endoscopy (CE) is a non-invasive technology that visualizes the entire small intestine. It is a small capsule-shaped camera that is swallowed by the patient. The camera records a video of the tract for more than 8 hours and produces about 60,000 frames. Reviewing videos is time consuming and relies heavily on the physician's experience and focused attention, which could take up to two hours.

With a reliable computer-aided diagnosis (CAD) system, physicians are enabled to simply confirm the detection identified by the program. An endoscopy CAD system should consist of two functions: categorizing images into their respective organs (i.e., video segmentation) and detecting abnormalities. The gastrointestinal tract beyond esophagus can be divided into three main organs: stomach, small intestine, and large intestine. There exist thousands of images in each of these categories. Learning and classifying organ images is inevitably affected by the large number of images [17]. When detecting abnormalities, the images containing suspicious signs is submerged among thousands of images of normal views. The much greater number of normal views imposes an implicit bias

A. Ell Hassanien et al. (Eds.): AMLTA 2012, CCIS 322, pp. 285–294, 2012.

to the learning algorithm. In addition, the massive amount of images requires high computational resources and suffers longer training time.

We proposed the idea of combining sampling with ensemble learning in [1]. In this paper, we propose a multi-class boosting method (SampleBoost) that employs an intelligent weighted sampling in training iterations, for improved classification of CE images. After training each weak classifier the weights of examples are updated such that higher weights are assigned to misclassified examples. The training set is then down-sampled to a predetermined size based on the weights. Experimental results demonstrate the effectiveness and robustness of our SampleBoost method in avoiding early termination and in achieving improved accuracy and higher efficiency compared to AdaBoost and single classifier. Moreover, it circumvents biased decisions in imbalanced scenarios. The aim of this paper is not to identify the best feature selection method or the best base classifier. In fact, it provides an ensemble learning framework that can employ a variety of feature selection methods and weak classifiers. SampleBoost is a significant improvement on the way of achieving a fully automated detection system for CE videos.

The rest of this paper is organized as follows. In Section 2, we review the related work. In Section 3, we first analyze the error propagation among classical boosting methods, which is a cause of early termination. We then describe our SampleBoost method. In Section 4, experimental results on CE videos are discussed. In Section 5, we conclude the paper with a summary of our method.

2   Related Work

Most of the methods developed to improve classification of CE videos aim at extracting different types of features. Coimbra et al [5] employed MPEG-7 visual descriptors to search for abnormalities in the endoscopy images. Kodogiannis and Boulougoura [10] used texture and color histogram features in an adaptive neurofuzzy framework for automated diagnosis of images. Magoulas et al [16] developed a two stage unsupervised k-windows clustering method to classify CE images and detect Tumors. Gallo and Torrisi [8] selected Haar features from CE images in a cascaded AdaBoost framework for intestinal lumen detection.

Despite the success of boosting methods in improving classification accuracy, they were not commonly used for CE classification because of the videos' massive size. AdaBoost [6] is one of the most successful ensemble classification method. It was first introduced as a binary classification method. The weights of the sample points adaptively change in accordance to the decision of each weak classifier. Several other boosting methods were introduced using different weighting mechanisms and loss functions. Details can be found in [2,7,11–13]. Relying on the success of AdaBoost, extensions were also introduced for multi-class classification. Adaboost.M1, Adaboost.M2 [6] and Adaboost.MH [14] were proposed for multi-class problems. In dealing with multi-class cases, the problem was converted to several binary problems. Stagewise Additive Modeling using Multiclass Exponential loss function, SAMME, was introduced in [18], where a simple addition to the loss function and the error bound resulted in an effective multi-class boosting method. Our work is built upon the ideas presented in AdaBoost.M1 and SAMME.

In real world applications, particularly bleeding and tumor detection in CE videos, imbalanced data sets are very common. To solve this problem, methods were introduced to modify decision boundaries of different classifiers or to manipulate the data examples distribution using down-sampling or up-sampling. Chawla [3] introduced SMOTE; a method that adds synthetic examples to the minority class to balance the classes of the data set. Later ideas involving sampling in a boosting framework were introduced to balance data sets. Chawla et al. [4] introduced SMOTEBoost as a combination of SMOTE and AdaBoost. Other boosting methods employing random under-sampling to balance the binary imbalance problem can be found in [9,15].

3 Methodology

3.1 Weighted Error Analysis of AdaBoost

In this section, we provide our analysis of the evolution of weighted error. AdaBoost trains a weak classifier in every iteration. The combination of the decisions of all weak classifiers results in a strong combined decision. After training each weak classifier, AdaBoost and its multi-class extensions adjust the data distribution. Based on the updated weights, each classifier is assigned a weight that determines its contribution to the overall decision. Since the same dataset is used to train the weak classifier in every iteration, this may result in repetition of the misclassified examples. The weights of these examples increase significantly and eventually force the weighted error to pass the maximum bound. When it occurs, the boosting algorithm terminates. This termination exists because adding more classifiers does not improve the performance; instead, it results in negative classifier weights. The analysis follows the algorithms in [6,18] and provides a general boosting form that can easily be converted to AdaBoost, AdaBoost.M1 and SAMME. Our analysis shows that if the same number of examples is repeatedly misclassified, the boosting algorithm terminates rapidly regardless of the weak classifier accuracy.

Assume we are given a training data set $(x_1, y_1), \ldots, (x_N, y_N)$, where $x_i \in \mathcal{X}$ and $y_i \in \mathcal{Y} = \{1, \ldots, C\}$. N is the total number of examples and C is the total number of classes. Each example has an initial weight $w_1(i) = 1/N$.

Assuming m examples were misclassified after the first training, where $m \in \{1, \ldots, N\}$. Hence, the weighted error is $\epsilon_1 = \frac{m}{N}$. Assume that the same m examples are misclassified again after the second iteration. Weights will hence be updated and normalized for the m misclassified examples to

$$w_2 = \frac{e^{\alpha_1}}{NW_2} \tag{1}$$

And for the $N - m$ correctly classified examples to

$$w_2 = \frac{e^{-\alpha_1}}{NW_2} \tag{2}$$

W_2 represents the summation of the example weights after the second iteration. $W_2 = \sum_1^N w_2 = \frac{m}{N}e^{\alpha_1} + \frac{N-m}{N}e^{-\alpha_1}$. α is the weight assigned to a weak classifier based on its performance.

$$\alpha_1 = \frac{1}{2}\log(\frac{1-\epsilon_1}{\epsilon_1}) + \frac{1}{2}\log(\gamma) \qquad (3)$$

γ is a factor that is equal to 1 for AdaBoost and AdaBoost.M1, and to $C-1$ for SAMME algorithm. Then the weighted error after the second training is

$$\epsilon_2 = \frac{\frac{m}{N}e^{\alpha_1}}{\frac{m}{N}e^{\alpha_1} + e^{-\alpha_1} - \frac{m}{N}e^{-\alpha_1}} = \frac{e^{2\alpha_1}}{e^{2\alpha_1} + \frac{N}{m} - 1} \qquad (4)$$

After substituting with the values of ϵ_1 and α_1, the weighted error can be simplified to

$$\epsilon_2 = \frac{[\frac{N}{m} - 1][\gamma]}{[\frac{N}{m} - 1][\gamma] + \frac{N}{m} - 1} \qquad (5)$$

The weighted error is then

$$\epsilon_2 = 1 - \frac{1}{\gamma + 1} \qquad (6)$$

After substitution with the value of γ, the final weighted error is

$$\epsilon_2 = \begin{cases} 0.5 & \text{AdaBoost} \\ 0.5 & \text{AdaBoost.M1} \\ 1 - \frac{1}{C} & \text{SAMME} \end{cases} \qquad (7)$$

In this case the weighted error reaches the error bound for all three algorithms and the boosting process terminates rapidly.

3.2   SampleBoost Framework

Our SampleBoost is a multi-class boosting method that employs a novel intelligent weighted sampling strategy. It uses a portion of the whole training set in each step. This strategy has several benefits. It improves the accuracy and reduces the training time yet takes advantage of the availability of more examples. It avoids early termination of the typical boosting algorithms by changing the data distribution using sampling. It also evens the number of examples in each class to avoid biased decisions towards majority classes in imbalanced scenarios.

After each iteration, the algorithm down-samples the training examples of each class into a predetermined size s. The examples are selected and trained based on their weights. That is, the weight of each sample represents its probability of being selected in the next round training set. Misclassified examples then have higher probability of being selected. Each weak classifier is then evaluated using the whole training set. Based on the evaluation, a weight α is assigned to each weak classifier to determine its contribution to the overall classification process. The decisions of all weak classifiers are then combined using weighted

---

Algorithm 1. SampleBoost

1: initialize data distribution with $w_1(i) = 1/N$
2: **for** $t = 1, \ldots, T$ **do**
3:    Select a subset $S \subseteq D$ according to the examples distribution
4:    Train a weak classifier f_t with S

$$f_t = \arg\min_{f_t \in F} \sum_{i=1}^{N} w_t(i) \mathcal{I}[y_i \neq f_t(x_i)]$$

5:    **if** $\epsilon_t > \frac{\gamma}{\gamma+1}$ **then** $\alpha_t = 0$
6:    Compute α_t for current weak classifier

$$\alpha_t = \log(\frac{1 - \epsilon_t}{\epsilon_t}) + \log(\gamma)$$

7:    Update the data distribution weights

$$w_t \Leftarrow w_t e^{\alpha_t [\![y_i \neq f_t(x_i)]\!]}$$

8:    Normalize w_t
9: **end for**
10: Combine classifiers f_t into $F(x)$

$$F(x) = \arg\max_y \sum_{t=1}^{T} \alpha_t f_t(x)$$

---

majority voting. Our SampleBoost is presented in Algorithm 1. The indicator function $[\![\cdot]\!]$ returns 1 if true and -1 otherwise while the indicator function $\mathcal{I}[.]$ returns 1 if true and 0 otherwise.

In case of balanced classification, the number of selected examples per class s can be specified by the user. The total size of a training set S is $S = s * C$. Based on our experiments we do not recommend using a very small size since it affects the performance or a very large size since it degrades efficiency. In case of a severely imbalanced training set, classes with more examples are down-sampled to match the size of the smallest class. Let $|s_i|$ be the smallest class size. Following the example distribution, a subset of examples s_a is selected from each of the other classes so that $|s_a| = |s_i|$. That transforms the imbalanced scenario into a balanced classification. The selected examples from the majority and minority classes form the new training subset S for each iteration.

$$S = \{\cup s_{ip}, \cup s_{aq}\} \tag{8}$$

In case of imbalanced multi-class classification, p represents the number of minority classes and q represents the number of majority classes.

4   Experimental Results

Capsule endoscopy videos of 8 patients were collected. Each video consists of 40,000 to 60,000 frames. The classification process is divided into two steps. The first step categorizes the images into one of the three main regions of the gastrointestinal tract, stomach, small intestine, and large intestine. 1400 images were randomly selected for each of the three classes in a balanced classification problem. The second step classifies the images as normal or abnormal. The normal class contains 4150 images. Abnormal images might suffer from erosion, ulcer, or erythema. The abnormal class lacks availability of images. For the 8 patients, 50 abnormal images were available which creates a severe imbalanced classification of a ratio of 83:1. The collected images are divided into two sets for a two-fold cross validation. All training images were preprocessed using Principal Component Analysis (PCA). PCA is a classicial feature selection method that reduces the dimensionality linearly by projecting the images into a space with lower dimensions referred to as the eigenspace. The principal components represent the axes of this space. The projected examples preserve discriminant information of the original set. Test images are projected on the training eigenspace before tested. Decision Trees (DT) with early pruning is used as the base classifier in AdaBoost, SAMME, and SampleBoost and each ensemble consists of 20 classifiers.

Table 1. Number of training samples/class (S/C), average error rate (Err.%), efficiency in seconds (Eff.), and the average number of effective weak classifiers (WC) in CE categorization

CE	Single	AB.M1	SAMME	SB-50		SB-150		SB-350	
		$\alpha = 1$	$\alpha = 2$	$\alpha = 1$	$\alpha = 2$	$\alpha = 1$	$\alpha = 2$	$\alpha = 1$	$\alpha = 2$
S/C	700	700	700	50	50	150	150	350	350
Err.%	53.83	53.8	53.8	40.61	41.54	37.85	39.81	41.78	44.16
Eff.	27.47	388.18	404.87	16.45	13.71	37.15	37.54	143.69	150.77
WC	1	2.5	1.5	6	20	20	20	20	20

Figure 1 presents the per-class error rate of the balanced categorization process. Figure 1 shows the error rates with results when $\gamma = 1$ in top panel and when $\gamma = C - 1$ in the bottom panel. Single classifier, AdaBoost.M1, and SAMME show very close performance with a difference of less than 0.1%. Their results are mostly overlapped and depicted as one curve in the figure. The three methods achieved the highest error rate for the stomach and large intestine classes. The large intestine class suffers from the worst accuracy between the classes. SampleBoost with sample sizes of 50, 100, and 150 show a significant improvement in accuracy. Using SampleBoost, the improvement reaches 52% for the large intestine class. SampleBoost with 50 samples has very small increase in the error rate compared to AdaBoost.M1, SAMME, and single classifier for both γ values for the small intestine class. On the contrary, it can be noticed

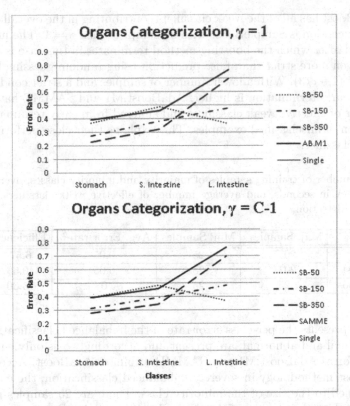

Fig. 1. Per-class error rate of categorizing CE images into stomach, small intestine, and large intestine with $\gamma = 1$ and $\gamma = C - 1$ (*top and bottom*). SB-50, SB-150, SB-350 represent SampleBoost with sample sizes of 50, 150, and 350 respectively.

that as the number of samples increases for SampleBoost, the improvement in the large intestine classification performance is lower. This can be attributed to the fact that many patients have stools in some parts of the large intestine. The colors and shapes of these parts vary significantly as the number of samples increases. These variations result in a degradation of performance. Changing the γ value does not show significant effect. The limited effect of changing γ can be attributed to the low classes number. For the balanced experiments γ is either 1 or 2.

Table 1 shows the efficiency, average error rate, and the number of weak classifiers that contributed in the boosting decision, i.e., the average total number of non-zero α. It can be seen that all SampleBoost experiments have an average error rate that is significantly lower than all other methods. Training time of SampleBoost experiments is significantly lower compared to AdaBoost.M1 and SAMME. As the number of samples increases the training time also increases. SampleBoost with 50 samples has a training time ratio of approximately 1:26 on average compared to AdaBoost.M1 and SAMME methods. It is also more efficient than training a single classifier with all samples.

SampleBoost has all of the weak classifiers contributing in the overall decision. The only exception is SampleBoost with 50 samples when $\gamma = 1$. The maximum error bound after which the boosting method terminates in this case is 0.5. This bound is even more strict than false prediction using random guessing for three classes, i.e., $(1 - 1/3)$. With a lower number of samples and a strict condition the chances of early termination is higher. AdaBoost.M1 and SAMME have a very low number of effective weak classifiers and suffered from early termination due to repetition of misclassified examples. This explains their close performance to the single classifier.

Table 2. Number of training samples of majority and minority classes, average error rate, efficiency in seconds, and average number of effective weak classifiers (WC) in abnormality detection

CE	Maj. Samples	Min. Samples	Avg. Error rate%	Efficiency	WC
Single	2075	25	0.05	6.57	1
AdaBoost	2075	25	0.05	40.63	1
SampleBoost	25	25	0	13.00	20

Figure 2 presents the per-class error rate of the imbalanced classification. Two classes, normal and abnormal, are present and accordingly γ is only equal to 1. This transforms AdaBoost.M1 and SAMME to binary AdaBoost. According to SampleBoost methodology in severely imbalanced classification, the classes are down-sampled to the size of the minority class. There are 25 samples per class for training. The performance of the single classifier and AdaBoost are very close and their error plots are mostly merged into one. The error rate of the majority class is very small 0.05%; whereas the error rate of the minority class is 98%. With an imbalanced ratio of 83:1 the single classifier and AdaBoost decisions are biased to a great extent to favor the majority class. Our SampleBoost shows a significant improvement in the minority error rate. The error rate achieved for both the majority and the minority classes is 0%. SampleBoost evened the classes resulting in an unbiased decision with a great improvement.

In Table 2 the average error rate of the single classifier, AdaBoost, and SampleBoost is very close. Average error rate is a not a fair metric in this case. With a 2-fold cross validation, 2075 samples were used to test the majority class and 25 samples to test the minority. A fair metric here is the error rate of individual classes or the sensitivity (1 - the error rate of the minority) and specificity (1-average error rate of the majority). A 68% improvement in efficiency is also evident using SampleBoost compared to AdaBoost. In this case single classifier is the most efficient method with a very poor performance on the minority class. It can be seen that again all the 20 weak classifiers were effective in case of SampleBoost and only one on average for AdaBoost.

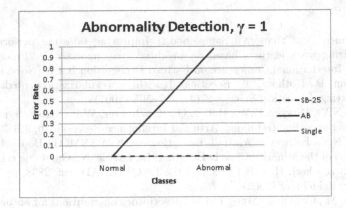

Fig. 2. Per-class error rate of abnormality detection. SB-25 represent SampleBoost with sample size of 25. Single represents single classifier and AB refers to AdaBoost.

5   Conclusion

Capsule endoscopy is a relatively new way to visualize unseen parts of the gastrointestinal tract. Thousands of frames need to be analyzed by physicians in a process that requires a lot of experience and concentration. A fully automated analysis requires two parts. The first categorizes images into three main parts of the tract, stomach, small intestine, and large intestine in a balanced classification scenario. The second part detects the images that reveal abnormal regions in a binary imbalanced scenario. Improvement of the classification process using boosting methods is not widely used for CE videos due to the massive amount of data that requires a lot of training time. Additionally, repetition of misclassified examples maximizes the weighted error to the maximum error bound that causes the algorithm to terminate. The early termination causes boosting algorithms to perform very closely to single classifiers. Moreover, imbalanced training achieves predictions that are biased towards the majority class.

SampleBoost is a great advance on the road of achieving a fully reliable automated system for CE classification. A novel intelligent sampling strategy is employed that selects a subset of the training data to train each weak classifier. The selection process focuses on hard examples by assigning them higher probability of selection. The suggested methodology also balances uneven classes to avoid biased decision. The experiments of the multi-class CE categorization and the imbalanced abnormality detection show the superiority of the suggested method. SampleBoost improves the accuracy, achieves higher efficiency, and avoids early termination. In future work, the system can be modified to classify the CE images into detailed parts of the tract. It can also be used to classify between different types of abnormalities since SampleBoost supports multi-class classification.

References

1. Abouelenien, M., Yuan, X.: Sampleboost: Improving boosting performance by destabilizing weak learners based on weighted error analysis. In: Proceedings of the 21st International Conference on Pattern Recognition ICPR (November 2012)
2. Buhlmann, P., Hothorn, T.: Boosting algorithms: regularization, prediction and model fitting. Statistical Science 22(4), 477–505 (2007)
3. Chawla, N.V., Bowyer, K.W., Hall, L.O., Kegelmeyer, W.P.: Smote: Synthetic minority over-sampling technique. Artificial Intelligence Research 16, 321–357 (2002)
4. Chawla, N.V., Lazarevic, A., Hall, L.O., Bowyer, K.W.: SMOTEBoost: Improving Prediction of the Minority Class in Boosting. In: Lavrač, N., Gamberger, D., Todorovski, L., Blockeel, H. (eds.) PKDD 2003. LNCS (LNAI), vol. 2838, pp. 107–119. Springer, Heidelberg (2003)
5. Coimbra, M., Cunha, J.: Mpeg-7 visual descriptorscontributions for automated feature extraction in capsule endoscopy. IEEE Transactions on Circuits and Systems for Video Technology 16(5), 628–637 (2006)
6. Freund, Y., Schapire, R.E.: A decision-theoretic generalization of on-line learning and an application to boosting. Journal of Computer and System Sciences 55, 119–139 (1997)
7. Freund, Y., Schapire, R.E.: A short introduction to boosting. Journal of Japanese Society for Artificial Intelligence 14(5), 771–780 (1999)
8. Gallo, G., Torrisi, A.: Boosted wireless capsule endoscopy frames classification. In: The Third International Conferences on Pervasive Patterns and Applications, pp. 25–30 (2011)
9. Geiler, O.J., Hong, L., Yue-Jian, G.: An adaptive sampling ensemble classifier for learning from imbalanced data sets. In: International MultiConference of Engineers and Computer Scientists, vol. 1 (March 2010)
10. Kodogiannis, V.S., Lygouras, J.N.: Neuro-fuzzy classification system for wireless-capsule endoscopic images (2007)
11. Meir, R., Rätsch, G.: An Introduction to Boosting and Leveraging. In: Mendelson, S., Smola, A.J. (eds.) Advanced Lectures on Machine Learning. LNCS (LNAI), vol. 2600, pp. 118–183. Springer, Heidelberg (2003)
12. Schapire, R.E.: Theoretical views of boosting and applications. In: Tenth International Conference on Algorithmic Learning Theory (1999)
13. Schapire, R.E.: The boosting approach to machine learning: An overview. In: MSRI Workshop on Nonlinear Estimation and Classification (2003)
14. Schapire, R.E., Singer, Y.: Improved boosting algorithms using confidence-rated predictions. In: Machine Learning, pp. 80–91 (1999)
15. Seiffert, C., Khoshgoftaar, T.M., Hulse, J.V., Napolitano, A.: RUSBoost: A hybrid approach to alleviating class imbalance. IEEE Transaction on Systems, Man, and Cybernetics, Part A: Systems and Humans 40(1) (January 2010)
16. Unsupervised, U.T., Magoulas, G.D., Plagianakos, V.P., Tasoulis, D.K., Vrahatis, M.N.: Tumor detection in colonoscopy. In: Fourth European Symposium on Biomedical Engineering, pp. 25–27 (2004)
17. Yuan, X., Giritharan, B., Panchakarala, S.: Learning from large data set – segmentation of capsule endoscopy videos. International Journal of Functional Informatics and Personalized Medicine (in press)
18. Zhu, J., Zou, H., Rosset, S., Hastie, T.: Multi-class adaboost. Statistics and Interface 2(3), 349–360 (2009)

Advanced Parallel Genetic Algorithm with Gene Matrix for Global Optimization

Abdel-Rahman Hedar[1], Amr Abdelsamee[2], Ahmed Fouad[3], and Sherif Tawfik Amin[2]

[1] Department of Computer Science, Assiut University, Assiut 71526, Egypt
hedar@aun.edu.eg
[2] Department of Mathematics, Faculty of Science, Assiut University, Assiut 71516, Egypt
amr.abdelhafez@science.au.edu.eg, sherif.t.amin@gmail.com
[3] Department of Computer Science, Faculty of Computers and Information,
Suez Canal Univ., Ismailia 41522, Egypt
afar1111@yahoo.com

Abstract. In this paper we address the parallelization of genetic algorithm (GA) as a tool to solve optimization problems. The proposed method which is called Parallel Genetic Algorithm with Gene Matrix (PGAGM), is a new parallel genetic algorithm technique that is based on distributed model for high dimensional problems. In this algorithm, Gene Matrix (GM) operator is used as an automatic termination criterion in order to assure that sufficient exploration of the search space has been conducted. The resulting technique shows excellent results with low execution time for finding the optimal solution.

Keywords: Genetic algorithms, Distributed Computing, Hybrid Meta-heuristic, Global optimization, MPI.

1 Introduction

Genetic algorithms (GAs) is known to be both an efficient and effective means of solving optimization problems, because they do not use domain specific knowledge in their search procedure. GAs are characterized by using a population of solutions to perform the search through many different areas of the problem space at the same time [9]. GAs also has weak points like slow convergence and time consuming [5], especially when being applied to a high dimensional problems with many parameters and subsequently an enormous search space.

Parallelism is of interest in optimization because many optimization problems are expensive to solve [11]. This turn to concurrent programming was motivated by a variety of factors one of it is the need for solution to high dimensional problems. Nowadays the availability of highly powerful machines which steadily increase in power and scope let us address the massively parallel computation and have made the solution of such problems possible. Furthermore it generated interest in new types of problems that were not addressed in the past.

In our proposed method we optimize the search process in an efficient GA known as GAMCP [6], by injecting it with Gene Matrix (GM) [7], [8] termination criteria that gets modified during each iteration so that the search process gets improved through

A. Ell Hassanien et al. (Eds.): AMLTA 2012, CCIS 322, pp. 295–303, 2012.

a self-check procedure that will judge how much exploration has been done and assure maintenance of the population diversity. Then we speed up the search process by parallelizing the GAMCP approach through the adding of more population's dedicated processors to the execution pool and by applying a special type of mutation technique called Mutagenesis [8], which is used to alter some chromosomes in each iteration (generation). We will then recollect the GM into one global matrix in order to pin point the genes that haven't been updated enough in order to apply Mutagenesis to them.

The remainder of the paper is organized as follows. In Section 2, we address the structured models of PGAGM. In Section 3, Numerical Experiments presented to show the efficiency of PGAGM working on different number of processors. In the last section, we summarize our results and notes in the conclusion.

2   Parallel GA with Gene Matrix

In this section, a new modified version of Parallel genetic algorithms (PGAs) is presented, the main components of PGAGM are introduced below before presenting the formal PGAGM algorithm at the end of this section.

2.1   Mutagenses [8]

The Mutagenses operator is a special type of a directed mutation defined to achieve more efficient and faster exploration and exploitation processes. This operator selects randomly zero position in GM and alter some survival individuals which can maintain diversity and elitism.

2.2   Parallel Architecture

Our parallel model is based on the Distributed model described on [1], in this model, the population is structured into smaller subpopulations relatively isolated one from the others. Regardless, individuals occasionally migrate between one particular island and its neighbors, PGAs based on this paradigm are sometimes called multi-population or multi-deme GAs.

2.3   Migration

Distributed genetic algorithm (dGA) behavior is strongly determined by the migration mechanism [2], [3]. Migration operator is proposed to exchange the individuals between the subpopulations of the parallel distributed GAs so this will improve the gene pool and hence increase the diversity and accelerate the convergence of the algorithm. Our migration topology is based on Ring topology, the Ring topology used for the dGA ensures local communications between subpopulations. We set the migration rate to be 5% of the best found solutions, but this parameters should be adapted according to the problem type since migration has nonlinear effect on algorithm efficiency.

2.4   PGAGM Algorithm

PGAGM algorithm is described as follows, starts with multiple subpopulations equals to the number of processors available, each chromosome in the search space consists of n genes. Each subpopulations coded as a matrix of size $\mu \times n$ called population matrix (*PM*) and distributed to the corresponding processor. The formal detailed description of PGAGM is given in the following algorithm.

Algorithm 21. *PGAGM Algorithm*

For all workers do:
1. *Initialization.* *Set values of m, μ, ν, η, and (l_i, u_i), for $i = 1, \ldots, n$ as shown in Table 1. Set the crossover and mutation probabilities $p_c \in (0, 1)$ and $p_m \in (0, 1)$, respectively. Set the generation counter $t := 0$. Initialize GM as the $n \times m$ zero matrix, and generate an initial population P_0 of size μ and code it to a matrix PM_0.*
2. *Parent Selection.* *Evaluate the fitness function F of all individuals in P_t. Select an intermediate population $\widetilde{P}_t$ from the current population P_t and code it to a matrix PM_t.*
3. *Partitioning and Genetic Operations.* *Partition $\widetilde{\mathrm{PM}}_t$ into $\nu \times \eta$ sub-matrices . Apply the following for all sub-matrices.*
3.1. *Crossover.* *Associate a random number from $(0, 1)$ with each row in $\widetilde{\mathrm{PM}}_t^{(i,j)}$ and add this individual to the parent pool if the associated number is less than p_c. Apply Crossover Procedure to all selected pairs of parents and update $\widetilde{\mathrm{PM}}_t^{(i,j)}$.*
3.2. *Mutation.* *Associate a random number from $(0, 1)$ with each gene in $\widetilde{\mathrm{PM}}_t^{(i,j)}$. Mutate the gene which their associated number less than p_m, and update $\widetilde{\mathrm{PM}}_t^{(i,j)}$.*
4. *Migration to other GAs.* *if an interval of K generations is reached, then send and receive migrants, if this migrant is better than the worst one in $\widetilde{\mathrm{PM}}_t^{(i,j)}$ then add migrant Otherwise, go to Step 5.*
5. *Stopping Condition.* *If GM is full, then go to Step 7. Otherwise, go to Step 6.*
6. *Survivor Selection.* *Evaluate the fitness function of all corresponding children in $\widetilde{\mathrm{PM}}_t$, and choose the μ best individuals from the parent and children populations to form the next generation P_{t+1}. Set $t = t + 1$, and go to Step 2.*

For worker 0 do:
7. *Intensification.* *Apply a local search method to the best solution obtained over all the subpopulations in the previous search stage.*

3   Numerical Experiments

Both PGAGM and it's serial version was implemented in C++ and MPICH 2 in the Linux environment on distributed-memory parallel computer, this choice was because C++ compilers available for virtually every platform and operating environment.

3.1   Cluster System

The PGAGM is applied to seven test functions on distributed-memory cluster system. Our cluster consists of sixteen personal computers running Red Hat Enterprise Linux 5 Edition, each one having a Quad-Core AMD Opteron 2.3 GHz processor and 2 Gb of memory. The machines are interconnected by a Gigabit-Ethernet (100 Mbps) network.

3.2   Parameter Setting

In Table 1, PGAGM parameters are summarized with their assigned values. These values are based on the common setting in the literature or determined through our preliminary numerical experiments. In the final intensification process we applied local search by Powell's method [10] with max of $5n$ iterations for all the test functions to the best solution obtained over all the subpopulations out of the main cycle of PGAGM operators.

Table 1. Parameter Setting

Parameters	Definitions	Values
$Popsize$	Population size	420
nop	No. of Processors	16
μ	Number of individuals in each subpopulation	Popsize / nop
ν	No. of individual partitions	$\mu/5$
η	No. of gene partitions	$n/5$
p_c	Crossover probability	0.6
p_m	Mutation probability	$0.1/n$
m	No. of GM columns	$Popsize/4$
ϵ		0.0001
α	Gene Matrix percentage	$24 \log n \log \mu$
K	Migration Interval	30

3.3   Results

We have analyzed the results of minimization experiments on a set of standard benchmark test functions f_1 - f_7 with different properties, since f_1 - f_4 are multimodal functions where the number of local minima increases with the problem dimension and f_5 - f_7 are unimodal functions, the benchmark functions are listed in table 2. The dimension of the search space that chosen for evaluation was 30, 100 and 1000. The presented results are the average of first 50 executions times for dimensions 30, 100 and 30 executions times for dimension 1000, the execution time (σ) in seconds. The results are reported in Tables 3, 4 and 5 for 2, 8 and 16 processors respectively.

3.4   Performance Analysis

PGAGM Speed-up: Figure 1 shows that PGAGM has superlinear Speed-up in lower dimensions since less dimension leads to smaller GM. Hence, when we increase the

Table 2. Benchmark functions

Function Name		Definition	Range
f_1	Rastrigin Function	$10n + \sum_{i=1}^{n} \left(x_i^2 - 10\cos\left(2\pi x_i\right) \right).$	$[-5.12, 5.12]^n$
f_2	Ackley Function	$f_2(\mathbf{x}) = 20 + e - 20e^{-\frac{1}{5}\sqrt{\frac{1}{n}\sum_{i=1}^{n} x_i^2}} - e^{\frac{1}{n}\sum_{i=1}^{n}\cos(2\pi x_i)}.$	$[-32, 32]^n$
f_3	Griewank Function	$\frac{1}{4000} \sum_{i=1}^{n} x_i^2 - \prod_{i=1}^{n} \cos\left(\frac{x_i}{\sqrt{i}}\right) + 1.$	$[-600, 600]^n$
f_4	Sphere Function	$\sum_{i=1}^{n} x_i^2.$	$[-100, 100]^n$
f_5	Schwefel 1.2 Function	$\sum_{i=1}^{n} (\sum_{j=1}^{i} x_j)^2.$	$[-100, 100]^n$
f_6	Schwefel 2.22 Function	$\sum_{i=1}^{n} |x_i| + \Pi_{i=1}^{n}|x_i|.$	$[-10, 10]^n$
f_7	Sum Squares Function	$\sum_{i=1}^{n} i.x_i^2.$	$[-100, 100]^n$

Table 3. Results for 2 processors

Function	Dimension	Function Values	σ	S	ψ
	30	0	0.92	1.78	0.89
f_1	100	0	4.44	1.52	0.76
	1000	0	61.23	1.69	0.86
	30	2.04E-33	0.93	1.63	0.82
f_2	100	0	4.30	1.77	0.88
	1000	0	55.02	1.44	0.72
	30	0	1.02	1.53	0.77
f_3	100	0	4.97	1.62	0.81
	1000	0	65.30	1.39	0.70
	30	1.77E-30	0.74	2.06	1.03
f_4	100	0	4.27	1.43	0.71
	1000	0	51.10	1.45	0.72
	30	0	0.89	1.92	0.96
f_5	100	0	5.12	1.62	0.81
	1000	0	59.43	1.65	0.83
	30	4.05E-24	0.70	2.98	1.49
f_6	100	0	3.86	1.30	0.65
	1000	0	49.78	1.32	0.66
	30	0	0.72	2.45	1.22
f_7	100	0	3.95	1.83	0.92
	1000	0	49.32	1.77	0.89

Table 4. Results for 8 processors

Function	Dimension	Function Values σ		S	ψ
f_1	30	0	0.38	4.32	0.54
	100	0	1.55	4.36	0.55
	1000	0	21.28	4.87	0.61
f_2	30	0	0.39	3.90	0.49
	100	0	1.64	4.64	0.58
	1000	0	22.69	3.49	0.44
f_3	30	0	0.41	3.80	0.48
	100	0	1.44	5.59	0.70
	1000	0	22.15	4.10	0.51
f_4	30	0	0.25	6.08	0.76
	100	0	1.57	3.89	0.49
	1000	0	21.35	3.47	0.43
f_5	30	0	0.47	3.64	0.45
	100	0	1.73	4.79	0.60
	1000	0	23.95	4.09	0.51
f_6	30	0	0.25	8.08	1.01
	100	0	1.61	3.12	0.39
	1000	0	21.54	3.05	0.38
f_7	30	0	0.23	7.65	0.96
	100	0	1.34	5.40	0.67
	1000	0	20.84	4.19	0.52

Table 5. Results for 16 processors

Function	Dimension	Function Values σ		S	ψ
f_1	30	0	0.23	7.13	0.45
	100	0	1.05	6.44	0.40
	1000	0	12.87	8.05	0.50
f_2	30	0	0.23	6.61	0.41
	100	0	1.16	6.56	0.41
	1000	0	14.50	5.46	0.34
f_3	30	0	0.21	7.43	0.46
	100	0	1.11	7.25	0.45
	1000	0	13.42	6.76	0.42
f_4	30	0	0.17	8.94	0.56
	100	0	1.14	5.36	0.33
	1000	0	12.70	5.83	0.36
f_5	30	0	0.28	6.11	0.38
	100	0	1.69	4.91	0.31
	1000	0	13.74	7.14	0.45
f_6	30	0	0.18	11.22	0.70
	100	0	1.10	4.56	0.29
	1000	0	13.89	4.73	0.30
f_7	30	0	0.15	11.73	0.73
	100	0	1.02	7.09	0.44
	1000	0	11.92	7.32	0.46

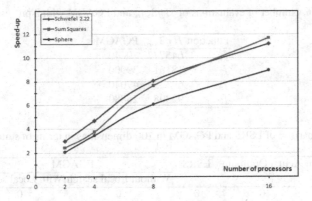

Fig. 1. Speed-up in terms of number of processors for 30 dimensions

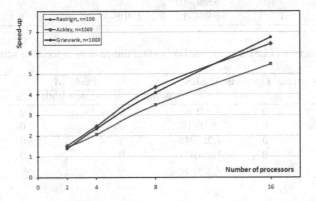

Fig. 2. Speed-up in terms of number of processors for 100, 1000 dimensions

number of processors this increases the gene exploration which fills gene matrix positions more fast and hence ends the execution more fast with wide exploration and higher solution quality. At higher dimensions, PGAGM achieve sublinear Speed-up as shown in figure 2, since higher dimensions leads to bigger GM which takes more execution time in addition to communication time to check the gene diversity and explore the search space.

3.5   Numerical Comparisons

In order to show the efficiency of our algorithm, we compared the results obtained by two recent methods. The first model is Hypercube3 (Hy3) Parallel model described in [2] and the second is Line Search Re-Start (LSRS) described in [4].

We have four test functions (f_1, f_3, f_4, f_5) in common with Hy3, the comparisons of function evaluations found in tables 6. We tested PGAGM with 4 processors on the same functions with the same domain used in LSRS, we compared the average of the first 50 results of solution quality obtained with the average of the results obtained by

Table 6. Number of evaluations of $Hy3_{syn}$ and PGAGM with 8 processors

Function	$Hy3_{syn}$	PGAGM
f_1	645777	80640
f_3	181614	39900
f_4	691239	47040
f_5	92308	26880

Table 7. Comparison of LSRS and PGAGM in 100 dimensions in terms of solution quality

Function	Actual Optimum	LSRS	PGAGM Without Local search	With Local search
f_1	0	0	0	0
f_2	0	-6.5E-19	0	0
f_4	0	6.94E-16	1.62E-32	0
f_6	0	3.98E-10	0	0
f_7	0	6.98E-16	1.40E-45	0

Table 8. Comparison of LSRS and PGAGM in 1000 dimensions in terms of solution quality

Function	Actual Optimum	LSRS	PGAGM Without Local search	With Local search
f_1	0	0	0	0
f_2	0	1.3E-18	0	0
f_4	0	1.25E-18	5.82E-34	0
f_6	0	1.12E-17	0	0
f_7	0	7.35E-33	0	0

LSRS on dimensions 100, 1000 in tables 7, 8. The comparisons shows that PGAGM obtained solution quality better than LSRS and Hy3, and was enable to reach global minimum in most of the test functions even without local search and with cheap time and less number of evaluations than the other methods.

4   Conclusions

In this paper, we include a further study on parallelizing a sequential algorithm called GAMCP. The new model has been called PGAGM, also we discussed the design and the implementation of this coarse grained model that is both flexible and stable on distributed-memory parallel machines.

Our contribution aims at overcoming the drawback of the expensive computational time and function evaluation of GAs specially in high dimensional problems with a parallel approach. The experimental results show that PGAGM is a memory efficient algorithm which simple to be implemented in massively parallel distributed-memory architecture and the efficiency of our proposed method for finding the optimal solution with respect to high dimensional problems.

References

1. Alba, E.: Parallel Metaheuristics: A New Class of Algorithms. A John Wiley & Sons, Inc., USA (2005)
2. Alba, E., Luna, F., Nebro, A.J., Troya, J.M.: Parallel heterogeneous genetic algorithms for continuous optimization. Parallel Computing 30, 699–719 (2004)
3. Alba, E., Troya, J.M.: Influence of the migration policy in parallel distributed GAs with structured and panmictic populations. Appl. Intell. 12(3), 163–181 (2000)
4. Grosan, C., Abraham, A., Hassainen, A.E.: A line search approach for high dimensional function optimization. Telecommun. Syst. 46, 217–243 (2011)
5. He, K., Zhengb, L., Donga, S., Tangc, L., Wud, J., Zhenge, C.: PGO: A parallel computing platform for global optimization based on genetic algorithm. Computers & Geosciences 33, 357–366 (2007)
6. Hedar, A., Ali, A.F.: Genetic algorithm with population partitioning and space reduction for high dimensional problems. In: Proceeding of the International Conference on Computer Engineering & Systems (ICCES 2009), Egypt, pp. 151–156 (2009)
7. Hedar, A., Ong, B.T., Fukushima, M.: Genetic algorithms with automatic accelerated termination, Technical Report 2007-002, Department of Applied Mathematics and Physics, Kyoto University (2007)
8. Hedar, A., Ong, B.T., Fukushima, M.: Genetic algorithms combined with accelerated mutation and automatic termination (submitted)
9. Luque, G., Alba, E., Dorronsoro, B.: Parallel Genetic Algorithms. In: Alba, E. (ed.) Parallel Metaheuristics: A New Class of Algorithms. John Wiley & Sons, Inc., Hoboken (2005)
10. Press, W.H., Bethe, H.A., Vetterling, W.T., Flannery, B.P.: Numerical Recipes: The Art of Scientific Computing, 3rd edn. Cambridge University Press, USA (2007)
11. Wang, N.: A parallel computing application of the genetic algorithm for lubrication optimization. Tribology Letters 18(1) (2005)

Combining Multiple K-Means Clusterings of Chemical Structures Using Cluster-Based Similarity Partitioning Algorithm

Faisal Saeed[1,2,*], Naomie Salim[1], Ammar Abdo[3], and Hamza Hentabli[1]

[1] Faculty of Computer Science and Information Systems, Universiti Teknologi Malaysia, Malaysia
[2] Information Technology Department, Sanhan Community College, Sana'a, Yemen
[3] Computer Science Department, Hodeidah University, Hodeidah, Yemen
alsamet.faisal@gmail.com

Abstract. Consensus clustering methods have been used in many areas to improve the quality of individual clusterings. In this paper, graph-based consensus clustering, Cluster-based Similarity Partitioning Algorithm (CSPA), was used to improve the quality of chemical structures clustering by enhancing the ability to separate active from inactive molecules in each cluster and improve the robustness and stability of individual clusterings. The clustering was evaluated using Quality Partition Index (QPI) measure and the results were compared with the Ward's clustering method. The chemical dataset MDL Drug Data Report (MDDR) database was used for experiments. The results obtained by combining multiple K-means clusterings showed that graph-based consensus clustering, CSPA, can improve the quality of individual chemical structure clusterings.

Keywords: 2D Fingerprint, Compound Selection, Consensus Clustering, K-Means, Molecular Datasets, Ward's Method.

1 Introduction

In chemoinformatics, there are many approaches for compound selection and the cluster-based compound selection (clustering) is the most commonly used. The main objective of clustering is to organize a collection of data items into some meaningful clusters, so that the items within a cluster are more similar to each other than the items in the other clusters. There are many studies on individual clustering techniques that have been used for chemical structures clustering [1-3].

Brown and Martin [3] considered the Ward's clustering method to be the most efficient clustering method in cluster-based compound selection. However, as it is known, no clustering method is capable of correctly finding the best clustering results for all datasets and applications. So, the idea of combining different clustering results (consensus clustering) is considered as an alternative approach for improving the quality of the individual clustering algorithms [4].

---

* Corresponding author.

A. Ell Hassanien et al. (Eds.): AMLTA 2012, CCIS 322, pp. 304–312, 2012.
© Springer-Verlag Berlin Heidelberg 2012

Consensus clustering involves two main stages: (i) partitions generation (also known as an ensemble generation) and (ii) combination using the consensus function. In the partitions generation step, as many as possible individual partitions will be generated. There are no constraints about how the partitions must be generated. Therefore, different generation mechanisms can be applied including: (i) different object representations; (ii) different individual clustering methods; (iii) different parameters initialisation for clustering methods; and (iv) data resampling. In the second stage, there are two main approaches: the objects co-occurrence-based and median partition-based consensus functions. Graph-based consensus clustering is widely used for the first approach.

Fred and Jain [5] used the K-means algorithm to generate an ensemble of clusterings by random initializations of cluster centroids. Then, data partitions present in these clusterings were mapped into a new similarity matrix between patterns, based on a voting mechanism. Fred and Jain [5] and Topchy et al. [6] summarised that consensus clustering can improve the robustness, consistency, novelty and stability of individual clusterings.

In chemical structures clustering, it is most unlikely that any single method will yield the best classification under all circumstances, even if attention is restricted to a single type of application [7]. The combination procedure, data fusion, has been used in virtual screening [8-10]. Over the last few years, data fusion has become accepted as a simple way of enhancing the performance of existing systems for ligand-based virtual screening, by combining the results of two or more screening methods. In some cases, the fused search may be better than even the best individual screening method when averaged over large numbers of searches [9].

Chu et al. [7] used consensus similarity matrix clustering methods on sets of chemical compounds represented by 2D fingerprints (ECFP_4) and they concluded that consensus methods can indeed out-perform the Ward's method, the current standard clustering method for chemoinformatics applications. However, based on the implemented methods, it was not the case if the clustering is restricted to a single consensus method. In this paper, the graph-based consensus clustering methods, CSPA, was applied to combine multiple runs of K-means algorithm to evaluate the effectiveness of consensus clustering for chemical structures. The K-means algorithm was used for ensemble generation because it is one of the simplest clustering algorithms and it is computationally efficient.

2   Materials and Methods

2.1   Dataset

Experiments were conducted over the MDL Drug Data Report (MDDR) database [11]. This database consists of 102516 molecules. Two datasets (DS1-DS2) were chosen from the MDDR database. These datasets have been used for many virtual screening experiments [12-14]. The dataset DS1 contains ten homogeneous activity classes (5083 molecules) and the dataset DS2 contains ten heterogeneous activity classes (8568 molecules). Details of these two datasets are presented in Tables 1-2. Each row in the tables contains an activity class, the number of molecules belonging to the class, and the diversity of the class, which was computed as the mean pairwise

Tanimoto similarity calculated across all pairs of molecules in the class. For the clustering experiments, two 2D fingerprint descriptors were used, which were developed by Scitegic's Pipeline Pilot [15]. These were 120-bit ALOGP and 1024-bit extended connectivity fingerprints (ECFP_4).

Table 1. MDDR Activity Classes for Low Diverse DS1 Dataset

Activity Index	Activity class	Active molecules	Pairwise Similarity
			Main
07707	Adenosine (A1) Agonists	207	0.229
07708	Adenosine (A2) Agonists	156	0.305
31420	Renin Inhibitors 1	1300	0.290
42710	CCK Agonists	111	0.361
64100	Monocyclic Lactams	1346	0.336
64200	Cephalosporins	113	0.322
64220	Carbacephems	1051	0.269
64500	Carbapenems	126	0.260
64350	Tribactams	388	0.305
75755	Vitamin D Analogous	455	0.386

Table 2. MDDR Activity Classes for High Diverse DS2 Dataset

Activity Index	Activity class	Active molecules	Pairwise Similarity
			Main
09249	Muscarinic (M1) Agonists	900	0.111
12455	NMDA Receptor Antagonists	1400	0.098
12464	Nitric Oxide Synthase Inhibitors	505	0.102
31281	Dopamine Hydroxylase Inhibitors	106	0.125
43210	Aldose Reductase Inhibitors	957	0.119
71522	Reverse Transcriptase Inhibitors	700	0.103
75721	Aromatase Inhibitors	636	0.110
78331	Cyclooxygenase Inhibitors	636	0.108
78348	Phospholipase A2 Inhibitors	617	0.123
78351	Lipoxygenase Inhibitors	2111	0.113

2.2   Partitions Generation

Every consensus clustering method is made up of two steps: partitions generation and consensus functions. In this paper, multiple runs of K-means algorithm were used to generate the ensemble with size n=5-50 with 5-times step. The values of k 500, 600, 700, 800, 900 and 1000 were used to generate partitions with different number of clusters. The molecule-cluster similarity was calculated using the Euclidean metric between the molecule's fingerprint and the centroid of the cluster, where the centroid is the arithmetic mean of the fingerprints of the molecules currently contained in the cluster.

2.3   Cluster-Based Similarity Partitioning Algorithm

The Cluster-based Similarity Partitioning Algorithm, proposed by Strehl and Gosh [16], was used to obtain the consensus partition from ensembles generated in the previous step. The algorithm was developed based on transforming the set of clusterings into a hyper-graph representation. By using CSPA, a clustering signifies a relationship between objects in the same cluster and can thus be used to establish a measure of pairwise similarity. The algorithm was coded by the published cluster ensemble package that is available on (www.strehl.com).

The similarity matrix is generated so that each two objects have a similarity of 1 if they are in the same cluster and a similarity of 0 otherwise. The process is repeated for each run of K-means clustering (5-50 times). A $n \times n$ binary similarity matrix $\mathbf{S}$ can be created where n is the total number of objects in the dataset. The entries of $\mathbf{S}$ are divided by r, which is the number of runs of K-means clustering. Now, we can use the similarity matrix to recluster the objects using any reasonable similarity-based clustering algorithm. Here, we view the similarity matrix as graph (vertex = object, edge weight = similarity) and partition it using METIS [17], because of its robust and scalable properties, in order to obtain the consensus partition.

2.4   Performance Evaluation

The results were evaluated based on the effectiveness of clustering methods to separate active from inactive molecules using Quality Partition Index (QPI) measure, which was devised by Varin et al. [18]. As defined by [7], an active cluster is a non-singleton cluster for which the percentage of active molecules in the cluster is greater than the percentage of active molecules in the dataset as a whole. Let p be the number of actives in active clusters, q be the number of inactives in active clusters, r be the number of actives in inactive clusters (i.e., clusters that are not active clusters) and s be the number of singleton actives. The high value occurs when the actives are clustered tightly together and separated from the inactive molecules. Then the QPI is defined to be:

$$QPI = \frac{p}{p+q+r+s} \tag{1}$$

Then, the results will be compared with the Ward's clustering method, the standard clustering method for chemoinformatics applications.

3   Results and Discussion

The generation process was done by multiple runs of K-means algorithm, each with random initialisation of cluster centroids. The number of partitions generated in this step was ranged between n=5 to n=50, with 5-times step. Then, all the generated partitions were combined using CSPA to obtain the consensus partition. This process is done for each fingerprint (ALOGP and ECFP_4) in DS1 and DS2.

Table 3. Effectivenss of clustering of low diverse dataset DS1: ALOGP Fingerprint

Clustering Method		No. of clusters					
		500	600	700	800	900	1000
	N=5	69.76	71.1	74.44	75.56	77.08	78.87
	N=10	70.33	72.02	74.55	76.97	77.43	80.06
	N=15	70.17	73.03	74.02	76.42	79.76	80.21
	N=20	69.75	72.27	73.13	75.20	78.74	80.70
	N=25	72.41	73.16	77.10	77.52	80.61	82.78
Consensus	N=30	73.16	76.56	78.30	80.14	81.25	83.15
(CSPA)	N=35	74.85	79.04	78.81	81.30	83.99	85.01
	N=40	75.71	79.18	80.52	82.37	85.03	85.24
	N=45	**78.02**	**79.88**	81.01	82.18	84.06	**86.73**
	N=50	76.77	78.28	**81.10**	**83.54**	**85.85**	85.70
Individual	Wards' Method	71.78	73.43	75.07	76.46	77.97	79.96

The mean of QPI values were averaged over the ten activity classes of the datasets DS1-DS2. Tables 3-6 show the effectiveness of MDDR dataset clustering using ALOGP and ECFP_4 fingerprints. The best QPI value of consensus clustering methods for each column was bold-faced for ease of reference.

Table 4. Effectivenss of clustering of high diverse dataset DS2: ALOGP Fingerprint

Clustering Method		No. of clusters					
		500	600	700	800	900	1000
	N=5	49.87	51.04	53.26	55.77	58.33	59.87
	N=10	50.79	53.20	54.25	55.44	59.35	61.24
	N=15	50.88	54.43	54.83	55.61	59.60	61.21
	N=20	**52.62**	53.36	54.64	56.07	60.39	**62.09**
	N=25	51.86	53.44	55.24	56.72	59.48	61.47
Consensus	N=30	51.30	52.99	54.59	**57.72**	60.20	61.40
(CSPA)	N=35	52.12	**54.49**	54.94	56.89	59.14	61.29
	N=40	52.38	53.96	53.88	56.97	**60.48**	61.96
	N=45	51.23	52.99	**55.46**	57.70	59.42	61.02
	N=50	51.36	53.31	54.85	57.27	60.00	61.65
Individual	Ward's Method	39.01	41.83	44.49	46.03	47.89	49.45

Visual inspection of QPI values in Tables 3-6 enables comparisons to be made between the effectiveness of consensus clustering of MDDR datasets and the Ward's method. In addition, ten sets of consensus clustering, for each fingerprint in DS1-DS2, were observed in order to study the effectiveness of consensus clustering with different ensemble sizes. The results in Table 3-4 show that CSPA consensus clustering obtained robust and novel result when K-means algorithm was run 20-50 times using ALOGP. The performance of consensus clustering for two datasets outperformed the Wards' method.

Table 5. Effectivenss of clustering of low diverse dataset DS1: ECFP_4 Fingerprint

Clustering Method		No. of clusters					
		500	600	700	800	900	1000
	N=5	81.03	83.78	83.95	87.20	88.00	87.89
	N=10	82.45	85.36	85.96	89.04	88.84	90.31
	N=15	83.74	85.83	85.69	88.16	89.66	90.48
	N=20	84.13	83.95	86.84	87.92	88.28	90.52
	N=25	84.91	86.37	86.96	88.40	88.87	90.55
Consensus	N=30	**85.11**	86.66	**88.58**	**89.30**	89.87	91.29
(CSPA)	N=35	85.09	**86.80**	85.53	88.25	89.56	90.87
	N=40	82.79	85.19	87.11	88.19	88.93	90.46
	N=45	83.42	85.96	87.55	88.48	**90.12**	**91.32**
	N=50	84.36	85.04	86.66	87.44	89.55	90.66
Individual	Ward's Method	87.68	88.95	89.68	90.54	91.23	92.42

For consensus of two datasets which were represented by ECFP_4 fingerprint, as shown in Tables 5-6, the best QPI values of consensus clustering were also obtained from ensembles of size n = 20-50. The performance of consensus clustering obtained robust results which were better than overall performance of individual clusterings. The values of QPI in both datasets for consensus clustering were closer to the Ward's method especially for low diverse dataset.

Moreover, the CSPA consensus clustering provides stable clusters by decreasing the sensitivity to noise and outliers. The average percentages of singleton clusters of individual clusterings compared to consensus clustering are shown in Tables 7-8 for both fingerprints in DS1-DS2. The results show that consensus clustering partition the datasets with average percentage of singleton equal to zero, which is better than individual clusterings and the Ward's method. For example, 1.67% of molecules of DS1 were clustered as singletons when Ward's method was applied on ALOGP fingerprint with partition size equal to 1000 clusters.

Table 6. Effectivenss of clustering of high diverse dataset DS2: ECFP_4 Fingerprint

Clustering Method		No. of clusters					
		500	600	700	800	900	1000
	N=5	57.28	60.62	61.80	64.03	68.73	71.30
	N=10	57.07	60.84	62.82	66.64	69.47	**74.39**
	N=15	58.90	61.82	63.53	64.14	69.15	73.17
	N=20	58.30	**63.47**	62.91	65.07	70.64	72.64
Consensus	N=25	57.96	62.42	64.48	66.21	70.00	72.35
(CSPA)	N=30	58.54	62.57	63.60	67.25	70.33	73.20
	N=35	58.27	62.92	64.16	66.87	69.57	73.33
	N=40	59.18	61.32	64.46	**67.66**	69.48	72.74
	N=45	59.96	63.29	**64.53**	66.07	**71.87**	73.73
	N=50	**60.41**	63.25	63.35	66.29	70.56	72.94
Individual	Ward's Method	64.86	68.89	74.12	76.09	79.13	82.23

Table 7. The percentages of singleton clusters for low diverse dataset DS1

Clustering Method			No. of clusters					
			500	600	700	800	900	1000
		Kmeans (Avg)	0.13	0.27	0.52	0.84	1.20	1.69
	ALOGP	Wards	0.32	0.53	0.63	0.83	1.26	1.67
Individual (Avg)		Kmeans (Avg)	0.07	0.15	0.25	0.42	0.67	1.00
	ECFP_4	Wards	0.00	0.02	0.10	0.24	0.45	0.65
Consensus (Avg)			0.00	0.00	0.00	0.00	0.00	0.00

Table 8. The percentages of singleton clusters for high diverse dataset DS2

Clustering Method			No. of clusters					
			500	600	700	800	900	1000
		Kmeans (Avg)	0.00	0.01	0.02	0.04	0.05	0.09
	ALOGP	Ward' method	0.21	0.27	0.35	0.39	0.50	0.61
Individual (Avg)		Kmeans (Avg)	0.01	0.01	0.03	0.04	0.07	0.09
	ECFP_4	Ward's method	0.00	0.00	0.00	0.00	0.02	0.04
Consensus (Avg)			0.00	0.00	0.00	0.00	0.00	0.00

4   Conclusion

The results of the experiments show that similarity-based partitioning algorithm, CSPA, can improve the effectiveness of chemical structures clustering. The best performance was obtained when the ensemble was generated by 20-50 multiple runs of K-means algorithm. The performance of CSPA consensus clustering is more robust, novel, stable and out-performs the Ward's method in case of using ALOGP fingerprint. When ECFP_4 fingerprint is used, it provides more robust and stable clustering and gives results that are closer to the Ward's clustering. The experiments suggest that the graph-based consensus clustering, CSPA, can improve the robustness and stability of chemical structures clustering for both low and high diverse datasets by combining multiple runs of K-means algorithm. In the future work, more graph-based consensus clustering methods will be examined with different partitions generation mechanisms.

Acknowledgment. This work is supported by Ministry of Higher Education (MOHE) and Research Management Centre (RMC) at the Universiti Teknologi Malaysia (UTM) under Research University Grant Category (VOT Q.J130000.7128.00H72). We also would like to thank MIS-MOHE for sponsoring the first author.

References

1. Adamson, G.W., Bush, J.A.: A method for the automatic classification of chemical structures. Information Storage and Retrieval 9, 561–568 (1973)
2. Downs, G.M., Barnard, J.M.: Clustering of Chemical Structures on the Basis of Two-Dimensional Similarity Measures. Journal of Chemical Information and Computer Science 32, 644–649 (1992)
3. Brown, R.D., Martin, Y.C.: Use of structure-activity data to compare structure-based clustering methods and descriptors for use in compound selection. J. Chem. Inf. Comput. Sci. 36, 572–584 (1996)
4. Vega-Pons, S., Ruiz-Schulcloper, J.: A survey of clustering ensemble algorithms. International Journal of Pattern Recognition and Artificial Intelligence 25(3), 337–372 (2011)
5. Fred, A.L.N., Jain, A.K.: Combining multiple clustering using evidence accumulation. IEEE Trans. Patt. Anal. Mach. Intell. 27, 835–850 (2005)
6. Topchy, A., Jain, A.K., Punch, W.: A mixture model of clustering ensembles. In: SIAM Int. Conf. Data Mining, pp. 379–390 (2004)
7. Chu, C.-W., Holliday, J., Willett, P.: Combining multiple classifications of chemical structures using consensus clustering. Bioorganic & Medicinal Chemistry (March 10, 2012)
8. Salim, N., Holliday, J.D., Willett, P.: Combination of Fingerprint-Based Similarity Coefficients Using Data Fusion. J. Chem. Inf. Comput. Sci. 43, 435–442 (2003)
9. Willet, P.: Enhancing the Effectiveness of Ligand-Based Virtual Screening Using Data Fusion. QSAR Comb. Sci. 25, 1143–1152 (2006)
10. Chen, B., Mueller, C., Willett, P.: Combination Rules for Group Fusion in Similarity-Based Virtual Screening. Mol. Inf. 29, 533–541 (2010)
11. Moffat, K., Gillet, V.J., Whittle, M., Bravi, G., Leach, A.R.: A Comparison of Field-Based Similarity Searching Methods: CatShape, FBSS, and ROCS. J. Chem. Inf. Model. 48, 719–729 (2008)

12. Abdo, A., Chen, B., Mueller, C., Salim, N., Willett, P.: Ligand-Based Virtual Screening Using Bayesian Networks. J. Chem. Inf. Model. 50, 1012–1020 (2010)
13. Abdo, A., Salim, N.: New Fragment Weighting Scheme for the Bayesian Inference Network in Ligand-Based Virtual Screening. J. Chem. Inf. Model. 51, 25–32 (2011)
14. Abdo, A., Saeed, F., Hentabli, H., Ali, A., Salim, N., Ahmed, A.: Ligand expansion in ligand-based virtual screening using relevance feedback. Journal of Computer-Aided Molecular Design 26, 279–287 (2012)
15. Sci Tegic Accelrys Inc. (September 1, 2012), http://www.http//accelrys.com/
16. Strehl, A., Ghosh, J.: Cluster Ensembles - A Knowledge Reuse Framework for Combining Multiple Partitions. J. Machine Learning Research 3, 583–617 (2002)
17. Karypis, G., Kumar, V.: A fast and high quality multilevel scheme for partitioning irregular graphs. SIAM J. Scient. Comput. 20, 359–392 (1998)
18. Varin, T., Saettel, N., Villain, J., Lesnard, A., Dauphin, F., Bureau, R., Rault, S.J.: Enzyme Inhib. Med. Chem. 23, 593 (2008)

Part V

Data Classification and Clustering Theory and Applications

Soft Flexible Overlapping Biclustering Utilizing Hybrid Search Strategies

Mohamed A. Mahfouz[*] and Mohamed A. Ismail

Department of Computer and Systems Engineering,
Faculty of Engineering, University of Alexandria, Egypt
{m.a.mahfouz,drmaismail}@gmail.com

Abstract. Biclustering is powerful data mining technique that allows identifying groups of genes which are co-regulated and co-expressed under a subset of conditions for analyzing gene expression data from microarray technology. Possibilistic biclustering algorithms can give much insight towards different biological processes that each gene might participate into and the conditions under which its participation is most effective. This paper proposes an iterative algorithm that is able to produce k-possibly overlapping semi-possibilistic (or soft) biclusters satisfying input constraints. Several previous possibilistic approaches are sensitive to their input parameters and initial conditions beside that they don't allow constraints to be put on the residue of produced biclusters and can work only as refinement step after applying hard biclustering. Our semi-possibilistic approach allows discovering overlapping biclusters with meaningful memberships while reducing the effect of very small memberships that may participate in iterations of possibilistic approaches. Experimental study on Yeast and Human shows that our algorithm can offer substantial improvements in terms of the quality of the output biclusters over several previously proposed biclustering algorithms.

Keywords: Possibilistic clustering, fuzzy clustering, biclustering, bi-dimensional clustering, gene expression analysis.

1 Introduction

Biclustering plays an important role in analyzing the huge amount of valuable data produced by microarrays. Microarrays are molecular biology tools by which the expression patterns of thousands of genes can be monitored simultaneously. The gene expression data are organized as matrices where rows represent genes, columns represent various samples such as tissues or experimental conditions, and numbers in each cell characterize the expression level of the particular gene in the particular sample. Biclustering can be defined as identifying a k possibly overlapping biclusters where a bicluster can be viewed as a group of correlated genes with respect to a group of conditions. Discovery of such biclusters is essential in revealing the significant connections in gene regulatory networks.

---

[*] Corresponding author.

A. Ell Hassanien et al. (Eds.): AMLTA 2012, CCIS 322, pp. 315–326, 2012.

A biclustering survey is given in [1] and [16] where a categorization of the different heuristic approaches is shown, such as iterative row and column clustering divide and conquers strategy, greedy search, exhaustive biclustering enumeration, distribution parameter identification and others. Several biclustering algorithms aimed at discovering biclusters with coherent values [2]-[7]. Other biclustering algorithms focus on the relative order of the columns in the bicluster rather than on the uniformity of the actual values in the data matrix [18].

The concept of residue is introduced in [2] as a similarity score to measure the coherence of the rows and columns in a bicluster and to quantify the difference between the actual value of an entry and the expected value of an entry predicted from the corresponding gene base, condition base, and the bicluster base. The mean square residue (MSR) is defined as the average of squared residues of all entries of the bicluster. Several biclustering algorithms are based on iteratively minimizing the mean square residue while maximizing the size of biclusters. MSR is used in several approaches such as [2], [3], [5] and [6]. The algorithm CC [2] identifies one bicluster at a time, mask it with random numbers, and repeat the procedure in order to eventually find other biclusters. Several enhancements to CC are proposed in FLOC [3]. FLOC starts from a set of seeds (initial biclusters) and carries out an iterative process to improve the overall quality of the biclustering.

Other algorithms are based on maximizing the average similarity between rows/columns of a biclusters such as the correlation based algorithms BISOFT [4] and BCCA [15]. In BISOFT, after all biclusters are generated, memberships are assigned to genes only using simple formula. Both algorithms start from initial bicluster and continuously add rows and columns to initial biclusters that resulting in the average similarity between rows/columns above a threshold whereas sometime removing previously added rows/columns may allow more rows and columns to be added. Correlation based algorithms can be easily modified to use any other (dis)similarity measure (http://gedas.bizhat.com/dist.htm) but such algorithms suffer high complexity.

In [10] an exhaustive enumeration biclustering algorithm is proposed that is based on closed itemsets enumeration algorithm termed BIMODULE. It start by normalizing and discretizing the data matrix into L levels and the discretized data are given as input to closed itemsets miner in a form of transaction items with support equals to the minimum accepted number of genes in a bicluster. In [11] an iterative algorithm termed BIDENS is presented that approximates a number of k possibly overlapping biclusters, their discretization is done using histogram and a level corresponding to several contiguous bins. The bicluster model in [11] extends the model in [12] to a generalized noise tolerant bicluster model using the concepts introduced in [14], but unlike [12], their proposed iterative procedure can mine coherent biclusters. The most recent related work is the hyper-graph based geometric biclustering (HGBC) algorithm [17] that uses the Hough transform (HT) to find sub-biclusters which correspond to the linear structures in column-pair spaces then build a hypergraph model to merge the sub-biclusters into larger ones.

The above algorithms produce crisp biclusters. It is desirable to have fuzzy biclusters that provide a degree of participation of genes, and the conditions under which its participation is most effective as well. One of the early fuzzy biclustering algorithms is PBC [5]. The algorithm PBC is based on the possibilistic clustering paradigm [8]. It formulates the biclustering problem as optimization of objective function to enables different degrees of membership of each gene or condition into different biclusters. In algorithm EPBC [6] the objective function of PBC is modified to allow missing values and the derivative of this objective function is accurately computed also the number of input parameter is reduced. Algorithm DPBC [7] generalizes and extends the idea of PBC to be applied using other (dis)similarity measures. These algorithms are sensitive to their initial conditions and input parameters. Also they do not allow constraints on the produced biclusters.

The previously explained drawbacks motivate us to propose soft biclustering algorithm based on randomized search termed SOFTFLOC. The proposed algorithm follows of a technique of building biclusters instead of breaking the whole matrix into smaller biclusters [1]. This is achieved through initiating the solution with k bicluster each of them contains only a randomly selected entry of the input gene expression matrix, and iteratively changing the memberships of rows and columns in a bicluster in randomized search manner by a small step in [0,1] until sequence of pre-specified number of iterations fail to satisfies the criterion of having the mean squared residue of all produced biclusters below a pre-specified threshold. The randomized search approach improves its performance over exhaustive approach such as BISOFT and BCCA. Also its alternating search strategy [19] and the small step used in changing the memberships of rows/columns (instead of changing the membership from 0 to 1 or from 1 to 0 as in CC and FLOC) reduces the possibility that the algorithm stuck in local minimum earlier and allow producing much larger biclusters than those produced by FLOC and CC. Experimental results show that the proposed algorithm is able to start from very small initial bicluster and is not sensitive to initial conditions compared to possibilistic algorithms such as PBC and EPBC. Also it is able to deal with null values in seamless manner and can support several future constraints at nearly no extra cost. The superior capability of clustering by SOFTFLOC over a number of other algorithms, namely, CC, FLOC, PBC and EPBC is demonstrated through experiments with datasets that are publicly available. Various issues related to the characteristics of the algorithm are also discussed.

2   The Proposed Model

2.1   A Bicluster

Gene expression data is organized as matrices where each entry x_{ij} in a gene expression matrix corresponds to the logarithm of the relative abundance of the mRNA of a gene i under a specific condition j, and may have a null value. Given a data matrix X with set of rows R of size n and set of columns C of size m, Biclustering can be defined formally as identifying a k possibly overlapping biclusters $B_i = (I_i, J_i)$ where I_i subset of R and J_i subset of C such that each bicluster B_i satisfies some specific characteristics of homogeneity. A fuzzy formulation of the problem can help to better model the bicluster and also to improve the optimization process. In [5], the concept of biclustering is generalized in a fuzzy set theoretical approach. The Authors assign two vectors of membership for each bicluster, one for the rows and one other for the columns, denoting them respectively a and b. The membership u_{ij} of an entry x_{ij} to a bicluster can be obtained by an integration of its row and column memberships. While in a crisp set framework row i and column j can either belong to the bicluster ($a_i = 1$ and $b_j = 1$) or not ($a_i = 0$ or $b_j = 0$) i.e. an entry x_{ij} of X belongs to a bicluster if both $a_i = 1$ and $bj = 1$ and its membership u_{ij} to the bicluster is $u_{ij} = $ and(a_i, b_j). In fuzzy approach, a_i and b_j are allowed to belong in the interval [0, 1]. In this paper the membership u_{ij} of an element x_{ij} is chosen as the product of the memberships of its row and column as follows:

$$u_{ij} = a_i b_j \qquad \text{(Product)} \qquad (1)$$

The product is more reasonable than the average of a_i and b_j [5]. For example, it gives a higher membership for entry having $a_i=0.2$ and $b_j=0.8$ over another entry having $a_i=0.01$ and $b_j=0.99$ while both entries have the same average membership 0.5.

2.2   Scoring a Bicluster

The proposed algorithm should iteratively maximize the average size while minimize the mean squared residue MSR of the resulting biclusters. By minimizing MSR, thus privileging biclusters with co-regulated gene expression values both across their genes and conditions. The score of a bicluster could be defined as a linear combination of the following two factors:

1) its mean square residue MSR   and   2) its volume (size) v.

The residue r_{ij} of an entry x_{ij} in a bicluster (I, J) is defined in [3] as follows:

$$r_{ij} = x_{ij} - x_{iJ} - x_{Ij} + x_{IJ} \qquad (2)$$

Where x_{iJ} is the average of the not null entries x_{ij} in row i for all columns $j \in J$. x_{Ij} is the average of the specified entries x_{ij} in column j for all rows $i \in I$. x_{IJ} is the average of the specified entries x_{ij} of the sub-matrix defined by all rows $i \in I$ and all column $j \in J$. If x_{ij} is null then $r_{ij}=0$.

From (1), the residue r_{ij} of an entry x_{ij} in the fuzzy paradigm can be computed as follows:

$$r_{ij} = x_{ij} - (\sum_{j=1}^{m} b_j x_{ij} / \sum_{j=1}^{m} b_j) - \sum_{i=1}^{n} a_i x_{ij} / \sum_{i=1}^{n} a_i + \sum_{i=1}^{n}\sum_{j=1}^{m} a_i b_j x_{ij} / \sum_{i=1}^{n}\sum_{j=1}^{m} a_i b_j \qquad (3)$$

The mean square residue MSR of the whole bicluster B= (a,b) is

$$MSR \ (B) = (\sum_{i=1}^{n} \sum_{j=1}^{m} a_i b_j r_{ij}^2) / \sum_{i=1}^{n} \sum_{j=1}^{m} a_i b_j \qquad (4)$$

The volume of a bicluster is the number of defined entries (not null) in the bicluster and can be calculated as follows:

$$v = \sum_{i=1}^{n} \sum_{j=1}^{m} a_i b_j \qquad (5)$$

Calculating the volume as in (5) has an advantage over other approaches that weights the relative number of genes and relative number of conditions separately [5], [18]. In equations (3)-(5) we can deal with null values in seamless manner by excluding null entries from computations.

2.3   A Graph Abstraction

The process of finding k possibly overlapping biclusters in a given data matrix X with set of rows R of size n and set of columns C of size m can be viewed abstractly as searching through a certain graph as in [13]. In this graph a node is represented by the set of k biclusters $\{(I_i, J_i), i=1,2,..k, I_i \subset R, J_i \subset C\}$. Two nodes are neighbors (i.e connected by an arc) if and only if one of the k biclusters represented by these nodes differs by only one object (row or column). Neighbors of a node can be derived from it by either adding (or removing) single row or column to (from) one of its biclusters. Each node has an associated two lists of values representing the mean squared residue and the size of the k biclusters. Each edge can be assigned a weight representing the cost differential between the two neighbors. Alternatively, the weight can represent the benefits deferential (gain) between neighbors measured as a function of the amount of increase in size and the amount of decrease in mean squared residue of the bicluster that differs in the two nodes.

It is obvious that biclustering algorithms such as CC and FLOC can be viewed as a search for maximum on the previous graph. While they iteratively adds or removes rows/columns i.e. change their memberships between 0 and 1 and compute the gain of such change as function of the amount of decrease in the relative MSR and increase in the relative volume. The proposed algorithm, instead, changes the memberships between set of fixed values for example (0, 0.25, 0.5, 0.75, 1). Each time the membership is changed, the gain of this change is efficiently computed as explained in the following sections. While the size of the graph increases as the step decreases, the number of neighbors of a node has an upper bound $2k$ $(n+m)$. Using this smaller step increases the number of possible good transitions on the graph which reduces the possibility that the algorithm gets stuck on local minimum earlier. Although the proposed algorithm for searching the graph is basically a hill-climbing algorithm, exploration is necessary [19] since it might be stuck in a local minimum at the very beginning. Therefore at each iteration, a pre-specified number of actions are selected from the best actions (actions yielding the best improvements) to be applied to current biclustering. Several modifications to the way this graph is searched in FLOC are proposed in this study to allow the proposed algorithm to produce much larger biclusters than FLOC within the same preset threshold.

2.4   Computing Edge Weight

Changing the membership of a row/column h in a bicluster $B(a, b)$ by δ is considered an action. In order to compute the gain of an action we need to compute the mean square residue MSR and the volume of a bicluster v after executing such action. Based on (3) the new residue of an entry x_{ij} after changing the membership of a row h by δ can be calculated as follows:

$$r_{ij} = x_{ij} - (\sum_{j=1}^{m} b_j x_{ij} / \sum_{j=1}^{m} b_j) - ((\delta x_{hj} + \sum_{i=1}^{n} a_i x_{ij})/(\delta + \sum_{i=1}^{n} a_i)) + (\delta \sum_{j=1}^{m} b_j x_{hj} + \sum_{i=1}^{n} \sum_{j=1}^{m} a_i b_j x_{ij})/(\delta \sum_{j=1}^{m} b_j + \sum_{i=1}^{n} \sum_{j=1}^{m} a_i b_j) \qquad (6)$$

Similarly the new residue after changing the membership of a column h by δ can be calculated as follows:

$$r_{ij} = x_{ij} - (\delta x_{ih} + \sum_{j=1}^{m} b_j x_{ij})/(\delta + \sum_{j=1}^{m} b_j) - (\sum_{i=1}^{n} a_i x_{ij}/\sum_{i=1}^{n} a_i) + (\delta \sum_{j=1}^{n} a_j x_{jh} + \sum_{i=1}^{n}\sum_{j=1}^{m} a_i b_j x_{ij})/(\delta \sum_{j=1}^{n} a_j + \sum_{i=1}^{n}\sum_{j=1}^{m} a_i b_j) \qquad (7)$$

Using (5), the new volume v_{new} after changing the membership of a row h by δ can be calculated from the old volume v_{old} (before the change) as follows:

$$v_{new} = \delta \sum_{j=1}^{m} b_j + \sum_{i=1}^{n}\sum_{j=1}^{m} a_i b_j = \delta \sum_{j=1}^{m} b_j + v_{old} \qquad (8)$$

Similarly the new volume after changing the membership of a column h by δ is:

$$v_{new} = \delta \sum_{j=1}^{n} a_j + \sum_{i=1}^{n}\sum_{j=1}^{m} a_i b_j = \delta \sum_{j=1}^{n} a_j + v_{old} \qquad (9)$$

Here we present a pre-specified threshold α, which are used to limit the mean squared residue of produced biclusters. This threshold controls the amount of co-regulation among gene/condition subsets in each bicluster the user may need. The gain of an action c is defined similar to [3] as follows:

$$\text{gain} = msr_{old}(msr_{old} - msr_{new})/\alpha^2 + (v_{new} - v_{old})/v_{old} \qquad (10)$$

Where msr_{new}, msr_{old} are the mean square residue of a bicluster $B(a,b)$ before and after executing the action c. Similarly v_{old}, v_{new} are the volumes of the bicluster before and after executing the action c. α is the maximum accepted MSR of produced biclusters.

An efficient method for computing the gain in (10) is to re-compute only the gene and condition bases affected by the action [3]. The values that need to be maintained along the run in the proposed algorithms are: $\sum_{j=1}^{m} b_j x_{ij}$ for each row i, $\sum_{i=1}^{n} a_i x_{ij}$ for each column j, $\sum_{i=1}^{n} a_i$, $\sum_{j=1}^{m} b_j$ and $\sum_{i=1}^{n}\sum_{j=1}^{m} a_i b_j$ for each baluster k.

3   Algorithm

3.1   Algorithm Description

This section describes the proposed algorithm with its input, output and temporary data structure. In the initialization phase, each bicluster are initialized by selecting a random entry x_{ij}. Memberships of all rows and columns in each bicluster are set to 0 and their sign are set to 1 except the selected row i and column j their memberships are set to 1 and their corresponding sign is set to -1 (to allow decreasing their memberships later). In the initialization phase, gene/condition bases and other data structure are initialized according to initial memberships.

After initialization, the algorithm proceeds into series of iterations in each iteration *max_trials* actions are tried. In steps 1B(a)-(d) a row or a column and a bicluster are selected randomly and the gain of this action is computed. In step 1B(e) if the gain less than zero the value of the *sign* of this row/column is reversed to allow the inverse of the action to be tried the next time this row/column is selected. The *max_best* actions with maximum gain are stored in *bestaction* array (steps 1B(f)-(g)). In step 1C, the *max_best* actions are applied sequentially to the current biclustering resulting in a new biclustering. In step 1C(a), gene/conditions bases are updated according to the change in memberships.

Applying an action may raise the MSR of its bicluster above the threshold α (*overcnt* > 0), if this was the case, the current biclustering is marked as not accepted and the number of failures *failures* is incremented and this action is stored in structured array termed *failed*. Otherwise if all biclusters within the threshold (*overcnt*=0) and the total gain from the last accepted biclustering is greater than zero then the current biclustering is considered a better biclustering and *failures* is set to 0. The small step taken by the proposed algorithm (instead of adding or removing) allows next actions to compensate before *max_neighbor* actions failed. The algorithm stops if *failures* reaches the *max_neighbor*. Step 2 of the algorithm is concerned with rolling back the last *max_neighbor* actions stored in *failed* array by updating the memberships stored in *a, b* by the negative value of the step that is previously applied by these actions. Finally in step 3, the *k* biclusters are returned as the two vectors *a* and *b* representing the memberships of rows and columns of each bicluster respectively.

Algorithm Input:

X : is *n* by *m* matrix with possibly missing elements

α: threshold controls MSR (dataset dependent)

step: a number beween 0 and 1, suitable value is 0.25

k: is the number of biclusters to be found.

max_neighbor: is the maximum number of failures default $(n+m)$

max_trials: is the no. of trials before selecting best actions default *k*

max_best: is the best actions selected from max_trials $(1+step)/step$

Output:

a, b: two arrays of size *k* by *n* and *k* by *m* holds rows, columns memberships of *k* biclusters

Temporary:

sign: array *of* $n+m$ by *k*, used in updating memberships (value -1 to decrease and 1 to increase)

failures: no. actions applied since last accepted biclustering

failed: structured array holds the data of failed actions

cv, pv, cr, pr and totalgain: holds the current and previous average volume *v* and average MSR

of last accepted biclustering and the gain computed using them respectively.

overcnt: the no. biclusters having MSR greater than α

bestaction: structured array of size *max_best* holds maximum gain actions

Gene/condition bases: defined in the previous section to allow efficient computation of the gain

Initialization:

1. Initialize each bicluster c by random entry from the matrix X and set corresponding entries in *a, b to 1* , *sign to -1* and over to false.
2. Set *cs, ps* to 1 and *ch, ph, cv, pv, overcnt* and *failures* to 0

Steps:
1. Repeat
   A. Set *bestaction*[*j*].*gain* to small negative value, *j*=1..*max_best*
   B. For *i* = 1 to *max_trials* do
      a. Set *d* to random number in [1, *n*+ *m*],
      b. Set c to random number in [1, *k*]
      c. Set *signofd* to *sign*[c][d]
      d. If (*d* ≤ *n*) Then   // if row
         If not ((*a*[*c*][*d*]+ *signofd* * *step*) in [0,1]) Then   *signofd*=-*signofd*   End If
         Compute *gain* using (6), (8), (10) with δ=*signofd**step
         Else   //if column
         If not((*b*[*c*][*d-n*]+ *signofd* * *step*) in [0,1]) Then   *signofd* = - *signofd*   End If
         Compute *gain* using (7), (9), (10) with δ= *signofd* *step
         End If
      e. If (*gain*<0) Then *sign*[c][d] = - *signofd* else *sign*[c][d] = *signofd* End If
      f. Find *j* such that *gain* > *bestaction*[*j*].*gain*
      g. Store *gain*, *d*, *signofd*, c in *bestaction*[*j*].
      End For
   C. For *j*=1 to *max_best* do
      a. Apply *bestaction*[*j*] by updating *a*, *b*, *cv*, *cr*, *overcnt* and gene/condition bases.
      b. totalgain= *pr*(*pr*−*cr*)/ α² +(*cv*− *pv*)/ *pv*

      c. If (*totalgain*>0 and *overcnt*=0) then   //accepted biclusering
            num_failure=0, *pv*=*cv*, *pr* =*cr*
         Else
            store *bestaction*[*j*] in *failed*[*failures*]
            failures= *failures* +1
         End If
      End For
   Until (*failures* > *max_neighbor*)
2. Undo last *maxneighbor* actions that are stored in *failed*.
3. Return a and b

3.2   Complexity Analysis

The proposed algorithm is a series of iterations. During each iteration, *max_trials* actions needs to be considered then *max_best* actions of them need to be applied. The complexity of computing the new MSR using gene/condition bases is O (*n*×*m*). Updating the gene/condition bases after applying an action on a row is O(*m*) while for an action on a column is O(*n*). Since row/column are selected randomly then the probability of choosing a column is *m*/(*n*+*m*) which can be approximated to *m*/*n*. The average time complexity to apply an action is O (*m*+*n*×*m*), which implies that the complexity of the proposed algorithm is O((*m*× *max_best* + (*max_trials*+ *max_best*) *n*×*m*) ρ) where ρ is the number of iterations till termination (ρ ≥ *n*+*m*). The complexity of FLOC, is O (*k n*×*m*(*n*+*m*) ρ) where ρ is the number of iterations till termination (ρ≥1). While the complexity of BISOFT is O (*k*×*n*×*m* (*n*+*m*)²). DPBC is

$O(k \times \rho \times \rho' \times n \times m(n+m))$ where ρ' is the number of iterations that are needed to compute the zeros of the objective function. PBC has the lowest complexity which is $O(k \times \rho \times n \times m)$ whereas BCCA has the highest complexity which is $O(n^5)$.

4   Experimental Results

The proposed algorithm is compared with FLOC [3] and CC [2] using two real datasets:

1) YEAST [11]: contains 2884 genes under17 conditions.
2) HUMAN [11]: contains 4026 genes under 96 conditions.

The average size of produced biclusters and the average MSR is used as an evaluation measure of the respective algorithms. The bigger the average size of biclusters and the lower the average MSR the better is the output biclustering. Both algorithms are used to find 100 largest biclusters in YEAST and HUMAN datasets (http://arep.med. harvard.edu/network discovery) whose residue is less than 300 and 800 respectively (the value of the threshold α in [2] and [3]). A procedure for estimating a proper value for α that can be used for other datasets and is based on computing histogram is described in [5].

In the following tables 1-3 the results correspond to the average of 20 runs of the algorithm for the same configuration. To be noted that the standard deviation for both average size and MSR of produced biclusters in the 20 runs when alternating search strategy is used (*max_best*>1) is smaller than the purely greedy situation (*max_best*=1). Also compared to CC and FLOC the proposed algorithm is less sensitive with respect to initial conditions than both algorithms.

One of our objectives is to keep the complexity of the proposed algorithm below the complexity of FLOC so in order to use a step less than 1 without decreasing the rate of bicluster enlargement we have two choices either decrease the number of trials or keep the max_trials equals to k and raise the *max_best* to accommodate the change in the *step*.   Experimental studies show that appropriate value for max_neighbor is $n+m$, *max_trials* is k and for a given value of the step parameter the *max_best* is set to 1/*step*.

4.1   YEAST Dataset

In table 1 the values of the SOFTFLOC parameters are set as follow *step*=0.25, *max_best*= 4, *max_trials*=k and max_neighbor=n+m.   The results show that the proposed algorithm is able to run much longer time than FLOC and able to produces much larger biclusters than FLOC within the same preset threshold in this time. Also in 70% of the average time taken by FLOC (Time=490 sec.), the proposed algorithm produces biclusters having average size greater than 1.17 the average size of FLOC with lower average MSR. This can allow choosing much easier stopping criteria such as reaching a certain average mean squared residue or certain runtime.

Table 1. Performance comparison on yeast dataset

Algorithm	time	avg. MSR	avg. size	avg. gene.	avg. cond.
CC	1360	204.29	1576	167	12
FLOC	760	187.54	1825	195	12.8
SOFTFLOC	490	177.29	2148	186	12.82
SOFTFLOC	760	180.20	2578	211	12.90
SOFTFLOC	1470	198.49	4362	312	14.45
SOFTFLOC	5410	251.04	9309	657	14.55

Table 2 shows memberships assigned by SOFTFLOC and FLOC for bicluser 95 of the biclusters reported by CC[2] on YEAST where *max_neighbor*=*n*+*m*, *max_trials*=*k*, *max_best*=4 and *step*=0.25. The six genes reported by CC have been removed from the table because they are produced by both algorithms with membership one. The proposed algorithm was able to add eight more genes to this bicluster with memberships greater than or equal 0.5. The more interesting is that genes numbered 217,616 and 1476 are also reported by FLOC. Genes numbered 58, 59 and 1623 are reported by FLOC but not reported by the proposed algorithm instead 105, 862, 1320, 1389 and 2087 are added. Other genes with membership equals 0.25 can be considered candidate genes that may participate in this bicluster if for example a higher residue threshold is specified. The same two conditions that are added by FLOC are also added by the proposed algorithm namely conditions 0 and 9.

Table 2. Memberships Assigned By SOFTFLOC for bicluster 95 of CC on YEAST

Gene No.	SOFTFLOC	FLOC	Gene No.	SOFTFLOC	FLOC
105	0.5	0	1184	0.25	0
217	0.5	1	1286	0.25	0
457	0.25	0	1320	0.50	0
541	0.25	0	1350	0.25	0
616	0.75	1	1389	0.50	0
862	0.50	0	1476	0.75	1
931	0.25	0	1868	0.25	0
1076	0.25	0	2087	0.50	0

4.2   HUMAN Dataset

In table 3 the proposed algorithm is also compared with [2] and [3]. The chosen values for *max_trials, max_best, max_neighbor and step* were *k*, 4, *n*+*m* and 0.25 respectively. The results of the proposed algorithm are produced by running it for the same time taken by FLOC. The proposed algorithm shows higher average size and lower average MSR. If the algorithm is allowed to run for longer time, it would be able to produce biclusters with average size greater than 7000 with average residue < 800.

Table 3. Performance comparison on HUMAN dataset

Algorithm	avg. MSR	avg. volume	Avg. gene	Avg. cond.
CC	850.04	4456.43	269.22	24.5
FLOC	795	5859.68	276.4	26.5
SOFTFLOC	789	5992.70	280.94	28.21

4.3 Gene Ontology (GO)

By running the proposed algorithm using the previous setting of the input parameters for the average time taken by FLOC, the proposed algorithm was always able to produce better biclustering in terms of average mean square residue and size. However, low average residue biclusters are of no interest to a biologist if those are not biologically relevant. Therefore, tests have been performed on the yeast genome to assess the number of biclusters significantly enriched by GO annotations, and the algorithm SOFTFLOC proved its aptitude to detect biologically relevant biclusters. Out of the 100 produced biclusters, 84 were enriched by annotations. All enriched biclusters found by our algorithm had annotations with very low p-values. None of them is higher than 0.1 percent, and therefore, they are highly significant.

5   Conclusions

This paper proposes an iterative semi-possibilistic approach for biclustering based on randomized search. The proposed algorithm starts from small initial biclusters and iteratively minimizes the average mean squared residue while maximizes the size of biclusters using randomized search approach with alternating search strategy. From experimental results and algorithm analysis, the following points can be concluded:

1) Possible actions on biclusters are not limited to addition and deletions such as FLOC and CC or only addition such as BISOFT. This flexibility allows producing much larger biclusters within the same preset threshold.
2) The complexity analysis for the proposed algorithm along with the experimental results shows that the algorithm compares favorably to FLOC. Also it has much lower complexity than algorithms based on average similarity [4] due to its randomized search approach.
3) Unlike PBC, EPBC, our iterative approach allows constraints to be put on produced biclusters.
4) The hybrid search strategy reduces the sensitivity of the proposed algorithm to input parameters and initial conditions than algorithms PBC, EPBC and FLOC.

References

1. Sara, C.M., Arlindo, L.O.: "Biclustering Algorithms for Biological Data Analysis: A Survey. IEEE Trans. Computational Biology And Bioinformatics 1 (2004)
2. Cheng, Y., Church, G.: Biclustering of expression data. In: Proc. Eighth Int'l Conf. Intelligent Systems for Molecular Biology (ISMB 2000), pp. 93–103 (2000)

3. Yang, J., Wang, W., Wang, H., Yu, P.: Enhanced Biclustering on Expression Data. In: Proc. Third IEEE Conf. Bioinformatics and Bioeng., pp. 321–327 (2003)

4. Sharara, H., Ismail, M.A.: BISOFT: A novel algorithm for clustering gene expression data. In: Proceedings of the 7th IEEE International Conference on Bioinformatics and Bioengineering, BIOCOMP 2008, pp. 974–981 (2007)

5. Filippone, M., Masulli, F., Rovetta, S., Mitra, S., Banka, H.: Possibilistic Approach to Biclustering: An Application to Oligonucleotide Microarray Data Analysis. In: Priami, C. (ed.) CMSB 2006. LNCS (LNBI), vol. 4210, pp. 312–322. Springer, Heidelberg (2006)

6. Mahfouz, M.A., Ismail, M.A.: Enhanced Possibilistic Biclustering Algorithm. In: Proceedings of the 3rd IEEE International Conference on Bioinformatics and Biomedical Engineering, Beijing, China, pp. 1–6 (2009)

7. Mahfouz, M.A., Ismail, M.A.: Distance Based Possibilistic Biclustering Algorithm. In: Proceedings of the 3rd IEEE International Conference on Bioinformatics and Biomedical Engineering, Beijing, China, pp. 1–4 (2009)

8. Baraldi, A., Blonda, P.: A survey of fuzzy clustering algorithms for pattern recognition systems. IEEE Transactions on Man, and Cybernetics, Part B 29(6), 778–785 (1999)

9. Selim, S.Z., Ismail, M.A.: Soft Clustering of multidimensional data A semi-fuzzy approach. Pattern Recogn. 17(5), 559–568 (1984)

10. Okada, Y., Fujibuchi, W., Horton, P.: Module Discovery in Gene Expression Data Using Closed Itemset Mining Algorithm. IPSG Transactions in Bioinformatics 48, 39–48 (2007)

11. Mahfouz, M.A., Ismail, M.A.: BIDENS: Iterative Density Based Biclustering Algorithm with Application to Gene Expression Analysis. Proceedings of World Academy of Science, Engineering and Technology 37, 342–348 (2009)

12. Liu, G., et al.: Distance Based Subspace Biclustering with Flexible Dimension Partitioning, pp. 1250–1254. IEEE (2007)

13. Ng, R.T., Han, J.: Efficient and effective clustering methods for spatial data mining. In: Proceedings of the 20th VLDB Conference, Santiago, Chile, pp. 144–155 (1994)

14. Pei, J., et al.: Fault-tolerant frequent pattern mining: Problems and challenges. In: Workshop on Research Issues in Data Mining and Knowledge Discovery (2001)

15. Anindya, B., Rajat, K.: Bi-correlation clustering algorithm for determining a set of co-regulated genes. Bioinformatics 25(21), 2795–2801 (2009)

16. Tchagang, A.B., et al.: Biclustering of DNA Microarray Data: Theory, Evaluation, and Applications. In: Handbook of Research on Computational and Systems Biology: Interdisciplinary Applications, pp. 148–186 (2010)

17. Zhiguan, W., Chi, W.: Hypergraph based geometric biclustering algorithm. Pattern Recognition Letters 33(12), 1656–1665 (2012)

18. Christinat, Y., et al.: Gene Expression Data Analysis Using a Novel Approach to Biclustering Combining Discrete and Continuous Data. IEEE/ACM Transactions on Computational Biology And Bioinformatics 5(4) (2008)

19. Ismail, M.A., Kamel, M.S.: Multidimensional data clustering utilizing hybrid search strategies. Pattern Recognition 22(1), 75–89 (1989)

Semi-possibilistic Biclustering Applied to Discrete and Continuous Data

Mohamed A. Mahfouz[*] and Mohamed A. Ismail

Department of Computer and Systems Engineering, Faculty of Engineering,
University of Alexandria, Egypt
{m.a.mahfouz,drmaismail}@gmail.com

Abstract. In contrast to hard biclustering, possibilistic biclustering not only has the ability to cluster a group of genes together with a group of conditions as hard biclustering but also it has outlier rejection capabilities and can give insights towards the degree under which the participation of a row or a column is most effective. Several previous possibilistic approaches are based on computing the zeros of an objective function. However, they are sensitive to their input parameters and initial conditions beside that they don't allow constraints on biclusters. This paper proposes an iterative algorithm that is able to produce k-possibly overlapping semi-possibilistic (soft) biclusters satisfying input constraints. The proposed algorithms basically alternate between a depth-first search and a breadth-first search to effectively minimize the underlying objective function. It allows constraints, applicable to any acceptable (dis)similarity measure for the type of the input dataset and it is not sensitive to initial conditions. Experimental results show the ability of our algorithm to offer substantial improvements over several previously proposed biclustering algorithms.

Keywords: Possibilistic biclustering, biclustering, subspace biclustering, gene expression analysis, high dimensional data.

1 Introduction

Biclustering plays an important role in analyzing the huge amount of valuable data produced by microarrays. Microarrays are molecular biology tools by which the expression patterns of thousands of genes can be monitored simultaneously. Gene expression data are organized as matrices where rows represent genes, columns represent various samples such as tissues or experimental conditions, and numbers in each cell characterize the expression level of the particular gene in the particular sample. Biclustering is a clustering technique that aims to detect a group of correlated genes with respect to a group of conditions. Discovery of such biclusters is essential in revealing the significant connections in gene regulatory networks.

A survey on biclustering techniques are given in [14] where a categorization of the different heuristic approaches is shown, such as iterative row and column biclustering,

---

[*] Corresponding author.

A. Ell Hassanien et al. (Eds.): AMLTA 2012, CCIS 322, pp. 327–338, 2012.

divide and conquers strategy, greedy search, exhaustive biclustering enumeration, distribution parameter identification and others. Several biclustering algorithms are aimed at discovering biclusters with coherent values such as CC [3], FLOC [18]. Other biclustering algorithms focus on the relative order of the columns in a bicluster [17] rather than on the uniformity of the actual values in the data matrix.

The CC algorithm identifies one bicluster at a time, mask it with random numbers, and repeat the procedure in order to eventually find other biclusters. Whereas FLOC starts from a set of seeds (initial biclusters) and carries out an iterative process to improve the overall quality of the biclustering. In [12] an exhaustive enumeration biclustering algorithm that is based on closed itemsets enumeration algorithm is proposed termed as BIMODULE. It starts by normalizing and discretizing the data matrix into levels and use support equals to the minimum accepted number of genes in a bicluster. In [8] an iterative algorithm is presented termed BIDENS that approximate a number of k possibly overlapping biclusters but unlike BIMODULE, their discretization is done using histogram and extends the model in [7] to a generalized noise tolerant bicluster model using the concepts introduced in [13] and can mine coherent biclusters.

Correlation based algorithms such as BISOFT[2] and BCCA[15] start with initial bicluster and iteratively add a new row/column to the current bicluster such that the added row/column satisfy the criterion of having the average homogeneity within the bicluster above a pre-specified threshold for each dimension. In BISOFT, after all biclusters are generated, memberships are assigned to genes only using simple formula. Both algorithms suffer high complexity.

The most recent related work is the hyper-graph based geometric biclustering (HGBC) algorithm [1] that uses the Hough transform (HT) to find sub-biclusters which correspond to the linear structures in column-pair spaces then build a hyper-graph model to merge the sub-biclusters into larger ones.

The above algorithms produce crisp biclusters. It is desirable to have fuzzy biclusters that provide a degree of participation of genes, and the conditions under which its participation is most effective as well. One of the early fuzzy biclustering algorithms is PBC [4]. PBC is based on the possibilistic clustering paradigm [4]. PBC has low computational complexity but it is sensitive to its input parameters and initial conditions and can work only as a refinement step. In EPBC algorithm [9] several enhancements to PBC are proposed, while DPBC [10] generalizes and extends the idea of PBC to be applicable to (dis)similarity measures other than residue. In PBC, EPBC and DPBC, it is not possible to put constraints on the produced biclusters.

The previously explained drawbacks motivate us to propose soft [16] biclustering algorithm based on randomized search termed as BISOFTNS. The randomized search approach improves its performance over exhaustive approach such as BISOFT and BCCA. Also its alternating search strategy [6] reduces its sensitivity to input parameters and initial conditions compared to algorithms that uses single search strategy such as CC and FLOC. The proposed algorithm is applicable to both discrete and continuous dataset using any acceptable definition for (dis)similarity between rows and columns. Also the algorithm deals with null values in seamless manner and can support several future constraints at nearly no extra cost. The superior capability of clustering by BISOFTNS over a number of other algorithms, namely, CC, FLOC, PBC and DPBC is demonstrated through experiments with datasets that are publicly available. Various issues related to the characteristics of the algorithm are also discussed.

2   The Proposed Model

2.1   Bicluster

The gene expression data is organized as matrices where each entry x_{ij} in this matrix corresponds to the logarithm of the relative abundance of the mRNA of a gene i under a specific condition j, and may have a null value. Given a data matrix X with set of rows R of size n and set of columns C of size m, Biclustering can be defined formally as identifying a k possibly overlapping biclusters $B_i = (I_i, J_i)$ where I_i subset of R and J_i subset of C such that each bicluster B_i satisfies some specific characteristics of homogeneity. In [4], the concept of biclustering is generalized in a fuzzy set theoretical approach. The Authors assign two vectors of membership for each bicluster, one for the rows and one other for the columns, denoting them respectively a and b. In a crisp set framework row i and column j can either belong to the bicluster ($a_i = 1$ and $b_j = 1$) or not ($a_i = 0$ or $b_j = 0$). An element x_{ij} of X belongs to the bicluster if both $a_i = 1$ and $bj = 1$, i.e., its membership u_{ij} to the bicluster is $u_{ij} = and(a_i, b_j)$. A fuzzy formulation of the problem can help to better model the bicluster and also to improve the optimization process. The membership u_{ij} of an entry to a bicluster can be obtained by an integration of its row and column memberships. In this paper the membership u_{ij} of an element x_{ij} is chosen as the product of the memberships of its row and column as follows:

$$u_{ij} = a_i b_j \qquad \text{(Product)} \qquad (1)$$

Another formula may be the average of a_i and b_j [4]. The product is more reasonable, for example, it gives a higher membership for entry having $a_i=0.2$ and $b_j=0.8$ over another entry having $a_i=0.01$ and $b_j=0.99$ while both entry having the same average membership 0.5.

2.2   Graph Abstraction

The process of finding k possibly overlapping biclusters in a given data matrix X with set of rows R of size n and set of columns C of size m can be viewed abstractly as searching through a certain graph as in [11]. In this graph a node is represented by the set of k biclusters $\{(I_i, J_i), i=1,2,...k, I_i \subset R, J_i \subset C\}$. Two nodes are neighbors (i.e connected by an arc) if and only if one of the k biclusters represented by these nodes differs by only one object (row or column). Neighbors of a node can be derived from it by either adding or removing only one row or column to one of its biclusters. Each node has an associated two lists of values representing the average (dis)similarity and the size of the k biclusters. Each edge can be assigned a weight representing the cost differential between the two neighbors, alternatively, the weight can represent the benefits deferential(gain) between neighbors measured as a function of the amount of increase in size and the amount of decrease in average dissimilarity (or increase in average similarity) of the bicluster that differs in the two nodes.

It is obvious that biclustering algorithms such as CC, FLOC, can be viewed as a search for maximum on the previous graph. While FLOC iteratively adds or removes rows/columns i.e. change their memberships between 0 and 1 and compute the gain of such change as the sum of the amount of decrease in the relative residue[18] and increase in the relative size. The proposed algorithm, instead, changes the memberships between set of fixed values for example (0, 0.25, 0.5, 0.75, 1). Each time the membership is changed, the gain of this change is efficiently computed as explained in the following sections. While the size of the graph increases as the step decreases, the number of neighbors of a node has an upper bound $2k(n+m)$. Using this smaller step increases the number of possible good transitions on the graph which reduces the probability that the algorithm gets stuck on local minimum earlier. Although the proposed algorithm for searching the graph is basically a hill-climbing algorithm, exploration is necessary since it might be stuck in a local minimum at the very beginning. Therefore, at each iteration a pre-specified number of actions are selected from the best actions to be applied to current biclustering. Several modifications to the way this graph is searched in FLOC are proposed in this study.

2.3   Scoring Biclusters

Here we present two pre-specified thresholds α_h and α_v, which are used to limit the average dissimilarity of each bicluster in horizontal and vertical direction respectively, below a certain value. This value or threshold controls the amount of co-regulation among gene/condition subsets in each bicluster the user may need. The score of a bicluster can be defined as a linear combination of the horizontal (between rows) average dissimilarity (h), vertical (between columns) average dissimilarity (v) and bicluster size(s) where

$$h = (1 / \sum_{i=1}^{n} \sum_{j}^{j>i} a_i a_j) \sum_{i=1}^{n} \sum_{j}^{j>i} a_i a_j d(r_i, r_j) \qquad (2)$$

$d(r_i, r_j)$ is the dissimilarity between row i and row j and a_i, a_j are the memberships of rows i and j respectively. Similarly the vertical average dissimilarity v is:

$$v = (1 / \sum_{i=1}^{m} \sum_{j>i}^{m} b_i b_j) \sum_{i=1}^{n} \sum_{j}^{j>i} b_i b_j d(c_i, c_j) \qquad (3)$$

$d(c_i, c_j)$ is the dissimilarity between column i and column j. b_i and b_j are the memberships of columns i and j respectively. To be noted that the vertical dissimilarity is not defined in case of discrete data as will be explained latter. The size of a bicluster, s, from equation (1) is:

$$s = \sum_{i=1}^{n} \sum_{j=1}^{m} a_i b_j \qquad (4)$$

Calculating the size this way allows dealing with null values in seamless manner unlike other approaches that weights the relative number of genes and conditions separately. The proposed algorithm should iteratively maximize the average size s, minimize the average horizontal dissimilarity h and minimize the average vertical dissimilarity v of the resulting biclusters. If a similarity measure is used instead the task will be maximizing h, v and s.

2.4   Derivation of New Average Dissimilarities and Size

In the proposed model, an action is considered to be changing the membership of a randomly selected row/column on a bicluster by a small value δ in [0, 1]. The gain of an action needs to be computed as a function of the new and old average dissimilarities and size in order to select best actions to be applied. This section shows how the new average dissimilarities h, v and size s can be computed in incremental manner from the old values of h, v, s and the change in membership δ. The new horizontal (between rows) average dissimilarity after changing the membership of a row h by δ (i.e. a_h set to $a_h + \delta$) can be computed as follows:

$$h_{new} = (1/(\sum_{i=1}^{n}\sum_{j>i}^{n}a_i\,a_j + \delta\sum_{i\neq h}^{n}a_i))(\sum_{i=1}^{n}\sum_{j>i}^{n}a_i\,a_j\,d(r_i,r_j) + \delta\sum_{i\neq h}a_i\,d(r_i,r_h)) \tag{5}$$

Whereas the new vertical (between columns) average dissimilarity of columns after changing the membership of a row h by δ is

$$v_{new} = (1/(\sum_{i=1}^{m}\sum_{j>i}^{m}b_i\,b_j))\sum_{i=1}^{m}\sum_{j>i}^{m}b_i\,b_j\,d(c_i,c_j)_{new} \tag{6}$$

$d(c_i,c_j)_{new}$ in the above equation represents the new dissimilarity between column i and j after a membership of a row h is changed.

Based on (1) the new size s_{new} after changing the membership of a row h by δ is:

$$s_{new} = \delta\sum_{j=1}^{m}b_j + \sum_{i=1}^{n}\sum_{j=1}^{m}a_i b_j = \delta\sum_{j=1}^{m}b_j + s_{old} \tag{7}$$

Similarly the new horizontal (between rows) average dissimilarity after changing the membership of a column h by δ is

$$h_{new} = (1/\sum_{i=1}^{n}\sum_{j}^{j>i}a_i\,a_j)\sum_{i=1}^{n}\sum_{j}^{j>i}a_i\,a_j d(r_i,r_j)_{new} \tag{8}$$

$d(r_i,r_j)_{new}$ in the above equation represents the new dissimilarity between row i and j after a membership of a column h is changed. The new vertical (between columns) average dissimilarity of columns after changing the membership of a column h by δ is

$$v_{new} = (1/(\sum_{i=1}^{m}\sum_{j>i}^{m}b_i\,b_j + \delta\sum_{i\neq h}^{m}b_i))(\sum_{i=1}^{m}\sum_{j>i}^{m}b_i\,b_j\,d(c_i,c_j) + \delta\sum_{i\neq h}b_i\,d(c_i,c_h)) \tag{9}$$

And the new size after changing the membership of a column h by δ can be calculated as follow

$$s_{new} = \delta \sum_{j=1}^{n} a_j + \sum_{i=1}^{n} \sum_{j=1}^{m} a_i b_j = \delta \sum_{j=1}^{n} a_j + s_{old} \tag{10}$$

In the following sections $d(r_i, r_j)$ will be represented as a function of the memberships of columns b and the values of entries in X. Similarly $d(c_i, c_j)$ but using the memberships of rows a.

2.5   Applying the Proposed Model to Discrete Data

For discrete data the vertical average dissimilarity has no meaning as the values of the discretized matrix can be considered as categorical data. The dissimilarity between two rows $d(r_i, r_j)$ in (2) can be calculated as follows:

$$d(r_i, r_j) = (1/\sum_{h=1}^{m} b_h) \sum_{h=1}^{m} b_h \, d(x_{ih}, x_{jh}) \tag{11}$$

$$if \; x_{ih} \neq x_{jh} \quad d(x_{ih}, x_{jh}) = 1 \quad otherwise \quad d(x_{ih}, x_{jh}) = 0 \tag{12}$$

The gain of executing an action on a bicluster c can be computed as follows:

$$\text{Gain} = h_{old}(h_{old} - h_{new})/\alpha_h^2 + (s_{new} - s_{old})/s_{old} \tag{13}$$

Where h_{new}, h_{old} are the horizontal average dissimilarity between rows of a bicluster c before and after executing the action c. similarly s_{old}, s_{new} are the size of the bicluster c before and after executing the action respectively.

In [12] a procedure for normalizing and discretizing input data matrix is described and an efficient algorithm for dealing with discrete data is discussed that is based on frequent itemset mining termed BIMODULE but algorithms based on frequent itemset are sensitive to noise [8].

2.6   Applying the Proposed Model to Continues Data

To use Euclidian distance the input data matrix need to be normalized using the normalization scheme in [5] in two steps. First divide each column by its mean then each row of the resulting data matrix is normalized such that, its mean vanishes and its norm is one. The squared euclidian distance between two rows in fuzzy clustering paradigm is

$$d(r_i, r_j) = (1/\sum_{h=1}^{m} b_h) \sum_{h=1}^{m} b_h (x_{ih} - x_{jh})^2 \tag{14}$$

The gain will be computed same as equation (13) with the addition of new term corresponds to the vertical dissimilarity as follows:

$$\text{Gain} = h_{old}(h_{old} - h_{new})/\alpha_h^2 + v_{old}(v_{old} - v_{new})/\alpha_v + (s_{new} - s_{old})/s_{old} \tag{15}$$

Where h_{old}, h_{new} are the horizontal average dissimilarity between rows of a bicluster c before and after executing the action c. Similarly v_{old}, v_{new} are the vertical average dissimilarity between columns of the bicluster before and after executing the action and s_{old}, s_{new} are the size of the bicluster before and after executing the action. α_h and α_v are the maximum accepted average dissimilarity between rows and columns of a bicluster respectively. The most common measures in the field of bioinformatics are similarity measures related to correlation coefficient. Most of them have corresponding dissimilarity measures (http://gedas.bizhat.com/dist.htm). However we need to derive this measure in the fuzzy paradigm. A simpler dissimilarity measure is the one that corresponds to the un-centered correlation coefficient and its distance falls in [0, 1].

3   Algorithm

3.1   Algorithm Description

This section describes the proposed algorithm with its input, output and temporary data structure. In the initialization phase each bicluster is initialized by a random entry x_{ij}. In step 1B(a)-(d), a row or a column and a bicluster are selected randomly and the gain of this action is computed using equation (13) or (15) depending on the type of the input data. In step 1A(e) if the gain less than zero the value of the sign of this row/column is reversed to allow reverse action to be tried the next time this row/column is selected. The *max_best* actions with maximum gain are stored in *bestaction* array (steps 1B(f) and 1B(g)). In step 1C, the *max_best* actions are applied sequentially to the current biclustering resulting in a new biclustering. Applying these actions may result in one or more biclusters having average dissimilarity above threshold(*overcnt* >0) if this was the case the current biclustering is marked as not accepted and the number of failures *failures* is incremented and the action is stored in structured array termed as *failed*. Otherwise if all bicluster within thresholds (*overcnt*=0) and the total gain from the last successful iteration is greater than zero the current biclustering is considered a better biclustering and *failures* is set to 0. The small step taken by the proposed algorithm (instead of adding or removing) allows next actions to compensate before *max_neighbor* actions failed. The algorithm stops if *failures* reaches the *max_neighbor*. The last step concerned with rolling back the last *max_neighbor* actions stored in *failed* array. This is done by updating the memberships stored in a, b by the negative value of the step that is previously applied by these actions. Finally the k biclusters are returned as the two vectors a and b representing the memberships of rows and columns of each bicluster respectively. The computation of the gain in (13) can be done efficiently in incremental manner by updating the following values according to the change in memberships along the run for each bicluster $\sum_{j=1}^{m} b_j$, $\sum_{i=1}^{n} a_i$, $\sum_{i=1}^{n}\sum_{j=1}^{m} a_i a_j$, $\sum_{i=1}^{n}\sum_{j=1}^{m} a_i a_j d(r_i, r_j)$ and $\sum_{i=1}^{n}\sum_{j=1}^{m} a_i a_j d(x_{ih}, x_{jh})$ for each column h. Also $\sum_{i=1}^{n}\sum_{j=1}^{m}b_i b_j$ and $\sum_{i=1}^{n}\sum_{j=1}^{m}b_i b_j\,d(r_i,r_j)$ of each bicluster, can be updated

for efficient computation of the gain in (15). This data structure are termed as gene/condition bases in the temporary section of the following algorithm description and computed initially in the initialization phase and updated incrementally in step 1C(a) of the proposed algorithm.

Algorithm Input:
X : is n by m matrix with possibly missing elements
α_h , α_v : thresholds control the average dissimilarity
step: a number beween 0 and 1, suitable value is 0.25
k: is the number of clusters to be found.
max_neighbor: is the maximum number of failures
max_trials, max_best: no. of trials *max_trials* before selecting the best *max_best* actions
Output:
k biclusters, represented by a and b (two arrays of size k by n
and k by m holds rows, columns memberships respectively)
Temporary:
sign: array *of* $n+m$ by k, used in updating memberships has value 1 or -1 default 1.
failures: no. actions applied since last accepted biclustering
failed: structured array holds the data of failed actions
cs, ps, ch, ph, cv, pv and totalgain: holds the current and previous average size s and dissimilarities h, v of last accepted biclustering and the gain computed using them respectively.
overcnt: the no. biclusters having average dissimilarity> *threshold*
bestaction, array of size *max_best* holds maximum gain actions
Gene/condition bases
Initialization:
1. Initialize each bicluster c by random entry from the matrix X and set corresponding entries in a, b to 1 , *sign to -1* and over to false.
2. Set cs, ps to 1 and ch, ph, cv, pv, overcnt and *failures* to 0
Output: k biclusters represented by a and b.
Steps:
1. **Repeat**
   A. Set *bestaction[j].gain* to small negative value, j=1..*max_best*
   B. For $i = 1$ to *max_trials* do
      a. Set d, c to two random number in $[1, n+m]$, $[1, k]$ respectively
      b. Set *signofd* to *sign[d]*
      c. If $(d \leq n)$ Then   // if row
         If not $((a[c][d]+ signofd * step)$ in $[0,1])$ Then *signofd=-signofd* End If
         Compute new h, v and s using (5)-(7) with δ=*signofd*step*
         Else   //if column
         If not$((b[c][d-n]+ signofd * step)$ in $[0,1])$ Then *signofd = - signofd* End If
         Compute new h, v and s using (8)-(10) with δ= *signofd *step*
         End If
      d. Compute *gain* using (13) for discrete data otherwise use (15)
      e. If $(gain<0)$ $sign[d]$ = - *signofd* End If

    f. Find j such that $gain > bestaction[j].gain$

    g. Store $gain, d, signofd, c$ in $bestaction[j]$

End For

C. For $j=1$ to max_best do

        a. Apply $bestaction[j]$ by updating $a, b, cs, ch, cv, overcnt$ and gene/condition
bases.

    b. totalgain= $ph(ph-ch)/\alpha_h^2 + pv(pv-cv)/\alpha_v^2 + (cs-ps)/ps$

    c. If ($totalgain>0$ and $overcnt=0$)   //accepted biclusering

       $num\_failure=0, pv=cv, ph =ch, ps = cs$

      Else

        store $bestaction[j]$ in $failed[failures]$.

        $failures= failures +1$

      End If

  End For

Until ($failures > max\_neighbor$)

2. Undo last $maxneighbor$ actions that are stored in $failed$.

3. Return a and b

3.2   Complexity Analysis

The proposed algorithm is a series of iterations. During each iteration, max_trials actions needs to be considered then max_best actions of them need to be applied. Equations (5) and (9) is $O(nm)$ while equations (6) and (8) of $O(m^2)$ and $O(n^2)$ respectively. Since row/column are selected randomly then the probability of choosing a column is $m/(n+m)$ which can be approximated to m/n. The average time complexity to perform an action (which is the same as to compute the gain of that action) is $O(m^2+nm)$, which implies that the complexity of the proposed algorithm is $O((max\_best +max\_trials) (m^2+nm) \rho)$ where ρ is the number of iterations till termination. While the complexity of BISOFT is O $(k \times n \times m (n+m)^2)$.The complexity of FLOC, is $O(k\rho nm(n+m))$ where ρ is the number of iterations till termination. BCCA has the highest complexity which is $O(n^5)$.

4   Experimental Results

In our experimental study both algorithms are used to find 100 largest clusters in the YEAST dataset. The YEAST dataset and the results of CC and FLOC are reported in (http://arep.med.harvard.edu/network discovery). It contains 2884 genes under 17 conditions. The average size of produced biclusters and the average MSR is used as an evaluation measure of the respective algorithms the bigger the average size of biclusters and the lower MSR the better is the output biclustering. In the following section BISOFTNS-DSC, BISOFTNS-ECD and BISOFTNS-COR correspond to the proposed algorithm applied on discrete data, using Euclidian distance and using correlation coefficient respectively. For BISOFTNS-DSC, the original data is discretized [12] into three levels.

The threshold of average dissimilarity between rows/columns α_h, α_v respectively is dataset dependent and can be estimated using histogram as in [10]. For discrete data, the threshold value is in [0,1] and should be proportional to the noise induced by discretization. A proper value is found to be 0.20 for YEAST with number of levels equal 3. For continues data, if Pearson correlation coefficient is used then the value is in [-1,1] a suitable value is found to be 0.85 for both directions while if distance measures that corresponds to Pearson coefficient is used, a value of 0.15 is appropriate. For squared Euclidian, a suitable value of the horizontal and vertical threshold are found to be 0.0005. One of our objectives is to keep the complexity of the proposed algorithm below the complexity of FLOC so in order to use a step less than 1 without decreasing the rate of bicluster enlargement we have two choices either decrease the number of trials or keep the *max_trials* equals to k and raise the *max_best* to accommodate the change in the step. Experimental studies show that appropriate value for *max_neighbor* is $n+m$, *max_trials* is k and for a given value of the step parameter the *max_best* is set to 1/*step*. In the following experiments the values of the BISOFTNS parameters are set as follows: *step*=0.25, *max_trials*=k, *max_best*=4 and *max_neighbor* =n+m.

In table 1 the proposed algorithm is compared with FLOC and CC. Experimental study with the proposed algorithm BISOFTNS-COR and BISOFTNS-ECD shows that they are able to execute much more iterations than FLOC resulting in much larger bicluster size within the same preset threshold (up to 5 times that produced by FLOC with residue below 275). The results show that the proposed algorithm BISOFTNS-COR is able to produce larger biclusters than using Euclidian distance with the smallest MSR. The runtime for Euclidian distance is 3.56 the time needed by FLOC but it is less than for correlation because gene/condition bases can be used for efficient computation of the gain while Pearson correlation coefficient needs to be recomputed and BISOFTNS-COR takes 5.12 the time of FLOC. If both algorithms BISOFTNS-COR and BISOFTNS-ECD allowed to run for only the same average runtime taken by FLOC (760 sec) they are also able to produce larger biclusters with smaller average MSR than FLOC.

Table 1. Performance comparison on yeast dataset

Algorithm	Avg. MSR	Avg. size	Avg. gene	Avg. cond.
CC	204	1576	167	12
FLOC	187	1825	195	12.8
BISOFTNS-DSC	289	1136	189	6.82
BISOFTNS-ECD	273	7895	548	14.26
BISOFTNS-COR	248	8251	567	14.92

BISOFTNS-DSC has the lowest average size and the highest average MSR but at the same time it the most efficient and it takes only 15% of the runtime of FLOC to produce this results. However, since data discretization reduces the level of information, relying only on discrete data is unsafe. Therefore, unless the discretization is extremely accurate, an algorithm on continuous data is mandatory. The key idea is to use the result of biclustering on discrete data as a starting point for biclustering on continuous data. The main advantage of the proposed model is that the same algorithm is applicable for both discrete and continuous data.

Low average MSR biclusters are of no interest to a biologist if those are not biologically relevant. Therefore, tests have been performed on the yeast genome to assess the number of biclusters significantly enriched by GO annotations, and the algorithm BISOFTNS-COR proved its aptitude to detect biologically relevant biclusters. Out of the 100 produced biclusters, 82 were enriched by annotations. All enriched biclusters found by our algorithm had annotations with very low p-values. None of them is higher than 0.1 percent, and therefore, they are highly significant.

5   Conclusions

This paper proposes an iterative semi-possibilistic approach for biclustering based on randomized search. The proposed algorithm starts from small initial biclusters and iteratively minimizes the average dissimilarity while maximizes the size of biclusters by changing the memberships of rows/columns by small step. From experimental results and algorithm analysis, the following points can be concluded:

- The proposed algorithm is applicable to both discrete and continues data using any acceptable definition for dis(similariy). Euclidian distance gives a lower performance than correlation.
- Possible actions on biclusters are not limited to addition and deletions such as FLOC and CC. This flexibility allows producing much larger biclusters within the same preset thresholds.
- The proposed approach allows constraints to be put on accepted biclusters.
- A low variance among the 20 runs used in computing the results shows that the hybrid search strategy reduces the sensitivity of the proposed algorithm to input parameters and conditions.
- The randomized search approach reduced the complexity of the proposed algorithm.
- The ability of the proposed algorithm of not being stuck in local minima early such as in FLOC can allow a user friendly stopping criteria.

References

1. Zhiguan, W., Chi, W.: Hypergraph based geometric biclustering algorithm. Pattern Recognition Letters 33(12), 1656–1665 (2012)
2. Sharara, H., Ismail, M.A.: BISOFT: A novel algorithm for clustering gene expression data. In: Proceedings of the 7th IEEE International Conference on Bioinformatics and Bioengineering, BIOCOMP 2008, pp. 974–981 (2007)
3. Cheng, Y., Church, G.M.: Biclustering of expression data. In: Proc. Eighth Int'l Conf. Intelligent Systems for Molecular Biology (ISMB 2000), pp. 93–103 (2000)
4. Filippone, M., Masulli, F., Rovetta, S., Mitra, S., Banka, H.: Possibilistic Approach to Biclustering: An Application to Oligonucleotide Microarray Data Analysis. In: Priami, C. (ed.) CMSB 2006. LNCS (LNBI), vol. 4210, pp. 312–322. Springer, Heidelberg (2006)
5. Getz, G., et al.: Coupled Two-Way Clustering Analysis of Gene Microarray Data. Proc. Natural Academy of Sciences, US, 12079–12084 (2000)

6. Ismail, M.A., Kamel, M.S.: Multidimensional data clustering utilizing hybrid search strategies. Pattern Recognition 22(1), 75–89 (1989)
7. Liu, G., et al.: Distance Based Subspace Biclustering with Flexible Dimension Partitioning, pp. 1250–1254. IEEE (2007)
8. Mahfouz, M.A., Ismail, M.A.: BIDENS: Iterative Density Based Biclustering Algorithm with Application to Gene Expression Analysis. Proceedings of World Academy of Science, Engineering and Technology 37, 342–348 (2009)
9. Mahfouz, M.A., Ismail, M.A.: Enhanced Possibilistic Biclustering Algorithm. In: Proceedings of the 3rd IEEE International Conference on Bioinformatics and Biomedical Engineering, Beijing, China, 6 pages (2009)
10. Mahfouz, M.A., Ismail, M.A.: Distance Based Possibilistic Biclustering Algorithm. In: Proceedings of the 3rd IEEE International Conference on Bioinformatics and Biomedical Engineering, Beijing, China, 4 pages (2009)
11. Ng, R.T., Han, J.: Efficient and effective clustering methods for spatial data mining. In: Proceedings of the 20th VLDB Conference, Santiago, Chile, pp. 144–155 (1994)
12. Okada, Y., et al.: Module Discovery in Gene Expression Data Using Closed Itemset Mining Algorithm. IPSG Transactions in Bioinformatics 48, 39–48 (2007)
13. Pei, J., et al.: Fault-tolerant frequent pattern mining: Problems and challenges. In: Workshop on Research Issues in Data Mining and Knowledge Discovery (2001)
14. Sara, C.M., Arlindo, L.O.: Biclustering Algorithms for Biological Data Analysis: A Survey. IEEE Trans. Computational Biology and Bioinformatics 1 (2004)
15. Anindya, B., Rajat, K.: Bi-correlation clustering algorithm for determining a set of co-regulated genes. Bioinformatics 25(21), 2795–2801 (2009)
16. Selim, S.Z., Ismail, M.A.: Soft clustering of multidimensional data A semi-fuzzy approach. Pattern Recogn. 17(5), 559–568 (1984)
17. Christinat, Y., et al.: Gene Expression Data Analysis Using a Novel Approach to Biclustering Combining Discrete and Continuous Data. IEEE/ACM Transactions on Computational Biology And Bioinformatics 5(4) (2008)
18. Yang, J., et al.: Enhanced Biclustering on Expression Data. In: Proc. Third IEEE Conf. Bioinformatics and Bioeng., pp. 321–327 (2003)

A Comparative Study of Localization Algorithms in WSNs

Mahmoud Nabil, Rabie A. Ramadan, Hamed ElShenawy, and Adel ElHennawy

mahmoudgendy@gmail.com, a.hennawy@hotmail.com,
rabie@rabieramadan.org, hamed_elshenawy@yahoo.com

Abstract. Wireless Sensor Networks (WSNs) are the type of networks that are currently used in many applications. Some of these applications are critical and their information is very sensitive e.g. battle field and health care monitoring. Any transferred data has to be known from where it comes. In other words, most of the WSNs applications depend mainly on the location of each node in the network. In fact, the location may affect the decision to be made. The importance of localization is not only due to location identification but also it provides the base for routing, density control, tracking, and number many of other communication network aspects. Therefore, it is very important that each node reports its location accurately. Unfortunately, GPS is not suitable for WSNs due to its cost in terms of nodes consumed energy as well as its availability. Many localization algorithms are proposed for WSNs; however, their accuracy is the main concern. This paper is designated to help the WSNs designers in selecting suitable localization algorithm for their applications. The paper presents as well as implements different localization algorithms and evaluate them.

Keywords: Localization, DIL, HiRLoc, SeRLoc, PTA, RAL.

1 Introduction

With the advanced of MEMS technology, sensing devices became smarter and compact. Sensors are capable to auto-configure themselves and form a wireless network. In addition, WSNs are used in many critical applications including health care, military, and environmental monitoring. Accurate sensors' locations represents as one of the important parameters that is reported with each message to the base station (sink node). GPS is one of the technologies that are used for location identification. However, GPS is still an expensive technology; at the same time, it consumes large amount of energy from the sensor nodes. In addition, GPS is not available in many places in which it limits the usage of WSNs.

Other than the GPS, there are many schemes/algorithms that are recently proposed for localization in WSNs. These schemes could be classified into range-based and range-free schemes as shown in Figure 1. Our interest in this paper is the range-free algorithms and we focus only on some of the recent algorithms that are widely used in

A. Ell Hassanien et al. (Eds.): AMLTA 2012, CCIS 322, pp. 339–350, 2012.

many applications. The paper discusses DIL, HiRLoc, SeRLoc, PAT, and RAL schemes. In addition, the paper shows our implementation to these algorithms and our point of view on the efficiency of such schemes. In this paper, the localization error is considered as the main criteria for evaluating these schemes.

The paper is organized as follows: in the next section elaborates on the different localization algorithms; section 3 explores the performance evolutions in terms of different case studied; finally the paper concludes in section 4.

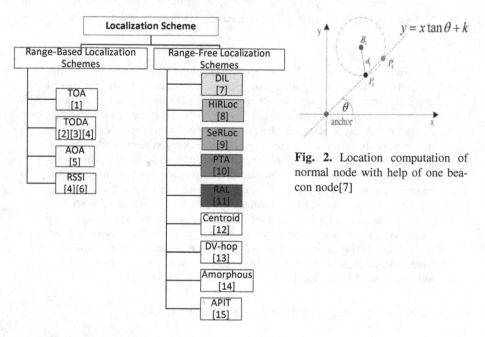

Fig. 2. Location computation of normal node with help of one beacon node[7]

Fig. 1. Localization schemes

2   Localization Algorithms

Fortunately, there are many localization algorithms proposed to solve the problem of sensor location determination. As mentioned, the algorithms could be classified to range-based and range-free algorithms as given in Figure 1. In range-based algorithms, the node could estimate its location according to: 1) Time of Arrival (TOA) in which the node location depends on propagation time[1]; 2) Time Difference of Arrival (TDOA) [2][3][4] in which the location information is estimated based the distance between two nodes given the time difference between arriving of different messages; 3) Angle of Arrival (AOA) where sensors locations are computed based on estimate the angle between two neighbor nodes[5]. 4) Received Signal Strength

Indicator (RSSI) that estimates the location by translates signal strength to distance and consider multi-path fading and interference [4][6]. These methods are not suitable for WSNs due to either the usage of GPS which is expensive and not available everywhere or due to the required hardware for nodes to apply the previous techniques.

2.1   Range-Free Localization Schemes

The main advantage of Range-free algorithms is minimizing the localization error without any additional hardware cost. The range-free algorithms, in most of the cases, estimate the location of normal nodes (which location is unknown) from the signals sent by locator and beacon nodes (which locations is known). There are many parameters that directly affect estimation error in range-free localization algorithms:

1- Node density(ND)
2- Anchors heard (AH)
3- Anchors to node range ratio (ANR)
4- Anchor percentage (AP)
5- Degree of irregularity (DOI)

In the following subsections, we focus on the most recent algorithms as well as the most used in WSNs. We briefly explore the operations of DIL, HiRLoc, SeRLoc, PAT, and RAL algorithms.

2.1.1   Distributed Localization (DIL) Algorithm

DIL algorithm proposed in [7] considers three types of nodes normal nodes (have no location information), beacon nodes (have location information), and anchor or locator nodes (have angle information). Normal and beacon nodes are assumed that they are deployed randomly over the network while anchor nodes are deployed manually or randomly as well. In addition, the WSN is divided into several clusters with each one should be have at least one anchor.

For the algorithm to operate, it assumes a rectangular outdoor monitoring region and it assumes that normal nodes get their angle information from anchor nodes. Moreover, nodes are assumed to be deployed on m × n monitored area and the communication range of the anchor node is double the sensing range, $R_A = 2R_s$, where R_s is the sensing range of each normal node.

DIL is simply described in Algorithm 1. More details of Algorithm 1 is discussed by explaining the distance measurement and computing the coordinates steps.

- **Distance Measurement**

DIL uses the received signal strength indicator (RSSI) to obtain the distance between the beacon nodes and normal nodes. Certainly, due to the usage of RSSI, the wireless communication channel could be affected by fading and shadowing. Therefore, average path loss is computed according to the Equation (1).

Algorithm 1:	Setup: Waiting time Tn;
Initialize:	**Do**
Waiting time T_n for each normal node;	{
All fields of coordinate table = { Φ };	**Listen** to the network;
Start: Node deployment strategy;	**If** (any beacon packet is received)
Do	**Translate**: RSSI into Distance;
{	**Start location computation;**
For each Anchor node:	Update the coordinate table;
Check: Neighbors of each normal node;	**End If**
Measure: Angle information for	} **While** (T_n is not expired);
each neighbor of normal nodes;	Calculate: Final result from all entries of the
Transmit: Angle information to each normal node;	table;
For each Beacon node:	Output: Normal node's location;
Broadcast the beacon packets;	}
For each Normal node:	**End**

$$P_r(d) = P_t(d_0) - 10\,n\,\log\left(\frac{d}{d_0}\right) + X_\sigma \tag{1}$$

where n is the path loss exponent, which depends on the specific propagation environment, d is the distance between Transmitter and Receiver, P_r (d) represents the received signal strength indicator (RSSI), P_t (d_0) represents the transmission power at reference distance (d_0), and $X\sigma$ is a random variable, which accounts for the random variation of the shadowing effect and is supposed to be Gaussian distribution with zero mean random variable (in dB) with standard deviation σ (also in dB).

From equation (1) we can deduce equation (2) to calculate the distance d as follow:

$$d = d_0 * 10^{-\left(\frac{Pt(d0)-Pr(d)-X\sigma}{10n}\right)} \tag{2}$$

- **Coordinate Computation**

As assumed, normal node must have received location information from at least one beacon node and angle information from one anchor node to calculate its own location. In addition, normal node must wait for a predefined timeout T_n units to receive RSSI value from beacon node. Based on this information, Figure (2) explains the location information computation process.

According to [6], let (x, y) be the coordinate of the normal node, (x_1, y_1) be the location of a beacon node B1, and (x_a, y_a) be the location of an anchor node. Distance between the beacon and normal node is d_1.

Let the angle between the anchor node's x-axis and the line joining the normal and anchor node be θ. Based on these information, we can obtain two equations as follow:

$$y = x \tan\theta + k \tag{3}$$

where k is a constant, which is obtained by substituting location of the anchor node.

$$k = y_a - x_a \tan\theta \tag{4}$$

Taking communication range of a beacon node as a uniform circular disc, Equation (5) can be obtained as follows:

$$(x - x_1)^2 + (y - y_1)^2 = d_1^2 \tag{5}$$

Substituting Equation (3) in Equation (5) and upon simplification, Equation (6) can be obtained.

$$(1 + tan^2\theta)x^2 - (2x_1 + 2y_1 \tan\theta - 2k \tan\theta)x + R = 0 \qquad (6)$$

where, R is

$$R = x_1^2 + k^2 - 2ky_1 + y_1^2 - d_1^2 \qquad (7)$$

Since Equation (6) is a simple quadratic equation, x coordinate of the location of the normal node can be calculated easily. Now y coordinate of the location can be obtained by substituting value of x in Equation (3).

2.1.2 HiRLoc: High-Resolution Range Independent Localization Scheme

In this section we will discuss the HiRLoc scheme [8] that allows sensors to determine their location with high accuracy even in the presence of security threats. However, we are not interested in the security threats discussed by HiRLoc. Our interest here is the localization techniques proposed in HiRLoc. The algorithm considers that there are two types of nodes: locator/anchor nodes which transmit beacons with location information and normal nodes (unknown location nodes).

The algorithm considers that normal nodes determine its own location by received beacon signal from locator. The beacon signal transmitted by locator node contains locator coordinates, angle of directional antenna, and locator communication range. Locator nodes updated this information every time and retransmit it to normal nodes.

Normal nodes can define Locator sector area $S_i(j)$ based on beacon information. Let $LH_s(j)$ denotes the set of locators heard by a sensor s during the jth transmission round. By collecting beacons from the locators $L_i \in LH_s(j)$, the normal node or sensor can compute its location as the Region of Intersection (ROI) of all the sectors $S_i(j)$. The ROI after the mth round of beacon transmissions can be expressed as the intersection of all the sectors corresponding to the beacons available at each sensor as given by the following equation:

$$ROI(m) = \bigcap_{j=0}^{m}\left(\bigcap_{i=1}^{|LH_s(j)|} S_i(j)\right) \qquad (8)$$

From equation (8), the sensor position is located inside ROI. Therefore, localization error can be reduced by reducing the size of ROI. This can be done by reducing the size of the sector areas $S_i(j)$ and, increasing the number of intersecting sectors $S_i(j)$. In our implementation to the reduction of ROI will be considered by varying the direction of their antennas, and varying the communication range via power control.

There are two different methods to determine the ROI as follow: 1) by computing the intersection between all locator sectors, and 2) by estimating ROI after every round and the intersection with the previous ROI. These two methods are called by HiRLoc-I and HiRLoc-II.

In HiRLoc-I, the estimation of the ROI is computed by collecting all beacons transmitted by each locator over time, intersecting all sectors of each locator and then intersecting the outcome as given in equation (9).

$$\text{ROI}(m) = \bigcap_{|LH_S|} \left(\bigcap_{j=0}^{m} S_i(j) \right) \tag{9}$$

The algorithmic steps performed for HiRLoc-I is summarized in Algorithm 2 and described as follows:

Step 1: **Initial estimate of the ROI:** in this step, the sensor determines the set of locators LHs that will be used to determine the location of sensor.

Step 2: **Beacon collection:** here, sensors are updated by changes in antenna orientation and locator communication range by the beacons signal.

Step 3: **Determination of the ROI:** it means achieving computation of ROI based on the boundary lines of locator to reduce the computational complexity.

In HiRLoc-II, the sensor computes the ROI by intersecting all collected information about locator at each transmission round as per equation (8). At a transmission round m the sensor intersects the newly acquired sectors as described in step 3 of Algorithm 1, and computes ROI_m using equation (10).

$$\text{ROI}_m = \bigcap_{i=1}^{|LH_s(j)|} S_i(m) \tag{10}$$

Then, the sensor intersects the ROI_m with the previous estimate $ROI\,(m-1)$ to acquire the current estimate, $ROI\,(m) = ROI_m.$

2.1.3   SeRLoc: A Secure Localization Scheme

In this Section we describe SeRLoc scheme [9]that enables sensors to determine their location based on beacon signal containing location information transmitted by the locators. Again the algorithm considers two types of nodes which are normal nodes and anchor or locator nodes.

The idea is that each locator transmits beacon signal contains locator coordinates, and angle of antenna to determine location sensors as shown in Figure 3.

As shown in Figure 3(a), a sensor s is able to hear four locators which are L_1, L_2, L_3, and L_4. Sensor s determines its position by executing a four step algorithm as follows:

Step 1: the sensor hears from different locators and collects the beacons signals transmitted from locators.

Step 2: the sensor determines an approximate search area within which it is located based on the coordinates of the locators heard.

Step 3: the sensor computes the overlapping antenna sector region using a majority vote scheme.

Step 4:   the sensor determines its location as the center of gravity of the overlapping region.

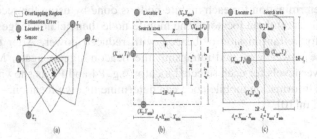

Fig. 3. (a) Locators L1 – L4 transmit beacons at each sector and sensor s estimates its location, (b) Determination of the search area, a rectangular area of size less than R^2, (c) A rectangular area of size greater than R^2 [9]

2.1.4 Power Tuning of Anchors (PTA)

In PTA algorithm [10] it is assumed that all the locators are capable to tune their transmission power and transmit beacon signals at different power levels starting from maximum to minimum received by the normal nodes or sensors. Once more, the algorithm considers two types of nodes which are normal nodes and locator or anchor nodes. In addition, the algorithm assumes the mobility of normal nodes.

Algorithm 2:

$L_i :$ **broadcast** $\left\{ (X_i, Y_i) \parallel \left(\theta_{i,1}(1), \theta_{i,2}(1) \right) \parallel R_i(1) \right\}$

$s :$ **define** $LH_s = \{ L_i : \parallel s - L_i \parallel \geq R_i(1) \}$

$s :$ **define** $A_s = [X_{max} - R_i(1), X_{min} - R_i(1),$
$Y_{max} - R_i(1), Y_{min} + R_i(1)]$

$s :$ **store** $S \leftarrow S_i(1) : \{ (X_i, Y_i) \parallel \left(\theta_{i,1}(1), \theta_{i,2}(1) \right) \parallel R_i(1) \},$

$\forall L_i \in LH_s$

$j=1$

for k=1 : Q−1

    for ω = 1: N − 1

    j++

    L **reduce** $R(j) = R(j-1) - \frac{R(1)}{N}$

    L : **broadcast** $\left\{ (X_i, Y_i) \parallel \left(\theta_{i,1}(j), \theta_{i,2}(j) \right) \parallel R_i(j) \right\}$

    $s : S \leftarrow S_i(j) : \{ (X_i, Y_i) \parallel \left(\theta_{i,1}(j), \theta_{i,2}(j) \right) \parallel R_i(j) \},$

    $\forall L_i : \parallel s - L_i \parallel \leq R_i(j) \cap L_i \in LH_s$

End for

    j++

$R_i(j) = R_i(1), \quad \forall L_i \in LH_s$

    L **rotate** $\theta_i(j) = \left\{ \theta_{i,1}(j-1) + \frac{2\pi}{MQ}, \theta_{i,2}(j-1) + \frac{2\pi}{MQ} \right\}$

    L **broadcast** $L_i : \left\{ (X_i, Y_i) \parallel \left(\theta_{i,1}(j), \theta_{i,2}(j) \right) \parallel R_i(j) \right\}$

    $s :$ **store** $S \leftarrow S_i(j) : \{ (X_i, Y_i) \parallel (\theta_1(j), \theta_2(j)) \parallel R_i(j) \},$

    $\forall L_i : \parallel s - L_i \parallel \leq R_i(j) \cap L_i \in LH_s$

End for

$s :$ **compute** $ROI = \cap_{i=1}^{|S|} S_i$

Location determination for each mobile node is done by using the received beacon signals from different three locators. The mobile node then acknowledges the locators and requests for retransmission of beacon with reduced power. After that, locators will reduce the power level and retransmit the beacon signals again. Mobile nodes select two power levels for each selected locator(e.g. P4 and P5 as shown in Figure 4) ; based on this information mobile node can determine its own location.   More details could be found in[10].

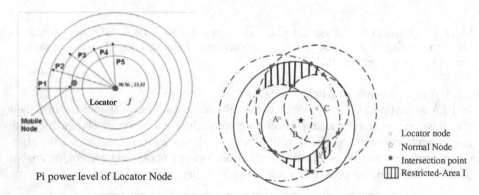

Pi power level of Locator Node

Fig. 4. Beacon Packet Transmission with Different Power Levels [10]

Fig. 5. Restricted-area I [11]

2.1.5   Restricted Area Based Localization (RAL) Algorithm
RAL algorithm algorithm considers two types of nodes which are normal nodes and locator or anchor nodes.   Location determination for normal node is done by measuring the received signal at normal node according to different power levels for locator and using radio connectivity and principle of perpendicular bisectors are used to form restricted-area I as shown in Figure 5. More details could be found in [11].

3   Performance Evaluation

After the implementation of the four algorithms, DIL, HiRLoc, PTA, and RAL, the comparison of between these algorithms is introduced in this section.   The main criterion for the comparison is the localization error of each algorithm in compared to others with different network settings.   Five case studies are explored in this section; in the first case study, the impact of locator radius on the localization error is studied. In the second case study, the effect of changing the number of the used beacons on the localization error is investigated. In the third case study, the localization error is computed when the beacons radiuses are changed. The experienced location error is also computed when locator beam width changed in case study 4. In case study 5, a comparison has been made between all of the algorithms in terms of the possibility of location detection and execution time.

Throughout these experiments, a deployment field of 549 x 514 units is considered. In addition, the number of deployed nodes in this area is 200 nodes. The results of these case studies are the average over 10 runs with different problem settings. A snapshot of our simulator which is a modification to the simulator is shown in Figure 6.

Before going through the cases studies, we summarized the characteristics of the four localization algorithms in Table 1.

Table 1. Characteristics of the different algorithms

Parameter	DIL	HiRLoc	PTA	RAL
Locator Antenna type	Directional	Directional	Omni-directional	Omni-directional
Mobility	N/A	limitation the mobility of locators within the range of sensor	No limitation for mobility	No limitation for mobility
Possibility of location detection	Low	high	medium	high
Execution time(complexity)	low	high	medium	low

Case Study 1: Localization Error vs. Locator Radius

In our first case study, we study the impact of locator radius on the localization Error. The locators' radiuses change from 250 to 500 units as shown in Figure 7. The average results show that average localization error seems to be fixed for all algorithms but RAL. RAL turns to be inefficient in terms of localization error with changing the locators' radius. However, its performance seems reasonable with very low locators' radiuses. The results only show that DIL is the most stable algorithm with different locators' radiuses. In addition, PTA and HiRloc works fine till the locators' radius reaches a certain point, 400 in our case, then the error percentages suddenly increases. After deeply investigating these algorithms, we found that when the radius of the locator increases more than the radius of the sensors, the error percentages increases sharply.

Case Study 2: Localization Error vs. Number of Beacons

Here, we study the impact of number of beacons on the localization Error. As shown in Figure 8, the number of beacons varied from 10 to 60. The average results shows that HiRLoc and RAL having almost the same error rate and they are stable with the increasing the number beacons. On the other hand, PTA shows a large error rate almost all the time and it is slightly increasing with the increase of number of beacons. Another conclusion can be drawn from the presented result is that DIL may experience unexpected error fluctuation with increasing the number of beacon.

Case Study 3: Localization Error vs. Radius of Beacons

In this test case the radius of the beacon itself is changed. As shown in Figure 9, the beacon radius is varied from 40 to 90 units. As can be seen in the Figure, the localization error is almost fixed in all algorithms; however, the minimum localization error in this case is reported by HiRLoc algorithm.

Case Study 4: Localization Error vs. Locator Beam Width

Figure 10 depicts the relation between the variations of locator beam width in the localization Error. In this set of experiments, the beam width is changed from 15 units to 60 units.   Again, the most stable algorithms in terms of location error are HiRLoc and RAL. In addition, PTA algorithm is stable as well with high location error. However, DIL seems to fluctuate with beam width changing.

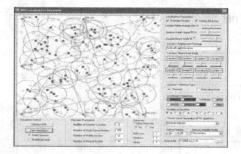

Fig. 6. Simulator snapshot

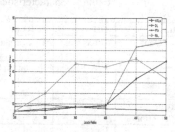

Fig. 7. Impact of Locator Radius in Localization Error

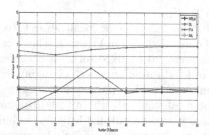

Fig. 8. Impact of number of Beacons in Localization Error

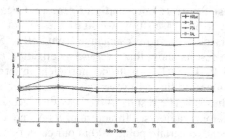

Fig. 9. Impact of Radius of Beacons in Localization Error

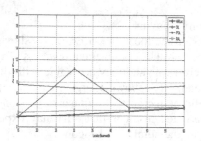

Fig. 10. Impact of locator beam width in Localization Error

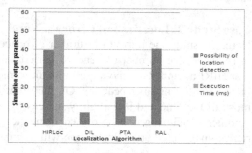

Fig. 11. Comparative chart between simulation output parameter

Case Study 5: Possibility of Location Detection and Algorithm Execution Time of all Algorithms
In this case study, we compare between all algorithms in terms of possibility of location detection and algorithm execution time. In this set of experiments, a large number of simulation cases are merged including different problem settings. Figure 11 shows the average results of the comparison. As can be seen, although DIL almost has the lowest running time but its possibility to detect nodes location is very low. On the other hand, it seems that RAL, on average, has best performance among all of the algorithms since it has the lowest running time and the best percentage of locating the nodes. Although HiRLoc has a very good percentage of location the nodes but its execution time is the worst.

4   Conclusion and Future Work

In this paper, we implemented four of the main localization algorithms and compared among them with different problem settings. Our comparison will be helpful for WSNs designers in selecting the best localization algorithm to use. In our future work, we will study the effect of different mobility models on these algorithms.

References

[1]   Wellenhoff, B.H., Lichtenegger, H., Collins, J.: Global Positions System: Theory and Practice, 4th edn. Springer (1997)

[2]   Harter, A., Hopper, A., Steggles, P., Ward, A., Webster, P.: The anatomy of a context-aware application. In: Proceedings of MOBICOM 1999, Seattle, Washington (1999)

[3]   Priyantha, N.B., Chakraborty, A., Balakrishnan, H.: The Cricket Location-Support System. In: Proceedings of MOBICOM 2000, New York (August 2000)

[4]   Bahl, P., Padmanabhan, V.N.: RADAR: An In-Building RF-Based User Location and Tracking System. In: Proceedings of the IEEE INFOCOM 2000 (March 2000)

[5]   Niculescu, D., Nath, B.: Ad Hoc Positioning System (APS) using AoA. In: INFOCOM 2003, San Francisco, CA (2003)

[6]   Hightower, J., Boriello, G., Want, R.: SpotON: An indoor 3D Location Sensing Technology Based on RF Signal Strength, University of Washington CSE Report #2000-02-02 (February 2000)

[7]   Sahoo, P.K., Hwang, I.-S.: Collaborative Localization Algorithms for Wireless Sensor Networks with Reduced Localization Error. Open Access Sensors 11, 9989–10009 (2011)

[8]   Lazos, L., Poovendran, R.: High-resolution Robust Localization for Wireless Sensor Networks, CTA form ARL, DAAD19-01-2-2011; ONR award, N00014-04-1-0479; ARO grant, W911NF-05-1-0491

[9]   Lozas, L., Poovendran, R.: Secure Range-Independent Localization for Wireless Sensor Networks, pp. 21–30. ACM (October 2004)

[10] Jabbar, S., Aziz, M.Z., Minhas, A.A., Hussain, D.: A Novel Power Tunning Anchors Localization Algorithm for Mobile Wireless Sensor Nodes. In: 2010 10th IEE International Conference on Computer and Information Technology (CIT 2010), pp. 2241–2446 (2010)

[11] Wang, C., Liu, K., Xiao, N.: A Range Free Localization Algorithm Based on Restricted-Area for Wireless Sensor Networks. In: 3rd International Multi-Conference on Computing in the Global Information Technology, pp. 97–101. IEEE (2008)

[12] Bulusu, N., Heidemann, J., Estrin, D.: GPS-less Low Cost Out-door Localization for Very Small Devices. IEEE Personal Communications Magazine 7(5), 28–34 (2000)

[13] Niculescu, D., Nath, B.: DV Based Positioning in Ad hoc Net-works. Journal of Telecommunication Systems (2003)

[14] Nagpal, R.: Organizing a Global Coordinate System from Local Information on an Amorphous Computer. A.I. Memo1666. MIT A.I. Laboratory (August 1999)

[15] He, T., Huang, C., Blum, B.M., Stankovic, J.A., Abdelzaher, T.: Range-Free Localization and Its Impact on Large Scale Sensor Networks. ACM Transactions on Embedded Computing Systems 4(4), 877–906 (2005)

Sentiment Classification Using Graph Based Word Sense Disambigution

Abbas Jalilvand and Naomie Salim

Faculty of Computer Science and Information Systems
Universiti Teknologi Malaysia, Johor Bahru
jabbas2@live.utm.my, naomie@utm.my

Abstract. Sentiment classification is the most active field in opinion mining that aims to determine whether an opinionated text expresses a positive, negative or neutral opinion. Existing lexicon based sentiment classification methods are unable to deal with context or domain-specific words. To solve this problem, Word Senses Disambiguation (WSD) is useful to identify the most related meaning (sense) of a word in a sentence. In this paper, a sense level sentiment classification method is proposed that determine the sentiment polarity of words using graph based WSD algorithm and a multiple meaning (sense) sentiment lexicon. To evaluate the impact of WSD on sentiment classification, the proposed method compared against a baseline method using two subjectivity lexicons, namely the MPQA and SentiWordNet. Experimental results using a benchmark dataset show that the WSD is effective for sentiment classification.

Keywords: opinion mining, sentiment classification, word sense disambiguation, context dependent word.

1 Introduction

In recent years, with the rapid growth of social media, such as forums, blog, discussion boards and social networks, people can freely express and respond to opinion on variety of topics. Thus, a very large amount of user-generated content has been available on the Web. However, the high volume of reviews makes it difficult for individuals and organizations to read and understand all of them. To solve this problem, a hot research area has recently emerged, which is called opinion mining and sentiment analysis. Sentiment classification is the most active field in opinion mining that aims to determine whether an opinionated text expresses a positive, negative or neutral opinion. Sometimes, subjectivity classification is used as an input data pre-processing step for sentiment classification. Sentiment classification is applied at word-level, sentence-level, document-level and feature/aspect-level using different methods ranging from unsupervised to supervised approaches that can be categorized into two main methodologies: semantic-orientation and machine learning approaches[1-4]. In the semantic-orientation approach, a text is classified based on average polarity of words/phrases containing positive or negative sentiment using a sentiment lexicon

A. Ell Hassanien et al. (Eds.): AMLTA 2012, CCIS 322, pp. 351–358, 2012.
© Springer-Verlag Berlin Heidelberg 2012

and linguistic rules. This lexicon consists of a list of opinion words and their polarity (positive, negative or neutral). In fact, this approach works at word-level to classify at sentence or document-level. One of the shortcomings of these methods is that they are unable to deal with context or domain-specific words. For example, the word "fight" expresses a positive sentiment in "the football team was full of fight" while is negative in "the people are always fighting". Words have different meaning (sense) in different context, and their sentiment polarities are different. Thus, to have better result in classification, it should be applied at sense-level rather than word-level. In this paper, a sense-level sentiment classification method is proposed. In this method, first, the most related sense of word is found according to its context and then the sentiment of word is determined using the multiple meanings sentiment lexicon. To find the related sense of words, WSD method is useful. WSD is an active field of natural languages processing to identify more related meaning of a word in a sentence. The graph based WSD algorithm builds a graph corresponding to a word sequence from WordNet [5] and then finds the stronger link as a related sense [6]. In this research, this algorithm is used for sentiment classification due to its high accuracy of performance. By using this strategy the problem of context dependent will be solved in sentiment classification. The remainder of the paper is organized as follows: Section 2 provides a review of related work on sentiment classification methods. Section 3 provides the research design. Section 4 shows the experimental results. Finally, Section 5 outlines conclusions.

2   Related Works

In the semantic-orientation approach, a text is classified based on average polarity of words/phrases containing positive or negative sentiment using a sentiment lexicon incorporated to syntactic rules. In recent years, two kinds of approaches have been proposed to build a sentiment lexicon: thesaurus and corpus based. Thesaurus based approach aims to grow a small set of seed opinion words using their synonyms, antonyms, and hierarchies in a thesaurus, e.g., WordNet [5] to generate a sentiment lexicon based on a bootstrapping process [7-10].

WordNet is an online lexical reference system whose design is inspired by psycholinguistic theories of human lexical memory. The WordNet lexicon contains nouns, verbs, adjectives, and adverbs. Lexical information is organized in terms of word meanings, rather than word forms. Senses in the WordNet database are represented relationally by synonym sets (synsets) that sets of all words sharing a common sense.

In this essence, Kim and Hovy [7] adopted the method which is based on synonym and antonym lists originated from WordNet to calculate the probability of sentiment polarity of words. Kamps et al. [11] used a hypothesis that synonyms have similar sentiments. They used related synonyms from the thesaurus in order to construct a lexical network; consequently, the sentiment of the word can be measured with the distance from seed words ("good" and "bad"). Furthermore, Hu and Liu [8] improved the method of Kamps et al. by using both synonyms and antonyms in order to construct lexical network. After that, Esuli and Sebastiani [12]found the sentiment of words according to the glosses of subjective terms.

MPQA [13] and SentiWordNet [9, 10] are also two popular sentiment lexicon. MPQA lexicon consists of over 8,000 subjective single-word clues. SentiWordNet is Built upon WordNet. In SentiWordNet each synset of WordNet is automatically annotated with three sentiment scores regarding their positivity, negativity, and objectivity. Many researchers have used SentiWordNet as the sentiment lexicon.

Corpus-based approaches expand a seed list of opinion words using syntactic or co-occurrence patterns in a large corpus[1, 14]. Since the corpus-based approach is inherently context based, it can handle domain and context-specific opinion words; unlike the thesaurus based approach. On the other hand, thesaurus-based approach is more effective than corpus-based, because it is difficult to prepare a huge corpus.

Recently some researchers have addressed the context dependent problem for words such as "high, small, low, and etc." Ding et al. [3] proposed a holistic lexicon-based approach that deals with context dependent opinion words using three rules based on contextual information in other reviews and sentences in same domain. Shortcoming of this approach is that, it is limited to a specific domain. Wanton et al. [15] used WSD-based method in a corpus of newspaper quotations. They worked on two-word phrases as ambiguity terms, and used the sources of SentiWordNet [10] and General Inquirer (GI) [16] to calculate the sentiment polarity. The weaknesses of this method are that it is unable to disambiguate words in sentence and used sources are not annotated based on sense polarities.

Wu and Wen [17] focused on 14 adjectives such as "large, small, many, few, high, low, and etc.", as Dynamic sentiment ambiguous adjectives (DSAAs). They defined the semantic expectation for nouns that shows the tendency of polarity. They predicted semantic expectation for nouns using search engine, and determined the sentiment of word based on semantic expectation and DSAAs. The performance of this method is depending on search engine.

3   Research Design

The proposed method aims to determine the sentiment of words based on the most related sense of words. In order to develop this method, a multiple meanings sentiment lexicon is needed. To construct this lexicon, a bootstrapping technique is applied that start with a list of seed words and uses the synonyms and antonyms of words to enlarge this list from WordNet. In this paper, SentiWordNet is used as a multiple meanings sentiment lexicon.

Firstly, in this method the most related sense of word is found according to its context and then, the sentiment of the word is determined using the multiple meanings sentiment lexicon. To find the related sense of words, graph based WSD algorithm [6] is used.

This algorithm builds a graph corresponding to words sequence from WordNet and then finds the stronger link as a related meaning (sense) of target word. Figure 1 illustrates the framework of proposed approach.

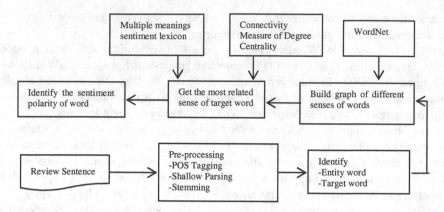

Fig. 1. Framework of WSD Based Sentiment Classification

For example, consider the sentence "people are always fighting". In the first step, preprocessing (POS Tagging, Shallow Parsing and Stemming) will be applied. After preprocessing, "people" and "fight" as entity and target words are identified respectively. Then, all different senses of "people" and "fight" words are extracted from WordNet which are four and nine respectively. To build the graph of words, four different senses of "people" in WordNet and the important words in their glosses are connected to "people". Then these words are followed leading to "fight" using depth-first search (DFS). To assign the most related senses of "fight", the shortest path between the two words is found using connectivity measure of degree centrality[6]. After finding the appropriate sense for "fight", its sentiment polarity is determined using multiple meanings sentiment lexicon[10].

4   Experiments and Result

In this section, experimental results are presented and discussed. To evaluate the impact of WSD method on sentiment classification, the proposed method is compared against a baseline method that determines sentiment of a review, using aggregated sentiment score of its words based on two different sentiment lexicons. Results evaluated using standard evaluation measures accuracy based on same data set.

4.1   Dataset Description

Two publicly available datasets will be used in this research. The movie review (MR)[1] crawled from the IMDB movie archive consists of 1000 positive and 1000 negative movie reviews [2], and the multi-domain sentiment(MDS)[2] used by Blitzer et al.[18] crawled from Amazon.com containing four different types of product reviews (Book, DVD, Electronics and Kitchen). This dataset contains 1000 positive and

---

[1] http://www.cs.cornell.edu/people/pabo/movie-review-data
[2] http://www.cs.jhu.edu/~mdredze/datasets/sentiment/index2.html

1000 negative examples for each domain. Pre-processing was performed on both of the datasets. Firstly, punctuation, numbers, non-alphabet characters and stop words were removed. Secondly, Porter's stemmer[19], Stanford POS tagger[3] and parser[4] were performed to identify phrases in the form of a pair of head term and modifier. Summary statistics of the datasets before and after preprocessing are shown in Table 1.

Table 1. Dataset in the number of words

Dataset	MR	MDS			
		Book	DVD	Electronic	Kitchen
Corpus size(before pre-processing)	674,662	214,350	212,413	146,159	129,587
Corpus size(after pre-processing)	450,032	120,553	119,887	74,996	64,443

4.2 Baseline Method

In this method, first, positive and negative words are extracted from review documents and then simply assign a score +1 and -1 to positive and negative words respectively based on sentiment lexicon. A document is classified as positive if the sum of score is above zero and as negative if is below zero. This method was implemented using two subjectivity lexicons, namely the MPQA[13] and SentiWordNet[10]. MPQA subjectivity lexicon contains 2,718 positive and 4,911 negative words. SentiWordNet is a multiple meaning sentiment lexicon. It is automatically annotated from WordNet. In SentiWordNet, each synset has three sentiment scores regarding how positive, negative, and objective. Since, in this method work based on single meaning of words, the first sense of words which is more important sense is considered as opinion words. It should be noted that these lexicons are domain-independent.

4.3 Proposed Method

In contrast to the baseline method, our method considers different sentiment polarities for words based on their different meanings in the context. To find the related meaning (sense) of words, graph based WSD algorithm [6] is used. After finding the appropriate sense, sentiment polarity is determined using multiple meanings sentiment lexicon. In this paper, SentiWordNet is used as a multiple meanings sentiment lexicon. Because each word in SentiWordNet has multiple senses, we calculated the sentiment polarity of each sense from the three polarity scores (positive, negative, and objective) using a sentiment polarity calculation strategy adopted from previous literature [20] (Figure 2).

---

[3] http://nlp.stanford.edu/software/tagger.shtml
[4] http://nlp.stanford.edu/software/lex-parser.shtml

If (score(sense)$_{objective}$ > 0.5 or (score(sense)$_{positive}$ = (score(sense)$_{negative}$
    Sentiment polarity (sense) =neutral
Else
    If (score(sense)$_{positive}$ > (score(sense)$_{negative}$
        Sentiment polarity (sense) =positive
    Else
        Sentiment polarity (sense) =negative

Fig. 2. Sentiment polarity calculation strategy

4.4   Results

Table 2 gives the experimental results for sentiment classification at document level using the baseline and proposed methods. The standard evaluation measures of accuracy used to evaluate performance of methods. From table 2, we observe that the proposed method yield results better than baseline method in different experiment. This improvement shows that WSD is useful to determine the sentiment polarity of words at sense level using the multiple meanings sentiment lexicon.

Table 2. Experimental results for baseline and proposed methods(accaracy%)

Method	MR	MDS			
		Book	DVD	Electronic	Kitchen
MPQA	65.90	61.95	63.40	60.30	61.85
SentiWordNet	60.60	59.50	59.75	58.25	59.30
Graph based WSD	67.15	63.70	65.60	63.80	64.60

5   Discussion and Conclusion

In this study, a sense level sentiment classification method was presented. However, words have different meanings (senses), but they don't necessarily represent the same sentiment polarity. The existing methods only consider one of the different senses for words; thus, they cannot deal with context dependent problems. The proposed method determines the sentiment polarity of each word based on its most related sense in the context; therefore, has better result in comparison with current lexicon based sentiment classification approach. To find the most related sense of words, a graph based WSD algorithm is applied. The proposed method was compared to a baseline method using two subjectivity lexicons (MPQA and SentiWordNet). The experimental results is shown the proposed method outperform the current method. It can be concluded

WSD can be a useful part of an opinion mining system. We plane to apply WSD in machine learning sentiment classification approach.

Acknowledgment. This work is supported by ministry of higher education and research Management Centre at Universiti Teknologi Malaysia (UTM) under Research University grant Category GUP (VOT Q.J130000.7128.00H72).

References

1. Turney, P.D.: Thumbs up or thumbs down? Semantic orientation applied to unsupervised classification of reviews. In: Proceedings of the 40th Annual Meeting of the Association for Computational Linguistics (ACL), Philadelphia, pp. 417–424 (2002)
2. Pang, B., Lee, L., Vaithyanathan, S.: Thumbs up?: sentiment classification using machine learning techniques. In: Proceedings of Conference on Empirical Methods in Natural Language Processing, EMNLP 2002 (2002)
3. Ding, X., Liu, B., Yu, P.: A holistic lexicon-based approach to opinion mining. In: Proceedings of the Conference on Web Search and Web Data Mining, WSDM 2008 (2008)
4. Abbasi, A., France, S., Zhang, Z., Chen, H.: Selecting attributes for sentiment classification using feature relation networks. IEEE Transactions on Knowledge and Data Engineering (99), 1 (2011)
5. Felbaum, C.: Wordnet, an Electronic Lexical Database for English. MIT Press, Cambridge (1998)
6. Navigli, R., Lapata, M.: An experimental study of graph connectivity for unsupervised word sense disambiguation. IEEE Transactions on Pattern Analysis and Machine Intelligence 32(4), 678–692 (2010)
7. Kim, S., Hovy, E.: Determining the sentiment of opinions. In: Proceedings of International Conference on Computational Linguistics, COLING 2004 (2004)
8. Hu, M., Liu, B.: Mining and summarizing customer reviews. In: Proceedings of ACM SIGKDD International Conference on Knowledge Discovery and Data Mining, KDD 2004 (2004)
9. Esuli, A., Sebastiani, F.: SentiWordNet: a publicly available lexical resource for opinion mining. In: Proceedings of Language Resources and Evaluation, LREC 2006 (2006)
10. Baccianella, S., Esuli, A., Sebastiani, F.: Sentiwordnet 3.0: An enhanced lexical resource for sentiment analysis and opinion mining (2010)
11. Kamps, J., Marx, M., Mokken, R.J., Rijke, M.: Using WordNet to measure semantic orientation of adjectives. In: Proceedings of LREC 2004, 4th International Conference on Language Resources and Evaluation, Lisbon, PT, vol. IV, pp. 1115–1118 (2004)
12. Esuli, A., Sebastiani, F.: Determining the semantic orientation of terms through gloss classification. In: Proceedings of ACM International Conference on Information and Knowledge Management, CIKM 2005 (2005)
13. Wilson, T., Wiebe, J., Hoffmann, P.: Recognizing contextual polarity in phrase-level sentiment analysis. In: Proceedings of the Human Language Technology Conference and the Conference on Empirical Methods in Natural Language Processing, HLT/EMNLP 2005 (2005)
14. Read, J., Carroll, J.: Weakly supervised techniques for domain-independent sentiment classification. ACM (2009)
15. Martın-Wanton, T., et al.: Word sense disambiguation in opinion mining: Pros and cons. Special issue: Natural Language Processing and its Applications, 119 (2010)

16. Stone, P.J., Dunphy, D.C., Smith, M.S.: The General Inquirer: A Computer Approach to Content Analysis (1966)
17. Wu, Y., Wen, M.: Disambiguating dynamic sentiment ambiguous adjectives. Association for Computational Linguistics (2010)
18. Blitzer, J., Dredze, M., Pereira, F.: Biographies, bollywood, boom-boxes and blenders: Domain adaptation for sentiment classification (2007)
19. Porter, M.F.: An algorithm for suffix stripping. Program (1980)
20. Dang, Y., Zhang, Y., Chen, H.: A lexicon-enhanced method for sentiment classification: An experiment on online product reviews. IEEE Intelligent Systems 25(4), 46–53 (2010)

Test Cases Automatic Generator (TCAG): A Prototype

P.N. Boghdady, N.L. Badr, M.A. Hashim, and M.F. Tolba

Faculty of Computer and Information Sciences, Ain shams University, Cairo, Egypt

Abstract. Light has been shed recently on the usage of requirements-based testing where requirements-based models, specifically UML models, are used in proposing test cases' generation models. In this paper, an automated prototype called "Test Cases Automatic Generator" (TCAG) is proposed, implementing an introduced enhanced technique for generating reduced, hybrid coverage and multi-testing types test cases from activity diagrams with a minimum user intervention. After their generation, the final test cases are captured using one of the well known automatic capture-replay tools and are executed generating summary reports. A traceability matrix called "Test cases Traceability Matrix" (TTM) is proposed and used by one of the well known requirements management tools to trace the final generated test cases to their initial requirements. Qualitative and quantitative evaluation of the proposed prototype is made, under different processing speeds, showing the improved performance over its previous releases and over a closely related prototype as well.

Keywords: Requirements-Based Testing (RBT), Category partitioning, Test cases generation, Automatic capture-replay, Requirements management.

1 Introduction

Requirements-Based Testing (RBT) refers to the type of testing process that focuses on deriving a test model using different types of requirements models as formal models, then converting this test model into a concrete set of test cases [1], [2]. The requirements models can be behavioral, interactional, or structural models. During the past decade, many researchers have been trying to automate the generation of test cases from different models [3]. Activity diagram is an important type of diagrams among 13 other diagrams supported by UML 2.0. It is used for business modeling, control and object flow modeling, complex operation modeling etc. The main advantage of this model is its simplicity and ease of understanding the flow of logic of the system.

To ensure a full coverage of respective requirements, the generated test paths require a metric that can tell whether they are of high coverage of not. The cyclomatic complexity metric developed by McCabe (1976) [4] measures the complexity of a program or module by determining the number of independent paths achieving by that the full line coverage rather than the full path coverage, which is practically impossible.

Test data is required for the execution of test cases. There exist several partition testing methods like Equivalence Partitioning, Category Partition, and Domain Testing

A. Ell Hassanien et al. (Eds.): AMLTA 2012, CCIS 322, pp. 359–368, 2012.

[5]. They depend on building a model that partitions the input space of the test object into subsets/partitions based on the assumption that all points in the same subset result in a similar behavior from the test object. Once the final test cases are generated, they are ready for capturing and execution. There are many commercial and non-commercial tools that automatically or manually execute test cases [6-15]. Tracing the test cases to their corresponding use cases eases the handling of continuous change requests. Many commercial requirements management tools [16], [17] can be used to create several traceability matrices.

This paper is structured as follows: the second section discusses some related work. In the third section, the proposed model's architecture is explained. In the fourth section, an implementation of the proposed prototype is explained supported with a case study. In the fifth section, an experimental evaluation of the proposed prototype is shown. The last section includes the conclusion.

2   Related Work

Many researchers during the last decade have implemented tools that generate test cases from different models whether UML models or other types. Since the UML models are the concern of this paper, tools related to them are presented as follows:

UMLTGF is a tool that generates test cases from simple activity diagrams [6] that ensure executing loops at most once. However, it restricted having only pairs of branches, merges and fork-join structures. Besides, any fork node can only have two outgoing edges. Moreover, there is no proof that the conditional threads in the fork-join structures were handled. Cow Suite is another tool that generates test cases from UML models but according to structural coverage criteria [7]. It covers a wide range of functional areas but without guaranteeing the coverage of all of them.

Conformiq Designer is a Commercial tool implemented in Eclipse where models can be created as UML State Machines and in Qtronic Modeling Language (QML) [8]. PyModel is one more tool that supports offline and online testing. It uses a composition of scenario control and coverage being met by test cases generated [9]. Test Designer tool is the successor of BZ-Testing-Tools and Leiros Test Generator, and now is a commercial product, where the system under test is first represented with UML models enriched with OCL constraints [10]. SCOOTER tool is another tool that generates test cases using UML models. It builds an intermediate model called State Collaboration TEst Model (SCOTEM) mentioned in [11], [12] from UML collaboration diagrams and state machines, and then generates tests from it according to various control-flow criteria.

Furthermore, the testing process does not stop at the test cases generation. There are many companies that released commercial test capturing and executing tools that use the automatic capture-replay technology to generate script-based or keyword-based test cases. Some of those commercial tools are: Automated QA Test Complete tool [13], IBM Rational Robot [14] and IBM Functional tester [15]. They are automated testing environments that depend on capturing and recording all the users' actions and storing them as scripts which are considered the test cases procedures that can be replayed again on other versions of the application under test.

3   The Proposed Architecture

The proposed model is an enhancement of our previous initial model [18] that was modified in [19] then in [20]. The enhanced architecture is shown in Fig. 1. The proposed enhanced architecture is composed of four modules for test cases generation which are: "XML Parse", "ADG Generation", "Test Paths Generation" and "Test Cases Generation". Each module is composed of sub modules. After the analyst prepares the activity diagrams using any UML 2.0 Drawing tool (e.g. Enterprise Architect, IBM Rational Modeler and Visual Paradigm) and stores them in the activity diagrams' database, they are converted into XML files using any XML Creator tool (e.g. Enterprise Architect and Visual Paradigm) and stored in an XML database. The XML files are considered the main building block in launching the automated methodology, i.e. the four modules, of generating test cases.

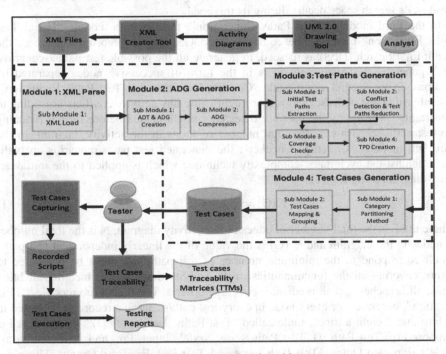

Fig. 1. The Proposed Model Architecture

In the first module, "XML Parse" each XML file is being loaded in the sub module "XML Load" and then parsed to extract all different kinds of nodes in the activity diagram and categorize them. The second module: "ADG Generation" is composed of two sub modules: "ADT & ADG Creation" and "ADG Compression". In the first sub module, a special table called the "Activity Dependency Table (ADT)" is created that contains records for every activity/action only. Each record is composed of nine attributes: "Symbol", "Activity Name", "Entity", "Node Type", "Dep.", "Input", "Pre-conditions", "Post-conditions" and "Output". Besides the activity name, a symbol and the entity performing each activity are included. The "Node Type" column differentiates the sequential from the concurrent activities. All the pseudo nodes are not included in the ADT reducing its size. However, in order not to lose essential activities or effect the logic of the diagram, the guard conditions or conditional threads resulting from those removed nodes, objects as well as the input/output pins are all reformed in introduced logical expressions that use simple AND and OR operations. Those expressions are then stored in the Pre- and Post-conditions columns. Moreover, the activities are connected using the "Dep." column. Both external inputs and outputs are accompanied by every activity as well.

From the generated ADT, a directed flow graph called "Activity Dependency Graph (ADG)" is created. A node for every different activity/action in the ADT is created and the dependencies between them are used to create the transitions between the nodes. The generated ADG is reduced in size due to only including the activities/actions. The second sub module, "ADG Compression" further reduces the ADG's size by combining the sequential activities in single nodes. This further reduction in the ADG's search space occurs during its traversal.

In the third module, "Test Paths Generation", the first sub module "Initial Test Paths Extraction" traverses the compressed ADG, using an algorithm that uses the Depth First Search (DFS) as its seed, to generate all the possible test paths/scenarios. Each generated test path/scenario is in the form of successive nodes separated by commas. In the second sub module "Conflict Detection and Test Paths Reduction", any infeasible test paths/scenarios that might cause any activity conflicts according to constraints specified by the user are detected and eliminated before further reducing the test paths/scenarios by the total number of loops in the activity diagram. In the third sub module, "Coverage Checker", the generated test paths/scenarios are validated against the cyclomatic complexity technique which is applied to the initial activity diagram using Eq. (1).

$$V(G) = E - N + 2 \tag{1}$$

Where the E is the total number of edges in the activity diagram, N is the total number of nodes in the diagram and V (G) is the value of the linearly independent test paths which correspond to the minimum number of test paths that must be generated to ensure covering all the functionalities in the activity diagram and meeting all basis paths, all branches and all predicates coverage criteria. The fourth sub module, "TPD Creation", generates for every node in every test path/scenario a record to be stored in an introduced eight-attribute table called "Test Paths' Details (TPD)". Every record is composed of: Test Path ID, Test Path Node, Node's Input, Pre- and Post-conditions, Node's Expected Output, Test Path Input and Test Path Expected Output. These details can help the tester perform unit and integration testing easily where s/he can easily trace the values of the internal variables during the execution of each test path/scenario.

The fourth module, "Test Cases Generation", is composed of two sub modules: "Category Partitioning Method" and "Test Cases Mapping & Grouping". The "Category Partitioning Method" sub module implements the category partitioning method

[5] to generate the required test data which is an important aspect of any test case. In the second sub module, "Test Cases Mapping & Grouping", the category partitioning method has been enhanced to include a simple mapping process that maps each test case to the corresponding test path/scenario that should be executed. Besides, a grouping process has been also added which creates groups according to the different outputs of test cases. The form of the test case record is as follows: The Test Cases Group ID, The Test Case Input which are the values of the external input parameters, Internal Conditions and Objects which are the logical expressions representing the guard conditions and conditional threads. Objects are included as well, each in a column storing the values of its changing states assigned to it during the execution of each activity/action, the Test Case's Expected Output and finally the Test Path ID of the corresponding test path to be executed in each test case. An example of the final suite of test cases is shown in Table 1; its form can help the tester perform system as well as acceptance testing easily.

Table 1. The Final Test Cases

Test Cases Group ID	Test Case Input: Input Parameters	Internal Conditions and Objects									Test Case Expected Output	Test Path ID
	i1: Input	A	B	C	D	E	F	G	obj: o1	obj: o2		
1	100-200	T	-	-	-	-	-	-	-	-	o1: Output	2
2	201-400	F	T, F	F	-	-	-	-	-	-	o2: Output	1
3	401-600	F	F	T	T	T	T	T	State 1, Sate 2	State 1, State 2, State 3	o3: Output	3
	401-600	F	F	T	T	T	T	F	State 1, Sate 2	State 1, State 2, State 3		4
	401-600	F	F	T	T	F	T	T	State 1	State 1, State 2, State 3		5
	401-600	F	F	T	T	F	T	F	State 1	State 1, State 2, State 3		6
...	...	...	...	...	...	...	...	...	...	...	...	...

The final test cases are eventually stored in our test cases database before the tester can capture each one automatically, using the Test Complete tool [13] as one of the well known automatic capture-replay tools. Moreover, an introduced matrix called Test cases Traceability Matrix (TTM) can be generated using IBM Rational Requisite Pro [17], one of the well known requirements management tools to trace the generated test cases to their initial requirements.

Different aspects have been enhanced in the proposed model as follows: the form and size of the ADG, dealing with the concurrent activities, applying the Category Partitioning Method and the reduction in the number of generated test cases before and mapping and grouping them.

4   The Proposed Prototype: TCAG

The proposed model is automated, with a minimum user intervention, and a prototype tool called "Test Cases Automatic Generator" (TCAG) has been built. The TCAG performs all the four modules until the final suites of test cases are generated and stored in the test cases' database. A screen shot from the TCAG is shown in Fig. 2(a). After the generation process is completed, on the right side of the form, all the final generated test cases and the TPD are displayed. Beside each test case, the specific test path that is to be executed is displayed. On the left side all the generated test paths/scenarios for each activity diagram are displayed. On clicking the "Test Cases

Capturing" button, the TCAG prototype integrates with the capture-replay tool called "Test Complete by Automated QA" [13] that is used to capture the final test cases on the system under test. The capturing process converts the test cases into test scripts that have the form shown in Fig. 2(b). During the execution of the scripts, the changes in the values of the internal variables in the form of the logical expressions or objects' states can be monitored in the TPD table compared to their expected values. After the execution is done, we can obtain testing reports as shown in Fig. 2(c). On clicking the "Test Cases Traceability" button, IBM Rational Requisite Pro [17] is opened and the Test cases Traceability Matrix (TTM) is created tracing each test case to its initial use case as shown in Fig. 2(d).

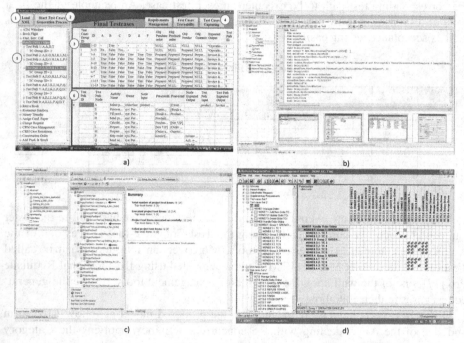

Fig. 2. a) TCAG Screen Shot, b) Test Script, c) Testing Summary Report, d) Test cases Traceability Matrix (TTM)

5   Experimental Evaluation

The proposed TCAG prototype is evaluated both quantitatively and qualitatively using different case studies in different domains [21-25]. The TCAG is evaluated against a closely related prototype. The proposed prototype has three previous beta releases before the release currently discussed in this paper; all releases are run under different processing speeds and their performance is compared proving that the enhancements made on our model that lead to this current release improved time efficiency, performance and coverage as well as space effectiveness as follows:

5.1   Performance

The performance of the TCAG prototype and a closely related protoype called "UMLTGF" [6] are calculated using Eq. 2 [26], [27] and Eq. 3 [27].

$$T = N * c / f \tag{2}$$

Where T is the total processing time elapsed by the processor to execute the proposed algorithm for generating the final test cases, N is the total number of instructions in the proposed algorithm, c is the number of CPU clock cycles per instruction and f is the number of CPU clock cycles per millisec.

$$P = IPC * f / N = 1 / T \tag{3}$$

Where P is the performance in the form of reciprocal of T, which is the total elapsed time to complete the execution of the proposed algorithm. f is the number of cycles per millisec, IPC is the number of instructions per cycle and N is the total number of instructions to be executed. The calculation was made for Intel Core 2 Duo processor 4 GB RAM and 2.80 GHz. Fig. 3 shows the performance of TCAG against UMLTGF where TCAG's performance outstands the other tool. Moreover, UMLTGF does not deal with complex activity diagrams.

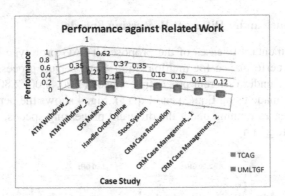

Fig. 3. Performance vs Related Work

5.2   The Search Space

The search space of the ADG is reduced; yet it still covers all the activity diagram's functionalities. Table 2, columns 2, 4 and 6, shows the reduction percentages of the search space in every release of the TCAG where the search space is further reduced in every release.

5.3   The Number of Generated Test Cases

The enhanced proposed model reduces the number of test paths before starting the test cases generation phase by detecting the conflicting test paths and eliminating them.

Table 2, columns 3, 5 and 7, shows the reduction percentages of the number of test paths generated in every release of the TCAG. Then it further reduces the generated test cases through the application of the category partitioning method. Although the enhanced proposed model generates a reduced set of test cases, they still meet a hybrid coverage criterion by meeting all branches, all predicates and all basis paths coverage criteria.

Table 2. Comparing the Search Space and Test Paths Reduction Percentage in every Release of TCAG

Case Study	Release 1		Release 2		Release 3		Release 4	
	Search Space Reduction %	Test Paths Reduction %	Search Space Reduction %	Test Paths Reduction %	Search Space Reduction %	Test Paths Reduction %	Search Space Reduction %	Test Paths Reduction %
ATM 1	21.4 %	0.0 %	50.0 %	40.0 %	50.0 %	40.0 %	64.3 %	40.0 %
ATM 2	11.1 %	0.0 %	44.4 %	43.0 %	44.4 %	43.0 %	55.6 %	43.0 %
CPS Make Call	27.0 %	0.0 %	54.0 %	36.4 %	70.3 %	36.4 %	75.7 %	36.4 %
Handle Order Online	9.0 %	0.0 %	36.4 %	52.6 %	45.4 %	52.6 %	59.0 %	52.6 %
Stock System	2.1 %	0.0 %	15.0 %	18.2 %	29.8 %	18.2 %	66.0 %	18.2 %
CRM Case Resolution	7.8 %	0.0 %	8.0 %	35.5 %	44.7 %	35.5 %	68.4 %	48.4 %
CRM Case Manage 1	9.0 %	0.0 %	9.1 %	55.4 %	45.4 %	55.4 %	68.2 %	64.1 %
CRM Case Manage 2	13.3 %	0.0 %	6.7 %	56.0 %	42.2 %	56.0 %	69.0 %	64.5 %

5.4   Performance under Different Processing Speeds

The four complementary releases of the proposed TCAG prototype are subjected to calculating their performance for multiple Intel Core 2 Duo processors with 4 GB RAM and running under different processing speeds (1.20, 2.00, 2.80 and 3.33). The calculations were made using Eq. (2) and Eq. (3). Fig. 4 shows the performance of the four different releases running under the different processing speeds, each processing speed in a separate graph.

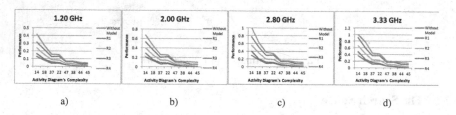

a)   b)   c)   d)

Fig. 4. Performance of Different Releases under Different Processing Powers

6   Conclusion

This paper proposes an automated prototype, with a minimum human intervention, called "Test Cases Automatic Generator" (TCAG) for generating hybrid coverage reduced test cases that can be applied to different types of testing using UML activity diagrams. The generated test cases can be applied to unit, integration, system as well as acceptance testing. The generated test cases are captured using one of the well known automatic capture-replay tools; Test Complete by Automated QA and traced to their initial requirements in an introduced traceability matrix called Test cases Traceability Matrix (TTM) using IBM Rational Requisite Pro, a well known requirements management tool. An experimental evaluation of the proposed prototype is made proving its reduced test cases, search space and elapsed time, as well as hybrid coverage and improved performance even under different processing speeds.

References

1. Berenbach, B., Paulish, D., Kazmeier, J., Rudorfer, A.: Software and Systems Requirements Engineering in Practice. The McGraw-Hill Companies Inc., USA (2009)
2. Boghdady, P.N., Badr, N., Hashem, M., Tolba, M.F.: Test Case Generation and Test Data Extraction Techniques. Inter. J. Electr. Comput. Sci. 11(3), 87–94 (2011)
3. Hasling, B., Goetz, H., Beetz, K.: Model Based Testing of System Requirements using UML Use Case Models. In: International Conference on Software Testing, Verification, and Validation, April 9-11, pp. 367–376. IEEE Computer Society, Washington DC (2008)
4. McCabe, T.J.: A Complexity Measure. IEEE Trans. Softw. Eng. 2(4), 308–320 (1976)
5. Ostrand, T.J., Balcer, M.J.: The category-partition method for specifying and generating fuctional tests. Commun. ACM 31(6), 676–686 (1988)
6. Linzhang, W., Jiesong, Y., Xiaofeng, Y., Jun, H., Xuandong, L., Guoliang, Z.: Generating test cases from UML Activity diagram based on gray-box method. In: 11th Asia-Pacific Software Engineering Conference, November 30-December 3, pp. 284–291. IEEE Computer Society, Busan (2004)
7. Basanieri, F., Bertolino, A., Marchetti, E.: The Cow_Suite Approach to Planning and Deriving Test Suites in UML Projects. In: 5th International Conference on the Unified Modeling Language - the Language and its Applications UML, Dresden, Germany, September 30-October 4, pp. 383–397 (2002)
8. Huima, A.: Implementing Conformiq Qtronic. In: 19th IFIP International Conference on Testing of Communicating Systems and 7th International Workshop on Formal Approaches to Testing of Software, Tallinn, Estonia, June 26-29, pp. 1–12 (2007)
9. Jacky, J.: PyModel: Model-based testing in Python. In: The Northwest Python Day Event Hosted by SCCC IT Program, Seattle Central Community College (January 30, 2010)
10. Bouquet, F., Grandpierre, C., Legeard, B., Peureux, F.: A test generation solution to automate software testing. In: 3rd International Workshop on Automation of Software Test, May 10-18, pp. 45–48. ACM, Leipzig (2008)
11. Ali, S., Briand, L.C., Jaffar-Ur Rehman, M., Asghar, H., Iqbal, M.Z.Z., Nadeem, A.: A State-based Approach to Integration Testing based on UML Models. Inf. Softw. Technol. J. 49(11-12), 1087–1106 (2007)
12. Srivastava, P.R., Puyalnithi, T., Verma, B., Raghurama, G.: State Oriented Software Integration Testing for Object Oriented Applications. Eur. J. Sci. Res. 20(3), 483–495 (2008)
13. Test Complete v.8.0 (July 2012),
   http://www.automatedqa.com/products/testcomplete/
14. IBM Rational Robot (July 2012),
   http://www._01.ibm.com/software/awdtools/tester/robot/
15. IBM Functional Tester (July 2012),
   http://www._01.ibm.com/software/awdtools/tester/functional/

16. HP-Requirements-Management (July 2012),
    `http://www8.hp.com/us/en/software/software-product.html?`
    `compURI=tcm:245-937050&pageTitle=requirements-management`
17. IBM RequisitePro (July 2012),
    `http://www_01.ibm.com/software/awdtools/reqpro/`
18. Boghdady, P.N., Badr, N., Hashem, M., Tolba, M.F.: A Proposed Test Case Generation Technique Based on Activity Diagrams. Int. J. Eng. Technol. 11(3), 37–57 (2011)
19. Boghdady, P.N., Badr, N., Hashem, M.A., Tolba, M.F.: An Enhanced Test Case Generation Technique Based on Activity Diagrams. In: 7th International Conference on Computer Engineering and Systems, November 29-December 1, pp. 289–294. IEEE Xplore, Cairo (2011)
20. Boghdady, P.N., Badr, N., Hashem, M.A., Tolba, M.F.: An Enhanced Technique for Generating Hybrid Coverage Test Cases Using Activity Diagrams. In: 8th International Conference on Informatics and Systems, May 14-16, pp. 20–28. IEEE Xplore, Cairo (2012)
21. Ye, N., Chen, X., Jiang, P., Ding, W., Li, X.: Automatic Regression Test Selection based on Activity Diagrams. In: 5th International Conference of Secure Software Integration & Reliability Improvement Companion, June 27-29, pp. 166–171. IEEE Xplore, Jeju Island (2011)
22. Nayak, A., Samanta, D.: Synthesis of test scenarios using UML activity diagrams. Softw. Sys. Model. 10(1), 63–89 (2011)
23. Sommerville, I.: Software Engineering, 7th edn., Harlow, England (2004)
24. Microsoft Dynamics Course 8913: Applications in Microsoft Dynamics CRM 4.0 (2008)
25. Agarwal, B.B., Tayal, S.P., Gupta, M.: Software Engineering and testing. Infinity Science Press, Jones and Bartlett, Hingham, Toronto (2010)
26. Sedgewick, R., Wayne, K.: Algorithms. Addison Wesley, Princeton University, US (2011)
27. Allen, A.O.: Introduction to Computer Performance Analysis with Mathematica. Morgan Kaufmann Pub., California (1994)

Support Vector Machines with Weighted Powered Kernels for Data Classification

Mohammed H. Afif, Abdel-Rahman Hedar,
Taysir H. Abdel Hamid, and Yousef B. Mahdy

Faculty of Computers & Information
Assiut Univ.
Assiut 71526, Egypt

Abstract. Support Vector Machines (SVMs) are a popular data classification method with many diverse applications. The SVMs performance
depends on choice a suitable kernel function for a given problem. Using
an appropriate kernel; the data are transform into a space with higher
dimension in which they are separable by an hyperplane. A major challenges of SVMs are how to select an appropriate kernel and how to find
near optimal values of its parameters. Usually a single kernel is used by
most studies, but the real world applications may required a combination of multiple kernels. In this paper, a new method called, weighted
powered kernels for data classification is proposed. The proposed method
combined three kernels to produce a new combined kernel (WPK). The
method used Scatter Search approach to find near optimal values of
weights, alphas and kernels parameters which associated with each kernel. To evaluate the performance of the proposed method, 11 benchmark
are used. Experiments and comparisons prove that the method given acceptable outcomes and has a competitive performance relative to a single
kernel and some other published methods.

Keywords: Support Vector Machine, Scatter Search, Classification.

1 Introduction

Classification can be defined as a process of placing objects into predefined
groups [7]. The aim of classification can be identified as prediction and data
simplification [8]. Many classification techniques are proposed in literature some
of them was a Kernel-based approaches or Kernel-based algorithm [1] (such as
Support Vector Machines (SVMs) [9], which are a promising machine learning algorithms. SVMs were widely employed in different domains like pattern
recognition [2], text classification [13], and bioinformatics [19]. SVMs have some
problems which limited their usage on the academic and industrial platforms
[21]. The goal of SVMs is to produce a model which forecasts target value of
data elements in the testing set that are given only the features. The training
phase involved optimization of a convex function. If the data set is separable
SVMs can be found an optimal hyperplane which maximize margin between

A. Ell Hassanien et al. (Eds.): AMLTA 2012, CCIS 322, pp. 369–378, 2012.

classes, while if the data set is non separable kernel trick is required to project the data in a space with higher dimension. The major problems that are en-counter in kernel-based method are how to select a suitable kernel as well as tune its parameters. The task of kernel trick was to transformed the data into a higher dimension feature space to avoiding the difficulties when deal with non separable data. Standard kernel based methods only employed a single kernel; no golden rules can be follow when choice kernels, and its still an open question. Most studies selected the kernel based on the literature. Furthermore, the real applications may required combined more than one kernel to develop a classifier with good outcomes. In [5] authors combined more than one kernel. The basic idea of combination depends on assigned weights values for each kernel. Weights are determined by using genetic algorithms to find near optimal values. Three kernels(Linear, Polynomial, RBF) were used in a linear combination to produce a new combined kernel ECK. Yue and $et\ al$ [12] proposed KGEP-SVMs method for kernel construction based on Gene expression programming. The suggested method used GEP algorithm to automatically constructed kernel function for SVMs to solving the kernel selection problem. The method improve the average of accuracy rate by 4%. Researchers in [6] proposed a method to automatically generated and adapted a kernel combination based on the data. The combination can be linear or non-linear, weighted or un-weighted according to the problem at hand. The method called kernel of kernel (KoKs). The authors used genetic programming (GP) to generated the KoKs, which was consists of mixed between standard kernels (RFB, Sigmoid, Polynomial) and some coefficient like weights.

This paper introduces a new method, called WPK-SVMs support vector ma-chines with weighted powered kernel for data classification. The method combined three kernels (Gaussian, Laplaican, Cauchy) to produce WPK a new combined kernels as in equation 8. The Scatter Search method was employed to find near optimal values of weights, alphs and kernels parameters. The SS methodology was used due to its flexibility since each of its steps can be implemented in a variety of ways and degrees of sophistication [17]. In addition, SS can found solutions of a higher average quality earlier during the search than other methods of search like GA [18].

To measure the performance of the proposed method, its results on 11 selected datasets are present. The obtained outcomes have shown that the WPK-SVMs method was promising and competitive with some other methods published in literature. The paper is organized as follows. Next two sections give a brief description about the SVMs, kernel and SS. Section 4 describes the proposed method steps in details. Section 5 reports numerical experiments and results. Section 7 listed the application of the method on hepatitis diagnosis with its experiments results. Finally, the conclusions make up Section6.

2   Brief Introduction about Support Vector Machines and Kernels

SVMs was initially proposed to solve binary classification problems. The basic idea of SVMs was to implicitly mapped the training data into a high-dimensional feature space. A hyper-plane was constructed in this feature space, which maximizes the margin of separation between the hyper-plane and the points lying nearest to it (called the support vectors) [20]. The hyper-plane can be used as a basis for classifying vectors of uncertain type. In a case of linearly separable data, the problem of two category classification is stated as the following. Suppose that there are N training pair (x_i, y_i) where x_i is an object and y_i is a class label (± 1), and $i = 1 \ldots N$. The hyper-plane is defined by a discriminate function 1,

$$f(x) = w^T \cdot x + b = 0 \qquad (1)$$

where the vector w of dimension equals to that of x and scalar b are chosen such that

$$w^T \cdot x_i + b \geq 0 \quad if \quad y_i = +1, \qquad (2)$$

$$w^T \cdot x_i + b \leq 0 \quad if \quad y_i = -1. \qquad (3)$$

Classification of an unknown vector x into class label y (± 1) is done using the discriminate function and defined as in equation 4:

$$y = sign(f(x)). \qquad (4)$$

How about the nonseparable case? The basic idea in design the nonlinear SVMs was to mapped input vectors $x \in \mathbf{R}^n$ into vectors $\Phi(x)$ of a higher dimensional feature space with m features (where $\Phi : \mathbf{R}^n \rightarrow \mathbf{R}^m$). Then, solve a linear classification problem in this new feature space. To avoid an explicit representation $\Phi(x)$ of the feature space, kernel trick is applied. Kernel function $K(X, Z) = (\Phi(X) \cdot \Phi(Z))$, is a function that perform mapping from input space into higher dimension feature space. After that, a linear machine is used to classify the data in the feature space. Several kernel functions are proposed to help the SVMs in obtaining the optimal solution, but the most frequently used kernel functions are the Polynomial, Sigmoid, Gaussian and Radial Basis Function (RBF). The RBF and Gaussian kernels are frequently used by most studies [11,23,15,4,16]. The selection of a suitable kernel for a given problem is not easy task and still an open question. This work proposed a new method to combined three kernels Gaussian (K_1), Laplaican (K_2), Cauchy (K_3) to produce a new combined kernel called WPK. The aim of combining more than one kernel is to enhance the performance of SVM classifier. Equations for all kernels are illustrated in equations 5, 6, 7 and 8.

$$K_1(X, Z) = \exp(\frac{-||X - Z||^2}{2\sigma^2}) \qquad (5)$$

$$K_2(X, Z) = \exp(\frac{-||X - Z||}{\sigma}) \qquad (6)$$

$$K_3(X, Z) = \frac{1}{1 + \frac{||X-Z||^2}{\sigma}} \qquad (7)$$

$$K_{WPK}(X, Z) = \sum_{i=1}^{k} w[i] \times (K_i(X, Z))^{alph[i]} \tag{8}$$

where the σ is the kernel parameter, $w[i]$ is the weight for a specific kernel, $alph[i]$ is the alph for a specific kernel, k represent the number of kernels.

3   Scatter Search (SS)

Scatter Search is a population-based algorithm. In 1998 [17,14] Glover published the SS template, which represented an algorithmic description of the SS method. This template for implementing SS, and can be described as follows:

- *Diversification Generation Step:* Generates a collection of diverse trial solutions.(POP).
- *Improvement Step:* Transforms a trial solution into one or more enhanced trial solutions. In this study this step is ignored.
- *Reference Set Update Step:* Chooses an initial *RefSet* from population *POP* and also updates the *RefSet* in each iteration.
- *Subset Generation Step :* Generates subsets of *RefSet* as an initial stage to produce a subset of its solutions as a basis, for creating combined solutions.
- *Solution Combination Step:* Transforms a given subset of the solutions produced by the subset generation method into one or more combined solution vector [17,14].

4   The Proposed Method

4.1   Solution Representation and Solution Quality Measure

In WPK-SVMs, the solution was represent as vector with dimensions equal to the number of trail solutions. Equation 10 depicts the solution representation of WPK-SVMs, where P_1 represent kernel parameter; P_2, P_3, P_4 are weigths while the reminder represent the alphs. Accuracy rate was used in WPK-SVMs to measure the quality of solution, which called the fittness function(fit). Accuracy rate for binary and multiple class calculated as in equation 9

$$Accuracy = (TP + TN)/(TP + TN + FP + FN) \tag{9}$$

where, TP (True Positive) is the positive cases that classified correctly as positive, TN(True Negative) is the negative cases that classified correctly as Negative, while, FP (False Positive) some cases with negative class classified as positive, and FN (False Negative) is the cases with positive class classified as negative [10,22].

$$X = [P_1, P_2, P_3, P_4, P_5, P_6, P_7] \tag{10}$$

4.2   Diversification Generation Step and Reference Set Update Step

A Population with $POP_{Size} = 25$ solutions (value for kernel parameter, weights and alphs) are generated randomly in this step. Each solution X_{sol} in POP was generated as in equation 11

$$X_{sol} = LB + (UB - LB) \times Rand, \tag{11}$$

where the LB: is the lower bound of the parameter, UB: is the upper bound of the parameter and $Rand$: is a random value in $(0,1)$. An initial reference set $Refset$ is constructed to has the best $b = 5$ solutions from POP.

4.3   Subset Generation Step and Solution Combination Step

This step generates all pairs of solutions in the $Refset$, where the maximum number of subsets are $b \times (b - 1)/2$. A number of new solutions are generated from each subsets of parents X_1 and X_2 as following:

$$X_1 = X_1 + (X_2 - X_1) \times r_1, \tag{12}$$

$$X_2 = X_1 + (X_2 + X_1) \times r_2, \tag{13}$$

$$X_3 = X_1 + X_2 \times r_3, \tag{14}$$

where r_1, r_2 and r_3 are random numbers in $(0,1)$. After that, solutions are put in pool together with solutions in the $Refset$ in order from the best one to worst.

4.4   Reference Set Update Method

In this step, the $Refset$ is updated to has the best $b_1 = 4$ solutions from the pool and the $b_2 = 1$ diverse solutions where $b_1 + b_2 = b$. Diverse solution is selected, which depends on calculating the Euclidean distance for each solution in the $Refset$ and solutions in the pool. The b_2 solution with the maximum distance is selected as diverse one. After that, the subset generation, solution combination and $Refset$ update steps, are repeated until one of the termination conditions is satisfied. The termination conditions are :

-First : When no $Refset$ update is achieved.
-Second : When the accuracy rate gets up to 100% for at least one solution.
-Third : When the iteration exceeds to the maximum iteration, $I_{max} = 15$.

Figure 1 display the steps of the WPK-SVMs method.

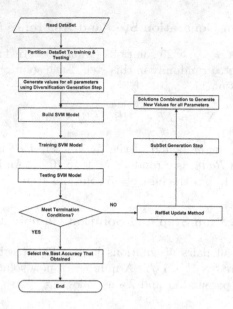

Fig. 1. Flowchart of the WPK-SVMs Method

5   Numerical Experiments

The WPK-SVMs approach was implemented on PC with Core2Due 2.93 Ghz CPU, 2GB of RAM, and windows XP Professional OS. Visual Studio 2008−Visual C♯ and Accord.net framework were used in development. To verify the quality of the WPK-SVMs method 11 datasets from LibSVM tool webpage [3] were used, as shown in Table 1.

Table 1. Datasets Information

Dataset	ID	Features	Instances	Classes	Dataset	ID	Features	Instances	Classes
Australian	AU	14	690	2 class	Breast Cancer	BC	10	683	2 class
Heart disease	HD	13	270	2 class	Ionosphere	IO	34	351	2 class
Liver	LI	6	345	2 class	Glass	GL	9	214	6 class
Segment	SE	19	2310	7 class	Sonar	SO	60	208	2 class
wine	WI	13	178	3 class	Vehicle	VE	18	846	4 class
Vowel	VO	10	528	11 class					

5.1   Parameter Setting

Table 2 summarize all parameters setting used in WPK-SVMs method with their assigned values. These chosen values are based on our numerical experiments.

Table 2. WPK-SVMs Parameters

Parameter Symbol		Interval	Parameter Symbol		Interval
P_1	Sigma(σ)	[0.0001, 1.5]	P_2	weight[1]	[0.5, 0.9]
P_3	weight[2]	[0.6, 0.8]	P_4	weight[3]	[0.7, 0.85]
P_5	Alph[1]	[0.21, 0.75]	P_6	Alph[2]	[0.23, 0.86]
P_7	Alph[3]	[0.3, 0.98]			

5.2   Results and Discussion

The *WPK-SVMs* approach used k−flod cross validation method for portioning the datasets, where the k value is usually set to 10. Therefore, the datasets is split into 10 parts. Nine data slices were applied in the training process, while the remaining one was utilized in the testing process. The program is run 10 times to enable each part of data to take a turn as testing data. The accuracy for testing and error rate for training phase are calculated by summing the individual accuracy rates and error rates for each time of run, and then it is divided by 10. While holdout method is used in case of multiple class. The data is split into two parts: one for training and the second for testing with size 70% and 30%, respectively. Table 3 lists results of experiments which conducted. The table contains in the first column accuracy rate for testing (ACC.Testing), and the remainder columns contain standard deviation for accuracy of testing (STDEV.Testing), accuracy rate for training (ACC. Training), standard deviation for error rate of training phase(STDEV.Err.TR), the last two columns are the sensitivity and specificity. The sensitivity reflects the proportion of the cases with positive class that are classified as positive (true positive rate, expressed as a percentage). While, specificity is the proportion of cases with negative rate class, classified as negative (true negative rate, expressed as a percentage). Sensitivity and specificity reflect how well the classifier discriminates between case with positive and with negative class[10]. The differences between the accuracy rate for training and testing is reasonable and acceptable for most datasets. This proves that the WPK-SVMs method does not suffer from over-fitting problem, according to the fact that there was no large difference between the training and testing accuracy [4]. Furthermore, the classification outcomes obtained by WPK-SVMs approach were compared with results of other published approaches[6] and [5]. Tables 4 and 5 list comparisons. From comparisons can be noted that the WPK-SVMs method gives promising results in all phases training and testing for all datasets from a single kernels methods as in table 4. Also, the WPK-SVMs method given acceptable results relatively to KoKs and ECK methods. There are some differences between the KoKs[6] and WPK-SVMs method, such as KoKs proposed two methods (KTS (Terminal Set) and MTS(Mixed Terminal Set)) for combination; where genetic programming (GP) was used to generated combined kernel from a set of standard kernels (RBF,Sigmoid,and Polynomial) and a set of weights and shifting coefficients, the number of datasets that used are 8 all binary class datasets. In addition to, the method divided the datasets into two parts only

Table 3. WPK-SVMs Results Using WPK

ID	ACC. Testing	STDEV. Testing	ACC. Training	STDEV. Err.TR	Sensitivity	Specifictiy
AU	88.69	0.04623	92.74	0.01109	91.35	86.32
BC	98.52	0.0155	99.39	0.00668	99.04	98.24
HD	88.148	0.0546	96.74	0.0129	89.09	86.39
IO	97.428	0.021	99.49	0.00163	99.16	94.52
LI	73.82	0.0626	87.18	0.083	57.48	87.58
GL	93.23	0.06338	96.14	0.0643	97.34	83.83
SE	99.32	0.014312	99.63	0.007711	98.95	99.67
SO	91.5	0.0818	100	0	89.93	93.94
WI	99.09	0.0156	100	0	98.214	100
VE	91.07	0.1374	98.65	0.0279	87.11	96.11
VO	99.77	0.0123	99.97	0.00198	99.87	99.74

Table 4. Testing Accuracy of WPK-SVMs Compared With Three Single Kernels

ID	K_1	K_2	K_3	WPK
AU	85.65	85.94	86.37	88.69
BC	97.35	96.61	96.91	98.52
HD	82.96	82.96	83.70	88.148
IO	94.28	96.80	96	97.428
LI	60.29	68.5	67.35	73.82
SO	89.5	87	87	91.5

Table 5. Testing Accuracy Of WPK-SVMs Compared With Those Of Approaches Developed By L.Diosan,*et al*[6],[5]

ID	WPK	KTS[6]	MTS[6]	ECK(0,k)[5]	ECK(-k,k) [5]	KGEP[12]
AU	88.69	-	-	-	-	-
BC	98.52	97.8	98.03	98.54	100	75
HD	88.148	86.98	86.98	85.18	87.037	-
IO	97.428	86.11	91.67	98.59	98.59	93
LI	73.82	-	-	-	-	-
GL	93.23	-	-	-	-	76
SE	99.32	-	-	-	-	-
SO	91.5	81.25	81.25	61.90	76.19	-
WI	99.09	-	-	-	-	90
VE	91.07	-	-	-	-	-
VO	99.77	-	-	-	-	-

80% for training and the rest for testing. Also, some differences are found between the WPK-SVMs and ECK [5] method which is in the range of the weights values, where the ECK was perform two type of experiments each ones has new range where the weights value are generated in range $(0, k)$ and $(-k, k)$ where

k is the number of kernels. In addition to, the method uses only 4 datasets, as well as the kernel that used were (Linear,Polynomial, RFB), also the datasets that used are divided into parts one for training and another for testing. From comparisons, one may conclude that the obtained results by the WPK-SVMs method are very acceptable and given competitive performance relatively to some published methods[6], and [5].

6 Conclusions and Future Works

This paper proposed the *WPK-SVMs* method for data classification based on combined three different kernels. The *WPK-SVMs* was used scatter search for finding near optimal values of weights, alphs and kernel parameters that associated with each kernel. Comparisons of the obtained results with single kernel and other published approaches prove that the proposed approach could improve the classification accuracy. Experimental results on 11 benchmark datasets demonstrated that the WPK-SVMs method has very promising performance. In future works, other public datasets and real world problems can be tested to verify and extend this approach, as well as may added more kernels function in combination.

References

1. Abbasnejad, M.E., Ramachandram, D., Mandava, R.: A survey of the state of the art in learning the kernels. Knowledge and Information Systems 31(2), 193–221 (2012)
2. Burges, C.J.: A tutorial on support vector machines for pattern recognition. Data Mining and Knowledge Discovery 2, 121–167 (1998)
3. Lin, C.-J., Chang, C.-C.: Libsvm: a library for support vector machines, http://www.csie.ntu.edu.tw/~cjlin/libsvm (visted in February 5, 2012)
4. Chen, S.C., Linb, S.W., Chou, S.Y.: Enhancing the classification accuracy by scatter-based ensemble approach. Applied Soft Computing, 1–8 (2010)
5. Dioşan, L., Oltean, M., Rogozan, A.: Improving SVM Performance Using a Linear Combination of Kernels. In: Beliczynski, B., Dzielinski, A., Iwanowski, M., Ribeiro, B. (eds.) ICANNGA 2007, Part II. LNCS, vol. 4432, pp. 218–227. Springer, Heidelberg (2007)
6. Diosan, L., Rogozan, A., Pecuchet, J.-P.: Improving classification performance of support vector machine by genetically optimising kernel shape and hyperparameters. Applied Intelligence 36(2), 280–294 (2012)
7. Fielding, A.H.: Cluster and Classification Techniques for the Biosciences. Cambridge University Press (2007)
8. Gordon, A.D.: Classification. Chapman & Hall/CRC (1999)
9. Hsu-Wei, C., Chang, C.-C., Lin, C.-J.: A practical guide to support vector classification. Technical Report, Department of Computer science, National Taiwan University, pp. 1–12 (2003)
10. Huang, C.-L., Wang, C.-J.: A ga-based feature selection and parameters optimization for support vector machines. Expert Systems with Applications 31, 231–240 (2006)

11. Jia, Z.-Y., Ma, J.-W., Wang, F.-J., Liu, W.: Hybrid of simulated annealing and svm for hydraulic valve characteristics prediction. Expert Systems with Applications 38, 8030–8036 (2011)
12. Jiang, Y., Tang, C., Li, C., Li, S., Zheng, H.: Automatic svm kernel function construction based on gene expression programming. In: Proceedings of Inernational Conference on Computer Science and Software Engineering (2008)
13. Joachims, T.: Learning to classify texts using support vector machines: methods, theory and algorithms. Kluwer Academic Publishers, Dordrecht (2002)
14. Laguna, M., Marti, R.: Scatter search methodology and implementations in C. Kluwer Academic (2003)
15. Li-Xia, L., Yi-Qi, Z., Xue-Yong, L.: Tax forecasting theory and model based on svm optimized by pso. Expert Systems with Applications 38, 116–120 (2011)
16. Lin, S.W., Chen, S.C., Lin, K.C., Lee, Z.J.: Particle swarm optimization for parameter determination and feature selection of support vector machines. Expert Systems with Applications 35, 1817–1824 (2008)
17. Marti, R., Laguna, M., Glover, F.: Principles of scatter search. Operational Research 169, 359–372 (2006)
18. Marti, R., Laguna, M., Glover, F., Campos, V.: An experimental evaluation of a scatter search for the linear ordering problem. Global Optimization 21, 397–414 (2001)
19. Nobel, W.S.: Support vector machine applications in computational biology. In: Schoekkopf, B., Tsuda, K., Vert, J.-P. (eds.) Kernel Methods in Computational Biology, pp. 71–92. MIT Press, Cambridge (2004)
20. Palaniswami, M., Shilton, A., Ralph, D., Owen, B.D.: Machine learning using support vector machines. In: Proceedings of International Conference on Artificial Intelligence in Science and Technology (2000)
21. Ren, Y., Bai, G.: Determination of optimal svm parameters by using ga/pso. Journal of Computers 5(8), 1160–1168 (2010)
22. Samadzadegan, F., Soleymani, A., Abbaspour, R.A.: Evaluation of genetic algorithm for tuning svm parameters in multi-class problems. In: CINTI 2010 - 11th IEEE International Symposium on Computational Intelligence and Informatics, pp. 323–327 (2010)
23. Sartakhti, J.S., Zangooei, M.H., Mozafari, K.: Hepatitis disease diagnosis using a novel hybrid method based on support vector machine and simulated annealing (svm-sa). Computer Methods and Programs in Biomedisine, 1–10 (2011)

Named Entity Based Document Similarity with SVM-Based Re-ranking for Entity Linking

Ayman Alhelbawy[1,2] and Rob Gaizauskas[1]

[1] Computer Science Department, University of Sheffield, Sheffield UK
[2] Information Science Department, Fayoum University, Fayoum Egypt
Ayman@dcs.shef.ac.uk, R.Gaizauskas@sheffield.ac.uk

Abstract. In this paper we present a novel approach to search a knowledge base for an entry that contains information about a named entity (NE) mention as specified within a given context. A document similarity function (NEBSim) based on NE co-occurrence has been developed to calculate the similarity between two documents given a specific NE mention in one of them. NEBsim is also used in conjunction with the traditional cosine similarity measure to learn a model for ranking. Naive Bayes and SVM classifiers are used to re-rank the retrieved documents. Our experiments, carried out on TAC-KBP 2011 data, show NEBsim achieves significant improvement in accuracy as compared with a cosine similarity approach. They also show that re-ranking using learn to rank techniques can significantly improve the accuracy at high ranks.

Keywords: NEBsim, Entity Linking, Supported Vector Machine, Learn to Rank, SVM-map, SVM-rank, Naive Bayes.

1 Introduction

As the amount of data published on the internet increases every day, it has become extremely difficult for users to find precisely the information they are looking for. Knowledge bases are becoming one of the most important references for information seekers. The best known semi-structured knowledge base is Wikipedia, which acts as a main source of information for many different user needs. Also, Wikipedia is widely used for a range of applications for text mining and search engines. Since a massive amount of new data is added to the internet every day (e.g. news, research, blogs), the need for new technologies to automatically link this data to existing knowledge bases is becoming more important. One obvious way to do this is to try to find and link named entities in new data to the existing entries in knowledge bases about these entities.

A named entity (NE) expression is a pointer to a real world entity such as a person, location, or organization. However, these pointers are ambiguous: one NE expression may refer to more than one real world entity; one real world entity may be referred to by more than one NE. Searching for the knowledge base entry that talks about a NE mentioned within a specific context is a very important task. In this task a query NE mention E_M within a query document Q_D must be searched for in a knowledge base to find the appropriate entry in the KB; if there is no corresponding entry in the KB then

A. Ell Hassanien et al. (Eds.): AMLTA 2012, CCIS 322, pp. 379–388, 2012.
© Springer-Verlag Berlin Heidelberg 2012

NIL should be returned. This task has been defined as the "entity linking task" in the Knowledge Base Population (KBP) track of the Text Analysis Conference (TAC)[1].

The main objective in this paper is to present a new document similarity function (NEBsim) based on the named entity mentions found in the two documents being compared and show how it can contribute in disambiguating the different named entities for entity linking. Also, different re-ranking techniques are tested to compare the performance of NEBsim measure against the normal cosine similarity measure.

KB entries contain a mix of semi-structured information (e.g. infoboxes) and free text (e.g. the Wikipedia article). While all this information may be useful in search, we here treat the problem as one of document retrieval, i.e. we treat the KB as a document collection and the task as that of returning the correct document given the query mention and query document. Posing the problem this way, it is natural to explore a vector space model approach as a baseline. We do this here, considering several query formulation strategies. However, analysis of poor results using this approach led us to the observation that it is other NEs co-occurring with the query mention that are most helpful in disambiguating the query mention. Building on this insight, we have developed a novel similarity function to search the KB documents based on statistical co-occurrence between NEs. We evaluate our approach on the TAC-KBP 2011 dataset. Comparison with a vector space model baseline approach based on cosine similarity with TF-IDF weighting shows our NE based search can indeed improve performance significantly.

2   Related Work

The task of named entity disambiguation is highly related to the current task since for a given ambiguous named entity and an ambiguous set of canonical named entities, one of the canonical named entities should be selected as the correct one. Normally, this ambiguous set is constructed from a knowledge base. In this case, the ambiguous set definitely contains the correct candidate. Bunescu and Pasca define a similarity function that compares the NE mention context to Wikipedia categories[2]. Cucerzan extends this work by adding some richer features to the similarity comparison [3]. Another paradigm uses semantic relatedness to disambiguate named entities. A graph-based method was proposed by Han et al. [4]. They model the global interdependence between different named entities then use a collective inference algorithm to disambiguate all name entities found in the document.

Entity linking is a more generalized task since the named entity is not necessarily found in the ambiguous set (e.g. it may be not entered in the knowledge base yet).

The bag of words (BOW) model [5] is the traditional method to disambiguate named entities. There are different approaches to tackle the named entity linking task; one approach proposed by Zheng et al. uses a classifier to identify the Nil linked entities and then uses a supervised model with SVM ranking to rank the remaining candidates [6]. They used the contextual comparison between the KB documents and the query mention in addition to any ambiguous pages in Wikipedia.

Traditional search methods consider the NE mention terms plus some selected terms from the query document according to the query formulation scheme. But, not all of these terms are useful in search. So, some research has modelled the dependency between named entities and other document terms to weight the terms differently based on the query NE mention [7,8,9].

Named entity based search has improved retrieval performance in different tasks like cross-language retrieval [10] and event detection [11]. But, such an approach has not been investigated for the entity linking task. Instead many approaches to entity linking adopt a vector space model using cosine similarity with the TF-IDF weighting scheme, exploring various query formulation strategies using as a query, e.g., just the query mention, the sentence containing the query mention, a window of words surrounding the query mention and a selected set of words (see, e.g., Reddy B et al. [12]).

3 Named Entity Based Search

NE mentions other than the query NE itself extracted from the query document appear more useful than other query document terms. The following example was taken from TAC-2011 query documents[1]. The Bold style words are named entities identified by the Stanford NER Tagger where the underline style named entities are classified as "Locations" and the only Bold style are classified as a "Person".

Barak tries to calm Syrian nerves over **Israeli** drill. '**Israel** has no intentions of launching any such operation," says. defense minister in public bid to allay **Damascus** concerns scheduled. nationwide exercise foretelling of aggressive **Israeli** intent.

Barak's deputy, **Matan Vilnai**, will brief the government on Sunday on. the course of the exercise. All State offices are also expected to. take part in the drill..

The query mention is "Barak". This is very ambiguous; it could be "Barack Obama", "Ehud Barak", "Barak Moshe" or "Barak Valley". It is clear from the example that most of the other non-NE words in the query document are unlikely to help in identifying the correct "Barak"; however, "Matan Vilnai" is very useful indeed. Thus, the joint relation between different named entities mentions appears to be a promising factor for NE mention disambiguation.

Our NE-based document retrieval is based on the assumption that NEs co-occurring with a specific NE in the same context will help in ranking the documents that contain information about this NE. The first stage in our proposed system is to model the statistical relation between all NE mentions recognized in the Wikipedia KB documents. The second stage is to score each candidate document – which contains the NE mention – using a similarity function based on this statistical relation.

3.1 Document Collection Indexing

In this phase, all knowledge base documents are converted into a NE pseudo-documents where each KB document is represented in terms of the set of named entities in it, as

---

[1] TAC-2011 file: eng-NG-31-143446-10242486.sgm

extracted by the Stanford NER Tagger. Stanford NER Tagger [2] is used with three class pre-trained model to identify and label all named entities of types (Person, Organization, Location). The new NE pseudo-document is represented in a vector space model with TF-IDF weighting scheme using the Lucene Indexer [3].

3.2   Modelling KB Named Entities

In the second phase, the named entity model θ is built given a set of Wikipedia pseudo-documents $D = \{d_1, d_2, ..., d_m\}$ and a set E of mentions of named entities mentioned in the documents in D where $\forall d \in D \exists E_d$ where $E_d = \{e_1, e_2, e_3, ..., e_{nd}\}$. The conditional probability between any two distinct named entity mentions $e_i, e_j \in E_d$, i.e. the probability that e_i occures in document d given that e_j occurred in document d, is estimated using the following formula as:

$$p(e_i) = \frac{\sum_{d \in D} in(d, e_i))}{\|D\|} \tag{1}$$

$$p(e_i, e_j) = \frac{\sum_{d \in D} in(d, e_i \wedge e_j)}{\|D\|} \tag{2}$$

$$p(e_i|e_j) = \frac{p(e_i, e_j)}{p(e_j)} \tag{3}$$

where the function $in(d, e)$ returns 1 if the NE mention e occurs in d and 0 otherwise and $in(d, e_i \wedge e_j)$ returns 1 if $in(d, e_i) = in(d, e_j) = 1$, 0 otherwise.

3.3   Searching and Scoring

In this phase, all knowledge base pseudo-documents are searched for the query mention e_m given the query document. The query document is converted into our standard pseudo-document which contains all named entities extracted by the NER tagger. All KB pseudo-documents that contain the query mention named entity e_m will be retrieved as candidate documents that describe the query named entity mention e_m. As a rule of thumb, the document that describes a named entity must contain a mention of the named entity while not all documents mentioning a named entity describe it. This candidate set is huge and highly ambiguous. For each document, a numerical score is assigned to the candidate document using our document similarity function. The basic concept is to use the relative information gained from the NE mentions in the query document and the document collection. Two similarity functions are proposed and their performance compared.

The first similarity function is based on the information theoretic definition of similarity proposed by [13]:

$$IT\text{-}Sim(A, B) = \frac{I(Common(A, B))}{I(Description(A, B))} \tag{4}$$

---

[2] http://nlp.stanford.edu/software/CRF-NER.shtml
[3] http://lucene.apache.org/java/docs/

where $I(Common(A, B))$ is the information content of the statement describing what A and B have in common and $I(Description(A, B))$ is the information content of the statement describing what A is and what B is. In this paper, the elementary units of a document are taken to be the NE mentions recognized in it.

- let A be the query document containing a set of NE mentions E_a .
- let B be a KB document containing a set of NE mentions E_b.
- let e_m be the query NE mention
- let E_{ab} be the set of NEs common to A and B, i.e. $E_{ab} = E_a \cap E_b$.

$$NEBsim1(A, B) = \frac{\sum_{e \in E_{ab}} p(e \mid e_m)}{\sum_{e \in E_a} p(e \mid e_m) + \sum_{e \in E_b} p(e \mid e_m)} \tag{5}$$

This similarity function has a problem since it is affected by the relative weight of the candidate document NEs which are not in common with the query document. So the denominator will change for each candidate. As a kind of normalization, the relative weight of the KB document is removed in the second similarity function, based on the assumption that the weight of all related named entities found in the KB document which is $Description(B)$ is not important in scoring the candidate. According to this assumption, we get the following formula:

$$NEBsim2(A, B) = \frac{\sum_{e \in E_{ab}} p(e \mid e_m)}{\sum_{e \in E_a} p(e \mid e_m)} \tag{6}$$

4   Learning to Rank Documents

Learning to rank is a popular topic in document retrieval. For the task of entity-linking, re-ranking is necessary to get the correct document at the top of the list of candidate KB documents. Learn-to-rank approaches are categorized into three approaches: pointwise, pairwise and listwise [14]. In this paper the three approaches are used to re-rank the candidate documents.

The pointwise approach is the simplest learn-to-rank approach. A Naive Bayes classifier is used where each instance is classified into relevant or non-relevant. The pointwise approach is used to discard some of the non-relevant documents.

The pairwise approach focuses on the relative order between two instances. So, it can be considered as a classification on instance pairs, and the objective function is to minimize the number of misclassified pairs. Each pair of instances (a, b) is labelled as a is more relevant than b, or b is more relevant than a. Then a trained classication model is used for ranking. SVM-rank [15,16] is used to build a pairwise ranking model and to re-rank the candidate documents.

The listwise approach tries to optimize the value of the evaluation measure, averaged over all queries in the training data. SVM-map [17] is used learn the ranking by using mean average precision (MAP) to calculate the listwise loss function.

Different experiments were carried out using different features. The cosine-similarity scores were used with the different query schemes, as was NEB-similarity, to train learn to rank models (Naive Bayes, SVM-map and SVM-rank) but there was no significant improvement. Another set of experiments, mentioned in this paper, were carried out using both cosine-similarity and NEB-similarity scores with different query schemes.

5   Experimental Results and Discussion

To evaluate the performance, the TAC-KBP 2011 data set was used to carry out different experiments. The dataset contains 2231 query documents containing 2250 query mentions. There are 1126 query mentions that have no entry in the knowledge base and 1124 query mentions that do have an entry in the knowledge base. The Wikipedia 2008 dump was used as a reference knowledge base.

5.1   Similarity Function (NEBsim) Experiments

In this set of expirements, NEBsim are evaluated separately without re-ranking the results. For each query mention, the highest 100 scored documents are retrieved and the performance checked at different ranks, i.e. at rank 1, 5, 10 ,30, 50 and 100. Accuracy is used as the performance measure. Cosine similarity with TF-IDF weighting is used with the following query formulation schemes as a baseline approach to search the knowledge base document text.

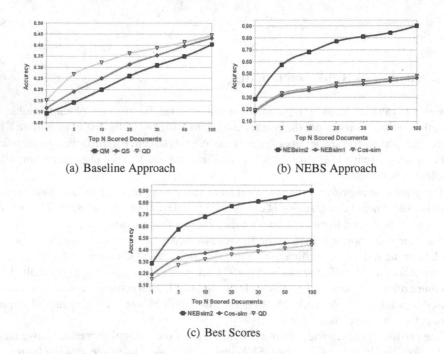

(a) Baseline Approach   (b) NEBS Approach

(c) Best Scores

Fig. 1. A Graph representation for the accuracy of baseline and NEB-similarity approaches

QM: Query mention terms alone are used.
QS: All terms in the sentence(s) containing the query mention in the query document are used as a query.
QD: All terms in the query document are used in conjunction with the query mention.

Figure1(a) shows the accuracy of the baseline approach at different ranks; i.e. the percentage of queries for which the correct document is found at or above the specified rank. These results show the QD scheme which considers all query document terms as a query achieves a better result than the QS scheme which uses the sentences containing the query mention as a query. On the other hand, the QM scheme which considers only the query mention does not perform nearly as well. From Figure 1(a) we can conclude that the information in the near context of the query mention is likely to be more useful than all the information in the query document.

To study the effect of using only NE pseudo-documents instead of the original documents, the NE pseudo-documents, created while modelling the NEs, are indexed using the Lucene search engine. Queries were constructed using the NEs identified in the query document conjoined with the query NE mention itself.

Three experiments were carried out to compare the different similarity functions' performance as follows:

NE cos-sim: The rank retrieved by lucene whose default similarity function is cosine similarity with TF-IDF weighting.
NEBsim1: using the NEBsim1 similarity function to evaluate the similarity between the query document and each of the documents retrieved by lucene.
NEBsim2: using the NEBsim2 similarity function to evaluate the similarity between the query document and each of the documents retrieved by lucene.

Figure 1(b) shows the accuracy results graphically at all ranks and Table (1) summarizes experimental results at ranks 1,5,10,20,30,50 and 100. Figure 1(c) shows the results of the best three approaches, two using the NE pseudo-documents and NE queries (NEBsim2 and cos-Sim) and one using the original KB documents and query mention document (QD). cos-sim between the NE pseudo-documents outperforms the QD approach which considers the query document terms to search the KB document text though overall the difference between these two approaches is not significant ($p > 0.05$ using unpaired(independent) two-sample student t-tests with two tails and unequal variances). NEBsim2 achieves a significant improvement over the best query scheme against full documents (QD) where $p < 0.05$. Also, ignoring the relative weight of the candidate

Table 1. Results for Baseline and NE approaches

Method	A@1	A@5	A@10	A@20	A@30	A@50	A@100
QM	0.09	0.14	0.20	0.26	0.31	0.35	0.40
QS	0.12	0.19	0.25	0.31	0.35	0.40	0.43
QD	0.15	0.27	0.32	0.36	0.39	0.41	0.44
NE cos-sim	0.19	0.33	0.37	0.41	0.43	0.46	0.48
NEBsim1	0.18	0.32	0.36	0.39	0.41	0.44	0.46
NEBsim2	0.28	0.57	0.68	0.77	0.81	0.84	0.90

document in similarity function NEBsim2 improves performance significantly over the NEBsim1, $p < 0.0001$.

5.2   Re-ranking Experiments

To study the effect of using different learn-to-rank approaches, one algorithm is used for each approach and tested using the different query schemes. For each query scheme

Table 2. The accuracy after re-ranking

Method	A@1	A@5	A@10	A@20	A@30	A@50	A@100
Query scheme: QM							
svm-map	53.48	76.48	86.82	94.31	95.60	96.89	98.19
svm-rank	78.29	93.79	96.12	98.70	99.48	99.74	99.74
Naive bayes	58.65	81.65	90.69	95.09	96.89	97.41	98.96
Query scheme: QS							
svm-map	54.31	75.88	86.04	93.90	95.17	96.70	98.22
svm-rank	78.93	93.40	96.70	98.22	98.98	99.74	99.74
Naive bayes	58.88	80.96	90.35	94.67	96.95	97.46	98.98
Query scheme: QD							
svm-map	62.27	81.13	91.73	96.64	97.41	97.93	98.44
svm-rank	75.19	91.98	97.15	98.44	98.96	99.48	100.0
Naive bayes	65.37	85.78	94.05	96.12	97.67	97.67	98.44

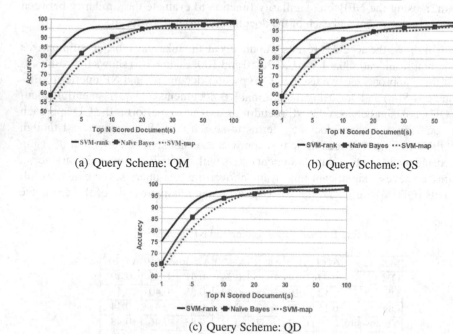

(a) Query Scheme: QM   (b) Query Scheme: QS

(c) Query Scheme: QD

Fig. 2. Learning To Rank Results

the features used for training are all cosine similarity scores and our NEB-similarity score.

Table (2) summarizes the results of using different learn-to-rank approaches with different features generated by using different query schemes. Figure 2 shows a graphical representation for our experiment results. In figures 2(a),2(b),2(c) we can see that SVM-rank outperforms both Naive Bayes and SVM-map approaches while Naive Bayes outperforms SVM-map. Because the relation between the different approaches remains the same along different query schemes, we can conclude that pairwise approach achieves the best results, whereas the listwise approach achieves the worst results, as compared with other tested approaches.

6 Conclusions

In this paper, we claimed that named entities occurring with the query mention in the same context are helpful to improve the search results in a knowledge base. We presented a document similarity function based on NEs in both query document and KB document. The results show the correctness of the conjecture that the NEs co-occurring with a specific NE can disambiguate it in a useful way. Our similarity function achieves a significant improvement over the cosine similarity measure. There are reliable relations between NEB-similarity and cosine-similarity that can be learned using the SVM-rank algorithm. Various extensions to this approach are possible. One is to ignore NEs which have a low co-occurring ratio. Another is to use query expansion techniques to find the different mentions for the same NE in the KB document. Finally testing other learning to rank algorithms that implement the listwise ranking approach is worth investigating.

Acknowledgments. The first author would like to acknowledge the Egyptian Government and the faculty of Computers and Information in Fayoum university for PhD studentship funding that made this research possible.

References

1. McNamee, P., Dang, H.T.: Overview of the TAC 2009 knowledge base population track. In: Text Analysis Conference TAC (2009)
2. Bunescu, R.C., Pasca, M.: Using Encyclopedic Knowledge for Named entity Disambiguation. In: Proceedings of EACL, vol. 6 (2006)
3. Cucerzan, S.: Large-scale named entity disambiguation based on Wikipedia data. In: Proceedings of EMNLP-CoNLL (2007)
4. Han, X., Sun, L., Zhao, J.: Collective entity linking in web text: a graph-based method. In: Proceedings of the 34th International ACM SIGIR Conference on Research and Development in Information (2011)
5. Bagga, A., Baldwin, B.: Entity-based cross-document coreferencing using the vector space model. In: Proceedings of the 17th International Conference on Computational Linguistics, vol. 1 (1998)

6. Zheng, Z., Li, F., Huang, M., Zhu, X.: Learning to link entities with knowledge base. In: Human Language Technologies: The 2010 Annual Conference of the North American Chapter of the Association for Computational Linguistics (2010)
7. Petkova, D., Croft, W.B.: Proximity-based document representation for named entity retrieval. In: Proceedings of the Sixteenth ACM Conference on Conference on Information and Knowledge Management, pp. 731–740 (2007)
8. Gottipati, S., Jiang, J.: Linking Entities to a Knowledge Base with Query Expansion. In: Empirical Methods in Natural Language Processing, EMNLP (2011)
9. Han, X., Sun, L.: A generative entity-mention model for linking entities with knowledge base. In: Proceedings of the 49th Annual Meeting of the Association for Computational Linguistics: Human Language Technologies, vol. 1 (2011)
10. Mandl, T., Womser-Hacker, C.: The effect of named entities on effectiveness in cross-language information retrieval evaluation. In: Proceedings of the 2005 ACM Symposium on Applied Computing (2005)
11. Kumaran, G., Allan, J.: Text classification and named entities for new event detection. In: Proceedings of the 27th Annual International ACM SIGIR Conference on Research and Development in Information Retrieval (2004)
12. Reddy, B.K., Kumar, K., Krishna, S., Pingali, P., Varma, V.: Linking Named Entities to a Structured Knowledge Base. International Journal of Computational Linguistics and Applications 1(1-2), 121–136 (2010)
13. Lin, D.: An Information-Theoretic Definition of Similarity. Morgan Kaufmann (1998)
14. Liu, T.Y.: Learning to rank for information retrieval. Morgan Springer-Verlag New York Inc. (2011)
15. Joachims, T.: Optimizing search engines using clickthrough data. In: Proceedings of the Eighth ACM SIGKDD International Conference on Knowledge Discovery and Data Mining (2002)
16. Joachims, T.: Training linear SVMs in linear time. In: Proceedings of the 12th ACM SIGKDD International Conference on Knowledge Discovery and Data Mining (2002)
17. Yue, Y., Finley, T., Radlinski, F., Joachims, T.: A support vector method for optimizing average precision. In: Proceedings of the 30th Annual International ACM SIGIR Conference on Research and Development in Information Retrieval (2007)

Part VI

Cloud Computing and Recommender Systems

Cloud Model—A Bidirectional Cognition Model between Concept's Extension and Intension

Guoyin Wang[1,2,3,*] and Changlin Xu[1,3]

[1] Chongqing Key Laboratory of Computational Intelligence, Chongqing University of Posts and Telecommunications, Chongqing, 400065, China
[2] Institute of Electronic Information Technology, Chongqing Institute of Green and Intelligent Technology, CAS, Chongqing, 401122, China
[3] School of Information Science and Technology, Southwest Jiaotong University, Chengdu, 610031, China
wanggy@ieee.org, xuchanglin83@gmail.com

Abstract. The expressing and processing of uncertain concepts is a fundamental problem in artificial intelligence. Several theoretical models have been proposed for solving this problem, such as probability theory, fuzzy sets, rough sets, cloud model, et al. Unfortunately, human deals with uncertain concepts based on words (concept intension), while computer based on sample set (concept extension). Many data mining and machine learning methods have been developed for extracting knowledge from data sets in recent years. These methods are unidirectional cognitive computing models from extension to intension. In this paper, a bidirectional cognitive computing model, cloud model, will be introduced. In the cloud model, forward cloud generator and backward cloud generator are designed for the bidirectional transformations between concept's intension and extension. Some experiment results will be discussed to show the validity and efficiency of cloud model for bidirectional cognitive computing.

Keywords: cognitive computing, cloud model, bidirectional cognition, granular computing.

1 Introduction

Cognition is a group of mental processes that includes attention, memory, producing and understanding language, solving problems, and making decisions [1]. Cognitive science is the interdisciplinary scientific study of the mind and its processes [2]. It examines what cognition is, what it does and how it works. It includes research on intelligence and behavior, especially focusing on how information is represented, processed, and transformed (in faculties such as perception, language, memory, reasoning, and emotion) within nervous systems (human or other animal) and machines (e.g. computers). Cognitive science consists of multiple research disciplines, including psychology [3], artificial intelligence(AI)

---

* Corresponding author.

A. Ell Hassanien et al. (Eds.): AMLTA 2012, CCIS 322, pp. 391–400, 2012.

[4], philosophy [5], neuroscience [6], linguistics [7], anthropology [8], sociology and education [2]. It spans many levels of analysis, from low-level learning and decision mechanisms to high-level logic and planning; from neural circuitry to modular brain organization.

Artificial intelligence is the intelligence of machines and a branch of computer science [4], [9], [10]. Artificial Intelligence is the area of computer science focusing on creating machines that can engage on behaviors that humans consider intelligent. The ability to create intelligent machines has intrigued humans since ancient times, and today with the advent of the computer and 60 years of research into AI programming techniques, the dream of smart machines is becoming a reality [10].

There are three main AI paradigms for studying of cognition, that is, symbolism AI, connectionism AI and behaviorism AI [11]. Between the late 1960s and the mid-1980s, virtually all research in the field of AI and cognitive science was conducted in the symbolic paradigm. This was due to the highly influential analysis of the capabilities and limitations of the perceptron[11], [12]. The physical symbol system hypothesis is introduced by Newell and Simon [13], [14]. They think cognition is a kind of symbolic processing, and the processes of human thinking can be computed by symbol[11]. In the mid-1980s a renaissance of neural networks took place under the new title of connectionism [15], [16] challenging the dominant symbolic paradigm of AI. The 'brain-oriented' connectionist paradigm claims that research in the traditional symbolic paradigm cannot be successful since symbols are insufficient to model crucial aspects of cognition and intelligence [12]. The connectionist paradigm thinks that the basic unite of human thinking is neuron, and the intelligence is the results of interconnected neurons' competition and collaboration[11]. The behaviorism paradigm uses cybernetics to study AI [11]. Its main idea is that intelligence depends on the perception and behavior; Intelligent behavior can be manifested through interaction between real-world and surrounding environment; "Perception-action" mode was proposed [11].

The expressing and processing of uncertain knowledge are key issues for both human brain intelligence study and artificial intelligence study [11], [17], [18]. Artificial intelligence with uncertainty is a new research field in AI in the 21st century [11]. There are many kinds of uncertainties in knowledge, such as randomness, fuzziness, vagueness, incompleteness, inconsistency, etc. Randomness and fuzziness are the two most important and fundamental ones [19], [20], [21]. There are many theories about randomness and fuzziness developed in the past decades, such as probability & statistics [19], fuzzy set [20], rough set [21], interval analysis [22], cloud model [23], grey system [24], set pair analysis [25], extenics [26], etc.

Machine learning, knowledge extraction and data mining are three popular research fields in AI [27], [28], [29]. Unfortunately, they are all unidirectional cognitive computing process from data (extension of concept) to knowledge (intension of concept). Languages and words are powerful tools for human thinking, and the use of them is the fundamental difference between human intelligence and the other creatures' intelligence. We need to study the relationship between the human brains (computing based on intension of concept) and machines (computing based on extension of concept) [11]. To describe uncertain knowledge by concepts is more natural and more generalized than to do it by mathematics. Prof D.Y. Li proposed a qualitative quantitative transformation model of uncertainty based on the traditional fuzzy set theory and probability statistics, cloud model, which can realize the uncertain transformation between qualitative concepts (concept intension) and quantitative values (concept extension) [23]. Cloud model, a new cognitive model [30], is used to simulate the bidirectional cognitive computing between intension and extension of concept through the forward cloud generator (FCG) and backward cloud generator (BCG). In this paper, the cloud model is used to study and analyze the bidirectional cognitive process.

The remainder of this paper is organized as follows. Section 2 introduces the definition of the second-order normal cloud model and the FCG and BCG algorithms are presented. A bidirectional cognitive process between concept extension and intension will be studied in Section 3. Final remarks and future perspectives will be discussed in Section 4.

2   Cloud Model and Cloud Generator

Cloud model is a cognition model to transform between quantitative data and qualitative concepts, which express a concept with three numbers.

Definition 2.1 (cloud) [11]: Let U be a universal set described by precise numbers, and C be the qualitative concept related to U. If there is a number $x \in U$, which randomly realizes the concept C, and the certainty degree of x for C, i.e. $\mu(x) \in [0,1]$, is a random value with steady tendency: $\mu(x) : U \to [0,1]$ $\forall x \in U$ $x \to \mu(x)$, then the distribution of x on U is defined as a *cloud*, and each x is defined as a *cloud drop*, noted $Drop(x, \mu)$.

Definition 2.2 (normal cloud) [11]: Let U be a universal set described by precise numbers, and C be the qualitative concept containing three numerical characters Ex, En, He related to U. If there is a number $x \in U$, which is a random realization of the concept C and satisfies $x = R_N(Ex, y)$, where $y = R_N(En, He)$, and the certainty degree of x on U is $\mu(x) = e^{-\frac{(x-Ex)^2}{2y^2}}$, then the distribution of x on U is a *second-order normal cloud*. Where $y = R_N(En, He)$ denoted a normally distributed random number with expectation En and variance He^2.

The key point in definition 2.2 is the second-order relationship, i.e. within the two normal random numbers. If $He = 0$, then the distribution of x on U will become a normal distribution. If $He = 0, En = 0$, then x will be a constant Ex and $\mu(x) \equiv 1$. In other words, certainty is the special case of the uncertainty. If He is large, the distribution of random variable X will have a heavy tail, which can be used in economic and social researches.

2.1   Forward Cloud Generator (FCG)

FCG algorithm [11] transforms a qualitative concept with three numerical characters Ex, En and He into a number of cloud drops representing the quantitative description of the concept. It depicts the process from thought to practice. Due to the universality of normal distribution, we mainly focus on second-order normal cloud model. According to the definition 2.2, the FCG algorithm is as follows.

Algorithm [11]: Forward normal cloud generator—**FCG**(Ex, En, He)
Input: Ex, En, He and the number of cloud drops n.
Output: n cloud drops and their certainty degrees, i.e. $Drop(x_i, \mu(x_i)), i = 1, 2, \cdots, n$.
Step 1: Generate a normally distributed random number y_i with expectation En and variance He^2, i.e. $y_i = R_N(En, He)$.
Step 2: Generate a normally distributed random number x_i with expectation Ex and variance y_i^2, i.e. $x_i = R_N(Ex, y_i)$.
Step 3: Calculate certainty degree $\mu(x_i) = e^{-\frac{(x_i - Ex)^2}{2y_i^2}}$.
Step 4: x_i with certainty degree $\mu(x_i)$, i.e. $Drop(x_i, \mu(x_i))$ is a cloud drop in the domain. Repeat the step 1 to step 4 until n cloud drops are generated.

2.2 Backward Cloud Generator (BCG)

The BCG is an algorithm based on probability statistics. It is used to transform a number of cloud drops (sample data) into three numerical characters representing a concept. In 2004, Liu proposed a BCG algorithm based on the sample variance and the first-order sample absolute central moment as following [31].

Algorithm [31]: Backward normal cloud generator—**BCG1**
Input: Drops$(x_i), i = 1, 2, \cdots, n$.
Output: (Ex, En, He) representation of a qualitative concept.
Step 1: Calculate the sample mean, sample variance and the first-order sample absolute central moment from the random sample $x_1, x_2, \cdots, x_n$, respectively, i.e.

$$\hat{Ex} = \bar{X} = \frac{1}{n}\sum_{i=1}^{n} x_i, S^2 = \frac{1}{n-1}\sum_{i=1}^{n}(x_i - \bar{X})^2, E|X - \hat{Ex}| = \frac{1}{n}\sum_{i=1}^{n}|x_i - \bar{X}|.$$

Step 2: According to the character of the second-order normal cloud distribution, Liu got the following equations:

$$S^2 = En^2 + He^2, E|X - Ex| = \sqrt{\frac{2}{\pi}}En. \tag{1}$$

Calculate the estimates of En and He from (1) respectively, i.e.

$$\hat{En} = \sqrt{\frac{\pi}{2}} \times \frac{1}{n}\sum_{i=1}^{n}|x_i - \hat{Ex}|, \quad \hat{He} = \sqrt{S^2 - \hat{En}^2}.$$

In addition to the BCG1 given by Liu, Dr.L.X. Wang proposed another backward cloud generator algorithm according to the sample variance and the fourth-order sample central moment as following, denoted by BCG2, the detailed algorithm see the reference [32], [33]. In 2012, G.Y. Wang, etc. proposed a multi-step backward cloud generator algorithm as follows [33].

Algorithm [33]: Multi-step backward cloud generator—**BCG3**
Input: Drops$(x_i), i = 1, 2, \cdots, n$
Output: (Ex, En, He) representation of a qualitative concept.

Step 1: Calculate the sample mean $\hat{Ex} = \bar{X} = \frac{1}{n} \sum\limits_{k=1}^{n} x_k$ from $x_1, x_2, \cdots, x_n$.

Step 2: Obtain the new sample from $x_1, x_2, \cdots, x_n$, that is, make the sample data $x_1, x_2, \cdots, x_n$ divide into m groups randomly, and each group will have r samples (i.e. $n = m \cdot r$ and n, m, r are positive integers). Calculate the sample variance $\hat{y}_i^2 = \frac{1}{r-1} \sum\limits_{j=1}^{r} (x_{ij} - \hat{Ex}_i)^2 (i = 1, 2, \cdots, m)$ from each group, where, $\hat{Ex}_i = \frac{1}{r} \sum\limits_{j=1}^{r} x_{ij} (i = 1, 2, \cdots, m)$. So, $y_1, y_2, \cdots, y_m$ are seen as a new random sample from a $N(En, He^2)$ distribution.

Step 3: Calculate the estimates of En^2 and He^2 from the new sample $y_1^2, y_2^2, \cdots, y_m^2$. We have

$$\hat{En}^2 = \frac{1}{2}\sqrt{4(\hat{EY}^2)^2 - 2\hat{DY}^2}, \hat{He}^2 = \hat{EY}^2 - \hat{En}^2. \qquad (2)$$

Where, $\hat{EY}^2 = \frac{1}{m} \sum\limits_{i=1}^{m} \hat{y}_i^2, \hat{DY}^2 = \frac{1}{m-1} \sum\limits_{i=1}^{m} (\hat{y}_i^2 - \hat{EY}^2)^2$. The estimates $\hat{En}$ and $\hat{He}$ are obtained from the formula (2).

3   The Bidirectional Cognition Experiment

According to the FCG and the above three BCGs, we will study the bidirectional cognitive computing process of human cognition for concepts. The initial concepts are divided into three kinds, that is, clear concept, uncertain concept and confusing concept. They can be expressed as a cloud concept with three numerical characters (Ex, En, He) respectively.

In order to facilitate the calculation, let (25, 3, 0.1) express a clear concept, (25, 3, 0.55) express an uncertain concept and (25, 1, 0.8) express a confusing concept. There is no clear boundaries for the three concepts due to the uncertainty of concept. In this paper, the different concept is determined by the atomized feature of cloud concepts [34]. Different cloud generators represent different people to conduct cognitive computing. So, the BCG1, BCG2 and BCG3 represent three kinds of people with different cognitive thinking respectively. One time cognition and many times cognition of different people for a concept are illustrated by the following two experiments respectively.

1) One time cognition process of different people for a concept

One time cognition process of three different kinds of people for a concept is like this: generate the concept extension by FCG form a given initial concept intension with numerical characters (Ex, En, He), and then three different kinds of people (that is, three BCGs) generate a new concept intension respectively, finally, the extensions are generated by FCG for the three new concepts again.

The results of new concept's intensions, which are generated by one time cognition of three different kinds of people for the above three concepts, are shown in Table 1 respectively. Their extensions are shown in Figure 1, Figure 2 and Figure 3 respectively.

Table 1. One time cognition results

Initial concept (Ex, En, He)	BCG1	BCG2	BCG3
Clear concept (25, 3, 0.1)	(24.96, 2.98, 0.28)	(24.96, 2.95, 0.21)	(24.96, 3.01, 0.09)
Uncertain concept (25, 3, 0.55)	(25.02, 3.01, 0.54)	(25.02, 3.02, 0.52)	(25.02, 3.01, 0.54)
Confusing concept (25, 1, 0.8)	(24.98, 1.25, 0.53)	(24.98, 1.04, 0.78)	(24.98, 0.98, 0.81)

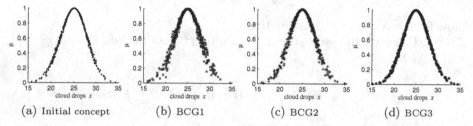

(a) Initial concept   (b) BCG1   (c) BCG2   (d) BCG3

Fig. 1. One time cognition results of the clear concept (25, 3, 0.1)

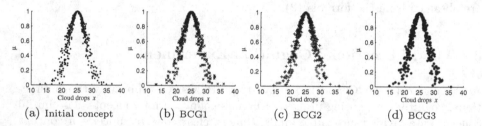

(a) Initial concept   (b) BCG1   (c) BCG2   (d) BCG3

Fig. 2. One time cognition results of the uncertain concept (25, 3, 0.55)

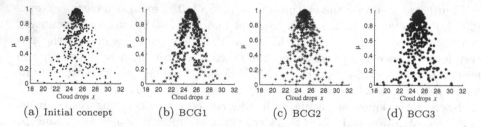

(a) Initial concept   (b) BCG1   (c) BCG2   (d) BCG3

Fig. 3. One time cognition results of the confusing concept (25, 1, 0.8)

From Table 1, and Figure 1 to Figure 3, we can find that when the initial concept is quite clear, the cognition results of BCG1 and BCG2 have some excursion, while BCG3's cognition result is very good. When the initial concept is uncertain in some degree, the cognition results of BCG1, BCG2 and BCG3 are similar. When the initial concept is confusing, BCG1's cognition result has much excursion, but the cognition results of BCG2 and BCG3 are quite good. These results show that the cognition of different people for different concept is different indeed.

2) Many times cognition process of different people for a concept

Many times cognition process of each kind of people with similar cognitive thinking for a concept will be studied in this section. We select 50 people in each kind of people with similar cognitive thinking, and each people's cognition process from the extension of a concept to its intension and then back to its extension is treated as one time cognition. So, 50 people's cognitions for the same concept are 50 times cognition in each kind of people with similar cognitive thinking. Where, the process from the concept's intension to its extension is implemented by FCG, and the process from the concept's extension to its intension is realized by human cognition, that is, BCG. The 50 times cognition processes (L=1 to 50) of each kind of people with similar cognitive thinking for the above three concepts are shown in Figure 4(a),(b),(c) respectively. Figure 4 expresses the changing process of new concept numerical characters (Ex, En, He) which are generated by cognition of 50 people in each kind of people with similar cognitive thinking. The concept's intensions obtained by the 50th cognition of three kinds of people with different cognitive thinking for the above three concepts

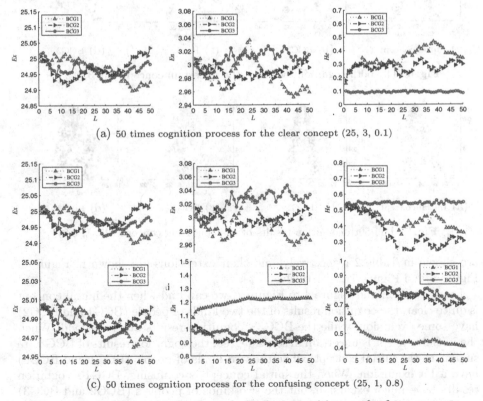

(a) 50 times cognition process for the clear concept (25, 3, 0.1)

(c) 50 times cognition process for the confusing concept (25, 1, 0.8)

Fig. 4. Three different kinds of people 50 times cognition results for a concept

Table 2. The 50th cognition's numerical characters

Initial concept (Ex, En, He)	BCG1	BCG2	BCG3
Clear concept (25, 3, 0.1)	(24.92, 2.96, 0.34)	(24.92, 2.98, 0.30)	(24.92, 3.01, 0.09)
Uncertain concept (25, 3, 0.55)	(24.93, 2.96, 0.36)	(24.93, 3.01, 0.31)	(24.92, 3.03, 0.54)
Confusing concept (25, 1, 0.8)	(25.03, 1.25, 0.41)	(25.03, 0.96, 0.83)	(25.03, 1.02, 0.78)

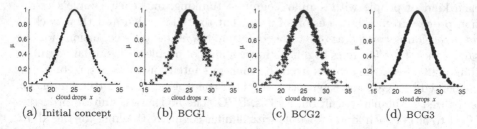

(a) Initial concept (b) BCG1 (c) BCG2 (d) BCG3

Fig. 5. The 50th cognition results of the clear concept (25, 3, 0.1)

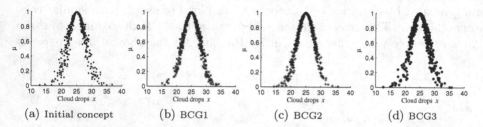

(a) Initial concept (b) BCG1 (c) BCG2 (d) BCG3

Fig. 6. The 50th cognition results of the uncertain concept (25, 3, 0.55)

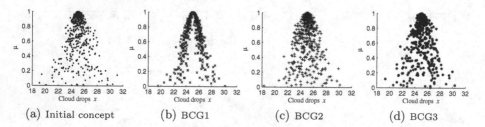

(a) Initial concept (b) BCG1 (c) BCG2 (d) BCG3

Fig. 7. The 50th cognition results of the confusing concept (25, 1, 0.8)

are shown in Table 2 respectively, and their extensions are shown in Figure 5, Figure 6 and Figure 7 respectively.

From Table 2, and Figure 4 to Figure 7, we can find when the initial concept is quite clear, the cognition results of the two kinds of people (BCG1 and BCG2) have some excursion, while the BCG3's cognition results are very good. When the initial concept is uncertain in some degree, the cognition results of BCG3 are similar to the initial concept, while the two kinds of people (BCG1 and BCG2) have a bit excursion. When the initial concept is confusing, BCG1's cognition results have much excursion, but the two kinds of people's (BCG2 and BCG3) cognition results are quite good.

4   Conclusions and Prospects

In this paper, the relationship of cognitive science and artificial intelligence is studied. A bidirectional cognitive computing model based on cloud model is introduced. Some experiment results are discussed to show the validity and efficiency of cloud model for bidirectional cognitive computing.

At the same time, there are still some problems to be further studied:

- Bidirectional cognitive computing process with increasing knowledge.
- Many people's mutual cognition process for a concept.
- Multi granularity bidirectional cognitive computing.

Acknowledgments. This paper is supported by National Natural Science Foundation of P.R. China under grants 61073146 and 61272060.

References

1. Coren, S.: Sensation & Perception. Harcourt College Publish (1999)
2. Thagard, P.: Cognitive Science(The Stanford Encyclopedia of Philosophy). The Metaphysics Research Lab Center for the Study of Language and Information. Stanford University (2011)
3. Feist, G.J., Rosenberg, E.L.: Psychology: Making Connections. McGraw-Hill Humanities/Social Sciences/Languages (2009)
4. Russell, S.J., Norvig, P.: Artificial Intelligence: A Modern Approach. Prentice Hall (2009)
5. Kim, J.: Problems in the Philosophy of Mind. Oxford University Press, Oxford (1995)
6. Gazzaniga, M.S.: The Cognitive Neurosciences III. The MIT Press (2004)
7. Croft, W., Alan, C.D.: Cognitive Linguistics. Cambridge University Press, Cambridge (2004)
8. D'Andrade, R.: The Development of Cognitive Anthropology. Cambridge University Press, Cambridge (1995)
9. Nilsson, N.: Artificial Intelligence: A New Synthesis. Morgan Kaufmann Publishers (1998)
10. Neapolitan, R., Jiang, X.: Contemporary Artificial Intelligence. Chapman & Hall/CRC (2012)
11. Li, D.Y., Du, Y.: Artificial Intelligence with Uncertainty, 1st edn. Chapman and Hall/CRC, London (2007)
12. Hoffmann, A.: Paradigms of Artificial Intelligence—A Methodological and Computational Analysis. Springer (August 1998)
13. Newell, A., Simon, H.A.: Computer Science as Empirical Inquiry: Symbols and Search. Communications of the ACM (19), 113–126 (1976)
14. Simon, H.A.: The Sciences of the Artificial, 3rd edn. MIT Press, Cambridge (1997)
15. Hopfield, J.J.: Neural Networks and Physical Systems with Emergent Collective Computational Abilities. Proceedings of the National Academy of Sciences (79), 2554–2558 (1982)
16. Rumelhart, D.E., Hinton, G.E., Williams, R.J.: Learning Internal Representations by Backpropagating Errors. Nature 323(99), 533–536 (1986)

17. Kanal, L.N., Lemmer, J.F.: Uncertainty in Artificial Intelligence. Elsevier Science publishing, New York (2008)
18. Wang, G.: Rough Set Based Uncertain Knowledge Expressing and Processing. In: Kuznetsov, S.O., Ślęzak, D., Hepting, D.H., Mirkin, B.G. (eds.) RSFDGrC 2011. LNCS, vol. 6743, pp. 11–18. Springer, Heidelberg (2011)
19. Wang, Z.K.: Probability Theory and Its Applications. Beijing Normal University Press, Beijing (1995)
20. Zadeh, L.A.: Fuzzy Sets. Information and Control 8(3), 338–353 (1965)
21. Pawlak, Z.: Rough Sets. International Journal of Computer and Information Sciences 11(5), 341–356 (1982)
22. Moore, R.E.: Interval Analysis, pp. 25–39. Prentice-Hall, Englewood Cliffs (1966)
23. Li, D.Y., Meng, H.J., Shi, X.M.: Membership Clouds and Cloud Generators. Journal of Computer Research and Development 32(6), 15–20 (1995)
24. Deng, J.L.: Grey Systems. China Ocean Press, Beijing (1988)
25. Zhao, K.Q.: Set Pair Analysis and Its Primary Application. Zhejiang Science and Technology Press, Hangzhou (2000)
26. Cai, W.: The Extension Set and Non-compatible Problems. Journal of Science Explore (1), 83–97 (1983)
27. Bishop, C.M.: Pattern Recognition and Machine Learning. Springer, New York (2006)
28. LOD2 EU Deliverable 3.1.1 Knowledge Extraction from Structured Sources, http://static.lod2.eu/Deliverables/deliverable-3.1.1.pdf
29. Fayyad, U., Piatetsky-Shapiro, G., Smyth, P.: From Data Mining to Knowledge Discovery in Databases. AI Magazine, 37–54 (1996)
30. Li, D.Y., Liu, C.Y., Gan, W.Y.: A New Cognitive Model: Cloud Model. International Journal of Intelligents Systems 24, 357–375 (2009)
31. Liu, C.Y., Feng, M., Dai, X.J., Li, D.Y.: A New Algorithm of Backward Cloud. Journal of System Simulation 16(11), 2417–2420 (2004)
32. Wang, L.X.: The Basic Mathematical Properties of Normal Cloud and Cloud Filter. Personal Communication (May 3, 2011)
33. Wang, G., Xu, C., Zhang, Q., Wang, X.: A Multi-step Backward Cloud Generator Algorithm. In: Yao, J., Yang, Y., Słowiński, R., Greco, S., Li, H., Mitra, S., Polkowski, L. (eds.) RSCTC 2012. LNCS (LNAI), vol. 7413, pp. 313–322. Springer, Heidelberg (2012)
34. Liu, Y., Li, D.Y.: Statistics on Atomized Feature of Normal Cloud Model. Journal of Beijing University of Aeronautics and Astronautics 36(11), 1320–1324 (2010)

An Enhanced Cloud-Based View Materialization
Approach for Peer-to-Peer Architecture

M.E. Megahed[1], R.M. Ismail[2], N.L. Badr[2], and M.F. Tolba[2]

[1] Faculty of Information Technology, Information Systems Department,
Misr University for Science & Technology, Egypt
mohammed_ezzat@live.com
[2] Faculty of Computer and Information Sciences, IS Department, Ain Shams University, Egypt
rashaismail@yahoo.com, {dr.nagwabadr,fahmytolba}@gmail.com

Abstract. Cloud computing is becoming increasingly popular as it enables
users to save both development and deployment time. It also reduces the
operational costs of using and maintaining the systems. Moreover, it allows the
use of any resources with elasticity instead of predicting workload which may
be not accurate, as the data warehousing environments can benefit from this
trend. In this paper, a cloud-based view allocation algorithm is presented to
enhance the performance of the data warehousing system over a Peer-to-Peer
architecture. The proposed approach improves the placement of the
materialized views. It also reduces the cost of the dematerialization process
more than any other policies. Furthermore, the proposed algorithm saves the
transfer cost by distributing the free space on the peers based on the required
space to store the views.

Keywords: Data Warehouse, Cloud computing, Materialized views, Peer-to-
peer Cloud.

1 Introduction

Cloud computing is the term of using any computer resources as a service; it is a very
successful service oriented computing paradigm, and it has a lot of features like:
infinite scalability, elasticity, reliability and pay-per-use etc. [1] and [2]. Infrastructure
as a Service (IaaS), Platform as a Service (PaaS), and Software as a Service (SaaS)
are the most popular cloud paradigms [3]. One of the cloud computing architectures is
Peer-to-Peer cloud architecture on which our proposed algorithm is based [4] and [5].

Data warehouse is considered one of the solutions for storing large amounts of data
to be used in decision making or supporting analysis. Data warehouse has a very large
size and can be geographically distributed leading to the occurrence of some
performance and storage problems. So, data warehouse can be distributed to data
marts which allow users to pose queries to these data marts directly instead of the data
warehouse. This will distribute the workload, make balance, and avoid single points
of failure [6],[7], [8].

A. Ell Hassanien et al. (Eds.): AMLTA 2012, CCIS 322, pp. 401–412, 2012.

View materialization is the process of computing and saving the result of a query in the data warehouse, in order to save processing cost. Every time the query is asked, the processing cost is saved, if the result of the query (the view) is materialized. It is not possible to materialize all the views because it costs a lot of storage. So we have to select some views to be materialized, the views which have the highest frequency of queries. There are two ways of view selection: static and dynamic. Static view selection is a traditional way to select views to be materialized based on prediction, but it has two main weaknesses. First, the workload of the queries is not easy to be predicted. The Second problem is the periodically changes of the workload [9],[10],[11]. Thus, the dynamic view selection could be considered better than the static view selection, especially in our case (cloud computing environment).

View materialization in a peer-to-peer cloud has some challenges. First, the evaluation of the views is to select some of them to be materialized. Second, is to decide where the materialized views should be allocated on the peers of the cloud to get the most enhanced performance, considering the transfer cost between the peers and the processing cost of the queries [9].

In this paper, a cloud dynamic view allocation algorithm is proposed to allocate the materialized views at the suitable peers in order to reduce the storage cost (Utilizing the elasticity of the cloud), transfer cost, query processing cost, and the dematerialization of the already materialized views.

2   Related Work

Recent researches applied an approach to materialize views in P2P data warehousing systems [7],[9],[12]. They provided two placement policies: Isolated Policy: Which places each materialized view in the peer with the highest frequency of queries based on that view. In case of no storage available to save the materialized view, the replacement policy will make dematerialization free enough space to store the new materialized view. The second policy is Voluntary policy: which is based on placing the materialized view in the peer which has enough space to store the materialized view, then select the peer which has the highest frequency of queries based on this view. If there is no peer having free enough space to store the materialized view, then it is necessary to dematerialize some materialized views to free enough space to store the new materialized view which is more beneficial.

In [13] they proposed the DynaMat system that makes dynamic materialization. It aims to unify the problems of view selection and maintenance, taking into consideration the maintenance restrictions, such as the views updating and available space. The main approach of the system is to monitor the incoming queries to get the frequencies and materialize the views of the more frequent queries. In DynaMat system, there is no dynamic detection of the redundancies (common views between queries); it is done by the data warehouse administrator.

Furthermore, others proposed cloud view distributed data processing system which allows users to define the required views to be maintained [14]. In cloud view, users can define the orientation of their applications. Based on the users' descriptions, the system generates the required jobs and distributes them to a set of nodes to be executed. The queries from the clients are served and executed by using the materialized and time versioned views in less time than the traditional queries.

However, in [12] they Presented PeerOLAP system which supports the Online Analytical Processing queries, based on P2P network, each end client containing a cache with the most asked queries results. If a query cannot find the result on its peer, it will distribute through the network until finding the result at the peer which contains it. The query answer may be located in more than one peer and this answer will be constructed from these peers.

In [15] they presented PeerDW system, which apply the DW upon P2P architecture, they also presented a stable hybrid P2P network structure for the PeerDW to adapt the DW and the P2P nature. The dynamic caching peer materialized views algorithm are also presented as materialized views distributed and cached dynamically in the peer side in order to reduce the query response time and increase the system throughput.

In [16] and [17] they presented an ASM-based approach to data warehouses dynamic design and OLAP systems with a foundational approach to data-intensive software services. Technically, data warehouse and OLAP features can be considered as an instantiation of an abstract state service. They explained this view and provided examples to clarify their idea.

Therefore our dynamic allocation methodology addressed a different algorithm as it considers the view materialization based on cloud computing not a traditional network. Besides, it utilizes the cloud features to improve the placement of the materialized views.

3   The Proposed Dynamic View Allocation Architecture

Our proposed methodology proposes a new architecture as shown in fig. 1 to improve the placement of the materialized views. Moreover, our placement policy keeps the materialized views and reduces the cost of the dematerialization process (dematerialization process waste processing cost as the views may be need to be materialized again with a new cost) more than any other policies. It also saves the transfer cost. The architecture consists of the following modules:

- **Module1:The Materialization module:**
The main challenge of view materialization that is based on peer-to-peer cloud is to select the best combination set of views to be materialized, considering query performance over the cloud, the overall processing time and the maintenance cost of views. Thus, each view should be evaluated before the selection process; this evaluation is based on the calculation of the saved cost if this view is materialized. The cost saved $CS_{(V_j)}$ could be calculated as follows:

$$CS_{(V_j)} = \Sigma \; f_{(q_j)} * Ct_{(V_j)} \tag{1}$$

Where $f_{(q_j)}$ is the frequency of Query q , and $Ct_{(V_j)}$ is the total cost of materializing view V. The total cost $Ct_{(V_j)}$ is calculated as follows:

$$Ct_{(V_j)} = Ce(vj) + PeerCost(pi \rightarrow cp) * Size\ (vj) \qquad (2)$$

Where $Ce(vj)$ is the processing cost of view v and PeerCost($pi \rightarrow cp$) the transfer cost from peer pi to the cloud peer. The view maintenance cost of the view could be calculated using the following equation:

$$CM_{(V_j)} = \sum\ F_{Br_{Pi}} * Cm_{(V_j)} \qquad (3)$$

Where $F_{Br_{Pi}}$ is the Relation update frequency of the view relations (tables) and $Cm_{(V_j)}$ is the maintenance cost of each update (i). The views will be ranked based on their goodness,

$$Goodness(Vj) = CS_{(V_j)} - CM_{(V_j)} \qquad (4)$$

Then the system can make combinations of these views and calculate the benefits of these combinations. Finally, it materializes the set of views which achieve the most benefits of the materialization process. The second challenge is the view placement on the peers considering the utilization of the materialized views, the query processing cost and transfer cost between the peers.

- **Module2: The Placement Module:**

In this module, a candidate peer is selected to store the materialized view. This selection is done according to the predefined equations. The placement phase is based on utilizing some of the cloud computing features to avoid wasting materialized views and reduce the transfer cost in the cloud.

The policy is based on placing the new materialized view at the peer which has the highest frequency of accessed queries. This reduces both the transfer and query processing cost.

- **Module3: The Resource allocation Module:**

The resource allocation is one of the main challenges in the cloud environment. As if there is no enough space to store the view at the peer, the free space of the other peers can be used. The materialized view will not be transferred to these peers. But, a resource reallocation process will be done (by doing resource allocation) and the required free spaces are located in the peer which has the highest use of this view utilizing the elasticity feature of the cloud. So, the peer can have enough free space to this view to be materialized and placed on it. Therefore, the network transfer cost will be saved.

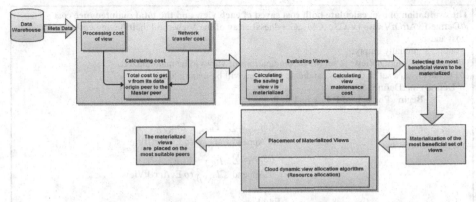

Fig. 1. The Proposed Dynamic View Allocation Architecture

4   The Cloud-Based Dynamic View Allocation Approach

The proposed approach allocates the materialized views at the suitable peers in order to reduce the storage cost (utilizing the elasticity of the cloud), transfer cost, query processing cost, and the dematerialization of the already materialized views. The algorithm is based on our proposed dynamic view allocation architecture as shown in the following pseudo code.

The cloud Dynamic View Allocation Algorithm

calculate the total cost of each view at the cloud

//Define P int "Number of Peers in the Cloud" ;

//Define PeerCost $_{(pi \rightarrow cp)}$ Cost between any peer and cloud Peer;

//Define FBr$_{pi}$ The update frequency of base relation Br at Peer p;

//Define Q = {q1,q2,......q$_T$} query Workload , T is the total number of queries;

//Define f$_{pi}$(q$_j$)The access frequency of query j at peer i;

//define Cm(v$_i$) The maintenance cost of query v$_i$;

//Define Cp(v$_i$) The processing cost of view v$_i$;

//Define Ct(v$_i$) The total cost of view v$_i$;

//Define Goodness(v$_i$) "A value Reflects the efficiency of materializing v$_i$;

//Define Vc Set of candidate Views;

//Define Cs(v$_i$) "The saving cost if View v$_i$ is materialized";

//Define CM(v$_i$) The Maintenance cost of view VI

//Define I,J int;

//Define Size[v$_i$, Size] " Array of views and their sizes";

//Define TotalCostArray [v$_i$, Ct(v$_i$)]"Array of views and their total cost";

Begin

  Begin For i=1 to P

        For j= 1 to P$_i$

          $Ct_{(v_j)} = Ce(vj) + PeerCost(pi \rightarrow cp) * Size\ (vj)$

        Next j

        End For

// Append vj & ct(vj) in TotalCostArray

        Next i

        End For End

The evaluation phase: calculate both cost saved of each view and the total maintenance cost
//Define EvArrOfViews [V,CS$_{Vj}$,CM$_{Vj}$,Goodness] array of the Views and their Saving cost , maintenance cost and
goodness : initially empty;
//Define AllCombOfView: A set of all combinations of views to be materialized.
//Define Cv$_{Final}$ a set of the final candidate view that will be materialized.
// Define i int; Define j int

> **Begin   For i=1 to P For j= 1 to P$_i$**

$$CM_{(V_j)} = \sum F_{Br_{P_i}} * Cm_{(V_j)}$$
// Append $CM_{(V_j)}$ to EvArrOfViews
$$CS_{(V_j)} = \sum f_{(q_j)} * Ct_{(V_j)}$$
// Append $CM_{(V_j)}$ to EvArrOfViews
Next j
End For

> Next i
> **End For**
End

Determine the final candidate views to be materialized
//Define EvArrOfViews [V,CS$_{Vj}$,CM$_{Vj}$,Goodness] array of the Views and their Saving cost , maintenance cost and goodness : initially
//Define AllCombArray: Array of sets of all combinations of views to be materialized: initially empty;
//Define Cnt int : total number of the available combinations of views in the AllCombArray array
//Define Cv$_{Final}$ a set of the final candidate view that will be materialized;

> **Begin**

> **For each View V ∈ EvArrOfViews**
> Goodness(V$_j$) = $CS_{(v_j)} - CM_{(V_j)}$
> //Append$Goodness_{(v_j)}$ to the EvArrOfViews
> **End For**
> //Create all combinations of views to be materialized
> // Append each of the combinations to the AllCombArray

For i=1 to Cnt Do

> CV$_i$=Max of $\sum$ Goodness(v$_j$) in AllCombArray[i]
> //append CV$_i$ to the CV
> Next i

> **For each CV$_i$ in CV**
> CV$_{Final}$[i]= Min Number of Views in CV[i]
> //Append CVi to CV$_{Final}$

> Next

> **End For**

End For
> **End**

View placement phase

// Define Cv$_{Final}$ [{V$_1$,Size$_1$},{V$_2$,Size$_2$},......} array of the final candidate views that will be materialized and its sizes;

// Define Q$_{pi}$={q$_1$,q$_2$,......} a set of quires at peer (i);

// Define [P$_i$,FreeSpace(P$_i$)] array of Peers in the cloud and the free space for each;

// Define CntQuery(V$_j$) int number of quires that access view (j);

// Define MaxPeerView[{V$_j$,P$_i$}] Array of peers id in which view(j) is mostly accessed by query initially empty;

> **Begin**
> **For each** $v_k \in \{vc_{final}\}$ **Do;**

```
                             ViewPeerNo(Vk)={Ø}; X=0;
                             For i 1 To P;
                             CntQuery(Vk) = 0;
                             For j=1 To P(i);
                             CntQuery(Vk) = CntQuery(Vk)+ Count(Qj for Vk);
                             Next J;
             End For;

                             If X > CntQuery(Vk);
                             ViewPeerNo = [i];
                             Next i;
                             End if;
                     Return ViewPeerNo(Vk);
                     Append Both Vk and ViewPeerNo(Vk)in MaxPeerView Array;
Resource allocation phase
For Each View (Vk) in MaxPeerView;
                     Check the Free Space [Pi,FreeSpace(Pi)],
                     If FreeSpace in Pi > Size (Vk);
                     Locate Vk At Pi;
                     Else //Enter Cloud De-fragmentation Phase Defragment The Cloud
                     Adding extra space for Pi
End For;          End;
```

5   Experimental Results

A simulated cloud environment has been developed with the help of VMWare workstation [18] to test the proposed cloud dynamic view allocation algorithm. It simulates the cloud peers which contain the data marts and the cloud super peer which contains the data warehouse and where the system is run.

The cloud simulation contains 3 peers and the cloud super peer. TPC-H database [19] is used as a dataset (scale factor 1) and 6 sets of queries had been run. These queries come from the each one contains a number of queries (20, 100, 200, 500, 1000, and 2000).These sets of queries are posed to the cloud on each peer randomly.

In order to evaluate the performance of our policy, the proposed cloud dynamic view allocation algorithm is compared to the two algorithms of [9], the isolated policy and the voluntary policy. The saving transfer cost, processing time and space usage are calculated and compared for the three polices through three simulation experiments. The algorithms are tested using [20].

Experiment-1: measures the transfer cost. Fig.2 shows that the comparison between the cloud view allocation algorithm , the isolated policy and the voluntary policy against the transfer cost based on four sets of queries (20,100,200 and 500), and it shows that the cloud view allocation algorithm saves the transfer cost especially in the two cases 200 and 500 query sets.

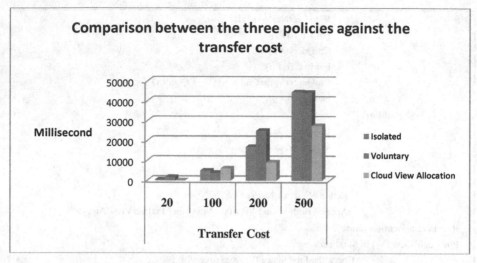

Fig. 2. Comparison between the three policies against the transfer cost

Fig. 3 shows the transfer cost savings of the three policies for all the 6 queries sets (20, 100, 200, 500, 1000, and 2000 queries). It shows that our policy saved the transfer cost by about 79.3%, while, the voluntary policy saved it by about 63.2%, and the isolated policy saved it by about 73.6%. This result is based on our cloud dynamic view allocation algorithm that saved the transfer cost by allocating the views in the peer with the highest frequency of queries. In case of no free space, additional space is added to the peer from the other peers on the cloud by utilizing the elasticity of the cloud.

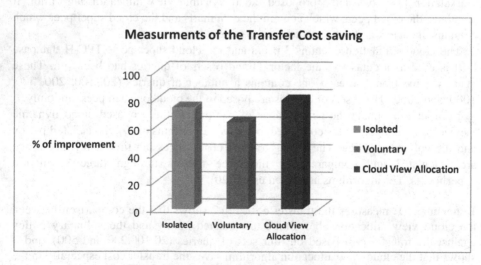

Fig. 3. Measurements of the saved transfer cost

Experiment-2: measures the processing cost. Fig. 4 shows the comparison between the cloud view allocation algorithm, the isolated policy and the voluntary policy against the processing cost based on four sets of queries (20,100,200 and 500) and it shows that the cloud view allocation algorithm saves more processing time than the two other policies.

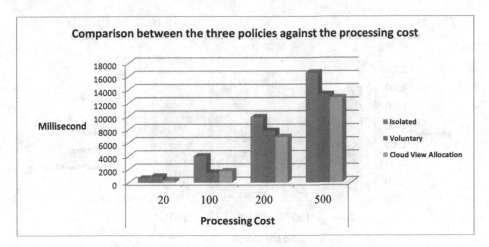

Fig. 4. Comparison between the three policies against the processing cost

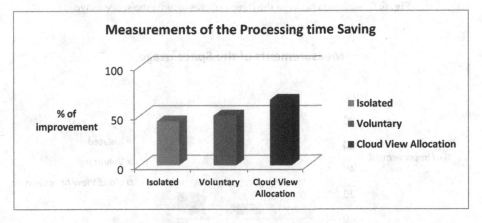

Fig. 5. Measurements of the saved processing time

Fig.5 shows the processing cost savings of the three policies for all the 6 queries sets (20, 100, 200, 500, 1000, and 2000 queries). It shows that our dynamic allocation policy enhanced the processing cost by about 66%, while the voluntary policy enhanced it by about 50.2%, and the isolated enhanced it by about 44.4%.

This result was expected because the processing cost is based on the transfer cost between the peers to get the data from the relations (the tables which the views are based on), and the transfer cost of the views themselves.

Experiment-3: measures the space usage of the cloud. Fig. 6 shows the comparison in space usage between the three policies, and it shows that in 3 of 4 sets the cloud view policy used space more than the other two policies but it is not the huge different and it is accepted compared to the improvement in the saving of transfer cost and processing cost.

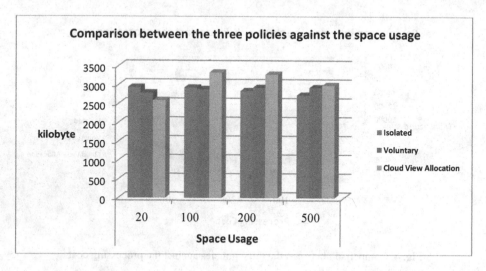

Fig. 6. Comparison between the three policies against the space usage

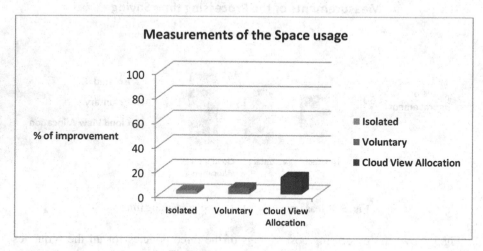

Fig. 7. Results of Space Usage

Fig.7 shows that using the cloud dynamic view allocation algorithm increased the space usage by about 13.8%, while, the voluntary policy increased it by about 5%, and the isolated increased it by only 3%.

So, our policy keeps the materialized views, increases the space usage of the cloud and reduces the transfer cost by distributing the free space on the peers based on the required space to store the views.

6   Conclusions

View materialization in a peer-to-peer cloud has some challenges, such as the evaluation of the views that will be selected to be materialized. Moreover, it decides where the materialized views should be allocated on the peers of the cloud to get the most enhanced performance, considering the transfer cost between the peers and the processing cost of the queries. Our proposed methodology overcomes the previously mentioned challenges. In this paper, the cloud dynamic view allocation algorithm is introduced to improve the data warehouse system over peer-to-peer cloud computing architecture. The main idea of the proposed approach is based on the view materialization of the most accessed queries on its peer by utilizing the cloud computing features especially the elasticity. The performance of the database system is based on the query processing time as well as the transferring time between the peers and the space utilized of the views. Our proposed methodology improved them by about 66%, 79% and 14% respectively.

References

1. Daniel, J.A.: Data Management in the Cloud: Limitations and Opportunities. IEEE Data Eng. Bull. 32(1), 3–12 (2009)
2. Divyakant, A., Sudipto, D., Amr, E.A.: Big data and cloud computing: new wine or just new bottles? VLDB 3(1-2), 1647–1648 (2010)
3. Bhaskar, P.R., Eunmi, C., Ian, L.: A Taxonomy and Survey of Cloud Computing Systems. In: NCM 2009 Fifth International Joint Conference on INC, IMS and IDC, pp. 44–51. IEEE Computer Society, Washington (2009) ISBN 978-0-7695-3769-6
4. Ozalp, B., Moreno, M., Michele, T.: Design and Implementation of a P2P Cloud System, University of Bologna, Mura Anteo Zamboni 7, 40127 Bologna (2011)
5. Mell, P., Grance, T.: The NIST Definition of Cloud Computing (Draft)–Recommendations of the National Institute of Standards and Technology, Gaithersburg (MD) (January 2011)
6. Ismail, R.M.: Maintenance of materialized views over peer-to-peer data warehouse architecture. In: Proceedings of the International Conference on Computer Engineering and Systems (ICCES), Cairo, Egypt, pp. 312–318 (2011)
7. Ismail, R.M., Karam, O.H., El-Sharkawy, M.A., Abdel-Wahab, M.S.: Streaming Real Time Data In Data Warehouses For Just-in-time Views Maintenance. In: The Proceedings of the IADIS International Conference on Applied Computing, Rome, Italy, pp. 101–108 (2009)
8. Zhao, J., Schewe, K.-D., Köhler, H.: Dynamic data warehouse design with abstract state machines. Journal of Universal Computer Science 15(1), 355–397 (2009)
9. Bellahsene, Z., Cart, M., Kadi, N.: A Cooperative Approach to View Selection and Placement in P2P Systems. In: Meersman, R., Dillon, T.S., Herrero, P. (eds.) OTM 2010, Part I. LNCS, vol. 6426, pp. 515–522. Springer, Heidelberg (2010)

10. Krompass, S., Dayal, U., Kuno, H.A., Kemper, A.: Dynamic workload management for very large data warehouses: Juggling Feathers and Bowling Balls. In: VLDB, pp. 1105–1115 (2007)
11. Chen, G., Wu, Y., Liu, J., Yang, G., Zheng, W.: Optimization of sub-query processing in distributed data integration systems. Journal of Network and Computer Applications 30, 1035–1042 (2010)
12. Panos, K., Wee, S.N., Beng, C.O., Ng, B., Chin, O., Dimitris, P., Kian-lee, T.: An adaptive peer-to-peer network for distributed caching of OLAP results. In: International Conference on Management of Data, pp. 25–36. ACM SIGMOD (2002) ISBN 1-58113-497-5
13. Yannis, K., Nick, R.: DynaMat: a dynamic view management system for data warehouses. In: International Conference on Management of Data, pp. 371–382. ACM SIGMOD (1999) ISBN 1-58113-084-8
14. Dehui, Z., Liang, Z., Tianyu, W., Junbin, K.: CloudView: Describe and Maintain Resource View in Cloud. In: Second International Conference on Cloud Computing, pp. 151–158. IEEE (2010)
15. Ismail, R.M., Karam, O.H., El-Sharkawy, M.A., Abdel-Wahab, M.S.: An Adaptive Peer-to-peer Network For Distributed Data Warehouse Views. The International Journal of Intelligent Computing and Information Sciences (IJICIS) 8(9) (June 2009)
16. Hui, M., Klaus-Dieter, S., Bernhard, T., Qing, W.: Cloud Warehousing. Journal of Universal Computer Science 16(8), 1183–1201 (2010)
17. Rizwan, M., Patrick, M., Jose, L.V.: Provisioning data analytic workloads in a cloud. Future Generation Computer Systems (2012), doi:10.1016/j.future.2012.01.008
18. VMware, http://www.vmware.com/
19. Transaction processing and database benchmark, http://www.tpc.org/tpch/
20. Boghdady, P.N., Badr, N.L., Hashem, M.A., Tolba, M.F.: An Enhanced Test Case Generation Technique Based on Activity Diagrams. In: Proceedings of the International Conference on Computer Engineering and Systems (ICCES), Cairo, Egypt, pp. 289–294 (November 2011)

An Enhanced Resource Allocation Approach
for Optimizing Sub Query on Cloud

E.A. Maghawry, R.M. Ismail, N.L. Badr, and M.F. Tolba

Faculty of Computer and Information Sciences, Ain Shams University, Cairo, Egypt
{e_maghawry,rashaismail}@yahoo.com,
{dr.nagwabadr,fahmytolba}@gmail.com

Abstract. Cloud computing is the latest evolution of computing. It provides services to numerous remote users with different requests. Managing the query workload in cloud environment is a challenge to satisfy the cloud users. Improving the overall performance and response time of the query execution can lead to users' satisfaction. In this paper, we examine the problem of the slow query response time. Sub query merging and query resource allocation approaches are proposed to minimize the query execution time.

The main aim of this paper is to exploit the shared data among the sub queries and minimize communication overhead on cloud. This paper proposes a new architecture to enhance the query execution time by applying the sub queries optimization and merging approach before implementing the query allocation approach. The results improving the query execution time as well as improving query allocation time.

Keywords: Cloud computing, query workload, query execution.

1   Introduction

As cloud computing is becoming more popular, this leads to increasing the number of applications needs to access and process data from multiple distributed sources [2]. The workloads generated by queries can change very quickly; so this can lead to a poor performance (e.g. query processing time) depending on the type and the number of requests made by users. The challenge is how to provide a fast and efficient access to database during queries execution over distributed data sources [5]. As Clouds are generally built over wide-area networks, query execution performance can be improved by minimizing communication cost because high communication over clouds can lead to a slow query response time [2]. Each query submitted from the user is transformed to a query plan which consists of a set of sub-queries formulated over the data sources and operators specifying how to combine results of the sub-queries to answer the user query [2]. The challenge in this paper is how to exploit and optimize the shared data among the sub queries to minimize the query response time. This paper presents an architecture to enhance the query execution time by applying the sub

A. Ell Hassanien et al. (Eds.): AMLTA 2012, CCIS 322, pp. 413–422, 2012.

queries optimization and merging approach before implementing the query allocation approach.

The paper is organized as follows. Section 2 reviews related works. Section 3 presents our proposed query workload architecture. Section 4 describes the mechanism used to implement our architecture. Section 5 presents the experimental environment. Section 6 presents the results. Conclusion and future work are discussed in section 7.

2   Related Work

In [2] they presented Merge-Partition (MP) query reconstruction algorithm. Their work is related to IGNITE system proposed in [6]. The algorithm is able to exploit data sharing opportunities among the concurrent sub- queries. This can reduce the average communication overhead. In [1] they proposed resource selection module to limit the search space by selecting a subset of resources and applying ranking function to improve the performance and optimization time. In [3] they presented an architecture to achieve workload balance during queries execution. In [4] they presented several techniques to respond to load imbalance by dynamically redistributing processor load assignments throughout a computation to take account of varying resource capabilities. In [4] they introduced five adaptively strategies, such as strategy proposed in [12]; they presented Flux(Fault-tolerant Load-balancing eXchange) which is placed between producer consumer stages in a dataflow pipeline to repartition stateful operators while the pipeline is still executed under memory loads. In [13] they presented DITN (Data In Network), a new method of parallel querying based on dynamic outsourcing of join processing tasks to non-dedicated and heterogeneous computers. In [5] they presented an approach that combines proprietary cloud based load balancing techniques and density-based partitioning for efficient range query processing across relational database-as-a-service in cloud computing environments. In [8] they described the use of utility functions to coordinate adaptations that assign resources to query fragments from multiple queries, and demonstrate how a common framework can be used to minimize overall query response times and to maximize the number of queries meeting quality of service goals. Besides, in [10] they described how utility functions can be used to make explicit the desirability of different workload evaluation strategies, and how optimization can be used to select between such alternatives. Their approach is illustrated for workloads consisting of workflows or queries. In [9] they examined the problem of provisioning resources in a public cloud to execute data analytic workloads. The goal of their provisioning method is to determine the most cost-effective configuration for a given workload. In [11] they proposed a workload management system for controlling the execution of individual queries based on realistic customer service level objectives. In [14] they proposed a low complexity resource scheduler algorithm that allows for partitioned parallelism for use in a distributed query processor over heterogeneous machines. In this paper, we focused on the work proposed in [1] and [2] that targets only one of the two issues: query allocation or sub query optimization and merging, but not both. The proposed work considers both issues.

3   The Proposed System's Architecture

Our proposed architecture overcomes the challenge of slow query response time by optimizing and merging the sub queries. Furthermore, it assigns the sub queries to the appropriate resources. In addition, it manages queries execution to respond to any load imbalance before retrieving the results of queries to the users.

Our proposed architecture which is shown in Fig.1 involves three subsystems: the first subsystem is the *Query Optimization* which accepts queries from users. The output of this subsystem is the list of the resources that is responsible for queries execution. The second subsystem is the *Workload Manager* which manages queries execution on resources and responds to any load imbalance that may occur through the execution. The third subsystem is *Integrator* which is responsible for collecting the queries results from the resources and retrieving them to the users.

The *Query Optimization subsystem* is responsible for discovering data sharing among the sub queries of accepted queries from users. Then it determines the ordering of queries execution. Finally, it allocates the query to the appropriate resources. The main advantage of this subsystem is minimizing the query execution time.

- **Query Optimization subsystem contains the following main processes:**

— Transform Queries to Abstract Query Tree(AQT): accept queries from users and transform each query to abstract query tree.
— Optimize Sub Queries: traverse AQTs and determine which sub queries that have shared data.
— Merge Queries: construct new merged queries from the group of optimized sub queries that have shared data among them.
— Schedule Query: determine the ordering of queries execution.
— Resource Allocation: an AQT is traversed to find candidate hosts for each operation in the AQT, then apply the ranking function. The host with the highest rank is chosen as the provider of the base relation [1].

The *Workload manager subsystem* is responsible for managing the queries execution through handling any failure during query execution. The main advantage of this subsystem is the improvement of query execution performance.

- **Workload Manager subsystem contains the following main processes:**

— Monitor/Observer: collects information as a source of notifications of queries execution, such as the processing cost of a tuple and communication cost of an outgoing buffer of tuples.
— Diagnoser: performs the assessment phase; it determines if there is an issue with the current execution (e.g., workload imbalance).
— Responder: receives notifications from the diagnoser about issues of execution (e.g., workload imbalance) in the form of proposed enhanced workload distribution.

The *Integrator subsystem* is responsible for collecting the results of queries from the resources then returning the results to the users.

- **Integrator subsystem contains the following main processes:**

— Collector: is responsible for collecting answers of non-merged and merged queries from the resources.
— Retrieve Results: for non-merged queries, it returns the result directly to the users. In merged queries, it first gets the answers of the original queries from the result of merged queries then returns the final result to the users.

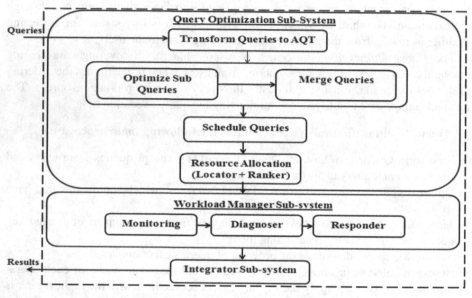

Fig. 1. Proposed Enhanced Query Workload Architecture

4   The Implementation of the Proposed System

The proposed system accepts the queries from the remote users. Each query is transformed to an abstract query tree (AQT) generated by parser which generates query execution plan as a tree. The tree consists of internal nodes that have the operations of the query, such as select operation, and the relations used in the operation put in the leaves of the tree. We assume that the queries submitted are select-project query in the form of $\Pi_L (\sigma_p (R))$ where L is the list of output attributes, P is the selection predicate, and R are queried relations.

Traversing the AQTs to optimize the sub queries: (i) check if the operation in internal node is "table scan" then check the name of the relation which will be scanned, (ii) examine if there are sub queries which will select tuples from the same relation. This mean that data can be shared among them so the sub queries can be merged (i.e. either parameterized queries or non-parameterized queries).

The set of the new queries are reconstructed by this query reconstruction mechanism to eliminate data redundancy among the sub-queries being processed [2].

Example: For a given submitted query q: $\Pi_L (\sigma_p (R))$.

Let us assume the following assumptions:

- $L^o(q_i)$ be the set of output attributes.
- $P(q_i)$ be these lection predicates of q_i.
- $L^c(q_i)$ be the set of attributes that appear in $P(q_i)$.

For two queries qi and qj, let $R(qi \cap qj)$ be their common answer. In Non-Parameterized query, sub queries can be merged in the case of the three conditions presented in [2] that can all be satisfied:

- $L^c(q_i) \subseteq Lo(q_i)$
- $L^c(q_j) \subseteq L^o(q_j)$
- $L^o(q_i) = L^o(q_j)$.

After optimizing and merging the sub queries into new merged queries, the new merged queries are transformed into abstract query tree. The first in first out (FIFO) algorithm is used for scheduling and determining the ordering of the query execution.

All the cloud resources' information (such as: RAM amount, CPU speed, relations size,..) is stored on a database. Each internal node in AQT of merged or non merged queries is traversed to select the appropriate resource based on ranking function to execute its operation.

$$
\begin{aligned}
rank_{ij} = \ & \frac{(mips_{ij} - min(mips)) \times w_{cpu}}{max(mips) - min(mips)} \\
& + \frac{(ram_{ij} - min(ram)) \times w_{ram}}{max(ram) - min(ram)} \\
& + \frac{(count_{ij} - min(count)) \times w_{count}}{max(count) - min(count)} \\
& + \frac{w_{wk}}{(wk_{ij} - min(wk))/(max(wk) - min(wk)) + 1} \\
& + \frac{w_{TLR}}{((TLR_{ij} - min(TLR))/(max(TLR) - min(TLR)) + 1}
\end{aligned}
\tag{1}
$$

Where:

- $mips_{ij}$: MIPS (Million Instructions Per Second) of Hi j
- w_{mips}: weight of MIPS
- ram_{ij} : RAM amount at H_{ij} (MB)

- w_{ram}: weight of RAM
- $count_{ij}$: number of relations that are involved in a query and maintained by H_{ij}
- TLR: is an index of a host's transmission capacity
- w_{count}: weight of count
- wk_{ij} : current workload of H_{ij} (0 means idle and 1 means fully utilized)
- w_{wk} : weight of workload.

TLR is not be computed because we assumed that the queries are Select-Project, so there is no transition between the resources during query execution. After computing ranks of all candidate hosts, the host with the highest rank is chosen as the provider of the relation.

5   Experimental Environment

TPC-H database [7] is used as a dataset (scale factor 1). The TPC-H database has eight relations: REGION, NATION, CUSTOMER, SUPPLIER, PART, PARTSUPP, ORDERS, and LINEITEM. The cloud environment is simulated with the help of VMWare workstation which is the global leader in virtualization and cloud infrastructure [15]. Three virtual machines are deployed as Table 1 shows their capabilities and the relations distribution among them. Ten queries are used with different combinations to test our experiment. Table 2 shows an example of the queries used.

Table 1. Capabilities of each VM with relations distribution

	VM1	VM2	VM3
Relations	Orders Region supplier	Orders Lineitem nation	Orders Lineitem Part Partsupp Customer
RAM (MB)	512	128	256
MIPS	1600	1830	1830

Table 2. Example of four queries used in our experiment

Query1	Select L_OrderKey, L_LineNumber,L_Quantity from lineitem where L_Quantity > 20
Query2	Select L_OrderKey, L_LineNumber,L_Quantity from lineitem where L_Quatity > 40
Query3	Select O_OrderKey, O_TotalPrice, O_OrderDate from orders where O_TotalPrice > 10000
Query4	Select O_OrderKey, O_OrderDate, O_TotalPrice from orders where O_OrderDate > '1996-01-12'

Microsoft Structured Query Language Server (MS SQL server) is used as a parser and to deploy TPC-H database.

6   Evaluations

Experiment1: Measure the queries resource allocation time

Table 3 shows the new merged queries after applying optimizing and merging the sub queries approach. Table 4 presents the resources selected to execute the new merged queries. Table 5 presents the resources selected to execute the four queries without merging. The execution time of the queries allocation is measured five times by different queries using sub query optimization and query resources allocation then the average execution time is computed, and the experiment is repeated using query resources allocation only as proposed in [1]. The results are shown in Table 6 and Fig.2.

Table 3. The new merged queries in sub query optimization and merging approach

Q1	Select L_OrderKey, L_LineNumber,L_Quantity from lineitem where L_Quantity > 20
Q2	Select L_OrderKey, L_LineNumber,L_Quantity from lineitem where L_Quantity > 40
New Merged Query	Select L_OrderKey, L_LineNumber,L_Quantity from lineitem where L_Quantity > 20
Q3	Select O_OrderKey, O_TotalPrice, O_OrderDate from orders where O_TotalPrice > 10000
Q4	Select O_OrderKey, O_OrderDate, O_TotalPrice from orders where O_OrderDate > '1996-01-12'
New Merged Query	Select O_OrderKey, O_OrderDate , O_TotalPrice from orders where O_TotalPrice > 10000 or O_OrderDate > '1996-01-12'

Table 4. The resources selected to execute the new merged queries

Queries	Assigning Virtual Machine
New Merged Query1	VM2
New Merged Query2	VM3

Table 5. The resources selected for the four queries without optimizing or merging

Queries	Assigning Virtual Machine
Query1	VM2
Query2	VM2
Query3	VM3
Query4	VM3

Table 6. The average execution time of the queries resource allocation

Approaches	Average Execution Time(Sec)
Without Merging/ Optimization (Query Allocation Approach [1])	0.064079
With Merging/Optimizing Queries (Our Approach)	0.042797

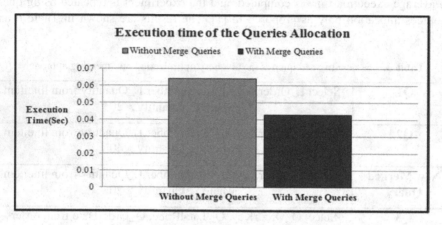

Fig. 2. The average execution time of the queries resource allocation

Experiment2: Measure the overall queries execution time

The total execution time of the queries is measured five times by different queries using sub query optimization and query resources allocation then the average execution time is computed, and the experiment is repeated using query resources allocation only as proposed in [1]. The results are shown in Table 7 and Fig.3.

Table 7. The average of measuring the queries execution time three times

Approaches	Average Execution Time(Sec)
Without Merging/Optimization (Query Allocation Approach[1])	156.0819
With Merging/Optimizing Queries(Our Approach)	82.46665

The results show that applying the sub query optimization and merging approach before the query resource allocation reduces overall query execution time by 52% and reduces query allocation time by 66%.

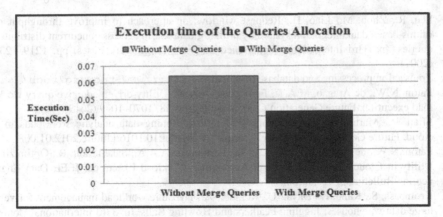

Fig. 3. The average overall queries execution time

7   Conclusion and Future Work

In this paper, a new architecture is proposed to minimize the overall query response time in cloud computing environment. The first subsystem of the proposed architecture is implemented and the results show that applying optimization and merging of the sub queries approach before the query allocation improves the execution time of the queries by 52% and improves query allocation time by 66%.

In our future work, the merging approach will be extended to handle joint and multiple predicates in the query. In these cases, the queries may become more complex, which needs to compute the sub query delay and improve query scheduling. The workload manager subsystem of the architecture will be implemented to improve the query execution performance by responding to the workload imbalance.

References

1. Liu, S., Karimi, A.H.: Grid query optimizer to improve query processing in grids. Future Generation Computer Systems 24, 342–353 (2008)
2. Chen, G., Wu, Y., Liu, J., Yang, G., Zheng, W.: Optimization of sub-query processing in distributed data integration systems. Journal of Network and Computer Applications 34, 1035–1042 (2011)
3. Gounaris, A., Smith, J., Paton, N.W., Sakellariou, R., Fernandes, A.A.A., Watson, P.: Adapting to Changing Resource Performance in Grid Query Processing. In: Pierson, J.-M. (ed.) VLDB DMG 2005. LNCS, vol. 3836, pp. 30–44. Springer, Heidelberg (2006)
4. Paton, N.W., Buenabad, J.C., Chen, M., Raman, V., Swart, G., Narang, I., Yellin, D.M., Fernandes, A.A.A.: Autonomic query parallelization using non-dedicated computers: an evaluation of adaptivity options. VLDB 18, 119–140 (2009)
5. Guabtni, A., Ranjan, R., Rabhi, A.F.: A workload-driven approach to database query processing in the cloud. J. Supercomput. (2011), doi:10.1007/s11227-011-0717-y

6. Lee, R., Zhou, M., Liao, H.: Request window: an approach to improve throughput of rdbms-based data integration system by utilizing data sharing across concurrent distributed queries. In: 33rd International Conference on Very Large Data Bases, pp. 1219–1230 (2007)
7. Transaction processing and database benchmark, http://www.tpc.org/tpch/
8. Paton, N.W., de Aragão, M.A.T., Fernandes, A.A.A.: Utility-driven adaptive query workload execution. Future Generation Computer Systems 28, 1070–1079 (2012)
9. Mian, R., Martin, P., Vazquez-Poletti, J.L.: Provisioning data analytic workloads in a cloud. Future Generation Computer Systems (2012), doi:10.1016/j.future.2012.01.008
10. Paton, N.W., de Aragão, M.A.T., Lee, K., Fernandes, A.A.A., Sakellariou, R.: Optimizing Utility in Cloud Computing through Autonomic Workload Execution. IEEE Data Engineering Bulletin 32, 51–58 (2009)
11. Krompass, S., Kuno, H., Dayal, U., Kemper, A.: Dynamic workload management for very large data warehouses: Juggling Feathers and Bowling Balls. In: 33rd International Conference on Very Large Data Bases, Vienna, Austria, pp. 1105–1115 (2007)
12. Shah, M.A., Hellerstein, J.M., Chandrasekaran, S., Franklin, M.J.: Flux: an adaptive partitioning operator for continuous query systems. In: 19th International Conference on Data Engineering, pp. 25–36. IEEE Press (2003)
13. Raman, V., Han, W., Narang, I.: Parallel Querying with Non-Dedicated Computers. In: 31st International Conference on Very Large Databases, Trondheim, Norway, pp. 61–72 (2005)
14. Gounaris, A., Sakellariou, R., Paton, N.W., Fernandes, A.A.A.: A novel approach to resource scheduling for parallel query processing on computational grids. Distributed and Parallel Databases 19, 87–106 (2006)
15. VMware, http://www.vmware.com/

Food Recommendation Using Ontology and Heuristics

M.A. El-Dosuky[1], M.Z. Rashad[1], T.T. Hamza[1], and A.H. EL-Bassiouny[2]

[1] Dep. of Computer Sciences, Faculty of Computers and Info. Mansoura University, Egypt
{mouh_sal_010,magdi_12003,Taher_Hamza}@mans.edu.eg
[2] Dep. of Mathematics, Faculty of Sciences, Mansoura University, Egypt
el_bassiouny@mans.edu.eg

Abstract. Recommender systems are needed to find food items of one's interest. This paper reviews recommender systems and recommendation methods, then propose a food personalization framework based on adaptive hypermedia and extend Hermes framework with food recommendation functionality. Moreover, it combines TF-IDF term extraction method with cosine similarity measure. Healthy heuristics and standard food database are incorporated into the knowledgebase. Based on the performed evaluation, we conclude that semantic recommender systems in general outperform traditional recommenders systems with respect to accuracy, precision, and recall, and that the proposed recommender has a better F-measure than existing semantic recommenders.

Keywords: Ontology, Semantics-Based Recommendation, Heuristics.

1 Introduction

Recommender systems are needed to find food items of one's interest. Challenges in building nutrition recommender systems can be classified as those concerning the user, and those concerning the algorithms used [1]. Different models are proposed [2] to deal with the missing or incorrect data from food recording measurements. Other challenges have a trade-off between them such as the perfect databases size and the cold-start problem. The cold-start problem can be solved by using information about the user's previous meals to calculate similarity measures to recommend new recipes [3]. Challenges about user compliance can benefit from many suggested strategies[4]. Users need nutrition heuristics to help develop a bias toward eating healthfully [5].

Section 2 reviews the previous attempts in building food recommenders and recommendation approaches. Section 3 presents our solution and the evaluation of the proposed framework. We conclude in Section 4 with plans for future work.

2 Previous Work

First efforts of designing automated systems to plan a meal based on personal nutritional needs utilize case-based planning such as CHEF [6] and JULIA [7]. A recipe recommender system usually employs similarity measures to recommend

A. Ell Hassanien et al. (Eds.): AMLTA 2012, CCIS 322, pp. 423–429, 2012.
© Springer-Verlag Berlin Heidelberg 2012

recipes that are most similar to meals the user likes [3]. User ratings are core for the recommender system [8], taking into account heuristics indentified by health care providers [9]. A system that analyses shopping receipts and then recommends healthier food choices is proposed [10]. To calculate the nutritional content of meals, Smart Kitchen [11] is proposed. Computer vision can be applied to analyze pictures of meals to predict the nutritional content [12]. Other systems focus on analysing the written form of nutritional content ([13], [14]). Recent attempts try to improve recipe recommendations by understanding the user's tastes [15].

There are four types of recommender approaches: content-based, semantics-based, collaborative filtering, and hybrid [16], but we restrict our discussion to the first two only. Content-based recommenders make use of Term Frequency-Inverse Document Frequency (TF-IDF)[17] and cosine similarity to compare the similarity between documents. Semantics is concerned only with concepts, and employing approaches such as concept equivalence [18], binary cosine [18], Jaccard [19], and semantic relatedness [20]. Next section shows how these approaches can be implemented.

3   Proposed Framework

The proposed framework is shown in fig. 1.

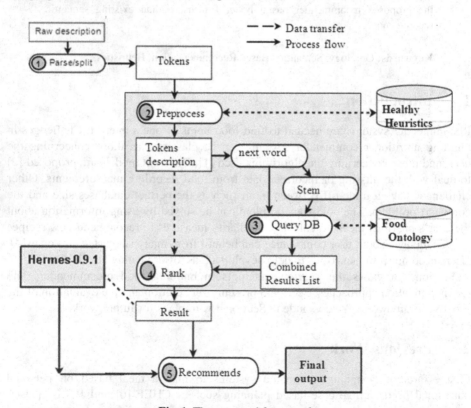

Fig. 1. The proposed framework

The first step is to take the raw description directly from the user or from his profile. Stop words are removed, followed by stemming words back to the root and removing punctuation and converting to lower case. To develop a bias toward healthful food, examined nutrition heuristics are collected [5]. The effectiveness of the collected heuristics was clear. Heuristics (e.g., *eat a hot breakfast*) are easy to comply with and more effective in making better food choices, such as suggesting *hot*-tagged items for any query with *breakfast*-related items.

The next stage is to match the description or the output of the rule to the knowledgebase entries. The knowledge base is a domain ontology consisting of classes, relationships and instances of classes. For instance the sample ontology used as an example in this paper 'Fruit' and 'Juice' are classes and between them there exists a relation like 'hasForm' and its inverse 'isFormedBy'. We define a concept as being a class or an instance of a class, such as 'Banana' is an instance of 'Fruit'.

User profile is constructed by calculating TF-IDF values for each term. We determine the term frequency (TF) $f_{i,j}$ for a term t_i within an recipe a_j:

$$tf_{i,j} = \frac{n_{i,j}}{\sum_k n_{k,j}} \tag{1}$$

dividing $n_{i,j}$, the number of occurrences of term t_i in recipe by a_j, the total number of terms in the document. Then the inverse document frequency (IDF):

$$idf_i = \log \frac{|A|}{|\{a : t_i \in a\}|} \tag{2}$$

dividing the total number of food items by the number of food items containing term t_i. The final value is computed by multiplying TF and IDF:

$$tfidf_{i,j} = tf_i \times idf_i \tag{3}$$

Semantic measures benefit from the ontology that is defined by a set of concepts:

$$C = \{c_1, c_2, c_3, \cdots, c_n\} \tag{4}$$

The food recipe can be defined by a set of p concepts:

$$A = \{c_1^a, c_2^a, c_3^a, \cdots, c_p^a\} \tag{5}$$

The user profile, U, consists of q concepts found in the food items read by the user:

$$U = \{c_1^u, c_2^u, c_3^u, \cdots, c_q^u\} \tag{6}$$

The similarity between a food recipe and the user profile can be computed by:

$$Similarity(U, A) = \begin{cases} 1 & \text{if } |U \cap A| \triangleright 0 \\ 0 & \text{otherwise} \end{cases} \tag{7}$$

We can employ binary cosine to compute the similarity:

$$B(U, A) = \frac{|U \cap A|}{|U| \times |A|} \tag{8}$$

by dividing the number of concepts in the intersection of the user profile and the unread food recipe by the product of the number of concepts in respectively U and A.

Similarly, Jaccard computes the similarity between two sets of concepts:

$$J(U,A) = \frac{|U \cap A|}{|U \cup A|} \tag{9}$$

Semantic neighborhood of c_i is all concepts directly related to c_i including c_i:

$$N(c_i) = \{c_1^i, c_2^i, c_3^i, \cdots, c_n^i\} \tag{10}$$

A food item a_k, which consists of m concepts is described as the following set:

$$A_k = \{c_1^k, c_2^k, c_3^k, \cdots, c_m^k\} \tag{11}$$

To compare two new items n_i and n_j, a vector can be created:

$$V_l = \left(\left\langle c_1^l, w_1^l \right\rangle, \cdots, \left\langle c_p^l, w_p^l \right\rangle\right) \qquad l \in \{i,j\} \tag{12}$$

where w_i is the weight of c_i. The similarity between food items a_i and a_j is :

$$\text{SemRel}(a_i, a_j) = \cos(V_i, V_j) = \frac{V_i \cdot V_j}{\|V_i\| \times \|V_j\|} \in [0,1] \tag{13}$$

The proposed framework is implemented in Java. It allows the user to formulate queries and execute them to retrieve relevant food items. We use the approach applied to adaptive hypermedia [21] and Hermes framework[22]. Hermes framework was originally used for building personalized *news* services. We extend Hermes with food recommendation functionality. It utilizes OWL[23] for representing the ontology.

Performed tests are based on a corpus of 300 food items extracted from the United States Department of Agriculture (USDA) [24] as shown in Table 1.

We have used 5 users with different but well-defined interests in our experiments. An example of a user interest is "Fruits". Each user has manually rated the food items as relevant or non-relevant for his interest. For each user we split the food items

Table 1. Food database

Group	No. of items	Group	No. of items
American Indian	165	Lamb and Veal	345
Baby Foods	329	Legumes	386
Baked Products	497	Nut and Seed	128
Beef Products	757	Pork Products	340
Beverages	284	Poultry Products	388
Breakfast Cereals	408	Restaurant and Meals	121
Cereal Grains	184	Sausages and Luncheon	234
Dairy and Egg	253	Snacks	169
Fast Foods	385	Soups and Sauces	510
Fats and Oils	220	Spices and Herbs	61
Finfish	258	Sweets	341
Fruits and Juices	329	Vegetables	814

Table 2. Evaluation results

	Accuracy	Precision	Recall	Specificity	F-Measure
TF-IDF	90%	90%	45%	99%	60%
B. Cosine	47%	23%	95%	36%	37%
Jaccard	93%	92%	58%	99%	71%
Sem. Rel.	57%	26%	92%	47%	41%
Proposed	94%	93%	62%	99%	74%

corpus in two different sets: 60% of the food items are the training set and 40% of the food items are the test set. Recommenders compute the similarity between the food items and previously computed user profile. If the computed similarity value is higher than a predefined cut-off value the food item is recommended and ignored otherwise. Evaluating the recommenders is done by measuring accuracy, precision, recall, specificity, and F-measure. This is done by calculating a confusion matrix for each user. Table 2 shows the results of the evaluations and Fig. 2 visualizes them.

The best recommenders for accuracy is the proposed framework, for precision is the proposed framework, for recall is binary cosine, for specificity are TF-IDF, Jaccard, and the proposed framework, and for F-measure is the proposed framework. The proposed algorithm scores well on accuracy as it makes relatively small amount of errors for both recommended food as well as discarded food items. For precision, the proposed algorithm scores the best for precision as most recommended food items

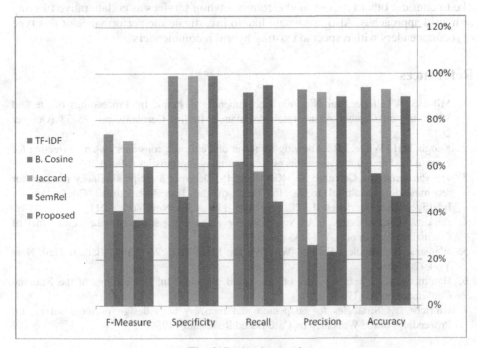

Fig. 2. Evaluation results

are relevant. The good results for recall obtained by the concept equivalence are due to the optimistic nature of the algorithm: any food item which involves previously viewed concepts is recommended. TF-IDF, Jaccard, and the proposed framework score well on specificity as these algorithms do not recommend most of the non-relevant food items.

4   Conclusion and Future Work

The framework can be used for building a personalized nutrition service. Based on a set of concepts, selected by the user, it is able to determine which items are relevant.

The knowledge base is a domain ontology consisting of classes, relationships and instances of classes. The knowledge base has initially been extracted from the United States Department of Agriculture (USDA) provided a comprehensive food database. Based on the performed evaluation, we conclude that semantic recommender systems in general outperform traditional recommenders systems with respect to accuracy, precision, and recall, and that the proposed recommender has a better F-measure than existing semantic recommenders.

In the future we plan to extend the querying language by defining its grammar, and applying it for extracting deep knowledge from food ontology. Another possible research direction relates to the advanced traditional weighting schemes that other than TF-IDF such as logarithmic TF functions [25]. Another research direction is the considered similarity function. We would like to evaluate alternatives for cosine similarity as Lnu.ltu [26] which seem to remove some of the cosine similarity bias favoring long documents over short documents. As additional further work we would like to consider other types of food recommendation services as collaborative filtering or hybrid approaches. Also, we would like to investigate the performance of this type of recommenders with respect to existing hybrid recommenders.

References

1. Mika, S.: Challenges for Nutrition Recommender Systems. In: Proceedings of the 2nd Workshop on Context Aware Intel. Assistance, Berlin, Germany, pp. 25–33 (October 2011)
2. Keogh, R.H., White, I.R.: Allowing for never and episodic consumers when correcting for error in food record measurements of dietary intake. Biostatistics (March 2011)
3. van Pinxteren, Y., Geleijnse, G., Kamsteeg, P.: Deriving a recipe similarity measure for recommending healthful meals. In: Proc. of the 16th International Conference on Intelligent User Interfaces, IUI 2011, pp. 105–114. ACM, New York (2011)
4. Becker, M.H., Maiman, L.A.: Strategies for enhancing patient compliance. Journal of Community Health 6(2), 113–135 (1980)
5. Wansink, B.: Mindless Eating—Why We Eat More Than We Think. Bantam-Dell, New York (2006)
6. Hammond, K.: Chef: A model of case-based planning. In: Proceedings of the National Conference on AI (1986)
7. Hinrichs, T.: Strategies for adaptation and recovery in a design problem solver. In: Proceedings of the Workshop on Case-Based Reasoning (1989)

8. Freyne, J., Berkovsky, S.: Intelligent food planning: personalized recipe recommendation. In: Proceedings of the 15th International Conference on Intelligent User Interfaces, IUI 2010, pp. 321–324. ACM, New York (2010)

9. Aberg, J.: Dealing with malnutrition: A meal planning system for elderly. In: AAAI, Spring Symposium on Argumentation for Consumers of Health Care (2006)

10. Mankoff, J., Hsieh, G., Hung, H.C., Nitao, E.: Using Low-Cost Sensing to Support Nutritional Awareness. In: Borriello, G., Holmquist, L.E. (eds.) UbiComp 2002. LNCS, vol. 2498, pp. 371–378. Springer, Heidelberg (2002)

11. Chi, P., Chen, J., Chu, H., Lo, J.: Enabling calorie-aware cooking in a smart kitchen. In: Proc. of the 3rd International Conference on Persuasive Technology, June 04-06 (2008)

12. Kitamura, K., de Silva, C., Yamasaki, T., Aizawa, K.: Image processing based approach to food balance analysis for personal food logging. In: 2010 IEEE International Conference on Multimedia and Expo (ICME), pp. 625–630 (July 2010)

13. Karg, G., Bognar, A., Ohmayer, G.: Nutrient content of composite food: a survey of methods. In: Proceedings of European Seminar of EOQC Food Section, Budapest, pp. 148–179 (1986)

14. Powers, P.M., Hoover, L.W.: Calculating the nutrient composition of recipes with computers. J. Am. Diet. Assoc. 89, 224–232 (1989)

15. Freyne, J., Berkovsky, S.: Intelligent food planning: personalized recipe recommendation. In: Proceedings of the 15th International Conference on Intelligent User Interfaces, IUI 2010, pp. 321–324. ACM, New York (2010)

16. Adomavicius, G., Tuzhilin, A.: Toward the Next Generation of Recommender Systems: A Survey of the State-of-the-Art and Possible Extensions. IEEE Transactions on Knowledge and Data Engineering 17(6), 734–749 (2005)

17. Salton, G., Buckley, C.: Term-Weighting Approaches in Automatic Text Retrieval. Information Processing and Management 24(5), 513–523 (1988)

18. IJntema, W., Goossen, F., Frasincar, F., Hogenboom, F.: Ontology-Based News Recommendation. In: EDBT/ICDT International Workshop on Business Intelligence and the Web (BEWEB 2010). ACM (2010)

19. Jaccard, P.: Étude Comparative de la Distribution Florale dans une Portion des Alpes et des Jura. Bulletin del la Société Vaudoise des Sciences Naturelles 37, 547–579 (1901)

20. Getahun, F., Tekli, J., Chbeir, R., Viviani, M., Yetongnon, K.: Relating RSS News/Items. In: Gaedke, M., Grossniklaus, M., Díaz, O. (eds.) ICWE 2009. LNCS, vol. 5648, pp. 442–452. Springer, Heidelberg (2009)

21. Bra, P.D., Aerts, A.T.M., Houben, G.J., Wu, H.: Making General-Purpose Adaptive Hypermedia Work. In: World Conference on the WWW and Internet (WebNet 2000), pp. 117–123 (2000)

22. Borsje, J., Levering, L., Frasincar, F.: Hermes: a Semantic Web-Based News Decision Support System. In: 23rd Annual ACM Symposium on Applied Computing, SAC 2008, pp. 2415–2420 (2008)

23. Bechhofer, S., van Harmelen, F., Hendler, J., Horrocks, I., McGuinness, D.L., Patel-Schneider, P.F., et al.: OWL Web Ontology Language Reference W3C Recommendation, February 10 (2004)

24. http://ndb.nal.usda.gov/ndb/foods/list (accessed July 24, 2012)

25. Buckley, C., Allan, J., Salton, G.: Automatic Routing and Retrieval Using Smart: TREC-2. Information Porcessing and Management 31(3), 315–326 (1995)

26. Singhal, A., Buckley, C., Mitra, M.: Pivoted Document Length Normalization. In: 19th Annual International ACM SIGIR Conference on Research and Development in Information Retrieval (SIGIR 1996), pp. 21–29. ACM (1996)

A Population Based Feature Subset Selection Algorithm Guided by Fuzzy Feature Dependency

Ahmed Al-Ani and Rami N. Khushaba

Faculty of Engineering and Information Technology, University of Technology,
Sydney, Ultimo NSW 2007 Australia
ahmed@eng.uts.edu.au, Rami.Khushaba@uts.edu.au

Abstract. Population-based (or evolutionary) algorithms have been attracting an increased attention due to their powerful search capabilities. For the particular problem of feature selection, population-based methods aim to produce better "or fitter" future generations that contain more informative subsets of features. It is well-known that feature subset selection is a very challenging optimization problem, especially when dealing with datasets that contain large number of features. Most of the commonly used population-based feature selection methods use operators that do not take into account relationships between features to generate future subsets, which can have an impact on their capabilities to properly explore the search space. We present here a new population-based feature selection method that utilize dependency between features to guide the search. In addition, a novel method for estimating dependency between feature pairs is proposed based on the concept of fuzzy entropy. Results obtained from datasets with various sizes indicate the superiority of the proposed method in comparison to some of the well-known methods in the literature.

1 Introduction

Most of the real-life classification problems are highly challenging, and hence, require informative feature sets to achieve the desired performance. The inclusion of irrelevant, noisy and redundant features may have a negative impact on the classification performance. Feature selection is usually employed to identify feature subsets that can achieve optimal performance for the considered classification task. The two most important components in feature selection are the evaluation measure and search strategy. Evaluation measures are used to estimate the goodness of subsets, while search strategies are needed to generate candidate subsets [1]. In this paper we will focus on the search strategy, while the classification performance will be adopted as the evaluation measure, i.e., a wrapper approach.

Many search strategy approaches have been proposed in the literature. The stochastic population-based (or evolutionary) search strategies have in particular attracted a lot of attention, where it has been found that including some randomness in the population search process makes it less sensitive to the dataset

A. Ell Hassanien et al. (Eds.): AMLTA 2012, CCIS 322, pp. 430–438, 2012.

[1], and hence helps avoid local minima. Some of the famous stochastic methods used in feature selection are: simulated annealing [2], Genetic Algorithm (GA) [3], Ant Colony Optimization (ACO) [4] and Particle Swarm Optimization (PSO) [5]. However, most of these methods do not utilize relationships between features in guiding the search. In some attempts, local search and evaluation have been included to enhance the performance of some evolutionary-based feature selection algorithms. For example, the hybrid genetic search algorithm (HGA) [6] uses embedded local search to fine tune the search implemented using GA. This modification proved to give good results when used on datasets with small number of features (less than 100) [6]. However, for larger datasets that consist of thousands of features, this method becomes impractical to run.

We have proposed in [7] a population-based search strategy that utilizes dependency between feature pairs to guide the search in the feature space. The method proved to produce better results than other population-based feature selection algorithms, however it has two main limitations: (i) the computational cost for estimating the mutual information between feature pairs can be quite high for large subsets, and (ii) the method requires the desired number of features to be specified, i.e., can only search for subsets of the same size. In this paper, we refine the algorithm and generalize it, such that the algorithm would itself search for the desired number of features and hence consider subsets of different sizes. Moreover, a new fuzzy feature dependency estimation is proposed to reduce the computational complexity of the algorithm.

The paper is organized as follows: the next section presents our new fuzzy-based feature dependency estimation approach. Section 3 describes the proposed search strategy. Experimental results are presented in section 4, and a conclusion is given in section 5.

2   Fuzzy Feature Dependency Estimation

The proposed dependency estimation is based on the concept of fuzzy entropy, that was first coined by De Luca and Termini [8]. Let $X = \{x_1, x_2, ..., x_n\}$ be a discrete random variable with a finite alphabet set containing n symbols, and let $\mu_A(x_k)$ be the membership degree of element x_k to fuzzy set A, and let F be a set to point mapping $F : G(2^X) \rightarrow [0, 1]$. F is considered as an entropy measure if it satisfies the following axioms [8]:

1. $F(A) = 0$ iff $A \in 2^x$, where A is a non-fuzzy set and 2^x indicates the power set of set A.
2. $F(A) = 1$ iff $\mu_A(x_k) = 0.5$ for all k,
3. $F(A) \leq F(B)$ if A is less fuzzy than B, i.e., if $\mu_A(x_k) \leq \mu_B(x_k)$ when $\mu_B(x_k) \leq 0.5$ and $\mu_A(x_k) \geq \mu_B(x_k)$ hen $\mu_B(x_k) \geq 0.5$.
4. $F(A) = F(A^c)$,

where $A^c = (1 - \mu_A(x_1), ..., 1 - \mu_A(x_n))$. One possible entropy measure that satisfies the above axioms is the well-known Shannon entropy which for a discrete random variable X with a probability mass function $p(x_k)$ is given as $H(X) = -\sum_k p(x_k)\log_2 p(x_k)$.

A new non probabilistic entropy measure is then introduced in the context of fuzzy memberships, i.e., by replacing $p(x_k)$ by $\mu(x_k)$. Various approaches for the membership estimation were proposed in the literature including the kNN approach, the fuzzy C-means clustering approach, and other simple fuzzy membership measures [9]. In order to simplify the computations, we used here the fuzzy membership measure from [9]. Denote the mean of the data samples that belongs to class i as $\overline{x}_i$ and the radius of the data as $r = \max \|\overline{x}_i - x_k\|_\sigma$.

Then the fuzzy membership μ_{ik}, denoting the membership value that the kth vector has in the ith class can be calculated as

$$\mu_{ik} = \left(\frac{\|\overline{x}_i - x_k\|_\sigma}{r + \epsilon} \right)^{\frac{-2}{m-1}} \tag{1}$$

where m is the fuzzification parameter, and $\epsilon > 0$ is a small value to avoid singularity, and σ is the standard deviation involved in the distance computation. Using the proposed membership function in Eq. 1, we construct c-fuzzy sets along each specific feature f, each of these will in turn reflect the membership degree of the samples in each of the c problem classes. Denote the membership of all of the samples along the first feature f_1 in each of the c-fuzzy sets as A (with a size of $c \times n$). The fuzzy equivalent to the marginal probability density of all of the training patterns along each feature f in the c-sets is then given as

$$P(f) = \frac{\sqrt{AA'}}{n} \tag{2}$$

where n is the total number of patterns. The above approach employs a fuzzy approximation to the concept of histograms utilized usually in mutual information estimation. In simple words, rather than assigning each of samples to one of the bins of a histogram, we define a membership degree for that sample in each of the c-fuzzy sets. Then the marginal probability is simply defined by the summation of the memberships in each of the c-fuzzy sets. Then the fuzzy marginal entropy along each single feature f is found by

$$H(f) = -\sum \sum P(f) \log P(f) \tag{3}$$

where the logarithmic operator is applied element-wise and the two summations account for the sum across the columns and rows.

In order to compute the joint entropy of two features, say $H(f_1, f_2)$, we refer back to Eq. 1 again. Denote the membership of all of the samples along the first feature f_1 in each of the c-fuzzy sets again as A (with a size of $c \times n$), and similarly the membership of all of the samples along the second feature in the corresponding c-fuzzy sets along that feature as B (with a size of $c \times n$). Then the joint entropy $H(f_1, f_2)$ can be calculated as

$$H(f_1, f_2) = -\sum \sum (\frac{\sqrt{AB'}}{n}) \log(\frac{\sqrt{AB'}}{n}) \tag{4}$$

After computing the joint entropy $H(f_1, f_2)$, the mutual information between the two features f_1 and f_2 can be computed as

$$I(f_1; f_2) = H(f_1) + H(f_2) - H(f_1, f_2) \tag{5}$$

A Matlab code implementation was made available for the reader to simplify the understanding of the proposed fuzzy entropy and mutual information measures[1].

3   The Proposed Search Strategy

The proposed search strategy, which is termed as DSS (Dependency-based Search Strategy), is implemented as shown in Fig. 1. The detailed implementation steps are as follows:

1. Randomly initialize subsets of the first generation such that they have different sizes, sz_i, that are bounded by upper and lower limits. Sort the subsets according to their fitness values to identify the K best subsets
2. For each subset, S_i, of the current generation
   - Make a copy of S_i, which will be denoted as S_i'
   - Randomly choose one of the K best subsets, S_k
   - Set the size of the newly generated subset $sz_i' = round((sz_k + sz_i)/2 \pm rand() \times M)$, where M is an integer that enables generating subsets of slightly different sizes. Let $d = sz_i - sz_i'$. If $d > 0$, then d features need to be removed. If $d < 0$, then we need to add d features. On the other hand, there is no change in the subset size when $d == 0$.
   - When removing features from a subset, randomly take out d features after ensuring that the subset does not contain highly dependent features.
   - When adding features to a subset, form a vector by concatenating features of the best K subsets. Remove from it duplicated features and one of each two highly dependent ones. Randomly add d features of the vector given that each one of them is not highly dependent on any of the existing features of S_i'. If there are no enough features in the vector, then randomly select the remaining features from the original feature set, given that they are not highly dependent on the existing features of S_i'.
   - Feature f_{ij}' of S_i' can be replaced by: (i) one of the F features, (ii) f_{kl}, which is one of the S_k features, (iii) one of the F features that surrounds f_{kl} in terms of dependency. Each of the three alternatives is assigned a certain probability. Only features that are not highly dependent on other features of S_i' are considered to be potential replacement features. If non of the three alternatives is executed, then f_{ij}' will not be replaced. The maximum number of features that can be replaced is $\min(sz_k, sz_i)$.
   - Evaluate the newly formed subset S_i'. If the fitness of S_i' is better than that of S_i, then replace S_i with S_i'. Otherwise, keep S_i unchanged.
3. Re-identify the K best subsets.
4. Continue till the termination criterion is met.

---

[1] http://www.mathworks.com/matlabcentral/fileexchange/31888-fuzzy-entropy-and-mutual-information

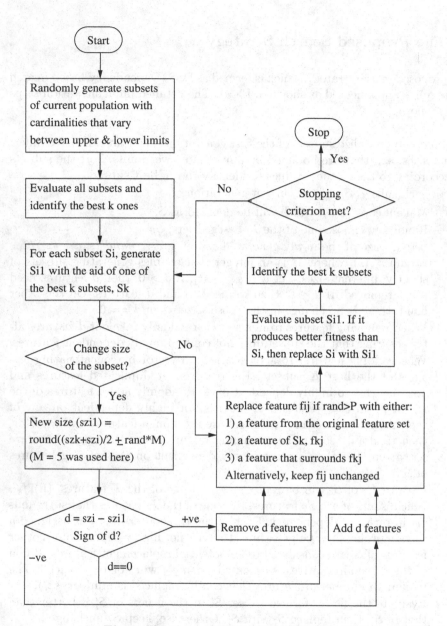

Fig. 1. Flowchart of the proposed DSS algorithm

The rationale behind considering the third replacement alternative is because we can not presume that f_{kl} is the absolutely best feature when combined with other features of S'_i. However, instead of randomly choosing any feature from the original feature set $\mathcal{F}$, it is more logical to consider features located in the space that surrounds f_{kl}. The first replacement alternative has still been considered to allow the algorithm considering features that have not been considered yet.

4   Experimental Results

Four classification datasets are used to compare the performance of the proposed DSS algorithm with that of GA- and PSO-based feature selection. The considered datasets contain different number of features, classes and samples, as shown in table 1.

Table 1. Description of the datasets employed

Dataset	# Features	# Classes	# Samples
EEG	168	2	406
Madelon	500	2	2600
9Tumors	5726	9	60
BrainTumor1	5920	5	90

An enhanced variant of GA that attempts to increase diversity between population members to avoid local minima was adopted here [10]. It is implemented using binary strings with probability of crossover $= 0.8$, and probability of mutation $= 0.05$. Feature selection using PSO was implemented using binary strings as well. It uses particles' best and global best values to guide the search. The proposed DSS is implemented as explained in the previous section. A reasonable value of K is found to be around 10% of the population size. Probabilities for the three alternatives to replace feature f'_{ij} are assigned the values of 0.03, 0.3 and 0.3 respectively. As alternative one is not expected to have major influence on the slection of informative features, it hence has been assigned a low probability. If non of the three replacements have been implemented, then f'_{ij} would remain unchanged. In order to identify the optimal subset size, the algorithm does not change the size of each subset of the population in the first 30% of the total number of iterations. For the remaining iterations, changes in subset sizes are implemented as explained in the previous section.

For all experiments described below, a population size of 50 was used by the three feature selection methods. In addition, all of the three methods have the same stopping criterion, which is reaching a pre-defined maximum number of iterations.

Figure 2(a) shows the averaged classification accuracy (over 20 runs) obtained using an LDA classifier versus number of iterations for the three feature selection methods when applied to the EEG dataset. One can notice that GA converged faster than DSS and PSO, however, it made very minimal improvement after the first 100 iterations. On the other hand, the performance of both DSS and PSO continued to improve despite of their relatively slow start. By the end of the 600 iterations, PSO almost achieved the same performance of GA, however, the performance of DSS was noticeably better than both GA and PSO. The final classification accuracies achieved by the three methods, which are shown in Figure 2(b), indicate that PSO had quite a high fluctuation in performance, while DSS achieving better and relatively more consistent performance than both GA and PSO.

The three algorithms selected subsets of different sizes, which were on average 37, 30 and 58 for DSS, GA and PSO respectively. As mentioned earlier, DSS does not change subset sizes in the first 180 iterations (30% of the total number of iterations), rather it attempts to enhance the performance of each subset while maintaining its size. Subset sizes are allowed to change afterwads. Because of this, DSS maintained larger subset size variability. This enabled DSS to explore more space and helped in avoiding local minima.

For the madelon dataset, which contains 500 features, classification accuracy obtained using a kNN classifier was used to evaluate candidate subsets. The three feature selection methods were used to search for the optimal subset and the maximum number of iterations was set to 300. The averaged classification accuracies (over 10 runs) for the best subset found in each iteration are shown in Figure 2(c). Despite its slow start, DSS managed to outperform GA and PSO after the first 100 iterations, while GA outperformed PSO after the first 40 iterations. The slow start of DSS can be justified by not allowing subset sizes to change in the first 90 iterations. It is also important to mention that the GA algorithm was altered by assigning noticeably higher weights to smaller subsets than big ones. Without doing so, GA was not able to converge close to the optimal subset size.

Accuracies of the final selected subsets by the three methods are shown in Figure 2(d). The figure indicates that DSS had a better and more consistent performance, followed by GA and finally PSO.

The classification for both 9-Tumors and Brain-Tumor1 was implemented using a 10-fold cross validation approach due to the limited number of samples. A linear SVM classifier was used for both datasets. Due to the large number of features in both datasets, an upper subset size of 250 for the initial population was enforced. For the 9-Tumor dataset, accuracies of best feature subsets achieved by the three feature selection methods in each iteration (averaged over 10 runs) are shown in Figure 2(e). Results indicate that DSS achieved "perfect" performance for this dataset. The performance of GA was noticeably better than PSO, but not as goos as that of DSS. For the Brain-Tumor1 dataset, DSS had a slow start, but it outperformed GA after 300 iterations, as shown in Figure2(g). The performance of PSO was not as competitive, which indicates that PSO could not handle very well the search for optimal subsets in datasets containing large number of features.

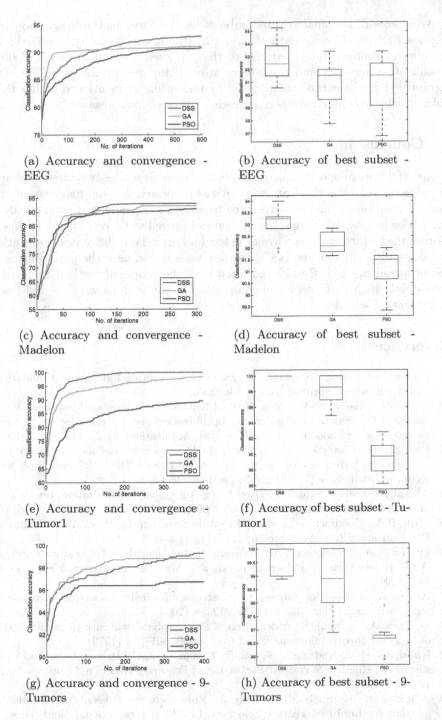

(a) Accuracy and convergence - EEG

(b) Accuracy of best subset - EEG

(c) Accuracy and convergence - Madelon

(d) Accuracy of best subset - Madelon

(e) Accuracy and convergence - Tumor1

(f) Accuracy of best subset - Tumor1

(g) Accuracy and convergence - 9-Tumors

(h) Accuracy of best subset - 9-Tumors

Fig. 2. Accuracy of DSS, GA and PSO for the EEG, Madelon, Tumor1 and 9-Tumors datasets

Accuracies of the final selected subsets by the three methods are shown in Figures 2(f) (the 9-Tumor dataset) and 2(h) (the Brain-Tumor1 dataset). Those two figures confirm the superiority of the proposed method in terms of both classification accuracy and consistency when compared to GA and PSO. The second best performance was achieved by GA, while as mentioned earlier PSO did not achieve competitive performance for those two datasets.

5   Conclusion

A powerful feature selection algorithm that utilizes dependency between features to guide the search in the feature space was proposed. A novel fuzzy-based mutual information method was presented to estimate dependency between feature pairs. The proposed feature selection method proved to be very successful in exploring the feature space and avoiding local minima. Four different classification problems with different dataset sizes were used to evaluate the performance of the proposed method. Results indicated that the proposed method achieved a consistently high performance in comparison to the well-known GA- and PSO-based feature selection.

References

1. Guyon, I., Gunn, S., Nikravesh, M., Zadeh, L.A.: Feature Extraction: Foundations and Applications. Springer, New York (2006)
2. Lin, S.-W., Tseng, T.-Y., Chou, S.-Y., Chen, S.-C.: A simulated-annealing-based approach for simultaneous parameter optimization and feature selection of back-propagation networks. Expert Systems with Applications 34(2), 1491–1499 (2008)
3. Frohlich, H., Chapelle, O., Scholkopf, B.: Feature Selection for Support Vector Machines by Means of Genetic Algorithms. In: Proc. IEEE Intl. Conf. Tools with Artificial Intelligence (ICTAI 2003), pp. 142–148 (2003)
4. Al-Ani, A.: Feature Subset Selection Using Ant Colony Optimization. Int. Journal of Computational Intelligence 2, 53–58 (2005)
5. Firpi, H.A., Goodman, E.: Swarmed Feature Selection. In: Proc. Applied Imagery Pattern Recognition Workshop, pp. 112–118 (2004)
6. Oh, I.S., Lee, J.S., Moon, B.R.: Hybrid Genetic Algorithms for Feature Selection. IEEE Transactions on Pattern Analysis and Machine Intelligence 26(11), 1424–1437 (2004)
7. Al-Ani, A.: A dependency-based search strategy for feature selection. Expert Systems with Applications 36(10), 12392–12398 (2009)
8. De Luca, A., Termini, S.: A definition of a nonprobabilistic entropy in the setting of fuzzy set theory. Information and Control 20, 301–312 (1972)
9. Khushaba, R.N., Kodagoda, S., Lal, S., Dissanayake, G.: Driver Drowsiness Classification Using Fuzzy Wavelet-Packet-Based Feature-Extraction Algorithm 58(1), 121–131 (2011)
10. AlSukker, A., Khushaba, R., Al-Ani, A.: Enhancing the Diversity of Genetic Algorithm for Improved Feature Selection. In: IEEE International Conference on Systems, Man, and Cybernetics, SMC 2010 (2010)

Adapting Voting Techniques for Online Forum Thread Retrieval

Ameer Tawfik Albaham and Naomie Salim

Faculty of Computer Science and Information Systems,
Universiti Teknologi Malaysia, Skudai, Johor, Malaysia
ameer.tawfik@gmail.com, naomie@utm.my

Abstract. Online forums or message boards are rich knowledge-based communities. In these communities, thread retrieval is an essential tool facilitating information access. However, the issue on thread search is how to combine evidences from text units(messages) to estimate thread relevance. In this paper, we first rank a list of messages, then score threads by aggregating their ranked messages' scores. To aggregate the message scores, we adopt several voting techniques that have been applied in ranking aggregates tasks such as blog distillation and expert finding. The experimental result shows that many voting techniques should be preferred over a baseline that treats threads as a concatenation of their messages' text.

Keywords: Forum thread search, Ranking aggregates, Voting techniques.

1 Introduction

Online forums are virtual places(communities) that facilitate seeking and sharing knowledge through in depth discussions. A user starts a discussion through posting an initial message, then other users read the initial message and answer it through reply messages. The initial message and its replies form a threaded discussion(thread).

One challenge in accessing information in forums is information overload. Thread retrieval is one way to tackle it. However, the actual contents are not the threads but the messages. Therefore, given a query, a retrieval system must infer the thread relevance using the message text. In that aspect, thread retrieval resembles ranking aggregates tasks such as blog feed retrieval[14,4,6] and expert finding[7]. In these tasks, given a query, the objective is to rank aggregates(blogs, experts) by leveraging associated text units(blogs' postings, experts' writings)[8]. An analogy between ranking aggregates and thread retrieval is that threads are the aggregates, and messages are the associated texts or documents.

Voting techniques performed well in ranking aggregates tasks [7,6,8]. However, the effectiveness of each voting technique varies between tasks and datasets [8]. In addition to that, threads have a conversational structure that does not exist in other ranking aggregates contexts. In threads, the meaning of a message is

A. Ell Hassanien et al. (Eds.): AMLTA 2012, CCIS 322, pp. 439–448, 2012.

fully understood within its discussion context. Furthermore, messages are mostly replies, hence they tend to be shorter than blogs' postings and experts' writings. In other words, that might alter the performance of voting techniques. In this paper, we review several voting methods and investigate their performance on thread retrieval.

2   Voting in Thread Retrieval

Voting techniques were first proposed by [7] to the expert finding task. In voting techniques, we first rank a list of documents(e.g. expert's writings) based on their relevance to the given query. Then, we rank aggregates(e.g. the experts) based on their scores obtained from fusing their ranked documents' scores or ranks. Similarly, in this work, given a query $Q = \{q_1, q_2, ..., q_n\}$, we first rank a list of messages R_Q with respect to Q. Then, we score threads by aggregating their ranked messages' scores or ranks. In addition, threads are ranked based on their aggregated scores in a descending order.

In estimating the relevance between the query Q and a message M, we employ the query language model[12] assuming term independence, uniform probability distribution for M and Dirichlet smoothing as follows[17]:

$$P(Q|M) = \prod_{q \in Q} \left(\frac{n(q, M) + \mu P(q|C)}{|M| + \mu} \right)^{n(q,Q)} \tag{1}$$

where q is a query term, μ is the smoothing parameter. $n(q, M)$ and $n(q, Q)$ are the term frequencies of q in M and Q respectively, $|M|$ is the number of tokens in M and $P(q|C)$ is the collection language model. The outputs of $P(Q|M)$ and $P(Q|C)$ are probabilistic values.

To rank threads, the twelve aggregation methods proposed by [7] are adapted: Votes, Reciprocal Rank(RR), BordaFuse, CombMIN, CombMAX, CombMED, CombSUM, CombANZ, CombMNZ, expCombSUM, expCombANZ and exp-CombMNZ. In addition to these methods, this study uses CombGNZ— the geometric mean of the relevance scores. We use this method because it is the aggregation method employed by [5,13].

In these methods, the relevance between a thread T and Q, $rel(T, Q)$, is the score obtained through the aggregation of all T's ranked messages R_T as shown below:

$$rel_{\text{Votes}}(Q, T) = |R_T| \tag{2}$$

$$rel_{\text{RR}}(Q, T) = \sum_{M \in R_T} \frac{1}{rank(Q, M)} \tag{3}$$

$$rel_{\text{BordaFuse}}(Q, T) = \sum_{M \in R_T} |R_Q| - rank(Q, M) \tag{4}$$

$$rel_{\text{CombMIN}}(Q, T) = MIN_{M \in R_T} P(Q|M) \tag{5}$$

$$rel_{\text{CombMAX}}(Q,T) = MAX_{M \in R_T} P(Q|M) \tag{6}$$

$$rel_{\text{CombMED}}(Q,T) = Median_{M \in R_T} P(Q|M) \tag{7}$$

$$rel_{\text{CombSUM}}(Q,T) = \sum_{M \in R_T} P(Q|M) \tag{8}$$

$$rel_{\text{CombANZ}}(Q,T) = \frac{1}{|R_T|} \times \sum_{M \in R_T} P(Q|M) \tag{9}$$

$$rel_{\text{CombGNZ}}(Q,T) = \left(\prod_{M \in R_T} P(Q|M) \right)^{\frac{1}{|R_T|}} \tag{10}$$

$$rel_{\text{CombMNZ}}(Q,T) = |R_T| \times \sum_{M \in R_T} P(Q|M) \tag{11}$$

$$rel_{\text{expCombSUM}}(Q,T) = \sum_{M \in R_T} \exp(P(Q|M)) \tag{12}$$

$$rel_{\text{expCombANZ}}(Q,T) = \frac{1}{|R_T|} \times \sum_{M \in R_T} \exp(P(Q|M)) \tag{13}$$

$$rel_{\text{expCombMNZ}}(Q,T) = |R_T| \times \sum_{M \in R_T} \exp(P(Q|M)) \tag{14}$$

where $rank(Q,M)$ is the rank of the message M in R_Q, $|R_Q|$ is the size of R_Q, and $|R_T|$ is the number of T's ranked messages.

As an illustrative example, let $R_Q = \{M_1, M_2, M_3, M_4, M_5, M_6\}$ denote a list of ranked messages, where there are 3 threads associated with these messages T_1, T_2 and T_3; and, M_1 belongs to T_1; also, M_2 and M_3 belong to T_2; lastly, M_4, M_5 and M_6 belong to T_3. In addition, let the relevance scores between the user query and these messages assigned by query language relevance model to be 0.06, 0.05, 0.04, 0.03, 0.02 and 0.01 respectively, whereas the ranks of these messages are 1,2,3,4,5 and 6 respectively. Then, we calculate the relevance between the given query Q and the thread T_3 using the Votes, CombSUM and BordaFuse aggregation methods as follows: $rel_{\text{Votes}}(Q, T_3) = |R_{T_3}| = 3$, $rel_{\text{CombSUM}}(Q, T_3) = P(Q|M_4) + P(Q|M_5) + P(Q|M_6) = 0.03 + 0.02 + 0.01 = 0.06$, $rel_{\text{BordaFuse}}(Q, T_3) = 6 - rank(Q, M_4) + 6 - rank(Q, M_5) + 6 - rank(Q, M_6) = 2 + 1 + 0 = 16$.

3 Related Studies

The voting techniques approach to the ranking aggregates tasks are inspired by works on data fusion(meta search)[15,11,1]. A meta search algorithm aims to combine several ranked lists of documents into a unified list [1]. These ranked lists are generated by various retrieval methods. The essences of the data fusion are two folds[16]. First, the more retrieval methods retrieve a particular document, the more the document is expected to be relevant to the user query. Second, a document that is ranked at top ranking positions by many retrieval methods might be more relevant than a one that was found at the bottom of several ranked lists. Data fusion methods can be categorized into score based and rank based aggregation methods. The score based methods — such as [15]'s CombMAX, CombMIN, CombMED and CombSUM methods, use the relevance scores of documents, whereas the rank based methods, [1], utilize the ranking positions of these documents on the ranked lists.

[7,6] approached the problem of ranking aggregates as a data fusion problem: each document is an evidence about its parent aggregate's relevance to the query. Generally, the the voting approach was found to be statistically superior to baseline methods [7,6]. However, the performance of each voting technique was not consistent across tasks[8]: the CombMAX method, which performed well on the expert finding setting, was significantly worse than the baseline methods on the blog distillation setting[6]. Therefore, how will these methods perform on the thread retrieval task is the focus of this study.

Several combination techniques have been proposed to address evidences combination for thread retrieval. [5] proposed two strategies to rank threads: inclusive and selective. The inclusive strategy utilizes evidences from all messages in order to rank parent threads. Two models from previous work on blog site retrieval [4] were adapted to thread search: the large document and the small document models. The large document model creates a virtual document for each thread by concatenating the thread's message texts, then it scores threads based on their virtual document relevance to the query. In contrast, the small document model defines a thread as a collection of text units (messages). Then, it scores threads by adding up their messages' relevance scores. In contrast to the inclusive strategy, [5]'s selective strategy treats threads as a collection of messages; and it uses only few messages to rank threads. Three selective methods were used. The first one is scoring threads using only the initial message relevance score. The second method scores threads by taking the maximum score of their message relevance scores. The third method is based on the Pseudo Cluster Selection(PCS) method[14]. PCS scores threads in two steps: it scores a list of messages, then it ranks threads by taking the geometric mean of the top k ranked messages' scores from each thread. Generally, it was found that the selective models are statistically superior to the inclusive models[5,3]. Our work extends this selective strategy by investigating more aggregation methods. In addition, PCS focuses on the top k ranked messages, whereas we focus on all ranked messages. Applying voting techniques as aggregation methods in PCS is an interesting problem, but we leave it for a separate study.

Another line of research is the multiple context retrieval approach proposed by [13]. This approach treats a thread as a collection of several local contexts— types of self-contained text units. Four contexts were proposed: posts— identical to messages, pairs, dialogues and the entire thread. The thread and post contexts are identical to [5]'s virtual document and message based representations. In the pair and the dialogue contexts, the conversational relationship between messages is exploited to build text units. In the pair context, for each pair of messages m_i, m_j that have a reply relationship— m_j is a reply to m_i, a text unit is built by concatenating their texts. In the dialogue context, for each chain of replies that starts by the initial message; and, there is a reply relation between each message and its neighbour in the chain, a text unit is built by concatenating the chain's message texts. To rank threads using the post, pair and dialogue contexts, PCS was used. It was observed that the retrieval using the dialogue context outperformed retrieval using other contexts. Additionally, the weighted product between the thread and the dialogue contexts achieved the best performance. In our work, we are focusing on how to combine the ranked contexts' relevance scores. Therefore, our work is complementary to [13]'s work.

The third line of work is the structure based document retrieval proposed by[2]. In this approach, a thread consists of a collection of structural components: the title, the initial message and the reply messages set. In this representation, the thread relevance to the user query is estimated using [10]'s inference network framework. Our work can be applied to [2]'s representation as well. We could use [2]'s inference based relevance score the same way the thread context score was used in [13].

4 Experimental Design

Thread retrieval is a new task and the number of test collections is limited. In this study, we used the same corpus used by [2]. It has two datasets from two forums— Ubuntu[1] and Travel[2] forums. The statistics of the corpus is given in Table 1. Text was stemmed with the Porter stemmer, and stopword removal was applied at the ranking stage. In conducting the experiments, we used the Indri retrieval system[3].

Table 1. Statistics of test collection

	Ubuntu	Travel
No of threads	113277	83072
No of users	103280	39454
No of messages	676777	590021
No of queries	25	25
No of judged threads	4512	4478

As for evaluation, we use [5]'s virtual document model VD as a baseline. This model has been used as a strong baseline in previous studies [5,13,2]. For each query, we calculated the standard used measures on Ad Hoc retrieval [9]: Precision at 10 (P@10), Normalized Discounted Cumulative Gain at 10 (NDCG@10),

---

[1] ubuntuforums.org

[2] http://www.tripadvisor.com/ShowForum-g28953-i4-New York.html

[3] http://www.lemurproject.org/indri.php

Mean Reciprocal Rank(MRR) and Mean Average Precision (MAP). In all experiments, we used the same relevance protocol followed in [2,13], a thread is considered as relevant if its relevance level is greater or equal to 1— if it is partially or highly relevant; and, it is irrelevant if the relevance level is zero.

As for parameter estimation, we estimated the smoothing parameters, μ, for the virtual document and message language models. In addition, for all voting techniques, we estimated the size of the initial ranked list of messages R_Q. To estimate μ, we varied its value from 500 up to 4000; adding 500 in each run. To estimate the size of R_Q, we varied its value from 500 up to 5000 adding 500 in each run. Then, an exhaustive grid search was applied to maximize MAP using 5-fold cross validation.

5   Result and Discussion

Table 2 and Table 3 present the retrieval performance of voting methods on thread retrieval for the Ubuntu dataset and the Travel dataset respectively. Several observations can be found from the data shown in these tables. The first observation is the performance of the aggregation methods as compared to the "baseline method"— the virtual document(VD) model. In high precision measures (P@10 and NDCG@10), RR, BordaFuse, CombSUM, CombMNZ, expCombSUM, expCombSUM and expCombMNZ are able to produce better or comparable result with respect to VD. These methods favour threads with highly ranked messages. In contrast, CombGNZ, CombMED, CombANZ, CombMIN

Table 2. Retrieval performance of voting methods on the Ubuntu dataset

Method	MAP	MRR	P@10	NDCG@10
VD	0.3437	0.7258	0.4200	0.3284
CombGNZ	$0.2272^\triangledown$	$0.4974^\blacktriangledown$	$0.2760^\triangledown$	$0.1971^\triangledown$
Votes	$0.2749^\triangledown$	0.6550	0.4680	0.3551
RR	0.3313	0.6287	$0.4600^\blacktriangle$	0.3428
Bordafuse	0.3153	0.6913	0.5080	0.3778
CombMIN	$0.1779^\triangledown$	$0.5000^\blacktriangledown$	$0.2600^\triangledown$	$0.1849^\triangledown$
CombMAX	$0.3074^\triangledown$	0.6420	0.4480	0.3257
CombMED	$0.2212^\triangledown$	$0.5021^\blacktriangledown$	$0.2760^\triangledown$	$0.1927^\triangledown$
CombSUM	0.3100	0.6667	0.4720	0.3633
CombANZ	$0.2314^\triangledown$	$0.4971^\blacktriangledown$	$0.2800^\triangledown$	$0.1991^\triangledown$
CombMNZ	0.3108	0.6933	0.4880	0.3720
expCombSUM	0.3088	0.6933	0.4840	0.3676
expCombANZ	$0.2315^\triangledown$	$0.4971^\blacktriangledown$	$0.2800^{\ \triangledown}$	$0.1991^\triangledown$
expCombMNZ	0.3088	0.6933	0.4840	0.3676

The symbols $\triangle$ and $\blacktriangle$ denote statistically significant improvements over the virtual document model (VD) at p-value < 0.01 and 0.05 respectively using paired randomization test. Similarly, $\triangledown$ and $\blacktriangledown$ denote statistically significant degradations over (VD) at p-value < 0.01 and 0.05 respectively.

Table 3. Retrieval performance of voting methods on the Travel dataset

Method	MAP	MRR	P@10	NDCG@10
VD	0.3774	0.6967	0.4800	0.3549
CombGNZ	$0.2001^\triangledown$	$0.4838^\blacktriangledown$	$0.3320^\triangledown$	$0.2319^\triangledown$
Votes	$0.3066^\triangledown$	0.7491	0.5080	0.4063
RR	$0.3155^\triangledown$	0.6120	0.4520	0.3431
BordaFuse	0.3630	0.7547	0.5640	0.4350
CombMIN	$0.1574^\triangledown$	$0.4843^\blacktriangledown$	$0.3040^\triangledown$	$0.2199^\triangledown$
CombMAX	$0.2724^\triangledown$	0.5754	0.4360	0.3216
CombMED	$0.2004^\triangledown$	$0.4841^\blacktriangledown$	$0.3480^\triangledown$	$0.2388^\triangledown$
CombSUM	0.3668	0.8000	0.5560	$0.4440^\blacktriangle$
CombANZ	$0.2065^\triangledown$	$0.4841^\blacktriangledown$	$0.3400^\triangledown$	$0.2346^\triangledown$
CombMNZ	0.3575	0.7790	0.5280	0.4205
expCombSUM	0.3513	0.7937	0.5200	0.4109
expCombANZ	$0.2065^\triangledown$	$0.4841^\blacktriangledown$	$0.3400^\triangledown$	$0.2346^\triangledown$
expCombMNZ	0.3513	0.7937	0.5200	0.4109

The symbols $^\triangle$ and $^\blacktriangle$ denote statistically significant improvements over the virtual document model (VD) at p-value < 0.01 and 0.05 respectively using paired randomization test. Similarly, $^\triangledown$ and $^\blacktriangledown$ denote statistically significant degradations over (VD) at p-value < 0.01 and 0.05 respectively.

and expCombANZ might be effected by threads that have a lot of low scored messages. This behaviour was also reported in applying voting techniques to expert finding[6]. Therefore, based on [7]'s conclusion, we assert that highly ranked messages are good indicators of relevant threads.

To confirm this conclusion, the effects of varying the size of the initial ranked list was studied. As Figure 1 and Figure 2 show, the retrieval performance decreases as the size gets relatively big (more than 1000). In addition, one can see that almost all methods suffer from this problem except RR and CombMAX. This is expected because RR and CombMAX address the problem of low scored messages inherently. RR adds up the inverse of the messages' ranks, thus it penalizes threads with a lot of low ranked messages. In the case of CombMAX, it takes only the best scoring message; therefore, if no threads are introduced as the size increases, the order of threads will not change. That explains the convergence of CombMAX and RR and the consistent decrement of the other methods. This was replicated with other measures such as P@10 and NDCG@10(Not shown in this paper) as well. This indicates the importance of highly ranked messages to thread retrieval.

Another observation is the importance of utilizing non score signals. For instance, the Votes method's performance is relatively good as compare to other methods. Similarly, CombMNZ ,which makes use of the number of ranked messages in addition to sum of scores, has similar performance as well. All of these methods leverage information that is not coming from scores: the number of ranked messages. Nevertheless, exhaustive emphasis on these signals will hurt the

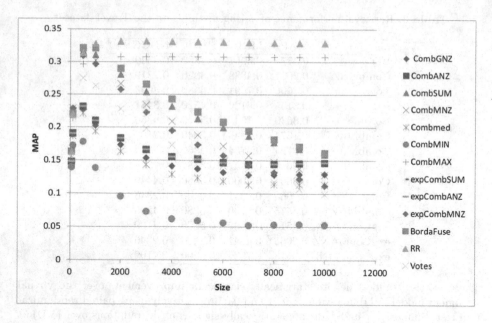

Fig. 1. The performance of aggregation methods as the size of the initial ranked list increases on the Ubuntu dataset

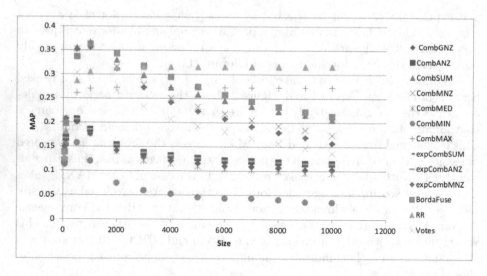

Fig. 2. The performance of aggregation methods as the size of the initial ranked list increases on the Travel dataset

performance. One could see that from fast decrement of Votes and CombMNZ methods as size increases. One possible reason is that adding up low scores has less impact than multiplying by the number of these messages; CombSUM's decrement is always less than those of the Votes and CombMNZ methods.

Although the voting methods improvements are not statistically significant, they are consistent on both datasets and require only using the message index. That gives the voting approach an extra advantage over the virtual document model because it coincides with what users contribute, hence it frees the retrieval system from re-concatenating messages into a virtual document whenever a new message is created or edited.

6   Conclusion

In this paper, we studied applying voting techniques to online forums thread retrieval. We used thirteen voting methods that aggregate ranked messages scores or ranks in order to score the parent threads. The experimental result shows that voting techniques—RR, BordaFuse, CombSUM, CombMNZ, expCombSUM, ex-pCombSUM and expCombMNZ, that favour threads with highly ranked messages produced comparable or better performance as compare to baselines; and, none of them is a winning method. Although the observed improvements were not statistically significant, we recommend using voting methods because their improvements are consistent across datasets, and they coincide with what user contributes.

Nevertheless, this experiment has motivated us to further study the effects of voting techniques when aggregating only the top k messages. Another future direction is incorporating these voting methods into [13]'s multiple context models. Similar approach will be applied to incorporate the structural component representation of [2].

Acknowledgements. This work is supported by Ministry of Higher Education (MOHE) and Research Management Centre (RMC) at the Universiti Teknologi Malaysia (UTM) under Research University Grant Category (VOT Q. J130000. 7128. 00H72).

References

1. Aslam, J.A., Montague, M.: Models for metasearch. In: Proceedings of the 24th Annual International ACM SIGIR Conference on Research and Development in Information Retrieval, SIGIR 2001, pp. 276–284. ACM, New York (2001)
2. Bhatia, S., Mitra, P.: Adopting inference networks for online thread retrieval. In: Proceedings of the Twenty-Fourth AAAI Conference on Artificial Intelligence, Atlanta, Georgia, USA, July 11-15, pp. 1300–1305 (2010)
3. Elsas, J.L.: Ancestry.com online forum test collection. Technical Report CMU-LTI-017, Language Technologies Institute, School of Computer Science, Carnegie Mellon University (2011)
4. Elsas, J.L., Arguello, J., Callan, J., Carbonell, J.G.: Retrieval and feedback models for blog feed search. In: Proceedings of the 31st Annual International ACM SIGIR Conference on Research and Development in Information Retrieval, SIGIR 2008, pp. 347–354. ACM, New York (2008)

5. Elsas, J.L., Carbonell, J.G.: It pays to be picky: an evaluation of thread retrieval in online forums. In: Proceedings of the 32nd International ACM SIGIR Conference on Research and Development in Information Retrieval, SIGIR 2009, pp. 714–715. ACM, New York (2009)
6. Macdonald, C., Ounis, I.: Key blog distillation: ranking aggregates. In: Proceedings of the 17th ACM Conference on Information and Knowledge Management, CIKM 2008, pp. 1043–1052. ACM, New York (2008)
7. Macdonald, C., Ounis, I.: Voting techniques for expert search. Knowl. Inf. Syst. 16(3), 259–280 (2008)
8. Macdonald, C., Ounis, I.: Learning Models for Ranking Aggregates. In: Clough, P., Foley, C., Gurrin, C., Jones, G.J.F., Kraaij, W., Lee, H., Mudoch, V. (eds.) ECIR 2011. LNCS, vol. 6611, pp. 517–529. Springer, Heidelberg (2011)
9. Mark, S.: Test collection based evaluation of information retrieval systems. Foundations and Trends in Information Retrieval 4, 247–375 (2010)
10. Metzler, D., Croft, W.B.: Combining the language model and inference network approaches to retrieval. Inf. Process. Manage. 40(5), 735–750 (2004)
11. Ogilvie, P., Callan, J.: Combining document representations for known-item search. In: Proceedings of the 26th Annual International ACM SIGIR Conference on Research and Development in Informaion Retrieval, SIGIR 2003, pp. 143–150. ACM, New York (2003)
12. Ponte, J.M., Croft, W.B.: A language modeling approach to information retrieval. In: Proceedings of the 21st Annual International ACM SIGIR Conference on Research and Development in Information Retrieval, SIGIR 1998, pp. 275–281. ACM, New York (1998)
13. Seo, J., Bruce Croft, W., Smith, D.: Online community search using conversational structures. Information Retrieval 14, 547–571 (2011), 10.1007/s10791-011-9166-8
14. Seo, J., Croft, W.B.: Blog site search using resource selection. In: Proceedings of the 17th ACM Conference on Information and Knowledge Management, CIKM 2008, pp. 1053–1062. ACM, New York (2008)
15. Shaw, J.A., Fox, E.A., Shaw, J.A., Fox, E.A.: Combination of multiple searches. In: The Second Text REtrieval Conference (TREC-2), pp. 243–252 (1994)
16. Spoerri, A.: Authority and ranking effects in data fusion. J. Am. Soc. Inf. Sci. Technol. 59(3), 450–460 (2008)
17. Zhai, C., Lafferty, J.: A study of smoothing methods for language models applied to information retrieval. ACM Trans. Inf. Syst. 22(2), 179–214 (2004)

On the Use of Data Mining Techniques in Vehicular Ad Hoc Network

Yazan Alaya AL-Khassawneh and Naomie Salim

Faculty of Computer Science and Information Systems
University Technology Malaysia, Malaysia
yakhassawneh@yahoo.com, naomie@utm.my

Abstract. As vehicles become more intelligent, it is predictable that in the near future they will be outfitted with a wireless comparison. This will allow the construction of vehicular networks, commonly referred to as VANETs, as an example of mobile ad hoc networks where cars are the mobile nodes. VANETs (Vehicular Ad hoc Networks) are vastly mobile wireless ad hoc networks and will cooperate an imperative role in public safety communications and commercial applications. Mobilization of these VANETs aim of the mission and duties for the rapid changes in topology and dynamics of high-speed car. Position based routing protocols are becoming trendy due to development and accessibility of GPS devices. One of the major VANETs question often leads to rupture of the corridor high-speed vehicle dynamics, which leads to a broken step, which leads to low throughput and high overhead costs. VANET has become a dynamic spot of research in the last years; one of the important and promising research topics is applying data mining techniques to extract useful patterns from VANET, such as clustering, association, classification, and more. Therefore this paper surveys some of VANET applications that used data mining techniques.

1 Introduction

An example of an ad hoc network application is Vehicular Ad Hoc Networks (VANET). In order to enable short-range communication between vehicles on the road such as vehicle-to-vehicle (V2V) communication, integration of ad hoc networking with the modern wireless network is done. Aimed to ensure passengers' safety and comfort on the road, a platform for intelligent wireless services is developed through projects such as the CAR-2-CAR communication consortium, CarLink as well as Fleetnet. Furthermore, devices such as Global Positioning System (GPS) providing the ability to track the positioning of the vehicle, the direction of a vehicle in motion including the speed of the motion is now widely equipped in modern vehicles. Any vehicle can become a node of the network and start receiving and relaying messages if it is equipped with wireless communication device such as Onboard Unit (OBU), the transmission signal range is 100 to 300 meters and when vehicles fallout of the signal range other vehicles can join the network [1, 2]. The road side units allows the vehicles to

A. Ell Hassanien et al. (Eds.): AMLTA 2012, CCIS 322, pp. 449–462, 2012.

connect to external networks such as internet, RSUs are separated and working infrequently as a junction point between vehicular nodes and nodes of central authority (CA) who are responsible for maintaining the network [3]. The three categories of architectures proposed for VANETs include 1) The Wireless Wide Area Network (WWAN) in which the access points of the cellular gateways are fixed allowing direct communication between the vehicles and the access points. These access points however, require costly installation which is also not feasible, 2) The Hybrid Wireless Architecture in which HWAN access points are used at certain points while an ad hoc communication provides access and communication in between those access points, and 3) The Ad Hoc V2V Communication which does not require any fixed access points in order for the vehicles to communicate. Equipped with wireless network card, spontaneous setting up of an ad hoc network can be done for each vehicle.

The purpose of Vehicular Ad hoc NETworks (VANETs) is to allow wireless communication between vehicles on the road including the road-side wireless sensors enabling the transfer of information to ensure driving safety and planning for dynamic routing, allow mobile sensing as well as provide in-car entertainment. As VANETs have uniqueness in their characteristics which include dynamic topology, frequent disconnection of the networks and varying environments for the communication, the routing protocols for traditional Mobile Ad hoc NETworks (MANETs) such as Dynamic Source Routing (DSR) [4], Ad hoc On-demand Distance Vector (AODV) [5], Distributed Dynamic Routing (DDR) [6] Optimized Link State Routing (OLSR) [7], Fisheye state routing (FSR) [8] are not directly usable for VANETs. Researchers have developed various efficient routing protocols for VANETs including Greedy Perimeter Stateless Routing (GPSR) [9], Greedy Perimeter Coordinator Routing (GPCR) [10], Connectivity Aware Routing (CAR) [11], Road-Based using Vehicular Traffic-Reactive (RBVT-R) [12], Greedy Traffic-Aware Routing (GyTAR) [13], and GeoCross [14]. The current issue however, is that the range of the wireless sensors on vehicles are limited to a few hundred meters at most and the conditions of the traffic in a vehicular urban environment often change dynamically. Other than that, VANET routing protocols also face other problems including the issue of unstructured roads, the difference in the sizes of the intersections in a certain area, the sharp curves of the roads, the uneven slopes and other obstacles such as large buildings, traffic lights, trees and sign boards. As it is impractical to spend excess cost on rebuilding or restructuring the existing roads in urban environments, a routing protocol for the purpose of larger distance of data communication in one-to-one and one-to-many transfers specific for VANETs need to be developed.

The paper is organized as follows: the following section explains the VANETs applications; Section (3) discusses the VANETs data mining techniques. A deep comparative analysis between data mining techniques for VANETs is given in section (4). Finally the paper concludes in section (5).

2 Applications of VANETs

Vehicular network applications range from road safety applications oriented to the vehicle or to the driver, to entertainment and commercial applications for passengers, making use of a plethora of cooperating technologies. The primary vision of vehicular networks includes real-time and safety applications for drivers and passengers, providing safety for the latter and giving essential tools to decide the best path along the way. These applications thus aim to minimize accidents and improve traffic conditions by providing drivers and passengers with useful information including collision warnings, road sign alarms, and in-place traffic view. According to B. Mishra, et al 2011 [15] and Rezwana Karim [16], VANETs applications can be categorized as the following:

- *Safety applications:* Road safety can be improved by VANETs by sharing the valuable information between vehicles about road and weather conditions and car accidents. Warning messages will be sending to the vehicles in the range of the accident by the vehicles involved in the accident, so more drivers will be notified about the accident before reaching it. Furthermore by slowing down the speed, or using the electric break lights, or when there is a landslides, road curve or turn conflict, the accidents could be prevented by spreading warning messages to the vehicles on that road. Fig 1 is an example of these applications.

Fig. 1. A VANET in a city scenario. Vehicles are warned of the truck blocking the road and find alternate routes [17].

- *Convenience applications:* If the neighboring vehicles slow down the speed, that means there is a road congestion, so the traffic management vehicles pass this information to other vehicles on the network to take an alternative way. Also in this application there are some techniques can help vehicles to find a free (available) place in the parking areas, and also it can help to collect the toll without stopping for long time. Also in this type of applications, it's important to avoid collision domains especially at an intersection. [18]. Fig 2 illustrates how this application is used to avoid the chain collision (multi car pile-ups).

Fig. 2. A VANET preventing a multi-vehicle collision [17]

- *Commercial applications:* The overall objective of these applications to improve passenger's comfort and efficiency of traffic. May include the nearest POI (Points of Interest) settlement, and the current traffic or weather information and interactive communication. Can be applied to all types of applications, which may work on top of TCP/IP stack, for example, online games or instant messaging. Another application is receiving data from commercial vehicles and infrastructure on the side of the road for their actions (propaganda radio). Companies (shopping malls, fast food, gas stations and hotels) can set up the gates for the transfer of fixed marketing data to potential customers passing by. Moreover, this can be integrated with electric payment services. Important advantage of these applications is that they should not overlap with safety applications. In this scenario prioritization of traffic and use of detached physical channels is a workable solution.

3   Data Mining Techniques for VANETs

3.1   Association Techniques

Association Rules have been used to obtain information about the incidence of certain events based on the minimum value of support provided in the foundation of criteria for how the data mining will be delicate process [19] and [21]. These Association Rules can be used to detect common features or liaison among juveniles or objects, as long as they appear under the same domain of the given dataset [22]. Rezgui and Cherkaoui, 2011 [23], have suggested a new approach for the detection of false and noxious vehicles based on data mining techniques, and this is significant to insure the dependability and efficiency of safety applications through VANETs, since it relies on the reliability of contacts between vehicles. For the detection of faulty and / or adverse vehicles (vehicles that are not linked to the district pursuant to the Association Rules), this approach proposed a mechanism called VANET Association Rule- based (VARM), this mechanism has to maintain all the information about each single vehicle and transport in the neighboring for the extraction of rules temporal relations between all vehicles involved in the area of transmission. The proposed approach is the first one of its kind that reveals the defects / adverse vehicles through the generation of Association Rules on the activities of vehicles. For the detection of anomalies using the method of VARM, each vehicle stores the transmitted data (data received from a routine message) in the base transaction data temporarily and then VARM uses a data structure tree-based called itemset-tree (enhancement the idea of FP-tree [24] and Cats-tree [25]) to generate the local general rules on this event, which can be produced by the vehicle, VARM then merge the local rules to for the establishment of global rules and then analyze these global rules for the discovery of defective or malignant vehicles. When VARM disclosure a false information from defective or adverse vehicle it will uses (1: N) technique which is a spare relationships resorted to re-establish the validety of the data collection between vehicles in the same network. To demonstrate the idea to the discovery of defective /adverse vehicles capture the next instance of a local sequential association rule:

$$(m_1 \Rightarrow m_3, m_4, m_5, m_6, 93\%, \alpha) \tag{1}$$

It means that there is a 93 percent opportunity that if we get an episode from vehicle m1 then we'll get the same episode from vehicles m_3, m_4, m_5 and m_6 within α units of time but if we don't get the predictable episode from one of the those vehicles then it is a defective or adverse vehicle i.e. it is not interrelated with vehicles in the neighborhood. The results of the simulation technique for the effective performance when compared VARM itemset-tree structure with the other two structures (FP-tree [24] and Cats-tree [25]) in terms of compactness (the original size versus the size of advanced structure) in the itemset-tree and was more compact than other structures. Bae and Olariu 2010 [26], have also taken exploitation of Association Rules Mining in an Applications for VANETs. In their work, Association Rules Mining was used to extract the rules governing the system of linguistic information in the context of their proposed science driving assistance system that helps to prevent traffic accidents. Based on the current vehicle status information and the extracted rules, a mechanism similar to the pattern is used to find a relationship between the current events and those in the information system, which led to accidents or death. Using this mechanism, the system can provide drivers with the most efficient procedures and secure, should be taken to avoid the accidents or to reduce the impact of an accident like this occurring. A. F. Merah, et al [27] proposed a data mining method to extract models that show the vehicles crossing movements during their journey between the source and final destination. This style form of movements is a subset or special case of a well-known data mining method known as sequential models. The objective of this proposed system is the application of the rules of the movement models to predict the path of a specific vehicle, such as this expectation is very useful in the following cases: (1) Discovering the shortest path a vehicle can take; (2) Predicting the easy and habitual routes taken by criminals, so it becomes easy for the police forces to catch them at the time, and (3) Helping to find alternative roads for the cars in the case of congestions or accidents.

In order to derive traffic patterns, proposed approach begins with the preparation of the operation of data collection for all routes the vehicles cross and store this information in a movement database. To achieve this, the approach displays two mechanisms to prepare the data, Road-Side Units (RSU) scheme and Newest-Edge vehicle scheme. Both of the schemes gather the information paths for each vehicle through the registration of each edge the experience of the vehicle and the information received from vehicles (partial path) will be stored in the movement database, will create a full working path when the vehicle reaches its final distention a and the vehicle remove all the edges stored in the path information except for the last edge (the current edge) to be used for the journey ahead. The Newest-Edge vehicle based scheme has the same idea of the RSU scheme with two major differences: (1) In Newest-Edge vehicle based scheme vehicles are responsible for transmission the information while in the other scheme the RSU handle the sending scheme. and (2) In Newest-Edge vehicle based scheme the vehicles send their edge information only when and edge modify occurs while in RSU scheme the vehicles send edge information every x seconds which will cause message overhead since there might be slow vehicles that will remain on the edge after x seconds. To estimate the functioning of the scheme the authors used the SUMO simulator and two measurements which assess the cumulative number of message exchanged in each flow and the volume of the messages exchanged.

3.2   Clustering Techniques

Vehicle ad networks are a unique version of MANETs (Mobile Ad hoc NETworks), where the mobile nodes are the means of movement with the qualities of both deterministic and random. The deterministic aspects of vehicles movements include, following the speed of the front vehicles and driving within the speed limits. While random aspects include: changing lane, passing other vehicles, radical changing the speed because of an accident or the appearance of heavy traffic and excessive speed. A clustered network has an ample motivation because of there are many challenges within the VANETs. VANETs have a huge problem caused by routing in an intensive and rapid movement environment and also have a problem with invisible terminals. Overcrowding and the problem of invisible terminals can be mitigated by clustering the network. Furthermore to be easy for VANETs to cope with delayed information and safety messages, a

Quality-of-Service (QoS) required being included within this network. Clustering techniques have the ability to handle QoS requirements, as discussed in [28].

Many researches were done in the field of clustering VANETs. Wang and Lin [29] suggested three proficient reflexive clustering-based techniques to advance the routing act in VANETs, called VPCs; the suggested plans take advantage of a significant characteristic of the native clustering technique which is to limit the public expenditure in the discovery of roots. The VPC techniques aimed at identifying the occasion vehicle to take part discovering a rout, to do so it employs three standards to help identifying the proper vehicle to become a cluster-head or gateway. The standards are: (1) *Vehicle density:* the base standard of VPC1, the main goal for this standard is for choosing a proper cluster-head or gateway, the intensity of vehicle should be taken in to consideration, the vehicle with more numbers of neighbors is a good choice since this node will decrease the delivery delay, (2) *Link quality:* a cluster-head or gateway is chosen depending on this standard which is base of VPC2 designing; the connected link should be trust-worthy, (3) *Link sustainability:* to assess the sustainability of a link, VPC3 has been designed based on this standard, for increasing the proportion of packet delivery the routing protocol ought to select a more permanent paths consisting of constant links.

The donation of this approach is that it is the first one to assess the impact of techniques on the characteristics of VANET on the pc. For the assessment process of the VPCs protocols, compareing to the traditional Passive Clustering technique the simulation showed better results for packet delivery ratio, end-to-end delay and network throughput. Dornbush and Joshi, 2007 [30] have suggested a smart system of traffic in the street to detect jams and broadcast vehicles using Vehicular Ad-Hoc Networks (VANETs). The major purpose of the system is to provide a method for saving the wasted time and fuel spent in travelling through traffic jams through the discovery and spread of patterns of traffic jams.

Providing more accurate real time about jams information and the ease and cheap of implementation on all types of the roads, is the main differences between this system and other systems that offer data about traffic jams. To efficiently discover and spread the traffic patterns, and because of the high mobility of VANETs, the proposed system uses circulated clustering techniques with high performance communications. The system uses Global Positioning System (GPS) and peer-peer wireless communication medium (801.11 or 801.15). Every vehicle creates its own map based on noticing the speed of other vehicles moving around within the chosen roads, and all vehicles after that can exchange the speed maps with each other. Any vehicle through the network can get the speed map for every road even if it is not using these roads. The suggested system represents the traffic as a set of clusters of slow traffic, every node in the network maintains a summary statistics about clusters of every other node, the node only communicate when recorded speed is outside the variance of expected speed on that road segment. Nodes exchange the statistics by the epidemic communication and each node calculate the higher level cluster using its local statistics and those gathered from the network.

Simulation has showed that the system is effective in a challenging environment with non stationary data and high mobile nodes since smart system do not require constant connectivity. Because traffic jam problem is big issue nowadays specially in the major cities, many studies were done in this field. G. Thakur, 2011, et al [31] suggested a new scheme to mine image data of vehicles for measuring traffic jam and a new scheme for vehicular traffic data collecting from general traffic web cams. This scheme collects image data foe vehicles using the web cams installed on the roads of traffic jam and intersections in 10 different cities for several months. The collected data being used to analyze the attitude in traffic in these cities. The collected data was an ample dataset includes the movement of the vehicles, around 7.5 Terabytes of vehicle movements and vehicle images, which reached to 125 million images, as well as a set of driving time and distance between consequent pairs of sites using geographical coordinates of the cameras, thus this scheme considered the first one in this area that applies data mining techniques to extract the knowledge and information form huge datasets to approximate the intensity of traffic. This approach has two steps to calculate the driving distances and consequent time for the pairs of sites in every city, after that it applies a special type of data mining techniques called Spatio-temporal to analyze the dataset on three chosen cities (Connecticut, London, Sydney). The first step is to analyze the dynamics structural of the cities by making a comparison between driving distances and consequent driving time because there is a relation between both of them. The findings showed that if a short distance takes more than expected time regarding to the statistics then that part is highly susceptible to overcrowding (low to negative correlation), on the contrary (the values of high correlation) show overcrowding-free traffic and even distribution of traffic speed on that part. The second step is to apply the special data mining technique spatio-temporal and analyze the traffic intensity known from mining imagery dataset. The dataset is an aggregation statistics from all cameras during different hours of the day, because of that the analysis showed that it was very difficult to approximate the traffic model for a city. The results showed that the traffic approximates of 42 days was stabilized for various hours, also the results showed that the traffic jam has a high relation for 1-2 hours (80%), while it has a low correlation for 4 hours (25%-30%). Based on spatial data mining from GPS, Lima and Ferreira 2009 [32] suggested an algorithm for extracting automatic road network. This approach creates a powerful new way of infrastructure for remote sensing in order to obtain spatial data through networks of vehicles VANETs. To create this, it uses the information from the GPS receivers installed in the modern vehicles and the free communications infrastructures to get the information gathered by vehicles. This new approach provides an important geographic information such as topological connectivity, status of traffic and speed patterns, temperatures and humidity of roads, air contamination levels, as well as the occurrence of potholes on the road, all of that is provided in an truthful, low-cost and up to date manner, also it enhances the maps of the roads and update the road networks. From different road networks, millions of points collected in GPS receivers in VANETs, this approach automatically uses this dataset, and uses spatial SQL queries to gather the data from many GPS to form a weighted-mean of road maps. The algorithm needs a huge dataset for accomplishment; more than 30 million points collected by a vehicle tracking company were used to build the road map of Arganil city in Portugal. To get a valuable input data, the algorithm used three filters to reduce wrong and changeable data from GPS. Referring to [32] when the directional road maps for Arginal city created by the proposed algorithm being compared to Google Maps for the same city, the results showed the presence of minute overlap of the road network. A comparison between the automatic road extraction form this algorithm and the traditional approaches were done for the purpose of process evaluation, based on chiropractic to aerial images using three measurements: how many kilometers in Arginal city were extracted, how many kilometers have been matched with Portugal geographic map and how many kilometers were not found in Portugal geographic map because of the updating of the map. Comparing to the traditional approaches, this algorithm has many advantages: (1) This approach provides an important geographic information such as topological connectivity, status of traffic and speed patterns, temperatures and humidity of roads, air contamination levels, as well as the occurrence of potholes on the road, all of that is provided in an truthful, low-cost and up to date manner, also it enhances the maps of the roads and update the road networks; (2) the ability to discover roads that are invisible in aerial images; (3) inexpensive and updated representation of all details on the road due to the use of large number of GPS traces, and (4) the ability to supply low-cost means to perform and accurate update maps.

3.3 Classification Techniques

Through this technique of data mining a model being created for describing a group of predefined categories from a group of tuples called training group. This technique is designed to identify a group of unfamiliar organisms according to some characteristics of this unfamiliar organism. This technique needs the input to be entered by the user, which means it's a supervised technique. In this case the input is the training group, which is being used to build and train the classified model [20]. To assist the security needed for many applications in VANETs, the authors in [33] tried to provide an approach for this case. To obtain this goal, the authors suggested using classification mining techniques for analyzing a broad range of applications in VANETs, classifying based on the safety necessities (such as high level of verification needed, return potential attack, etc), and offer a safety answer for every class in the application. By the use of the suggested model, a new implementation can be evaluated on the basis of the necessities of the safety procedures and suitable safety actions could be applied. T. Kim, et al 2010 [34] proposed a nomination form to differentiate between fake (invalid) and lawful (valid) messages, to enhance road safety in view of the fact that harmful message may cause serious cases that could conduct to accidents through the dissemination of false alarms or restrict the security serious alarms. The suggested approach offers a construction for detecting of

Ref	Objective	Data Mining Technique	Dataset used	Main contribution	Benefits
[23]*	Detecting faulty and malicious vehicles in VANETs using rule based communications data mining to guarantee the reliability of VANETS's safety applications.	Build association rules to analyze the behavior of vehicles and detect faulty or malicious ones.	The authors compared the itemset-tree with other two structures (FP-tree and cats-tree) using sparse and dense benchmark transaction databases found in [1]	The first approach to detect malicious and faulty vehicles in VANETs based on communication data mining.	1. The correlated correlation and association rules are easy to understand and easy to log by humans. 2. Improve the storage and mining to react to positive detections
[29]	Propose three efficient pc-based techniques called VPCs to improve the routing performance in VANETs	Clustering The proposed schemas are based on the famous clustering technique.	Simulation model	Providing extensive evaluations of influence of VANET characteristics on the PC-based techniques under Diverse scenarios.	Achieve better results for packet delivery ratio, end-to-end delay and network throughput compared to the traditional Passive Clustering technique.

* R. Lin, E. Khalastchi and G. A. Kaminka, "Detecting anomalies in unmanned vehicles using the Mahalanobis distance", in Proc. of ICRA, pp. 3038-3044, 2010.

Fig. 3. Comparison between data mining techniques for VANETs

VANET misconduct which exploits several sources of information accessible in a VANET background to empower the on board unit (OBU) to differentiate between harmful alerts from lawful alerts.

The sources of information are formerly individual instrument for detecting misconduct, they are five sources listed as the follows: (1) *Cryptographic Authentication:* for checking the digital signature if it's included with the message or not for confirmation reason; (2) *Source Location:* for checking the sender location to make sure that he can send the message to other vehicles or not; (3) *Local Sensor:* for checking the ability of the local sensors to support the alert; (4) *Infrastructure Validation:* for checking the ability of the road side unit (RSU) to support the message and (5) Sender Reputation: for checking if any previous messages from the sender were harmful messages.

The on board unit OBU merge the supplementary sources of information and according to the combined results from the applicable ones, it can filter out bad messages. The model relies on two central elements: (1) *The threshold curve:* to determine the importance of events to the driver based on the distance between the driver and the event, the more near events are more important than far ones, and (2) *COE curve:* to illustrate the confidence of actions, the OBU of a vehicle be able to choose the authority of a convinced incident based on the number of the applicable messages established.

If the OBU received the alert message from many vehicles, that means the event in this message is valid, because the hypothesis of this approach is that minority opportunities for harmful drivers. When the driver arrives the real event location the CEO value become more and the driver will be warned about the event when he crosses the threshold curve, because the OBUs will generate an alarm at that time. In the simulation the authors applied the detection techniques to detect the behavior to the EEBL (electronic emergency break light) application using the NS2 simulator by measuring the collision percentage the results were very good.

[30]	Saving the wasted time and fuel spent in travelling through traffic congestion by discovering and disseminating traffic congestion patterns using VANETs	Uses clustering as a data aggregation techniques to combine related recordings of unusual speed	Used maps from TiggerLine approach For the simulation cars drive random paths through a Manhattan grid on Baltimore area road	New method for collecting accurate real time congestion information for which there is a great need.	1. Lower cost compared to approaches for collecting live traffic information. 2. Each node tries to do analysis of the gathered statistics not just the central node. 3 Distributed clustering algorithm that does not require constant connectivity and function using an epidemic diffusion model. 4. Reduce communication load by only transmitting useful information (only exchange summary information on areas of unexpected traffic).
[31]	Measuring traffic congestion and identifying patterns and predictions to current traffic problems by providing a comprehensive knowledge of the city structure and the traffic distribution on its important intersections.	K-midoid Clustering Spatio_temporal data mining techniques to analyze the structural dynamics of the monitored cities and their vehicular traffic density distribution	Collection of vehicular mobility traces with 7.5 Terabytes of data and 125 million vehicular images collected during several months from 2709 traffic webcams in 10 different cities, plus a collection of driving distance and corresponding driving time between pairs of cameras for each city using the geo-coordinates of cameras.	1. Novel approach of collecting vehicular traffic information using online vehicular traffic cameras. 2. Identifying patterns and prediction for traffic problems using spatio-temporal analysis and correlation. 3. Providing the research community with the largest and most extensive library if vehicular density	1. Provide helpful information about planning future cities. 2. The first approach on traffic issues that apply data mining rules on a large data set to profile cities and estimate traffic densities.

Fig. 4. Comparison between data mining techniques for VANETs

[32]	Constructing road networks based on GPS traces collected from vehicular networks to provide better and enhance geographical information	Clustering spatial SQL queries to aggregate data from multiple GPS traces inorder to porovid a weighted-mean geometry of road axles	Since the algorithm require a large dataset for implementaion the authores used more then 30 millions points collected by a vehicle tracking company to construct the roadmap of Arganil city in portogal Reaching a total of 371600 KM of vehicular traces	First powerful approach of remote sensing geographical information to automatically extract road networks using GPS traces from vehicular networks	1. It is able to discover roads that are not visible from aerial images due to tree shadows or clouds. 2. The ability of extracting the geometric representation of tiny details on the road in an inexpensive and updated manner. 3. The ability of the algorithm to provide a low-cost and accurate way of performing cartographic updating. 4. The ability to provide characterization of the roads in terms of topological connectivity ,traffic conditions and speed patterns, temperatures and wetness of roads, and presence of potholes
[34]	Filtering model to distinguish spurious (invalid) message from legitimate (valid) messages, to improve road safety.	Classification	Data model for simulation	The first approach that provides a framework for VANET misbehavior detection exploiting multiple sources of information available in a VANET environment to enable the on board unit (OBU) to distinguish between malicious alerts from legitimate alerts.	1. Reduce the number of Malicious alerts even in environment without attacker. 2. Not expensive comparing to other projects. 3. The system provides fast notifications for nearby events, and that give the enough time to the driver to react against the event.

Fig. 5. Comparison between data mining techniques for VANETs

4   Comparison between Data Mining Techniques for VANETs

The main feature of the approaches discussed in the previous section given in Figures [3-5]. The comparison is based on the objectives of the approach, as well as the use of methods of data mining, the dataset used, the main contribution and benefits.

5   Conclusions

Vehicular networking is the enabling technology that will support several applications varying from global Internet services and applications up to active road safety applications. Data mining techniques have been applied in VANETs to extract useful patterns and information to achieve better performance, improve the vehicle and road safety, and save the wasted resources. The studies discussed in this paper are the main works in this area.

References

[1] Papadimitratos, P., de La Fortelle, A., Evenssen, K., Brignolo, R., Cosenza, S.: Vehicular Communication Systems: Enabling Technologies, Applications, and Future Outlook on Intelligent Transportation. IEEE Commun. Mag. 47(11), 84–95 (2009)

[2] Hartenstein, H., Laberteaux, K.P.: A Tutorial Survey on Vehicular Ad Hoc Networks. IEEE Communications Magazine 46(6), 164–171 (2008)

[3] Sakib, R., Reza, B.: Security issues in vanet, April 16 (2010)

[4] Johnson, D.B., Malts, D.A.: Dynamic source routing in ad hoc wireless networks. Mobile Company, 153–181 (1996)

[5] Perkins, C., Belsing-Rower, E.M., Das, S.: Ad Hoc On Demand Vector (AODV) Routing, IETF Internet Draft, draft-ietf-manet-aodv-09-txt (July 2003)

[6] Nikaein, N., Laboid, H., Bonnet, C.: Distributed Dynamic Routing Algorithm (DDR) for mobile ad hoc networks. In: Proceedings of the MobiHOC 2000: 1st Annual Workshop on Mobile Ad Hoc Networking and Computing (2000)

[7] Jacquet, P., Muhletaler, P., Qayyum, A., Laouiti, A., Viennot, L.: Optimized Link State Routing Protocol. In: IEEE INMIC, Pakistan (December 2001)

[8] Mario, G.P., Gerla, M., Chen, T.-W.: Fisheye State Routing: A Routing Scheme for Ad Hoc Wireless Networks. In: Proceeding of the International Conference on Communications, New Orleans, USA, pp. 70–74 (June 2000)

[9] Karp, B., Kung, H.T.: GPSR: greedy perimeter stateless routing for wireless networks. In: Proceeding of the 6th Annual International Conference on Mobile Computing and Networking (Mobicom 2000), Boston, Massachusetts, pp. 243–254 (2000)

[10] Lochert, C., Mauve, M., Fussler, H., Hartenstein, H.: Geographic routing in city scenarios. Proceedings of the SIGMOBILE 9(1), 69–72 (2005)

[11] Naumov, V., Gross, T.R.: Connectivity-Aware Routing (CAR) in Vehicular Ad-hoc Networks. In: Proceedings of INFOCOM 2007: The 26th IEEE International Conference on Computer Communications, Anchorage, AK, May 6-12, pp. 1919–1927 (2007)

[12] Nzouonta, J., Rajgure, N., Wang, G., Borcea, C.: VANET Routing on City Roads Using Real-Time Vehicular Traffic Information. IEEE Transactions on Vehicular Technology 58(7) (September 2009)

[13] Jerbi, M., Senouci, S.M., Rasheed, T.: Towards Efficient Geographic Routing in Urban Vehicular Networks. IEEE Transactions on Vehicular Technology 58(9), 5048–5059 (2009)

[14] Lee, K.-C., Cheng, P.-C., Gerla, M.: GeoCross: A geographic routing protocol in the presence of loops in urban scenarios. Ad Hoc Networks 8, 474–488 (2010)

[15] Mishra, B., Nayak, P., Behera, S., Jena, D.: Security in Vehicular Adhoc Networks: A Survey. In: ICCCS 2011, Proceedings of the 2011 International Conference on Communication, Computing & Security, New York, USA, pp. 590–595 (2011)

[16] Karim, R.: Superior System for Content Distribution in Vehicular Ntwork Applications. In: Rutgers University Conference, pp. 1–8 (March 2010)

[17] Car 2 car communication consortium, http://www.car-2-car.org

[18] Yin, J., ElBatt, T., Yeung, G., Ryu, B., Habermas, S., Krishnan, H., Talty, T.: Performance evaluation of safety applications over dsrc vehicular ad hoc networks. In: VANET 2004: Proceedings of the 1st ACM International Workshop on Vehicular ad Hoc Networks, pp. 1–9. ACM, New York (2004)

[19] Jian, W., Xing Ming, L.: A Novel Algorithm for dynamic Mining of Association Rules. In: Proceedings of WKDD, pp. 94–99 (2008)

[20] Han, J., Kamber, M.: Data Mining: Concepts and Techniques, 2nd edn. Morgan Kaufmann Publisher (2006)

[21] Sayad, S.: An Introduction to data Mining, Data Mining Group, University of Toronto (2010), http://chem-eng.utoronto.ca/datamining

[22] Samarah, S.: Knowledge Discovery for Behavioral Patterns in Wireless Sensor Networks. PhD thesis, University of Ottawa (2008)

[23] Rezgui, J., Cherkaoui, S.: Detecting Faulty and Malicious Vehicles Using Rule based Communications Data Mining. In: LCN 2011, pp. 827–834 (2011)

[24] Han, J., Pei, J., Yin, Y.: Mining frequent patterns without candidate generation. In: Proc. of the ACM-SIGMOD Intl. Conference on Management of Data, Dallas, Texas, pp. 1–12 (2000)

[25] Cheung, W., Zaiane, O.: Incremental mining of frequent patterns without candidate generation or support constraint. In: Proc. of the Seventh International Database Engineering and Applications Symposium (IDEAS), Hong Kong, China (2003)

[26] Bae, I.-H., Olariu, S.: A Tolerant Context-Aware Driver Assistance System for VANETs-Based Smart Cars. In: 2010 IEEE Global Telecommunications Conference (GLOBE- COM 2010), December 6-10, pp. 1–5 (2010), doi:10.1109/GLOCOM.2010.5684041

[27] Merah, A.F., Samarah, S., Boukerche, A.: Vehicular Movement Patterns: A Prediction-Based Route Discovery Technique for VANETs. University of Ottawa, Canada

[28] Ramanathan, R., Steenstrup, M.: Hierarchically-organized, multihop mobile wireless networks for quality-of-service support. Mobile Networks and Applications 3(1), 101–119 (1998)

[29] Wang, S.-S., Lin, Y.-S.: Performance Evaluation of Passive Clustering Based Techniques for Inter-vehicle Communications. In: Proceedings of the 19th Annual Wireless and Optical Communications Conference (WOCC 2010), Shanghai, China, May 14-15 (2010)

[30] Dornbush, S., Josh, A.: StreetSmart Traffic: Discovering and Disseminating Automobile Congestion Using VANET's. In: VTC 2007-Spring: Proceedings of the 65th IEEE Vehicular Technology Conference, pp. 11–15 (April 2007)
[31] Thakur, G., Hui, P., Ketabdr, H., Helmy, A.: Spatial and Temporal Analysis of Planet Scale Vehicular Imagery Data. In: 2011 11th IEEE International Conference on Data Mining Workshops, pp. 905–910 (2011)
[32] Lima, F., Ferreira, M.: Mining Spatial Data from Gps Traces for Automatic Road Network Extraction. In: 6th International Symposium on Mobile Mapping Technology, Presidente Prudente, São Paulo, Brazil, July 21-24 (2009)
[33] Kargl, F., Ma, Z., Schoch, E.: Security Engineering for VANETs. In: 4th Workshop on Embedded Security in Cars, escar 2006 (November 2006)
[34] Kim, T.H.-J., Studer, A., Dubey, R., Zhang, X., Perrig, A., Bai, F., Bellur, B., Iyer, A.: VANET Alert Endorsement Using Multi-Source Filters. In: VANET 2010, Proceedings of the Seventh ACM International Workshop on Vehicular Internetworking, pp. 51–60 (2010)
[35] Lin, R., Khalastchi, E., Kaminka, G.A.: Detecting anomalies in unmanned vehicles using the Mahalanobis distance. In: Proc. of ICRA, pp. 3038–3044 (2010)

Part VII

Case-Based Reasoning and Data Processing

Comparative Study of Data Quality Dimensions
for Data Warehouse Development: A Survey

Munawar, Naomie Salim, and Roliana Ibrahim

Dept. of Information System, Universiti Teknology Malaysia
Johor Bahru, Malaysia
an_moenawar@yahoo.com, {naomie,roliana}@utm.my

Abstract. Due to the increasing complexity of data warehouse (DW), continuous attention must be paid for evaluation of their quality throughout their
design and development. DW quality depends on the quality of all requirements, conceptual, logical and physical models used for DW design. Therefore,
identification of various data quality (DQ) dimensions in those phase of DW
development are very much needed.

In this paper, we surveyed and evaluated the literature related to the DQ
dimension in every phase of DW development and proposed an integrated approach for incorporating DQ in DW development in order to minimize risk of
DW project failure.

Keywords: data quality, dimension, data warehouse, integration.

1   Introduction

A data warehouse (DW) is a special database used for storing enormous amounts of
data, gathered from heterogeneous data sources in order to satisfy decision-making
requests [20]. DWs are increasingly being used by many organizations in many sectors to improve their operations and to better achieve their objectives. DW enables
executives to access the information they need to make informed business decisions
[33]. Therefore DW has to deliver highly aggregated, high quality data from heterogeneous sources to decision makers [15]. However, many DW projects fail for many
reasons, all of which can be traced to a single cause: non quality [2]. There should be
a way of guaranteeing that the data in the sources is the same data that reached the
DW, and the DQ is improved; not lost [26].

In the data warehousing process, data passes through several stages each one causing different kind of changes to the data to finally reach the user in a form of a chart
or a report. All these stages of data warehousing are responsible for DQ in the DW.
Understanding the key DQ dimensions in every stage of DW development phase is
the first step to DQ improvement [30].

Even though many papers have been written, there is still no consensus on a development method yet. Most methods agree on the opportunity of distinguishing between
the following phases: requirements analysis, conceptual design, logical design, and
physical design. In order to meet the DQ requirements in those phases, it is essential

A. Ell Hassanien et al. (Eds.): AMLTA 2012, CCIS 322, pp. 465–473, 2012.

to determine the DQ dimensions that are important to each phase and to identify ways of improving DQ in every phase of DW development.

Organizations are often aware of DQ problems. However, their improvement efforts generally focus narrowly on only the accuracy of data, and ignore the many other DQ attributes and dimensions that are important [26]. This paper describes an empirical study of DQ in a DW development. A conceptual framework for understanding the relationships between DW development phase and categories of DQ dimensions was developed from an analysis of the DQ and data warehouse literature.

This paper will be organized as follows: section 2 will be briefly survey the DQ dimension for DW. Section 3 descibes the DW development. Section 4 discusses the conceptual framework for understanding relationships between DW development phase and categories of DQ dimensions. And final section contains some concluding remarks.

2   Data Quality Dimension for Data Warehouse

DW is one of the most complex information system projects. The main contribution of a DW is its capability of turning data into strategic information, accessible to

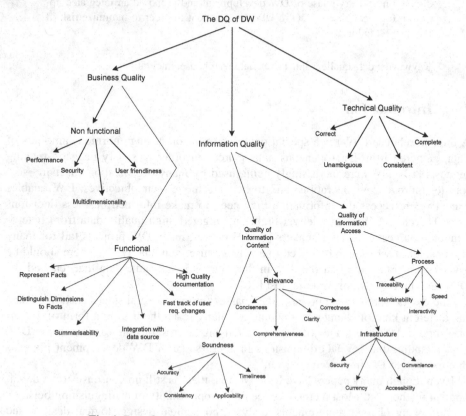

Fig. 1. Data Quality Dimension for Data Warehouse [21; 22]

decision-makers in the highest level of an organization [24]. Effective business decision-making depends on good quality data, and poor DQ can be costly and sometimes disastrous [26]. A key factor in the success of data warehousing is the quality of the data provided [16]. Organizations therefore need to understand DQ, and establish procedures to assure the quality of data in DWs.

There is consensus that quality involves several dimensions [1]; [2]; [13]; [28]; [26], but there is no general agreement on what the set of dimensions should be. [1] included accuracy, timeliness and completeness; although they have pointed out that other dimensions may also be relevant. Author of [13] grouped DW quality dimensions into design and administration quality dimensions (e.g. correctness, completeness, minimality, traceability, interpretability and metadata evolution), data usage quality dimensions (e.g. responsiveness, timeliness, interpretability, security and availability) and DQ dimensions (e.g. accuracy, completeness, consistency, credibility and data interpretability). A complete set of DQ dimension is presented in fig. 1.

3   Data Warehouse Development Phase

Basically, classical model describes the whole design process of DW starting from requirements analysis, conceptual design, logical design and physical design. During all this process DQ dimensions can be incorporated in order to minimize risk of DW project failure. Detail process of DW development can be seen in figure 2.

4   Proposed Data Quality Dimensions for Each Phase of Data Warehouse Development

Due to the increasing complexity of DW, continuous attention must be paid for evaluation of their quality throughout their design and development. DW quality depends on the quality of all requirements, conceptual, logical and physical models used for DW design. Therefore, identification of various DQ dimensions in those phase of DW development are very much needed.

[21;22] proposed a useful framework for integrating DQ into the DW development. However, their model does not provide a detail explanation about DQ dimension in every phase of DW development. Understanding DQ dimensions that are important to each phase of DW development is so critical to identify ways of improving DQ in DW.

It is true that, in the relevant literature, we can find several initiatives for the inclusion of DQ dimension in DWs [13;15;24-26]. However, none of them considers DQ dimension aspects which incorporate all stages of the DW development cycle. We have analyzed research work done in the DW development (fig. 2) and its related issues in DQ dimension (fig. 1). A brief tabular has been provided below in table 1, to the DQ dimensions in every phase of DW development.

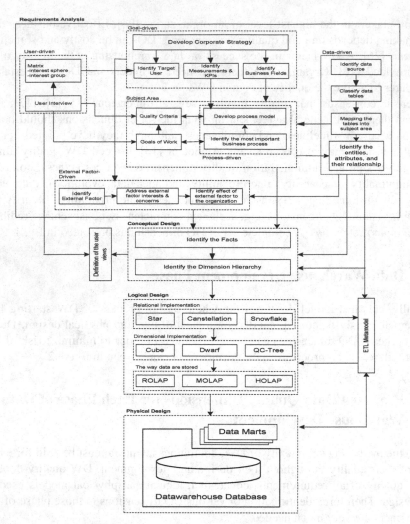

Fig. 2. Data Warehouse Development Phase [14]

In a DW where data is processed in stages, and where the quality of data at one stage is dependent on the DQ measurements in preceding stages, the use of a framework for managing DQ is very much needed [21]. Within a framework, DQ dimension can be treated as a continuous improvement in the whole phase of DW development. Furthermore, DQ can be assessed and monitored continuously in order to guarantee high quality levels.

In requirements phase, the DQ is often defined as 'fitness for use'. The assessment of DQ dimensions should consider the degree to which data satisfy requirements' needs. In order to evaluate the DQ with respect to requirements phase, DQ dimensions must be associated with specific dimensions. Only a few subsets of dimensions, such as consistency and timeliness can be used in external-driven. However, some dimensions such as conciseness, it is not possible to define an objective measure for user-driven. Consequently, quality assessment must be based on the subjective perception of users.

In order to analyze the requirements from the perspective of decision makers and organization (goal-driven), the approach does not covering the analysis on technical dimensions. Therefore, decision making often refer to information that does not exist in required form and must be derived from data sources.

Within data-driven, technical dimensions are very dominant aspects. But, we can not use this alternative wherenever a deep analysis of data sources is unfeasible

Table 1. Data quality dimension for every phase of DW development

Data Quality Dimension				Requirements Analysis					Conceptual		Logical	Physical	ETL
				UD	GD	ED	DD	PD	MD	SC			
Business Quality [9;11;34]	Non Functional [3;25]		Performance		[27;35]				[10]				
			Security		[27;35]				[10]		[13]		[13]
			Multidimensionality		[35]				[30;10]	[30]	[31]	[31]	[31]
	Functional [3;24]		User Friendliness	[8]	[35]			[8]	[30;10]	[30]	[8]		[8]
			Represent Fact		[35]		[24;30]		[30;10;8]	[30]	[31]	[31]	[31]
			Distinguish Dimensions to facts		[35]		[24;30]		[30;10;8]	[30]	[31]	[31]	[31]
			Summarisability		[35]		[24;30]		[30;10]	[30]			[30]
			Integration with Data Source	[8]	[35]		[23;24]	[8]	[30;10;8]	[30;8]	[31]	[31]	[23;30;31]
			Fast Track of User Req. Changes		[35]		[24;30]		[30;10]	[30]	[31]	[31]	[30;31]
			High Quality Documentation				[24]		[10;13]	[13]	[13]		[13;30]
Information Quality [9;11;34]	Content [6]	Soundness	Accuracy	[26;8]	[27]		[12;23;14;29]	[12;8]	[14;29;8]	[8]		[13]	[7;12;23;30;14;29;36]
			Consistency	[12;26;8]	[12]	[12]	[12;23;30;14;29]	[12;8]	[14]	[14]	[8]	[13]	[12;23;30;14;29;8]
			Applicability	[26]									[30]
			Timeliness	[12;26;8]	[12]	[12]	[12;23;30;14;29]	[12;8]	[30;14;8]	[30;14]	[8]	[14]	[12;23;30;14;29;8]
		Relevance	Conciseness								[8]		[30;8]
			Comprehensiveness	[26]									[30]
			Clarity	[26]									[30]
			Correctness	[26]			[30]		[13]	[13]	[13]		[30;36]
	Access [6]	Infrastructure	Security	[8]							[13]		[13;35]
			Currency				[14]		[14]	[14]	[8]	[14]	[30;14;8]
			Accessibility	[8]			[14]		[14]	[14]	[13;8]		[13;15;16;19;14;8]
			Convenience	[8]							[8]		[8]
		Process	Traceability	[8]	[26]			[8]	[13;8]	[13;8]	[13]		
			Maintainability		[26]							[13]	[18;30;32]
			Interactivity		[26]								
			Speed	[8]	[26]			[8]	[8]	[8]	[8]		[30;8]
Technical Quality [9;11;34]	Correct [17]						[17;30]		[13]	[13]	[13]		[17;36]
	Unambiguous [17]						[17]						[17]
	Consistent [17]						[17]						[17]
	Complete [17]			[8]			[1;2;17;23;14;29]	[8]	[13;14;8]	[13;14;8]	[13;8]	[13]	[7;12;17;23;30;14;29;8;36]

Legend : UD-User Driven; GD-Goal Driven; ED-External Driven; DD-Data Driven; PD=Process Driven; MD-Multidimensional Modeling; SC-Star/ Snowflake Schema (e.g. if the DW is fed from an ERP system, whose logical schema is huge and hardly understandable), or data sources reside on legacy systems whose inspection and normalization is not recommendable.

In a process-driven, what the decision makers actually need is a view of their business processes and its data, which allows them an extensive analysis of their data. Therefore, accuracy, consistency, timelines, traceabilty, speed, completeness, integration with data sources & user friendlines are main dimensions that should be considered.

In terms of DW quality, the conceptual model defines a theory of the organization. Actual observation can be evaluated for quality factors such as functional, nonfunctional, accuracy, timeliness, completeness with respect to this theory. Moreover, the fact that DW views intervene between client views and source views can have both a positive and a negative impact on information quality.

The logical perspective conceives a DW from the view point of the actual data models involved. Researchers and practitioners following this perspective are the ones that consider a DW simply a collection of materialized views on top of each other, based on existing information sources.

The physical perspective interprets the DW architecture as a network of data stores, data transformers and communication channels, aiming at the quality factors of reliability and performance in the presence of very large amounts of slowly changing data.

In data warehousing, ETL (Extract, Transform, and Load) processes are in charge of extracting the data from the data sources that will be contained in the DW. Due to their relevance, the quality of these processes should be formally asessed in order to avoid populating the DW with incorrect data. Unfortunately, to the best of our knowledge there is no proposals evaluates the quality of ETL processes. Therefore, we attempts to assure the quality of ETL process by evaluating quality dimensions in ETL process. DQ refers that data is exactly fit for the purpose of business use; that it is consistent, accurate, complete and unambiguous. Cleaning of data refers to an activity which determines and detects the unwanted, corrupt, inconsistent and faulty data to enhance the quality of data.

5   Conclusions and Future Works

In this paper we have seen that several approaches have been proposed by various authors to determine the DQ for DW development, but none of the approaches determine DQ dimensions for requirements level to final implementation.

DQ is an important factor in the success of data warehousing projects. This paper has proposed a framework for understanding DQ dimensions in every phase of DW development and integrates them into each phase of DW development. Our future research is determining the DQ measurement in every phase of DW development in order to identify ways of improving DQ in DW development.

References

1. Ballou, D.P., Tayi, G.K.: Enhancing Data Quality in Data Warehouse Environments. Communications of the ACM 42(1), 73–78 (1999)
2. Cowie, J., Burstein, F.: Quality of data model for supporting mobile decision making. Decision Support Systems 43, 1675–1683 (2007)
3. Dubielewicz, I., Hnatkowska, B., Huzar, Z., Tuzinkiewicz, L.: Feasibility Analysis of MDA-based Database Design. In: Proceedings of the International Conference on Dependability of Computer Systems (DEPCOS-RELCOMEX 2006). IEEE (2006) 0-7695-2565-2/06
4. ElGamal, N., Bastawissy, Galal-Edeen, G.: Towards a Data Warehouse Testing Framework. In: 2011 Ninth International Conference on ICT and Knowledge Engineering. IEEE (2011)
5. English, L.P.: Improving Data Warehouse and Business Information Quality (Methods for Reducing Costs and Increasing Profits). John Wiley and Sons, Inc., New York (1999)
6. Eppler, M.J.: Managing Information Quality: Increasing the Value of Information in Knowledge-Intensive Products and Processes, 2nd edn. Springer (2006)
7. Foshay, N., Mukherjee, A., Taylor, A.: Does Data Warehouse End-User Metadata Add Value? Communications of the ACM 50, 70–77 (2007)
8. Giannoccaro, A., Shanks, G., Darke, P.: Stakeholder Perceptions of Data Quality in a Data Warehouse Environment. In: Proc. 10th Australian Conference on Information Systems (1999)
9. Gosain, A., Singh, J.: Towards Data warehouse Business Quality through Requirements Elicitation. IEEE 978-1-4244-2624-9/08 (2008)
10. Golfarelli, M.: From User Requirements to Conceptual Design in Data warehouse Design. IGI Global (2010), doi:10.4018/978-1-60566-756-0.ch001
11. Hadley, L.: Data Warehouse Quality Management (1998), http://www.users.qwest.net/~lauramh/resume/dwqual.htm
12. Helfert, M., von Maur, E.: A Strategy for Managing Data Quality in Data Warehouse Systems. In: The Proceedings of the International Conference on Information Quality, Boston, MA (2001)
13. Jarke, M., Jeusfeld, M., Quix, C., Vassiliadis, P.: – Architecture and Quality in Data Warehouses: An Extended Repository Approach. Information Systems 24(3), 229–253 (1999)
14. Jarke, M., Vassiliou, Y.: Data Warehouse Quality: A Review of the DWQ Project. In: Proceedings of the 2nd Conference on Information Quality, Cambridge, MA (1997)
15. Jeusfeld, M.A., Quix, C., Jarke, M.: Design and Analysis of Quality Information for Data Warehouses. In: Ling, T.-W., Ram, S., Li Lee, M. (eds.) ER 1998. LNCS, vol. 1507, pp. 349–362. Springer, Heidelberg (1998)
16. Kimball, R., Reeves, L., Thornthwaite, W., Ross, M., Thornwaite, W.: The Data Warehouse Lifecycle Toolkit: Expert Method for Designing, Developing, and Deploying Data Warehouses. John Wiley & Sons, Inc. (1998)
17. Kimball, R., Caserta, J.: The Datawarehouse ETL Toolkit: Practical techniques for Extracting, Cleansing, Conforming and Delivering Data. Wiley Publishing, Inc., IN (2004) ISBN: 0-764-56757-8
18. March, S., Hevner, A.: Integrated decision support systems: A data warehousing perspective. Decision Support Systems 43(3), 1031–1043 (2007)

19. Marco, D.: Building and Managing the Meta Data Repository: A Full Lifecycle Guide. Willey and Sons, Inc., New York (2000)
20. Marotta, A., Ruggia, R.: Data Warehouse Design: A schema-transformation approach. In: SCCC 2002, Chile (2002)
21. Munawar, Salim, N., Ibrahim, R.: Toward Data Quality Integration into the Data Warehouse Development. In: Ninth IEEE International Conference on Dependable, Autonomic and Secure Computing. IEEE Computer Sociaty (2011a), 978-0-7695-4612-4/11, doi:10.1109/DASC.2011.194
22. Munawar, Salim, N., Ibrahim, R.: Toward Data Warehouse Quality through Integrated Requirements Analysis. In: ICACSIS 2011 (2011b) ISBN: 978-979-1421-11-9
23. Nemani, R.R., Konda, R.: A Framework for Data Quality in Data Warehousing. In: Yang, J., Ginige, A., Mayr, H.C., Kutsche, R.-D. (eds.) UNISCON 2009. LNBIP, vol. 20, pp. 292–297. Springer, Heidelberg (2009)
24. Paim, F.R.S., Castro, J.B.: DWARF: An Approach for Requirements Definition and Management of Datawarehouse Systems. In: Proceedings of the 11th IEEE International Conference on Requirement Engineering, pp. 75–78 (2003)
25. Paim, F.R.S., Castro, J.B.: Enhancing Data Warehouse Design with the NFR Framework. In: 5th Workshop on Requirements Engineering (WER 2002), Valencia, Spain, November 11-12, pp. 40–57 (2002)
26. Prakash, N., Singh, Y., Gosain, A.: Informational Scenarios for Data Warehouse Requirements Elicitation. In: Atzeni, P., Chu, W., Lu, H., Zhou, S., Ling, T.-W. (eds.) ER 2004. LNCS, vol. 3288, pp. 205–216. Springer, Heidelberg (2004)
27. Prakash, N., Gosanin, A.: An Approach to Engineering the Requirements of data Warehouses. Springer, London (2007), doi:10.1007/s00766-007-0057-x
28. Pipino, L., Lee, Y., Wang, R.: Data Quality Assessment. Commun. ACM 45, 4 (2002)
29. Piprani, B., Ernst, D.: A Model for Data Quality Assessment. In: Meersman, R., Tari, Z., Herrero, P. (eds.) OTM-WS 2008. LNCS, vol. 5333, pp. 750–759. Springer, Heidelberg (2008)
30. Singh, R., Singh, K.: A Descriptive Classification of Causes of Data Quality Problems in Data Warehousing. IJCSI International Journal of Computer Science Issues 7(3(2)) (May 2010) ISSN : 1694-0784
31. Solodovnikova, D.: Metadata to support Data Warehouse Evolution. Information System Development, 627–635 (2010) 10.1007/b137171_65
32. Solomon, M.: Ensuring a successful data warehouse initiative. IS Management 22(1), 26–36 (2005)
33. Sumathi, S., Sivanandam, S.N.: Data Marts and Data Warehouse: Information Architecture for the Millennium. SCI, vol. 29, pp. 75–150. Springer, Heidelberg (2006)
34. Thomann, J., Wells, D.: Data warehouse quality management. In: The Data Warehousing Institute's Fourth Annual Implementation Conference, Anaheim, CA, February 14-19 (1999)
35. Van, L.A.: Goal-oriented requirements engineering: a guided tour. Invited paper for RE 2001, Proceedings of 5th IEEE International Symposium on Requirements Engineering, Toronto, pp. 249–263 (August 2001)
36. Vetterli, T., Vaduva, A., Staudt, M.: Metadata Standards for Datawarehousing: Open Information Model vs Common Warehouse Metamodel (2000)
37. Celko, J., McDonald, J.: Don't warehouse dirty data. Datamation 41(19), 42–53 (1995)

38. Giblett, P.B.: Data Quality: The Key to Managing the Successful Data Warehouse Project (2002),
    http://www.ontariocio.com/Data_Quality_key_to_successful_BI_project_20020501.pdf (retrieved 20 April, 2010)
39. Rizzi, S., Abelló, A., Lechtenbörger, J., Trujillo, J.: Research in data warehouse modeling and design: Dead or alive? In: Proceedings of the 9th ACM Int. Workshop on Data Warehousing and OLAP (DOLAP 2006), pp. 3–10. ACM Press (2006)

A General Framework for Measuring Information and Communication Technology Investment
Case Study of Kingdom of Saudi Arabia

Farrukh Saleem[1,2], Naomie Salim[1], Ayman G. Fayoumi[2], and Abdullah Alghamdi[2]

[1] Faculty of Computer Science and Information Systems,
Universiti Teknologi Malaysia, 81310, Skudai, Johor, Malaysia
farrukh800@yahoo.com, naomie@utm.my
[2] Faculty of Computing and Information Technology,
King Abdulaziz University, Jeddah, Kingdom of Saudi Arabia
ayman.fayoumi@gmail.com, aalmalaise@kau.edu.sa

Abstract. Growing concerns of decision makers about measuring Information and Communication Technology (ICT) investments has increased the wide interest in developing and analyzing the return on investment (ROI) methodologies. Researchers and professionals have presented several models for accessing return on ICT investment from the financial and non-financial perspectives. Due to disperse dimensions of investment and its measuring return, still the government and ICT investors are puzzled to opt the best comprehensive evaluation strategy which can help them out for entire evaluation phases. Conceptually ROI can be divided into two types of measuring returns; financial and non-financial value. In this paper, we aim to develop the framework for building return methodology which can deal with both values. Therefore, we investigate the relationship between types of ICT investment and its returns value type. Stakeholder analysis and value measuring variables give strength to our proposed model and increase its feasibility. Overall the methodology has six stages to evaluate ICT investment which are dependent on its investment type, evaluation type, value measuring variables and stakeholders.

Keywords: ICT Investments, Return on Investment, Value on Investment, Value Measuring Variables, Stakeholder.

1   Introduction

The fast growth of ICT has built more pressure on the emerging organizations like; education, hospitals, banks, and other industries to adopt and upgrade ICT resources timely. Currently, the competitive environment not allows the organization to waste money and time, therefore, the ICT investor are more worried about the methods of measuring return from investments. One of such method is to study "return public value" from the investments, which considers non-financial measuring factor. This method was initiated by Gartner [1] who introduced the concept of measure Value on

A. Ell Hassanien et al. (Eds.): AMLTA 2012, CCIS 322, pp. 474–486, 2012.

Investment (VOI); return from list of intangible benefits. According to Gartner, VOI model is based on five basic measureable values, (i) business process reinvention, (ii) cultivation, management of knowledge assets, (iii) impact on communities, (iv) organizational performance, and (v) leadership quality. In addition, three other primary dimensions; (i) Scope of the investment, (ii) Organizational Impact, and (iii) Organizational Dynamics. There are several other research articles in which scholars discussed VOI concept as an ICT investment measuring method such as [3, 8]. The complex issues associated with VOI method are its scattered measurements which are ultimately link with the public value. Since the public value can calculates from the shared resources use by citizens of the particular organization or country. Anthony et al. [6] illustrated the public value measurement is a combination of values which extracting out of; the stakeholders, the technology investments, and government programs & operations. It shows the boundaries of VOI calculation are boundless and stretch around ICT strategy, stakeholders, and government programs.

In this study, we proposed a general framework for the evaluation of ICT investments. We concentrate on classifying the taxonomies of measuring ICT investment techniques, types of ICT investment, and types of stakeholders respectively. Further, the context of ICT investment and return value type will enhance the model's applicability and reusability in different environment.

The succeeding sections of this study outlined as follow: Related work on measuring return on investment is discussed in Section 2. In Section 3 the proposed model and conceptual work presented under the methodology part. Final discussion on this study is described in Section 4. In the end we presented the conclusion and future work.

2   Related Work

The previous literature illustrate that there have been several discussions on return on ICT investments. As long as ROI has discussed and improved around the world many times [6-8] is considers most common method in building evaluation model. Apart from ROI which deals with only financial matrix and has criticized in many researches [4, 7, 9] the focal point in this research is to enhance the ROI (return financial value) with the essence of VOI (return public value). REDF Network [8] used the social return on investments (SROI) to understand the social and environmental value being produced by enterprises in addition to the financial value created. It is a purposeful method for measuring the extra-financial value from the investment using stakeholder's analysis who receives the value. The major constraint in SROI is the assessment of only social values. While the public value (non-financial) may apply on other dimensions also as described in methodology section. Also it's a private network which not supposes to perform the tasks for all government technology programs.

These related works highlights good examples for initiating the same kind of work in KSA. The major limitations of these works are the restricted list of public value and stakeholders covered in assessment phase. In this study we are classifying the steps of building comprehensive framework and enhancing previous models. The major concern of this study is not to reject the previous methodologies but to enhance and modify them under the environment and culture of KSA. Also the government programs, policies and investment size vary from country to country. Therefore, our geographical concern in this study is to design the methodology which highlights the public values of KSA.

3   Methodology

Since the previous discussion on proposing the general framework for evaluation of ICT investment in KSA, in this section we will discuss the methodology for the proposed model (depicted in Figure 1). Therefore, we discussed the possible stages (section 3.3) for evaluation the ICT investments. Before presenting the proposed model following we are presenting the need of this framework under the circumstances of KSA.

3.1   The Purpose of Proposed ICT Investment Assessment Model – Case Study of Kingdom of Saudi Arabia

In related work we presented several examples from developing countries who have built the ICT investment evaluation model to provide better government services, and to make good relation in between government and citizens. Currently, KSA ICT market has astonishingly reached at the top in the Gulf and Middle East region. Specially, ICT industries and telecommunication represent around 55% and 51% of the total Middle East market respectively. [12]. The total ICT spending reached at Saudi Riyal (SR) 83 billion in 2011 and is forecast to increase by 10% more until the end of 2012 [13]. Further details of ICT spending in different industries and projects can be found in [2].

According to our findings, we found short progress made in KSA regarding assessment and calculation of return on investment from the huge amount of spending in government technology program/projects. Yesser e-government program [14] has one of the objectives to work for increase in ROI. But no comprehensive framework for evaluation has been available yet as compare to [5, 8] which can assess the public value (non-financial). Moreover, we have studied several official reports [2, 12, 15] published by higher authorities of KSA but not successful to get such methods. Therefore, in this study we proposed a model for measuring ICT investment under the conditions of KSA.

3.2   How to Measure Return from ICT Investment

Measuring return from the ICT investment has never been an easy task for the implementation. Conceptually, it has been divided into two forms; ROI uses to calculate financial return from the invested amount [16], on the other side VOI (also known as public value) considers to measure the non-financial [1]. But both play essential role for completing the evaluation strategy as discussed in section 2. ROI measurement can perform using quantitative analysis (financial factors) which is comparatively easy to implement, but VOI as its qualitative behavior (non-financial factors), which makes it more complex. In looking over the previous methodologies, from ROI perspective they are complete. But from VOI perspective, the shortened analysis on public value may generate incomplete results. Also, deficient relationship between ICT investment and its value receivers (stakeholders) can mislead the final assessment. We conclude this section on the description of essential factors (described in table-1) selected for proposed model (section 3.3) for ICT investment evaluation. The conceptual framework using overall methodology and Table-1 description presented in Figure-2.

Table 1. Essential Factors to be used in Proposed Model

Stages	Descriptions	Prototypes
1. Context of ICT Investment (CI)	Examine the background, risks, reasons, and goals of the ICT investment/project; (Improve Services, Political Concerns, and Government Establishment etc).	CI
2. Type of ICT Investment (TI)	According to the (CI) and purpose behind investment select the (TI); (Government, Public Service, Political, Social, etc). It will help finally in selection of (TE).	CI → TI
3. Stakeholder Analysis (SA)	Who will receive the value from investment according to (CI & TI); (Investor, Vendor, Government, and Citizen, etc).	CI + TI → SA
4. Value Measuring Variables (VMV)	List of value measuring variables/impact factors will be updated after (SA) analysis; (Operational Efficiency, Targeted Goals, etc).	SA → VMV
5. Type of Evaluation (TE)	With the help of (TI), select the type of evaluation for final assessment; (Strategic Value, Financial Return, etc).	TI + VMV → TE
6. Return Value (RV)	The final result of the evaluation strategy.	VMV+TE → RV

3.3   Proposed Framework – Stepwise Description

In this section we will discuss the proposed model which constructed using stepwise (Stage 1 – 6) strategy (demonstrated in Figure-1), where each step extracted by covering comprehensive literature review. Measuring public value from the ICT investment is a type of measurement need proper evaluation framework. A framework which must cover the maximum boundaries of the invested amount such as described in figure-1. The subsequent subsections provide the complete review process for building the model and its stage wise description. In this study we are not rejecting the previous methodologies, but enhancing to provide complete evaluation system in KSA. In future it will be improved through observations, questionnaires and testing on different cases.

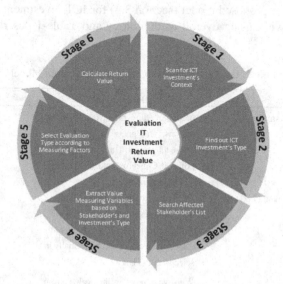

Fig. 1. Stepwise Demonstration of Proposed Model

Stage 1: Examine the Context of ICT Investment. Every process requires fine start to get the best output. Therefore, this stage regards as the backbone of the complete evaluation strategy. Evaluation process has to begin from somewhere to collect the utmost information for further procedure as Anthony [17] described this stage as initiator for assessment of ICT investment. In this phase, examine the context of ICT investment will provide the sufficient amount of information before proceeding to the further steps. It will help for the best classification of value receiving stakeholder as well as to get the information regarding goals and its limitations.

Justification. Anthony [17] explained the ICT evaluation is context-dependent. The complete procedure has to have the complete information about the investment; public value, goals, and limitations of the investment, which can collect by analyzing the context of ICT investment. Therefore, this stage plays a significant role for having the favorable results in the end.

Deliverables. There are several deliverables of Stage-1 as follows:

- The complete background, information, and stakeholders of the ICT investment.
- Goals, limitations of the investment which will be helpful to precede next step.

How to Obtain. There will be many questions to be answered to obtain the said deliverables such as (but not limited to):

- In which project invest the amount? Who will receive the value?
- What is the level of risk factor, reasons and goals behind the investment?

Stage 2: Types of ICT Investment. Using the previous step deliverables, illustrate in this stage the type of investment. The type of investment such as, strategic, political, financial, and etc, will help to set the goals of the investment. According to the goal, then value measuring variable will be defined. The investigation in this stage will help to select the measuring variables or impact factors, in addition the type of evaluation to be applied in the end.

Justification. To justify this phase we maintained the type of ICT investment taxonomy (Table-2) based on the previous applied methodologies. These are the possible types of investment we prepared form the literature review, possible enhancement will be applied accordingly. It shows the importance of choosing type of ICT investment in the evaluation process. It will help to finalize the value measuring variables to assess the investment, and list of stakeholders; who will be impacted directly or indirectly.

Deliverables. The possible deliverables are defined as follows:

- Gathered information will assist to choose the evaluation strategy.
- There are several internal and external stakeholders need to be identified properly.

How to Obtain. Following are some points will be used to obtain the desired results:

- Using the context of ICT investment. Who will affect by the investment?
- Conduct interview with the investors.
- The impact factors (table-2) will be measured in evaluation phase, using questionnaires and financial returns after the investment.

In the following taxonomy factors; types, list of possible stakeholders, goals and value measuring variables has extracted using 'Referenced' (the last column) model. There can be less or more information in all extracted features by observation and test implementation. The list of stakeholder showed the direct and indirect impacted elements. Measuring variables also described according to the methodology but it will be based on the respective government. For example, under the KSA environment the measurements factors can depend on Kingdom Royalty, Muslim world, Hajj (pilgrim) Management, and Oil reserves. The main purpose of this taxonomy is to identify the major factors work behind every ICT investment.

Stage 3: Classification of Stakeholders. The evaluation process of ICT investment does not complete without analysis of public value impact during value creation phase; the value receiver stakeholders. Anthony et al. [6] described stakeholders that, every ICT investment has its direct and indirect impacts on different kinds of internal and external stakeholders. In this phase the stakeholder analysis helps to collect the

Table 2. Taxonomy – Types of ICT Investment (Using Previous Literature)

Types	Possible Stakeholders	Goals (Possible Outcomes)	Value Measuring Variables / Impact Factors (to assess the investment)	Ref.
Strategic Government- Invest amount for the sake of government agencies, policies to initiate, modify and implement strategies. Real beneficiaries in this investment are government's associated group.	Government Investors Vendors Partners	The goal is to provide the facilities to government employees, agencies, investors and other related collaborative groups. To upgrade the business process and technology.	Efficient Process. Common Facilities. Special Services. Profitable Business. Fresh Environment.	[5]
Strategic Public- Government ICT strategy program are part of it. Reasons behind the investment are efficient public services, update technology, and to provide modern facilities.	Citizens Government Partners	Increase the service level high. Provide public resources, current technology and better living standards. Ultimately this investment will support government.	Quick services. Online Facilities. Customer Satisfaction. Workforce Power. Profitable Operation. Human Resources.	[1] [10]
Development: Investment amount which require in developing and maintaining ICT project. Development is necessary to provide updated technology/resources to the citizens/employees.	Citizens Government Investor Vendors	Develop and maintain the business processes and technological factors. The new technology will support the program in better way.	Efficiency. Effectiveness. Updated Facilities. Availability.	[3]
Political: The investment amount for political affairs, such as marketing and elections campaigns. The current government has the right to use this investment in their benefits.	Citizens Government Investors	To get personal, communal & tribal support for all type of government actions and policies. It will support political affairs to make the status stronger for current and futures angle.	Overall Responses. Public Benefits. Loyalty. Trust.	[5] [11]
Social: Investment for making corporate and social life stronger. It will provide facility to the citizens and investors to build good social and business relationships.	Citizens Investors Vendors Government	Affect in increasing the social and corporate links. Specially use for building relationship, profiles, personal identification and social communities.	Social Development Social Responsibility. Corporate Responsibility. Trusty Environment.	[8]

Table 2. (*continued*)

Environmental: Government makes this investment for building safe and healthy environment in the order to better living and doing business for respective citizens and investors.	Citizens Investors Partners	Impact on increasing in the artificial and natural resources to provide best atmosphere for living.	Environmental Development. Safe Environment. [8]
Cultural: Investment for organizing Cultural and religious activities. It will help to remind the cultural and religious responsibilities.	Citizens Investors Partners	Cultural and religious activities are major part of every society. It will help to make the society stronger and more social.	Cultural Activities. Religious Activities. Social Activities. [8]

value measuring variables through the impacts of investments. This process consists on in depth knowledge of investment's context (stage-1).

Justification. The justification of this stage can be extracted through the list of stakeholders (Table-3). This table has proper definition of each stakeholder. Furthermore, we created the possible relationship between each stakeholder to its related type of investment, and value measuring variables. The taxonomy has built from the reference of previous literature explained in table-2, where we explained the investment's type.

Deliverables. In this stage the deliverables are as follows:

- Generate the stakeholders list by using the in depth knowledge of investment's context.
- It will help to ·maintain the value measuring variables, and ultimately complete evaluation strategy.

How to Obtain. Obtaining methodology is as follows:

- Using the information collected from previous two stages.

Stage 4: Value Measuring Variables / Impact Factors. This is the critical point of the overall methodology. Point out the value measuring variables is a difficult task as the wrong selection may lead to the inaccurate result. With the help of measuring variables, we can measure the invested costs and its return benefits. There are different approaches to select these factors, in table-3 using the literature review we illustrated the taxonomy of stakeholders and their corresponding possible impact factors (which affected by investment). Those factors are useful entities for evaluation the assessment depend on the "Level of affection" rates "High" or "Low".

Justification. Every evaluation strategy has impact factors or value measuring variables to generate the analytical outcome. [17] described the measuring variable are the important factors for the evaluation of investment. It may consist of several kind of measuring variables such as; Efficiency Measures, Impact Measures, Risk Analysis, Cost Effectiveness, finally measuring cost. Moreover, SROI [8] model calculate social value, enterprise index of return, and blended index of return in evaluation phase of ICT investment. It clearly justifies the importance and use of measuring variable in evaluation process.

Table 3. Taxonomy – Types of Stakeholder (Reference from Table-2)

Type of Stakeholder (Direct and indirect value receivers)	Possible Related ICT Investment (What is related ICT investment; who impact on the stakeholder)	Value Measuring Variables (Factors which can use for evaluation of expected value)
Citizens: In stakeholder's list, citizens of any country receive the great impact of ICT investment. The population of a country has impact on the budgeting too.	Citizens receive impact from almost every kind of ICT investment. They play essential role in the success and failure of any investment.	Service Performance Value Impact Online Facilities Customer Satisfaction Human Resources
Government: In ICT investment government role is essential. The Government agencies, employees, and partners receive larger impact from the investment.	Government has big relation and control on any kind of investment. They do invest as a whole or provide space to collaborative work with investors and vendors.	Risk Factors Return Value Value Impact Operational Efficiency Strategic Establishment
Investors: Investors may have different categories (i.e. Vendor and partners). We described all of three as different entity to construct proper variable/evaluation.	This category may also involve in almost every kind of investment. The investor or businessman invests money as a large stakeholder.	Return Value Efficient Business Process Value Impact Secure and wide space Risk Factors
Partners: They work as an association with the government and other private organizations. This type of stakeholders can invest as local or foreign citizen.	Strategic Government (partially). Cultural. Strategic Public. Environmental.	Return Value Risk Factors Business Satisfaction Value Impact Business Process
Vendors: Vendors are those personnel who involve as a dealer, seller, wholesaler, and retailer. They invest partially and fully with the support of government agencies and policies.	Strategic Government (partially). Development. Social.	Return Value Risk Factors Value Impact Trust on Government Policies Protected Environment

Deliverables. The possible outcomes of this analysis are as follows:

- Depends on the types of ICT investment and its stakeholders it will generate possible list of measuring variables.
- The extracted variables such as; social value, strategic establishment, operational efficiency, customer satisfaction, which will help to interpret the return of the investments.

How to Obtain. The following methodology will be used to obtain the result:

- There is no proper format or method to generate the variables who impacted the stakeholders in value generation phase.
- Stakeholder analysis and list of question will help to finalize the measuring variables. The example questions used in different methodology described in [8, 3].

Stage 5: Evaluation Value(s) Type. Once we obtain the all previous features defined from stage (1-4). Now, it's time to select and apply the evaluation strategy. In this section we identify the relationship between ICT investment and its evaluation strategy (depicted in Table-4) with the help of stakeholders list the measuring variable already identified. This table is illustrated from the combination of Table (2-3), where we observed the previous methodologies and their way of processing the evaluation. These observations will be maintained through practical implementation of the proposed model using case studies of KSA in future work.

Justification. This is the final stage of proposing the evaluation strategy which is composed from the previous four phases already described in detail. The relationship between the ICT investment and how the investment will be evaluated depicted in table-4, which shows the overall procedure the measure the investment. In future, new investment type will cause of generate new evaluation strategy. This procedure is basically making the evaluation more organized.

Deliverables. This phase will generate the following results:

- Select the type of evaluation strategy will be applied accordingly.
- Calculate value measuring variables and final return using stakeholder's data.

Table 4. Relationship between Investment and Evaluation Type (Ref. Table: 2-3)

(TI) Investment Type	(SA) Stakeholder Type	(VMV) Value Measuring Variables	(TE) Evaluation (s) Value Type
Strategic – Government	Government	Risk Factors	Strategic Value
	Investors & Vendors	Value Impact & Loyalty	Financial Return
Strategic– Public	Citizens	Service Performance	Strategic Value
	Government & Partners	Value Impact/Satisfaction	Financial Return
Development	Citizens	Efficiency & Effectiveness	Development Value
	Government & Investor	Updated Facilities	Financial Return
Political	Citizens	Overall Responses	Political Value
	Government & Investor	Public Benefits & Loyalty	Financial Return
Social	Citizens & Government	Social Development	Social Value
	Investors/Vendors	Social Responsibility	Financial Return
Environmental	Citizens	Environmental Development	Environmental
	Investors & Partners	Safe Environment	Financial Return
Cultural	Citizens	Cultural Activities	Cultural Value
	Investors/Partner	Religious/Social Activities	Financial Return

How to Obtain. Following are the points for obtain the final outcomes:

- The financial return value will calculate by collecting all financial data.
- Qualitative analysis will be applied on non-financial data to calculate return value.
- Surveys and questionnaires will be used to obtain the feedback from the stakeholders.

Stage 6: Final Return Value. Final return value calculated in the previous stage. In this phase reports and analysis will be generated to get to know about the status of ICT investment. Proper evaluation will provide the success and failure rate of ICT investment. Future investment can be based on the final return value. Following is the figure-2 illustrated the conceptual framework describing the overall flow of the presented methodology.

4   Discussion

This section describes the discussion on the methodology and conceptual framework presented in the previous section. This study will assist the ICT investors and decision makers of KSA; which known as a largest ICT investor in the Gulf and Middle East religion. The methodology and framework can provide detailed analysis on previous invested amount and will help to take decision for future investments. The presented model can assess the numerous measurement factors such as; service performance, risk factors, utilization of resources, financial return, public value and etc.

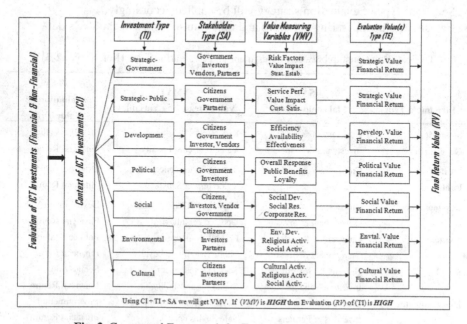

Fig. 2. Conceptual Framework for Evaluation of ICT Investments

Basically, the presented methodology is step wise general approach to build the evaluation strategy for invested amount in any environment. Start from analyzing the context of ICT investment, stakeholder analysis which will help to extract the value measuring variables. Finally, the last step is help to select evaluation strategy and calculate return value. The detailed description of each stage, its deliverables, and list of steps to obtain the outcome are proposed guidelines which will help in evaluation. In addition, proposed conceptual framework acquired using defined methodology will help to understand the flow of working on different tasks. This study is not rejecting the previous methodologies, but the main concern is to build and enhance such strategies like [5, 8], under the conditions of KSA. In last, we found in this study that, wide boundaries of measuring the ICT investment are still open to work on building new evaluation strategy using stakeholder's analysis and their value measuring factors.

5   Conclusion and Future Work

This study describes the several phases involved in evaluation of ICT investment. It's a basic approach which leads the ICT investment decision until its proper evaluation using different measuring factors and stakeholder's perspective. Larger investments and lack of evaluation methodology applied in KSA, this study will create a new boom in this field. The proposed framework will provide the secure environment to the decision makers for new ICT investment and projects. Continuous improvement through feedback and survey strategies from the official authorities and stakeholders will help to make this framework in better form.

The proposed model showed the stepwise approach consists of the six stages. In future the case based implementation on Saudi governmental organization will guide to improve the model. The measuring variables and list of stakeholders has identified using the previous methodologies, the future task is to apply it on Saudi organization to test and validate the proposed model.

References

1. Hurley, D.: Changing the View of ROI and VOI – Value on Investment. Gartner Research Note (November 2011)
2. Communication and Information Technology Commission (CITC) IT Report: CITC Report, Kingdom of Saudi Arabia (2010)
3. Val IT Framework for Business Technology Management: Information Systems Audit and Control Association (ISACA), USA (2009)
4. Benaroch, M., Kauffman, R.: Justifying Electronic Banking Network Expansion Using Real Options Analysis. MIS Quarterly 24(2), 197–225 (2000)
5. Value Measuring Methodology (VMM), How-to-Guide: CIO Council Best Practices Committee, Washington D.C., pp. 1–116 (2002)
6. Cresswell, A.M., Brian Burke, G., Pardo, T.A.: Advancing Return on Investment, Analysis for Government IT, A Public Value Framework. Center for Technology in Government, University at Albany (September 2006)

7. McShea, M.: Return on Infrastructure, the New ROI. Phillips Healthcare, IT Pro Magazine (July-August 2009)
8. SROI Methodology: Analyzing the Value of Social Purpose Enterprise Within a Social Return on Investment Framework, Roberts Enterprise Development Fund (REDF), California, San Francisco, pp. 1–93 (2001)
9. Forrer, D.A., Anderson, T.A.: The Dichotomy of Measurement: Information Technology Return on Investment in the Public Sector. In: Proceedings of the 12th Annual Conference of the Production and Operations Management Society, Orlando, Florida, pp. 1–10 (2001)
10. Demand and Value Assessment Methodology (DVAM): for better Government Services, Proposed by Information management Office, Australian Government (2003)
11. IDA Value of Investment: Final Report European Commission DG Enterprise (ECDGE), Gothenburg, Sweden, pp. 1–60 (2003)
12. Saudi Arabian General Investment Authority (SAGIA) Report: ICT Sector Success stories. SAGIA, KSA (2011)
13. Saudi Arabia ICT Spending, http://www.datacentres.com/news/saudi-arabias-ict-spending-reaches-sr83-billion-2011-grow-12-2012 (last accessed date June 25, 2012)
14. Yesser, http://www.yesser.gov.sa (last accessed July 1, 2012)
15. The National Communications and Information Technology Plan (NCITP), The Vision Towards the Information Society. Ministry of Communication and Information Technology (MCIT), Kingdom of Saudi Arabia (2005)
16. Dadayan, L.: Measuring Return on Government IT Investments. In: 13th European Conference on IT Evaluation, Italy, September 28-29 (2006)
17. Cresswell, A.M.: Return on Investment in Information Technology: A Guide for Managers, Center for Technology in Government, Albany, USA (August 2004)

Learning and Applying Range Adaptation Rules in Case-Based Reasoning Systems

Dina A. Sharaf-Eldeen, Ibrahim F. Moawad, Khalid El Bahnasy, and M.E. Khalifa

Faculty of Computer and Information Sciences, Ain Shams University, Abbasia, Cairo, Egypt
{dina_ali,ibrahim_moawad,khaled.bahnasy,esskalifa}@cis.asu.edu.eg

Abstract. The retrieval-only Case-Based Reasoning (CBR) systems do not provide acceptable accuracy in critical domains such as medical. Besides, the case adaptation process in CBR is often a challenging issue as it has been traditionally carried out manually by domain experts. In this paper, a new case-based approach using transformational adaptation rules called "range adaptation rules" is proposed to improve the accuracy of a retrieval-only CBR system. The range adaptation rules are automatically generated from the case-base. In this approach, after solving each new problem, the case-base is expanded and the range adaptation rules are updated automatically. To evaluate the proposed approach, a prototype is implemented and experimented in agriculture domain to classify the IRIS plant types. The experimental results show that the proposed approach increases the classification accuracy comparing with the retrieval-only CBR system.

Keywords: Case-based reasoning (CBR), Case adaptation, IRIS plant classification, Range adaptation rules.

1   Introduction

Case-Based Reasoning (CBR) is a reasoning methodology that simulates human reasoning using past experiences to solve new problems [1]. The classical model of the CBR problem solving cycle consists of four steps [2]: (1) RETRIEVE step that is responsible for retrieving one or more similar cases to the new problem (a new case);(2) REUSE step that is responsible for reusing the solution of the most similar case to the new case. It may include the adaptation task in which the solution of the retrieved case is adapted to fit the new case; (3) REVISE step that is responsible for revising the suggested solution for confirmation and (4) RETAIN step that is responsible for retaining the learned case for future use.

CBR has been successfully applied in various domains [1, 3-6]. However, adaptation is often a challenging issue and has been traditionally carried out manually by domain experts [7]. Besides, most retrieval-only CBR systems fail to solve some of the new problems, so they do not provide convincing accuracy in critical domains like medical. In this paper, a new case-based approach using range transformational adaptation technique is proposed to improve the retrieval-only CBR system accuracy. This

A. Ell Hassanien et al. (Eds.): AMLTA 2012, CCIS 322, pp. 487–495, 2012.

approach has three main objectives. Firstly, extracting range transformational adaptation rules from the case-base automatically. Secondly, exploiting and updating these range adaptation rules in the CBR cycle dynamically. Thirdly, evaluating the proposed approach by implementing a prototype to classify the IRIS plant types. This evaluation shows that the proposed approach increases the accuracy of retrieval-only CBR system.

The rest of this paper is organized as follows. Section 2 reviews some recent related CBR systems. The approach conceptual view is introduced in section 3. Section 4 presents how the range adaptation rules are extracted from the case-base. Section 5 shows IRIS plants classification example and experimental evaluation. Finally, section 6 concludes the paper.

2   Related Work

In the past 20 years, Case-based reasoning (CBR) methodology has attracted much attention since the underlying idea of reusing the experiences of solving previous problems is a powerful and frequently used way of human problem solving [8]. CBR systems may use adaptation technique to solve more new problems [9]. In general, adaptation knowledge describes how the feature-value differences between the new case and the retrieved similar cases affect the differences in their solutions [10]. There are four types of adaptation techniques: Null adaptation, Transformational adaptation, Derivational adaptation, and Compositional adaptation [11].

Adaptation is becoming increasingly important to ensure that cases remain relevant over time [12]. Huan Li et al [8] proposed a method for learning adaptation rules and applied them on a case-base of plants and flowers. However, their method generates a lot of adaptation rules, which are needed to be refined before being used in the CBR cycle.

On the other hand, CBR has many different applications in the medical and health domains. Adaptation is often a challenging issue in the health sciences and has been carried out manually by physicians/experts of the domain. According to Shahina Begum et al [7] and Yusof and buckingham [9], only some of the recent medical CBR systems [13, 14, and 15] adopted and explored different approaches of automatic and semi-automatic adaptation strategies. Although these systems apply adaptation, the adaptation knowledge remains static during the CBR life cycle.

In this paper, a new case-based approach using range transformational adaptation rules technique is proposed to improve the retrieval-only CBR system accuracy. The range adaptation rules are automatically learned from the case-base and they are dynamically updated during the CBR life cycle.

3   Approach Conceptual View

Figure (1) shows the conceptual view of the proposed case-based approach. The approach develops the classical CBR by integrating an additional module called Range Adaptation Rules Generation Module. Initially, based on the case-base, the Range Adaptation Rules Generation module is responsible for extracting the range adaptation rules. After that, the CBR process life cycle starts when a new problem needs to be solved. In the **RETRIEVE** step, similar cases to the new problem are retrieved from the case-base. In the **REUSE/ADAPT** step, the solution of the retrieved similar case is either reused to the new problem or adapted using the range adaptation rules to fit the new problem as a suggested solution. In case of adaptation process failure, the solution of the most similar case is returned as a suggested solution. In the **REVISE** step, the suggested solution is revised to be confirmed and the confidence value of range adaptation rules may be updated. In case of adaptation, if the adapted solution is suitable, the range adaptation rules are updated by increasing the confidence value of the used range adaptation rule. Otherwise, if the adapted solution is not suitable for the current problem, a more suitable solution is provided by a domain expert and the confidence value of the used range adaptation rule is decreased. In the **RETAIN** step, the case-base is expanded by adding the new learned case. Because of a new learned case, the Range Adaptation Rules Generation module may add new/update range adaptation rules.

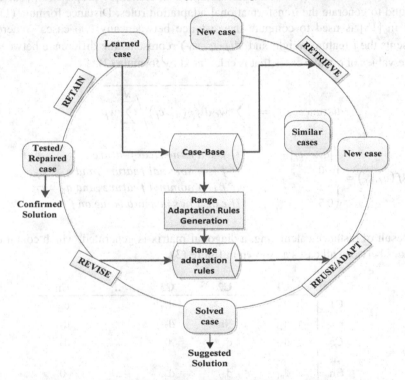

Fig. 1. The Approach Conceptual View

4   Range Adaptation Rules Generation Module

The range adaptation rules relate the changing of the problem feature value ranges to the changing in the solution feature value. Figure (2) shows a general form of the range adaptation rule in IF-THEN format.

> **Rule :**RangeRule1 *Confidence value: c1*
> **IF** PFeature$_1$ *CHANGES FROM* [min_1 , max_1] *TO* [min_2 , max_2] **AND** PFeature $_2$ *CHANGES*
> *FROM* [min_3 , max_3] *TO* [min_4 , max_4] **AND**...etc.
> **THEN** SolFeature$_1$ *CHANGES FROM* X TO Y

Fig. 2. Range adaptation rule general form

The Range Adaptation Rules Generation module extracts the range adaptation rules in three steps: Case-Pair Comparison, Transformational Adaptation Rules Generation, and Range Adaptation Rules Generation.

Step1: Case-Pair Comparison
The first step of range adaptation rules generation module is to calculate the dissimilarity between all cases. The case-pair comparison technique proposed in [16, 17] is exploited to generate the transformational adaptation rules. Distance formula (1) proposed in [18] is used to compute the distance between any two cases. Where W_f represents the f feature weight and $dif(q_f, c_f)$ represents the difference between the feature values of q and c cases that is calculated by formula (2).

$$distance(q,c) = \sqrt{\sum_{f=1}^{N} w_f\, dif^2(q_f, c_f) \bigg/ \sum_{f=1}^{N} w_f} \qquad (1)$$

$$dif(q_f, c_f) = \begin{cases} |q_f - c_f| & , & \textit{if f is a numerical feature} \\ 0 & , & \textit{if f is a nominal feature, and } q_f = c_f \\ 1 & , & \textit{if f is a nominal feature, and } q_f \neq c_f \\ 0.5 & , & \textit{if c or q has missing value on f} \end{cases} \qquad (2)$$

As a result of distance calculating, a diagonal matrix is generated, which contains the distances between all cases as shown in figure (3).

	C1	C2	C3	..	Cn
C1	0	d_{12}	d_{13}	..	d_{1n}
C2	d_{21}	0	d_{23}	..	d_{2n}
C3	d_{31}	d_{32}	0	..	d_{2n}
..	..	..	..	..	..
Cn	d_{n1}	d_{n2}	d_{n3}	..	0

Fig. 3. Case-pair distances matrix

Step2: Transformational Adaptation Rules Generation
The transformational adaptation rules relate the changing of the problem feature values to the changing in the solution feature value. Figure (4) shows a general form of the transformational adaptation rule in IF-THEN format.

> **Rule :**Rule1   *Confidence value: c1*
> **IF** PFeature$_1$ *changes from val$_1$ to* val$_2$ **AND** PFeature$_2$ *changes from* val$_3$ *to* val$_4$ **AND**...etc.
> **THEN** SolFeature$_1$ *changes from* X *to* Y

Fig. 4. Transformational adaptation rules general form

After the case-pair distances matrix is derived in step 1, it is used to generate the transformational adaptation rules. The differences between the feature values of each pair of the compared cases are used to generate the antecedent part of the transformational adaptation rule, and the differences between the solutions in the compared cases become the rule consequent part. If the distance between any two compared cases is greater than a certain threshold value (t) which is determined by the domain expert, they are not used to generate a transformational adaptation rule.

Step3: Range Adaptation Rules Generation
The transformational adaptation rules generation step generates a lot of adaptation rules, so they need to be generalized to extract the range adaptation rules to be exploited during the CBR cycle. Figure (5) shows the range adaptation rules generation algorithm.

> **Input**: Transformational adaptation rules (AR)
> **Output**: Range adaptation rules
> *Cluster the adaptation rules (AR) based on the number of adaption rule conditions (CFCS)*
> *For each cluster C in (CFCS) clusters do*
> *Cluster the adaptation rules in cluster C based on adaption rule action (AFCS)*
> *For each cluster A in (AFCS) clusters do*
>   *For each condition feature (Fi) in adaption rule conditions do*
>   *Get minimum value of the from part (FromMin Fi)*
>   *Get maximum value of the from part (FromMax Fi)*
>   *Get minimum value of the to part (ToMin Fi)*
>   *Get maximum value of the to part (ToMax Fi)*
>   *Generate the feature Fi changing ranges:*
>   *from range of (Fi)=[FromMin Fi , FromMax Fi] and To range of (Fi)=*
>   *[ToMin Fi, ToMax Fi]*
>   *Generate the range adaptation rule Ri*
>   *Add Ri to the range adaptation rules*

Fig. 5. Range adaptation rules generation algorithm

5   Classification Example and Experimental Evaluation

In the following, to show how the presented approach works, IRIS plant classification example is illustrated in details. Besides, a prototype has been implemented to experimentally evaluate the approach using the IRIS plant case-base. In this example, the case-base contains the IRIS plant data set, which is obtained from UCI Machine Learning Repository [19]. It includes three classes, where each class contains 50 objects. Each class refers to a type of IRIS plant. Each case consists of four equally-weighted attributes (sepal length, sepal width, petal length, petal width) and the solution attribute, which is the IRIS plant type (Iris Setosa, Iris Versicolour or Iris Virginica).

5.1   IRIS Plant Classification Example

Table 1 shows a sample of the IRIS plant case-base. To solve an IRIS plant classification problem (sepal length= 7.0, sepal width=2.9, petal length=5.5, petal width =1.5), the presented approach went through two phase: range adaptation rules generation phase and IRIS plant classification phase.

Table 1. IRIS plant case-base sample

	Case 1	Case 2	Case 3	Case 4	Case 5	Case 6	Case 7
sepal length	4.3	4.8	5.7	6.0	6.0	4.9	7.9
sepal width	3.0	3.4	4.4	3.4	2.9	2.5	3.8
petal length	1.1	1.6	1.5	4.5	4.5	4.5	6.4
petal width	0.1	0.2	0.4	1.6	1.5	1.7	2
Class	Iris-setosa	Iris-setosa	Iris-setosa	Iris-versicolor	Iris-versicolor	Iris-virginica	Iris-virginica

Initially, during the range adaptation rules generation phase, the transformational adaptation rules were generated from the case-base and then the range adaptation rules were extracted to be used in the CBR cycle. By default, the confidence values of the range adaptation rules were set to 1. 9280 transformational adaptation rules were generated and 34 range adaptation rules were extracted. Table 2 shows a sample of the range adaptation rules generated from the case-base.

Table 2. Range adaptation rules sample

Name	Adaptation Rule
Range rule 1	**IF** [sepal length] changes from [5.9,6.5] to [6,7.2] **AND** [petal length] changes from [4.5,4.8] to [5,6] **THEN** [IRIS class] changes from 'Iris-versicolor' to 'Iris-virginica'
Range rule 2	**IF** [sepal length] changes from [4.9,7] to [4.3,5.8] **AND** [sepal width] changes from [2.2,3.4] to [2.9,4.4] **AND** [petal length] changes from [3.3,5.1] to [1,1.9] **AND** [petal width] changes from [0.1,1.8] to [0.1,0.5] **THEN** [IRIS class] changes from 'Iris-versicolo'r to 'Iris-setosa'
Range rule 3	**IF** [sepal length] changes from [4.3,5.4] to [5.4,7] **AND** [petal length] changes from [1.1,1.9] to [3.6,5] **AND** [petal width] changes from [0.1,0.5] to [1.3,1.8] **THEN** [IRIS class] changes from 'Iris-setosa' to 'Iris-versicolor'

Secondly, during the IRIS plant classification phase, the CBR cycle steps were invoked to solve this problem as follow.

● **RETRIEVE and REUSE/ADAPT Steps**

In the **RETRIEVE** step, the distances between the new problem and all cases in the case-base were calculated using formula (1). No case with distance 0 to the new problem, so the case with the smallest distance to the new problem was returned (case 5).

In the **REUSE/ADAPT** step, the retrieved solution of case 5 needs to be adapted to fit the new problem. To select the appropriate range adaptation rule to be used in **ADAPT** step, the difference attributes set between the retrieved case (case 5) and the new problem was derived using formula (3) [9].

$$\text{DiffAtt}(e, t) = \{a_e \in C_e \mid a_t \neq a_e, a_t \in C_t, e \in E, t \in T\}, \tag{3}$$

Where C_e is the attributes set of a case e, C_t is the attributes set of a target problem t, a_e denotes attribute of the case e, a_t denotes attribute of the target problem t, E is the retrieved cases space, T is the target problem space.

For this problem, the DiffAtt (Case 5, the new problem) = {"sepal length"," petal length"}. The range adaptation rules that include these difference attributes were chosen from the range adaptation rules set, and then they were ordered by their confidence values. Based on the attribute values transition range, the range adaptation rule 1 (presented in table 3) was chosen and the solution of Case 5 was updated to fit this problem by substituting the value of "class" attribute from 'Iris-versicolor' to 'Iris-virginica' and then returned. Therefore, this problem belongs to Iris-virginica class.

● **REVISE and RETAIN Steps**

By comparing the derived solution of the new problem with its original solution in the testing data set, it was correct. Therefore, the confidence value of the range adaptation rule 1 was increased by one. Also, a learned case was composed and added to the case-base. As a result of adding the new learned case, the range adaptation rules were updated if necessary.

5.2 Experimental Evaluation

To evaluate the presented approach, a prototype has been implemented to classify the IRIS plant types. One hundred and twenty cases (80%) were selected as a training data set and thirty cases (20%) were separated as a testing data set. The experiment was conducted in two steps:

1. **Applying retrieval-only CBR**: In this step, the testing data was tested using the classical CBR without applying the range adaptation rules.
2. **Applying the developed prototype:** In this step, the range adaptation rules were applied.

The developed prototype increased the classification accuracy comparing with the retrieval-only CBR systems. As shown in figure (6), the classification accuracy of the

494   D.A. Sharaf-Eldeen et al.

retrieval-only CBR system was 83.33 %, where the developed prototype classification accuracy was 100%. The classification accuracy was calculated using formula (4).

$$Classification\ accuracy = TC/TT \qquad (4)$$

Where TC is the total number of test cases classified correctly and TT is the total number of the test cases.

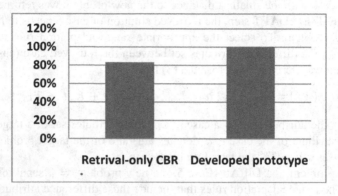

Fig. 6. Retrieval-only CBR vs. the developed prototype classification accuracy

In addition, the developed prototype achieved 100% classification accuracy versus one of the recent IRIS plant classification systems [20], which gave classification accuracy ranged from 83.33% to 96.66%.

6   Conclusion

In this paper, a new case-based approach using range transformational adaptation rules was proposed to improve the retrieval-only CBR system accuracy. The range adaptation rules are automatically extracted from the case-base. Also, after solving each new problem, the case-base is expanded and the range adaptation rules are updated dynamically. IRIS plants classification was presented as a case study to show how the developed approach prototype improved the classification accuracy of the retrieval-only CBR systems.

References

1. Kolodner, J.: Case based reasoning. Morgan Kauffman, San Mateo (1993)
2. Aamodt, A., Plaza, E.: Case-Based Reasoning: Foundational Issues, Methodological Variations and System Approaches. AICOM 7(1), 39–52 (1994)
3. Baumeister, J., Atzmüller, M., Puppe, F.: Inductive Learning for Case-Based Diagnosis with Multiple Faults. In: Craw, S., Preece, A.D. (eds.) ECCBR 2002. LNCS (LNAI), vol. 2416, pp. 28–42. Springer, Heidelberg (2002)
4. Hunt, J., Miles, R.: Hyprid case-based reasoning. The Knowledge Engineering Review 9(4), 383–397 (1994)

5. Lenz, M., Bartsch-Spörl, B., Burkhard, H.-D., Wess, S. (eds.): Case-Based Reasoning Technology. LNCS (LNAI), vol. 1400. Springer, Heidelberg (1998)
6. Macura, R.T., Macura, K.: Case-based reasoning: opportunities and applications in health care. Artificial Intelligence in Medicine 9(1), 1–4 (1997)
7. Begum, S., Ahmed, M., Funk, P., Xiong, N., Folke, M.: Case-Based Reasoning Systems in the Health Sciences: A Survey of Recent Trends and Developments. IEEE Transactions on Systems, Man, and Cybernetics–Part C: Applications and Reviews 41(4), 421–434 (2011)
8. Li, H., Li, X., Hu, D., Hao, T., Wenyin, L., Chen, X.: Adaptation rule learning for case based reasoning. Concurrency and Computation: Practice and Experience 21(5), 673–689 (2009)
9. Yusof, M., Buckingham, C.: Medical case-based reasoning: A review of retrieving, matching and adaptation processes in recent systems. In: Hamza, M.H. (ed.) Proceedings of the Artificial Intelligence and Applications, pp. 72–76. Innsbruck, Austria (2009)
10. Pal, S.K., Shiu, S.C.K.: Foundations of soft case-based reasoning. Wiley-Interscience, USA (2004)
11. Chang, C.G., Cui, J.J., Wang, D.W., Hu, K.Y.: Research on case adaptation techniques in case-based reasoning. In: Proc. of ICMLC 2004, pp. 2128–2133 (2004)
12. Holt, A., Bichindaritz, I., Schmidt, R., Perner, P.: Medical applications in case-based reasoning. The Knowledge Engineering Review 20(3), 286–292 (2006)
13. Huang, M.J., Chen, M.Y., Lee, S.C.: Integrating data mining with case-based reasoning for chronic diseases prognosis and diagnosis. Expert Systems with Applications 32(3), 856–867 (2007)
14. Schmidt, R., Gierl, L.: A prognostic model for temporal courses that combines temporal abstraction and case-based reasoning. International Journal of Medical Informatics 74(2-4), 307–315 (2005)
15. Schmidt, R., Vorobieva, O.: Case-based reasoning investigation of therapy inefficacy. Knowledge-Based Systems 19(5), 333–340 (2006)
16. Craw, S., Wiratunga, N., Rowe, R.C.: Learning adaptation knowledge to improve case-based reasoning. Artificial Intelligence 170(16-17), 1175–1192 (2006)
17. Hanney, K., Keane, M.: Learning Adaptation Rules from a Case-Base. In: Smith, I., Faltings, B.V. (eds.) EWCBR 1996. LNCS, vol. 1168, pp. 179–192. Springer, Heidelberg (1996)
18. Gu, M., Tong, X., Aamodt, A.: Comparing similarity calculation methods in conversational CBR. In: Proceedings of the 2005 IEEE International Conference on Information Reuse and Integration, Las Vegas, NV, pp. 427–432 (2005)
19. Machine Learning Repository-Iris Data Set, http://archive.ics.uci.edu/ml/datasets/Iris (accessed July 2012)
20. Swain, M., Dash, S.K., Dash, S., Mohapatra, A.: An Approach for IRIS Plant Classification Using Neural Network. International Journal on Soft Computing 3(1), 79–89 (2012)

Integration of Neural Network Preprocessing Model for OMI Aerosol Optical Depth Data Assimilation

A. Ali, S.E. Amin, H.H. Ramadan, and M.F. Tolba

Scientific Computing Department, Ain Shams University, Cairo, Egypt
ahmed4a@hotmail.com

Abstract. A regional chemical transport model assimilated with daily mean satellite and ground based Aerosol Optical Depth (AOD) observations is used to produce three dimensional distributions of aerosols throughout Europe for the year 2005. In this paper, the AOD measurements of the Ozone Monitoring Instrument (OMI) are assimilated with Polyphemus model. In order to overcome missing satellite data, a methodology for pre-processing AOD based on Neural Network (NN) is proposed. The aerosol forecasts involve two-phase process assimilation, and then a feedback correction process. During the assimilation phase, the total column AOD is estimated from the model aerosol fields. The model state is then adjusted to improve the agreement between the simulated AOD and satellite retrievals of AOD. The results show that the assimilation of AOD observations significantly improves the forecast for total mass. The errors on aerosol chemical composition are reduced and are sometimes vanished by the assimilation procedure and NN preprocessing, which shows a big contribution to the assimilation process.

Keywords: air quality, data assimilation, neural network, satellite observations, aerosol.

1   Introduction

Aerosols are small particles produced by natural and man-made sources that both reflect and absorb incoming solar radiation. Aerosol concentration and chemical properties are important parameters in climate change modeling, in studies of regional radiation balances and the hydrological cycle [1]. Using radiance observations from satellite instruments, it is possible to estimate the attenuation of solar energy as it passes through a column of atmosphere due to particulates, a quantity commonly known as (AOD). Since radiance intensity depends on AOD, deterministic forward simulation algorithms are used to "retrieve" AOD [2, 3]. These algorithms predict radiances for candidate aerosol types and amounts and select the types and amounts that most closely match the observed radiances. While deterministic algorithms provide accurate retrievals, they are computationally demanding, and this limits achievable spatial resolution and the ability to provide timely updates. To address these issues we are exploring a complementary statistical approach based on supervised learning.

A. Ell Hassanien et al. (Eds.): AMLTA 2012, CCIS 322, pp. 496–506, 2012.

In preliminary work, we used artificial neural networks (ANNs) to construct global aerosol predictors by learning from all available labeled aerosol data [4]. While the results were encouraging, the heterogeneous spatial-temporal nature of aerosol makes it unlikely that a single aerosol predictor could fully exploit distinct properties of specific spatial regions [4]. An alternative is to construct a number of local predictors, each specific to a given spatial area. While development of local models addresses the data heterogeneity problem, the scarcity of region-specific data could raise issues related to the choice of model complexity and over-fitting control in supervised learning. Therefore, integration of local and global models is an attractive alternative. In a more recent study, we proposed an integration approach where global and local neural network models were appropriately combined resulting in more accurate retrievals than provided by the component models in isolation.

In this paper, the AOD measurements of the OMI are investigated. Two algorithms are applied to retrieve aerosol parameters from OMI reactance measurements, referred to as the near- ultra violet (UV) algorithm and the multi-wavelength algorithm respectively. OMI aerosol optical thicknesses are better retrieved in the multi-wavelength retrieval than in the near UV [5]. Moreover, especially over land, the multi wavelength AOD shows a better correlation with ground observations than near-UV algorithm [6, 7]. In this paper, AOD with wavelength 440nm is used and applied afterward in all assimilation and validation processes.

In this paper, one uses a 3-D Chemical Transport Model (CTM) (Polair3D, [8]) coupled with a SIze-REsolved Aerosol Model (SIREAM, [9]) in the framework of the Polyphemus system [10]. The system has been evaluated for aerosol outputs of different Particular Matter (PM) (PM_{10}, $PM_{2.5}$ and chemical composition) and gas-phase species at the ground level for year 2005 over Europe [11] and over Greater Paris [12].

The paper is organized as follows: The ANN constructed for the preprocessing stage, and the assimilation technique is firstly described. In the second part, the regional 3D chemical transport model is described along with the assimilation algorithm used. The next section shows the main validation, and sensitivity analysis results of the assimilation process. Finally, the fifth section demonstrates the conclusion and the suggested issues.

2   Methodology

Data assimilation is a technique that allows an optimal use of observations of atmospheric compounds in a chemistry-transport model to derive global three-dimensional distributions of atmospheric species. Firstly, we describe the ANN used in the preprocessing stage.

2.1   Neural Network

Artificial Neural Network (ANN) can be used effectively to reconstruct non-linear relationship learning from training. An ANN model basically consists of processing elements (called neurons) and connections between elements. Every single neuron performs a weighted sum of inputs that receives from neighboring neurons, then uses an activation function to process data and passes results to following neurons. Neurons are structured in layers that can be of 3 different typologies: input layer (where input data enter the network), hidden layers (where real calculations are performed) and output layer (where final results are produced). Different possible Neural Network structures can be used, depending on the architecture of the network (number of layers, neurons, etc...), the model parameters, and the transfer function used. In this paper, a cascade-forward network with 2 layers is chosen, characterized by the following equations:

$$f(p) = \sum_{j=1}^{S} OW_j \cdot a_l + \sum_{i=1}^{R} w_i \cdot p_i + c \tag{1}$$

with

$$a_j = TF(\sum IW_{j \cdot i} \cdot p_i + b_j) \tag{2}$$

Where:

IW and OW are weight matrices of first and second layers; w is the weight vector of second layer coming from first layer input; b and c are network bias weights; S is the number of neuron of the first layer; R is the size of input vector; and TF is the

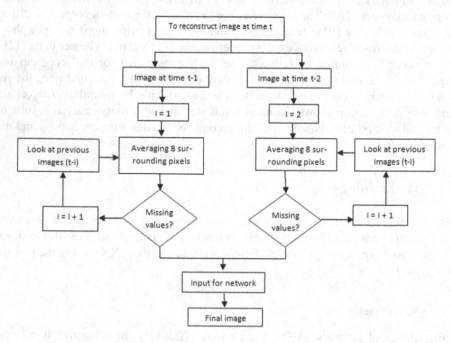

Fig. 1. The methodology used to reconstruct missing data using ANN

used Transfer Function. After ANN has been identified, the reconstruction of missing data using ANN is performed using algorithm shown in Fig. 1

2.2   Construction of a Global Neural Network Model

Given a set $\{x_i\}$ of satellite-based radiance observations, each data point x_i is represented as tuple $x_i = [t_i, lat_i, lon_i, x_{i1}... x_{iM}]$, where t_i is the time of the observation, lat_i and lon_i denote the spatial location, and $x_{ij}, j = 1...M$, are derived from the observed radiances and the corresponding geometric parameters which describe satellite camera view angles, and sun angle at time t_i. Given a set of K data points with observation attributes obtained from the deterministic algorithm over a period of time. Use them to construct a set of labeled points for training a regression model. ANNs have been successfully used in many applications and we use them here. Specifically, we use a feedforward neural network with a single hidden layer of sigmoidal units to predict AODs. The design objectives are feature selection, identification of an appropriate ANN structure, as well as choice of training algorithm to maximize prediction accuracy on out-of-the-sample test data. Prediction accuracy is measured by the coefficient of determination $R_2 = 1 - MSE/Var(y)$, where $Var(y)$ is the variance of the AOD target variable. OMI data provide a large number of informative attributes $[t_i, lat_i, lon_i, x_{i1}... x_{iM}]$ (M=111 in our case).This results in a neural network with a large number of weights, and requires significant training time. Under these circumstances, over fitting problems can result when learning from limited training data. Therefore, we used Principal Component Analysis (PCA) to reduce data dimensionality to $k < M$ attributes, and used the largest k principal components as inputs to our ANN. We determined the appropriate number of hidden units in our ANN, and the best training algorithm experimentally. We considered 5, 10, 15 and 20 units, and the following training methods: Bayesian regularization, Powell-Beale conjugate gradient, Polak-Ribiere conjugate gradient, scaled conjugate gradient, Levenberg-Marquardt and quasi-Newton back propagation.

2.3   Optimal Interpolation (OI)

In the OI method, observations, as soon as available, are used to produce an analysis. This analysis is supposed to be a better estimate of the true state. It replaces the current state of the model and it therefore serves as initial conditions for the next

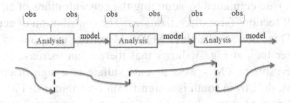

Fig. 2. Optimal Interpolation

model iterations. This procedure is repeated at the frequency of measurement as shown in Fig. 2.

The analysis is given by the best estimate (linear and unbiased) in the least squares sense. The analysis, or analyzed state vector, x_a, is solution of the minimization problem

$$x_a = \arg\min J \qquad (3)$$

Where J is the cost function defined by:

$$J(x) = (x - x_b)^T B^{-1}(x - x_b) + (y - H(x))^T R^{-1}(y - H(x)) \qquad (4)$$

xb is the background state vector, or a priori state vector (i.e., the AOD forecast provided by the model), y is the vector of observations (measured AOD), and H is an interpolation function that maps the state x to the observational data. B and R are the matrices of error covariance's matrices, for background and observations respectively. Upon minimization and under the assumption of the linearity of H, x_a is given by:

$$x_a = x_b + K(y - H(x)) \qquad (5)$$

where K is the so-called gain matrix defined as

$$K = BH^T(HBH^T + R^{-1}) \qquad (6)$$

During the assimilation period, the process is repeated each time the observations are available. So, at time h, the assimilation produces an analysis $x_a^{(h)}$, which serves as a new model state[13]. Starting from that new state, the model computes a forecast $x_f^{(h+1)}$ at time $h + 1$. This forecast is actually called background, x_b. The assimilation takes place to compute $x_a^{(h+1)}$, and so on and so forth.

2.4   Redistribution over Sections and Chemical Species

The correction applied to the simulated AOD at the ground is provided by the OI method. The controlled variable is thus the AOD concentrations over the whole horizontal domain, in the first layer only (in the reference configuration) or in more layers. Forecast AOD are computed by summing the concentrations of all aerosol species simulated over all sections (size discretization). The contribution of aerosol species on the value of AOD is shown in Table1. AOD/PM aerosol components are also shown in Fig. 3. A closer look at Fig. 3 shows that there is an increase in contribution of anthropogenic aerosols to PM - west to east sulfate is a significant anthropogenic component of PM, dust from south is a significant contributor to PM, primary contributors to AOD (fine mode aerosols) different from primary contributors to PM.

Table 1. Polyphemus basic Aerosol species contribution on AOD

Species	Refract index at 550nm	Mode radius [μm]	Stand. Dev. of size distribution	Particle density [g/cm³]	Extinction coefficient cm³ at 550nm[km⁻¹]	Single scattering albedo
Sulfate/nitrate R_h=70%	15.3-0.0055i	0.028	2.24	1.33	7.9 e-6	0.981
Mineral dust,	1.53-0.008i	0.471	2.51	2.0	8.5 e-3	0.73
Mineral dust, low hematite	1.53-0.0019i	0.471	2.51	2.0	8.5 e-3	0.891
Sea salt, accumulation	1.36-0i	0.378	2.03	1.2	3.14 e-3	1.0
Sea salt, coarse	1.36-0i	3.17	2.03	1.2	1.8 e-1	1.0
Biomass burning soot	1.63-0.036i	0.0118	2.0	1.0	1.5 e-7	0.698
Diesel soot	1.49-0.67i	0.0118	2.0	1.0	7.8 e-7	0.125
Transported minerals, high	1.53-0.0055i	0.5	2.2	2.6	5.86 e-3	0.837
Hematite	1.53-0.0019i	0.5	2.2	2.6	5.86 e-3	0.93

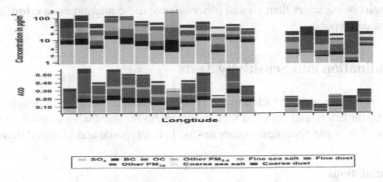

Fig. 3. AOD/PM aerosol components

3   Polyphemus

CTM components used in this paper and its stages are described in this section. In addition, because of the importance of system configuration, specific model configuration that was applied in the experiment is shown in much detail.

3.1   Polyphemus System and Experiment Configuration

Polyphemus system can deal with applications of passive tracers, radioactive decay, photochemistry, and aerosol dynamics from local to continental scales [10]. It is made of four distinct components: i) Preprocessing. ii) Eulerian chemistry-transport models (Polair3D and Castor) iii) Drivers for handling the models. iv) Postprocessing tools.

3.2   Comparison with Ground Observations

Ground observations are useful for validating the model simulations. They can be further used for quantifying the improvements due to satellite data assimilation. In this paper, the ground observations are from the *European Monitoring and Evaluation Programme* (EMEP) network. It provides the hourly and daily measurements of AOD in Europe. The important advantages of EMEP measurements are the common quality control standards applied and their station locations; the latter makes the measurements representative of regional background conditions, relatively unaffected by local emissions. Several other monitoring networks (urban, suburban, etc.) are not used here, since they would pose serious problems concerning criteria of data selection and treatment of uncertainties. An obvious disadvantage of the EMEP network is the rather sparse distribution of stations for AOD (totally 25 in 2005). The statistics are computed station per station and then averaged. The mean RMSE is 6.9 $\mu g\ m^{-3}$ between model and ground observations; the mean correlation is 0.62, indicating a good consistency between them. Model results are higher than ground observations on average: 12.4 $\mu g\ m^{-3}$ versus 8:1 $\mu g\ m^{-3}$, this difference is now discussed. The ground AOD is measured by sun photometer monitors and the values can be systematically overestimated because of interferences of other compounds [14]. However, with model results being larger than ground observations, these measurement errors cannot explain the discrepancy.

4   Validation and Sensitivity Tests

Several experiments are conducted to verify and validate the model prediction before and after assimilation, and with and without using ANN. The analysis assists to measure the correlation and root mean square errors, in both spatial and temporal domains.

4.1   Simulations

The aerosol model used in this paper is SIREAM [15], plugged to the chemistry-transport model Polair3D. SIREAM includes 16 aerosol species: 3 primary species (mineral dust, black carbon and primary organic species), 5 inorganic species (ammonium, sulfate, nitrate, chloride and sodium) and 8 organic species predicted with the Secondary ORganic Aerosol Model –SORGAM [16]. In the usual configuration, SIREAM includes 5 bins logarithmically distributed over the size range 0.01 μm–10 μm.

A previous study in [12], evaluated the model configuration for the year 2005 with comparisons to three databases (also used in this study and described hereafter) and with respect to the performance of other CTMs used in Europe (Chimere, EMEP, ...). Polyphemus shows a tendency to underestimate AOD, and to overestimate nitrate concentrations in wintertime. Other models also show similar behavior. The configuration of the simulations of this paper is essentially the same as in [12].

4.2   Operational Forecast

In operational conditions, at time t_0, only the data for the past is available. It is possible to assimilate the past data over a few days before t_0. The model results from (t_0

day) to (t_{0+1} day) are called one-day forecasts; the results from (t_{0+1} day) to (t_{0+2} days) are called two-day forecasts, etc. This operation can be repeated every day ("moving window"); one-day forecast and two-day forecast are then available every day. Table 2 summarizes the performance of the model without assimilation, and of the one-day and two-day forecasts, when compared to EMEP observations. Besides, in this table, the effect of applying ANN preprocessing is shown. It is noteworthy that, as expected, the one-day forecast clearly shows better statistics for PM10 and AOD than the simulation without assimilation, and much better with the ANN preprocessing. The decrease of the RMSE is 1.5 μgm^{-3} for PM_{10} and 1.4 μgm^{-3} for AOD, that is, about 10%. The increase of the correlation is more than 10% for PM_{10} and AOD. Mean Fractional Error (MFE) and Mean Fractional Bias (MFB) are also markedly improved; the improvement in MFE brings the model to satisfy the performance objective of 50% defined by Boylan and Russell [17] – see also Sartelet et al.[11]. Moreover, the effect of ANN preprocessing has significantly improved the assimilation process by another 10%, making a correlation value for both PM_{10} and AOD increase above 50%.

Table 2. of the simulations on the EMEP for PM10 and AOD. Period: 4 to 30 January 2005.

Species	Simulation	# stations	OBs. Mean $\mu g\ m^{-3}$	Sim. Mean $\mu g\ m^{-3}$	RMSE $\mu g\ m^{-3}$	Correl. %	MFE %	MFB %
PM$_{10}$	Model	156	21.8	17.4	16.6	35.7	55.3	-9.2
	One-day			18.7	15.1	46.8	49.9	-3.5
	One-day NN			20.1	14.5	53.2	46.2	-2.7
	Two-day			17.7	16.4	37.9	54.6	-8.2
	Two-day NN			18.5	14.4	44.6	50.1	-6.5
AOD	Model	8	19.8	15.8	15.0	30.2	57.9	-10.3
	One-day			16.9	13.6	43.2	53.3	-3.9
	One-day NN			19.1	13.0	51.8	47.8	-2.4
	Two-day			15.9	14.8	32.3	57.4	-9.4
	Two-day NN			17.0	13.5	45.8	51.2	-7.9

Since the OI method only changes the initial conditions, the model tends after all to its reference trajectory (without assimilation). Here, the two-day forecasts show a less obvious improvement. Two-day forecasts show slightly better statistics than the free-running model, but the decrease of the RMSE is only 0.2 μgm^{-3} and the increase of the correlation is 2%. The time period after which the corrections due to DA become essentially ineffective are discussed in the next section.

Figs. 4, 5, and 6 show the daily evolution (averaged over the period 4 to 30 January 2005) of the RMSE, the correlation and the mean concentrations respectively for the

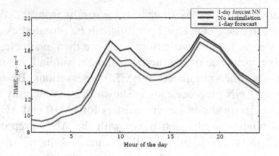

Fig. 4. Hourly evolution of the RMSE for the PM10 forecast without assimilation (blue line) and for the one-day forecast (green line), and for NN (red line)

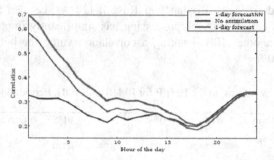

Fig. 5. Hourly of the correlation for the PM10 forecast without assimilation (blue line) and for the one-day forecast (green line), and for NN(black)

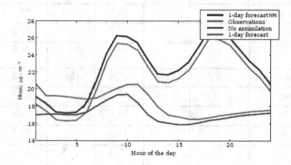

Fig. 6. Hourly of the mean concentration for the PM10 observations (red line), for the forecast without assimilation (blue line) and for the one-day forecast (green line), and for NN (black)

model without assimilation, one-day forecast and for the one-day forecast using ANN. These figures underline the tendency of the assimilation procedure to be almost ineffective after 24 h of forecast. Actually, after 12:00 UTC, the differences in RMSE and in mean concentration are lower than 1 μgm^{-3}, and the difference in correlation is about 2%. However, using ANN increases correlation value by 10%, reduces RMSE of one-day forecast, and makes the effect of assimilation process much longer. The fact that DA with the OI method has some influence only during such a short period of time (one day in this experiment) is not only a limit of the OI method. Actually, in air quality models, concentrations are not much influenced by initial conditions [18]. Besides, it depends on several parameters and on the pollutant. For ozone, the influence is a bit longer – see Wu et al.[19].

5   Conclusions

In this paper, we have performed the data assimilation of OMI AOD in the Polyphemus air quality system. Good consistency is presented in the comparisons of model simulation, satellite data and ground observations before assimilation. In order to enhance satellite image, ANN using multi layer perceptron is used to fill incomplete data grid. The optimal interpolation method is then applied to produce analysis of AOD. The assimilation is carried out with available satellite data in the studied period, and the next-day prediction is also performed. The model results from the reference simulation, assimilation and prediction) are compared with the EMEP ground observations for evaluation. It is found that in winter the RMSE between model and ground observations is less with assimilation than that without assimilation, reduced by 19% on average. The next-day predictions also show a better forecast of AOD with RMSE decreased by 15%. Therefore, OMI data assimilation has the potential to improve the forecast of surface aerosol concentrations in the cold season. The sensitivity tests show that, in this specific paper, the uncertainties on the condensation process might be greater than the uncertainties on the emissions. These uncertainties could originate from uncertainties in the concentrations of condensable gas species or in the modeling of the condensation process itself.

References

1. Ramanathan, V., Crutzen, P.J., Kiehl, J.T., Rosenfeld, D.: Atmosphere – Aerosols, climate, and the hydrological cycle. Science 294(5549), 2119–2124 (2002)
2. Diner, D.J., et al.: Level 2 Aerosol Retrieval Algorithm Theoretical Basis. Jet Propulsion Lab., Pasadena, CA, JPL Tech. Doc. D-11400 (2008)
3. Wen, G., Tsay, S.C., Cahalan, R.F., Oreopoulos, L.: Path Radiance Technique for Retrieving Aerosol Optical Thickness over Land. J. Geophys. Res. 104, 31321–31332 (1999)
4. Han, B., Braverman, A., Vucetic, S., Obradovic, Z.: Construction of an Accurate Geospatial Predictor by Fusion of Global and Local Models. In: 8th Int'l Conf. Information Fusion, Philadelphia, PA (2005)
5. Torres, O., Decae, R., Veefkind, J.P., de Leeuw, G.: OMI Aerosol Retrieval Algorithm. OMI Algorithm Theoretical Basis Document: Clouds, Aerosols, and Surface UV Irradiance 3(2) (2002)
6. Ali, A., Amin, S.E., Ramadan, H.H., Tolba, M.F.: Ozone monitoring instrument aerosol products: Algorithm modeling and validation with ground based measurements over Europe. In: The 2011 International Conference on Computer Engineering & Systems (ICCES 2011), Cairo, Egypt (2011)
7. Ali, A., Amin, S.E., Ramadan, H.H., Tolba, M.F.: Ozone Monitoring Instrument aerosol products: a comparison study with ground-based airborne sun photometer measurements over Europe. Int. J. Remote Sens. 33(20), 6321–6341 (2012)

8. Boutahar, J., Lacour, S., Mallet, V., Quelo, D., Roustan, Y., Sportisse, B.: Development and validation of a fully modular platform for numerical modelling of air pollution: POLAIR. Int. J. Environ. Pollut. 22(1/2), 17–28 (2004)
9. Debry, E., Fahey, K., Sartelet, K., Sportisse, B., Tombette, M.: Technical note: A new SIze REsolved Aerosol Model, Atmos. Chem. Phys. 7, 1537–1547 (2007)
10. Mallet, V., Quelo: Technical Note: The air quality modeling system Polyphemus. Atmos. Chem. Phys. 7, 5479–5487 (2007)
11. Sartelet, K.N., Debry, E., Fahey, K.M., Roustan, Y., Tombette, M., Sportisse, B.: Simulation of aerosols and gas-phase species over Europe with the Polyphemus system. Part I: model-to-data comparison for 2001. Atmos. Environ. 29, 6116–6131 (2007)
12. Tombette, M., Sportisse, B.: Aerosol modeling at a regional scale: Model-to-data comparison and sensitivity analysis over Greater Paris. Atmos. Environ. 41, 6941–6950 (2007)
13. Hollingsworth, A., Lonnberg, P.: The statistical structure of short-range forecast errors as de-termined from radiosonde data. Part I: the wind field. Tellus 38A, 111–136 (1986)
14. Dunlea, E.J., Herndon, S.C.: Evaluation of nitrogen dioxide chemiluminescence monitors in a polluted urban environment. Atmos. Chem. Phys. 7, 2691–2704 (2007)
15. Debry, E., Fahey, K., Sartelet, K., Sportisse, B., Tombette, M.: Technical note: A new SIze REsolved Aerosol Model. Atmos. Chem. Phys. 7, 1537–1547 (2007)
16. Schell, B., Ackermann, I.J., Hass, H., Binkowski, F.S., Ebel, A.: Modeling the formation of secondary organic aerosol within a comprehensive air quality model system. Journal of Geophysical Research 106, 28275–28293 (2001)
17. Boylan, J.W.: PM and light extinction model performance metrics, goals, and criteria for three-dimensional air quality models. Atmos. Environ. 40, 4946–4959 (2006)
18. Huneeus, N.: Assimilation variationnelle d'observations satellitaires dans un mod'ele atmosphérique d'aérosols, Ph.D. thesis, Université des Sciences et Technologies de Lille (2007)
19. Wu, D., Hartman, A., Ward, N., Eisen, J.A.: An Automated Phylogenetic Tree-Based Small Subunit rRNA Taxonomy and Alignment Pipeline (STAP). PLoS ONE 3(7), e2566 (2008), doi:10.1371

Part VIII

Authentication, Digital Forensics and Plagiarism Detection

Initial Study of the Content Authentication on Digital Preservation of Cultural Institutions

Zuraidah Abdul Manaf[1], Aliza Ismail[1], Noor Masliana Razlan[1],
Rusni Daruis[2], and Azizah Abdul Manaf[2]

[1] Faculty of Information Management
Universiti Teknologi Mara (UiTM), Shah Alam, Malaysia
{zuraidaham,alizai}@salam.uitm.edu.my, masliana0315@gmail.com
[2] Advanced Informatics School (AIS)
Universiti Teknologi Malaysia, Kuala Lumpur, Malaysia
{rusni,azizah07}@ic.utm.my

Abstract. The aim of this paper is to identify potential risks of digital cultural resources in Malaysia. Apart from that, it proposed watermarking as a way to authenticate digital items for future work. A multiple case studies approach is used to examine the potential risks of digital cultural resources in four (4) selected Malaysian cultural institutions. Data is collected through a structured interview with information professionals who are involved in digitisation works in the selected cultural institutions. Findings reveal that digital cultural heritage resources in Malaysia is at risk in terms of digitisation policies, selection criteria, cost, staffing, technology, storage, metadata management and copyright. This study is very significant to professionals who are involved in archiving the digital cultural heritage as it can be a guide for managing risks in preserving the valuable digital resources. The result of this study can be a practical tool of managing risks not only for digital cultural heritage but also to all documents in digital format. The study gives insight to other researchers to seriously investigate other risks of digital cultural resources besides the risks that have been identified in this study.

Keywords: Digital Resources, Risk management, Cultural Heritage Resources, Malaysia.

1 Introduction

The numbers of records created in electronic form is increasing because the organisations are too depending on digital technology to make, process, store, communicate, and use information in their activities. The technological challenge is compounded by the long-term expansion of information technology, creation the cultural heritage information increasingly more diverse and complex (Lim, Ramaiah & Pitt, 2003). Besides that, in Betts (1999) case study, he asserts that digital cultural heritage information is at possibility of disappearing of becoming unreachable because of the decline of storage media like magnetic tapes. Other concerns include ever-changing data

A. Ell Hassanien et al. (Eds.): AMLTA 2012, CCIS 322, pp. 509–515, 2012.

formats and the fact that software and hardware become obsolete quickly. The greatest challenge to electronic record keeping is the evolution of technology (Coombs, 1999). Therefore, in order to preserve this information, institutions must manage collections in a consistent and decisive manner. It is important to decide what should be preserved, in what priority, and with what techniques. Hence, they most often overlook the issue of sustainability of their materials that have been digitised.

Content authentication can be achieved through the use of watermarking algorithm (Raja, A & Ahmed, A, 2004). Two types of authentications exist: exact and selective authentication. Exact authentication can be achieved through the use of fragile watermark, embedded signatures and erasable watermark while selective authentication can be achieved by semi-fragile watermark, embedding semi-fragile signatures and tell-tale watermark (Raja, A & Ahmed, A, 2004).

In addition, there are a number of risks related issues that might be faced by cultural institutions if their digital files are not being managed accordingly. Zuraidah and Aliza (2009) describe in their findings that among the risks related issues that would be faced by cultural institutions if their digital resources are not managed accordingly would include availability and accessibility of information; authenticity and integrity of information; long-term storage of information; and information disaster recovery issues. The aim of this study is to identify the potential risks in preserving Malaysian digital cultural heritage information that are practiced by several cultural institutions in Malaysia.

2   Methodology

This research uses multiple case studies at four (4) public cultural institutions in Malaysia. The data were collected through interviews. The analysis methods included the descriptive and comparative analysis. For the purpose of this article, only comparative analysis is discussed. Purposive sampling is used in this study where only four (4) main cultural heritage institutions (CHIs) in Malaysia are selected. The four selected cases were chosen because they are the main cultural institution under Ministry of Information, Communication and Culture of Malaysia which have been involved in digitisation projects since 2000. The research unit of analysis is information professionals who are dealing with digitisation of cultural heritage resources in their organisations.

3   Findings and Discussions

Potential risks include selection criteria, digitisation policy, cost, staffing, technology, storage, metadata and copyright issues.

3.1   Selection Criteria

According to Puglia (1999), items selected for digital collections should fit into the scope, purpose, and audience of the project itself as stated on the project description form. The findings found that most of the cultural institutions select materials to be digitised based on these criteria (arranged by the most preferred criteria):

1. Cultural value
2. Historical value
3. Materials that allow copyright access
4. Materials that have digitisation procedures and standard
5. Frequently used by users
6. Help them to save space without considering the value of resources
7. Educational and research purpose

Majority of the cultural institutions select materials to be digitised which have cultural and historical value and materials that allow copyright access. These WIU Libraries Digitization Policies Committee (2009) and *Dasar Pendigitalan Koleksi Perpustakaan Negara Malaysia* (2010) support these findings where both of the policies highlight cultural and historical value are the most essential resources need to be digitised. As cultural institutions, all of the cases in this study are not at risk in selecting the right materials to be digitised since they totally select materials based on the main function of their organisation.

Hirtle, Hudson and Kenyon (2009) believed that copyright is an important issue to be considered in doing digitisation projects. It is found that all the respondents prefer to choose materials that are copyright free since they are not bounded with Copyright Act. However, as cultural institutions, they cannot limit to select materials that are only copyright free since there are a lot of resources out there which are valuable even though they are copyrighted. Hereby, majority of the cultural institutions are at risk as they only prefer to choose materials that are copyright free to avoid copyright problems without considering the value aspect of copyrighted materials.

The findings report that only two of the cases prefer to digitise materials that have digitisation procedures and standard. Another two cultural institutions do not consider this criterion because for them, they do not need specific standard and procedures in digitising the materials as their procedures are very simple. Nevertheless, these two cultural institutions should be aware that choosing the materials that already have the digitisation procedures and standard will minimise risk of accessibility of the digital resources later. The findings shows that our digital cultural information at risk since the cultural institutions do not really prefer to choose materials that do not have the digitisation procedures and standard.

3.2   Digitisation Policy

More than half of the cases in this study do not have a standard digitisation policy. Only CASE A has developed their digitisation policy and it was published in July 2010 namely *Dasar Pendigitalan Koleksi, Perpustakaan Negara Malaysia* (2010). It is a complete digitisation policy and was developed based on the best practices of international organisation which are involved in digitisation projects earlier. The best practices are such as National Library of Australia and NISO.

All cases in this study except CASE A do not have a digitisation policy. However, CASE B is developing their digitisation policy and it is estimated to be published in 2014. The ongoing process of digitisation policies shows that CASE B is aware pertain to the importance of having a digitisation policy. However, the other two (2) cultural institutions do not have any since for them their digitisation process are not complicated as others. The result indicates that not all cultural institutions in Malaysia have systematic procedures in digitising their resources. This is one of the risks for the digital resources since they are not produced in a proper way and this will affect the long-term accessibility of the resources.

The findings reveal that even though CASE B does not have a digitisation policy, they are able to minimise risks by following guidelines from NISO and NARA. According to CASE B, they choose to follow the international guideline because they want their digital resources to fulfill international standard requirement so that the resources can be accessed internally and externally.

3.3   Cost and Staffing

As stated in the findings, all of the cultural institutions are not allocated with specialised budget for digitisation. This condition is one of the barriers for Malaysian cultural institutions to excel and provide good digital collections. Majority of the cases in this study are given one-off budget if there is any projects that need them to digitise their collections. For instance, CASE B, which have been given large amount of budget for digitisation to support Economic Transformation Program (ETP) in 2010. Nevertheless, if the cultural institutions only get one-off budget for digitisation, this situation will limit them to digitise their collections since such a special projects should have their certain target, for instances, project given to CASE B should digitise two (2) billion collections only.

In addition, majority of the cultural institutions hire staffs based on academic achievement and experiences. These two (2) criteria are very important since staffs that have suitable academic qualification and at least minimal experience is capable to produce quality of works. Without knowledge, skills and the right attitude of the professionals, the initiatives will go nowhere and eventually collapse.

3.4   Technology, Storage and Scalability

Zuraidah (2006) asserts in her study that digitisation is a costly exercise requiring high investment usually from public funds. There are significant risks to these investments due to the adoption of inappropriate technologies and standards. This can result in creating resources which are quickly obsolete and unusable or which require the investment to be repeated within a short time frame.

Findings report that only one of the cases do not has a specialised system to manage the digital collections. This finding shows that three (3) of the institutions are aware the significance of having a digital resources management system. Another cultural institution is going to have a system in 2014 and now the system is still in developing process. As for storage, all of the cultural institutions store their digital resources in-house. They could not afford to keep the digital collections in service providers' servers. This is a risk for the cultural institution since they do not have other backup server outside the institutions if there is anything happened to their building and existence servers.

According to Mayesti, Rachman, and Yayan (2011), the computer storage capacity will determine how many data and files could be stored inside. Findings of this study found that only storage in one cultural institution is not scalable. Other storages in another three (3) institutions are scalable. Mayesti, Rachman and Yayan (2011) report that if the storage has only small capacity, the digital files that could be stored will be limited.

3.5   Metadata

The two aspects of cultural institutions data quality are the quality of the data in the objects themselves, and the quality of the metadata associated with the objects (Diallo, 2011). Low quality metadata can render an information institution almost unusable, while high metadata quality can lead to higher user satisfaction and increased use (Stvilia1 et al., n. d.). The finding of this study reveals that one of the cultural institutions has a metadata scheme. However, the metadata scheme that is used is not user friendly in term of managing metadata of their digital resources as the scheme is more suitable for profit making organisation, and not for non-profit organisation such as cultural institutions. This situation contributes risks for the digital resources since it will lead to loss of data and other consequences. If compared to other institutions, the risk that they have is much minimum rather than other cultural institutions which do not have metadata scheme.

All of cases in this study include the descriptive metadata for their digital resources. Descriptive metadata encompass a range of information from basic elements such as title and subject to more advanced elements such as geographic or temporal coverage and relationships (UMDM, 2011). There are three (3) of the cultural institutions include the technical metadata for their digital resources. According to IBM (2011), technical metadata is data about the processes, the tool sets, the repositories, the physical layers of data under the covers. However, findings shows that most of cultural institutions do not consider the technical metadata is important for them. In term of putting IPR, only one of the cases does not include it. Besides that, not all the cultural institutions consider that history metadata is an important part to be included.

3.6   Copyright

Copyright assessments play a defining role in digitising projects and must be addressed early in the selection process. Therefore, the use of watermarking technique can be used. A watermarking technique is to prevent digital images that belong to the rightful owners from being illegally commercialised or used, and it can ascertain the intellectual property right (Lee, Lin, Su & Lin, 2008). The findings reveal that most of cultural institutions embedded visible watermarking but only one of the institution embedded invisible watermarking. Invisible watermarking is more effective than visible watermarking even though digital watermarking cannot by itself prevent copying, modification, and re-distribution of documents, and furthermore if encryption and copy protection fail, watermarking allows the document to be traced back to its rightful owner and to the point of unauthorised use (Su, Hartung & Girod, 1998).

3.7   Sustainability Factors Adopted

In considering the suitability of particular digital formats for the purposes of preserving digital information as an authentic resource for future generations, it is useful to articulate important factors that affect choices. The sustainability factors that are taken as important consideration planned by Library of Congress are very systematic. The factors that are considered by them are applied in this study which consists of disclosure, adoption, transparency, self-documentation, external dependencies, impact of patents, and technical protection mechanisms. The findings show that Malaysian cultural institutions do not take the sustainability factors seriously. However, they are aware of the importance of technical protection mechanisms factor. Sustainability in the institutions maybe the factors have been applied by them without their awareness since the processes are in embedded in their routines processes. Besides that, they are not familiar with these specific factors.

4   Conclusion

It is reported in finding that in term of selecting criteria and storage, the digital cultural information in Malaysia are somewhat saved from hazardous risks. Selecting criteria that are considered by all the cultural institutions are totally based on their cultural and historical values of the resources. It can be concluded that digital cultural information in Malaysia is exposed to risks since most of the cultural institutions producing the digital resources are not managing digitization projects according to standard digitisation policy. Digitisation of resources is done based on their general skills and knowledge.

A part from that, the lack of skilled workers who produce the digital product is another risk which could not be ignored. This is a hazardous situation since digitisation process is extremely complex, difficult in manner and need highly qualified and experienced professional to do the job efficiently. Moreover, inappropriate metadata management of digital contents is another risk of Malaysian digital cultural resources management. The metadata associated with digital objects could affect the access to and usability of items in the collection. The process of digitisation in the cultural institutions do not take sustainability factors as important consideration due to the lack of understanding among them towards these factors.

Therefore, the management of digitisation process of the cultural information in Malaysia will not be in an excellent condition until the issues of the followings are resolved. One of the major issues is allocated budgets for digitization projects. Projects with sufficient budget will cover the installation of quality digital resources management system, recruiting sufficient number of skilled and knowledgeable staffs, having enough and sophisticated facilities, having a systematic and efficient metadata scheme and embedded both visible and invisible watermarking to the digital resources. In a nut shell, the requirement of a framework that show the potential risks that might be exposed to the digital cultural information is really necessary for cultural institutions so that they are always aware of it to avoid deterioration of the valuable information sources. In addition, a proposed watermarking algorithm could be used in order to authenticate the digital content.

References

Aliza, I.: Assessing the practice of trusted electronic records management in Malaysian government-controlled companies. PhD Dissertation (2010)

Betts, M.: Business worry about long-term data losses. Computerworld 33(38), 22–24 (1999)

Coombs, P.: The crisis in electronic government record keeping: a strategy for long-term storage. Library Computing 18(3), 196–202 (1999)

Hirtle, P.B., Hudson, E., Kenyon, A.T.: Copyright and cultural institutions: guidelines for digitization for U.S. libraries, archives, and museums. Cornell University Library, Ithaca (2009)

Kaufman, P., Watstein, S.B.: Library value (return on investment, ROI) and the challenge of placing a value on public services. Reference Services Review 36(3), 226–231 (2008), http://www.emeraldinsight.com (retrieved)

Lim, S.L., Ramaiah, C.K., Pitt, K.W.: Problems in the preservation of electronic records. Library Review 52(3), 117–125 (2003), http://www.emeraldinsight.com (retrieved February 14, 2011)

Malaysia Vacation Guide. Malaysia national heritage (2011), http://www.malaysiavacationguide.com/nationalheritage.html (retrieved February 6, 2011)

Perpustakaan Negara Malaysia. Dasar pendigitalan koleksi Perpustakaan Negara Malaysia (2010), http://www.pnm.gov.my/upload_documents/DasarPendigitalanKoleksiPerpustakaan.pdf (retrieved October 1, 2011)

Puglia, S.: The costs of digital imaging projects. RLG Digi-News 3, 20–23 (1999)

Raja, A., Ahmed, A.: A Fragile Watermarking Algorithm for Content Authentication. International Journal of Computing & Information Sciences 2(1), 27–37 (2004)

Su, J.K., Hartung, F., Girod, B.: Digital watermarking of text, image, and video documents. Computer & Graphics 22(6), 687–695 (1998)

UMDM. University of Maryland Descriptive Metadata (2011), http://www.lib.umd.edu/dcr/publications/taglibrary/umdm.html (retrieved December 1, 2011)

WIU Libraries Digitization Policies Committee. WIU libraries digitization policies recommendations (2009), http://www.wiu.edu/libraries/administration/policies/DigitizationPolicies_0809.pdf (retrieved December 1, 2011)

Zuraidah, A.M.: The State of Digitisation Initiatives by Cultural Institutions in Malaysia: An Exploratory Survey. Library Review 55(1) (2006)

Zuraidah, A.M., Aliza, I.: Malaysian cultural heritage at risk? A case study of digitisation projects. Library Review 59(2), 107–116 (2009), http://www.emeraldinsight.com (retrieved January 21, 2011)

Advanced Encryption Standard Algorithm: Issues and Implementation Aspects

Ahmed Fathy[1], Ibrahim F. Tarrad[2],
Hesham F.A. Hamed[3], and Ali Ismail Awad[1,4]

[1] Faculty of Engineering, Al Azhar University, Qena, Egypt
[2] Faculty of Engineering, Al Azhar University, Cairo, Egypt
[3] Faculty of Engineering, Minia University, Minia, Egypt
[4] Member of Scientific Research Group in Egypt (SRGE)
{ahmedf.abdelfatah,tarradif}@gmail.com, hfah66@yahoo.com, aawad@ieee.org

Abstract. Data encryption has become a crucial need for almost all data transaction application due to the large diversity of the remote information exchange. A huge value of sensitive data is transferred daily via different channels such as e-commerce, electronic banking and even over simple email applications. Advanced Encryption Standard (AES) algorithm has become the optimum choice for various security services in numerous applications. Therefore, many researches get focused on that algorithm in order to improve its efficiency and performance. This paper presents a survey about the cutting edge research conducted for the AES algorithm issues and aspects in terms of developments, implementations and evaluations. The contribution of this paper is targeted toward building a base for future development and implementation of the AES algorithm. It also opens door for implementing the AES algorithm using some machine learning techniques.

Keywords: Cryptography, Advanced Encryption Standard, FPGA, ASIC, Machine Learning.

1 Introduction

Cryptography is the process of transferring data into scrambled format, but at the same time, it allows the intended recipient to restore the original data by using a secret key. Encryption and decryption are the two major functions in any cryptography system. Encryption is transferring data into unintelligible format by secret key to guarantee the user privacy. Decryption is the opposite function used to recovery the original encrypted data by using secret key. Data encryption is an important process in almost all data transaction applications [1].

There are two classes of data encryption algorithms; symmetric key and asymmetric key [2]. In symmetric or private key algorithm, the communication is achieved by using only one key. In contrary, asymmetric key algorithm uses more than one key for data encryption and data restore. One key is a public

A. Ell Hassanien et al. (Eds.): AMLTA 2012, CCIS 322, pp. 516–523, 2012.

key, and it is used for data encryption, where the other key is a private key, and it is used for data decryption. The symmetric algorithms are much faster than asymmetric key which need bigger key and complex computation [1], [3].

Advanced Encryption Standard (AES) [4] algorithm is one of the symmetric key block ciphers with block size varies from 64 to 256 bits as the processors become more sophisticated. However, the AES can accept block size up to 256 bit, its speed still slow compared to the stream-based ciphers in the time of all applications are seeking for faster encryption process such as web servers and Automatic Teller Machines (ATMs). On the other hand, some AES applications are keep struggling for low implementation area such as smart card and cellular phone related hardware. Therefore, the encryption speed and implementation area are the two important factors of the real time deployment of AES algorithm. The problem of AES spreading out is the compromising between the encryption/decryption speed and the implementation area.

Field Programmable Gate Array (FPGA)[5] is an Integrated Circuit(IC) that can be repeatedly reconfigured as requested by the operated applications, and it can produce different behaviour by simple configuration changes [6]. According to the previous property and its low cost, FPGA is considered as a good environment for simulating the hardware implementation of the AES encryption algorithm [7]. This paper emphasizes the deployment of AES algorithm on the FPGA environment and focusing on the cutting edge approaches for enhancing the encryption speed and reducing the required implementation area. Due to their friability and inelegance, machine learning techniques are also good candidates for efficient AES development and cryptanalysis processes [8].

The contribution of this research lies on reporting the state-of-the art implementations of the AES algorithm over the FPGA modules, and get focusing on the raised implementation issues and aspects. This contribution is significant for any future developments and implementations of the AES encryption algorithm. It is considered as a ground truth information for evaluating any new AES developments by comparing the output results of the proposed approaches with the results reported in this research.

The rest of this paper is organized as follows. Section 2 presents the theoretical background of the AES algorithm with respect to algorithm's structure, data encryption and data decryption methodologies. Section 3 reports the cutting edge research about the AES implementation over the FPGA environment with speed and area considerations. Furthermore, the new machine learning implementation of AES are also reported in section 3. Conclusions and future work are reported in Section 4.

2   Advanced Encryption Standard Algorithm

Data Encryption Standard (DES) [9] was considered as a model for the symmetric key encryption which has a key length of 56 bits. but this key length is become small and can easily be hacked [10]. The National Institute of Standards

Table 1. Different AES keys and their attributes

	Key length (N_k) words	Block size (B_b) words	Number of round (N_r)
AES128	4.0	4.0	10.0
AES192	6.0	4.0	12.0
AES256	8.0	4.0	14.0

and Technology NIST [11] released a contest to choose a new symmetric crypto-graph algorithm that would be called Advanced Encryption Standard to replace the DES. A five algorithms have been chosen as Mars, RC6, Rijndael, Serpent and Twofish. After two years of detailed evaluation NIST announced Rijndael as a proposed AES [12], [13]. AES has length of bits 128 which can encrypt and decrypt with the three different key lengthes as 128 bit, 192 bit and 256 bit which known as AES128, AES192 and AES256 [14]. The key length, block size and the number of rounds for each AES mode (128, 192, and 256) are reported in Table 1.

The encryption operation is performed on a two dimensional array of bytes (Each block is organized as a 4 × 4 matrix of bytes) called State which consists of 4 rows of bytes and each row has N_b bytes. By considering AES 128 algorithm in which its initial round state is XOR with a selected key. The regular round consist from four main operations which called SubBytes, ShiftRows, MixColumns, and AddRoundKey. In the last round, only three operations are found while MixColumns operation is eliminated [15].

SubBytes are nonlinear transformation that uses 16 identical 256-byte substitution tables (S-box) for independently mapping each byte of State into another byte. S-box entries are generated by computing multiplicative inverses in Galois Field $GF(2^8)$ and applying an affine transformation. SubBytes can be implemented either by computing the substitution or using look up table. ShiftRows cyclically shifts the bytes in the second, third and fourth rows by one, two and three, respectively. This function requires no resource hardware and it can be executed on an FPGA as plain wiring [12]. MixColumns is a linear transformation and it is conducted on the State array column by column. The key scheduler of the AES generates a total of N_b ($N_r + 1$) words in order to complete the encryption and decryption processes [16], [17], [18].

The decryption process is the inverse operation of encryption which inverse the round transformations to obtain the original plain data. The round transformations of the decryption process have four functions: AddRoundKey, InvMixColumn, InvShiftRows and InvSubBytes, respectively. AddRoundKey is an XOR function. InvShiftRows have the same function as ShiftRows but only in the inverse direction. The first row is not changed, but the second is shifted by one, the third is shifted by two and last is shifted by three. The InvSubBytes transformation is done using a permutation table called InvS-box that has 256 numbers (from 0 to 255) [10]. It is worth notice that the AES algorithm can operate in four modes, Cipher Block Chain (CBC), Cipher Feedback (CFB), Output Feedback (OFB) and Electronic Code Block (ECB) [1], [19].

Table 2. AES restrictions and achievements by [20]

Target FPGA Device	Virtex XCV600 BG 560-6
Optimization goal	Speed
Maximum operating frequency	140.390MHz
Encryption/decryption throughput	352 Mbit/sec
Total memory usage	130248 Kbytes

3   FPGA Implementations

The FPGA toolkit consists of a matrix of programmable logic cells, known as configurable logic blocks (CLBs) with a grid of interconnecting lines and switches between them. The I/O cells exist around the perimeter and they work as interface between the interconnect lines and the chip's external pins [5]. The exact functionality of a logic cell varies with the manufacturer of the chip, but it is typically comprised of a small amount of functional logic and/or some register storage capability. Programming (configuring) the FPGA consists of specifying the logic function of each cell and the switches on the interconnecting lines.

3.1   AES Speed Optimization

Ghewari et al. [20] used iterative operations in order to reduce the consumed resources by the AES. The AES algorithm is implemented using VHDL language in Xilinx ISE 9.2 with Device XCV600 of Xilinx Virtex Family. The achieved encryption/decryption throughput is around 352 Mbit/s. The problem with this approach is a high memory consumption. Table 2 shows the restrictions and achievements of the mentioned algorithm.

Thulasimani et al. [21] developed a hardware architecture and implementation for AES128, AES192 and AES256 on the same hardware, and they used the iterative round technique to reduce the resource consumption. The AES has been implemented using the VHDL code running on Xilinx 9.2 with maximum throughput around 666.67 Mbit/s. The advantage of this approach is the low power consumption as the the implementation of three keys on single chip leads to consumed power reduction which is useful for applications such that radio software. The implementation results and achievements of this approach is shown in Table 3.

Table 3. AES restrictions and achievements by [21]

Target FPGA Device	XC2V6000BF957-6
Optimization goal	Speed
Maximum operating frequency	62.5MHz
Encryption/decryption throughput	666.67 Mbit/sec
Total memory usage	Not reported

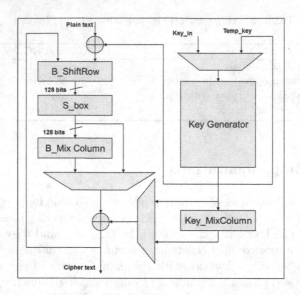

Fig. 1. Flowchart of the AES implementations over the ASIC chip

Yin et al. [22] proposed an implementation of the AES algorism on Application Specific Integrated Circuit (ASIC) which supports three key lengthes as 128, 192 and 256. The encryption/decryption processes are implemented using the same sequential architecture, but with more efficient control. The implementation flowchart is shown in Fig.1. The achieved throughput with different key lengths is shown in Table 4.

Liberatori et al. [23] used Spartan3 to implement AES algorism which have only 173 single ended I/O pins. Therefore, two buses of 64 bits have been used for input and output data and another 32 bus for encryption key and the remaining 13 pins have been used for managing the control signal. They have used Xilinx6.3i, ModelSim5.8 and ModelSim3.0SE plus for the implementation purpose. The achievements of the proposed approach are reported in Table 5.

The above reported researches are interested only in enhancing the encryption/decription speed regardless of the consumed FPGA area as some of these research did not even consider reporting the value of implementation area. Enhancing the encryption/decription speed does not optimize the overall deployment of AES as some applications are interesting in small implementation area. The following part reports the researches about optimizing the AES implementation area over the FPGA.

Table 4. AES throughputs with different key lengthes [22]

	Key length 128 bit	Key length 192 bit	Key length 256 bit
Data length 128 bit	1.03 Gbps	0.853 Gbps	0.73 Gbps

Table 5. AES restrictions and achievements by [23]

Target FPGA Device	Spartan 3 XC3s200FT256-5
Optimization goal	Speed
Maximum operating frequency	91.049MHz
Encryption/decryption throughput	224 Mbit/sec
Total memory usage	Not reported

3.2 AES Area Optimization

Hamalainen et al. [15] tried to reduce the implementation area (number of gates) by parallelizing the AES operations on FPGA. The high level architecture consists of byte permutation, `MixColumn` multiplier, parallel to serial converter, S-box and key scheduler. The proposed design is implemented on a 0.13 μm CMOS technology, therefore, this approach is appreciated for low cost and low power applications. The achieved results are shown in Table 6.

Another area improvement approach is introduced by Rady et al. [24]. The proposed AES core architecture consists of three units; controller unit, interfaces unit and the main Enc/Dec AES unit with the key expansion and storage. The proposed architecture introduced two ways to improve the AES area. The first way is by iterative the key expansion and ordinary round. The second way is by sharing specific resource in the ordinary round and key expansion. This design introduce improvement in area implementation of the Enc/Dec AES core by VHDL code with Spartan3(Xc3s400) FPGA kit using the iteration architecture and the resource sharing. This design consumes 2699 slices and two BRAM. It is simulated with the timing simulation of ModelSim V 6.0.

Away from the AES hardware implementations, machine learning techniques contribute very well not only for AES development, but also for encryption hacking and cryptanalysis operations. Siddeeq and Ali [25] used the Neural Networks technique for building and simulating the AES based cryptosystem. The initial weights for neural network representing the key used in both encryption and decryption processes. The simulation results prove that the performance of NN-AES is equivalent to the normal one. Albassal and Wahdan [26] used the neural networks for attacking and cryptanalysis of a Feistel type block cipher. The achieved results can be used in the future for filling some holes of encryption algorithm. They have also extended their work to include Genetic Algorithms as a machine learning techniques for cryptanalysis process [27].

Table 6. CMOS implementations of AES for area optimization [15]

	Width (bit)	Area (Kgates)	Freq. (MHz)	Power $\mu W/MHz$	Thro. Mbps
Area	8	3.1	152	37	121
Power	8	3.2	130	30	104
Speed	8	3.9	290	62	232

4   Conclusions and Future Work

Data encryption is a basic notion of information security, and it is used by almost all data transaction applications. The Advanced Encryption Standard (AES) is one of the most efficient encryption algorithms, and it has received great research attention due its simplicity and applicability. The AES related researches are focused in the encryption speed and the hardware implementation area as two important factors for algorithm's performance. This paper presented some cutting edge researches for enhancing the AES speed and implementation area. According to the reported results, it is clear that these is trade-off between the two factors. As a future work, we are going to continue this research in order to get the maximum encryption speed in limited implementation area. Moreover, some machine learning techniques can be used for simulating the AES encryption and cryptanalysis processes.

References

1. van Tilborg, H.C.A.: Encyclopedia of Cryptography and Security. Springer-Verlag New York, Inc., Secaucus (2005)
2. Nedjah, N., de Macedo Mourelle, L.: A Versatile Pipelined Hardware Implementation for Encryption and Decryption Using Advanced Encryption Standard. In: Daydé, M., Palma, J.M.L.M., Coutinho, Á.L.G.A., Pacitti, E., Lopes, J.C. (eds.) VECPAR 2006. LNCS, vol. 4395, pp. 249–259. Springer, Heidelberg (2007)
3. Paar, C., Pelzl, J.: Understanding Cryptography: A Textbook for Students and Practitioners, 1st edn. Springer Publishing Company, Incorporated (2009)
4. Burr, W.E.: Selecting the advanced encryption standard. IEEE Security and Privacy 1(2), 43–52 (2003)
5. Kilts, S.: Advanced FPGA Design: Architecture, Implementation, and Optimization. Wiley-IEEE Press (2007)
6. Gomes, O., Moreno, R., Pimenta, T.: A fast cryptography pipelined hardware developed in FPGA with VHDL. In: The 3rd International Congress on Ultra Modern Telecommunications and Control Systems and Workshops (ICUMT), pp. 1–6 (October 2011)
7. Mijalli, M.H.A.: Efficient realization of S-Box based reduced residue of prime numbers using Virtex-5 and Virtex-6 FPGAs. American Journal of Applied Sciences 8(8), 754–757 (2011)
8. Dileep, A., Sekhar, C.: Identification of block ciphers using support vector machines. In: International Joint Conference on Neural Networks, IJCNN 2006, pp. 2696–2701 (2006)
9. National Institute of Standards and Technology: FIPS PUB 46-3: Data Encryption Standard (DES) (October 1999),
    http://www.itl.nist.gov/fipspubs/fip186-2.pdf, supersedes FIPS 46-2
10. Hoang, T., Nguyen, V.L.: An efficient FPGA implementation of the advanced encryption standard algorithm. In: IEEE RIVF International Conference on Computing and Communication Technologies, Research, Innovation, and Vision for the Future (RIVF), pp. 1–4 (March 2012)
11. National Institute of Standards and Technology,
    http://www.nist.gov/index.html

12. Zambreno, J., Nguyen, D., Choudhary, A.: Exploring Area/Delay Tradeoffs in an AES FPGA Implementation. In: Becker, J., Platzner, M., Vernalde, S. (eds.) FPL 2004. LNCS, vol. 3203, pp. 575–585. Springer, Heidelberg (2004)

13. Wali, M.F., Rehan, M.: Effective coding and performance evaluation of the Rijndael Algorithm (AES). In: Student Conference on Engineering Sciences and Technology, SCONEST 2005, pp. 1–7 (August 2005)

14. Tillich, S., Feldhofer, M., Popp, T., Großschädl, J.: Area, delay, and power characteristics of standard-cell implementations of the AES S-Box. Journal of Signal Processing Systems 50(2), 251–261 (2008)

15. Hamalainen, P., Alho, T., Hannikainen, M., Hamalainen, T.: Design and implementation of low-area and low-power AES encryption hardware core. In: The 9th EUROMICRO Conference on Digital System Design: Architectures, Methods and Tools, DSD 2006, pp. 577–583 (2006)

16. Elumalai, R., Reddy, A.R.: Improving diffusion power of AES Rijndael with 8 × 8 MDS Matrix. International Journal of Scientific and Engineering Research 2(3) (March 2011)

17. Rais, M.H., Qasim, S.M.: Efficient fpga realization of S-Box using reduced residue of prime numbers. International Journal of Computer Science and Network Security (IJCSNS) 10(1), 74–96 (2010)

18. Huang, J., Seberry, J., Susilo, W.: A Five-Round Algebraic Property of the Advanced Encryption Standard. In: Wu, T.-C., Lei, C.-L., Rijmen, V., Lee, D.-T. (eds.) ISC 2008. LNCS, vol. 5222, pp. 316–330. Springer, Heidelberg (2008)

19. Yenuguvanilanka, J., Elkeelany, O.: Performance evaluation of hardware models of advanced encryption standard (AES) algorithm. The IEEE Southeastcon, 222–225 (April 2008)

20. Ghewari, P.B., Jaymala, M., Patil, K., Chougule, A.B.: Efficient hardware design and implementation of AES cryptosystem. International Journal of Engineering Science and Technology 2(3), 213–219 (2010)

21. Thulasimani, L., Madheswaran, M.: A single chip design and implementation of aes-128/192/256 encryption algorithms. International Journal of Engineering Science and Technology 2(5), 1052–1059 (2010)

22. Yin, H., Debiao, H., Yong, K., Xiande, F.: High-speed ASIC implementation of AES supporting 128/192/256 bits. In: International Conference on Test and Measurement, ICTM 2009, vol. 1, pp. 95–98 (December 2009)

23. Liberatori, M., Otero, F., Bonadero, J., Castineira, J.: AES-128 cipher. high speed, low cost FPGA implementation. In: The 3rd Southern Conference on Programmable Logic, SPL 2007, pp. 195–198 (Febraury 2007)

24. Rady, A., El Sehely, E., El Hennawy, A.: Design and implementation of area optimized AES algorithm on reconfigurable FPGA. In: Internatonal Conference on Microelectronics, ICM 2007, pp. 35–38 (December 2007)

25. Siddeeq, Y.A., Ali, H.M.: AES cryptosystem development using neural networks. International Journal of Computer and Electrical Engineering (IJCEE) 3(2), 309–314 (2011)

26. Albassal, A., Wahdan, A.M.: Neural network based cryptanalysis of a feistel type block cipher. In: International Conference on Electrical, Electronic and Computer Engineering, ICEEC 2004, pp. 231–237 (September 2004)

27. Albassal, A., Wahdan, A.M.: Genetic algorithm cryptanalysis of a feistel type block cipher. In: International Conference on Electrical, Electronic and Computer Engineering, ICEEC 2004, pp. 217–221 (September 2004)

Machine Learning Techniques for Fingerprint Identification: A Short Review

Ali Ismail Awad[1,2]

[1] Electrical Engineering Department, Faculty of Engineering
Al Azhar University, Qena, Egypt
[2] Member of Scientific Research Group in Egypt (SRGE)
aawad@ieee.org

Abstract. Fingerprint is considered as a dominant biometric trait due to its acceptability, reliability, high security level and low cost. Due to the high demand on fingerprint identification system deployments, a lot of challenges are keep arising in each system's phase including fingerprint image enhancement, feature extraction, features matching and fingerprint classification. Machine learning techniques introduce non traditional solutions to the fingerprint identification challenges. This paper presents a short survey that emphasizes the implementations of basic machine learning notions for compensating some fingerprint problems. This survey contributes as a ground truth for developing machine learning based algorithms for fingerprint identification in the near future.

Keywords: Biometrics, Fingerprints, Machine Learning Techniques.

1 Introduction

Biometrics technology is a way of personal identification using the phycological or the behavioural characteristics. Driven from the security needs for the electronically connected world, biometrics identification compensates some weaknesses of token- and knowledge-based identification in terms of loss, duplication and theft. Biometrics traits contain iris pattern, retinal scan, fingerprints, voice and signature. Fingerprint is one of the dominant biometrics traits that keeps spreading out because its uniqueness, acceptability, and low cost [1]. According to the biometrics market and industry report [2], Fig. 1 represents the total fingerprint revenue which is around 66% compared to the other biometrics technologies.

In spite of fingerprint identification provides high security level and it has large application domains, fingerprint identification system (will be explained in Section 2.2) is attacked by many challenges that lead to system performance degradation with respect to identification time and accuracy [3]. These challenges are found in fingerprint acquisition, fingerprint preprocessing and enhancement, feature extraction, fingerprint matching and fingerprint classification [4]. However, these problems have been tackled by many researches using different techniques in order to enhance the overall identification system performance, the ideal solutions for some of these problems are still unavailable.

A. Ell Hassanien et al. (Eds.): AMLTA 2012, CCIS 322, pp. 524–531, 2012.
© Springer-Verlag Berlin Heidelberg 2012

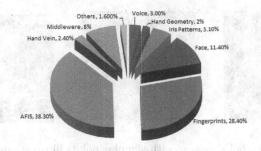

Fig. 1. Biometrics technologies deployment in 2009

Machine learning techniques such as Artificial Neural Networks (ANN), Support Vector Machine (SVM) and Genetic Algorithms (GA) [5] play an important role for presenting non traditional solutions for fingerprint identification problems. The idea behind these techniques is to build a feature vector and train (learn) the machine how to process that vector according to some particular rules. This way, machine learning techniques can process efficiently the complicated fingerprint data, and hence, contribute in solving some problems of the fingerprint identification system.

The contribution of this paper is to introduce a precise survey about some machine learning techniques that have been used in fingerprint identification. The survey can be used as ground truth for developing new machine learning based algorithms for fingerprint identification system. The methodology of this research is to consider only the most promising techniques in machine learning and their deployment in some phases of the fingerprint identification system.

The reminder part of this paper is organized as follows. Section 2 gives a preliminary information about the fingerprint identification system components staring from fingerprint acquisition phase and ending with fingerprint matching phase. Moreover, fingerprint structure has been explained as a first part of that section. Section 3 reports the research progress of deploying three machine learning techniques, namely, ANN, SVM and GA over fingerprint identification system. Finally, conclusions and future work have been reported in Section 4.

2   Fingerprint Identification

This section covers the fingerprint identification system in order to fully understand the implementations of the machine learning techniques in each phase.

2.1   Fingerprint Structure

Fingerprint is defined as the ridge and valleys formed on the fingertip [6]. It is constructed from harmonic patterns of alternating ridges and valleys. However, fingerprint ridges and valleys are parallel in most regions, several deforming features such as scars, cuts, cracks and calluses, are also present on the finger

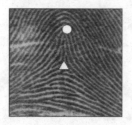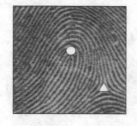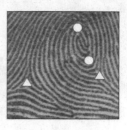

Fig. 2. Fingerprint global structure with singular points illustrations (Circles- for core points and Triangles- for delta points)

tip [7]. In common, there are three representation levels of fingerprints: (*i*) Global structure, (*ii*) Local structure, and (*iii*) Low level structure [8]. Fig.2 shows three different examples of fingerprint images with ridges and valleys representations.

The global fingerprint representation expresses the overall shape of the fingerprint. In global structure, a single representation is valid for the entire fingerprint image [9]. Another important feature of the global structure is the singular points (Circles and Triangles in Fig. 2) [10]. Singular points are unique for each fingerprint class, therefore, they are widely used as a feature for fingerprint coarse registration and classification [11]. The local fingerprint structure represents the ridges and valleys format at local interesting region. The most famous ridge property is ridge ending and ridge bifurcation (it is called Minutiae) [12], [13]. The local structure is mostly used in fingerprint matching because minutiae are the highest discriminant feature of fingerprint images. The low level (level-3) structure considers the sweat pores on the fingerprint skin. The low level structure is difficult to get captured as it needs properly environment with very high resolution sensor that requires high cost [8].

2.2   Fingerprint Identification System

Automatic Fingerprint Identification System (AFIS) has replaced human experts in fingerprint recognition as well as classification. It consists of two phases: (*i*) Enrollment phase and (*ii*) Identification phase. The enrollment phase is directed to register the individual identity in the database for future usage. While, the identification phase is responsible for extracting the individual identity from the database according to the user claimed identity [3].

Each phase is decomposed into the following sub-stages: (*i*) Fingerprint acquisition, (*ii*) Preprocessing, (*iii*) Feature extraction and (*iv*) Database storage. Fig. 3 shows the flowchart of fingerprint identification system. Generally speaking, fingerprint acquisition, preprocessing and feature extraction are the common stages for both enrollment and identification. However, fingerprint matching is an extra mandatory step for the identification phase to extract the claimed identity from the pre-collected database [1]. Processing time and identification accuracy are two import factors for increasing the system performance [3]. Machine

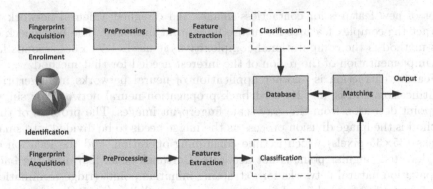

Fig. 3. A flowchart of fingerprint identification system (basic components)

learning techniques can be good contributors for enhancing the system performance as reported in Section 3.

3 Machine Learning Techniques

Machine learning systems are concerned with building fixable algorithms or techniques that their performance is automatically improved with experience (training) [14]. Machine learning system is first trained with source data, and following, it is used to perform required operations according to its acquired experience. The problem of machine learning techniques is related to their sensitivity to the training data and the training parameters as they may produce different results by changing the training data. However machine learning includes many techniques such as Artificial Neural Networks, Support Vector Machine, Genetic Algorithms, Bayesian Training and Probabilistic Models [15], we will stress only on the implementation of the first three techniques on fingerprint identification.

3.1 Artificial Neural Networks

Artificial Neural Networks is the most widely used algorithm of the machine learning system [16]. The quality assurance of the acquired fingerprint image is an important process before the feature extraction. Xie and Qi [17] designed a supervised back propagation neural network that uses the gray scale fingerprint image for continuous image quality estimation. The problems of this method are the lack of evaluation as it has been evaluated for small fingerprint images from Fingerprint Verification Competition 2002 (FVC2002)[18]. Moreover, the fingerprint image needs to be divided into blocks which is computationally expensive process before running the proposed method. Zhu et al. [19] used the neural network for quality estimation of the fingerprint images using fingerprint ridge orientation. The correct ridge orientation is estimated using the trained neural networks. Labati et al. [20] proposed the usage of neural network for image quality measurement in contactless fingerprint acquisition. They discovered a set of new features for contactless images and designed a neural network to extract the complex features for future fingerprint matching. The bottleneck of this method is the computational complexity as it needs 1.5 to 3.7 seconds for the implementation of the region of the interest needed for that method.

Feature extraction is another application of neural networks in fingerprint identification. Liu et al. [21] used back propagation neural network for singular point detection from the gray scale fingerprint images. The problem of this method is the image division process as the image needs to be divided into small blocks (35×35 pixels) which is time consuming operation, and the location of the detected singular point is not accurate. Bartunek et al. [22] used the back propagation natural networks for extracting minutiae points (ridge termination and bifurcation) from thinned fingerprint images. A sliding (5×5 pixels) window has been used to access the whole fingerprint image searching for minutia points. The problem with this method is the huge processing time to get the thinned image. Yang et al. [23] used the fuzzy neural networks for minutiae extraction from the gray scale image with high invariant to rotation and gray level changes.

Fingerprint classification is an important process for reducing the identification time. Sarbadhikari et al. [24] proposed two-stage fingerprint classifier. In the second stage, Multi-Layer Perceptron (MLP) feed forward neural network was used to classify the directional Fourier image. The achieved classification accuracy was around 84%. Mohamed and Nyongesa [25] proposed the usage of fuzzy neural networks as a classification mechanism due to its ability to work as an adaptive filter in order to produce reliable results. They constructed a feature vector using five different parameters including number of core points, number of delta points, directional image, core point direction, and the position of delta point. The algorithm achieved 85.0% for classifying the Left Loop class, and 98.35% for classifying the Whorl class. Kumar and Vikram [26] used multidimentional ANN (MDANN) for fingerprint matching using minutiae points. The algorithm achieved a maximum recognition rate as 97.37%.

Kristensen et al. [27] presented a comparative study on different neural networks and support vector machine. They implemented four types of neural networks including Multi-Layer Perceptron (MLP), Bidirectional Associative Memory (BAM), Hopfield and Kohonen neural networks, as well as the support vector machine. They concluded that MLP neural network achieved the best performance with an overall accuracy as 88.8% for the $5 - class$ problem. Support vector machine came in the second rank with classification rate about 87.0%, but both classifiers failed to classify most of Tented Arches class. In general, the other three classifiers could not perform well compared to multi-layer perceptron and support vector machine.

3.2 Support Vector Machine

Support Vector Machine is a training algorithm for linear classification, regression, principal component analysis and for non-linear classifications. The idea behind the support vector machine is to maximizing the margin between the training patterns and the decision boundary [16].

Liu et al. [28] used the support vector machine technique with five features vector length to determine the fingerprint image qulaity. fingerprint has been classified into high, medium and low quality images with the accuracy of 96.03%. The problem with Liu's method is the long processing time of the feature extraction step. Zhao et al. [29] implemented support vector machine for fingerprint image segmentation as it is an important step before feature extraction. They divided the image into (12 × 12 pixels) blocks, and five features have been used to construct the feature vector. These features are gray mean, gray variance, contrast, coherence and the main energy ratio. The proposed method is consider as robust for small scale evaluation. From the other side, Li et al. [30] used the support vector machine for fingerprint classification into 5 − *classes* with total achieved accuracy 93.5% with a combination of singular points and orientation image. However, using the orientation coefficients only produced 87.4%, and using singular point only produced 88.3% at maximum.

3.3   Genetic Algorithms

Genetic Algorithms are promising machine learning techniques for solving fingerprint related problems. Mao et al. [31] succeeded to use genetic algorithm for singular point extraction. They presented a new definition for core point location and orientation which is used as fitness function for the genetic algorithm. The challenge of this method is processing time is become higher with increased accuracy (1×1 pixels with 10° accuracy). Tan et al. [32] implemented genetic algorithm for fingerprint matching process using optimized minutiae transformation. However the genetic algorithm achieves promising matching results, the required times are 15 and 8 seconds for genuine and imposter matching, respectively. Therefore, an optimization process is become a crucial need.

Tan et al. [33] developed a classification algorithm based on some new learned features. In the proposed approach, they tried to find unconventional primitives from the orientation images using the Genetic Programming (GP) technique. The learned features might never be imagining by humans experts. Then, a Bayesian classifier was used for conducting the actual classification process. The proposed method was evaluated over the NIST-4 database [34]. The first 2000 images were used for the training process, and the second 2000 were used for the evaluation purposes. The total Percentage of Correct Classification (PCC) was about 93.3% and 91.6% for the 4 − *class* and the 5 − *class* classification problems, respectively.

4   Conclusions and Future Work

This paper introduced a precise survey on the usage of machine learning techniques for solving some fingerprint identification problems. The paper has focused on three important techniques which are Artificial Neural Networks, Support Vector Machine and Genetic Algorithms, and their implementations on image quality measurements, feature extraction and fingerprint classification. The review confirms the superiority of using machine learning for tackling different fingerprint identification problems. The future work will be targeted toward developing one of machine learning technique for tackling some pending fingerprint challenges such as processing time reduction and identification accuracy enhancement. Moreover, another biometrics traits like palmprints and iris patterns will be considered as an applications of machine learning techniques.

References

1. Jain, A.K., Bolle, R., Pankanti, S.: Biometrics Personal Identification in Networked Society. Springer (2009)
2. International Biometric Group: Biometrics Market and Industry Report 2009-2014 (2008), http://www.biometricgroup.com
3. Egawa, S., Awad, A.I., Baba, K.: Evaluation of Acceleration Algorithm for Biometric Identification. In: Benlamri, R. (ed.) NDT 2012, Part II. CCIS, vol. 294, pp. 231–242. Springer, Heidelberg (2012)
4. Jain, A.K., Ross, A.A., Nandakumar, K.: Introduction to Biometrics. Springer (2011)
5. Bishop, C.M.: Pattern Recognition and Machine Learning. Springer (2006)
6. Delac, K., Grgic, M.: A survey of biometric recognition methods. In: Proceedings Elmar 2004, the 46 th International Symposium on Electronics in Marine, pp. 184–193 (2004)
7. Jain, A.K., Pankanti, S.: Automated fingerprint identification and imaging systems. In: Lee, H.C., Gaensslen, R.E. (eds.) Advances in Fingerprint Technology, 2nd edn., pp. 275–326. CRC Press (2001)
8. Maltoni, D., Maio, D., Jain, A.K., Prabhakar, S.: Handbook of Fingerprint Recognition, 2nd edn. Springer (2009)
9. Jain, A.K., Flynn, P.J., Ross, A.A.: Handbook of Biometrics, 1st edn. Springer, New York (2007)
10. Srinivasan, V., Murthy, N.: Detection of singular points in fingerprint images. Pattern Recognition 25(2), 139–153
11. Awad, A.I., Baba, K.: Fingerprint Singularity Detection: A Comparative Study. In: Mohamad Zain, J., Wan Mohd, W.M.b., El-Qawasmeh, E. (eds.) ICSECS 2011, Part I. CCIS, vol. 179, pp. 122–132. Springer, Heidelberg (2011)
12. Amin, A., Neil, Y.: Fingerprint classification: a review. Pattern Analysis and Applications 7(1), 77–93
13. Espinosa-Dur, V.: Minutiae detection algorithm for fingerprint recognition. In: Proceedings of IEEE 35th International Carnahan Conference on Security Technology, pp. 264–266. IEEE (2001)
14. Mitchell, T.: Machine Learning. McGraw-Hill series in Computer Science. McGraw-Hill (1997)
15. Theodoridis, S., Pikrakis, A., Koutroumbas, K., Cavouras, D.: Introduction to Pattern Recognition: A Matlab Approach. Academic Press (2010)
16. Sivanandam, S.N.: Introduction To Neural Networks Using MATLAB 6.0. Tata Mgraw Hill (2009)
17. Xie, R., Qi, J.: Continuous fingerprint image quality estimation based on neural network. In: The International Symposium on Intelligent Signal Processing and Communication Systems, ISPACS (2010)
18. Maio, D., Maltoni, D., Cappelli, R., Wayman, J., Jain, A.K.: FVC2002: Second Fingerprint Verification Competition. In: Proceedings of 16th International Conference on Pattern Recognition (ICPR 2002), Quebec City, pp. 811–814 (2002)

19. Zhu, E., Yin, J., Hu, C., Zhang, G.: Quality Estimation of Fingerprint Image Based on Neural Network. In: Wang, L., Chen, K., S. Ong, Y. (eds.) ICNC 2005, Part II. LNCS, vol. 3611, pp. 65–70. Springer, Heidelberg (2005)
20. Labati, R., Piuri, V., Scotti, F.: Neural-based quality measurement of fingerprint images in contactless biometric systems. In: The 2010 International Joint Conference on Neural Networks, IJCNN (2010)
21. Yong-Xia, L., Jin, Q., Rui, X.: A new detection method of singular points of fingerprints based on neural network. In: The 3rd IEEE International Conference on Computer Science and Information Technology, ICCSIT (2010)
22. Bartunek, J., Nilsson, M., Nordberg, J., Claesson, I.: Neural network based minutiae extraction from skeletonized fingerprints. In: The 2006 IEEE Region 10 Conference, TENCON 2006 (2006)
23. Yang, G., Shi, D., Quek, C.: Fingerprint Minutia Recognition with Fuzzy Neural Network. In: Wang, J., Liao, X.-F., Yi, Z. (eds.) ISNN 2005, Part II. LNCS, vol. 3497, pp. 165–170. Springer, Heidelberg (2005)
24. Sarbadhikari, S.N., Basak, J., Pal, S.K., Kundu, M.K.: Noisy fingerprints classification with directional based features using MLP. Neural Computing & Applications 7, 180–191 (1998)
25. Mohamed, S.M., Nyongesa, H.O.: Automatic fingerprint classification system using fuzzy neural techniques. In: Proceedings of the 2002 IEEE International Conference on Fuzzy Systems, (FUZZ-IEEE 2002), vol. 1, pp. 358–362 (2002)
26. Kumar, R., Vikram, B.D.: Fingerprint matching using multi-dimensional ann. Engineering Applications of Artificial Intelligence 23(2), 222–228 (2010)
27. Kristensen, T., Borthen, J., Fyllingsnes, K.: Comparison of neural network based fingerprint classification techniques. In: Proceedings of the International Joint Conference on Neural Networks, (IJCNN 2007). IEEE, Orlando (2007)
28. Liu, L., Tan, T., Zhan, Y.: Based on svm automatic measures of fingerprint image quality. In: Pacific-Asia Workshop on Computational Intelligence and Industrial Application, PACIIA 2008 (2008)
29. Zhao, S., Hao, X., Li, X.: Segmentation of fingerprint images using support vector machines. In: Second International Symposium on Intelligent Information Technology Application, IITA 2008 (2008)
30. Li, J., Yau, W., Wang, H.: Combining singular points and orientation image information for fingerprint classification. Pattern Recognition 41(1)
31. Mao, K., Wang, G., Jin, Y., Yu, C.: Using genetic algorithms for fingerprint core point detection. In: The 6th International Conference on Fuzzy Systems and Knowledge Discovery, FSKD 2009 (2009)
32. Tan, X., Bhanu, B.: Fingerprint matching by genetic algorithms. Pattern Recogn. 39(3), 465–477 (2006)
33. Tan, X., Bhanu, B., Lin, Y.: Fingerprint classification based on learned features. IEEE Transactions on Systems, Man, and Cybernetics, Part C: Applications and Reviews 35(3), 287–300 (2005)
34. Watson, C., Wilson, C.: NIST special database 4, fingerprint database. U.S. National Institute of Standards and Technology (1992)

A Novel Watermarking Approach for Data Integrity and Non-repudiation in Rational Databases

N. Zawawi, R. El-Gohary, M. Hamdy, and M. F. Tolba

Ain Shams University, Cairo, Egypt
{Nourzawawi,fahmytolba}@gmail.com,
dr.raniaelgohary@fcis.asu.edu.eg, m.hamdy@cis.asu.edu.eg

Abstract. Keeping large scale data sets like data warehouse seems a vital demand of business organizations. Proving copyright, ownership, integrity and non-repudiation have a growing interest of database community. Many watermarking techniques have been proposed in the literature to address these purposes. This paper introduces a new technique WRDN (Watermarking Rational Database with Non-Repudiation) to protect the ownership of relational database by adding only one hidden column with a secret formula where it has the ability to know the latest updates made by users. The calculation of this formula is based on the values of other numeric and textual columns. Moreover, the proposed approach keeps track on the latest updates made to numeric and textual data by users. This approach is compared to two other alternative approaches. The proposed approach survives by 100% against insertion and deletion attacks.

Keywords: Relational Database, Database Security, Copyright protection, Digital Watermarking.

1 Introduction

The massive use of the Internet offers a wide range of web-based services, such as database as a service, digital repositories and libraries. All these kinds of services allow people to share a divest database content like images and videos over the internet. As a result, preserving the rights and roles of accessing this content in such environment becomes a challenging vital task. Privacy, illegal redistribution, ownership claiming and theft are the most common attacks against rational database contents. The techniques of digital watermarking provide promising solutions for protecting data inside relational databases from illegal copying and manipulation. These techniques embed directly the secret codes into the tables inside the databases. These secret codes called (watermarks), which can provide a better security for data protection, such as copyright protection, integrity checking, and fingerprinting.

In this paper, Digital watermarking for integrity and copyright is presented. A watermarking should not significantly affect the quality of original data and should not be destroyed easily. Moreover, watermarking aims to identify pirated copies of original data. Watermarking does not prevent copying, but it deters illegal copying by

A. Ell Hassanien et al. (Eds.): AMLTA 2012, CCIS 322, pp. 532–542, 2012.

providing a means of establishing the ownership of a redistributed copy. The digital watermarking for integrity verification is called fragile watermarking as compared to robust watermarking for copyright protection. Watermarking techniques apply to various types of host content. Here, one concentrates on relational databases.

In this paper, one proposes a novel technique WRDN (Watermarking Rational Database with Non-Repudiation). WRDN is based on changing database schema by adding a new column. The values inside depend on the values of related attributes, which are applied over a secret formula. WRDN adds the user fingerprint for each row to have the ability to recognize authorized from unauthorized users. The rest of this paper is organized as follows: Section 2 presents an overview of the related work. The proposed WRDN insertion and detection algorithm is presented in Section 3. Section 4 introduces a security analysis of WRDN in comparison with other algorithms. Finally, the conclusion of this paper with summaries is introduced in Section 5.

2   Related Work

Database watermarking consists of two basic processes; in the first Watermark Insertion: Watermark (W) is embedded into the relational database (D) with a secret key (K), and distributes the watermarked relational database (DW). In the second Watermark Detection: The watermarked database (DW) with the same secret key (K) will be extracted in order to recover the original watermark data (D). The watermarking techniques proposed [9] so far can be classified along various dimensions as follows:

— Data type: Different watermarking schemes embed different types of watermark information (e.g. image, text etc.) into the underlying data of the database.
— Distortion: Depends on whether the watermarking introduces any distortion to the underlying data.
— Sensitivity: Watermarking schemes can be classified into either robust or fragile according to their sensitivity to database attacks.
— Watermark information: The watermarking can be performed by modifying or inserting information at a bit level or a higher level.
— Verifiability: The detection/verification process may be performed publicly (by anyone) or privately (by the owner only).
— Data Structure: Different watermarking schemes are designed to serve different purposes depending on the structure model that data is built on.

In this paper, distortion as a classification technique is proposed. The watermarked database may suffer from various types of intentional and unintentional attacks, which may damage or erase the used watermarking. These attacks can be summarized into two types: the first type is attacks against watermark itself, where the attacker knows that there is a watermarking over this database and he is trying to destroy it. Moreover, the second type is attacks over data itself, where the attacker does not know that there is a watermarking in this data and he is just trying to add one's own watermarking to one's data.

The approaches handle these types of attacks, which are based on the two main categories of algorithms. These algorithms can be summarized as: the first algorithm is the distortion based algorithm, which introduces small changes in data values during embedding phase where changes are tolerable and should not make the data useless. The watermarking scheme proposed by [1], also known as AHK, is one of the pioneering research in database watermarking. The fundamental assumption is that the watermarked database can tolerate a small amount of errors in numeric data. Although the basic assumption of AHK scheme is that the relation has a primary key whose value does not change, Li et al. [15] suggest three different schemes to obtain virtual primary keys for a relation without primary key. Sion et. al [23] use the most significant bits of the normalized dataset instead of primary key. The work of Liu et al. [16] uses a hash function based on the private key and buyer's ID. Unlike the above mentioned watermarking schemes, the right protection scheme proposed by Sion et al. [24] is based on categorical type data. Database watermarking based on cloud model is proposed by Zhang et al. [25]. A fragile watermarking scheme is able to detect and localize any malicious modification made to a relational database and it can also recover the true data from modified cells [12].

The second algorithm is the distortion free, where the proposed model is considered to be one of them. There is no modification made to any data item and the digital watermarking is used for integrity verification. The watermarking scheme proposed by Y. Li et al. [14] was the first distortion free algorithm made. The Basic idea was that all tuples are securely partitioned into (g) groups. A different watermark is embedded in each group such that any modifications can be detected and localized into the group level with high probabilities. The watermarking scheme proposed by Li and Deng [13] is applicable for marking any type of data. The interesting feature of this scheme is that it does not use any secret key. Moreover, the unique watermarking key is used in both the creation and the verification phases. While, Kamel [10] suggested a way to improve the detection rate of malicious alteration by watermarking not only the relational tables (data records) but also all relevant indexes by proposing a fragile watermarking technique for protecting data integrity in databases and more specifically in R-tree data structures. The approach proposed in [21] aims to generate fake tuples and insert them erroneously into the database. The fake tuple creation algorithm takes care of candidate key attributes and sensitivity level of non candidate attributes, while in [8] they add only one hidden column, using a secret formula to relational database that contains only numeric values. Moreover, it locks this calculated column from any attacks or manipulations. However, the work done by [7] uses the same schema made in [8] but by applying it over a non-numeric data over the watermarking on a new row. The watermarking schemes, which are able to detect any modifications made in database relation, are proposed in [3- 4 -5]. Partitioning is based on categorical attribute values, after partitioning the tuple level and group level of hash values for each group are computed. Moreover, Cortesi et al [4] have removed the constraints on the presence at different categorical values and serve the purpose of temper detection of the associated partition. In addition, Cortesi et al [5] have concentrated on the integrity of the relational databases by using a public zero distortion authentication mechanism. They have generated a gray scale image to trace the verification of database integrity and employ a zero distortion public authentication mechanism to prove the owner-ship. All of the work cited so far assumed that attacks facing database are outsider attacks and the number of users does not affect the performance.

3   WRDN as an Approach

In this section, one proposes WRDN (Watermarking Rational Database with Non-Repudiation) approach to prevent the impacts of tampering dataset and localizing any changes made. WRDN has the ability to know the latest changes made by each user in the available database. The proposed approach gives the database owner more con-trol over his data. However, all other watermarking algorithms concentrated on prov-ing their ownerships or integrity of database against outsider attackers; but what if the attacker is from inside our organization? The previous related works fail to know if the attacker is from insider or outsider the organization. Although the proposed ap-proach tries to add a user fingerprint in order to be able to recognize the authorization from the unauthorized users. These developed steps added a new feature to the proposed watermarking algorithm where it becomes a non-repudiation approach. In subsection 3.1 WRDN insertion and detection mechanisms are introduced. The wa-termark insertion algorithm for WRDN is presented in Subsection 3.2. Subsection 3.3 presents the WRDN watermark detection algorithm and how to add a user fingerprint is described in Subsection 3.4.

3.1   WRDN Framework

Figure 1 shows the proposed WRDN framework. It can be summarized as follows: it relies on changing database schema; thus the structure of the database will be changed by adding a new column (altering the table). The function is used in constructing the

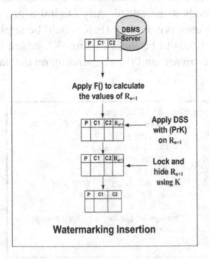
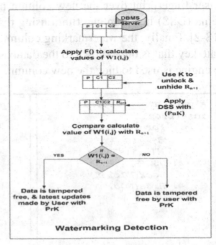

Fig. 1. Insertion and Detection mechanism of WRDN

Table 1. Notation and parameters

n	Number of attributes in the relation
m	Number of tuples in the relation
X	Number of users
PrK1..x	User private key
Rn+1	Watermarked column
W(i,j)	Watermark value of tuple i and attribute j
PuK 1..x	User public key
K	Database embedded key
F()	Special function used to calculate values in Rn+1
W1(i,j)	New column values calculated at detection phase

new record as well as a secret key (K) known only by the data owner; each user has a private key. The public key for each user is available in public, then applies user private key over Digital Signature Schema (DSS) to add user fingerprint. By adding user fingerprint, it gives the ability to differentiate authorized from unauthorized users. Finally, the proposed model combines some important features to database watermarking Non-Repudiation, Integrity and Copyright protection.

3.2   Watermark Insertion

Table I shows the notations and parameters used in this paper. Suppose database relation has a primary key (P) and (n) attribute, denoted by R (P, C1, C2, ..., Cn). WRDN algorithm does not need to have a primary key attribute.   A new column Rn+1 is added to the existing schema. Rn+1 holds value from a special function F() of any values. The special function F() does not need to take numeric values.

The watermarking insertion algorithm is shown in Algorithm 1.In step 1, the values of the new column need to be calculated. By applying all the corresponding attribute values over a special function F(), any mathematical formula can be used. In step 2, the user fingerprint over the new column needs to be added. Any Digital Signature Schema (DSS) insertion algorithm using the user private key (PrK) could be applied in [18-2]. Finally, the watermarking column needs to be locked using (K), which is a private key that is only known to the database owner, and then depending on the database engine is used to hide the new column.

```
Algorithm 1: Watermark
insertion
    1. For i=0 to m and
       j=1 to n
       W(i,j)=F(Ri)
    2. DSS(Rn+1,PrK)
    3. Lock(NCol,K)
    4. Hide(NCol)
```

```
Algorithm 2: Watermark detection
    1.   For i=0 to m & j=1 to n
         W1(i,j)=F(Ri)
    2.   UnHide(Rn+1)
    3.   UnLock(Rn+1,K)
    4.   DSS(W(i,j),PuK)
    5.   IF W1(i,j)= W(i,j)
         Data is accepted
    6.   Else
         Changes made at R(i) by
         User x
    7. Hide(NCol)
```

3.3   Watermark Detection

The watermark detection algorithm is shown in Algorithm 2. In steps 1 and 2, one needs to calculate the value of watermark for each tuple W1 (i,j); by applying the row values over the same mathematical formula which is used when inserting the water-marking. In steps 3 and 4, unhide and unlock the original watermark column are pro-posed. Then in step 5, one needs to check the user fingerprint over the watermarked attribute. This is applied by using the same DSS detection algorithm for all users pub-lic key (PuK).One will have the available watermarked value W (i,j) with the availa-ble information for the user who made the latest updates.   From step 6, one needs to compare the new calculated result with the original watermark result. If they match, then one will be able to know which user made the latest updates by proving the data-base ownership. Otherwise, it enables to prove which rows are changed and if the changes are made by an authorized or unauthorized user.

3.4   Adding User Fingerprint

Adding a user fingerprint or a digital signature is a mathematical scheme for demon-strating the authenticity of a digital message or document. It is equivalent to tradition-al handwritten signatures in many respects; properly implemented digital signatures are more difficult to forge than the handwritten type [20-17]. They must not be forge-able. Recipients must be able to verify them and Signers must not be able to repudiate them later. In addition, digital signatures cannot be constant and must be a function of the entire document it signs. The signature types may direct digital signature which involves only the communicating parties and arbitrated digital signature which involves a trusted third party or arbiter. The usage of digital signature is for three reasons authentication, Integrity and Non-repudiation. In a Public-key technique, the user applies the Secure Hash Algorithm (SHA) to the message to produce message digest [6]. Then User's private key is applied to message digest using Digital Signa-ture Algorithm (DSA) to generate signature [11-19]; it has the following parameters:

- M = message to be signed
- H(M) = hash of M using SHA
- M', S' = received versions of M, S
- X = User private key
- p, q, g, y = User public key
- K =n User per message secret key

Signing a message is done by the following steps:

$$r = (g^k \bmod p) \bmod q, \tag{1}$$

$$S = (H(M) + (X \times r))^{K-1} \bmod q \tag{2}$$

Verifying a sent message (S, r) is done by the following steps:

$$M' = ((g^{e1} \times y^{e2}) \bmod p) \bmod q. \tag{3}$$

Where:

$$e1 = (H (M') \times S') \bmod q \qquad (4)$$

$$e2 = r \times S' \bmod q \qquad (5)$$

If the value of Eq.3 is equal to the value of Eq.1, then the signature is valid.

4 Security Analysis

WRDN is resilient against attacks facing data itself to prove integrity and copyright. To compare WDRN with other schemas, the algorithms in [21] and [22] are chosen since both are distortion free algorithms and considered to be the basic structure for WRDN where it adds a new row / column as the database watermark. In [21] it is assumed that only one row will be added as a watermark. In the experiments, it is assumed that only one user is using the database. In the following subsections, one focuses on attacks facing data itself. Subsection 4.1 discusses results over insertion attacks. The Results after deletion attacks are presented in Subsection 4.2, and Subsection 4.3 introduces results after alternation attacks.

4.1 Insertion Attacks

Assume that an attacker adds new records over the existing dataset, as shown in Table III. Where (*) at watermark column represents new tuples added by the attackers. In The detection process, when watermark value is equal to zero then WRDN founds new unauthorized columns and drops them.

Figure 2 shows that both WRDN and Pourn algorithm [21] survive by 100% even if the number of new tuples is equal to the number of already available tuples over the dataset. Meanwhile, Prasann algorithm [22] starts decreasing when the number of inserted tuples increases over 75% of the number of available tuples.

Table 2. Values After Insertion Attacks

t_numb	R_indx	L_d	L_min	Lon_d	Lon_min	A
70	60	64	0	22	33	7.26913
75	60	64	3	22	3	7.21177
80	60	64	4	21	57	1.89074
90	60	64	9	22	1	7.85921
100	60	64	9	21	56	1.04897
1	89	87	55	89	54	0*
7	88	90	6	9	5	0*

4.2 Deletion Attacks

Assume that an attacker deletes some tuples. One will notice that in WRDN watermark value will be deleted at the same time with its tuples. Likewise, in the detection process, one will be able to detect all the available watermarks.

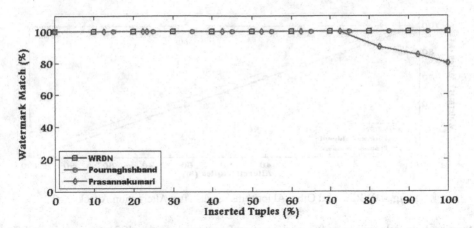

Fig. 2. WRDN and Other Algorithms results after Insertion Attacks

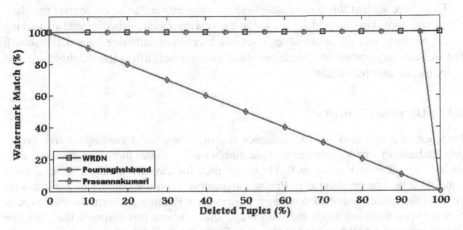

Fig. 3. WRDN and Other Algorithms results after Deletion Attacks

Figure 3 shows that WRDN survives by 100%, even if the attacker tries to delete 99% of available tuples. In the meantime, Pourn algorithm [21] starts to decrease if 99% of available tuples are deleted. Meanwhile, Prasann algorithm [22] decreases by 10% each time the number of deleted tuples increases.

4.3   Alteration Attacks

Assume that some attributes will be updated. The available watermark value will not match the calculated value, where the data will be rejected due to tampering. Therefore, it is noticed that WRDN can know which tuples have changed, where one could apply a backup mechanism to restore original data.

Figure 4 shows that WRDN decreases by 10% when the number of alternation increases. While Pourn algorithm [21] decreases by 5%, if 100% of tuples are changed,

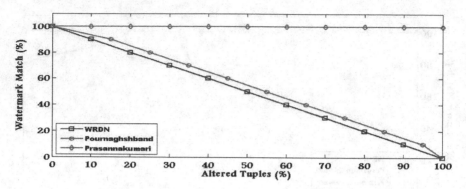

Fig. 4. WRDN and Other Algorithms results after Alternation Attacks

then both models will have 0% of detection. Prasann algorithm [22] survives by 100% against this type of attack, even if all tuples are altered.

To survive against this type of attack, some changes need to be made over the algorithm structure. One change is to use the encryption mechanisms instead of locking and applying it over the entire table. Thus, if a user is not authorized, the database will fail to make any update over data; but these changes will affect the database accessibility mechanism performance.

4.4   Overhead Matrices

Presence of a new attribute (A) occupies and increases the storage space required of the database. Figure 5 illustrates that the number of attributes increases the space consumed for watermarking as well. However, they increase by nearly a fixed amount equal to 0, 8. The opposite is in Prasann algorithm when the number of attributes increases, the space consumed decreases. However, in Pourn algorithm, there is no relation between these attributes and the storage space, where it is assumed that only one watermarked row will be added as shown in figure 5.

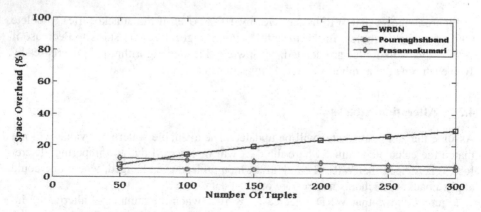

Fig. 5. Comparison between proposed model and other models

5   Conclusions

In this paper, the Watermarking Relational Database with Non-Repudiation (WRDN) approach is introduced. The embedded watermarks can detect and localize any modifications made to the database with the ability to know which user made that update. WRDN does not depend on any particular type of attributes (categorical, numerical). It only adds a hidden watermark record where its values are known only by the data owner. It focuses on attacks (by authorized and unauthorized users) that affect the constancy, integrity, and the content quality of rational databases. Moreover, WRDN is a Non- Repudiation approach, where it has the ability to know the latest updates made by authorized users. Nevertheless, it does not have sophisticated requirements or infrastructure on either database design or administration. Because it does not modify any database items, it is distortion free, which it survives by 100% against insertion and deletion attacks. However, in alteration attacks, it starts to fail by 10% when the number of changing tuples increases; so it needs changes in the framework which has been made.

References

1. Agrawal, R., Kiernan, J.: Watermarking relational databases. Very Large Database (2002)
2. Albluwi, Q., Kamel, I.: Watermarking Essential Data Structures for Copyright Protection. In: Pointcheval, D., Mu, Y., Chen, K. (eds.) CANS 2006. LNCS, vol. 4301, pp. 241–258. Springer, Heidelberg (2006)
3. Bhattacharya, S., Cortesi, A.: A distortion free watermark framework for relational databases. In: International Conference on Software and Data Technologies, ICSOFT (2009)
4. Bhattacharya, S., Cortesi, A.: A Generic Distortion Free Watermarking Technique for Relational Databases. In: Prakash, A., Sen Gupta, I. (eds.) ICISS 2009. LNCS, vol. 5905, pp. 252–264. Springer, Heidelberg (2009)
5. Bhattacharya, S., Cortesi, A.: Database authentication by distortion free watermarking. In: International Conference on Software and Data Technologies. ICSOFT, vol. 5 (2010)
6. Daemen, J., Rijmen, V.: The first 10 years of advanced encryption. IEEE Security and Privacy 8, 6 (2010)
7. El-Bakry, H., Hamada, M.: A Novel Watermark Technique for Relational Databases. In: Wang, F.L., Deng, H., Gao, Y., Lei, J. (eds.) AICI 2010, Part II. LNCS, vol. 6320, pp. 226–232. Springer, Heidelberg (2010)
8. Gamal, G., Rashad, M., Mohamed, M.: A simple watermark technique for relational database. In: Mansoura Journal for Computer Science and Information System (2008)
9. Halder, R., Pal, S., Cortesi, A.: Watermarking techniques for relational databases: Survey, classification and comparison. Journal of Universal Computer Science 16(22) (2010)
10. Kamel, I.: A schema for protecting the integrity of databases. Computers& Security 28 (2009)
11. Katz, J., Lindell, Y.: Introduction to Modern Cryptography, ch. 12. Chapman & Hall/CRC Press (2007)
12. Khataeimaragheh, H., Rashidi, H.: A novel watermarking scheme for detecting and recovering distortions in database tables. International Journal of Database Management Systems 2 (2010)

13. Li, Y., Deng, R.H.: Publicly verifiable ownership protection for relational databases. In: ACM Symposium on Information, Computer and Communications Security, ASIACCS (2006)
14. Li, Y., Guo, H., Jajodia, S.: Tamper detection and localization for categorical data using fragile watermarks. ACM (2004)
15. Li, Y., Swarup, V., Jajodia, S.: Constructing a virtual primary key for fingerprinting relational data. In: Digital Rights Management Workshop 2003 (2003)
16. Liu, S., Wang, S., Deng, R.H., Shao, W.: A Block Oriented Fingerprinting Scheme in Relational Database. In: Park, C.-s., Chee, S. (eds.) ICISC 2004. LNCS, vol. 3506, pp. 455–466. Springer, Heidelberg (2005)
17. Menezes, A., Smart, N.: Security of signature schemes in a multi-user setting. Des. Codes Cryptography 33, 3 (2004)
18. Narasimha, M., Tsudik, G.: Authentication of Outsourced Databases Using Signature Aggregation and Chaining. In: Li Lee, M., Tan, K.-L., Wuwongse, V. (eds.) DASFAA 2006. LNCS, vol. 3882, pp. 420–436. Springer, Heidelberg (2006)
19. Nikodem, M.: DSA Signature Scheme Immune to the Fault Cryptanalysis. In: Grimaud, G., Standaert, F.-X. (eds.) CARDIS 2008. LNCS, vol. 5189, pp. 61–73. Springer, Heidelberg (2008)
20. Olivier Blazy, D.P., Fuchsbauer, G., Vergnaud, D.: Signatures on randomizable ciphertexts. In: International Conference on Theory and Practice in Public Key Cryptography, PKC (2011)
21. Pournaghshband, V.: A new watermarking approach for relational data. In: ACM Southeast Regional Conference, pp. 127–131 (2008)
22. Prasannakumari, V.: A roubust tamperproof watermarking for data integrity in relational database. Research Journal of Information Technology 1, 115–121 (2009)
23. Sion, R., Atallah, M., Prabhakar, S.: Rights protection for relational data. IEEE Transactions on Knowledge and Data Engineering (2004)
24. Sion, R., Atallah, M., Prabhakar, S.: Rights protection for categorical data. IEEE Transactions on Knowledge and Data Engineering (2005)
25. Zhang, Y., Niu, X., Zhao, D.: A method of protecting relational databases copyright with cloud watermark. International Journal of Information Technology 1(3) (2004)

Fuzzy Semantic Plagiarism Detection

Ahmed Hamza Osman[1,2,*], Naomie Salim[1], Yogan Jaya Kumar [1],
and Albaraa Abuobieda[1,2]

[1] UniversitiTeknologi Malaysia, Faculty of Computer Science and Information Systems,
Skudai, Johor, Malaysia
[2] International University of Africa, Faculty of Computer Studies, Khartoum, Sudan
{ahmedagraa,albarraa}@hotmail.com, naomie@utm.my,
yogan@utem.edu.my

Abstract. This paper introduces a plagiarism detection scheme based on a Fuzzy Inference System and Semantic Role Labeling (FIS-SRL). The proposed technique analyses and compares text based on a semantic allocation for each term inside the sentence. SRL offers significant advantages when generating arguments for each sentence semantically. Voting for each argument generated by the FIS in order to select important arguments is also another feature of the proposed method. It has been concluded that not all arguments in the text affect the plagiarism detection process. Therefore, only the most important arguments were selected by the FIS, and the results have been used in the similarity calculation process. Experimental tests have been applied on the PAN-PC-09 data set and the results shows that the proposed method exhibits a better performance than the available recent methods of plagiarism detection, in terms of Recall, Precision and F-measure.

Keywords: Plagiarism Detection, Semantic Similarity, Semantic Role, Fuzzy Inference System, Rule Reduction.

1   Introduction

Paraphrasing is a technique to modify the structure of an original sentence by changing the sentence structure or replace some of the original words with its synonym. Without any proper citation or quotation marks, it can also be considered as plagiarism. The techniques used in current detection tools are not capable to detect the plagiarism mention above due to the differences of the fingerprint between original and plagiarize document. These incidents are much harder to detect, as semantic plagiarism is often a fuzzy process that is hard to search for, and even harder to stop as they usually cross international borders. This study proposes new method for plagiarism detection. These methods will be based on Semantic Role Labeling and Fuzzy Logic technique.

Semantic Role Labeling (SRL) is one of the Natural Language Processing techniques that were used in many fields such as text summarization [1]. An improved

* Corresponding author.

A. Ell Hassanien et al. (Eds.): AMLTA 2012, CCIS 322, pp. 543–553, 2012.

plagiarism detection scheme based on SRL was introduced recently by Ahmed et.al, [2]. The proposed method was trained to use an argument weighting scheme to study the behavior of the plagiarized user. In this paper, we are focusing on selecting the important arguments of plagiarized text using fuzzy rules and fuzzy inference system. Fuzzy logic techniques as a form of approximate reasoning provide decision-support and expert systems with powerful reasoning capabilities.

The rest of the paper is organized as follows: Section 2 provides a description of the related work in plagiarism detection. Section 3 discusses fuzzy logic technique. In Section 4, a full description of the underlying idea involved in our method is covered. Section 5 discusses the experimental design used in our proposed method. Corpus and dataset, including similarity detection and results discussion of the proposed approach, are presented in Section 6, whereas Section 7 concludes the paper.

2   Related Work

This section discusses several recently proposed plagiarism detection techniques. In ours Knowledge [2], a plagiarism detection based on SRL was proposed as a new semantic detection technique. The introduced method used a weight arguments scheme to improve a results that were obtained by SRL. Where the authors were studied the behaviours of the plagiarized user and selected just the arguments that can affect on plagiarism process.

The CHECK technique proposed by Si et al. [3] as a new mechanism for plagiarism detection is similar to SCAM. Both methods adopted information retrieval techniques and work on overlapping detection based on the frequency of words. The CHECK technique, which is built on an indexed structure known as structural characteristic (SC), is used to parse documents for building the SC. It captures plagiarism depending on the key words proportion of structural characteristic for the nodes. The CHECK covered the structured documents only while ignoring the unstructured documents. Another technique, Match Detect Retrieval (MDR), was proposed by Monostori[4]. With this technique, plagiarism can be detected using string matching similarity algorithms based on suffix trees. MDR concentrates on the copy-paste plagiarism, but its limitation appears when the plagiarized parts are modified by rewording or synonyms replacement. Another limitation appears when there is a need to build the suffix tree for the suspected documents.

A semantic plagiarism detection technique introduced by Alzahrani and Salim [5] uses fuzzy semantic-based string similarity. The method was developed in four main steps. The first step is pre-processing, which comprises tokenization, stop words removal and stemming. The second step is the retrieval of a list of candidate documents for each suspicious document using Jaccard coefficient and shingling algorithm. Suspicious documents are then compared sentence-wise with the associated candidate documents. This step entails the computation of the fuzzy degree of similarity that ranges between two edges: 0 for completely different sentences and 1 for identical sentences. Two sentences are marked as similar if they gain a fuzzy similarity score above a certain threshold. The last stage is post-processing in which consecutive sentences are joined to form single paragraphs or sections.

A different method of semantic-based plagiarism detection was proposed by Chow and Salim [6]. The proposed method calculates the similarity between the suspected and original documents according to the predicates of the sentences. Each sentence predicate is extracted using the Stanford Parser Tree (SPT). The degree of similarity between the extracted predicates was calculated using the WordNet thesaurus. The drawback of this method is that it does not cover all parts of the sentence, only subject, verb and object.

The literature review in this section has indicated many efforts that have been made in the past to detect the similarity between text documents. But, these methods still need to improve the detection capability in order to capture more plagiarized parts especially in semantically plagiarized parts.

The main difference between the proposed method in this paper and other techniques is that, the proposed method is a comprehensive plagiarism detection technique which focused on many types of plagiarisms, such as copy paste plagiarism, rewording or synonym replacement, changing of word structure in the sentences, modifying the sentence from passive voice to active voice and vice-versa.

3   Fuzzy Logic System

Fuzzy logic, initially introduced by Zadeh[7], was later on used for control of a simple laboratory steam engine by Mamdani[8]. It is a mathematical assumption of ambiguous reasoning that allows it to obtain decision-making models in linguistic terms. Recently, fuzzy logic has become one of the main successful technologies in many applications and sophisticated control systems.

Fuzzification is a fuzzy operation, in which the input values are translated into degrees of membership (in the [0;1] range) to the fuzzy sets of the linguistic terms by using a membership function. Equation (1) is a common fuzzification method of a set A, which is solved by keeping μ_i constant and converting x_i to a fuzzy set that depicts the expression about $x_i\,k(x_i)$ [9].

$$A = \frac{\mu_i}{x_i} x_i \in x \tag{1}$$

Where A is a Fuzzified set, X represents the universe of discourse and μ assumes values in the range from 1 to 0.

The fuzzy set K(x_i) is referred to as the kernel of fuzzification. The fuzzified set A is expressed as:

$$A = \mu_1 k(x_1) + \mu_2 k(x_2) + \cdots + \mu_n k(x_n) \tag{2}$$

The inference is the core part of a fuzzy system, which merges the facts obtained from the fuzzification part with a series of production rules to perform the fuzzy reasoning process.

4   Fuzzy Plagiarism Detection Based on SRL

Plagiarism detection using semantic roles labeling aims to detect the possible semantic similarity between two sentences. In this section, the idea of the proposed method is discussed.

Our proposed method is trained to solve text plagiarism detection based on several steps. First, a Semantic Role Labeling technique applies to text documents. There are three main activities performed in the preprocessing stage: Sentence Segmentation, Removing Stop Word and Word stemming. The process of dividing the text into meaningful units is called text segmentation. Text can be divided by sentences, words or topics. The technology of stop words removal for deleting meaningless words was used. The stemming algorithm was also applied to remove the affixes (prefixes and suffixes) in a word in order to generate its root word. The arguments similarity score is calculated based on SRL similarity measure that was proposed and described in [2]. Fuzzy used as arguments selector method to select all the important arguments that can affect the plagiarism detection process.

In our proposed method, we used the similarity scores between the suspected and original documents using features input of the Fuzzy Logic method. Each sentence (S) will be associated with a vector of the input arguments features, $S = \{A\_F1, A\_F2, A\_F1, A\_F3, ...\}$ where A_F1 represents argument feature 1 and so on. Values will be derived from the similarity between the documents. Next, the arguments score will be generated by the Fuzzy Logic method and then, a set of the highest argument score will be extracted as a final important arguments to enter with similarity detection based on the comparison.

4.1   Inference System and Membership Functions

In the proposed method, the input membership function was divided into two linguistic values, each input denoted as important and unimportant respectively. The important and unimportant similarity scores under fuzzy membership function for input and output were created by determining the similarity score values whereby, if the similarity score is greater or equal to 0.5 then the similarity score is important, otherwise the similarity score is unimportant. The membership function was determined by using the FIS Toolbox in MATLAB. This toolbox enables excellent model development for non-linear process in which fuzzy rules are automatically generated in the FIS environment.

4.2   Construct the Fuzzy IF-THEN Rules

Understanding the definition of fuzzy rules is an important task in working with an Inference Engine. The linguistic values of the intermediate and output variable discussed above are the result of the fuzzy rule base containing the IF-THEN rules. These IF-THEN rules extract the important arguments in accordance with our argument criteria.

A common technique for rule construction was applied to extract and build all the possible rules that could be generated according to input features. Suppose we has a a f input features, the number of possible rules will be generated according to the following equation:

$$R = f^n \qquad (3)$$

Where R is a number of rules; f is a number of input features; n is a possibility logic of the rule.

For instance, suppose we had a 5 inputs and each input had two logic outputs true and false. The number of the generated rules is equal to 32. Our proposed method used Equation 3 to generate all the possible rules that could support the inference system to differentiate between important and unimportant arguments.

A huge amount of rules was generated as a thousand documents were used to test our proposed method. Although representing all the generated rules in the fuzzy system was difficult, it was a very important issue. A way was needed to reduce a number of rules generated. Our proposed method solved this problem by using a combination method for rule reduction [10].

An objective of the proposed technique is to select the best and most important arguments that can exactly affect the plagiarism process and thus improving the detecting similarity score. One of the important parts in FIS is the fuzzy IF_THEN rule base. All possible rules were extracted before performing rule reduction. A Sample of IF_THEN rules with "AND" operator as shown in Figure 1.

IF (Similarity score of argument x in Sentence1 is Important) and (Similarity score of argument x in Sentence 2 is Important) and (Similarity score of argument x in Sentence 3 is Important) and (Similarity score of argument x in Sentence 4 is Important) and (Similarity score of argument x in Sentence 5 is Important) THEN (argument x is Important)

Fig. 1. Sample of IF_THEN Rules with "AND" Operator

The important arguments were selected for the second testing comparison process. Arguments that were selected as unimportant using FIS were ignored. Testing was done after the selection of the arguments. It was found that the score of similarity declined when compared to the results from the first test because the degree of similarity depends on the number of arguments extracted from the sentences, and, therefore, reducing the unimportant arguments consequently leads to increase of the similarity score. The similarity score was calculated by using the PAN-PC-09 plagiarism dataset for cross-checking. The details of similarity calculation are explained in the next sections.

4.3   Defuzzification

The last step in the Fuzzy Logic process is Defuzzification. During defuzzification, the inference system results are translated into a final score for each argument. The aggregate output of a fuzzy set is used as the input and results in an output represented as a single value. In order to create a single value output, the defuzzification process must be completed. There are many common techniques for defuzzification described by Mogharreban[11]. In this work we employed the Centroid method for defuzzification stage. The centroid defuzzification method was widely used in Natural Language Processing and Text Summarization fields [12-14]. The advantage of the centroid method is that used as good candidates for fuzzy reasoning systems [15].

5   Experimental Design and Dataset

The experiments were performed on 1000 suspected documents. Each one of these documents was plagiarized from one or more original documents according to the PAN-PC-09 dataset. The documents were divided into some groups with each group having a certain number of documents. The documents increased for each group with each testing of comparison. The process started with 5 documents in the first group. Then, 5 more were added to the first group and then 10, 20, 40 and 100 respectively. The aim of this grouping process is to study the behaviours of the plagiarized user for each argument so it can be trained. After studying the behaviours of the arguments, the experiments were applied cross 1000 documents. Each group was chosen as an input variable in FIS and all arguments as instances or record. Then the output is a total similarity score across these groups. The values of the input variable are a similarity score between any similar pair of arguments. The experiments were applied across these groups up to 100 documents as training of the data. Then the proposed method was tested across 1000 documents. It was observed that by using FIS, important arguments can be selected.

The similarity between the arguments of the suspected document and original document was calculated according to Jaccard coefficient that can be defined in the following equation:

$$Simialrity\left(c_i(argS_i, argS_j)\right) = \frac{C(argS_j) \cap C(argS_k)}{C(argS_j) \cup C(argS_k)} \qquad (4)$$

Where, C(ArgSj) = concepts of the argument sentence in the suspected document; Ci (ArgSk) = concepts of the argument sentence in the original document;.

We then calculated the similarity between the suspected document and original document based on the following equation:

$$Total\ simialrity\ (Doc1, Doc2) = \sum_{i=1,l} \sum_{\substack{j=1,m \\ k=1,n}} SimC_i(argS_j) \cap C(argS_k) \qquad (5)$$

Where, SimCi(ArgSj, ArgSk) is similarity between arguments sentence j in suspected document containing concept i and arguments sentence k in original document containing concept i, l = no. of concepts, m = no. of Arguments sentence in suspected document, n = no. of Arguments sentence in the original document.

6   Results and Discussion

The suspected documents were plagiarized in different ways of plagiarism such as a simple copy and paste, changing some terms with their corresponding synonyms, and modifying the structure of the sentences (paraphrasing). Three general testing metrics that are commonly used in plagiarism detection were applied as expressed in equations (6) to (8).

$$Recall = \frac{number\ of\ detected\ arguments}{total\ number\ of\ arguments} \tag{6}$$

$$Precision = \frac{number\ of\ plagirized\ arguments}{number\ of\ detected\ arguments} \tag{7}$$

$$F - measure = \frac{2 * Recall * Precision}{Recall + Precision} \tag{8}$$

Table 1. Results across the set of documents

Number of Documents in Set	A0	A0A1	A1	A1A0	A2	Verb	MNR	TMP	DIS	ADV	NEG	LOC	PNC	MOD	O	A3	A4	DIR	EXT
5	0.93	0.74	0.8	0.51	0.82	0.8	0.52	0.75	0	0	0	0.83	0	0	0	0	0	0	0
10	0.82	0.65	0.92	0.52	0.94	0.86	0	0.79	0	0.85	0	0.88	0	0	0.91	0.8	0	0	0
20	0.89	0.67	0.67	0.84	0.77	0.74	0.66	0.85	0.7	0	0	0.66	0.9	0	0.87	0.8	0	0	0
40	0.97	0.78	1	0.85	0.82	0.79	0.75	0.81	0	0.77	0	0	0	0	0.88	0	0	0	0
100	0.94	0.84	0.85	0.87	0.76	0.9	0	0.81	0	0.66	0	0.61	0	0	0.77	0	0	0	0

Table 1 illustrates the results obtained from the trains performed on the selected set of documents. Each row represents a group of documents that are used to explain the arguments during the similarity calculation.

As indicated in the columns in Table 1, there are 19 arguments that have been extracted using the SRL. Table 2 illustrates these types that appeared in Table 1.

Table 2. Argument types and their descriptions

Type	Description	Type	Description
Arg0	Agent	**NEG**	Negation marker
Arg1	Direct object/theme/patient	**LOC**	Location
Arg2–5	Not fixed	**PNC**	Purpose
V	Verb	**MOD**	Modal verb
MNR	Manner	**O**	Adjective
TMP	Time	**DIR**	Direction
DIS	Discourse connectives	**EXT**	Extent
ADV	General-purpose		

Table 3. Results after similarity calculation

Number of Documents in set	Recall	Precision	F-Measure
5	0.863158	0.586471	0.698409
10	0.826316	0.734412	0.777658
20	0.802632	0.61239	0.694722
40	0.807895	0.678677	0.73767
100	0.818421	0.642406	0.719809
1000	0.803415	0.652483	0.729875

Table 2 shows the types of arguments that were used in the experiments and their description or meaning. The results of the similarity calculation in term of recall, precision and f-measure are given in Table 3.

Table 3 shows the similarity between the suspected and original documents for each set of documents. It can be observed that all the score values in recall measure are above 0.80 while all the score value in precision and f-measure are more than 0.58. All the scores in Table 3 seem to give good results because they are greater than 0.5 but still attempts were made to improve these scores to obtain higher similarity values.

After the optimization process using FIS, it was noted that the plagiarizing user does not focus on all arguments of the sentences, hence some arguments are ignored. These arguments are called unimportant arguments. The results of FIS cross SRL sentences are given in Table 4.

Table 4 demonstrates the behaviours of the arguments after the optimization process; two types of arguments are depicted. The first type of arguments has a similarity score greater or equal than 0.5 and is selected as important arguments, while the second type has a similarity score less than 0.5 and is called unimportant arguments. The important arguments are selected to improve the similarity score by FIS process. On the other hand, unimportant arguments reduce the similarity score in order to reduce the overall similarity ratio between the suspected and original documents and therefore are ignored.

The arguments similarity score is calculated based on SRL similarity measure that was proposed and described by Osman et.al [2]. All the similarity scores between the arguments organized in one table called similarity scores table. The similarity scores table then used as a features input of the FIS. The features are represented by the arguments and total similarity between these arguments, where the instants of the dataset represented by the number of suspected and original documents that were used in the dataset. The target of the FIS is to generate a number of important arguments were used to improve the similarity scores in plagiarism detection.

For a plagiarized behaviour, users tried to focus on the important terms to modify them into their work. Only important arguments with a high affect of sentences should be targeted to change. Several target selection methods are available, all of them intending to predict the important targets of the data as possible. One of these methods is FIS.

Table 4. Behaviours of the arguments after optimization using FIS

5 inputs	Fuzzy Result	10 inputs	Fuzzy Result	20 inputs	Fuzzy Result	40 inputs	Fuzzy Result	100 inputs	Fuzzy Result	1000 inputs	Fuzzy Result	Rank
O	0.6403	O	0.6403	O	0.5287	O	0.5409	Verb	0.5068	Verb	0.5017	Important
LOC	0.6332	LOC	0.6332	A01	0.5251	A1	0.5361	TMP	0.5057	A2	0.5012	Important
Verb	0.6278	A0	0.6277	A0A1	0.5233	LOC	0.5359	ADV	0.5055	A0	0.5012	Important
A0	0.6277	A2	0.6254	Verb	0.5186	A0	0.5353	A2	0.5046	O	0.5011	Important
A2	0.6254	A1	0.6065	A1A0	0.5143	A2	0.5347	A0	0.5045	A0A1	0.5011	Important
A1	0.6065	TMP	0.6009	A0	0.5082	Verb	0.5309	O	0.5044	A1A0	0.501	Important
TMP	0.6009	MNR	0.597	TMP	0.5	ADV	0.526	A0A1	0.5041	A1	0.501	Important
MNR	0.597	A0A1	0.5936	ADV	0.5	TMP	0.5252	A1A0	0.5039	LOC	0.5	Important
A0A1	0.5936	PNC	0.5	LOC	0.5	A0A1	0.5194	A1	0.5038	TMP	0.4998	Unimportant
PNC	0.5	Verb	0.5	A2	0.5	A1A0	0.5078	MNR	0.5	MNR	0.4996	Unimportant
A1A0	0.4866	A1A0	0.4866	MNR	0.5	MNR	0.4948	LOC	0.5	DIR	0.4985	Unimportant
DIR	0.3935	DIR	0.3935	MOD	0.4541	PNC	0.4749	DIR	0.4941	PNC	0.4985	Unimportant
ADV	0.3614	ADV	0.3614	DIS	0.4411	DIS	0.4675	PNC	0.494	A4	0.498	Unimportant
DIS	0.3591	DIS	0.3591	NEG	0.4411	A3	0.4671	A4	0.4922	DIS	0.4979	Unimportant
NEG	0.3591	NEG	0.3591	DIR	0.4411	A4	0.4671	DIS	0.4919	NEG	0.4979	Unimportant
MOD	0.3591	MOD	0.3591	PNC	0.4364	MOD	0.466	NEG	0.4919	MOD	0.4979	Unimportant
A3	0.3591	A3	0.3591	A3	0.4357	NEG	0.4632	MOD	0.4919	A3	0.4979	Unimportant
A4	0.3591	A4	0.3591	A4	0.4324	DIR	0.4616	A3	0.4918	EXT	0.4978	Unimportant

The proposed method is evaluated and compared with some plagiarism detection algorithms in the PAN competition. The results from comparison are illustrated in Figure. 2.

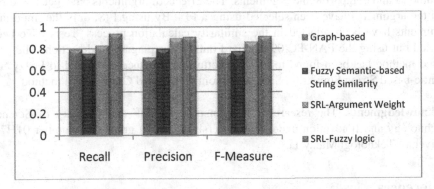

Fig. 2. Compare results with other plagiarism detection techniques

Figure. 2 shows the comparison between SRL-fuzzy logic method with fuzzy semantic-based string similarity [5], graph-based method [16] and SRL-Argument weight [2]. The Y-Axis denote to the evaluation score for the method and the X-Axis denote to the the evaluation measures that were used in the comparison.

We found that our proposed method achieved better results in terms of Recall, Precision and F-measure.

Table 4. Comparison between the proposed method and other techniques by time complexity

Algorithm	Time Complexity
Fuzzy Semantic-based String Similarity	$O(n^2)$
SRL-Argument Weight	$O(n^2)$
Graph-based Method	$O(V + E)$
SRL- Fuzzy logic	$O(n^2)$

Another evaluation criterion is time efficiency or time complexity. This measure is commonly used to evaluate the algorithms. The proposed method was evaluated based on time complexity. It was discovered that the proposed method belongs to the $O(n^2)$ Class. Table 4 demonstrates the results in terms of time complexity.

Table 4 demonstrates the time complexity comparison between the our proposed method with Fuzzy Semantic-based String Similarity, SRL-Argument weight and Graph-based method. The results show that the proposed method belongs to the $O(n^2)$ Class which is a famous widely accepted class for detection algorithms.

7   Conclusions

Semantic role labeling can be used for plagiarism detection by extracting sentence arguments and comparing the arguments. The effects of arguments have been studied, and the arguments have been selected using a FIS. By using FIS, only the important arguments have been selected in the similarity calculation process. Tests have been carried out using the PAN-PC-09 standard dataset for plagiarism detection. The proposed method has been found to achieve better performance compared to Fuzzy Semantic-based String Similarity, SRL-Argument weight and Graph-based method.

Acknowledgments. The researcher is sponsored by IDF and Ministry of Science Technology and Innovation under the university research grant vote number 01H74, Universiti Teknologi Malaysia.

References

1. Suanmali, L., Salim, N., Binwahlan, M.S.: Automatic Text Summarization Using Feature-Based Fuzzy Extraction. Jurnal Teknologi Maklumat 2(1), 105–155 (2009)
2. Osman, A.H., et al.: An Improved Plagiarism Detection Scheme Based on Semantic Role Labeling. Applied Soft Computing 12(5), 1493–1502 (2011)
3. Antonio, S., Leong, H.V., Rynson, W.H.L.: CHECK: a document plagiarism detection system. In: Proceedings of the 1997 ACM Symposium on Applied Computing, pp. 70–77. ACM, San Jose (1997)

4. Kriszti, et al.: Document overlap detection system for distributed digital libraries. In: Proceedings of the Fifth ACM Conference on Digital Libraries, pp. 226–227. ACM, San Antonio (2000)
5. Alzahrani, S., Salim, N.: Fuzzy Semantic-Based String Similarity for Extrinsic Plagiarism Detection. In: CLEF (Notebook Papers/LABs/Workshops) (2010)
6. Kent, C., Salim, N.: Web Based Cross Language Plagiarism Detection. In: Second International Conference on Computational Intelligence, Modelling and Simulation, pp. 199–204 (2010)
7. Zadeh, L.A.: Fuzzy sets. Information and Control 8(3), 338–353 (1965)
8. Mamdani, E.H.: Application of fuzzy algorithms for control of simple dynamic plant. Proceedings of the Institution of Electrical Engineers 121(12), 1585–1588 (1974)
9. Ibrahim, A.M.: Fuzzy logic for embedded systems applications. Newnes (2004)
10. Setnes, M., et al.: Similarity measures in fuzzy rule base simplification. IEEE Transactions on Systems, Man, and Cybernetics, Part B: Cybernetics 28(3), 376–386 (1998)
11. Mogharreban, N., Dilalla, L.F.: Comparison of Defuzzification Techniques for Analysis of Non-interval Data. In: Annual Meeting of the North American Fuzzy Information Processing Society, NAFIPS 2006 (2006)
12. Binwahlan, M.S., Salim, N., Suanmali, L.: Fuzzy swarm diversity hybrid model for text summarization. Inf. Process. Manage. 46(5), 571–588 (2010)
13. Suanmali, L., Binwahlan, M.S., Salim, N.: Sentence features fusion for text summarization using fuzzy logic. IEEE (2009)
14. Khoury, R., et al.: Semantic understanding of general linguistic items by means of fuzzy set theory. IEEE Transactions on Fuzzy Systems 15(5), 757–771 (2007)
15. Ting, Y., et al.: A fuzzy reasoning design for fault detection and diagnosis of a computer-controlled system. Engineering Applications of Artificial Intelligence 21(2), 157–170 (2008)
16. Osman, A.H., et al.: Conceptual Similarity and Graph-Based Method for Plagiarism Detection. Journal of Theoretical and Applied Information Technology 32(2), 135–145 (2011)

Development of Malaysian Digital Forensics Investigator Competency Identification Methods

Elfadil Sabeil[1,2], Azizah Abdul Manaf[1,3], and Zuraini Ismail[1,3]

[1] University Technology of Malaysia (UTM)
[2] Faculty of Computer Science & Information Systems
[3] Advance Informatics School (AIS), UTM International Campus,
AIS, 54100, Kuala Lumpur, Malaysia
azizah07@ic.utm.my

Abstract. Cyber Forensics Investigations and its training/education are relatively new. The nature of Cyber Forensics is complex that requires multidisciplinary skills, knowledge and abilities. Although there are proliferations training/ education programs, from a handful of day's workshop to Masters Degree in Cyber Forensics, the world lacks of Cyber Forensics Investigators due to some factors. Consequently, this paper focuses on Competency Identification Requirements. The majority of the respondents (average of 95.66%) agreed that various stakeholders should carry out the Competency Identification stage, while, 86.7% of the respondents supported the characteristics of Competency Identification. Moreover, there is a significant relationship between Competency Identification and Cyber Forensics Investigator Proficiency.

Keywords: Cyber Forensics Investigations (CFIs), Cyber Forensics Investigations Investigator, Information and Communications Technologies (ICTs), Cyber crimes, Skills, Knowledge an Ability (SKA), Competency Identification Participant and Competency Identification Characteristics.

1 Introduction

In the current era, the information and communication technologies (ICTs) dominate not only our life [1], but also our lifestyle, mostly in a series of beneficial contributions. The ICTs are considered as the backbone of the modern day development and the veritable driving force for most of the business environments today, in both the public and the private sectors without any shadow of doubt whatsoever as the influences of the ICTs are clearly manifest in all human transactions. On the other hand, these technologies also have their undesirable side effects which are mostly incorporated in most criminal and illegal activities. Carol T. [2] estimated over 85% of the criminal and civil prosecution cases have involved digital evidences in their illegitimate activities. In other words, they greatly contribute to various present day digital-crimes [3]. A digital-crime is defined as any criminal activity which involves the use of computers and networks or any other digital devices.

Nowadays, the digital-crimes have become more sophisticated in their protocol and technique due to the results of the rapid development in the technological fields. As

A. Ell Hassanien et al. (Eds.): AMLTA 2012, CCIS 322, pp. 554–565, 2012.
© Springer-Verlag Berlin Heidelberg 2012

the computer/digital resource assets are more valuable and widely available, they are thus considered as the best tools in most of the modern digital criminals.

Consequently, the computer/digital crimes have a massive impact on the world economics at large. Financial losses were found in most of the companies that had been struck by the digital offenders [4]. Securing information assets of organizations becomes more complex and is highly recommended as the ICTs resources are used in multi-sharing modern operations in business, government, military and academics. Therefore, information security and criminal evidence maintenance become most significant challenges in the ICTs management. Moreover, both service restoration and crime evidence maintenance are essentially required to incriminate the offenders [5].

Digital forensics can play a significant role in a computer and network security, information assurance, law enforcement, national defence, etc [6]. According to Luther [7], the Computer Emergency and Response Teams (CERT) announced their inability to handle all cases involving the cybercrime attacks that have been increasing dramatically, thus, necessitating more relevant professionals, with the appropriate skills and knowledge, who are urgently and badly needed to fight against these dastardly crimes.

Cyber forensic is defined as "legal aspects of computer investigation and involves the analysis of digital evidence covering the identification, examination, preservation and presentment of potential electronic evidence in a manner that would allow such evidence to be admitted in a court of law" [8].

The mission of Cyber forensics exceeds crimes combat. For example, Cyber forensic investigation (CFI) is a main pole when building business continuity and contingency planning, particularly on National Critical Corporations (NCC); such as Electricity Corporation, Health Organization, Military, Transportation and etc. This comes due to the fact that both service return and preserving crime evidence are required when systems are compromised [5]. In addition to that, the task of the CFI is not only a process of to investigate crimes but it also to present technically in adequate manner that should teach the laymen in court. So, the Cyber forensic investigators must be educated/trained, and skilfully with adequate experience in the relevant field in order to meet the examination fulfilments [9].

Although of the fact that the Cyber forensic goes backs to 30 years ago, training and education still new or rarely in most of the world countries. Studies have proven that most of the world countries lack Cyber forensic professionals [10-11]. The origin of the lack of professionalism in Cyber forensic backs to some factors. For instance, not exclusively, all Cyber forensics investigation training /education programs are totally new and immature. Secondly, most of these training/education programs are totally provided by vendors or producer of investigation tools. Thirdly, in addition to most of the training/education institutions concentrate on the system weakness or training trainees on how the use of specific tools or techniques, rather than focusing on skills, knowledge, ability (SKA) and assessment needs [12]. According to Elfadil et. al [13], there is lack of adequate competencies identification practices in most of Cyber forensic training programs. Furthermore, most of them are not qualified and verified by independent external and accreditation bodies [14]. Recently, specifically on 23 Feb 2012, Barbara [15] raised many questions regarding the DFIP.

As a consequence, the ideas of nationalizing the digital forensics certificates had been raised on different occasions in some countries around the world. Matthew M. and Marc R. [16] highlighted the importance of a national system for certifying the digital crime professionals. Nigel Jones [17] stated "The idea of countries having properly trained and equipped staff to combat digital crime was first recognized officially in a communique´ of the Justice and Interior Ministers of the G8 countries in December 1997".

Therefore, the USA, the UK, China, Australia etc., have begun to develop their own digital forensics training/educational programs in order to meet the industrial and government demands [10-11]. In contrast, in Malaysia, the Cybersecurity provides workshops in digital forensics investigation. The workshops are classified into digital forensics fundamental (5 days) and digital forensics intermediate (3 days) [18]. Ec-council Malaysia and UTM-AIS also provide a 5-day CHFI certification workshop. The APIIT University also delivers some courses for undergraduate programs. Some universities like (UTM and UPM) also intend to involve digital forensics courses in their master programs.

This paper proposes DFI competency identification method, as well as to test its relationship to Digital Forensics Investigator Proficiency (DFIP). It is formed with five main sections. The first section conveys the problem behind this paper. Section two is literature review, while, section three is research method. In section four, the authors discuss the result of the analysis, and section five summarizes the findings.

2   Literature Review

The SKAs is defined in several diverse points of views. Competence is the ability to apply knowledge and/or skills, where it is relevant and defines the personal attributes [19]. In other words, competency is the ability to apply knowledge and skills to produce the required outcome [20]. The Australian National Training Authority defines competency as the capability to carry out tasks and duties according to the job's expected standards [21]. The Qualifications and Curriculum Authority (QCA) in England defines competency through the National Vocational Qualifications (NVQs) that is based on occupational standards to describe the competencies of workers [21]. In brief, it is the ability to efficiently perform a piece of allotted work in the workplace.

Azmi [22] found that most of the countries around the world (USA, UK, Netherland, Germany, France, Italy, Belgium, Sweden, France and Poland) have been in the competency-based training/educational programs since 1980s. He also found that the Malaysian public service has been practicing competency-based human resource since 2002, in order to develop and upgrade the service quality level. The programs have included training and development, recruitment and selection, performance management and reward, and career development.

Nowadays, most of the professionals and authorities around the world recommend targeting competency when defining the jobs' needs [20]. They believe that it plays a significant role to ensure the workforce proficiency. In fact, competency-based concepts have being used by varieties of stakeholders in various fields according to their agendas. It is used by the Psychologists, Management theorists, Human resource managers, Politicians and Educationists to perform various functional commitments [23].

Irons [24] said "Whilst trainers may place more emphasis on skills and educators more on knowledge, together they agree that both are important for a digital investigator to carry out his job". Thus, the digital forensics training/educational programs should be built by combining training and educational characteristics in order to meet the required SKAs level.

This study has created itself a challenge due to the rare studies of competency-based training/educational programs in the Digital Forensics fields. The researcher would therefore extend the review to other matured fields of associated entities. According to Jason [25], although the fields differ, there are similarities in the workforce missions on the Digital Forensics and Medication. For example, the Digital Initial Responder assignment is similar to the job of the First Aid Responder on medication. The Digital Forensics Technician works just like a Nurse in a hospital. The Digital Forensics Analyst diagnoses the crime case just like a Doctor who diagnoses the patient's case wherein the Specialist's jobs are also consistent in both areas.

Competencies are likely built up from three procedures, namely, education, training and experience, as well as being delivered from the real jobs [20]. According to [20-21, 23, 26], the labor competency has various characteristics. Firstly, it should be approved in a standards form that consists of units defining the elements of competency, the performance criteria, the field of application and the knowledge required. Secondly, it should be organized on the levels of competencies in order to distinguish the degree of independence, the responsibility for resources, the implementation of basic knowledge, the range and scope of skills and the ability to perform a task under a variety of conditions, with the ability to handle contingencies. Thirdly, different stakeholders and experts from quite different sectors (private and public) should participate in its design. For instance, groups of worker experts or scientific working group on digital evidence (SWGDE), state representative members of the executive and legislative power, digital forensics professionals, law and juridical representatives, scientific and intellectual professionals from training and educational institutions, would all jointly and categorically define the workplace needs [27-28]. Fourthly, various competency identification methodologies should be used, such as, occupational analysis, functional analysis, development of curriculum (DACUM), a model (AMOD) and systematic curriculum and instructional development (SCID) [21, 29-31].

Finally, there are rare studies about relationship between Competency Identification Requirements and the DFIP. However, the researcher depended on other disciplines to assess the relationship between competency identification procedures and DFIP. For example, llhaamie [32] constructed the conceptual framework of competency based on the career development and performance management practices and service quality.

There is a need to establish consensus on the Digital Forensics Investigator's basic competencies (skill, knowledge and abilities). Thus, this research investigates the relationship between the Competency Identification Requirements and the DFIP, so that the hypothesis is:-

H0.   Competency Identification Requirements are not positively related to the Digital Forensics investigators' proficiency.

H1.   Competency Identification Requirements are positively related to the Digital Forensics investigators' proficiency.

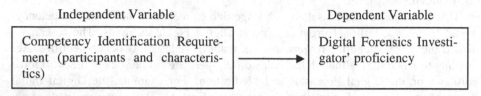

Independent Variable

Competency Identification Requirement (participants and characteristics)

Dependent Variable

Digital Forensics Investigator' proficiency

Fig. 1. The concept of the Relationship between the Digital Forensics Investigator Proficiency and Competency Identification procedures

3   Research Methodology

In this research, a census sampling was performed as the population was small and the variability within the population was very high [33]. The population consisted of around 33 respondents. They had different qualifications in both the academic and the digital forensics fields. They also worked in various Malaysian education/training providers, such as, the UTM, the UPM, the MMU, the Cybersecurity (Malaysia) and the Ec-council Malaysia. They also participated in delivering different types of digital forensics training/education programs, such as, a few days of workshop session for the undergraduate/master courses.

Essentially, self-completion questionnaires (online and paper) were used as primary data collection tools. Exploratory data analysis played essential roles in the data analysis and techniques in this research. In addition to Inferential statistical analysis is the analysis method used to test the relation between the research variable items.

4   Results and Discussions

Fig. 3 shows the descriptive analysis and presentation of the respondents' views regarding the Competency Identification participants' significances to identify the digital forensics workforce competencies. Based on the findings on Fig. 3, a majority of the respondents supported the participation of various stakeholders in the Competency Identification (CI) development as Development Expert Group (DEG).

All respondents (100%) agreed that the Digital Forensics Professionals are key members of the DEG committee. Most respondents also confirmed that the state representative members (96.9%), academic professionals (94%), workplace worker experts (93.6%) and Laws and Juridical representatives (87.8%) were the DEG key members.

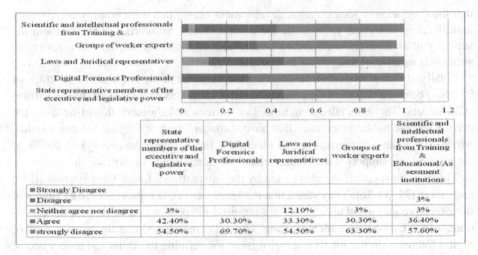

	State representative members of the executive and legislative power	Digital Forensics Professionals	Laws and Juridical representatives	Groups of worker experts	Scientific and intellectual professionals from Training & Educational/Assessment institutions
Strongly Disagree					
Disagree					3%
Neither agree nor disagree	3%		12.10%	3%	3%
Agree	42.40%	30.30%	33.30%	30.30%	36.40%
strongly disagree	54.50%	69.70%	54.50%	63.30%	57.60%

Fig. 2. Competency Identification Participants

Fig. 4 depicts the descriptive analysis and presentation of the respondents' support to Competency Identification characteristics.

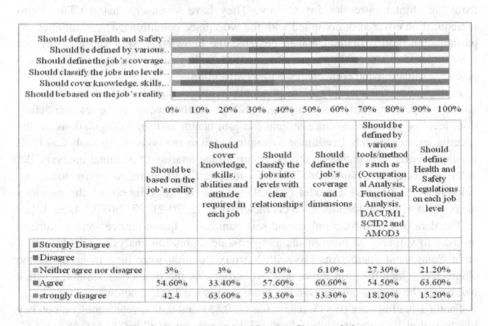

	Should be based on the job's reality	Should cover knowledge, skills, abilities and attitude required in each job	Should classify the jobs into levels with clear relationships	Should define the job's coverage and dimensions	Should be defined by various tools/methods such as (Occupational Analysis, Functional Analysis, DACUM1, SCID2 and AMOD3	Should define Health and Safety Regulations on each job level
Strongly Disagree						
Disagree						
Neither agree nor disagree	3%	3%	9.10%	6.10%	27.30%	21.20%
Agree	54.60%	33.40%	57.60%	60.60%	54.50%	63.60%
strongly disagree	42.4	63.60%	33.30%	33.30%	18.20%	15.20%

Fig. 3. Competency Identification Characteristics

It shows the similarities in the respondents' decision on Competency Identification Characteristics. From 90.9% of the respondents and over, agreed that the Competency Identification should be based on the job's reality, cover SKAs job's classification and job's conditional circumstances. While 72.7% of the respondents recommended that the Competency Identification development committee must employ competency identification analytical tools to define competencies. Similarly, 78.8% of them assumed that an awareness regarding health and safety in the digital forensics crime scene was significant and should have consideration.

Finally, the most important findings are the majority of the respondents (average of 95.66%) believed that the Competency Identification should be carried out by various stakeholders. The associated committees of various stakeholders should be from the private and the public enterprises that have a concern with the digital forensics fields, which can create a consensus on the outcomes. Furthermore, an average of 86.7% of the respondents supported the characteristics of Competency Identification.

This finding supports the idea raised by the International Labor Organization (ILO) and others [21, 34-36]. They stated that the leader and state representative members of the executive and legislative power are required to sponsor and to support the procedures of the Competency Identification. They also mentioned that the participation of digital forensics professionals is a major issue for defining the skills and ability needs. Moreover, contributions from the Laws and Juridical representatives are vital to define the legal requirements and ensure the training/education outcomes satisfy the Juridical expectations regarding the DFI qualification [35]. The Work Groups Experts participation is very significant to define the workplace needs and their expectation from the Digital Forensics Investigator. They have to ensure that the DFI training/education covered or complied with the workplace conditions. The academicians' participation is also fundamental to describe the knowledge, skill and abilities that were required in a specific job position, as well as they propose the methods of competency evaluation and competency-based curriculum.

Furthermore, the majority of respondents assumed that the definition of the required competency (skill, knowledge and ability) totally depend on the real job definition, level of job, circumstance around the job, health and safety regulations on the specific level of the job. In addition to employ various methods of job analytical tools to diagnosis the occupations, such as, occupational analysis, functional analysis, development of a curriculum (DACUM), Systematic Curriculum and Instructional Development (SCID) and a model (AMOD). These findings supported the previous ideas of Competency Identification characteristics [15, 20-21, 27, 29-30, 34, 36-40].

The data collected from online and self-completion questionnaire were factorized in order to validate the instruments and generate regression analysis variables. Principle Component Factor Analysis with Virmax Rotation were used to grouping the Competency Identification items into two groups as the prediction variables which will use in the regression analysis. For more details see Table 2 below.

Factor 1 loadings are (0.885, 0.839, 0.837, 0.831 and 0.829) represent Competency Identification Participants; while Factor 2 loadings are (0.872, 0.832, 0.687, 0.643, 0.423 and 0.336) represent Competency Identification Characteristics. Moreover, the Kaiser-Meyer-Olkin (KMO) Measure of Sampling Adequacy more than (- or +) 0.50 [41] and the Bartlett Test Sphericity significant ($p = 0.00 < 0.05$).

Table 1. Factor Analysis Result on Digital Forensics Investigator Competency Identification Requirements

Items	Factors	
	1	2
Laws and Juries representatives	**.885**	.320
Scientific and intellectual professionals from Training & Educational/Assessment institutions	**.839**	
State representative members of the executive and legislative power	**.837**	
Groups of workers experts	**.831**	.367
Digital Forensics Professionals	**.829**	.314
Should define Health and Safety Regulations on each job level	.397	**.336**
Should classify the jobs into levels with clear relationships		**.872**
Should define the jobs coverage and dimensions		**.832**
Should be based on the jobs reality		**.687**
Should cover knowledge, skills, abilities and attitude required in each job		**.643**
Should be defined by various tools/methods such as (Occupation Analysis, Functional Analysis, DACUM1, SCID2 and AMOD3	.372	**.423**
KMO	0.785	
Bartlett Test Sphericity significant (p = 0.00 < 0.05)		

Table 4 depicts the Digital Forensics Investigator Proficiency Characteristics factorization. The characteristics skills, knowledge and abilities were factorized to form the criterion variable for regression analysis. The loadings of the factor are (0.967, 0.948 and 0.857), while, the KMO is 0.667.

Table 2. Digital Forensics Investigator Proficiency Characteristics

Items	Factor1
knowledge	**.967**
skill	**.948**
ability	**.857**
KMO	0.667

Multiple regressions (Enter method) was used to determine the best linear combination of the predictor variables, namely, the Competency Identification Participants, Competency Identification Characteristics for forecasting the Digital Forensics investigators' proficiency. Tables 4 and 5 reveal the results of regressions analysis of each independent variable's component.

The findings show that the combination of the predictor variables has a significance achievement, (R^2 = 41.1%, $p < 0.05$), however, all the two variables together contribute significantly in the prediction of the dependent variables (DFIP). The VIF and Tolerance statistics are similar (=1 and < 10), which indicate there are no multi-collinearity problems [41].

Table 3. Statistical Stepwise Regression Analysis Coefficient

Dependent Variables	Independent Variables	Standardized Coefficients Beta	t	Sig.	Correlation Part	Collinearity Statistics	
Digital Forensics Investigator Proficiency (Skill, Knowledge and Ability)	Competency Identification Participants	0.573	4.017	.000	0.598	1.000	1.000
	Competency Identification Characteristics	0.288	2.019	.05	0.351	1.000	1.000

Table 4. Model Summary

Model	R	R^2	Adjusted R^2	F-Value	Sig.
1	0.641	0.411	0.370	10.106	0.000

The following analysis can define which of the variables have great contribution in the model of the Competency Identification methods.

Firstly, significant association between the Competency Identification Participants and the Digital Forensics investigators proficiency is indicated as (B = 0.573, R^2 = 0.357, $p < 0.05$). This indicates that 35.7% of the variance of the Digital Forensics Investigator Proficiency is explained by the Competency Identification.

Secondly, further analysis was also carried out in order to determine the relationship between the Competency Identification Characteristics and the Digital Forensics Investigator Proficiency. The significant association between them is indicated by (B = 0.288, R^2 = 0.123, $p < 0.05$). The result of this analysis indicates that 12.3% of the Digital Forensics investigator's proficiency is detected by the Competency Identification Characteristics.

5   Conclusions and Recommendation

In conclusion, this study describes the findings of the survey data analysis which shows the respondents supported the Digital Forensics Investigation Competency Identification Requirements. Moreover, it also concentrates on assessing the relationship between the Competency Identification Requirements items and the Digital Forensics investigator's proficiency. The findings confirm that the Competency Identification Participants and Competency Identification Characteristics have a great contribution on the Digital Forensics Investigator Proficiency. These results will have significant contribution in our next study Digital Forensics Investigator Competencies Standardization.

Acknowledgments. This work is of a research that has been done in Universiti Teknologi Malaysia (UTM), under support from Ministry of Science, Technology &Innovation, Malaysia.

References

1. Rogers: The future of computer forensics: A needs analysis survey. Computers & Security 23(1), 12–16 (2004)
2. Taylor, C., Endicott-Popovsky, B., Phillips, A.: Forensics Education: Assessment and Measures of Excellence. In: Proceedings of the Second International Workshop on Systematic Approaches to Digital Forensic Engineering (SADFE 2007), pp. 155–165. IEEE (2007)
3. John, D., Fernandez, S.S.M.G.D.K.: Computer forensics: a critical need in computer science programs. JCSC 20, 4 (2005)
4. Pidanick, R.: An Investigation of Computer Forensics. Information System Control Journal 3 (2004), http://www.isaca.org (last visit September 15, 2012)
5. Hopkins, D.: Innovative Corporation Solutions, Inc. (2006),
   http://www.michigantechnologyleaders.com/.../
   InnovativeNewsImportanceofComputerForensics.pdf
   (last visit 15 September 2012)
6. William Figg, Z.Z.: A computer forensics minor curriculum proposal. Journal of Computing Sciences in Colleges 22(4), 32–38 (2007)
7. Luther: Forensic Course Development. In: CITC4 2003. Proceedings of the 4th Conference on Information Technology Curriculum, pp. 265–269. ACM, New York (2003)
8. Hamzah, Z.: E-Security Law & Strategy. Kelana Jaya Malaysia, KL: Malayan Law Journal Sdn Bhd, 47301, 122 (2005) ISBN 967-962-632-6
9. Stephen, C.: How to be a Digital Forensic Expert Witness: Systematic Approaches to Digital Forensic Engineering. In: SADFE 2005 Proceedings of the First International Workshop on Systematic Approaches to Digital Forensic Engineering, pp. 69–85. IEEE Computer Society, Washington, DC (2005)
10. Huebner, D.B.: Computer Forensics Workshop for Undergraduate Students, Tenth Australasian Computing Education Conference (ACE 2008), Wollongong, vol. 78. Australian Computer Society, Inc. (2008)
11. Liu, Z.W., Ning: Developing a computer forensics program in police higher education. In: Proceedings of 2009 4th International Conference on Computer Science & Education, pp. 1431–1436. IEEE (2009)
12. Nance, K., Armstrong, H.: Digital Forensics: Defining an Education Agenda. In: 2010 43rd Hawaii International Conference on System Sciences (HICSS), pp. 1–10 (2010)
13. Sabeil, E., Manaf, A.B.A., Ismail, Z., Abas, M.: Cyber Forensics Competency-Based Framework - Areview. International Journal on New Computer Architectures and Their Applications (IJNCAA) 1(3), 1014–1023 (2011) ISSN: 2220-9085
14. Barbara, J.: Certification and Accreditation Overview. In: Handbook of Digital and Multimedia Forensic Evidence, pp. 23–45 (2008), http://www.springerlink.com/index/t5852u690qhv5512.p (last visit September 15, 2012), doi:10.1007/978-1-59745-577-0_3

15. Barbara, J.: ISO/IEC 17025:2005 Accreditation of the Digital Forensics Discipline. Digita Forensic Investigator News (DFI) (February 23, 2012), http://www.dfinews.com/print/6183 (last visit September 15, 2012)
16. Matthew: Computer Forensic: The Need for Standardization and Certification. International Journal of Digital Evidence 3 (2004), http://www.ijde.org
17. Jones, N.: Training and accreditation - Who are the experts? Digital Investigation 1, 189–194 (2004), http://www.elsevier.com/locate/diin
18. SyberSecurity Malaysia: Info Security Professional Development (2011), http://www.cybersecurity.my/en/services/training_outreach/training/calendar/main/detail/1376/index.html (last visit September 14, 2012)
19. EURIM: Supplying the Skills for Justice (2004), http://www.eurim.org/consult/e-crime/may_04/ECS_DP3_Skills_040505_web.htm (last visit 2010)
20. Trinder, J.C.: Competency Standards - A Measure of the Quality of Workforce. In: The International Archives of the Photogrammetry, Remote Sensing and Spatial Information Sciences, Beijing (2008)
21. Cinterfor, I.: How the competency-based training approach first applied (2011), http://www.build-project-management-competency.com/wp-content/uploads/2011/02/ILOs-FAQs-for-Competency-Development.pdf (last visit September 15, 2012)
22. Azmi, I.A.G.: Competency-based human resource practices in Malaysian public sector organizations. African Journal of Business Management 4(2), 235–241 (2010), http://www.academicjournals.org/ajbm
23. Hoffmann, T.: The Meanings of Competency. Journal of European Industrial Training 23(6), 275–285 (1999)
24. Irons, A.D., Stephens, P., Ferguson, R.I.: Digital Investigation as a distinct discipline: A pedagogic perspective, pp. 82–90 (2009)
25. Jason: Forensic Computing: Developing Specialist Expertise within the CS Curriculum. In: Proceedings of the 10th Colloquium for Information Systems Security Education, June 5-8, University of Maryland, University College, Adelphi (2006)
26. David Trejo, S., Elizabith: Framework for Competency and Capability Assessment for Resource Allocation. Journal of management in engineering (2002)
27. John, J., Digital, B.: evidence accreditation in the corporate and business environment. Digital Investigation 2(2), 137–146 (2005)
28. Stretton, A.: Australian competency standards. International Journal of Project Management 13(2), 119–123 (1995)
29. Norton, R.E.: Competency-Based Education via the DACUM and SCID Process: An Overview (2009), http://www.unevoc.unesco.org/e.../CBE_DACUM_SCID%20article2.pdf (last visit September 14, 2012)
30. CAA-01: IADC Competence Assurance Accreditation Program Form CAA-01 Overview & Accreditation Procedures (2010), http://www.iadc.org/competence/CAA-01%20Overview%20&%20Procedures_rev2010-0222.pdf (last visit September 15, 2012)
31. Curtain, R.: Implementing Competency-Based Training In The Workplace: A Case Study In Workforce Participation. Asia Pacific Journal of Human Resources 32(2), 133–143 (1993), http://www.curtain-consulting.net.au/download_controlled/Skill%20formation/CurtainOrmondCBT.pdf (last vist September 15, 2012)

32. Ilhaamie Abdul Ghani Azmi, Z.A.A.a.Y.Z.: Competency based Career Development and Performance Management Practices and Service Quality in Malaysian Public Organizations. African Journal of Business Management 4(2) (2010) ISSN 1993-8233, http://www.academicjournals.org/ajbm
33. Schindler, D.R.C.a.P.S.: Business Research Methods, 10th edn. McGraw-Hill/Irwan (2008)
34. Philip, C.: Training and Education in Digital Evidence. In: Handbook of Digital and Multimedia Forensic Evidence, pp. 11–22 (2008)
35. Michael, L.: Panel Topic: Education and Interdisciplinary Issues in Digital Forensics. Computer Science and Judicial Process (2007)
36. Stephens, P., Induruwa, A.: Cybercrime Investigation Training and Specialist Education for the European Union, pp. 28–37 (2007)
37. Huff-Eibl, R., Voyles, J.F., Brewer, M.M.: Competency-based hiring, job description, and performance goals. The Value of an Integrated System 51(7-8), 691 (2011)
38. Valli, C.: Establishing a vendor neutral skills based framework for digital forensics curriculum development and competence assessment. In: Proceedings of Australian Digital Forensics Conference, pp. 153–158. Edith Cowan University (2006), http://ro.ecu.edu.au/cgi/viewcontent.cgi?article=3097&context=ecuworks (last visit September 15, 2012)
39. Leibrock, L.R.: Duties, Support Functions, and Competencies. Digital Forensics Investigators (2007)
40. IOCE: IOCE Training and KSAs (2002), http://www.ioce.org/fileadmin/user../Training%20and%20KSAs.pdf (last visit 2010)
41. Hair: Multivariate Data Analysis, 7th edn. (2010)

A Holistic Approach to Duplicate Publication and Plagiarism Detection Using Probabilistic Ontologies

Pouya Foudeh and Naomie Salim

Faculty of Computer Science and Information Systems
Universiti Teknologi Malaysia, Johor Bahru
fpouya2@live.utm.my, naomie@utm.my

Abstract. Duplicate publication and plagiarism are two major problems in scholarly world and even they are called the cancer of academia. Plagiarism detection systems try to find similar publications of a specific article; yet, there is a little advance in holistic plagiarism detection systems. Text similarity services, without a human manual confirmation, are not capable to confirm duplication; nonetheless, it is achievable to develop a system that determines the probability of an infringement. In this paper we introduce a technique to develop such systems by using probabilistic ontologies and reasoning. The output of this system can be used for statistical surveys about rate of prevalence of plagiarism. As well, it can hit on the most probable cases of plagiarism for further investigation by human.

Keywords: plagiarism detection, duplicate publication, probabilistic ontologies, ontology reasoning, reasoning about uncertainties.

1 Introduction

Having publications is one of the priorities of academics and researchers because it is an important factor to assess the success on a research project. Usually the passion to have several publications make researchers work harder, but it sometimes leads to duplicate publication of their pervious researches or plagiarism from others.

Plagiarism and duplicate publication are the cancer of academia. They distract other researchers who read the papers, waste funding and grants and makes circumstances unjust in advancement in academia and earning funds and demoralize real researchers. In the digital era, plagiarism has become an easy task. Therefore, many plagiarism detection techniques have been developed to detect them.

Modern plagiarism detection systems are high-performing and find duplications easily even after a fair rewording or translating from another language. Nonetheless, they are still quite far from making plagiarism impossible.

Nowadays, editors and reviewers easily employ these systems to ensure the originality of a scientific paper. Despite that, plagiarism detection systems are still not able to retrieve plagiarized papers from millions of articles stored in a bibliographic database. Furthermore, plagiarism or duplication can only be confirmed, after

A. Ell Hassanien et al. (Eds.): AMLTA 2012, CCIS 322, pp. 566–574, 2012.
© Springer-Verlag Berlin Heidelberg 2012

investigation by human. High amount of similarity between two papers does not provide enough evidence as it may happen because of some justified reasons such as periodical updating or using the same texts from own previous works with the purpose of introducing a new research. On the other hand, some articles with lower similarity can be marked as duplicated after human investigation.

It is impossible to employ specialist human resources to compare tens of thousands of similar documents manually. Plagiarism detection systems are strong, when we ask: "give me what is similar to this article.", but they fail when we ask about duplicate publication and plagiarism rate in countries, universities, journals or even for a person with dozens of scientific papers under his/her name. Therefore, plagiarism detection based on holistic approach is in need.

Moreover, sometimes a plagiarism or duplication is not discovered by reviewers, either because of their fault or an excuse such as publication of two papers at a same time. These cases are unlikely to be discovered after publication, especially for duplication because, unlike plagiarism, owner of the first paper never cares about it.

An automatic information retrieval system is unable to definitely decide about duplication. Nevertheless, the system is able to determine the probability of plagiarism or duplication according to several parameters such as, but not limited to, the amount of similarity between them. If it is estimated with enough accuracy, the results are useful in statistical surveys. Besides, the most probable cases of plagiarism are extractable.

The current research is going to discuss about building a probabilistic ontology according to data coming from bibliographic databases and plagiarism detection systems and then using reasoning about such ontologies to develop information needed for holistic analysis of scientific misconducts, and also, to report the most probable cases of plagiarism to be investigated by human.

2   Related Works

2.1   Probabilistic Ontologies

An ontology is a controlled vocabulary of well-defined terms which their relations to each other are specified, and can be interpreted by computers as well as human. They can be used as the source of background knowledge for expert systems to process and answer user queries [1].

Human knowledge is limited. Therefore sometimes, information is incomplete or contradictory. It usually happens when data are resulted from unproven theories, when it is impossible to do experiment, or they are collected from different and entrusted sources, for instance, historical information. When we develop an ontology using such information, the ontology would be obviously inconsistent.

Inconsistency is unsustainable in any kind of knowledge and data bases, including ontologies. While data are inconsistent, there is no guarantee for system to be able to answer queries and update data. In short, an inconsistent knowledge base is worthless. Besides omitting some useful information from ontology to make it consistent, another strategy is adapting inconsistencies in form of probabilistic data [2-3].

Reasoning on ontologies enables systems to process and answer user queries which the answers are not directly stored in the ontology, but can be found after inference on available axioms and relations in the ontology.

Reasoning and query processing are the most challenging parts of probabilistic ontologies. In non-probabilistic ontologies, reasoning can be done by just applying some logical operators on a limited number of related relations and axioms.

In contrast, reasoning on probabilistic ontologies can be very complicated. All possible worlds, possible states of the database, must be computed before estimation the probability of a single entry, and several nodes will be affected from updating one node. This is not only in probabilistic ontologies, but also all structures for probabilistic data, more or less, suffer from this problem and even some algorithms in this area are in #P complete degree of complexity [4-6].

2.2   Multi Entity Bayesian Network

Probability is one of the available logics' interfaces for uncertain data while the belief functions, possibility measures (also called plausibility and is based on fuzzy logic) and relative likelihood are three other famous models. Each interface has its own illustration of ambiguous information and methods for reasoning about them [7].

Among many proposed interfaces for uncertain information, probability is the strongest, contender as a universal representation. Bayesian networks is based on probability theory. It is a graphical model, used for a vast domain of application fields, including probabilistic ontologies.

A Bayesian Network is a directed acyclic graph with an associated set of probability tables, loosely speaking. Each node is a random variable and the edges and tables define relations among them. In such networks, neither variables nor causal relations are deterministic [8].

Multi Entity Bayesian Network, MEBN, uses directed graphs for modeling too. It is an extension of Bayesian networks empowered with expressive first-order logic. MEBN logic, as a knowledge representation language, unifies logical foundation for the emerging collection of more expressive probabilistic languages [9].

Ontologies are usually represented with knowledge representation languages. OWL is an RDF/XML based language to represent regular ontologies and is endorsed by W3C. PR-OWL is an extension of OWL to represent probabilistic ontologies. It is based on MEBN. PR-OWL is still an ongoing standard since some problems are still open, including compatibility with OWL [6], [10-11].

2.3   Procurement Fraud Detection in Brazil

Office of the comptroller general is responsible of detecting government frauds in Brazil and one of the major concerns in this domain is procurements. According to laws, all procurements must be assigned in fair and competitive conditions. The most common corruption is where several companies competing for procurement actually belong to one, named front companies, where there is no real competition.

A front company is managed by a front man, person who usually has no role in the company but formally occupies the chair to conceal the actual owners. There are some rules to recognize front companies. For example it is unusual when, a large company is managed by a person who has little education or very low income. As well, when the managers of two different companies live in the same address, it looks like they have a family relationship. None of such or similar cases are criminal, but they are suspected and eligible to be investigated by comptroller general audits.

For further investigations, all proposals and auctions, public notices, have been transferred to computers with all details and after information gathering, they were stored on a database. A huge amount of papers were converted to huge amount of information in the computers, but they were not easy to investigate yet.

The research develops a probabilistic ontology according to the database. This ontology is designed using UnBBayes [12-13], a tool developed by the same research team to design and perform reasoning on Bayesian networks as well as MEBN. After reasoning according to particular rules, the system is able to provide the list of most probable cases of fraud in government procurements to be investigated by comptroller audits [14].

2.4   Déjà vu

eTBLAST [15] and Déjà vu [16] are two research projects in the innovation labs of Virginia Bioinformatics Institute. eTBLAST is a free text similarity service, available as a duplication detection system over MEDLINE, a famous biomedical bibliographic database containing about twenty million scientific papers, and several other bibliographic databases.

Déjà vu is a database having tens of thousands of records of similar MEDLINE articles, tagged by eTBLAST. Some records are also eyeballed and categorized manually as Duplicate/Different Authors (DA), Duplicate/Same Authors (SA), Duplicate/Update/Same Journal (SJ), Duplicate/Update/Different Journal (DJ), Duplicate Medline Issue (MI), Duplicate/Other, errata, false positive or no abstract, and many other records have only automatic similarity tags.

The database is available for free download and viewing in the website. There are also several statistical reports on the number of detected cases by their curators, languages, countries, institutes and journals. Déjà vu is a live project and its records are being constantly updated.

In the extension of this research, they set up an experiment aiming to mark out plagiarisms and duplications automatically. Again, MEDLINE was used as the data source and eTBLAST as the similarity service. Because of the huge amount of processing, they used only articles abstracts for similarity checking. Therefore, only records with abstracts, about half of the papers in MEDLINE, could participate in the experiment.

A set of 5313 papers were selected randomly. If we assume they are selected from ten million papers and one percent of papers are duplicated, then the probability of each one of them having a duplicate in the set is .01*.0005, almost nil. Hence, we can

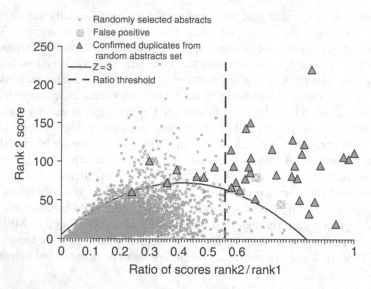

Fig. 1. The results of searching Medline with 5313 random citations as queries (small squares) are shown on a graph with Rank 2/Rank 1 score ratio versus the raw Rank 2 score, two measures used to classify a citation. Inspection of the 272 citation pairs that were above the Z-score=3 curve confirmed 37 as true duplicates (triangles) and 3 false true (crossed squares). Reproduced from Ref. [17] which published on behalf the international society for computational biology, by permission of Oxford University Press.

assume them non-duplicated. They also used another collection of papers, 171 visually confirmed duplications. These two sets of non-duplicated and duplicated paper were mixed and the system must separate them.

Each paper was compared to all other papers in the set using eTBLAST. For each article, the amount of similarity of the most similar item must be itself, named Rank1 and the amount of similarity of the second similar item, plagiarism candidate, named Rank2.

The results was plotted on a chart on Fig.1, small gray squares are presenting for non-duplicates and triangles for duplicates. Two threshold limits were used to separate duplicates. First is Z-score (normal score) above 3, that separate 272 papers but only 37 of them are real duplication. The second threshold limit is Rank2/Rank1 more than 0.56, which trades off between sensitivity and specificity, separates 30 duplicates with only 3 false positives.

The number of shared references in similar articles having either same authors or different, is another discussed issue in this research [17-18].

The next extension of the research introduced a new similarity method, named 'statistically improbable phrases', to improve the results that was taken by eTBLAST [19]. In another paper, they directed to journals that accepted duplicated works and their impact factors. They also had communicated with authors and journal editors of plagiarized and original papers and published some key points of these communications [20].

3   Methods

In Déjà vu, the tradeoff between sensitivity and specificity was costly in any manner, because the system either ignored many duplications or gave false positive to many non-duplications instead. It was caused from the deterministic nature of the system; this problem can be dealt with using probabilistic approach. The whole process is illustrated in Fig 2.

In some way, plagiarism is comparable with crimes. After presenting all evidences in the court, juries have only two choices: innocent or guilty. In plagiarism detection there is also two final statuses; either not duplication or duplication and then retraction. That is why when the position is near to threshold and the system is undecided, the probabilistic approach is more helpful than fuzzy.

3.1   Dataset

We will use Déjà vu database and the database that we will build as our dataset. Each record of Déjà vu contains the ID of two suspected papers in Medline, name of authors and date of publication for each one and the similarity ratio determined by eTBLAST. For our database, we retrieve almost the same information from bibliographic databases but not limited to medicine. In cases where full text is freely available; the system will determine the similarity amount of each section separately. It will raise the performances, for example, if two papers belong to one, it is common to have same structure or sentences in introduction. However, it will be different in the results or discussion.

Visualize confirmed duplications is an essential part of dataset to execute the learning process and to evaluate the performance of the system as well. Déjà vu has a small set of confirmed duplications and its website is open to receive reports of confirmed duplication to extend the list. All reports are double checked by the team members. With probabilistic approach, the system is more open to accept public participation. Everyone is able to get an ID, the old hand users who have been working in the system for a long time and with many confirmed correct reports, are more trustable so their reports are more probable to be true.

3.2   Probabilistic Ontology Development

Using the dataset, our database and Déjà vu, we develop the probabilistic ontology. Some probabilistic relationships, such as authorship of papers, are stored in the ontology, while some are not stored but can be deducted, including probability of a paper being plagiarized from others.

The actualized ontology according to this information must be fast updateable in consequence of frequent addition and updating of bibliographic information as well as visual confirmations of duplications by inspector users. Nevertheless, updating is very effortful for probabilistic ontologies, unlike regular ontologies; updating even one node may affect many others. In addition, it must be receptive to a very large ontology.

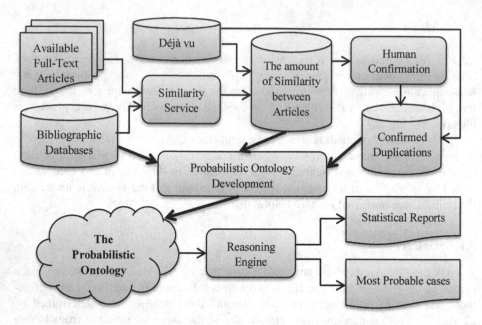

Fig. 2. The process of the proposed method

The uncertainties about the duplication of articles are not the only probabilistic entities in the ontology. For example, authors of papers may be uncertain as well. While, the name of an author is submitted in bibliographic databases in different formats, sometimes even according to their affiliation, system is not able to determine papers either belong to same person or not. In reverse, very common names have the same problem even when two authors' names are exactly the same. In short, the ownership of papers can be probabilistic data in the system. It is important in plagiarism detection because using own previous works are, more or less, justified if it is referenced accordingly.

3.3   Reasoning Engine

After constricting the probabilistic ontology, the system must be able to report trespass cases accompanying with the probability of affirmation for each one. Definition of rules for the reasoning engine is not an easy task. Criterions, such as normal amount of similarity between each section of paper or number of common references, are different from one domain to another. This problem was not so challenging in Déjà vu because all dataset was selected from one domain. But it would be more arduous when it is going to work in other domains such as art, humanity and engineering. If an adequate number of confirmed duplicates are available in each domain as the training data set, probabilistic threshold values can be determined using machine learning for each domain.

Other than text similarity, references are usable in detection of duplications. Having an ample number of common references between two papers is suspected. Fortunately nowadays, bibliographic databases are capable of linking papers and their references.

On the other hand, it is possible to do reasoning according to the authors' records. If one has some confirmed or a lot of high probable plagiarism or duplication cases, he or she is more likely to commit it again. The same argument can be applied to journals and conferences, who have accepted many plagiarized papers. In addition, their impact factor can be used as well.

4   Conclusion

Plagiarism and duplicate publication detection is a research area which has direct beneficial effects on academic society. In this paper, we proposed a method for automatic investigation of plagiarism and duplicate publication with a holistic approach.

In one hand, data which can be absorbed from biographic databases and Déjà vu is a great help. On the other hand, full text of most papers is not easily accessible. Additionally, probabilistic ontology is a new, ongoing and very challenging research area. Particularly, reasoning, updating and population algorithms for probabilistic ontologies are costly for processor and low performances. Aforementioned problems must be addressed to make the research goals achievable.

Acknowledgement. We would like to express our gratitude to the Universiti Teknologi Malaysia. This research is partially funded by research university grant (QJ13000.7128.00H72) of Universiti Teknologi Malaysia.

References

1. Encyclopedia of Database Systems, 1st edn. Springer (2009)
2. Poole, D., Smyth, C., Sharma, R.: Ontology design for scientific theories that make probabilistic predictions. IEEE Intelligent Systems 24(1), 27–36 (2009)
3. Haase, P., Völker, J.: Ontology Learning and Reasoning — Dealing with Uncertainty and Inconsistency. In: da Costa, P.C.G., d'Amato, C., Fanizzi, N., Laskey, K.B., Laskey, K.J., Lukasiewicz, T., Nickles, M., Pool, M. (eds.) URSW 2005 - 2007. LNCS (LNAI), vol. 5327, pp. 366–384. Springer, Heidelberg (2008)
4. Calì, A., Lukasiewicz, T., Predoiu, L., Stuckenschmidt, H.: Rule-Based Approaches for Representing Probabilistic Ontology Mappings. In: da Costa, P.C.G., d'Amato, C., Fanizzi, N., Laskey, K.B., Laskey, K.J., Lukasiewicz, T., Nickles, M., Pool, M. (eds.) URSW 2005 - 2007. LNCS (LNAI), vol. 5327, pp. 66–87. Springer, Heidelberg (2008)
5. Haarslev, V., Pai, H.-I., Shiri, N.: Uncertainty Reasoning for Ontologies with General TBoxes in Description Logic. In: da Costa, P.C.G., d'Amato, C., Fanizzi, N., Laskey, K.B., Laskey, K.J., Lukasiewicz, T., Nickles, M., Pool, M. (eds.) URSW 2005 - 2007. LNCS (LNAI), vol. 5327, pp. 385–402. Springer, Heidelberg (2008)

6. Foudeh, P., Salim, N.: Probabilistic ontologies and probabilistic ontology learning: Significance and challenges. In: 2011 International Conference on Research and Innovation in Information Systems (ICRIIS), pp. 1–4. IEEE (2011)

7. Halpern, J.Y.: Reasoning about uncertainty. MIT Press (2005)

8. Pearl, J.: Bayesian networks: A model of Self-Activated memory for evidential reasoning. In: Proceedings of the 7th Conference of the Cognitive Science Society, pp. 329–334. University of California, Irvine (1985)

9. Laskey, K.B.: MEBN: A language for first-order bayesian knowledge bases. Artificial Intelligence 172(2-3), 140–178 (2008)

10. Costa, P.C.G., Laskey, K.B.: PR-OWL: A framework for probabilistic ontologies. In: Proceeding of the 2006 conference on Formal Ontology in Information Systems: Proceedings of the Fourth International Conference (FOIS 2006), pp. 237–249. IOS Press, Amsterdam (2006)

11. Carvalho, R.N., Laskey, K., Costa, P.: Compatibility formalization between PR-OWL and OWL. In: First International Workshop on Uncertainty in Description Logics (2010)

12. Costa, P.C.G., Ladeira, M., Carvalho, R.N., Santos, L.L., Matsumoto, S., Laskey, K.B.: A First-Order bayesian tool for probabilistic ontologies. In: Proceedings of the Twenty-First International Florida Artificial Intelligence Research Society Conference, pp. 631–636. AAAI Press, Menlo Park (2008)

13. Carvalho, R.N., Ladeira, M., Santos, L.L., Matsumoto, Costa, P.C.G.: UnBBayes-MEBN: Comments on Implementing a Probabilistic Ontology Tool. In: Proceedings of the IADIS International Conference on Applied Computing, Algarve, Portugal, pp. 211–218 (2008)

14. Carvalho, R.N., Laskey, K.B., Costa, P., Ladeira, M., Santos, L.L., Matsumoto, S.: Probabilistic knowledge fusion for procurement fraud detection in Brazil (2009)

15. Deja vuresearch website, http://dejavu.vbi.vt.edu/dejavu

16. eTBLAST research website, http://etest.vbi.vt.edu/etblast3

17. Errami, M., Hicks, J.M., Fisher, W., Trusty, D., Wren, J.D., Long, T.C., Garner, H.R.: Déjà vu-a study of duplicate citations in medline. Bioinformatics 24(2), 243–249 (2008)

18. Errami, M., Sun, Z., Long, T.C., George, A.C., Garner, H.R.: Deja vu: a database of highly similar citations in the scientific literature. Nucleic Acids Research 37(Database issue), D921–D924 (2009)

19. Errami, M., Sun, Z., George, A.C., Long, T.C., Skinner, M.A., Wren, J.D., Garner, H.R.: Identifying duplicate content using statistically improbable phrases. Bioinformatics 26(11), 1453–1457 (2010)

20. Long, T.C., Errami, M., George, A.C., Sun, Z., Garner, H.R.: Scientific integrity responding to possible plagiarism. Science 323(5919), 1293–1294 (2009)

Novel Binary Search Algorithm for Fast Tag Detection in Robust and Secure RFID Systems

Marizan Yaacob[1] and Salwani Mohd Daud[2]

[1] Department of Electrical Engineering, School of Professional and Continuing Education,
Universiti Teknologi Malaysia, Kuala Lumpur, Malaysia
marizan@ic.utm.my
[2] Department of Software Engineering, Advanced Informatics School,
Universiti Teknologi Malaysia, Kuala Lumpur, Malaysia
salwani@ic.utm.my

Abstract. Novel binary search algorithm for fast tag detection (BSF1) and (BSF2) in robust and secure RFID systems is presented in this paper. These algorithms introduce fast tag detection with the new method of inquiry. Tags were grouped in two groups and tag collisions of each group were solved by implementing dynamic searching and backtracking procedure. By grouping the tags, time for solving collision was reduced. It performed fast detection in a robust situation, a group of tags with all possibilities of ID arrangements. Tags attached to the products of different manufacturers may considerably have robust ID. For the security of RFID system, the number of bit (n) will be increased to provide allocation of 2^n unique ID. The increasing number of bit and the uniqueness of ID will increase the security of the system from counterfeiting. However it will also increase time identification, but our algorithms will provide fast detection in the situation of high security.

Keywords: anti-collision, binary search, fast tag detection, secure RFID systems.

1 Introduction

Radio Frequency Identification (RFID) is an automatic identification technology that a reader recognizes object through wireless communication with tags attached to the objects. An RFID reader is capable of reading the information stored at tags located in its sensing range. Tag collisions occur when multi tags try to respond to a reader simultaneously. Various anti-collision algorithms have been devised and applied with various levels of performance in respect of the number of tags that can be handled and the time required in handling them. An effective algorithm for solving collision for fast tag detection is very important for enhancing the system performance.

Algorithm for tag collision resolution can be categorized as the probabilistic frame slotted ALOHA and deterministic tree based algorithm. The slotted ALOHA based algorithm reduces the probability of occurring tag collisions on how tags respond at

A. Ell Hassanien et al. (Eds.): AMLTA 2012, CCIS 322, pp. 575–582, 2012.

the different time but it has a problem that a specific tag may not be identified for a long time, leading to tag starvation problem. With the increasing number of tag, the identification performance will deteriorate sharply. The tree based algorithms split the group of colliding tags into subgroups until all tags are identified. Tree-based algorithms could achieve better read rate by using a binary search approach. RFID readers repeatedly split the set of tags into two subsets and labeled them by binary numbers until each subset has only one tag, thus the reader is able to identify all tags.

By research the binary search algorithm, the length of the parameter which sends with the command by the reader is as long as the length of the tag ID. The tags response to the reader, they send all the bits of their IDs without concerning whether the bits have been recognized or not. For the ID is usually very long, there will be too many data packet to be transmitted and it would waste a lot of time. Many researchers have proposed enhancement algorithm based on binary search algorithm. Dynamic binary search algorithm [1], [2], the reader need to transmit the bits of ID which already knows and the response to the reader the rest bit of ID. However, these algorithms implement backtracking to the root node of the tree, where the command parameter is as long as the lengths of tag ID, which tend to increase the inquiry time from reader to tag, if the bit number of ID is large.

For improved dynamic binary search algorithm [3], [4], [5], [6], they are adopted 4-ary [7], method of request for dynamic searching, which creating idle cycle if the number of tags is small or having robust ID. 4-ary request is beneficial for a group of large tags number which having a portion of similarities in tag ID. Meanwhile our algorithm considers in robust situation, covering small and large number of tags and detection can cope with any possibilities of tag ID arrangement. Probably that tag ID of a group of tags may not have a portion of similar, in case that tag may be attached to the product of different manufacturer or to the product of high security protection. Our novel BSF1 and BSF2 algorithms consider fast detection of multiple tags in robust situations by performing dynamic searching and backtracking procedure to speed up the identification.

2   Binary Search Algorithm

Binary search algorithm [8] involves the reader transmitting a serial number to tag, which they then compare against their ID. Those tags with ID equal to or lower than serial number respond. The reader than monitor tags reply bit by bit using Manchester coding, and once a collision occurs, the reader splits tags into subset based on collision bit. In Manchester coding system, if two (or more) transponders simultaneously transmit bits of different value then the positive and negative transitions of the received bits cancel each other out, so that a subcarrier signal is received for the duration of an entire bit. This state is not permissible in the Manchester coding system and therefore leads to an error. The reliability of the binary search algorithm is that all must remain accurate synchronization and transmit their sequence number at the same time. In binary search tree, when the tags are requested by reader, the reply of tags can be seen as pattern of logic 0, 1 and 'X' as in Fig. 1, where 'X' is a collision bit.

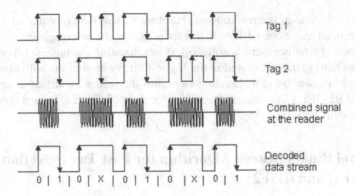

Fig. 1. Binary Search Algorithm

Table 1. Traditional Binary Search Algorithm

Tags ID		Command REQUEST		Received ID	Identified Tags
Tag 1	00100011	1.	(11111111)	(XXXXXXXX)	None
Tag 2	00110110	2.	(01111111)	(0XXX0XXX)	None
Tag 3	01000101	3.	(00111111)	(001X0X1X)	None
Tag 4	01110100	4.	(00101111)	(00100011)	Tags 1
Tag 5	11010110	5.	(11111111)	(XXXXX1XX)	None
Tag 6	11010111	6.	(01111111)	(0XXX01XX)	None
Tag 7	11011101	7.	(00111111)	(00110110)	Tags 2
		8.	(11111111)	(X1XXX1XX)	None
		9.	(01111111)	(01XX010X)	None
		10.	(01011111)	(01000101)	Tags 3
		11.	(11111111)	(X1X1X1XX)	None
		12.	(01111111)	(01110100)	Tags 4
		13.	(11111111)	(1101X1XX)	None
		14.	(11010111)	(1101011X)	None
		15.	(11010110)	(11010110)	Tags 5
		16.	(11111111)	(1101X1X1)	None
		17.	(11010111)	(11010111)	Tags 6
		18.	(11111111)	(11011101)	Tags 7

The procedure of the binary search algorithm is as shown in Table 1. The first ite-ration of the algorithm begins with the transmission of the command REQUEST by the reader. The reader send serial number 11111111 is the highest possible in the example system using 8-bit serial numbers. The serial numbers of all transponders in the interrogation zone of the reader must therefore be less than or equal to 11111111, so this command is answered by all transponders in the interrogation zone of the reader. Detecting whether there is collision, if yes, locating the highest bit position of the collision. Setting the bit located in the highest bit position of the collision as 0 and those located in lower bit as 1. Iterating step until the reader identified a tag and getting the next REQUEST parameter from the root node of the tree. Repeat step until all the tags are identified.

3   Novel Binary Search Algorithm for Fast Tag Detection (BSF1) and (BSF2)

The problem in the binary search tree algorithm has been addressed. In a robust situation when the response of tags through Manchester coding is XXXXXXX, all the bit of tags ID collide, time to solve the collision is long since after every tag selection, the next request is back to root node which is 11111111. Our novel BSF1 and BSF2 algorithms have new approach for solving the collisions, the tags are grouped in two groups, the first groups from ID 00000000 to 01111111 and second group from ID 1000000 to 1111111. This method is more effective, fast detection since tags are grouped in small number that can reduced time to solve the collision. By referring to Table 1, Table 2 and Table 3, binary search algorithm needs (log 2 N + 1) iterations, BSF1 needs (2N-1) and BSF2 (2N - 3) iterations, N is the number of tags. For BSF1, the program needs to recognize the position of collision bit (X) from MSB to LSB. The highest position is being solved first. For BSF2, the program need to recognize the position and the number of collision bit (L), if L = 1, then the reader will read two tags at the same time and reply with UNSELECT command to these tags to make it in 'silence' status.

Table 2. Binary Search Algorithm for Fast Detection (BSF1)

Command REQUEST	Received ID	Identified Tags
1. (0)	(XXX0XXX)	None
2. (00)	(1X0X1X)	None
3. (0010)	(0011)	Tags 1
4. (0011)	(0110)	Tags 2
5. (0)	(1XX010X)	None
6. (010)	(00101)	Tags 3
7. (011)	(10100)	Tags 4
8. (0)		None
9. (1)	(101X1XX)	None
10. (11010)	(11X)	None
11. (11010110)	(11010110)	Tags 5
12. (11010111)	(11010111)	Tags 6
13. (1)	(1011101)	Tags 7

Table 3. Binary Search Algorithm for Fast Detection (BSF2)

	Command REQUEST	Received ID	Identified Tags
1.	(0)	(XXX0XXX)	None
2.	(00)	(1X0X1X)	None
3.	(0010)	(0011)	Tags 1
4.	(0011)	(0110)	Tags 2
5.	(0)	(1XX010X)	None
6.	(010)	(00101)	Tags 3
7.	(011)	(10100)	Tags 4
8.	(0)		None
9.	(1)	(101X1XX)	None
10.	(11010)	(11X)	Tags 5, Tags 6
11.	(1)	(1011101)	Tags 7

For both algorithms, BSF1 and BSF2, the approaches reduce the inquiry steps and bits from the reader to tag. Instead of using request of full length of ID, the reader only send bit request as reflex by Manchester coding of collision bit. It will reduce the communication overhead between reader and tag. We also introduce a new approach of backtracking, if the tags are in the first group, i.e. the tag IDs in the range 0XXXXXXX, after each tag selection, the reader send request '0', for backtracking to the first group. After all tags from the first group are selected, then it is searching and backtracking to the second group i.e. the tag IDs are in the range of 1XXXXXXX.

3.1   List of Commands from Reader to Tag

REQUEST: Reader send request to the tags. Tags respond to the reader if the request bit is identical with tag's bit.

SELECT: For BSF1, this command sends by the reader if only one tag response. For BSF2, this command send if only one tag response or the number of bit collision, L = 1, to read both tags.

UNSELECT: This command cancels a selected tag and set it into 'silence' status. Tag is inactivated in this status and does not answer command of

REQUEST. In order to activate the tags, it must move out of the scope of reader.

3.2   Step of Request from Reader to Tag for BSF1

First step: reader sends the command REQUEST (0) and is responded by tags that are having the most significant bit (MSB) zero. According to Manchester coding, the collision occurs and the decoded data is $(X_6X_5X_40X_2X_1X_0)$. Then the parameter (00) is set as next REQUEST command.

Second step: reader sends the command REQUEST (00) to all the tags in the interrogation zone of the reader. This command REQUEST is responded by the tag 1 and tag

2. The decoded data is $1X_40X_21X_0$. The algorithm set X_4 to (0) and gets the parameter (0010) for the next request command.

Third step: reader sends the common REQUEST (0010) to all the tags in the interrogation zone of the reader. In this step only tag 1 responds, therefore no collision occurs. The reader send command SELECT. After implemented the data reading of tag 1, the reader transmits the command UNSELECT to tag 1 and make it in 'silence' status. The next request parameter is (1011), this proposed algorithm implement dynamic searching by replacing X_4 to (1).

Fourth step: reader sends the command request (1011). In this step only tag 2 responds and reader sends command SELECT. After implemented the data reading of tag 2, the reader transmits the command UNSELECT to tag 2 and make it in 'silence' status. The next request parameter is (0), this proposed algorithm implement backtracking by return to the root node of first group of tags.

Fifth step: reader sends the command REQUEST (0) and is responded by tags that are having the most significant bit (MSB) zeros. According to Manchester coding, the collision occur and the decoded data is $(1X_5X_4010X_0)$. Then the parameter (010) is set as next REQUEST command, X_5 is set to (0).

Sixth step: reader sends the command REQUEST (010) and only tag 3 responds, therefore no collision occurs and reader sends command SELECT. After implemented the data reading of tag 3, the reader transmits the command UNSELECT to tag 3 and make it in 'silence' status. The next request parameter is (011), this proposed algorithm implement dynamic searching by replacing X_5 to (1).

Seventh step: reader sends the command request (011). In this step only tag 4 responds and reader sends command SELECT. After implemented the data reading of tag 4, the reader transmits the command UNSELECT to tag 4 and make it in 'silence' status. The next request parameter is (0), backtracking to the root node of first group of tags.

Eighth step: reader sends the command REQUEST (0) to search other tags in the first group. There is no response since all tags in the first group have been selected. The next request is (1), searching for the tags in the second group.

Ninth step: reader sends the command REQUEST (1) and is responded by tags that are having the most significant bit (MSB) one. According to Manchester coding, the collision occur and the decoded data is $(101X_31X_1X_0)$. Then the parameter (11010) is set as next REQUEST command.

Tenth step: reader sends the command REQUEST (11010) to all the tags in the interrogation zone of the reader. This command REQUEST is responded by the tag 5 and tag 6. The decoded data is $(11X_0)$. The algorithm sets X_0 to (0) and gets the parameter (11010110) for the next request command.

Eleventh step: reader sends the command REQUEST (11010110) to all the tags in the interrogation zone of the reader. In this step only tag 5 responds. The reader send command SELECT. After implemented the data reading of tag 5, the reader transmits the command UNSELECT to tag 5 and make it in 'silence' status. The next request parameter is (11010111), this proposed algorithm implement dynamic searching by replacing X_0 to (1).

Twelfth step: reader sends the command request (11010111). In this step only tag 6 responds and reader sends command SELECT. After implemented the data reading of tag 6, the reader transmits the command UNSELECT to tag 6 and make it in 'silence' status. The next request parameter is (1), this proposed algorithm implement back-tracking by return to the root node of second group of tags.

Thirteenth step: reader sends the command REQUEST (1) and is responded by tags that are having the most significant bit (MSB) one. In this step only tag 7 responds and reader sends command SELECT. After implemented the data reading of tag 7, the reader transmits the command UNSELECT to tag 7 and make it in 'silence' status. The proposed algorithm closes the process since all the tags are identified.

3.3   Step of Request from Reader to Tag for BSF2

First step – Ninth step: same step as BSF1

Tenth step - the reader sends the command REQUEST (11010) to all the tags in the interrogation zone of the reader. This command REQUEST is responded by the tag 5 and tag 6. The decoded data is $(11X_0)$. Since the number of collision (L) is one, reader read their ID and sends SELECT to tag 5 and tag 6. The reader then sends UNSELECT command, to make it in 'silence' status.

Eleventh step: the reader sends the command REQUEST (1) and is responded by tags that are having the most significant bit (MSB) one. In this step only tag 7 responds and reader sends command SELECT. After implemented the data reading of tag 7, the reader transmits the command UNSELECT to tag 7 and make it in 'silence' status. The proposed algorithm closes the process since all the tags are identified.

4   Conclusions

In this work, we propose novel binary search algorithm for fast tag detection, (BSF1) and (BSF2) in robust and secure RFID systems. The approach of dynamic searching and backtracking mechanism is to save step and bit of inquiring and reducing time for solving collision. We introduce new backtracking method for solving collision by grouping the tag in two groups and the tag collision is solved group by group. It is proving that the step of inquiry is reduced even though all the tags collide. Therefor it is beneficially in reducing communication overhead and providing fast tag detection in the environment of robust and secure RFID systems. The further assessment will be on the performance of the algorithm due to the increasing number of tags and ID in secure RFID systems and how the algorithm can be adapted in the situation when the set of tags to be identified changes over time. Further discussion will be included in our future work.

Acknowledgment. The authors would like to express greatest appreciation to Ministry of Higher Education (MOHE), Malaysia and Universiti Teknologi Malaysia (UTM) particularly Advanced Informatics School (AIS) for providing the financial support to carry out this research work.

References

1. Cheng-Sen, B., Jiang, Z.: Research on an RFID Anti-Collision Improved Algorithm Based on Binary Search. In: IEEE International Conference on Computer Application and System Modeling, pp. 430–432 (2010)
2. Zheng, J., Qin, T.: A Novel Collision Arbitration Protocol for RFID Tag Identification. In: 2nd IEEE International Conference on Software Engineering and Service Science, pp. 100–103 (2011)
3. Liu, L., Xie, Z., Xi, J., Lai, S.: An Improved Anti-Collision Algorithm in RFID System. In: IEEE Conference on Mobile Technology, Applications and Systems, pp. 1–5 (2005)
4. Chen, Z., Liao, M.: An Enhanced Dynamic Binary Anti-Collision Algorithm. In: 5th IEEE International Conference on Computer Science and Education, pp. 961–964 (2010)
5. Yu, Z., Liu, X.: Improvement of Dynamic Binary Search Algorithm Used in RFID System. In: Conference on Cross Strait Quad-Regional Radio Science and Wireless Technology Conference, pp. 1046–1049 (2011)
6. Xie, X.M., Xie, Z.H., Lai, S.L., Chen, P.: Dynamic Adjustment Algorithm for Tag Anti-Collision. In: IEEE International Conference on Machine Learning and Cybernetics, pp. 443–446 (2011)
7. Ryu, J., Seok, Y., Kwon, T., Choi, Y.: A Hybrid Query Tree Protocol for Tag Collision Arbitration in RFID Systems. In: IEEE International Conference on Communications, pp. 5981–5986 (2007)
8. Finkenzeller, K.: RFID Handbook: Radio-Frequency Identification Fundamentals and application. John Wiley & Sons Ltd. (1999)

A New Dynamic Hash Algorithm in Digital Signature

Erfaneh Noroozi[1], Salwani Mohd Daud[1], Ali Sabouhi[2], and Hafiza Abas[1]

[1] Advanced Informatics School (AIS), Universiti Teknologi Malaysia
Kuala Lumpur, Malaysia
nerfaneh2@live.utm.my, {salwani,hafiza}@ic.utm.my
[2] Software Engineering of Computer Science
Kuala Lumpur, Malaysia
ali_sabouhi@yahoo.com

Abstract. This paper presents adoption of a new hash algorithm in digital signature. Digital signature presents a technique to endorse the content of the message. This message has not been altered throughout the communication process. Due to this, it increased the receiver confidence that the message was unchanged. If the message is digitally signed, any changes in the message will invalidate the signature. The comparison of digital signature between Rivest, Shamir and Adleman (RSA) algorithms are summarized. The finding reveals that previous algorithms used large file sizes. Finally the new encoding and decoding dynamic hash algorithm is proposed in a digital signature. The proposed algorithm had reduced significantly the file sizes (8 bytes) during the transferring message.

Keywords: Digital signature, public key, encoding, decoding, hash algorithm.

1   Introduction

Along with the thriving improvement of the technologies communication and information, systems of paper-based workflow is quickly substituted by the electronic-based medium in which all information and forms are digitally procedure such as e-government and e-commerce. In these systems, it is very significant to protect the sensitivity and security of digital object from malicious. Thus, how can this message be passed on so that only included or authentic parties obtain the comprehension of the message completely as it was transferred? The main objective in the field of cryptography is to make certain that the included parties communicate securely over a probably insecure channel. When an eavesdropper listens to a conversation between two parties, he should not be able to recognize the message. This can be attained by enciphering a message. This is a cryptographic primeval identified as encryption [1].

2   Digital Signature Schemes

Diffie and Hellman put out an explanation to this problem in their seminal paper entitled "New Direction in Cryptography" [2]. They primarily introduced the important

A. Ell Hassanien et al. (Eds.): AMLTA 2012, CCIS 322, pp. 583–589, 2012.

view of Public-Key Cryptography. The major proposal of public key cryptosystem is to utilize two different keys; for encryption a public key and for decryption a secret key, that are mathematically associated. The two keys are such that working out the secret key is infeasible from the public key. In fact, digital signature is a procedure that generates the same effects while a real signature and it is a mark where only the sender can create and other people can prove the signature simply. The digital signature is utilized to verify the content of the message by using asymmetric ciphering wherever a pair of keys that are public key and private key being considered. The keys used for digital signature are very long sequence of alphabetical and mathematical characters.

3   Signature and Public Key

Significant and private electronic mail be able to utilize digital signature to confirm that the e-mail is from the sender with approving secret key and the content of the e-mail has not been changed [3]. The scenario of digital signature is similar to this situation: a sender doesn't sign the main text directly but he gets a one way hash of the message and then signs the hash. Most digital signature algorithms don't encrypt the messages that are signed. The sender creates some processing based on the text and his private key to produce the signature. Then, the signature is appended to the main text. The receiver also will build an additional calculation based on the message, the signature and the sender's public key to confirm the signature. A stranger that doesn't distinguish the sender's private key can confirm the signature but can't produce a legal signature.

The Ron Rivest, Adi Shamir and Leonard Adleman(RSA) is a public-key cryptosystem and digital signature are generally deployed today and have developed into important building blocks for producing the emerging public-key communications (PKI) in e-government and e-commerce [4]. There are two kinds of RSA assumptions, which are used to make digital signature schemes; the usual RSA problem (ORSA) and the strong RSA problem (SRSA) which is an alteration of RSA by Bari and Pfitzmann; Fujisaki and Okamoto[5], [6]. On the other hand, a small number of digital signature schemes have been recommended based on the SRSA assumption. The Cramer-Shoup signature scheme (CS) is very interesting in that it is a useful and probably secured in a model of standard security [7].

In digital signatures with functionalities, there are numerous aspects used in e-commerce such as proxy signatures and blind signatures. Previously, with systems based on the standard (RSA) theory; there is no confirmed secure signature with additional functionalities such as an alternative signature or blind signature. Formerly, the signature is applied for individual signatures, in easy background, habitually with single two parties included in the connections, i.e. a signature is made on behalf of an individual. However, in numerous cases these days, a message produced for example by one association needs the approval of a number of members of this organization. Thus, raises the attempt of verification and the need of storages. The complex key to this problem is appearing with the aspect of a group-oriented signature scheme, which has been presented by Desmedt[8]. The point of group-oriented digital signature is to expand method in dealing with multi-signers and multi-verifiers.

There are a number of definitions for cryptosystem, including multi-signature schemes and the threshold signature schemes[9]. These secure signature schemes present attractive ways to recognize the aspect of the multi-signature and combined signature schemes. To check the validity of a group-oriented signature, it still requires the public keys of all participating signers. Furthermore, each key may come with an associated documentation signed by the Certificate Authority (CA), which must be conforming along with a generated multi-signature [10].

Accordingly, this means that it increases proportionally with the number of the participating signers. In coefficient block (CB-PKC), the group-oriented signature might not present significantly improved performance compared to conventional signature schemes [11]. Clearly, it still uses a signer's arbitrary public key which defeat the main suggestion of the group-oriented digital signature. It can be addressed by using the characteristics of signers rather than using the casual public keys.

4   Encoding and Decoding

4.1   Encoding Process

First step: In encoding process (Fig. 1) for an image a signature with $S = s_1, s_2, s_3, ...$ and the watermarked image with î, function E is the encoder processing, while imageI and a signature S is the input of the function The output is a new image with embedded watermark, becomes the watermarked image, and can be represented mathematically by,

$$E(I, S) = î \tag{1}$$

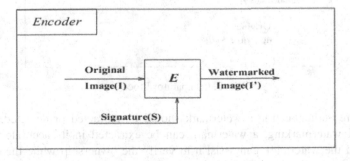

Fig. 1. Encoding Process

4.2   Decoding Process

Function D is the decoder procedure and image J (J can be a watermarked image) as input of the function and is represented as:

$$D(I, J) = S \tag{2}$$

where S' is the extracted signature from the image J.

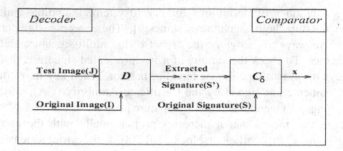

Fig. 2. Decoding Process

The extracted signature S, will be compared with the original owner signature S using comparator, C_σ. If both match to each other, the output will be 1 otherwise 0, as follows:

$$C_o(S,S) = \begin{cases} 1, & C \le \delta \\ 0, & otherwise \end{cases} \tag{3}$$

Figure 3 shows the function of comparator C. The correlation of two signatures δ, $x = C_\sigma(S,S)$ in watermarking scheme can be considered as a three options such as encoding, decoding and comparator.

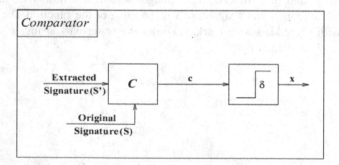

Fig. 3. Comparator Process

To ensure authentication a watermark should be extracted or detected. In a few schemes of watermarking, a watermark can be extracted in its accurate form; the detection of the watermark can assist it to verify the ownership while the extraction process can prove the owner of the message or image.

Main disadvantage using watermark for authentication of a message is the size of the file transfer is very large and will affect the speed of the process.

5   Proposed Algorithm with Hash Code

For the proposed algorithm, the hash code is applied instead of watermarking. The sender and the receiver compare the hash code and checks if it is genuine. The message is authentic when the message retrieved by the receiver is similar to the messages originally sent. Any changes to the data will affect the hash code which is sent with the data (Fig. 4). If the significance of the message processes after the encryption and decryption process is similar, then the message is not modified.

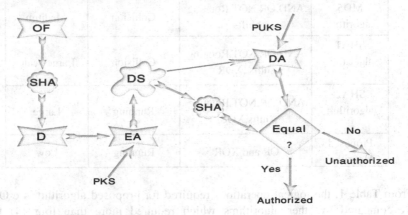

DA: Decryption Algorithm
PKS: Private Key of Sender
PUKS: Public Key of sender
EA: Encryption Algorithm
OF: Original File
D: Digest
SHA: Secure Hash Algorithm

Fig. 4. The Algorithm of Digital Signature

The procedures of the suggested algorithm are as follows, do a procedure in a package of 100 bytes. Every one of the byte has loaded from file and does the logical operation of OR with a byte of (00000001), after that setting the product passionate to character of the variable. Subsequent to the dealing out of initial 100 bytes, multiply all of the ORed outcome bytes and maintain them in variable of 32 bits. Utilize the 32 of chief bits development of the outcome. Afterward the second 100 bytes will be procedure through the similar action. Accordingly every 100 bytes of information are cutting to hashed information in 32 bits.

The next part is encryption of the information from the secret key belongs to sender. The private key is 16 bytes and applies for encryption of data. There are two characters of arrays, key $Key[0..15]$ and another is hashed. In encoding procedure, the initial byte of hashed $H[0]$ and key ($Key[0]$) will be XOR and place the result in the first byte of the key ($Key[0]$). Then at another time, $H[0]$ and the $Key[1]$ do the same operation until the end of the hashed message. At the end of the process, the result of this operation will be kept in an array of character.

Then we compared the proposed algorithms with other hash algorithms in terms of its logical operators and the complexity of the hardware involved as shown in Table 1.

Table 1. Comparison of Logical Operations, Current Status and Hardware Complexity

Algorithm	Logical operations	Current status	Hardware complexity
MD5 algorithm	AND,OR,NOT,Rotating shifts	Collision	Medium
SHA1 algorithm	AND,OR,NOT,Rotating shifts ,XOR	Collision	Large-scale
SHA2 algorithm	AND,OR,NOT,Rotating shifts,XOR	Running	Large
Proposed Algorithm	OR and XOR	Running	Low

From Table 1, the logical operations required for proposed algorithm are OR and XOR compared to other algorithms which required more than four (4) logical operations. The hardware complexity requirement is also lower compared to other algorithms.

Hardware complexity contains devices such as Logic Devices, Programmable and Gate Arrays and Application Specific Integrated Circuits. Then Table 2 compares the file size during transmission for these algorithms.

Table 2. Comparison of Size of File in Bytes

Size of original files (Byte)	MD5 algorithm (Byte)	SHA1 algorithm (Byte)	SHA2 algorithm (Byte)	Proposed algorithm (Byte)
14	32	40	64	8
18	32	40	64	8
72	32	40	64	8
1	32	40	64	8

(*SHA is Secure Hash Algorithm).

The proposed algorithm had reduced significantly the sizes of the file to be only 8 bytes for various original file sizes compared to other algorithms.

6   Conclusion

In hash function, a small number of bits are generated from a large size file. This mathematical one way encryption produces hash code or hashes. The hash code procedure is more desirable than any other process because the generation of the code is faster than any other methods. Cryptographic hash functions are used extensively due to its cheap construction. The function is further used for digital signatures in verification of the authentication of the data [12]. The proposed algorithm is adopted for applications which transfer messages with small file size (such as for multi agent systems), which is a fundamental benefit to improve an application to be fast, simple and secure.

In future works, the next process will be implemented are the extracting signature in order to remove any extra signature message and to decrease the encrypted image size and to reduce extra bandwidth in file transmission.

Acknowledgment. The authors would like to express greatest appreciation to Ministry of Higher Education (MOHE), Malaysia and Universiti Teknologi Malaysia (UTM) particularly Advanced Informatics School (AIS) for providing the financial support to carry out this research work.

References

1. Fridrich, J., Goljan, M.: Robust Hash Functions for Digital Watermarking. IEEE Information Technology, Coding and Computing, 178–183 (2000)
2. Diffie, W., Hellman, M.E.: New directions in cryptography. IEEE Transactions on Information Theory 22, 644–654 (1976)
3. Bellare, M., Desai, A., Pointcheval, D., Rogaway, P.: Relations among Notions of Security for Public-Key Encryption Schemes. In: Krawczyk, H. (ed.) CRYPTO 1998. LNCS, vol. 1462, p. 26. Springer, Heidelberg (1998)
4. Rivest, R., Shamir, A., Adleman, L.M.: A method for obtaining digital signatures and public key. Cryptosystems Communications of the ACM 21, 120–126 (1978)
5. Barić, N., Pfitzmann, B.: Collision-Free Accumulators and Fail-Stop Signature Schemes without Trees. In: Fumy, W. (ed.) EUROCRYPT 1997. LNCS, vol. 1233, pp. 480–494. Springer, Heidelberg (1997)
6. Fujisaki, E., Okamoto, T.: Secure Integration of Asymmetric and Symmetric Encryption Schemes. In: Wiener, M. (ed.) CRYPTO 1999. LNCS, vol. 1666, p. 537. Springer, Heidelberg (1999)
7. Merkle, R.C.: A Digital Signature Based on a Conventional Encryption Function. In: Pomerance, C. (ed.) CRYPTO 1987. LNCS, vol. 293, pp. 369–378. Springer, Heidelberg (1988)
8. Desmedt, J., Nguyen, T., Bourguet, M.: Electroencephalography and Clinical europhysiology/Evoked Potentials Section 68(1), 1–19 (1987)
9. Bellare, M., Ristenpart, T.: Multi-Property-Preserving Hash Domain Extension and the EMD Transform. In: Lai, X., Chen, K. (eds.) ASIACRYPT 2006. LNCS, vol. 4284, pp. 299–314. Springer, Heidelberg (2006)
10. Luo, H., Kong, J., Zerfos, P., Lu, S., Zhang, L.: Providing Robust and Ubiquitous Security Support for Mobile Ad-Hoc Networks. In: IEEE ICNP 2001 (2001)
11. Gordon, D.: A Survey of Fast Exponentiation Methods. Center for Communications Research 27(1), 129–146 (1998)
12. Vaudenay, S.: Secure Communications over Insecure Channels Based on Short Authenticated Strings. In: Shoup, V. (ed.) CRYPTO 2005. LNCS, vol. 3621, pp. 309–326. Springer, Heidelberg (2005)

Design of Adaptive IDS with Regulated Retraining Approach

Anazida Zainal[1], Mohd Aizaini Maarof[1], Siti Mariyam Shamsuddin[2],
and Ajith Abraham[3]

[1] Information Assurance and Security Research Group,
[2] Soft Computing Research Group,
Faculty of Computer Science and Information System
Universiti Teknologi Malaysia
81310 Skudai, Johor
[3] IT for Innovations, EU Center of Excellence, Technical University of Ostrava,
Czech Republic
{anazida,aizaini,mariyam}@utm.my, ajith.abraham@ieee.org

Abstract. Computer networks are becoming more insecure and vulnerable to intrusions and attacks as they are increasingly accessible to users globally. To minimize possibility of intrusions and attacks, various intrusion detection models have been proposed. However, the existing procedures suffer high false alarm, not adequately adaptive, low accuracy and rigid. The detection performance deteriorates when behavior of traffic is changing and new attacks continually emerge. Therefore, the need to update the reference model for any given anomaly-based intrusion detection is necessary to keep up with these changes. Severe changes should be addressed immediately before the performance is compromised. Available updating approaches include dynamic, periodic and regulated. Unfortunately, none considers severity of changes to trigger the updating. This paper proposed an adaptive IDS model using regulated retraining approach based on severity of changes in network traffic. Therefore, retraining can be done as and when necessary. Changes are denoted by ambiguous decisions and assumed to reflect insufficient knowledge of classifiers to make decision. Results show that the proposed approach is able to improve detection accuracy and reduce false alarm.

Keywords: adaptive, intrusion detection, dynamic, regulated.

1   Introduction

Information is becoming ubiquitous with Internet infrastructure and sensitive information exposure is inevitable. Studies covering the prevention, detection and the forensic aspect of computer network attacks have long being researched on. The prevention techniques such as encryption, Virtual Private Network (VPN) and firewall alone seem to be inadequate. It reduces exposure rather than monitors or eliminates vulnerabilities in computer systems (Ghosh et al., 1998). Therefore, it is important to have

A. Ell Hassanien et al. (Eds.): AMLTA 2012, CCIS 322, pp. 590–600, 2012.

a detecting and monitoring system to protect important data. The outraging incident of Morris Worm in 1988, Code Red in 2001 and followed by SQL Slammer in 2003 (Langin and Rahimi, 2010) had handicapped many organizations including business-es, military, education and others. The importance to safeguard network against confidentiality, integrity and availability (CIA) breaches is an important issue and intrusion detection plays vital role in ensuring a secure network. This increasing im-portance of computer network security motivates various aspects of security related research that provide new solutions, which might not be achievable by conventional security approaches.

An Intrusion Detection System (IDS) is an automated system that can detect a computer system intrusion either by using the audit trail provided by an operating system or by using the network monitoring tools. The main goal of intrusion detection is to detect unauthorized use, misuse and abuse of computers by both system insiders and external intruders (Kim, 2002; Kim et al., 2007). IDS does not eliminate any pre-ventive mechanism but provides the defense in safeguarding the computer system. In IDS, misuse and anomaly are the two types of detection approaches. Misuse detection can detect known attacks by constructing a set of signatures of attacks while anomaly detection recognizes novel attacks by modeling normal behaviors (Xu and Wang, 2005). The outcome of this modeling is called reference model. A significant devia-tion from the model of reference indicates a potential threat. Anomaly detection approach is popular because it is a possible approach to detecting unknown or new attacks (Denning, 1987; Forrest et al., 1996; Warrander et al., 1999). Unfortunately, anomaly detection approach suffers high false alarm especially when IDSs use pattern recognition algorithms in operational environments (Giacinto et al., 2003).

Two major problem characteristics of IDS are; trend in network traffic; and limita-tion of the existing IDS tools and techniques. Normal traffic patterns are changing due to changes in work practices and nature of intrusions usually polymorph and conti-nuously evolve (Wu and Banzhaf, 2010). Therefore, intrusion detectors must undergo frequent retraining to incorporate new normal traffic samples into the training data for classifying novel attacks and changes from existing normal behavior (Zhang and Shen, 2004). The periodic reconstruction of reference model can provide adaptation to the new environment (Tapiador et al., 2004) and this will ensure that the new learnt model is relevant. Modern IDS requires adaptability in order to respond to constantly changing threat environment (Shafi and Abbas, 2009). Unfortunately many of the existing intrusion detection methods (misuse detection and anomaly detection) are generally incapable of adapting detection systems to the change of circumstance, which causes a declination of detection precision and rise in false alarm rate and it remains a major problem in IDS (Hossain and Bridges, 2001; Giacinto et al., 2003; Yu et al., 2005; Yang et al., 2005; Xu and Wang, 2005). Traditional anomaly based methods commonly build a static (rigid) reference model based on training dataset during modeling and then utilize this model to predict on new network behavior data at detecting stage (Yang et al., 2005). With time, this reference model becomes irrele-vant and obsolete.

There are few major challenges in anomaly-based IDS and among the critical ones are high workload and inability to update reference model which has direct impact on accuracy of detection. The scope of this paper will focus workload reduction and adaptability.

The chapter is organized into six sections. Section 2 gives an overview on adaptive IDS and some existing approaches toward building adaptability into IDS and Section 3 explains the design of the proposed Adaptive IDS. Section 4 describes experimental procedure follows by Section 5 describing results obtained and discussion. Finally Section 6 summarizes and concludes the paper.

2   Adaptive Intrusion Detection System

Since the Normal network traffic patterns are changing and new attacks are continually evolved, IDS needs to be updated. Failure to update these changes may degrade its detection performance. This is undesirable as the network of computers needs to be protected and firewall alone is not sufficient. Adaptive IDS in the context of this work refers to the ability of an IDS to dynamically change the model of reference through relearning or retraining in addressing the dynamic nature of network traffic pattern.

A typical stationary anomaly-based IDS system requires only one-time training which is done at the beginning of IDS system development in order to obtain reference model. This model was then utilized to predict network behavior during detection stage (Yang et al., 2005). However, it is important to note that intrusions usually polymorph and continuously evolve (Wu and Banzhaf, 2010). Therefore, it resulted in poor performance. Besides associated with low detection rate, its inability to adapt to the changes that occur in both normal and attack traffic patterns, would cause high false alarms (Eskin et al., 2000; Hossein et al., 2003; Xu and Wang, 2005; Liu et al., 2007; Shafi and Abbas, 2009). Therefore, an intrusion detection system must be able to adapt to the changing environment while still recognizing abnormal activities (Hossain and Bridges, 2001).

Table 1 summarizes related researches on adaptive IDS from year 2000 to 2009. The issue is how to make IDS adaptive. Adaptive in this context refers to an ability to update in order to cope with the changes happen in the network traffic. Generally, the models are either rule-based or model-based.

In rule-based approach, a new rule will be added to the existing rule set and retraining is required in model-based approach.

Although an update can be instantly done, this approach has some drawbacks and they are:

1. the detection time is affected as the list grows
2. initial rule-sets must be comprehensive to avoid excessive rules add-on
3. lacks of flexibility as slight variation to the sequence may affect activity to rule comparison

Shafi and Abbas (2009) managed to curtail the list of rules to a predefined size. This was achieved by pruning less significant or less generalized existing rules and replaced by new significant and generalized rules. Usually changes in the environment were detected when sequence extracted from an instance does not match with any of the available rules as implemented in Fan and Stolfo (2002) and Shafi and Abbas (2009). Despite the automatic rule generation, human intervention is still required to confirm the label for sequence in the newly created rule before it can be updated. In contrast to the growing list of rules, model-based approach produces a model with consistent size. Therefore, detection time remains short and unchanged. However, it requires retraining using the whole training dataset together with the additional new training data in order to update the reference model.

The updating strategies as listed in first column of Table I can be classified as, periodic updating, regulated updating, dynamic updating and manual updating. The description of each strategy is given below.

Table 1. Related Works on Adaptive IDS

Updating Strategy	Researchers	Detection Techniques	Training & Testing Data
Periodic	Hofmeyr, 1999	Model-based (AIS)	subnet at CS Dept, Univ.of New Mexico
	Kim, 2003	Model-based (AIS)	Trouble shootout data
Regulated	Hossain et al., 2003	Similarity measure & rule-based	mail & web servers, MSU
	Liu et al., 2007	Model-based	KDDCup 1999 datasets
	Burbeck and Tehrani, 2007	Clustering	KDDCup 1999 datasets
Dynamic	Lee et al., 2000	Rule-based	LBL and IWSS16 datasets
	Fan and Stolfo, 2002	Rule-based (RIPPER)	1998 DARPA IDS Evaluation dataset
	Lee et al., 2002	Rule-based	LBB-CONN-7 (TCP/IP network traffic)
	Chavan et al., 2004	Rule-based	KDDCup 1999 datasets
	Yang et al., 2005	Rule-based	KDDCup 1999 datasets
	Lee et al., 2006	Incremental Clustering (+Kernel Method)	KDDCup 1999 datasets
	Jemili et al., 2007	Statistical (Bayesian Network)	KDDCup 1999 datasets
	Shafi and Abbas, 2009	Rule-based (UCSm)	KDDCup 1999 datasets
Manual	Eskin et al., 2000	Model-based (*manually set the period for model generation, based on weekly data collected*)	System calls
	Yu et al., 2005	Clustering & rule-based (*manually applied the rule mining algorithm to extract rules from cluster*)	KDDCup 1999 datasets
	[1]Xu and Wang, 2005	Model-based (*Notion of adaptive refers to dynamic composition of several classifiers*)	KDDCup 1999 datasets
	[2]Tang et al., 2008	Rule-based (*reordering the sequence of rules based on specified metric performance*)	KDDCup 1999 datasets

(a) Periodic Updating

Update is done in certain interval or time frame. A lifespan is imposed to a classifier and after it has expired, the same classifier will undergo retraining (with some additionally new data) as such the new model will reflect the new patterns of normal and attacks.

(b) Dynamic Updating

The changes are incorporated as and when they are detected. In rule-based, usually a newly created rule will be appended to the existing rule set.

(c) Regulated Updating

The update is triggered when a preset threshold is met and usually associated with changes. Usually the regulated updating can be divided into two type which are quantity-based and quality-based threshold. An example of quantity-based is the work of Liu *et al.* (2007).

(d) Manual Updating

Feedback by the system administrator is required especially when the IDS starts to produce false alarms such as in Burbeck and Tehrani (2007). Since manual update heavily relies on human intervention, it is not the interest of this study to cover this particular updating strategy.

Hofmeyr (1999) and Kim (2003) implemented periodic updating strategy mimicking human antibodies replenishment concept in Artificial Immune System (AIS). Both works imposed lifespan on the validity of the detectors (classifiers), where a new set of detectors were created when the previous detectors age expired. Periodic updating strategy is not suitable especially when the occurrence of changes to normal network traffic patterns and emergence of new attacks are unpredictable. Worst case scenarios of this approach are described in Section 2.6.4. Periodic updating approach does not require any triggering event because the updating is scheduled. Therefore, changes in the network traffic patterns are irrelevant. Meanwhile, dynamic updating requires continuous update if changes are rapid. One of the seminal works on adaptive IDS was done by Lee et al. (2000) started with rule-based adaptive IDS. The traditional association rule mining proposed by Lee et al. (2000) was replaced by recent rule-mining techniques such as Fuzzy Inference and Artificial Neural Network as done by Chavan et al. (2004) and Liao et al. (2007) and Genetic Algorithm and Learning Classifier System by Shafi and Abbas (2009). Dynamic updating strategy is pursued until now. Table 2.2 reveals that it is common to adopt dynamic updating approach when the proposed models are rule-based. Dynamic updating adds new rule when there is no rule match the tested instance. Another updating approach is regulated. This approach commonly requires threshold to trigger the update such as in Hossain et al. (2003), Liao et al. (2007) and Burbeck and Tehrani (2007). Hossain et al. (2003) used sliding window and changes are measured relative to the traffic captured in one window size. Assumption on gradual change denotes changes in Normal behavior have led to poor performance. Meanwhile, Liu et al. (2007) used amount of uncertain instances and Burbeck and Tehrani (2007) used amount of false alarms as a threshold to trigger updating. Usually model-based together with clustering are used in this regulated updating approach as in Liu et al. (2007) and Burbeck and Tehrani (2007).

3   The Proposed Adaptive Intrusion Detection Model

Most of the existing intrusion detection system suffers from several problems and among them are high resource consumption and high overhead, high false alarm, poor detection accuracy. The proposed model is designed to address the following issues:

(i) High overhead due to voluminous data. Some are unnecessary recognition.
(ii) Low detection accuracy and high false alarm due to obsolete model of reference.
(iii) Poor detection due to; vague boundary between normal and abnormal and imbalanced data problem.
(iv) Note: The issue of severe class imbalanced is not considered in this study.

In order to solve the above problem situations, two solution concepts are formulated and they are; improve data representation through feature selection and update the model of reference through regulated retraining.

The model comprises of three components; (i) Pre-detection, (ii) Detection and (iii) Training and Retraining as shown in Figure 1. The modular design focuses on solving two respective problems. **Predetection** focuses on reducing the workload of an IDS by performing feature selection which will reduce the dimension of the data itself. Currently, there are 41 attributes (based on Intrusion Detection KDDCup dataset) and reduction can speed up the detection time. Furthermore, using only significant features may also improve the detection accuracy. (Chebrolu *et al.*, 2005). Next stage of the model is called **Detection**. A supervised approach is used to classify the incoming instance. Weak decision which falls in the range of $L \leq \theta \leq U$ (where θ indicates the decision value) is also called ambiguous decision. This ambiguous decision will be assigned a weight corresponds to the degree of ambiguity (where decision 0 and 1 represent absolute *Yes* and *No* and decision value of 0.5 carries the highest degree of ambiguity). This is called Weight Mapping. Assumption made in the study is that ambiguity denotes changes. Weight Mapping is a component in **Training and Retraining** stage. The weight will be accumulated until it reaches a predefined threshold. Once the threshold is reached, a clustering technique will cluster the instances (traffic connections) with weak decisions ($L \leq \theta \leq U$) into the respective traffic classes (Normal, Probe, DoS, U2R and R2L). These instances later will be appended to the train datasets for each respected classes (Normal, Probe, DoS, U2R and R2L).

In the study, Linear Genetic Programming was used to do detection and Fuzzy c-Means was used to cluster the instances with ambiguous decision values. Normal, Probe and Dos were represented by 8 features, each with different feature subset. Meanwhile U2R and R2L were represented by 7 features. Similarly, they are different feature subset.

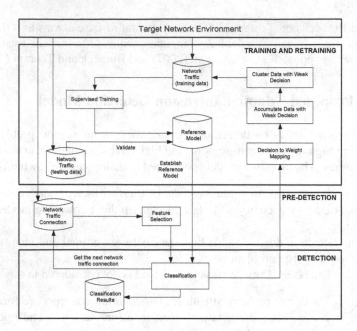

Fig. 1. Design of Adaptive IDS

4   Experiments

The dataset used in the experiments was obtained from 1998 DARPA Intrusion Detection Evaluation Program prepared by MIT Lincoln Labs also known as KDDCup 1999 datasets. These datasets were used in many of IDS works such as in Liu et al. (2007), Shafi and Abbas (2009) and Li et al., (2009). Tsai et al. (2009) reported there have been 30 major IDS studies used KDDCup 1999 datasets in their research. According to Wu and Banzhaf (2010), KDDCup 1999 dataset is the largest publicly available and sophisticated benchmarks for researchers to evaluate intrusion detection algorithms or machine learning algorithms. Figure 2 shows data used in the experiment.

Table 2. Distribution of Known dataset in windows unit

	Normal	Probe	DoS	U2R	R2L	Total
w-1	31,315	111	3,817	4	53	35,300
w-2	7,983	719	26,582	1	15	35,300
w-3	19,191	978	15,093	4	34	35,299
w-4	6,088	616	28,406	0	190	35,300
w-5	6,649	895	26,903	20	833	35,300
w-6	0	0	35,300	0	0	35,300
w-7	0	0	35,300	0	0	35,300
w-8	0	0	35,300	0	0	35,300
w-9	0	0	35,300	0	0	35,300
w-10	5,894	359	29,043	4	0	35,299
w-11	892	117	34,289	2	0	35,300
w-12	406	1	34,891	2	0	35,300
w-13	8,824	181	26,288	6	1	35,300
w-14	10,037	129	24,945	9	0	35,120

Original Data Distribution

Known Dataset — 494,020 data

Corrected Dataset — 309,428 data

Experimental Data

Training & Determination of Retraining for Classifier

Known Dataset — 388,300 data

(about 80% of the original Known Dataset size)

Testing on the Trained Classifier

Known Dataset — 494,020 data

Corrected Dataset — 309,428 data

Fig. 2. Data Distribution

5   Results and Discussion

Figure 3(a) to 3(c) graphically shows the number of retraining activated for different threshold values. When retraining is activated, it gains additional knowledge about the data since the previous instances with ambiguous decisions were part of the training data (after recommendation from clustering exercise).

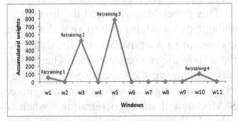

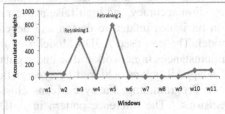

Fig. 3(a). Number of retraining when threshold is small

Fig. 3(b). Number of retraining when threshold is medium

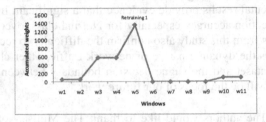

Fig. 3(c). Number of retraining when threshold is medium

Table 3(a). Confusion matrix for Adaptive IDS (A-IDS) Model on Known dataset

	Detection					Total	Accuracy
	Normal	Probe	DoS	U2R	R2L		(%)
A-IDS Model							
Actual	91,838	2672	1713	783	271	97,277	94.409
Normal	(94.41)	(2.75)	(1.76)	(0.80)	(0.28)		
	53	4,036	4	0	13	4,106	98.295
Probe	(1.29)	(98.30)	(0.10)	(0.00)	(0.32)		
	74	7	391,374	1	1	391,457	99.979
DoS	(0.02)	(0.002)	(99.98)	(0.00)	(0.00)		
	17	5	0	27	3	52	51.923
U2R	(32.69)	(9.62)	(0.00)	(51.92)	(5.77)		
	63	6	0	20	1,037	1,126	92.096
R2L	(5.60)	(0.53)	(0.00)	(1.78)	(92.10)		

In bracket is % ; Overall Accuracy = 98.85%; False Alarm Rate = 5.60% and Hit Rate = 99.95%

Table 3(b). Validation results for Adaptive IDS (A-IDS) Model on Corrected dataset

	Detection					Total	Accuracy
	Normal	Probe	DoS	U2R	R2L		(%)
A-IDS Model							
Actual Normal	56,635	249	3,553	1	156	60,594	93.466
	(93.47)	(0.41)	(5.86)	(0.00)	(0.26)		
Probe	675	3,484	0	0	7	4,166	83.629
	(16.20)	(83.63)	(0.00)	(0.00)	(0.17)		
DoS	6	0	229,847	0	0	229,853	99.997
	(0.003)	(0.00)	(99.997)	(0.00)	(0.00)		
U2R	32	2	0	19	17	70	27.143
	(45.71)	(2.86)	(0.00)	(27.14)	(24.29)		
R2L	7,137	46	0	5	9,159	16,347	56.029
	(43.66)	(0.28)	(0.00)	(0.03)	(56.03)		

In bracket is % ; Overall Accuracy = 96.179%; False Alarm Rate = 6.534% and Hit Rate = 96.865%

Small threshold for A-IDS requires frequent retraining and a large threshold makes the system suffers from low detection accuracy due to inadequate knowledge to predict but it requires less retraining. In summary, the regulated retraining approach with threshold set to medium value has triggered retraining twice. First retraining was done at the end of third window (w-3). The second retraining was performed at the end of fifth window (w-5). Adaptive IDS Model was tested on Known and validated on Corrected datasets. Its performance on Known dataset is summarized in Table 3(a) and validation performance on Corrected dataset is shown in Table 3(b).

6   Conclusion

The lack of adaptability leads to obsolete reference model which resulted in poor detection accuracy and high false alarm rate. This paper has described the investigation on issues related to design and development of an adaptive intrusion detection model. The proposed A-IDS Model used the concept to adaptively learn the dynamic circumstances in network traffic and regularly update the reference model. The notion of adaptability was achieved by synergistically combining the supervised Linear Genetic Programming, Fuzzy c-Means clustering and weight mapping on ambiguous decisions. The reference pattern in A-IDS Model will undergo retraining when a specified degree of changes has been accumulated. The accumulated weight will trigger the A-IDS Model for retraining either when a sudden significant change has happened or when accumulated small changes have hit the threshold limit. The proposed Adaptive IDS promotes retraining based on the severity of changes in the network traffic. The experimental results provide evidence that a significant improvement was achieved for the detection accuracy especially for Normal class, overall accuracy and false alarm. Findings from this study also confirm the difficulty to recognize U2R and R2L classes. Besides the dynamic nature of network traffic, other challenges in IDS are the imbalance dataset and the vague decision boundary between normal and abnormal traffic. This will be the focus of our future work.

Acknowledgment. The authors would like to thank The Ministry of Higher Education of Malaysia (MOHE) and Universiti Teknologi Malaysia (UTM) for funding this study.

References

Burbeck, K., Tehrani, S.N.: Adaptive real-time anomaly detection with incremental clustering. Information Security Technical Report 12, 56–67 (2007)

Chavan, S., Shah, K., Dave, N., Mukherjee, S., Abraham, A., Sanyal, S.: Adaptive neuro-fuzzy intrusion detection systems. In: IEEE Proceedings of International Conference on Information Technology: Coding and Computing (ITCC 2004), vol. 1, pp. 70–74 (2004)

Chebrolu, S., Abraham, A., Thomas, J.P.: Feature deduction and ensemble design of intrusion detection systems. Journal of Computers and Security 24(4), 295–307 (2005)

Denning, D.E.: An Intrusion-Detection Model. IEEE Transactions on Software Engineering SE 13(2), 222–232 (1987)

Eskin, E., Miller, M., Zhong, Z.D., Yi, G., Lee, W.A., Stolfo, S.: Adaptive Model Generation for Intrusion Detection System. In: Proceedings of the ACMCCS Workshop on Intrusion Detection and Prevention, Athens, Greece (2000)

Fan, W., Stolfo, S.: Ensemble-based Adaptive Intrusion Detection. In: Proceedings of 2nd SIAM International Conference on Data Mining (SDM 2002), Arlington, VA, April 11-13 (2002)

Forrest, S., Hofmeyr, S.A., Somayaji, A., Longstaff, T.A.: A sense of self for Unix Processes. In: IEEE Proceedings of Symposium on Security and Privacy, pp. 120–128 (1996)

Ghosh, A.K., Wanken, J., Charron, F.: Detecting Anomalous and Unknown Intrusions Against Programs. In: Proceedings of the 14th Annual Computer Security Applications Conference, AC-SAC (1998)

Giacinto, G., Roli, F., Didaci, L.: Fusion of multiple classifiers for intrusion detection in computer network. Pattern Recognition Letters 24(12), 1795–1803 (2003)

Hofmeyr, S.A.: An Immunological Model of Distributed Detection and Its Application to Computer Security. Ph.D. Thesis. Computer Science Dept of University of New Mexico, United States (1999)

Hossein, M., Bridges, S.M.: A Framework for an Adaptive Intrusion Detection System With Data Mining. In: Proceedings of the 13th Annual Canadia Information Technology Security Symposium, Ottawa, Canada (2001)

Hossein, M., Bridges, S.M., Vaughn, R.B.: Adaptive Intrusion Detection wit Data Mining. In: Proceedings of IEEE Conference on Systems, Man & Cybernetics, pp. 3097–3103 (2003)

Jemili, F., Zaghdoud, M., Ahmed, M.: A Framework for an Adaptive Intrusion Detection System using Bayesian Network. In: IEEE Proceedings of Intelligence and Security Informatics, New Brunswick, New Jersey, pp. 66–70 (2007)

Kim, J.: Integrating Artificial Immune Algorithms for Intrusion Detection. PhD Thesis, Department of Computer Science, University College of London (2003)

Kim, J., Bentley, P.J., Aickelin, U., Greensmith, J., Tedesco, G., Twycross, J.: Immune System Approaches to Intrusion Detection – A Review. Natural Computing 6(4), 413–466 (2007)

Langin, C., Rahimi, S.: Soft computing in intrusion detection: the state of the art. Ambient Intelligent and Humanized Computing 1, 133–145 (2010)

Lee, H., Chung, Y., Park, D.: An Adaptive Intrusion Detection Algorithm Based on Clustering and Kernel-Method. In: Ng, W.-K., Kitsuregawa, M., Li, J., Chang, K. (eds.) PAKDD 2006. LNCS (LNAI), vol. 3918, pp. 603–610. Springer, Heidelberg (2006)

Lee, W., Stolfo, S.S., Mok, K.W.: Adaptive Intrusion Detection: A Data Mining Approach. Artificial Intelligence Review. Issues on the Application of Data Mining 14, 533–567 (2000)

Li, Y., Jun, L.W., Zhi, H.T., Tian, B.L., Chen, Y.: Building lightweight intrusion detection system using wrapper-based feature selection mechanisms. Computers and Security 28(6), 466–475 (2009)

Liao, Y., Vemuri, V.R., Pasos, A.: Adaptive anomaly detection with evolving connectionist systems. Network and Applications 30(1), 60–80 (2007)

Liu, G., Yi, Z., Yang, S.: A hierarchical intrusion detection model based on the PCA neural networks. Neurocomputing 70, 1561–1568 (2007)

Shafi, K., Abbass, H.A.: An Adaptive Genetic-based Signature Learning System for Intrusion Detection. Expert Systems with Applications 36(10), 12036–12043 (2009)

Tang, W., Cao, Y., Xi, M.Y., Won, H.S.: Study on Adaptive Intrusion Detection Engine Based on Gene Expression Programming Rules. In: Proceedings of International Conference on Computer Science and Software Engineering, pp. 959–963 (2008)

Tapiador, J.M.E., Teodoro, P.G., Verdejo, J.E.D.: Anomaly Detection Methods in Wired Networks: A Survey and Taxonomy. Computer Communications 27(16), 1569–1584 (2004)

Tsai, C.F., Hsu, Y.F., Lin, C.Y., Lin, W.Y.: Intrusion Detection by Machine Learning: A Review. Expert Systems with Applications 36(10), 11994–12000 (2009)

Warrander, C., Forrest, S., Pearlmutter, B.: Detecting intrusions using system calls: alternative data models. In: IEEE Proceedings of Symposium on Security and Privacy, pp. 133–145 (1999)

Wu, X.S., Banzhaf, W.: The Use of Computational Intelligence in Intrusion Detection Systems: A Review. Applied Soft Computing 10(1), 1–35 (2010)

Xu, X., Wang, X.: An Adaptive Network Intrusion Detection Method Based on PCA and Support Vector Machines. In: Li, X., Wang, S., Dong, Z.Y. (eds.) ADMA 2005. LNCS (LNAI), vol. 3584, pp. 696–703. Springer, Heidelberg (2005)

Yang, W., Yun, X.C., Zhang, L.J.: Using Incremental Learning Method for Adaptive Network Intrusion Detection. In: Proceedings of the 4th International Conference on Machine Learning and Cybernetics, Guangzhou, August 18-21, pp. 3932–3936 (2005)

Yu, Z.X., Chen, J.R., Zhu, T.Q.: A Novel Adaptive Intrusion detection system Based on Data Mining. In: Proceedings of the Fourth International Conference on Machine Learning and Cybernatics, Guangzhou, August 18-21, pp. 2390–2395 (2005)

Zhang, Z., Shen, H.: Application of online-training SVMs for real-time intrusion detection with different considerations. Computer Communications 28(12), 1428–1442 (2005)

Author Index